Women Writers
of the Renaissance
and Reformation

omen Writers

of the Renaissance and Reformation

EDITED BY

KATHARINA M. WILSON

The University of Georgia Press
ATHENS AND LONDON

© 1987 by the University of Georgia Press
Athens, Georgia 30602
All rights reserved

Designed by Kathi L. Dailey
Set in 10 on 12 Mergenthaler Sabon
The paper in this book meets the guidelines for permanence
and durability of the Committee on Production Guidelines for
Book Longevity of the Council on Library Resources.

Typeset by The Composing Room of Michigan
Printed and bound by Cushing-Malloy

Printed in the United States of America

91 90   5   4   3   2

Library of Congress Cataloging in Publication Data

Women writers of the Renaissance and Reformation.

Bibliography: p.
Includes index.
1. European literature—Women authors. 2. European
literature—Renaissance, 1450–1600.
I. Wilson, Katharina M.
PN6069.W65W63   1987   809'.89287   86–3150
ISBN 0–8203–0865–X (alk. paper)
ISBN 0–8203–0866–8 (pbk.: alk. paper)

Contents

Introduction   ix
KATHARINA M. WILSON

PART ONE
Italy

Gaspara Stampa: Aphrodite's Priestess, Love's Martyr   3
FRANK J. WARNKE

Vittoria Colonna: Child, Woman, and Poet   22
JOSEPH GIBALDI

Veronica Gambara: A Renaissance *Gentildonna*   47
RICHARD POSS

Saint Catherine of Genoa: Mystic of Pure Love   67
DONALD CHRISTOPHER NUGENT

Saint Catherine of Bologna: Franciscan Mystic   81
JOSEPH R. BERRIGAN

PART TWO
France

Marguerite of Navarre: The *Heptameron*, a Simulacrum of Love   99
MARCEL TETEL

Louise Labé: Poet of Lyon   132
JEANNE PRINE

Dianne de Poitiers: The Woman Behind the Legend   158
SANDRA SIDER

Hélisenne de Crenne: Champion of Women's Rights   177
KITTYE DELLE ROBBINS-HERRING

Pernette Du Guillet: The Lyonnais Neoplatonist   219
ANN ROSALIND JONES

Les Dames des Roches: The French Humanist Scholars   232
ANNE R. LARSEN

Marie Dentière: A Propagandist for the Reform   260
THOMAS HEAD

PART THREE
German Principalities/Hapsburg Empire

Caritas Pirckheimer: The Nuremberg Abbess   287
GWENDOLYN BRYANT

Anna Owena Hoyers: A View of Practical Living   304
BRIGITTE EDITH ARCHIBALD

Helene Kottanner: The Austrian Chambermaid   327
MAYA C. BIJVOET

Margaret of Austria: Regent of the Netherlands   350
CHARITY CANNON WILLARD

PART FOUR
The Low Countries

Anna Bijns: Germanic Sappho   365
KRISTIAAN P. G. AERCKE

PART FIVE
Spain

Saint Teresa of Jesus: The Human Value of the Divine   401
CIRIACO MORÓN-ARROYO

PART SIX
Hungary

Lea Ráskai: A Dominican Author   435
SUZANNE FONAY WEMPLE

PART SEVEN
England

Margaret More Roper: The Learned Woman in Tudor England   449
ELIZABETH MCCUTCHEON

Mary Sidney: Countess of Pembroke   481
COBURN FREER

Elizabeth I: Queen of England   522
FRANCES TEAGUE

Mary Sidney: Lady Wroth   548
MARGARET PATTERSON HANNAY

Katherine Philips: The Matchless Orinda   566
ELIZABETH H. HAGEMAN

Appendix: Chronology of Literary and Historical Figures and
Major Events   609

Contributors   623

Index   627

Introduction

KATHARINA M. WILSON

> Well born and living at a propitious time for learning
> You seem inclined toward the Muses.
> May Heaven grant you such a desire
> For holy living, the only just [source of] pleasure,
> And the Daemon, who began the work,
> Guide so well the issue of your thought,
> That as a witness to posterity
> Of how much honor you will have merited,
> You may become immortal some day through your virtue,
> It is thus that I have always wished you to be.
> MADELEINE NEVEU, "Epistle to My Daughter"

With these lines, addressed to her daughter Catherine, Madeleine Neveu, Dame des Roches, concludes her epistle by extolling the merits of learning and writing as the glorious paths leading to virtue, fame, and immortality. Aware of the ambivalent attitude of her age toward learned women, Madeleine des Roches embraces a conciliatory, and politically and religiously conservative, brand of feminism that encourages woman's intellectual and literary endeavors within the ideological confines set by society and the Church. Her views are representative of a majority of Renaissance women writers—or, to be more specific, of those women whose works have survived—but they are by no means true for all fifteenth- and sixteenth-century women who wrote.[1] Indeed, while the Dame des Roches and many other ladies of similarly conciliatory modes of expression were widely celebrated for their literary accomplishments, the subversive and polemical texts of others earned them persecution, ridicule, and even martyrdom.

The present volume explores the lives and works of women writers of the European Renaissance, Reformation, and Counter-Reformation during the fifteenth and sixteenth centuries. A few women are included who wrote in the early seventeenth century but whose works were felt to be more akin to the spirit of the Renaissance and Reformation than to the Baroque. Many of the texts presented here are translated for the first time into English, and the inclusion of writers from Central and Eastern Europe as well as from Western Europe will, we hope, lend a representative focus to the collection.[2]

While for centuries the Burkhardtian definitions of the Renaissance have gone unchallenged, recent criticism has questioned the very existence of the Renaissance, particularly the concept of a Renaissance for women during the fifteenth and sixteenth centuries. In her essay "Did Women Have a Renaissance?," for example, Joan Kelly questions traditional assumptions about the experience of women.[3] She emphasizes, as other scholars have increasingly stressed, that women's historical experience often differs from men's regarding changing property relations, institutional control, religious and social ideologies, and that, therefore, period labels, applied prima facie to women's history, are often meaningless.[4] Her conclusions, leading to a negative answer to her question, are based on analyses of medieval and Renaissance literature, mostly written by men, that reflect on and formulate the Renaissance evolution of class relations, institutional policies, sexual and family relations, and political ideologies, all of which she interprets as representing a deterioration in the status and freedom of women in the Renaissance.[5] Their status in a particular historic period is only one of the difficulties that complicates our understanding of Renaissance women; problems of contextuality, the dearth of gender-specific critical works, and the distorting effects of the mirror phenomenon—that is, the investigation of female voices obscured through accreted layers of male aesthetic norms and male critical appraisal—are other obstacles in the way. Indeed, the metaphor of the mirror—its reverse sides and edges, its splintering and doubling effect—is now commonly used to describe female self-awareness controlled by the male gaze. It is a metaphor particularly applicable to the investigation of texts penned by early women writers, an investigation that involves the complicated process of delineating what Silvia Bovenschen has termed the "conquering and reclaiming, appropriating and formulating as well as forgetting and subverting" of male aesthetics in the woman writer's text.[6] In addition to the unscrambling of the mirror's distortions, we must also listen to the language of silence. As Gary F. Waller argues, the gender-specific (as well as culture-specific) nature of women's discourse makes it essential that we look not only at what *is* there but also at what *is not* there—the silences, margins, and absences in women's writings.[7] He draws a parallel between Foucault's theory of marginalized voices in a culture and the writings of Renaissance women:

> Foucault raises the question of how the excluded or marginalized voices of culture can be heard within the seemingly replete language constituted by specific discursive practices, as those voices struggle against the power of a dominant system which tries to organize all of a society's cultural activity. Above all, what power seeks to control is discourse since it is there that "reality" is defined by the society; further it is only through discourse that a society's speaking subjects may enter and participate in it.[8]

"So how do oppositional forces speak," he adds, "when the dominant language refuses them words? How are the voices of silence heard?"[9] Waller's observations and concerns are most applicable to Tudor women writers whose works are, indeed, predominantly religious and who, more than Continental women, were often limited in their literary pursuit to the practice of translations, but his emphasis on the importance of "silence" in women's discourse carries significant implications for the works of all early women writers.

The articles by Kelly, Bovenschen, and Waller and several recent symposia on the subject raise important issues and demonstrate to what significant extent the cross-fertilization of feminist scholarship, linguistic and literary criticism, and history have forced us to reconsider and even revise our understanding of the Renaissance.[10] An obvious and most welcome effect of the debate has been the recovery and examination of a large and varied body of materials, literary and historical, that have been hitherto ignored or overlooked. More important, the recovery of new materials and the new examination of existing, canonized texts has led to a reexamination of some fundamental aspects of Renaissance thought: the questions of authority and education; moral, intellectual, political, religious, and social values, as well as the roles institutions played in fostering or manipulating the arts.

The testimony of fifteenth- and sixteenth-century women writers is one element of the complex realities of Renaissance civilization that sheds significant light on the question of whether or not (and if so, in what manner) women did have a Renaissance during the Renaissance.[11] This volume attempts to present such evidence by providing the reader with a sampling of the manifold and varied contributions women made to intellectual history, contributions that reflect some of the epistemological and ontological complexities of female voices during the Renaissance. This construction of a Renaissance "City of Ladies" is by nature selective, since most women writers were members of a privileged elite (though they were not limited to the aristocracy) and are, therefore, not representative of women in all walks of life. They present far more (and far less) than the "feminine voice."[12] In each case this "voice" reflects (to a degree varying from writer to writer) general male aesthetic norms deeply internalized by the woman. No attempt has been made to subscribe to the essentialist argument and to label the works of women writers as original expressions of female experience *tout court*.[13] But even as a minute, highly specialized, and often constricted segment of the female population, fifteenth- and sixteenth-century women writers do offer some counterpoint to literature written by men, as they often give alternate views of contemporary reality and voice the concerns, aspirations, frustrations, and experiences of women, and as they celebrate their opportunities for self-expression. They are able to impart a sense of individuality and authenticity to their voices in spite of the fact that their works incarnate much of conventional Renaissance thought: the cult of antiquity, the concomitant predilection for ornate expression, the use of conventional topoi and forms, a love of balanced and polished diction, rare words, mythological references, and ideals of ancient moral philosophy, history, and letters. Not surprisingly, the women with the most authentic and individual voices are those not belonging to the upper nobility, those not related to literary men, and those who were affiliated with socially, politically, or religiously subversive groups (i.e., those whose voices are marginalized for grounds other than their sex).[14] While the works of fifteenth- and sixteenth-century women have not been incorporated into the mainstream literary tradition, the Renaissance fortunes of their works range from "bestseller" (Margaret More Roper, Marguerite of Navarre) to prohibited text (Marie Dentière); their own fortunes range from general acclaim and literary success to abject rejection and even persecution; and the sheer variety of their voices belies traditional assumptions concerning the homogeneity of "women's literature."

The plethora of genres utilized by women of the fifteenth and sixteenth centuries represented here include sonnets (Louise Labé, Vittoria Colonna, Gaspara Stampa, Mary Wroth, Les Dames des Roches, Veronica Gambara), chansons (Pernette Du Guillet, Margaret of Austria), elegies (Pernette Du Guillet, Louise Labé, Katherine Philips), epigrams (Pernette Du Guillet, Mary Sidney, Katherine Philips), odes (Veronica Gambara, Les Dames des Roches), madrigals (Veronica Gambara), ballads (Veronica Gambara), religious lyrics (Vittoria Colonna, Marguerite of Navarre, Anna Owena Hoyers), epithalamia (Katherine Philips), letters (Dianne de Poitiers, Margaret of Austria, Veronica Gambara, Caritas Pirckheimer), chronicles (Caritas Pirckheimer), memoirs (Helene Kottanner), polemic history (Marie Dentière), polemic counterreformational refrains (Anna Bijns), polemical reformational poems (Anna Owena Hoyers), novellas (Marguerite of Navarre), novels (Hélisenne de Crenne), sonnet sequences (Les Dames des Roches, Mary Wroth), translations (Mary Sidney, Margaret More Roper, Lea Ráskai, Elizabeth I), spiritual dialogues and mystical writings (Catherine of Genoa, Catherine of Bologna, Saint Teresa of Jesus), hagiographic *vitae* (Lea Ráskai), prose and poetic dialogues (Louise Labé, Les Dames des Roches), homilies and political orations (Elizabeth I).

The chronological limits of this volume are, by necessity, arbitrary. We have included women writers from 1400 to 1600 and two writers of somewhat later dates. In the selection of both texts and writers, we were guided by aesthetic principles as well as by the desire to provide a representative florilegium of Renaissance women's texts. The variety of the works and authors included is mirrored in the variety of critical approaches in the volume—in most cases the directions of the essays are dictated by their material. When arranging the texts, we opted for a geographic presentation but included chronological tables in the Appendix.

Italy is represented by three secular and two religious women. All but one were members of the upper nobility; they were not related to literary men; all were known for their poetic and/or mystic talents by their contemporaries, and the literary fortunes of some survived to posterity. The secular writers Vittoria Colonna (1492–1547), Veronica Gambara (1485–1550), and Gaspara Stampa (ca. 1524–1554) all composed lyric poetry of high quality, valued greatly by such outstanding humanists and artists as Pietro Bembo, Michelangelo, and Tiraboschi.[15] Gambara and Colonna were both *gentildonne,* married aristocratic ladies; Gaspara Stampa, on the other hand, was a cultivated *cortigiana onesta* of the Venetian bourgeoisie. All three (but especially Gambara and Colonna) infused the strict confines of the Petrarchan tradition with their own essentially personal perspectives: Veronica Gambara and Vittoria Colonna paid tribute to married love, and Gaspara Stampa depicted passionate and even obsessive love and its frustrations. Like the medieval *troubairitz,* these poets saw themselves as lovers, not as the beloved, and the two married poets, by singing of fulfilled love, burst the confines of the Petrarchan tradition dominated by the themes of betrayal and erotic frustration. Colonna and Gambara also wrote devotional poems; as well, both were noted patrons of the arts and presided over literary salons.

The two religious Italian writers included are Catherine of Genoa (1447–1510), mystic and exponent of the doctrine of annihilation, that is, the absorption of the human into the Divine, and Catherine of Bologna (1413–1463), an aristocratic lady of good education who chose a life of apostolic poverty as a Franciscan tertiary and later as a Poor Clare. Both were entirely orthodox and both advocated Church reform on the eve of the Reformation. A calligrapher and miniaturist as well as an author, Catherine of Bologna is especially representative of the disseminating efforts of the Renaissance religious woman.

Renaissance literature in France, coming from Italy and disseminating in part through the efforts of Marguerite of Navarre, is represented by the works of seven women. Unlike their Italian and English sisters, all the French ladies wrote secular works, even though Marguerite of Navarre also composed devotional texts; only a few women were related to literary men, several were of nonaristocratic origin, but all were acclaimed by their contemporaries. Those of aristocratic birth, Marguerite of Navarre (1492–1549) and Dianne de Poitiers (1500–1566), epitomize the secular virtues advocated and praised by their late medieval literary forerunner Christine de Pizan, with whose works both were familiar. They were skilled diplomats and negotiators, polished speakers, good politicians, generous patrons of the arts, and effective political thinkers. Marguerite of Navarre, in addition, experimented with the novelistic, dramatic, and lyric genres; her religious and secular plays were performed in the convent she founded. Her novella collection, examining the relationships of the sexes, is arranged in a dialectic framework, enabling her, thus, to offer interlocking sets of reflections on the narratives. The Dames des Roches (ca. 1520–1587; 1542–1587), Louise Labé (ca. 1515–1556), and Pernette Du Guillet (1520–1545), on the other hand, were members of the urban patriciate or middle class, and Hélisenne de Crenne belonged to the local gentry. The Dames des Roches, fully seizing the new opportunities of learning, won praise from their contemporaries for their erudition and defended single (secular) women who wished to pursue learning for its own sake, and Catherine des Roches infused the traditional Neoplatonic theme of the virtuously aloof mistress with the motif of the unfaithful lover. The Lyonnese Louise Labé, equally interested in women's education and a literary career, successfully adopted the classical elegy to sixteenth-century French language and themes. An elegant and erudite writer who enjoyed the admiration of her contemporaries, Labé has inspired many later poets, among them Rainer Maria Rilke. Pernette Du Guillet, also of Lyon, reshaped the conventional Petrarchan themes by deemphasizing the sufferings of the frustrated lover and insisting, instead, on the unity and tranquility of partnership in love. Finally, Hélisenne de Crenne (Marguerite Briet fl. 1525) transformed her autobiography into a sentimental novel and, while depicting the dangers of all-consuming passion so obsessive as to have the power to shock even today's reader, transcended those perils through her art. Popular during her lifetime (her collected *Oeuvres* appeared five times between 1543 and 1560), today she is no more than a name to the nonspecialist.

The German women writers included here, both members of the urban patriciate, represent the opposite poles of the religious movement. Caritas Pirckheimer (1467–1532), sister of the distinguished humanist Willibald and entirely orthodox in her Catholicism, worked as abbess of the Poor Clare convent in Nuremberg. Her erudition earned her comparison with the learned Cassandra Fidele, and her wide correspondence with the leading humanists of her age attests to her reputation for learning. Courageously and intelligently resisting the manifold pressures on her and her nuns to renounce the cloistered life, Caritas triumphed and recorded her experience for posterity. On the other hand, Anna Owena Hoyers (1584–1655), who may have been an Anabaptist herself, was a vocal supporter of the reformist movement, denouncing in her Low German dialect and with realistic, unflattering details the debauchery, drunkenness, and lechery of the local clergy.

From the Hapsburg Empire come two very different women writers:

Helene Kotanner (fl. 1400), chambermaid of Queen Elizabeth of Hungary and a very early representative of the initial stages of the Central European Renaissance, and Margaret of Austria (1480–1530), regent of the Netherlands for more than two decades. Kottanner, who was a member of the local gentry, presents in her *Memoirs* an absorbing picture of the period and depicts with sensitivity and sympathy the plight of the peasants in a noblemen's war. Though not very learned, she had a good sense of the dramatic and leaves us an eyewitness report that may be seen as an early, slow-paced precursor of the historical novel. Margaret of Austria, on the other hand, who was educated as was Louise of Savoy at the illustrious court of Anne of Beaujeu, was a woman of great learning. After a rather tragic early life, she wound up in Malines, where as regent for the Netherlands, she presided over a literary salon, collected art and books, and ruled the country with great political acuity. Her tremendous volume of correspondence bears testimony to the fascinating polarity between the public and the private woman. Stateswoman, patron, builder-educator, and peacemaker, she epitomizes the ideal qualities of queens and princesses enumerated by Christine de Pizan, of whom she was a devoted reader.

Anna Bijns (1496–1575), a Dutch schoolmistress and sworn enemy of Martin Luther and the Reformation, was the main speaker of the Counter-Reformation in Antwerp. Her defense of Catholicism is as vigorous and as passionate as is the Geneva author Marie Dentière's (fl. 1540) defense of the reform movement. Dentière, a former abbess of Augustinian nuns, exemplifies the active female involvement in the Geneva reformation. Advocating the right of women to preach and to interpret Scripture, Dentière epitomizes the reformers' nightmare about female ministerial participation in the church. Both Bijns and Dentière were very successful as polemicists; both, however, died poor, rejected, and unsupported by those whose ideological, political, and religious wars they had fought.

The Spanish Renaissance is represented by one of the best-known religious writers of the age. Saint Teresa (1515–1585), who was named, together with Saint Catherine of Siena, a doctor of the Church by Pope Paul VI, is one of Catholicism's most clairvoyant yet human mystics. Descended from a Jewish convert and showing from early childhood a disposition for martyrdom, Saint Teresa had spiritual experiences that were initially dismissed as inspired by the Devil. Epitomized as the embodiment of transcendence by Simone de Beauvoir, labeled by nineteenth-century psychiatrists as a hysteric, and immortalized by Bernini's magnificent rendering of her rapture, she has been recognized as a major exponent of holistic spirituality, preferring creative tension to comfortable dualism.

The Renaissance arrived in Eastern Europe from two directions. Both

the Polish and the Hungarian kings married Italian princesses who helped
them disseminate Italian humanism in their new countries, and Conrad
Celtis, German poet laureate and humanist, founded learned *sodalitates*
in Poland and Hungary. Lea Ráskai (fl. 1510–1525), a nun at the Rabbit's
Island convent in Buda, is the embodiment of the religious/humanist
movement in Hungary. Her efforts to translate, copy, and adapt Latin
texts constitute an important phase in the rise of the vernacular and the
growth of lay piety; her legends bear testimony to the intellectual and
literary activities of sixteenth-century Dominican convents in Hungary.

England is represented by five ladies, all of them learned, all but two
members of the upper nobility, and all but one related to learned and/or
literary men. Queen Elizabeth I (1533–1603), humanist and monarch of
remarkable intellectual and political talents, triumphant queen after a
long period of trials and tribulations, wrote orations, homilies, poems,
and translations, among them Marguerite of Navarre's *Mirror of the Sinful Soul.*[16] Like her famous father, who was noted for humanist interests
and respectable philological accomplishments, Elizabeth mastered the
rudiments of humanist learning. Similarly, Mary Sidney (1561–1621),
countess of Pembroke and sister of Sir Philip Sidney, was not only a literary patron of remarkably varied interests but also an outstanding translator whose works made a completely new range of opportunities for
expression available to her contemporaries.[17] Her philological accomplishments include introductions of new material and forms into English,
and "she is perhaps the first author in English to show a method of dramatic exposition working directly through poetry."[18] Whereas Mary
Sidney was almost universally acclaimed for her literary accomplishments, her niece, Lady Wroth (1586–ca. 1651), was castigated for her
composition of *Urania,* a pastoral tragicomedy of disillusioned love and
the first known full-length work of fiction by an Englishwoman. Indeed,
Lady Wroth was encouraged to follow the example of her pious aunt and
recreate (i.e., translate) rather than create. Margaret More Roper (1505–
1544), Sir Thomas More's daughter, was probably the most erudite of the
four. Indeed, Erasmus uses her example, together with that of the Pirckheimer girls, to demonstrate the value of education for women.[19] Praised
for her piety and learning during her lifetime, Margaret Roper exemplifies
the ideals of the new humanist learning for women, a learning that joined
moral probity with education. She was a noted philologist, writing with
facility in Greek and Latin and translating texts from both languages into
English. Finally, Katherine Philips (ca. 1631) represents the lyric and pastoral conventions of the late English Renaissance. A transitional figure,
singing of the precious bond of friendship between women and of
national/political concerns, Philips's poems conclude the volume by her-
alding a new age.

GENERALLY ACCLAIMED as an age of growth and expansion, the Renaissance was a period marked by various changes, social, religious, and moral: by the rise of national states in the wake of the Black Death; by the Reformist movement; and by the recovery of and reemphasis on the classical past. It was a period gloriously replete with new opportunities of which Renaissance men and women were joyfully aware. How did women writers of the fifteenth and sixteenth centuries avail themselves of these new opportunities? Did they have a distinctive voice? How did their contemporaries view them? It is quite clear that women, predominantly from the upper or well-to-do classes but also from other levels of society, contributed importantly and prodigiously to Renaissance letters and that many of them enjoyed contemporary literary success. However, while many women profited greatly from the availability of the new learning, it is also evident that, regardless of their talents or accomplishments, the full range of opportunities opened by the humanist movement were not available to them in the same manner or to the same extent as to men and that the vocational and moral goals of education enunciated by the humanists were almost invariably different for men and women. Clearly, the social (and economic) mobility made possible for male humanists through the pursuit of professional careers was not an available option to women.

Literary endeavors of men and women alike are not the results of poetic genius alone: education, some financial independence—either in the form of personal wealth, individual or institutional patronage—a modicum of leisure, access to source materials and books, some form of encouragement, and/or religious, political, or emotional zeal are also of significant import. Perhaps the most seminally important contribution of Renaissance humanism to the burgeoning of female literary activity was the availability, on a large scale, of a diversified education to laywomen fortunate enough to have had access to books and teachers. Indeed, the education of women was one of the most persuasively argued topoi in the famous Renaissance debate on woman's worth, the *querelle des femmes*.[20]

A prodigious appetite for learning and an eager delight in the fruits of philological endeavors created a large class of men and women that mastered the rudiments of humanist learning: proficiency in Latin, competency in Greek, knowledge of ancient and patristic literature, history, moral philosophy, as well as the conventions of Petrarchism and Ficinian Neoplatonism.[21] In particular, ladies of the upper classes and women relatives of the humanists profited from the humanist curriculum. In Italy, Isotta Nogarola, Laura Cereta, and Cassandra Fidele, among others, were esteemed for their learning.[22] The reputation of Cassandra Fidele spread far and wide, prompting Queen Isabella of Spain to invite her to her court and the Venetian senate, in turn, to proscribe her departure because she was deemed "too valuable" to lose.[23] In Spain, Isabella's Latin tutor,

Beatriz Galindo, famed for her learning, founded schools and may have written a commentary on Aristotle, while the Portuguese court also boasted a woman Latin tutor, Luisa Sigea, who penned a letter to Pope Paul III in five languages.[24] In France the literary salons of Catherine de Medicis and Marguerite of Navarre attracted leading poets and scholars; Marguerite of Navarre, educated with her brother Francis, the future king of France, was herself polyglot and wrote in many genres; the Dames des Roches consciously dedicated their lives to the pursuit of learning, and the Lyonnese school boasted such learned women as Louise Labé and Pernette Du Guillet. In England, Queen Elizabeth's philological training and knowledge of the classics dazzled the ambassadors at her court, and the erudition of Lady Jane Gray, Mary Sidney, and Margaret More Roper, to mention only a few, was eulogized by their contemporaries. Margaret Roper's philological expertise, for example, enabled her to offer an emendation to a passage in Saint Cyprian.[25] Katerina Jagellonica, queen of Sweden, demonstrated perhaps the widest linguistic range among Europe's rulers by corresponding with facility in seven languages.[26] Margaret of Austria and Louise of Savoy, both avid readers of the classics, ruled their realms with political and administrative acumen and their literary salons with erudition and wit. In Germany, Caritas Pirckheimer corresponded with the leading humanists of her day, and Margaret Peutinger corrected Erasmus on biblical texts.[27] In Central and Eastern Europe women (usually professed in orders) did much of the translating and copying work essential for the creation of literary vernaculars. Indeed, the growing emphasis on the education of women was reflected in the foundation in the early sixteenth century of a new order, the Ursulines, which was exclusively devoted to teaching girls.

How did education for women of the Renaissance differ from that for men and from medieval teaching? With slight variations, Renaissance curricula were the same for men and women (Latin, Greek, some Hebrew, some of the more useful vernaculars, a study of the classics, the Church Fathers, history, moral philosophy, poetry, grammar, music, some math, and some astrology) but differed in goal, application, and emphasis. For men, the goals of education were almost invariably public; for women, private.

Renaissance education for women also differed from that of the Middle Ages in scope and availability. Early medieval educational treatises written for a female audience as Saint Aldhelm's *De Virginitate* were usually addressed to nuns and stressed the importance of learning as secondary only to the monastic ideals of chastity and obedience.[28] Literacy and learning were the monopolies of convents and convent schools. Indeed, as Joan M. Ferrante observes, "religious schools produced virtually all the great intellectual women of the Middle Ages."[29] In the thirteenth and fourteenth centuries, profane didactic works written for women, such as Durand de Champaigne's *Speculum dominarum* and Robert of Blois's *Le Chastiement des dames,* made their appearance, which combined instruction in courtly behavior, social mores, grooming, and etiquette with Christian doctrine.[30] Almost all stressed a woman's social and religious duties to the detriment of "book learning" and strove to establish a religious foundation for moral behavior. Literacy had little or no place in such education, and authors like Philippe of Novare (1260) repeatedly stressed that only nuns should be taught how to read and write.[31] By the fourteenth century literacy was deemed while not essential, at least permissible. The Knight of La Tour Landry (1372), author of an educational treatise, even though most concerned with the reputation and marriageability of his daughters, did however encourage their reading so that they may learn from the exemplary lives of the saints.[32] Reflecting on the moral value of literacy, he says: "Hit is a noble and faire thinge for a man or a woman to see and beholde hem-self in the mirrour of auncient stories, the which hathe ben wretin bi oure Aunsetters forto shewe us good ensaumples that thei dede, to leue and to eschewe the euell."[33] In sum, education for secular women was utilitarian and private; it aimed at bringing girls up to be chaste, humble, and pious; literacy, when permitted, was placed in the service of moral improvement. On the other hand, excellent educational opportunities existed for some medieval women in the convents and occasionally at courts: "I study Latin grammar, I say my prayers and I write," says Saint Bridget, and, according to the saint's biography, the Virgin Mary declared that she should not give up any of these occupations.[34]

The late medieval/early Renaissance pioneer of advocating education for women, both lay and religious, was—not surprisingly—a woman: Christine de Pizan, a fourteenth-century French writer of Italian descent and the first woman in the West to make a living by her pen.[35] She is often identified as one of the first feminist thinkers and the initiator, as Joan Kelly remarks, of "a 400-year-old tradition of women thinking about women and sexual politics in European society."[36] "Feminist theorizing arose in the fifteenth century," Kelly adds, "in intimate association with and in reaction to the new secular culture of the modern European state."[37] Painfully aware of the fact that she was isolated in her intellectual pursuits in fourteenth-century France, Christine de Pizan emphatically asserted the potential intellectual equality of the sexes. In *The City of Ladies* (I.27.1) she says: "If it were customary to send little girls to school and to teach them the same subjects as are taught to boys, they would learn just as fully and would understand the subtleties of all arts and sciences. Indeed maybe they would understand them better. . . . If they understand them less it is because they do not go out and see so many different places and things but stay home and mind their own work. For there is nothing which teaches a reasonable creature so much as the experience of many different things."[38] Thus Christine cogently distinguishes between the two chief elements leading to the realization of one's full intellectual potential: the opportunity for education on the one hand, and the opportunity for experience and application on the other. The public (male) and private (female) spheres of daily life, she suggests, foster unequal intellectual developments.[39]

Education was of central interest to the Renaissance humanists, and their great contribution of making learning available to women cannot be overestimated. Theoretically, equal education was advocated for both sexes and for all social classes, but practically, formal education was restricted to the daughters, wives, and sisters of learned men, and to women of the nobility and the upper bourgeoise. Moreover, the emphasis on learning not for its own sake but as a means of moral improvement (or even for Castiglione's "pleasing affability") is almost omnipresent in the educational treatises written by men for women, underscoring, thus, a continuity of purpose with the medieval tradition. Erasmus stresses the importance of education (*Christiani matrimonii institutio* 17) for moral goals because "study busies the entire soul—it is not only a weapon against idleness but also a means of impressing the best precepts upon the girl's mind and of leading her to virtue."[40] Thomas More, similarly, joins moral probity with woman's learning:

> Since erudition in women is a new thing and a reproach to the sloth of men, many will gladly assail it. . . . If a woman (and this I desire and hope with you as their teacher for all my daughters) of eminent virtue of mind should add even moderate skill in learning, I think she will gain more real good than if she obtain the riches of Croesus and the beauty of Helen. Not because that learning will be a glory to her, though learning will accompany virtue as a shadow does a body, but because the reward of wisdom is too solid to be lost with riches or perish with beauty since it depends on the inner knowledge of what is right. (Letter 105)[41]

In addition, both emphasize the importance of woman's education as an aid in rearing and instructing children competently at an early age. As Ruth Kelso observes, "The training of the well-born girl was directed in every respect . . . toward fitting her to become a wife. . . . Marriage alone was held the proper vocation for women mainly because she was fitted only to learn the duties that belonged to her as a sort of junior partner to her husband."[42] Leonardo Bruni (1369–1444), in a treatise on the education of the daughter of Battista Montefeltro Malatesta, recommends the whole field of the new learning for women, making only one notable exception, the study of rhetoric. He maintains: "It was not decorous to see women speaking in public or taking on public functions. Study was perfectly appropriate to women but not the public display of learning."[43] Vives, in his influential *Instruction of a Christian Woman* (1523), stresses the importance of learning as a path to acquiring and maintaining feminine virtues—that is, chastity, modesty, plain living, and obedience to a husband.[44] For this very reason he advises against the reading of chivalric romances and books about erotic love. While most humanists consider the education of women as beneficial mostly in the private sphere, it is Agrippa d'Aubigné (1552–1630) who explicitly joins the public/private applications of female learning to the considerations of social standing. He draws a distinction between the desirability of education for upper-class ladies and others and warns against the "pitfalls" of education that waylay girls of the middle estate. In a letter to his daughters he writes:

> My daughters, your brother has brought you my summary of Logic in French, "Logic for girls," as M. de Boillon calls it. I am letting you have it on condition that you make use of it only for yourselves and not against your companions or superiors, as it is dangerous for women to use such things against their husbands. Moreover, I recommend that you conceal its art and terminology, . . . I do not blame your eagerness to learn with your brothers, but I would be loath either to discourage or encourage you. Still, if anything I would be more inclined to the former than the latter. . . .
>
> I have just given you my opinion of the advantages that women may derive from a superior education. However, I have nearly always found that such preparation turned out to be useless for women of middling rank like yourselves, for the more wretched among them rather abused than used their education, while the others, finding that their labor had been useless, bore out the common saying that when the nightingale has little ones, it sings no more. There is the fact, moreover, that a disproportionate elevation of the mind is very apt to breed pride. I have seen two bad effects issue from this: (1) contempt for housekeeping, for property, and for a husband less clever than oneself, and (2) discord. And so I conclude that I would be most reluctant to encourage girls to pursue book learning unless they were princesses, obliged by their rank to assume the responsibilities, knowledge, competence, administration, and authority of men. Then doubtless, as in the case of Queen Elizabeth, an education can stand girls in good stead.[45]

Education, Agrippa concludes, is useful for women in high (public) position, such as Queen Elizabeth and Marguerite of Navarre (who, as rulers, were legally considered men), but rather dangerous to women of less elevated birth and in the domestic sphere.

The exception to the general rule is provided by Agrippa of Nettelsheim ("De nobilitate et praecellentia foeminei sexus declamatio"), who affirms the absolute intellectual equality—regardless of sphere of application—of both sexes: "Women and men were equally endowed with the gifts of spirit, reason, and the use of words; they were created for the same end, and the sexual difference between them will not confer a different destiny."[46] In sum, while for the male humanists an awareness of and participation in political life and civic activities, including scholarship, constituted the goals of education, for women other than those of the highest nobility receiving a humanist education, such masculine goals were often irrelevant because they were unattainable. Though exceptions did exist. In Italy learned women such as Isotta Nogarola and Cassandra Fidele were chosen to deliver public addresses and the chair for Greek in Heidelberg may have been given to the Italian Fulvia Morate Olympia as was the chair of rhetoric to the Spanish Caterina Ribera at Salamanca and Alcala. But these were exceptions. Professional careers for women were great rarities up until the late eighteenth and early nineteenth centuries.[47]

Education for women of less elevated status was little changed from that of the Middle Ages. As a fifteenth-century Florentine bookseller observes, there were two rules for the behavior of women: "One: to bring up her children piously, and two: to be quiet in church, to which I myself would like to add: to be quiet everywhere else also."[48]

This strong "functional" distinction between the educational opportunities of royal and aristocratic ladies on the one hand and those of the rest of womankind on the other not only reflects the power-dynamics of historic reality but also addresses itself to the question of whether or not women indeed had a Renaissance. Never before (and seldom thereafter) was Europe ruled by so many learned ladies: Elizabeth of England, Mary of Scotland, Marguerite of Navarre, Catherine de Medicis and Louise of Savoy in France, Margaret of Austria, Mary of Hungary and Margaret of Parma in the Netherlands, Elizabeth of Hungary, Catherina Cornaro, queen of Cyprus, Eleanor of Aragon and Isabella of Spain. Some of the Italian principalities, too, were sometimes governed by ladies, among them, Veronica Gambara, Isabella d'Este, and Catherine Sforza. All these female rulers were exemplars of the new humanistic learning—stateswomen, patrons of the arts and writers, translators, writers, builders, educators, administrators, and peacemakers:[49] Elizabeth of England and Margaret of Austria, for example, counted the maintenance (or conclusion) of peace in their territories as their greatest triumphs. Indeed, the negotiation of the peace of Cambrai, also known as the Ladies Peace (since it was concluded by Margaret of Austria, Louise of Savoy, and Marguerite of Navarre), reminds one of Christine de Pizan's observation that queens and female regents are better suited than kings for making peace.[50]

Education, however, did not make these women queens or princesses. Study and formal training enabled them to develop their intellectual potential, but the future of that potential was predicated at and by birth.

Women of the "middling rank" or of the lower estates, on the other hand, lacked such opportunities, and neither group was free to pursue unidirectionally learning and scholarship. The meteoric rise of some men's careers, such as Sir Thomas More's through learning, from lawyer's son to royal chancellor, or Shakespeare's, through poetic talent from glover's son to court dramatist, is unparalleled when compared to the lives of Renaissance women scholars and writers. Very little, if any, opportunity existed in the power structure of Renaissance courts, principalities, universities, or professional organizations for the woman scholar to rise above her born position through education and intellectual accomplishments. Normality for her was tied to her sexual and social roles rather than to her mental abilities. Faced with these restrictions, fifteenth- and sixteenth-century women writers were nevertheless able to stretch their roles so as to encompass some of their talents. Mary Sidney, for example, used her role as translator and patron to foster the Reformist cause and to establish the cult of her brother as a Protestant martyr.[51] Marguerite of Navarre extended her protection toward reformers and expressed some "subversive" ideas in her *Miroir,* much to the dismay of the doctors at the Sorbonne.

As during the Middle Ages, so during the Renaissance, the most forceful and comprehensive arguments for equal education for men and women, as well as the advocacy of learning for learning's sake (rather than as the means to a moral end), come from the pen of women, women euphorically enthusiastic about the new freedom and autonomy that the availability of education provided. Significantly, these arguments most often took the form of a polemic; invariably they were penned by literate women of the new secular culture. Louise Labé, Laura Cereta, and the Dames des Roches, all advocate learning for women in attacks on women who scorn this opportunity and Maria de Zayas y Sotomayor embeds it in a polemic on the marital state. "Since a time has come," Louise Labé says, "when the strict laws of men no longer prevent women from applying themselves to the sciences and other disciplines, it seems to me that those of us who can should use this long-craved freedom to study and to let men see how greatly they wronged us when depriving us of its honor and advantages. And if any woman becomes so proficient as to be able to write down her thoughts let her do so and not despise the honor but rather flaunt it instead of fine clothes, necklaces and rings."[52] To Labé, as Anne Larson observes, "learning for women is not restricted to the bookish erudition, ornamental and passive in character, which was advertised for the courtly lady. Nor does she recommend learning solely to improve one's morals as did the majority of Renaissance humanists who favored female education. Her conception encompasses the Renaissance ideals of fame and freedom derived from liberal studies."[53]

In Italy the learned Laura Cereta vehemently attacks her own critics in particular and the misogynists in general with ferocity, and she provides us with some of the most rhetorically polished and cogently argued defenses of education for—and the educability of—women. She writes:

> You brashly and publicly not merely wonder but indeed lament that I am said to possess as fine a mind as nature ever bestowed upon the most learned man. You seem to think that so learned a woman has scarcely before been seen in the world. You are wrong on both counts, Sempronius, and have clearly strayed from the path of truth and disseminate falsehood. . . . You pretend to admire me as a female prodigy, but there lurks sugared deceit in your adulation. . . . I would have been silent, believe me, if that savage old enmity of yours had attacked me alone. For the light of Phoebus cannot be befouled even in the mud. But I cannot tolerate your having attacked my entire sex. For this reason my thirsty soul seeks revenge, my sleeping pen is aroused to literary struggle, raging anger stirs mental passions long chained by silence. With just cause I am moved to demonstrate how great a reputation for learning and virtue women have won by their inborn excellence, manifested in every age as knowledge, the (purveyor) of honor. Certain, indeed, and legitimate is our possession of this inheritance, come to us from a long eternity of ages past. . . . All of history is full of these examples. Thus your nasty words are refuted by these arguments, which compel you to concede that nature imparts equally to all the same freedom to learn.
>
> Only the question of the rarity of outstanding women remains to be addressed. The explanation is clear: women have been able by nature to be exceptional, but have chosen lesser goals. For some women are concerned with parting their hair correctly, adorning themselves with lovely dresses, or decorating their fingers with pearls and other gems. Others delight in mouthing carefully composed phrases, indulging in dancing, or managing spoiled puppies. Still others wish to gaze at lavish banquet tables, to rest in sleep, or, standing at mirrors, to smear their lovely faces. But those in whom a deeper integrity yearns for virtue, restrain from the start their youthful souls, reflect on higher things, harden the body with sobriety and trials, and curb their tongues, open their ears, compose their thought in wakeful hours, their minds in contemplation, to letters bonded to righteousness. For knowledge is not given as a gift, but is gained with diligence. The free mind, not shirking effort, always soars zealously toward the good, and the desire to know grows ever more wide and deep. It is because of no special holiness, therefore, that we women are rewarded by God the giver with the gift of exceptional talent. Nature has generously lavished its gifts upon all people, opening to all the doors of choice through which reason sends envoys to the will, from which they learn and convey its desires. The will must choose to exercise the gift of reason.[54]

Laura Cereta thus raises several problems facing learned women in the Renaissance. She delights in the fact that women can now avail themselves of education, but she strongly attacks the latent misogyny that prompts men to look upon learned women as prodigies, as isolated phenomena in the otherwise arid desert of female stultitude. Her eloquent defense of her sex, prompted by outrage, anticipates Virginia Woolf's reflections on the female creative genius and defies conventional wisdom and conventional authority by invoking the authority of *women's* past—the "long eternity" of female accomplishments.

Laura Cereta's text is rhetorical and conventional in its vitriolic denunciation of men who malign, belittle, or envy women; its Juvenalian sarcasm places the letter in the tradition of the vitriolic diatribe, and its inclusion of *exempla in bono* of female accomplishments from the past, reminiscent of Christine de Pizan's catalog, represents a clever fusion of the *de claris mulieribus* and the polemic traditions. Such a fusion, ostensibly a refutation of the conventional *exempla in malo* of female perfidy in misogynistic works, became a favorite mode of presenting the Renaissance *querelle des femmes* and advocating (predominantly in works penned by women) a full range of educational opportunities for women. Defying conventional (misogynistic) wisdom and hierarchical authority, these women writers construct their own *auctoritates* in cities of illustrious women from the past and the present. Their exempla of virtuous and erudite women illustrate the strengths, intelligence, and excellent qualities that the long tradition of misogynistic writers claimed *all* women lacked. These catalogs challenge authority by challenging the stereotype; they call patristic authorities into question by challenging the assumptions that their images of women, because they are familiar, are natural or necessarily true. Doing so, they inspire rethinking and reconsideration and perhaps even revision of the traditional view of women. Maria de Zayas y Sotomayor, writing at a later date but voicing the same concerns, begins her introduction to the first collection of her short stories by paying tribute to the illustrious women of the past and by expressing her dismay that in Spain, women's potential for writing had hitherto not been allowed to develop. In a charmingly visual passage and with a penchant for irreverent humor, she asserts the potential equality of the sexes (II.104): "But believe me that even if women are not Homers with skirts and petticoats or Virgils with chignons, at least they have the same souls, abilities, and feelings as men."[55] She also reflects on social conditioning (I.22.65): "The true reason that women are not learned is lack of opportunity, not lack of ability. . . . If in their education they were given books and preceptors rather than fine linens, working cases and sketches for embroidery frames, then they would be as capable as men of filling official posts and university chairs."[56] Zayas, like Laura Cereta, goes beyond advocating education for women and attacks the customs and institutions, as well as the men who propagated them, that misused their authorities by keeping women ignorant.

Men are not the sole targets of the woman scholar's ire. Laura Cereta, even more than the learned women of France, also scorns members of her own sex who disparage learned women and whose "empty-headed babbling" reeks of venomous envy: "One becomes disgusted with human failings and grows weary of these women who (trapped in their own mental predicament) despair of attaining possession of human arts when they could easily do so with the application of skill and virtue. For letters are not bestowed upon us or assigned to us by chance. Virtue only is acquired by ourselves alone; nor can those women ascend to serious knowledge who, soiled by the filth of pleasures, languidly rot in sloth. For those women the path to the knowledge is plain who see that there is certain honor in exertion, labor, and wakefulness."[57] Here she equates virtue with intellectual pursuits, and with personal autonomy, and with the laborious but rewarding process of acquiring knowledge.

Laura Cereta's letters summarize the major problems and aspirations of women humanists of the Renaissance: she observes that learned women had to face the authority of centuries of misogynistic literature—attitudes that prompted men to view them either as prodigies or as unnatural monsters unless, of course, their scholarly and creative energies were chaneled into religious or domestic outlets or into works traditionally considered female, such as translations and devotional texts.[58] Within those confines, their erudition lost its threat, and competition and/or envy could yield to paternalizing; without, their learning was deemed to foster promiscuity. Isotta Nogarola's anonymous accuser coined the maxim *nullam eloquentem esse castam,* which was to echo perennially in the attacks on learned single secular women.[59] It is not coincidental but rather a manifestation of the mirror phenomenon of the male gaze that Margaret More Roper, one of England's most learned women, was best known to posterity as the dutiful and loving daughter of Sir Thomas More rather than as an intellectual, that learned women such as Isotta Nogarola and Cassandra Fidele were more often praised for their chastity and virtue than for their erudition,[60] and that Louise Labé has generated avid critical interest, not because of her poetic genius or educational theories, but because of her romanticized biography.

Especially in Italy but to a lesser degree also north of the Alps, few learned women continued their studies after marrying. "Most were," as Patricia Lebalme observes, "like Ginevra Nogarola who gave up her studies when she gave up her *manus immaculata,* that immaculate hand with which she had copied ancient texts."[61] Those, on the other hand, who chose to continue their studies rather than marry did so at the inordinate cost of withdrawal from the world. As Margaret King points out, "The freedom of solitude permitted, in some cases, the learned woman to develop intellectual capacities—but that freedom . . . was purchased at the cost of solitude."[62] Distrust of single women was not restricted to learned ladies; during the witch crazes of the sixteenth and seventeenth centuries throughout the Holy Roman Empire illiterate women and poor widows and spinsters were persecuted in disproportionately much larger numbers than married women.[63]

Louise Labé, the Dames des Roches, and Laura Cereta boldly assess the learned woman's aspirations and responsibilities. Learning is a source of individuality, freedom, and everlasting pleasure; it leads to the attainment of *virtus*, virtue in the full humanist (and masculine) sense of intellectual and moral strength. Women must take advantage of the new opportunities for learning and demonstrate their worth by serious and sustained study, hard work and self denial, in order to reap the fruits of learning and thus gain honor and glory.

A SECOND and equally important phenomenon that was to affect the lives and writings of women during the Renaissance was the Reformist movement. The Protestant Reformation, articulating the resentments and aspirations of many people throughout Europe, found women participating in its political and economic turmoil. As had been the case in the early days of Christianity during the period of Christianization of the Germanic tribes and in the medieval reform movements, women were welcomed in the initial stages but were excluded from the decision-making process as soon as the movement triumphed and became institutionalized.[64] Both Martin Luther and John Calvin abhorred the idea that women might become ecclesiastical (as opposed to merely sacramental) participants in the church; only the Anabaptists—themselves universally persecuted and labeled as radicals—admitted all members, whether men or women, to priesthood.[65]

Luther's views on celibacy and monasticism and his high opinion of the married estate had complex repercussions for women. Those women who abandoned their convents left more than their vows behind them: monasticism had provided a certain autonomy and opportunity for women who, when leaving their convents, relinquished their positions of spiritual leadership and their opportunities for undisturbed devotion to religious and intellectual endeavors. On the other hand, for some women the Protestant Reformation did open avenues of influence in the secular world. Protestant ministerial households, as Clark and Richardson observe, "became the cultural, intellectual and social centers of their communities, providing models of human life which could be emulated by others. In these families, the wife and husband were partners. . . . Although these ministers' wives were hardly the independent professional women we admire today, they were the first of the non-aristocratic women to have an acknowledged position in secular life."[66]

Relying on the Old Testament depiction of the "Woman of Valor,"

Luther himself sketches a charming (albeit very busy) picture of the ideal burgher wife in his encomium on the wedded state:

> A pious, God-fearing wife is a rare treasure, more noble and precious than a pearl. Her Husband relies on her and trusts her in every respect. She gives him joy and makes him happy. . . . She handles flax and wool, likes to work with her hands; she benefits the house and resembles the merchant's ship which brings many goods from far-away countries. She rises early, feeds her servants and gives to the maids what is their due. She likes working and caring for what concerns her and does not busy herself with what is not her concern. She girds her loins and stretches her arms, works with energy in the house. She notices what is convenient and prevents damages. Her light is not extinguished at night. She puts her hand to the distaff and her fingers grip the spindle; she works with pleasure and diligence.[67]

Clearly the picture he presents is of an admirable helpmate and obedient lifelong partner to her husband whose activities are circumscribed by domesticity, a domesticity that, in contrast to medieval views, was greatly exalted. For Luther, as for the other reformers, the worth of woman was inextricably tied to her role of faithful wife and mother: "To bring up the children and to look after the house," he says, "these are the tasks to which she has been called, has been created by God."[68] Thus the urban Protestant schools that flourished in Germany in the sixteenth century could maintain, as did the one in Brunswick, that they would teach girls to be "useful, skillful, friendly, obedient, God-fearing and not self-willed housewives."[69] Even more than Luther, Calvin stressed the purpose of women as that of being companions to their husbands. As G. H. Tavard observes, however, while Calvin "teaches the companionship of man and woman, he maintains the subservience of woman to man."[70] She should be treated as a minor and should stay at home whether she is virgin, wife, or widow.[71] As in the Catholic tradition, domestic virtues were stressed and piety was singled out as a particularly feminine virtue in the Protestant setting. As a result, in the spheres of devotional literature, women were encouraged to express that piety by writing and translating.

EDUCATION, talent, experience, religious and political zeal, and emotional need largely determine the scope and nature of the artist's work. Social and/or functional identity, however, is also a determining factor. The women writers presented in this volume fall accordingly into six categories: the *grande dame,* the woman scholar, the nun, the religious or political activist, the *cortigiana onesta,* and the patrician. By and large, *grande dames* wrote secular and even public works, with lyric poetry, letters, translations, orations, and novelistic texts predominating, though some, notably Marguerite of Navarre and Vittoria Colonna, did compose devotional poems and Elizabeth I penned several homilies. By and large, they wrote in the vernacular, and almost invariably they were held in high literary esteem by their contemporaries. Second, the woman scholar, occupying perhaps the most Renaissance of the six categories, was almost invariably related to a literary man and was frequently of well-to-do but not necessarily aristocratic descent. Renaissance women scholars devoted themselves to philological pursuits: translations, essays, letters, dialogues, and even invectives, both in Latin and the vernacular. It is this group, together with the writers of the urban patriciate (that is, women for whom humanist education was not a matter of self-evident necessity) that seems most concerned with educational opportunities for women and with the obligations women have to take advantage of these new opportunities. Women scholars were occasionally attacked and ridiculed, and they were the most vociferous advocates that women should learn for learning's sake. Third, the nun, the major representative of medieval women writers, no longer occupied that preeminent position in Renaissance letters. Writing in Latin and the vernacular, she came from all social classes and her compositions include not only visions, revelations, and *vitae*, as in the Middle Ages, but also translations, biographies, and autobiographies. Fourth, the *cortigiana onesta,* the Italian Renaissance brand of the Greek hetaira, exemplifies the single woman's other alternative. Cultured, though rarely if ever of aristocratic descent, she most often wrote vernacular lyric poetry. Fifth, the religious political activist, militant descendant of the medieval Margery Kempe, often belonged to the urban poor, invariably wrote in the vernacular, and was seldom rewarded for her activism and pamphleteering. Finally, the gentlewoman writer: usually a member of the provincial urban patriciate, she was a Renaissance novelty. She is ordinarily learned as well as cultivated, she could be either single or married, she was rarely related to a literary man, and she composed almost always in the vernacular and in a variety of devotional or fictional forms. Conspicuously absent from this catalog of Renaissance women and their writings are the learned commentary or treatise and the original epic or secular drama.

In addition to their awareness of their social and functional identity, women writers, especially those not of the upper aristocracy, were also quite conscious of the relationship of their sex to their work. This concern lends their works a distinctive voice that must be seen in the context of the splintering, doubling effects of the mirror phenomenon, that is, as an incorporation of, as well as reaction to, male aesthetics. Most wrote of themselves as women; they explored their emotions, desires, frustrations, and aspirations in their texts; they advocated learning and even ecclesiastical ministry for women; they wrote defenses of women and elaborate catalogs of famous ladies and of female accomplishments of the past and the present. Even those women who eschewed direct and ostensible literary interest in women exhibited awareness of this relationship; they knew what they could or could not write. Margaret Tyler, translator of popular Spanish Catholic works, for example, protested the view that "women were intellectually unfit for anything but translation,"[72] and Anne Locke, translating Taffins's *Markes of the Children of God,* introduced her text by saying, "But because great things by reason of my sexe, I may not doe, and that which I may, I ought to doe, I have according to my duety, brought my poore basket of stones to the strengthening of the wals of that Jerusalem, wherof (by Grace) we are both Citizens and members."[73] Women were particular citizens and members of the Renaissance world, and their literary aspirations, albeit inherently ambiguous and restricted by the limited number of opportunities and modes of expression available to them, do leave us fascinating glimpses of the world of the fifteenth and sixteenth centuries.

BEFORE ADDRESSING the contribution women writers made to Renaissance literature, perhaps we should remind ourselves of the changing criteria of literary canonization. Much of what was considered the best of Renaissance letters was derivative in some sense. The sweeping prestige of classical antiquity, of the conventions of Petrarch, Boccaccio, and of Ficinian Neoplatonism fostered adaptations and reworkings of these sources. Classical erudition was deemed the fundamental prerequisite for literary endeavors; education and philological training, therefore, were necessarily the cornerstones of the canonized writer's literary path. By extension, editions, abridgements, collections, and adaptations were considered crowning achievements of humanist learning and literary skill, and translations and paraphrases were deemed useful and important endeavors. The many women translators, most well born, who wrote during the Renaissance, were profusely praised by their contemporaries. Translation, by and large, was considered a "feminine" (because nonoriginal) endeavor, best suited for women.[74] But Renaissance women translators, while discouraged from composing original texts, did often authenticate their works—if perhaps only marginally—by adding or shifting emphasis, coining new terms, extending metaphors, omitting phrases, and successfully adapting the source language into their native idiom. They played seminally important roles in creating the literary vernaculars. Mary Sidney, the countess of Pembroke, and Lady Ann Bacon, for example, were recognized for helping to forge the English literary vernacular in their translations, and Ann Bacon's translations continued to be used by the Anglican Church as standard texts well into the twentieth century; Elizabeth of Nassau Saarbrücken (1379–1456) and Eleonore of Austria (1433–1480) are credited with refining German courtly language by their translations of chivalric romances;[75] Margaret More Roper's translation of More's *De tristitia* won her almost universal acclaim; and Lea Ráskai's many translations of hagiographic and other sources not only aided lay piety but helped to establish Hungarian as a literary language.

Other works, perhaps considered derivative today, brought Renaissance women writers the same acclaim as they would have brought to male authors. Catherine des Roches's adaptation of Xenophon's *Panthee* was widely praised,[76] Katharina of Ostheim's abridgment of the *Chronicles of Limburg* and Countess Mathilda's collection of German poetry were hailed by their contemporaries as important achievements.[77] Marguerite of Navarre's quite radical adaptation of Boccaccio's *Decameron* and Maria de Zayas y Sottomayor's version of Marguerite's *Heptameron* were not considered any less immediate or fresh simply because they were based on well-known sources; nor would Renaissance critical theory fault them for it. The lyric poets, finally, working within the strict confines of the Petrarchan or Latin elegiac conventions, while also operating within the critical tenets of their age, left us personal expressions of their experience and imagination.

Not surprisingly, the most authentic and individual voices (at least in the modern sense) presented in this volume are the works of lesser known women of nonaristocratic descent and of lesser education. The scathing and passionate lines of Marie Dentière, the realism of Anna Owena Hoyers, the almost militant polemics of Anna Bijns, and the quotidian accounts of Helene Kottanner are far removed from the polished lines of their wealthier, better educated, and higher born sisters, but they appeal to modern sensibilities precisely because of their untamed vigor of expression and artless vitality.

Did women writers have a Renaissance during the Renaissance? Judged by the traditional definition of the availability of education, the secularization of instruction, the study of the classical past, the manifold opportunities of expression, and the emphasis on individuality, the answer to this question depends more on the woman's social position and familial circumstances than on her sex. The question, phrased in this conventional mold, however, does not address one of the most important aspects of education: its goals and the opportunities it provides. For those women who had a living of five hundred a year and "book-lined" cells of their own, Renaissance education provided a stupendous opportunity for personal and intellectual growth, a means for the realization of their potential; their decisions to write and to publish were their own and went beyond the expectations placed upon them. For those women, on the other hand, whose intellectual aspirations were generously fostered by the humanist learning but who were not born to public positions, scholarly endeavors frequently came to an abrupt halt when adulthood set in. No institutional and seldom personal patronage were available to single secular women, nor were the customary paths of administrative or advisory careers open to them. Ecclesiastical sponsorship of predominantly devotional literature by women was, as in the Middle Ages, a viable alternative for women, but the Renaissance shift from the educational protectorate of monastic institutions to royal and seignorial courts or enlightened home tutoring did not necessarily carry over into subsequent secular career opportunities. The learned Cassandra Fidele wrote as she reached her twenties:

> As for the utility of letters, enough said. Not only is this divine field, abundant and noble, amply useful, but it offers its copious, delightful, and perpetual fruits profusely. Of these fruits I myself have tasted a little and have esteemed myself in that enterprise more than abject and hopeless; and, armed with distaff and needle—women's weapons—I march forth to defend that belief that even though the study of letters promises and offers no reward for women and no dignity, every woman ought to seek and embrace these studies for that pleasure and delight alone that comes from them.[78]

In addition to the private pleasure derived from learning that, even if it afforded no professional rewards, could be the source of private satisfaction, those women in comfortable circumstances or those whose militant reformist or antireformist zeal could be employed in religious polemics who aspired to write, could do so and, in doing so, were often able to burst the confines placed upon their art.

Participation—any participation—in the shaping of language is social power. The written word as a signifier of status and power, is capable of bestowing parity to male and female in that privileged space. The literary labor of Renaissance women writers thus articulates a desire, however subliminal, for the status and power which that equity implies. Assuming the voice of the poet, engaging in the shaping, defining and ordering of experience, participating in constructing and creating, women of the fifteenth and sixteenth centuries could temporarily offset the hierarchies of gender and become the equals of men in the act of creation. The fruits of their labor, sampled here in the following selections, will, we hope, whet the appetite for more.

NOTES

1. Many texts have been destroyed or lost. King Henry apparently destroyed all of Dianne of Poitiers's love letters and almost all of her poetry. The poetry of the Renaissance Dubrovnik poet Cvijeta Zuzorić, though well received by her contemporaries, is now completely lost.

2. We have excluded most women writers of the seventeenth century from this collection as we plan a seventeenth-century volume for the near future.

3. Joan Kelly, "Did Women Have a Renaissance?" in *Becoming Visible: Women in European History*, ed. Bridenthal and Koonz, pp. 137–64.

4. Ibid., pp. 140ff.

5. Ibid., pp. 160–61.

6. Silvia Bovenschen, "Is There a Feminine Aesthetic?," trans. Beth Weckmueller, in *Feminist Aesthetics*, ed. Ecker, pp. 27ff.

7. Gary F. Waller, "Struggling into Discourse: The Emergence of Renaissance Women's Writing," in *Silent but for the Word*, ed. Hannay, pp. 238–56.

8. Ibid., p. 245.

9. Ibid.

10. The 1982 interdisciplinary symposium held at Yale University, "Renaissance Woman /Renaissance Man: Studies in the Creation of Culture and Society," for example, discussed such seminally important issues as how the growing power of city councils made it easier for women to enter the labor force in Renaissance Tuscany, or how Queen Elizabeth's cult of chastity reinforced patriarchal structures in Renaissance England.

11. Many excellent national or thematic collections are available. See, for example, *The Paradise of Women: Writings by Englishwomen of the Renaissance*, ed. Betty Travitsky; *Her Immaculate Hand: Selected Works by and About the Women Humanists of Quattrocento Italy*, ed. Margaret L. King and Albert Rabil; *Huit siècles de poésie féminine*, ed. Jeanine Moulin (Paris, 1975); *Deutsche Dichterinnen vom 16. Jahrhundert bis zur Gegenwart*, ed. Gisela Brinker-Gabler; and the abovementioned *Silent but for the Word*.

12. The only woman writer included here who faced constant financial difficulties was the Antwerp schoolmistress Anna Bijns. On feminist aesthetics, see Ecker, ed., *Feminist Aesthetics*.

13. As Ecker observes, the fact that "women took to painting flowers and still lifes (whilst excluded from nude classes); to handling 'useless' household materials in object arrangements (whilst being confined to their environment), that they took to writing drawing-room novels rather than adventure novels and using wool rather than marble; . . . still cannot sustain any essentialist argument" (*Feminist Aesthetics*, p. 16).

14. On the subject of a class-specific and gender-specific discussion of early women writers, see Sheila Delaney, *Writing Women: Women Writers and Women in Literature—Medieval to Modern*.

15. For example, Tiraboschi says: "Nothing shows us so well what was the common enthusiasm in Italy for the cultivation of vernacular poetry as the number of noble ladies who pursued it with such ardor and who valued nothing as much as the title of poet" (cited by Mary Agnes Cannon, *The Education of Women During the Renaissance*, p. 12). And Michelangelo writes to Vittoria Colonna: "O Lady who doeth bear / The soul through flood and fire to a bright shore, / Unto myself let me return no more" (also cited by Cannon, p. 15).

16. On Queen Elizabeth's translation of the *Mirror*, see the intriguing discussion of her omissions and additions by Anne Lake Prescott, "The Pearl of Valois and Elizabeth I: Marguerite de Navarre's *Miroir* and Tudor England," in *Silent but for the Word*, pp. 61–76.

17. On the works and patronage of Mary Sidney, see the following essays in *Silent but for the Word*: Diane Bornstein, "The Style of the Countess of Pembroke's Translation of Philippe de Mornay's *Discours de la vie et de la mort*," pp. 126–48; Margaret P. Hannay, " 'Doo What Men May Sing': Mary Sidney and the Tradition of Admonitory Dedication," pp. 149–65; and Beth Wynne Fisken, "Mary Sidney's *Psalmes*: Education and Wisdom," pp. 166–83.

18. Coburn Freer, the chapter on Mary Sidney in this volume.

19. See Rita Verbrugge, "Margaret More Roper's Personal Expression in the *Devout Treatise upon the Pater Noster*," in *Silent but for the Word*, pp. 30–42.

20. On the *querelle des femmes*, see L. McDowell Richardson, *The Forerunners of Feminism in French Literature of the Renaissance from Christine de Pisan to Marie de Gournay* (Baltimore, 1979). Linda Woodbridge, in *Women and the English Renaissance* (p. 326), offers an interesting observation on why women as a group did not try to assert themselves: "Renaissance women could not take group feminist action partly . . . because of the force of Christian doctrine, the Renaissance reverence for hierarchical authority and horror of civil disobedience . . . and partly because they must have believed what literature said about them. Women may not have dreamed of seeking power through uniting with other women because whenever women were considered as a group, as a sex they were seen to be feeble. Literature repeatedly took refuge in an unexamined paradox: while one bad woman 'shamed her sex' and served as an impetus to general misogyny, one good, strong, self-sufficient woman was dismissed as an exception to the general rule." In *First Feminists: British Women Writers, 1578–1799*, Moira Ferguson discusses several Renaissance women who showed awareness of women as a group and wrote consciously on their behalf.

21. On the Renaissance education of women, see Ruth Kelso, *The Doctrine for the Lady of the Renaissance*; Cannon, *The Education of Women*; and J. R. Brine, ed., *Female Scholars: A Tradition of Learned Women* (Montreal, 1980).

22. See King and Rabil, *Her Immaculate Hand*.

23. Ibid., p. 21.

24. Cannon, p. 55.

25. Verbrugge, "Margaret More Roper," p. 34.

26. Roland H. Bainton, "Learned Women in Europe of the Sixteenth Century," in *Beyond Their Sex: Learned Women of the European Past*, ed. Labalme, p. 171.

27. Cannon, p. 155.

28. "Carmen de virginitate," in *Aldhelm: Opera Omnia*, ed. R. Ehwald (Berlin, 1919).

29. Joan M. Ferrante, "The Education of Women in the Middle Ages in Theory, Fact, and Fantasy," in *Beyond Their Sex*, p. 12.

30. Robert of Blois, *Le Chastiement des dames*, ed. Barhanan, *Fabliaux et contes des poetes Franqois*, vol. 2 (Paris, 1808), pp. 184–219.

31. Philippe of Novare, *Les quatre âges de l'homme* (Paris, 1888).

32. *The Book of the Knight of the Tour Landry*, trans. Thomas Wright, EETS, O.S. 33 (London, 1868), p. 3. See also *The Goodman of Paris*, trans. Eileen Power (London, 1928). While both works emphasize obedience to husbands as the chief wifely virtue and advocate "sheltering" because of woman's innate intellectual weakness, they do see the ability to read as a tool for improving woman's morals.

33. *The Book of the Knight*, p. 4.

34. Cited by Germain Marc h'adour, "Thomas More and His Foursome of Blessed Holy Women," in *Jahrbuch der Thomas Morus Gessellschaft*, ed. Hermann Boventer (Düsseldorf, 1984), p. 123.

35. On Christine, see Charity Cannon Willard, *Christine de Pizan: A Biography* (New York, 1984), and Diane Bornstein, ed., *The Ideals of Women in Christine de Pizan* (Ann Arbor, 1981).

36. Joan Kelly, "Early Feminist Theory and the *Querelle des Femmes, 1400–1789*," p. 5.

37. Ibid.

38. *The Book of the City of Ladies*, trans. Earl Jeffrey Richards (New York, 1982), p. 63. Answering Christine's question as to why women, having equal minds with men, don't learn more, Lady Reason explains: "Because, my daughter, the public does not require them to get involved in the affairs which men are commissioned to execute . . . look at men who farm the flatlands or who live in the mountains. You will find that in many countries they seem

completely savage because they are so simple-minded. All the same, there is no doubt that Nature provided them with the qualities of body and mind found in the wisest and most learned men. All of this stems from a failure to learn. . . . Let me tell you about women who have possessed great learning and profound understanding and treat the question of the similarity of women's minds to men's" (pp. 63–64).

39. On Christine's ideas on education, see also Astrik L. Gabriel, "The Educational Ideas of Christine de Pizan," *Journal of the History of Ideas* 16 (1955): 3–22.

40. In his colloquy between an abbot and a learned woman, Erasmus stresses the importance of woman's learning as an aid to raising children properly (*Not in God's Image*, p. 183). Magdalene asks, "Is not a woman's business to mind the affairs of her family and to instruct her children?" Antonius replies, "Yes, it is." Magdalene says, "And do you think so weighty an office can be performed without wisdom? . . . This wisdom I learn from books."

41. For a discussion of More's ideas on education, see the chapter on Margaret More Roper in this volume.

42. Kelso, p. 78.

43. Bruni, *De studiis et literis*, trans. W. H. Woodward, in *Vittorino de Feltre and Other Humanist Educators: Essays and Versions*, p. 281, says: "To her neither the intricacies of debate nor the oratorical artifices of action and delivery are of the least practical use, if indeed they are not positively unbecoming. Rhetoric in all its forms . . . lies absolutely outside the province of women."

44. On Vives, see Cannon, pp. 78ff. and 107ff.; Foster Watson, *Vives and the Renaissance Education of Women*; and Julia O'Faolain and Lauro Martines, eds., *Women in History from the Greeks to the Victorians*.

45. From Agrippa d'Aubigné, *Oeuvres Complètes*, cited in *Not in God's Image*, p. 186.

46. *Not in God's Image*, p. 184.

47. Cannon, pp. 174, 5; Hannelore Sachs, *The Renaissance Woman* (New York, 1977), p. 18.

48. Cited by Sachs, p. 19.

49. In *The City of Ladies*, I.11.1, Lady Reason says to Christine: "In case anyone says that women do not have a natural sense for politics and government, I will give you examples of several great women-rulers who have lived in . . ." And in her letter to Jean de Montreuil, trans. Charity Cannon Willard, in *Medieval Women Writers*, ed. Katharina M. Wilson (Athens, Ga., 1984), p. 343, Lady Reason says: "For even if he and all his accomplices swear to it, let none take offense, there have nevertheless been, are now, and will always be women more valiant, more honest, better bred, and even wiser, and through whom more good has come to the world, than has ever come from him. And some are even more versed in the affairs of state and have more virtuous habits, some have been responsible for reconciling their husbands with their enemies and have borne their affairs . . . gently."

50. On Christine's detailed discussion of women as peacemakers, see *The Treasure of the City of Ladies*, trans. Sarah Lawson (Bungary, 1985), chapter 8.

51. Hannay, " 'Doo What Men May Sing,' " pp. 149–65.

52. From Louise Labé's dedicatory epistle, translated in *Not in God's Image*, p. 185.

53. Anne Larsen, "Louise Labé's *Débat de Folie d'Amour*: Feminism and the Defense of Learning," *Tulsa Studies in Women's Literature* 2, no. 1 (1983): 44.

54. King and Rabil, *Her Immaculate Hand*, pp. 81–84, reprinted with permission of the publisher. On Cereta, see also Margaret King, "Book-Lined Cells: Women and Humanism in the Early Italian Renaissance," in *Beyond Their Sex*, pp. 66–90; Margaret King "Thwarted Ambitions: Six Learned Women of the Italian Renaissance," *Soundings* 59 (1976): 280–304; and Albert Rabil, *Laura Cereta Quattrocento Humanist* (Binghamton, N.Y., 1981).

55. Sandra M. Foa, "Maria de Zayas y Sotomayor: Sibyl of Madrid," in *Female Scholars: A Tradition of Learned Women Before 1800*, ed. Brink, p. 58.

56. Ibid., p. 65.

57. King and Rabil, *Her Immaculate Hand*, pp. 85–86.

58. As Hannay observes in *Silent but for the Word*, pp. 8–9, "Denied the rhetorical training deemed necessary for public office and for original writing, women were encouraged to translate suitable works by men because such activity 'did not threaten the male establishments as the expression of personal viewpoints might.' Translations are 'defective and therefore all translations are reputed females,' John Florio declared, apologizing for his own labor in this degraded activity."

59. King, "Book-Lined Cells," p. 77.

60. See King and Rabil, *Her Immaculate Hand*, p. 12ff.

61. Labalme, p. 6.

62. King, "Book-Lined Cells," p. 69. King reflects on the phenomenon (p. 78): "I would suggest that when learned women (or men for that matter) themselves chose a celibate life, they did so at least in part because they sought psychic freedom; when on the other hand, men urged chastity upon learned women, they did so at least in part to constrain them. These fearful creatures of a third sex threatened male dominance in both the intellectual and the social realm. . . . Learning and chastity were indissolubly linked—for in undertaking the life of learning women repudiated a normal life of reproduction. *She* rejected a sexually active role for the sake of an intellectual life; *he* insisted on her asexuality because by means of intellect she had penetrated a male preserve."

63. On the frightening statistics of the Renaissance witch craze, see *Becoming Visible,* pp. 132–33. On the great disproportion of male to female witches, Jean Bodin (1530–96), a French jurist and magistrate, offers this most disconcerting explanation: "As I remarked before, it is clear from the looks of all who have written on witches that for every male witch there are fifty female witches. . . . In my opinion this is not due to the frailty of the sex—for most of them are intractably obstinate—it is more likely that what reduced them to this extremity was bestial cupidity. . . . And it is likely that this is why Plato placed woman between man and the brute beast. For one sees that women's visceral parts are bigger than those of men whose cupidity is less violent" (*Not in God's Image,* p. 209).

64. See, for example, Sherrin Marshall Wyntjes, "Women in the Reformation Era," in *Becoming Visible,* pp. 165–91. On women and the Reformation, see Roland H. Bainton's *Women of the Reformation,* vols. 1 and 2.

65. In his *Institutes,* Calvin is appalled at the notion of women baptizing, a practice common among Anabaptists (*Not in God's Image,* p. 202): "It is a mockery to allow women to baptize. Even the Virgin Mary was not allowed this."

66. Elizabeth Clark and Herbert Richardson, eds., *Women and Religion: A Feminist Sourcebook of Christian Thought* (New York, 1977), pp. 133–34.

67. "Praise of a Pious Wife," trans. by Sachs, in *The Renaissance Woman,* p. 13.

68. Sachs, p. 19.

69. Ibid., p. 18. In his *Table Talk,* Luther also remarks: "Men have broad shoulders and narrow hips, and accordingly they possess intelligence. Women have narrow shoulders and broad hips. Women ought to stay at home; the way they were created indicates this, for they have broad hips and a wide fundament to sit upon, keep house and bear and raise children" (*Not in God's Image,* pp. 196–97). See also Gerald Straus, *Luther's House of Learning: Indoctrination of the Young in the German Reformation* (Baltimore, 1978). He finds that the elementary training of boys and girls differed little but that professional training for girls of lower classes did not exist.

70. Tavard, p. 176.

71. Calvin especially stresses the importance of woman's domesticity even to the extent of interpreting the rape of Dina in that light. He comments: "Dina is kidnapped and raped because, having left her father's house, she went away and wandered in greater freedom than belonged to her. She should have stayed quietly at home, as the Apostle advises it (Titus 2:5)

and as nature itself teaches it, for this virtue, which a common proverb attributes to women, that they must be keepers of the house, applies to girls. For this reason the fathers are taught to keep their daughters under narrow watch if they want to protect them from all indignity" (cited by Tavard, p. 177).

72. Ferguson, p. 9. In the epistle introducing her translation of *The Mirrour of Princely Deedes and Knyghthood,* Margaret Tyler says: "But to returne whatsowever the truth is, whether that women may not at all discourse in learning, for men late in their claime to be sole possessioners of knowledge, or whether they may in some manner, that is by limitation or appointment in some kinde of learning my perswasion hath bene thus, that it is all one for a woman to pen a storie, as for a man to addresse his storic to a woman. But amongst all my ill willers, some I hope are not so straight that they would enforce me necessarily either not to write or to write of divinitie" (*First Feminists,* p. 56).

73. Cited by Bainton, "Learned Women in the Europe of the Sixteenth Century," p. 118.

74. Nicholas Breton's "An Old Mans Lesson," for example, advises: "If she be learned and studious, perswade her to translation, it will keep her from Idleness and it is a cunninge kinde taske" (cited in *Silent but for the Word,* p. 118).

75. See Brinker-Gabler, *Deutsche Dichterinner,* p. 26.

76. Keating, p. 51.

77. Cannon, p. 155. It was at Countess Matilda's instigation that her husband founded the University of Freiburg and her son the University of Tübingen. 78. Cassandra Fidele, "Oration in Praise of Letters," in *Her Immaculate Hand,* p. 77.

78. Cassandra Fidele, "Oration in Praise of Letters," in *Her Immaculate Hand,* p. 77.

BIBLIOGRAPHY

Adams, Robert P. *The Better Part of Valor: More, Colet, and Vives, on Humanism, War, and Peace, 1496–1535.* Seattle, Wash., 1962.

Bainton, Roland. *Women of the Reformation.* Vol. 1, *Germany and Italy.* Minneapolis, 1971. Vol. 2, *France and England.* Minneapolis, 1973. Vol. 3, *Spain and Scandinavia.* Minneapolis, 1977.

Becker-Contarino, Barbara. *(Social) Geschichte der Frau in Deutschland, 1500–1800: Ein Forschungsbericht.* Bonn, 1980.

Bornstein, Diane, ed. *Distaves and Dames: Renaissance Treatises for and About Women.* New York, 1978.

Bree, Germaine. *Women Writers in France.* New Brunswick, N.J., 1973.

Bridenthal, Renate, and Claudia Koonz, eds. *Becoming Visible: Women in European History.* Boston, 1977.

Brink, J. R. *Female Scholars: A Tradition of Learned Women Before 1800.* Montreal, 1980.

Brinker-Gabler, Gisela, ed. *Deutsche Dichterinnen vom 16. Jahrhundert bis zur Gegenwart.* Frankfurt, 1978.

Bush, Douglas. *Prefaces to Renaissance Literature.* Cambridge, Mass., 1965.

Camden, Caroll. *The Elizabethan Woman.* Houston, New York, and London, 1952.

Cannon, Mary Agnes. *The Education of Women During the Renaissance.* Washington, D.C., 1916. Reprint. 1981.

Carroll, Berenice A., ed. *Liberating Women's History: Theoretical and Critical Essays.* Urbana, Ill., 1976.

Clough, Cecil H., ed. *Cultural Aspects of the Italian Renaissance.* Manchester, Eng., 1976.

Davis, Natalie Zemon. "Gender and Genre: Women as Historical Writers, 1400–1820." In *Beyond Their Sex: Learned Women of the European Past,* ed. Patricia H. Labalme, pp. 153–82. New York and London, 1980.

_____. *Society and Culture in Early Modern France*. Stanford, 1975.

_____. "Women's History in Transition: The European Case." *Feminist Studies* 3 (1975–76): 84–103.

De Jean, Joan, "*The Female Tradition L'Esprit Createur* 23 (1983): 3–8.

De Lamar, Jensen. *Renaissance Europe: Age of Recovery and Renunciation*. Lexington and Toronto, 1982.

Delaney, Sheila. *Writing Women: Women Writers and Women in Literature—Medieval to Modern*. New York, 1983.

Dezon-Jones, Elyane. *Les Ecritures feminines*. Paris, 1983.

Dickens, A. G., ed. *The Courts of Europe: Politics, Patronage and Royalty*. New York, 1977.

Dunn, Catherine M. "The Changing Image of Woman in Renaissance Society and Literature." In *What Manner of Woman: Essays on English and American Life and Literature*, ed. Marlene Springer, pp. 15–38. New York, 1977.

Ecker, Gisela, ed. *Feminist Aesthetics*. Trans. Harriet Anderson. Boston, 1985.

Fahy, Conor. "Three Early Renaissance Treatises on Women." *Italian Studies* 12 (1965): 330–55.

Ferguson, Moira. *First Feminists: British Women Writers, 1578–1799*. Bloomington and Old Westbury, 1985.

Fitz, L. T. "What Says the Married Woman? Marriage Theory and Feminism in the English Renaissance." *Mosaic* 13 (1980): 1–22.

Freundlich, Elizabeth. *Sie wussten was sie wollten. Lebensbilder bedeutender Frauen aus drei Jahrhunderten*. Freiburg, 1981.

Frey, Linda, and J. Schneider, eds. *Women in Western European History: A Select Chronological, Geographical and Topical Bibliography from Antiquity to the French Revolution*. Westport, Conn., 1982.

Gabriel, Astrik L. "The Educational Ideas of Christine de Pisan." *Journal of the History of Ideas* (1955): 3–21.

Geranderie, M. M. de la. "Le Feminisme de Thomas More et d'Erasme." *Moreana* 10 (1966): 23–29.

Gilbert, Sandra, and Susan Gubar. "Sexual Linguistics: Gender, Language, Sexuality." *New Literary History* 16 (1985): 515–43.

Goulianos, Joan. *By a Woman Writt: Literature from Six Centuries by and About Women*. New York, 1973.

Greco, Norma, and R. Novotny. "Bibliography of Women in the English Renaissance." *University of Michigan Papers in Women's Studies* 1 (1974): 29–57.

Greenblatt, Stephen. *Renaissance Self-Fashioning from More to Shakespeare*. Chicago, 1980.

Hageman, Elizabeth H. "Recent Studies in Women Writers of Tudor England, Part 1: Women Writers, 1485–1603, Excluding Mary Sidney, Countess of Pembroke." *English Literary Renaissance* 14 (1984): 409–26.

Haigh, Christopher, ed. *The Reign of Elizabeth I*. Athens, 1985.

Hannay, Margaret P., ed. *Silent but for the Word: Tudor Women as Patrons, Translators, and Writers of Religious Works*. Kent, Ohio, 1985.

Hassauer, Friederike. "Konzept 'weiblicher Asthetik' als Gegenstand der Literaturwissenschaft." *Zeitschrift für Wissenschaft, Kunst und Literatur* 38 (1983): 925–32.

Hogrefe, Pearl. *Tudor Women: Commoners and Queens*. Ames, Iowa, 1975.

Irmscher, Johannes, ed. *Renaissance und Humanismus in Mittel und Osteuropa*. 2 vols. Berlin, 1962.

Jones, Ann Rosalind. "Assimilation with a Difference: Renaissance Women Poets and Literary Influences." *Yale French Studies* 62 (1981): 135–53.

————. "Writing the Body: Towards an Understanding of *L'Escriture Feminisme*." *Feminist Studies* 7 (1981): 247–63.

Kanner, Barbara, ed. *The Women of England from Anglo-Saxon Times to the Present.* Hamden, Conn., 1979.

Keating, Clark L. *Studies on the Literary Salon in France.* Cambridge, Mass., 1941.

Kelly, Joan. *Collected Essays.* Chicago, forthcoming.

————. "Did Women Have a Renaissance?" In *Becoming Visible*, ed. Renate Bridenthal and Claudia Koonz, pp. 139–64. Boston, 1977.

————. "Early Feminist Theory and the *Querelle des Femmes*, 1400–1789." *Signs: Journal of Women in Culture and Society* 8 (1982): 4–28.

————. "Notes on Women in the Renaissance and Renaissance Historiography." In *Conceptual Frameworks for Studying Women's History*, ed. M. Arthur et al., pp. 444–46. Bronxville, N.Y., 1975.

Kelso, Ruth. *Doctrine for the Lady of the Renaissance.* Urbana, Ill., 1956.

King, Margaret L., and Albert Rabil. *Her Immaculate Hand: Selected Works by and About the Women Humanists of Quattrocento Italy.* Binghamton, N.Y., 1983.

Klerk, Peter de, ed. *Renaissance, Reformation, Resurgence: Papers and Responses Presented at the Colloquium on Calvin and Calvin Studies.* Grand Rapids, Mich., 1976.

Krailsheimer, A. J., ed. *The Continental Renaissance.* Harmondsworth, 1971.

Labalme, Patricia H., ed. *Beyond Their Sex: Learned Women of the European Past.* New York and London, 1980.

Maclean, Jan. *The Renaissance Notion of Woman: A Study in the Fortunes of Scholasticism and Medical Science in European Intellectual Life.* Cambridge, Eng., 1980.

Mahl, Mary R. *The Female Spectator: English Women Writers Before 1800.* Bloomington, Ind., 1977.

Moore, Cornelia N. "Die adelige Mutter als Erzieherin: Erbauungs-literatur adeliger Mütter für ihre Kinder." *Europäische Hofkultur im 16. und 17. Jahrhundert*, ed. C. Wiedermann, pp. 505–10. Hamburg, 1981.

O'Faolain, Julia, and Lauro Martines, eds. *Not in God's Image: Women in History from the Greeks to the Victorians.* New York, San Francisco, and London, 1973.

Plowden, Alison. *Tudor Women: Queens and Commoners.* New York, 1979.

Radcliff-Umstead, Douglas. *The Roles and Images of Women in the Middle Ages and Renaissance.* Pittsburgh, 1975.

Richardson, Lula McDowell. *The Forerunners of Feminism in French Literature of the Renaissance.* Baltimore, 1929.

Rogers, Katharine. *The Troublesome Helpmate: A History of Misogyny in Literature.* Seattle and London, 1966.

Rose, Mary Beth, ed. *Women in the Middle Ages and the Renaissance.* Syracuse, N.Y., 1985.

Ruether, Rosemary, ed. *Religion and Sexism: Images of Women in the Jewish and Christian Traditions.* New York, 1974.

Spacks, Patricia Meyer. *The Female Imagination.* New York: Avon, 1972.

Spitz, Lewis W. *The Religious Renaissance of the German Humanists.* Cambridge, Mass., 1963.

Stock, Phyllis. *Better Than Rubies: A History of Women's Education.* New York, 1978.

Stone, Lawrence. *The Family, Sex, and Marriage in England, 1500–1800.* New York, 1977.

Symonds, John Addington. *Renaissance in Italy: Italian Literature.* 2 vols. New York, 1964.

Tavard, George H. *Women in Christian Tradition.* Notre Dame and London, 1973.

Travitsky, Betty, ed. *The Paradise of Women: Writings by Englishwomen of the Renaissance.* Westport, Conn., 1981.

Warnicke, Retha M. *Women of the English Renaissance.* Westport Conn., 1983.

Watson, Foster. *Vives and the Renaissance Education of Women*. London, 1912.

Weissweiler, Eva. *Komponistinnen aus 500 Jahren. Eine Kultur—und Wirkungsgeschichte in Biographien und Werkbeispielen*. Frankfurt, 1981.

Wiesner, Merry E. *Women in the Sixteenth Century: A Bibliography*. Sixteenth-Century Bibliography 23. St. Louis, 1983.

Wilkins, Ernes Hatch. *A History of Italian Literature*. Cambridge, Mass., 1962.

Woodbridge, Linda. *Women and the English Renaissance: Literature and the Nature of Womankind*. Urbana and Chicago, 1984.

Woodward, W. H. *Vittorino do Feltre and Other Humanist Educators: Essays and Versions*. Cambridge, Eng., 1897.

Wright, A. D. *The Counter-Reformation: Catholic Europe and the Non-Christian World*. London, 1982.

PART ONE

taly

APHRODITE'S PRIESTESS, LOVE'S MARTYR

aspara Stampa

FRANK J. WARNKE

Gaspara Stampa, the greatest woman poet of the Italian Renaissance, was born in Padua, probably in 1524. Her father, a jeweler, died while she was still a girl, and her family moved to Venice, where she spent the remainder of her short life. In both her life and her work she provides a dramatic contrast with another prominent woman poet of the time—Vittoria Colonna, great aristocrat and Platonic beloved of Michelangelo. Vittoria was noble; Gaspara bourgeoise. Vittoria was Roman; Gaspara, Venetian. Vittoria was a wife and chatelaine; Gaspara, a courtesan. Vittoria's poems embody the highest ideals of Christian Platonism; Gaspara's poems—except for the relatively small number of poems of Christian repentance with which her *canzoniere* closes—are devoted exclusively to obsessive sexual love, particularly to the torments of its frustration.[1]

In calling Gaspara Stampa a courtesan, I do not imply that she was in any sense an ordinary prostitute. She was, rather, a *cortigiana onesta*, or "respectable courtesan," and as such she enjoyed a social status of some dignity. The *cortigiana onesta* of Renaissance Italy—particularly of Venice, where the institution flourished especially—was a figure in some respects like the hetaira of classical Greece. Endowed not only with physical beauty but also with poetic and musical skills as well as a high degree of cultivation, such a woman did not bestow her favors thoughtlessly or promiscuously; she had dealings only with males from the privileged levels of society, and normally only with one—at least only with one during the period of the liaison. Marriage was not for such women, but in Venice they were admired, indeed respected, and their "protectors" often included great nobles, princes of the Church, and famous writers, painters, and intellectuals.

The institution of the *cortigiana onesta* was perhaps a response to a social situation in which marriage choices were normally determined by commercial or familial considerations rather than by mutual attraction or shared intellectual interest. The relation between *cortigiana* and protector was in some limited respects one of equality: the patron sought in the *cortigiana* intellectual and artistic qualities he would not demand in a wife. It is perhaps for this reason that, during the centuries of the Renaissance and the Baroque, so many distinguished women poets came from the class of the *cortigiane oneste:* it was an identity which, like that of the *grande dame* or the nun, at least made poetic creativity possible.[2]

Gaspara's status as an honest courtesan is not established beyond question. Her twentieth-century editor, Abdelkader Salza, is persuaded of it, but the contention has been hotly disputed by others. Justin Vitiello assumes the truth of the identification, and Fiora A. Bassanese, the author of a recent excellent study of the poet, regards it as possible but not certain beyond any doubt. We know little about Gaspara Stampa's life, and most of what we know comes from her poetry.[3]

We hear of her as a young woman in Venice, where she was, together with her brother Baldassare and her sister Cassandra, an artistic ornament of Venetian society. Baldassare was a poet (some of his work survives), Cassandra was a singer, and Gaspara was both poet and singer. We ought not, however, to picture these activities in twentieth-century terms. Cassandra would not be in a position to get an audition at the Met or a tryout for a Broadway musical, and Baldassare would not likely be offered a job as poet-in-residence at a university. They belonged to the brilliant Venetian demimonde, one populated by aristocrats, by high dignitaries of church and state. Music and poetry were not the only interests of that world.

Venice in the sixteenth century was a city remarkable for its prosperity, its sophistication, its love of luxury and pleasure, and its notable indifference to the more rigorous moral prescriptions of Christianity. It was a city of art and sensuality, and the links between the two were close. Sexuality was one of the pleasures most strenuously pursued by the Venetian upper classes (even the common prostitutes of Venice were famous throughout Europe for their beauty), but the more refined among them sought an ambience where sexuality was fused with art. The fusion of art and sexuality probably explains the presence of the bourgeois Stampa trio in a privileged social milieu.

Gaspara's position as a *cortigiana onesta,* far from subjecting her to opprobrium, assured for her a certain degree of esteem. The complimentary poems praising her beauty and her artistic gifts seem full of sincere admiration—even if they do betray at times a faintly leering quality (and Abdelkader Salza, in his edition, reprints a scurrilous contemporaneous epitaph taxing her with sexual vice).[4] It might well occur that a young

Venetian nobleman, powerful and respected, would establish a liaison
with such a woman—not marriage, to be sure, but nevertheless a liaison
of some solidity, duration, and mutual respect.

Count Collaltino di Collalto was the lover and protector of Gaspara
Stampa. On the evidence of her poems, he found her attractive enough to
be worth his time, and attractive—or importunate—enough to elicit
from him vows of eternal love and fidelity. On the same evidence, he was
the transfiguring love of Gaspara's life—not her first lover, it would seem,
nor her last, and yet her only true love. However obsessive love may have
been for Gaspara, it was not so for Collaltino. For him, apparently, sex
was fine in its place, but it was not nearly as interesting as war. He entered
the service of Henry II of France, who was at that time engaged in a series
of campaigns, and departed, promising to write. He didn't write.

> Hast du der Gaspara Stampa
> denn genügend gedacht, dass irgend ein Mädchen,
> dem der Geliebte entging, am gesteigerten Beispiel
> dieser Liebenden fühlt: dass ich würde wie sie?
> Sollen nicht endlich uns diese ältesten Schmerzen
> fruchtbarer werden? Ist est nicht Zeit, dass wir liebend
> uns vom Geliebten befrein und es bebend bestehn:
> wie der Pfeil die Sehne besteht, um gesammelt im Absprung
> *mehr* zu sein als er selbst. Denn Bleiben ist nirgends.[5]

> Have you thought of her enough,
> Of Gaspara Stampa, and that any girl
> Whose lover has left her might feel the exalted example
> Of that loving woman, and might feel: "May I be like her?"
> Isn't it finally time for these oldest of sorrows
> To become more fruitful for us? Isn't it time
> That we, loving, free ourselves from the beloved,
> And endure it, trembling, as the arrow endures the bow,
> That, collected in its leaping, it may be
> *More* than itself. For staying is no place.[6]

So wrote Rainer Maria Rilke in the first of his *Duino Elegies*
(1912/1922). The figure of Gaspara Stampa, like those of Louise Labé,
Heloise, the Comtesse de Die, Clara d'Anduze, and other women writers,
was of enormous importance for the great German poet. Elsewhere, in his
Aufzeichnungen des Malte Laurids Brigge (*Notebooks of Malte Laurids
Brigge,* 1910), Rilke discusses these figures again. Particularly interesting
is the passage in which he draws a distinction between the *Geliebte* and
the *Liebende*—between the "beloved" and the "loving one": the *Geliebte*
"lives poorly, and always in danger"; the *Liebende* is surrounded by "the
most complete certainty." The loving ones "fling themselves after the lost

one, but with the first step they overtake him, and *in front of* them is only God."[7]

The woman love poet is for Rilke, then, a crucial figure of the love that, transcending itself and any ego, becomes divine. To what extent is this a valid perception, and to what extent Rilke's projection of his own creation? With Gaspara Stampa, at least, it seems that Rilke has commented on what is truly in the text. For Gaspara has learned what Socrates taught to Phaedrus, what Thomas Mann's Aschenbach thinks "perhaps the tenderest, most mocking thought that ever was thought"—that the lover is nearer the divine than is the beloved.[8] Even in the early part of her *canzoniere,* before the abandonment, Gaspara's hyperbolic praises of Collaltino's superiority (for example, "Le doti preclare di lui forono le sue dolci catene") are interspersed with poems that, as Vitiello notes, assert the moral superiority conferred upon her by her pure love.[9]

There is much Petrarch in Gaspara, as in nearly all sixteenth-century love lyricists. The first of her sonnets, for example, is a pastiche of the first of Petrarch's *Rime,* and the second tells how she first saw Collaltino near Christmas, as Petrarch first saw Laura on Good Friday.[10] Given her gender, she is obliged often to modify the conventions of Petrarchanism, and one of the most important of her modifications is her insistence on the motif of the love that elevates the lover above the beloved. The following sonnet makes the point as well as any other:

Se, cosí come sono abietta e vile
donna, posso portar si alto foco,
perché non debbo aver almeno un poco
di ritraggerlo al mondo e vena e stile?

S'Amor con nove, insolite focile,
ov'io non potea gir, m'alzò a tal loco,
perché non puonon con usate gioco
far la pena e la penna in me simile?

E, se non può per forza di natura,
puollo almen per miracolo, che spesso
vince, trapassa e rompe ogni misura.
Come ciò sia non posso dir espresso;
io provo ben che per mia gran ventura
mi sento il cor di novo stile impresso.

If, being a woman so abject and vile,
I nonetheless can bear so high a flame,
Why should I not give to the world the same,
At least in part, in proper wealth and style?

If Love, with a new, unprecedented spark,
Could raise me to a place I could not reach,

Why cannot pain and pen combine to teach
Such arts as, never known, shall find their mark?

And if this does not lie in Nature's art,
Then let it be by miracle, whose power
Can conquer, transcend, and every limit break.
How this may be I cannot say for sure,
But well I know the fortune I partake,
And through it a new style engraves my heart.

It is not Collaltino who has made of Gaspara a poet; it is, rather, her "flame," the surpassing love she bears for him. Gaspara is her own Muse as, according to Robert Graves, Sor Juana Inés de la Cruz and other women poets were theirs.[11] The specific presence of art as theme in this sonnet is suggested by a possible allusion in the last line: the *novo stile* may refer to the *dolce stil novo* formulated by the Italian male poets of the later thirteenth century. The *dolce stil novo*, or "sweet new style," was distinguished by its elegance of diction and versification and by its concentration on the themes of the glorification of the beloved woman, her elevation to the role of spiritual guide, and the consequent ennobling of the spirit of the male lover-poet. Gaspara, in choosing the role of worshiper over that of object of worship, is staking a claim on the domains of art.

Art is, however, only one of her themes, and it would give a false impression of her lyric achievement if one were to imply that the entire *canzoniere* is dominated by that theme. Indeed, the very variety, inconsistency, and contradiction in the sequence bestow upon it its quality as a singularly accurate account of the turmoil of sexual love. In "She Will Be One Day Free; He, Too Late, Repentant," she shifts focus inexplicably, referring to her absent lover in the third person in the initial quatrain, then shifting to a direct address in which she predicts with sadistic glee the sorrows he will one day feel when he repents his cruelty. In "Holy Angels, I Don't Envy You," she compares her joy in seeing Collaltino with the joy felt by the angels on beholding the face of God. The consciously blasphemous identification of the love of God with the love of a human being is a recurrent feature of Gaspara's lyric work; the implied analogy between the speaker and Dante's Francesca is suggested later in the penitential sonnets.

In "She Does Not Fear Amorous Pain, But Rather Its End," the poet expresses her fear, not of the pains of love, but rather of the possibility of their cessation. In "O Great Exploit of Gentle Cavalier," she rages at her absent lover in a bitterly ironic manner, reminding him that his royal master, Henry II of France, does not scorn to follow Venus as well as Mars.

Another sonnet, "Send Back My Heart to Me, Relentless One," is interesting not only as an amorous complaint but also for its identification of Collaltino as her one-time source of "defense"—a term that may imply Gaspara's identity as a *cortigiana onesta*:

Rimandatemi il cor, empio tiranno,
ch'a sí gran torto avete ed istraziate,
e di lui e di me quel proprio fate,
che le tigri e i leon di cerva fanno.

Son pasati otto giorni, a me un anno,
ch'io non ho vostre lettre ed imbasciate,
contra le fé che voi m'avete date,
o fonte di valor, conte, e d'inganno.

Credete ch'io sia Ercol o Sansone
a poter sostener tanto dolore,
giovane e donna e fuor d'ogni ragione,
massimo essendo qui senza 'il mio core
e senza voi a mia difensione,
onde mi suol venir forza e vigore?

Venice plays a specific role in Gaspara's poetry, both as theme and as setting. Her "Elegiac Lament" in terza rima locates the poet specifically in that city on "the rich and blessed Adriatic shores" which is the "nest of love and nest of courtesy," and the sonnet "By Now This Waiting So Has Wearied Me" draws a vivid contrast between the waves of the maritime city—the element, as it were, of the female lover—and the inland hills on which the unfaithful Collaltino enjoys his martial sport. Here, as on several other occasions in the *Rime,* Gaspara utilizes a pun on her lover's name, which means literally "high hill."

Io son da l'aspettar omai sí stanca,
sí vinta dal dolor e dal disio,
per la sí poca fede e molto oblio
di chi del suo tornar, lassa, mi manca.

Che lei, che'l monde impalidisce e 'mbianca
con la sua falce e dá l'ultimo fio,
chiamo talor per refrigerio mio,
si'l dolor nel mio petto si rinfranca.

Ed ella si fa sorda al mio chiamare,
schernendo i miei pensier fallaci e folli,
come sta sordo anch'egli al suo tornare.
Cosí col pianto, ond'ho gli occhi miei molli,
fo pietose quest'onde e questo mare;
ed ei si vive lieto ne'suoi colli.

By now this waiting so has wearied me,
So vanquished am I by desire and grief
For him who, absent, grants me no relief,
So faithless, so forgetful, still is he.

That I turn and beg that she will give me ease,
Who with her sickle makes the world turn white
And gives to all the final blow; my plight
Such sorrow wrings from me, such anguished pleas.

But she is deaf to this my wretched crying,
And scorns my scattered thoughts disturbed and vain,
Like him who, deaf to me, grants no replying.
Thus with lament that from my eyes distills
I wake the pity of these waves, this main,
While he, lighthearted, lives among his hills.

In this complex poem the female deity evoked in the second quatrain is
clearly the moon, but she is equally clearly Death ("death" in Italian—*la
morte*—is a feminine noun). The double identity is explained further if we
consider the mythological reverberations of the moon image. In classical
myth the moon is identified with Diana (Artemis), the huntress, a goddess
dedicated to chastity. A version of the female archetype, she has, like the
moon, three aspects—as maiden, nymph, and crone. In her aspect as
crone she also bears the name of Hecate, goddess of the underworld and
hence of death (as so frequently in mythic discourse, one deity merges
with another—the triune Diana merges, as the crone Hecate, with the
maiden Persephone, ravished by Hades, and Persephone in turn tends to
merge with her mother Demeter, the goddess of fertility). The deity appealed to in Gaspara's sonnet is simultaneously the moon, the female
archetype, Diana, Hecate, and death. As the goddess of chastity, Diana
may be interpreted as spurning the poet's plea in punishment for her betrayal in having given herself to love. Gaspara Stampa's poems often have
this kind of complexity of resonance.

Finally Gaspara got tired of waiting and took another lover, who is
addressed in a number of later poems (he has been identified as Bartolomeo Zen).[12] Perhaps there was more than one. In any case, later experience did not trigger the intense emotion that the Collaltino affair did;
artistic expression comparable to that of the Collaltino poems appears
only in the poems of repentance with which the *canzoniere* concludes.

Of Gaspara Stampa's poems, only three sonnets were published during
her lifetime—in an anthology published in Venice in 1553.[13] Immediately
after her death her sister, Cassandra, saw to the publication of the entire
Rime, as a memorial to Gaspara and at the urging of the members of her

artistic circle. The volume did not gain much recognition, and the poet was largely forgotten until 1738, when Antonio Rambaldo reissued the poetic works in a handsome volume. Rambaldo was, curiously enough, a descendant of the family of Collaltino di Collalto and seems to have undertaken the publication out of a kind of family pride.

Rambaldo introduced the volume with an unauthenticated and probably fanciful biographical account of the poet, in which he identifies her as a descendant of a noble Milanese family and suggests that she died as the result of poison, administered either by herself or by an enemy. This is, as Bassanese notes, the stuff of legend, and before the eighteenth century was over, the figure of Gaspara Stampa was enshrined in Italian literary history as a kind of heroine of a Romantic tragedy.[14] In 1851 an epistolary novel purporting to be the actual letters of Gaspara to a female friend was published, and later in the century a number of plays were written with Gaspara as protagonist. New editions of her *Rime* were also published.

The sentimental legend was sharply challenged in 1913 by the scholar Abdelkader Salza, who, in his edition of her works, contended that Gaspara Stampa had been not an innocent young noblewoman but rather a member of the class of honest courtesans. The contention elicited considerable controversy, and throughout the first half of the twentieth century, the question of the poet's sexual virtue or lack of it seemed to be an issue of greater moment than the artistic quality of her work. New fictionalized biographies appeared, some of which, according to Bassanese, turned her into a kind of Violetta without Verdi's music.[15]

The issue remains unsettled, and perhaps it will always remain so. But more recent writing on Gaspara Stampa—such as the work of Bassanese, Guernelli, and Vitiello—focuses far more on the literary artist than on the human being, and the critical consensus is that she is a lyric poet of considerable stature, capable of speaking to us today with greater immediacy than many other lyric poets of the Renaissance. The heiress of a great, complex, and highly sophisticated poetic tradition, she was capable of modifying that tradition in such a way as to make it expressive of a female situation and sensibility. In so doing, she brought it once more to life, for she stands out like a beacon among the masses of Petrarchan lyricists of the *cinquecento*. Dealing with well-worn conventions, she imbued them with dramatic vitality and sincerity—or with the illusion of those qualities, which is, in art, the same thing. Among her immediate contemporaries, only Michelangelo was able to do more; among her immediate successors, only Tasso. And, in the sixteenth century, perhaps only these three lyricists are fully worthy of their master, Petrarch.

NOTES

Much of the material in this introduction was originally written for my volume *Three Women Poets: Renaissance and Baroque* (Lewisburg, Pa., forthcoming). The following translations also originally appeared in that volume: "The First Day of Her Love," "His Excellent Qualities Have Been Her Sweet Chains," "Love, Having Elevated Her to Him, Inspires Her Verses," "She Will Be One Day Free; He, Too Late, Repentant," "Holy Angels, I Don't Envy You," "She Does Not Fear Amorous Pain, But Rather Its End," "By Now This Waiting So Has Wearied Me," "With You My Heart Would Rove," "O Great Exploit of Gentle Cavalier," "Send Back My Heart to Me, Relentless One," "On Every Christmas Her First Love Returns to Her Mind," "Elegiac Lament, Her Love Being Far Away," "She Hopes for Divine Aid," and "Sweetest Lord, O Do Not Let Me Die." The critical material is used, and the poems are reprinted, with the kind permission of Bucknell University Press.

1. My use of first names in referring to these poets in no way implies the condescension involved in referring to Jane Austen as "Jane" or Emily Dickinson as "Emily." The usage is in accordance with Renaissance custom—as we refer to Buonarotti as "Michelangelo" and Da Vinci as "Leonardo."

2. See Frank J. Warnke, Introduction to *Three Women Poets*, for a fuller discussion of this point.

3. Justin Vitiello, "Gaspara Stampa: The Ambiguities of Martyrdom." Fiora A. Bassanese, *Gaspara Stampa*.

4. Gaspara Stampa/Veronica Franco, *Rime*, ed. Salza, p. 196.

5. Rainer Maria Rilke, *Werke*, ed. Allemann, vol. 1, pp. 442–43.

6. This selection has been translated by me. The complete *Duino Elegies* have been translated by J. B. Leishman and Stephen Spender (New York, 1963).

7. Rilke, vol. 3, p. 324.

8. Thomas Mann, "Death in Venice," in *Death in Venice and Other Stories*, pp. 45–46.

9. Vitiello, "Gaspara Stampa: The Ambiguities of Martyrdom."

10. See Bassanese, pp. 57–59, 75–77.

11. Robert Graves, *The Crowning Privilege*, p. 166.

12. See Bassanese, p. 19.

13. Ibid.

14. Ibid., pp. 24–32.

15. Ibid.

The First Day of Her Love

The day approached when He Who created all,
And Who, had He willed, could have remained on high,
In human form in virgin womb did lie,
Thence issuing, Himself full to reveal,

When my own noble Lord, who might have chosen
More lofty station, deigned to choose my heart
To make his nest, whence I've received such smart
That sighs innumerable from me have risen.

Joyfully I embraced this blessed chance
So rare and so exalted, just regretting
That eternal Providence so late did render
Me worthy of him. Each and every glance,
Each hope and thought of mine to him I tender,
Who is noble as is the sun rising or setting.

His Excellent Qualities Have Been Her Sweet Chains

An intellect angelic and divine,
A royal nature, of valorous deeds untiring,
Ardent desire, toward honored fame aspiring,
Sober in speech, and dignified in mien;

Of illustrious blood, to noble kings related,
Possessed of wealth inferior to few,
In the flower of his age and fair to view,
Mild in manner, in courtesy unbated;

A face more clear and radiant than the sun,
Where grace and beauty were by Love bestowed
To a degree that seen or heard was never:
Such are the chains that Love on me does load;
By sweet and honored war I am undone.
O may Love choose in these bonds to hold me ever!

Love, Having Elevated Her to Him, Inspires Her Verses

If, being a woman so abject and vile,
I nonetheless can bear so high a flame,
Why should I not give to the world the same,
At least in part, in proper wealth and style?

If Love, with a new, unprecedented spark,
Could raise me to a place I could not reach,
Why cannot pain and pen combine to teach
Such arts as, never known, shall find their mark?

And if this does not lie in Nature's art,
Then let it be by miracle, whose power

Can conquer, transcend, and every limit break.
How this may be I cannot say for sure,
But well I know the fortune I partake,
And through it a new style engraves my heart.

She Will Be One Day Free; He, Too Late, Repentant

If one day Love gives back to me my heart
And delivers me from this my impious lord,
My unwilling heart, which terror hath endured,
Such joy he takes in pains he can impart;

You'll call in vain upon my love unmeasured
And vast, and on my faith so freely given,
Repenting of your cruelty; unshriven
Of all, you'll rue the gifts that were untreasured.

While I, my liberty so gaily singing,
Released from bondage harsh and cruel, shall go
With springing step into my future state.
And if the heavens justice do bestow
On earnest prayers, I'll see a cruel hand wait
To seize your life, thus vengeance to me bringing.

Holy Angels, I Don't Envy You

Holy angels, I don't envy you
For all your glory and your bliss above,
And those desires that, filled, arouse still love,
You who have always highest God in view:

For my delights are such, and of such measure
That earthly hearts can't comprehend their size,
As long as I can see those candid eyes,
And justly sing and celebrate my treasure.

Just as your thirst is slaked for you in Heaven
By gazing always on His face divine,
Down here the infinite to me is given
As long as I can know my lover's mine.
In this alone your joy wins, to my sorrow:
Yours lasts forever; mine could end tomorrow.

She Does Not Fear Amorous Pain, But Rather Its End

Love, by your mighty arrows thus I swear,
And by the sacred, potent torch you carry:
Though the latter burn me, make my heart its quarry,
And the former wound me, still I do not care;

Delve in the past or in the future gaze,
You'll never find a woman who love's anguish
Could feel as I have, or like me could languish
In the arrow's sharpness, the torch's furious blaze;

For of these pains a special virtue is born,
Which dulls and conquers every sense of sorrow,
So that it doesn't hurt, does scarcely gnaw.
And that, which does both soul and body harrow,
Is the fear that leads me to my death forlorn:
That my fire may prove to be a fire of straw.

When Cupid with His Rays

When Cupid with his rays
Your beauty deep within my heart impressed,
He drew me from myself and in you placed;
Now that to you I'm made,
You are become with me a single one,
Whence you must always heed
My good, my ill, as if they were your own;
When all is said and done,
If you should choose to kill me with your pride,
Remember that you'll be a suicide.

By Now This Waiting So Has Wearied Me

By now this waiting so has wearied me,
So vanquished am I by desire and grief
For him who, absent, grants me no relief,
So faithless, so forgetful, still is he,

That I turn and beg that she will give me ease,
Who with her sickle makes the world turn white
And gives to all the final blow; my plight
Such sorrow wrings from me, such anguished pleas.

But she is deaf to this my wretched crying,
And scorns my scattered thoughts disturbed and vain,
Like him who, deaf to me, grants no replying.
Thus with lament that from my eyes distills
I wake the pity of these waves, this main,
While he, lighthearted, lives among his hills.

With You My Heart Would Rove

With you my heart would rove,
In your voyaging, my Lord,
But a heart I do not have,
Since, with your eyes, Love seized me as his ward.
But my sighs will be companions on your way
—My cries and sobbings too,
Comrades fair and true,
The only ones who stay—
And if you find yourself by them forsaken,
You'll know Death has me taken.

He Conquers All Others in Valor: She Conquers Him in Faith and Sorrow

Newest and rarest miracle of nature!
But neither new nor rare to that high lord,
Who is as Love by all the world adored,
Who masters every thing, beyond all measure:

The valor of my lord, which takes the prize
From every other, and does all valor vanquish,
Alas, is conquered only by my anguish,
Anguish that in no other bosom lies.

As much as he excels each other knight,
In beauty, fame, and valor all above—
Thus much he's conquered by the faith I have.

Miracle never known apart from love!
Pain that only the victim can believe!
Alas, I only conquer the infinite!

O Great Exploit of Gentle Cavalier

O great exploit of gentle cavalier:
To have carried off to France with him the heart
Of a rash young girl whom Love did from the start
Subdue when the splendor of his eyes came near!

At least if you had kept your promise keen
To salve my grief with one or two brief letters!
But you, my Lord, are one who chiefly betters
His honor, and all other vows are vain.

But in the ancient chronicles I've read
That the greatest heroes did not find it shame
To follow jointly Mars and Venus fair.
And of the King,* your master, it is said
Both love and war impose an equal claim,
Whence he is famed from east to western shore.

*Henry II, the French king whose service Count Collaltino had entered, was renowned as both a lover and a soldier.

The Pains of Love Are Blessed, Now That He Has Returned

I bless, O Love, the troubles manifold,
All of the injuries and all the tears,
All the distresses, whether new or old
You've made me feel so much, so many years.

I bless the many false, deceptive snares
In which you choose your followers to trap;
Now that I see again two loving stars
Restore my losses in one single step.

All my past sorrow I now put away,
Induced by those stars' new and lovely light,
Wherein alone is peace for my desire.

This light shall lead me by a pathway straight
To the contemplation of God and things on high
—Firm guide, high escort, ever-faithful fire.

Night of Love

O night to me more splendid and more blessèd
Than the most blessèd and most splendid days;
Night worthy of the most exalted praise,
Not just of mine, unworthy and distressèd;

You alone have been the faithful giver
Of all my joys; you've made the bitter taste
Of this life sweet and dear, for you've replaced
Within my arms the one who's bound me ever.

I just regret that I did not become
Lucky Alemena then, for whom the dawn
Postponed, against all custom, its returning;
But I can never say such good has come
From you, clear night, for even now my song
Cannot subdue the matter to its yearning.

Send Back My Heart to Me, Relentless One

Send back my heart to me, relentless one,
Who, tyrant-like, do hold and tear it so,
And do to it, and me, just what is done
By tigers and lions to the hapless doe.

Eight days have passed, at least a year to me;
No messages, no letters, do I get,
Despite the vows with which you were so free:
Fountain of valor, Count, and of deceit!

Am I Hercules or Samson, do you suppose,
To bear such sorrow now that we're apart?
I'm young, a woman, half out of my mind,
And, most of all, I'm here without my heart,
You being gone, in whom I used to find
Defense, who were for me strength and repose.

Elegiac Lament, Her Love Being Far Away

From the rich and blessèd Adriatic shores,
Nest of love and nest of courtesy,
Where sweet it is to live amid allures,
    A lady for her absent lord did cry,
And both at setting sun and at the dawn,
Made sad complaint with many a dismal sigh:
    Tell us, you shores, the burden of her moan;
"Faithful turtle-dove, belovèd spouse,
You who from branch to branch in vain have flown,
    Who know what pains both fear and love arouse,
When you, in flying here and there, come near
To where my love is, sing to him my cause,
    And with your voice of flame approach his ear:
Tell him how bitter my state is, how unsure,
Now that, alas, I find myself so far
    From him, and unjust fortune must endure.
And you, sweet nightingale, when you're impelled
To give vent in your lays to longing pure,
    With a voice whose singing cannot be excelled,
Tell him, complaining with all might and main,
That my life to darkest night has been compelled,
    Now that without those sweet rays I remain.
And Echo, you who dwell in grot and cave
Alone, take the harsh burden of my pain,
    And carry to his ears its bitter stave.
And you, sweet airs and zephyrs amorous,
The long procession of my sighs receive
    And bear them to my lord so generous.
You shady groves, prolonging a sweet spring,
You who often prove felicitous,
    To many a beast fair refuge offering,
Convey unto my lord, and speedily,
That my delights no pleasure to me bring,
    And my life is death, since he is not with me.
In leaving he took with him all my joy,
Which without him I nevermore shall see,
    But shall perforce meet death without delay.
'Tis hope alone gives meaning to my life,
Which boundless desire and endless pain destroy,

If he comes not back it soon will end its strife.
Those hours which I used to spend in bliss
And peace are now with bitter sorrow rife,
    Now that I must his dearest presence miss.
But oh, alas, all falsely they complain,
And cruel destiny condemn amiss,
    Who with free will consent to deadly pain.
Alas, I should with my incessant wails
Have kept him here, or used them to obtain
    That without me he would not raise his sails;
And thus I would not be lamenting ever,
Nor would the fear that in my heart prevails,
    This jealous fear, thus from myself me sever.
Correct, my dearest lord, my fault; return
To where your always desolated lover
    More than for life itself for you does yearn
And if the sun should ever bring that day,
Think nevermore of parting from this bourn,
For I would be beside you night and day;
Without you I see myself within the urn."

On Every Christmas Her First Love Returns to Her Mind

I never see return that blessed day,
When He was born, Himself the God of all,
And took on flesh that He might wipe away
Our father's sin against his Maker's will,

Without remembering the subtle skill
With which Love caught me, spreading out his net
Between the eyes and smile that haunt me still,
Eyes far away that I cannot forget;

And I cannot help but feel the ancient wound
Which Love gave to my heart and my desires,
So deep that wound was, and so harsh its pain,
Did reason not take up its arms again
To vanquish my senses, these consuming fires
Would be such that no succor could be found.

She Hopes for Divine Aid

"Impious sinner, turn your face to me,"
My Lord cries out, as on the cross He hangs;
His voice is filled with true compassion's pangs,
But my blind senses do not heed His plea,

So am I by my wretched Love transmuted,
And by such different fire my heart is seared;
Yet is my soul to true delight allured,
Which, once acquired, cannot be disputed.

Reason would follow fain its goal on high
With swift alacrity, but is misguided
By this frail flesh, which ever it opposes.
And thus my light remains from me divided,
Unless the sun of your grace itself imposes,
This dark and evil fog to drive away.

Sweetest Lord, O Do Not Let Me Die

Sad and repentant for my errors grave,
And the wild delirium that stole my sanity,
And for having spent the few years that I have
Of fleeting life in amorous vanity,

I turn to you, O Lord, who can make tender
The hardest hearts, and warm the coldest snow,
And who the harshest burden sweet can render
For those enkindled by your sacred glow.

And I pray that you'll extend your hand to me
And pull me from this stormy sea, whence I
Could never rise through efforts of my own.
You died for us, my Lord, you did atone,
Paying for all the human race the fee.
Sweetest Lord, O do not let me die!

BIBLIOGRAPHY

Primary Works

Gaspara Stampa/Veronica Franco. *Rime*. Ed. Abdelkader Salza. Bari, 1913.

Related Works

Bassanese, Fiora A. *Gaspara Stampa*. Boston, 1982.

Croce, Benedetto. *Conversazioni critiche*. 2d ed., pp. 223–33. Bari, 1924.

Donadoni, Eugenio. *Gaspara Stampa*. Messina, 1919.

Graves, Robert. *The Crowning Privilege*. London, 1955.

Guernelli, Giovanni. *Gaspara Stampa, Louise Labé y Sor Juana Inés de la Cruz: Tríptico Renacentista-Barroco*. San Juan, 1972.

Mann, Thomas. "Death in Venice." In *Death in Venice and Other Stories*, trans. H. T. Lowe-Porter, pp. 45–46. New York, 1954.

Rilke, Rainer Maria. *Werke*. Ed. B. Allemann. 3 vols. Frankfurt-am-Main, 1966.

Vitiello, Justin. "Gaspara Stampa: The Ambiguities of Martyrdom." *Modern Language Notes* 90 (January 1975): 58–71.

CHILD, WOMAN, AND POET

ittoria Colonna

JOSEPH GIBALDI

Ludovico Ariosto devotes one of his most famous digressions in *Orlando Furioso* to the many excellent women writers of his age—those who abandoned the needle and cloth and joined the Muses on Mount Helicon to quench their thirst at the sacred fountain (37.14). So numerous are these women, writes Ariosto, that to render a proper account of each would fill up an entire canto. He wonders if he should select only five or six to praise (and possibly offend the others), if he should be silent about them all, or if he should single out one from the many.

> I will choose only one, but will so choose
> that envy will be entirely confounded,
> for none of the others will be troubled
> if I pass over them and praise this one alone.
> This woman has not only made herself immortal
> with a sweet style that has not been surpassed;
> but whomever she speaks or writes about
> she can draw from the tomb and give eternal life.
>
> Just as Phoebus adorns his white sister
> with more brightness and gazes on her more
> than on Venus or Mercury or any other star
> that moves with the heavens or on its own:
> so he breathes into this woman more fluency
> and more sweetness than into any of the others;
> and he gives such power to her lofty words
> that in our time another sun ornaments the sky.
>
> Vittoria is her name, appropriate for one born
> amid victories; and no matter where she goes,
> embellished with trophies and with triumphs,
> Victory is with her, preceding and following.
>
> (37.16—18)

Vittoria Colonna, as Maud F. Jerrold has noted, was truly a "child of the Renaissance."[1] Born of illustrious parentage and witness to and participant in major historical events, Colonna was an influential political and intellectual leader, a friend and adviser to many of the greatest personalities of her age, and an outstanding poet admired and respected by her contemporaries.

The Colonnas were a noble Roman family that played an important military and political role in medieval and Renaissance Europe. Fabrizio (d. 1520), Vittoria's father, was a celebrated general and, in his later years, grand constable of Naples. Significantly, he figures among the renowned interlocutors in Niccolò Machiavelli's *The Art of War*. Colonna's mother, Agnese di Montefeltro (d. 1523), was the daughter of Duke Federigo of Urbino and Battista Sforza, and sister to Guidobaldo, at whose court Baldesarre Castiglione set his *Book of the Courtier*.

Vittoria was born in 1492 in the Colonna castle at Marino, south of Rome. Although little is known of her upbringing, it is clear that she received a comprehensive humanistic education. But her life was shaped by not only the intellectual but also the political forces of the age. In 1495 Ferdinand II (1469–1496), king of Naples, wishing to solidify his alliance with the Colonna family, induced Fabrizio to betroth his daughter to Ferrante Francesco d'Avalos, marquis of Pescara, a descendant of noble Spanish and Neapolitan families. Vittoria was three years old, Ferrante five. The wedding contract was signed in 1507; the marriage itself took place at Ischia, near Naples, two years later.

Though Colonna later protested to the contrary, the marriage seems not to have been a happy one. Pescara, like his father-in-law, was a military man. In 1510, one year after the wedding, he left Naples to join Fabrizio in fighting on the side of Pope Julius II and Spain against the French in northern Italy. Thereafter Colonna spent very little time with her husband, as he fought in one battle after another until his early death.

In 1512 Fabrizio and Pescara were both taken prisoner at the battle of Ravenna but were shortly released. The following year Pescara was fighting again in Lombardy. In 1521, after a brief truce, the war resumed, this time with Pope Leo X allied with Charles V of Spain against France, and with Pescara in command of the imperial infantry. Considerable military success followed. Pescara was victorious at Bicocca, near Milan, in 1522 and successfully held Cremona and Milan against the French in 1523. Then, after a defeat at Marseilles in 1524, the imperial forces defeated François I at Pavia in 1525, taking the French king himself as prisoner. At the height of his success, however, Pescara was gravely wounded and retired to Milan. He died there on November 25, 1525, at the age of thirty-five, leaving Vittoria Colonna a widow for the remaining twenty-two years of her life.

During her marriage Colonna resided chiefly at her home in the south. With no children of her own, she undertook the upbringing of her husband's orphaned cousin Alfonso d'Avalos, marquis of Vasto, who was to have a distinguished military and political career of his own. In Naples Colonna enjoyed the companionship of, among others, the famous poet Iacopo Sannazaro (d. 1530). At this time, too, her earliest poems apparently began to attract attention. In August 1515, Andrea di Asola dedicated to her his edition of Dante's *Divine Comedy,* alluding in his dedication to her beauty, her virtue, and her eloquence.[2] In 1519 the poet Girolamo Britonio similarly dedicated to Colonna his book of poems *Gelosia del Sole,* which included a sonnet ("Quando odo il vostro stile") praising her poetic style.[3]

There is little to document the details of Colonna's life during these years, but scholars are certain that she often traveled, with and without Pescara, to her parents' home in Marino and to nearby Rome. It was doubtless in the Rome of Leo X (r. 1513–1521) that she first met and formed lifelong friendships with three of the pope's secretaries: Giovan Matteo Giberti (d. 1543), later papal datary to Clement VII and bishop of Verona; Iacopo Sadoleto (1477–1547), the poet and subsequent bishop of Carpentras and cardinal; and, most important, Pietro Bembo (1470–1547), the famous poet and humanist who, in 1539, also became cardinal. Bembo served as a kind of mentor to Colonna the poet. He admired and encouraged her verse, and she in turn devoted a sonnet to him ("Spirto felice").[4] It was during this period, too, that Colonna may have met Ludovico Ariosto (1474–1533), who made frequent diplomatic missions to the court of Leo X on behalf of the Este family.

Bembo, a major figure in *The Book of the Courtier,* may also have introduced Colonna to Baldesarre Castiglione (1478–1529), who so respected the marchesa's literary taste that he sent her the manuscript of his famous work in 1524 for her opinion. Indeed, Colonna was the indirect cause of the book's publication, for she soon began to circulate the work with great enthusiasm—albeit without the author's permission—to Castiglione's considerable discomfiture. Fearful of the publication of a corrupt edition, Castiglione had the book printed himself in Venice in 1528.[5]

Immediately following her husband's death in 1525, the young widow went to live in the Convent of San Silvestro in Rome. Although she was to live in many convents during the remaining years of her life, Colonna never took the veil. She also did not marry again. Instead, she chose to live a full and independent "Renaissance life," combining secular interests and achievements together with the deepest piety.

Throughout her long widowhood, Colonna traveled considerably— Ferrara, Bologna, Florence, Lucca, Orvieto, and Viterbo, always return-

ing for lengthy stays in Rome and Marino as well as Naples and Ischia—
and everywhere she went, she attracted admiring and devoted friends.

In the early 1530s her cousin Cardinal Pompeo Colonna dedicated his
book *Apologia mulierum* to Vittoria and also included her in it as a modern counterpart to the virtuous women of antiquity.[6] It was around 1530,
too, that Ariosto added to canto 37 of the *Orlando Furioso* the glowing
passage, quoted above, on Colonna's illustrious reputation as woman and
poet. In addition, several Renaissance artists, including Sebastiano del
Piombo and Girolamo Muziano (Palazzo Colonna, Rome), painted por-
traits of the marchesa. Some believe that Paolo Veronese depicted her as
the Virgin in his *Marriage at Cana,* now at the Louvre in Paris.[7]

Colonna's literary circle in Naples at this time included the poets Galeazzo di Tarsia, Angelo di Costanzo, and Bernardino Rota. Tarsia
(1520–1553) devoted a poem ("Io benedico il dì") to Colonna's beauty.[8]
Many other literary figures, while traveling in southern Italy, also enjoyed
her company: the Latin lyricist and subsequent reformer Marcantonio
Flaminio, the historian Paolo Giovio, the literary theorist Antonio Min-
turno, and the poet Bernardo Tasso, father of Torquato. Bernardo (1483–
1569) wrote many sonnets, canzoni, and letters in praise of Colonna.[9]
Her Roman friends in later years included such poets and men of letters as
Giovanni Guidiccioni (who addressed three sonnets to the marchesa),
Francesco Maria Molza, Claudio Tolomei, Luigi Alamanni, Annibale
Caro, and Benedetto Varchi. Colonna also exchanged letters with the no-
torious Pietro Aretino (1492–1556) and the revered Marguerite of
Navarre (1492–1549).[10] Among her later spiritual advisers were the
powerful and influential cardinals Gasparo Contarini (1483–1542),
Giovanni Morone (1509–1580), and Reginald Pole (1500–1558). It was
not for nothing that Jacob Burckhardt called Vittoria Colonna "the most
famous woman of Italy" during the Renaissance.[11]

Yet of all her many famous acquaintances, Colonna's most celebrated
and doubtless her closest friend was none other than Michelangelo
Buonarroti (1475–1564). Their shared interests in art and poetry, their
profound religious sense, their Neoplatonic proclivities, and, obviously,
their complementary personalities made Colonna and Michelangelo the
most intimate of spiritual friends. Although they probably met earlier,
their friendship blossomed sometime during the 1530s and continued to
flourish until Colonna's death in 1547. During that decade or so, the two
wrote letters and poems to each other, with Michelangelo offering drawings and sketches to his friend, and they often saw each other. The Portuguese painter Francisco de Holanda has left a record of the friendship,
recounting in his *Diálogos de Roma* the visits he enjoyed with Colonna
and Michelangelo in the convent garden of San Silvestro in 1538.

Among the drawings that Michelangelo sent to Colonna around 1540 were a *Pietà with Angels* (Fenway Court, Boston) and a particularly striking *Christ on the Cross* (British Museum, London), in which the crucified Christ is depicted alive, looking up toward heaven, "triumphant over death."[12] Of the deposition, Colonna wrote to the artist: "I found it so wonderful that it surpassed my expectations in all ways; . . . it reaches the highest perfection in every point. . . . And I tell you that I am delighted that the angel on the right is so beautiful, because on the last day Michael will place you, Michelangelo, at the right hand of God. Meanwhile, I do not know how to serve you other than by praying for you to this sweet Christ, whom you have drawn so perfectly" (*Carteggio,* p. 209). The crucifixion pleased her even more: "It is impossible to find a figure more beautifully made, more lifelike, and more perfectly finished; I certainly can never express how subtly and marvelously it is done. . . . If it is truly yours, you must have patience, for I will never send it back to you. I have looked at it under the light and with a lens and with a mirror—I have never seen a more perfect thing" (*Carteggio,* p. 208).

For his part, Michelangelo wrote to Colonna, "I desire to do more for you than for anyone else I have ever known on earth" (*Lettere,* p. 275), while she speaks to him of "our secure friendship and most steadfast affection bound in a Christian knot" (*Carteggio,* p. 268). In his many verses devoted to Vittoria Colonna, Michelangelo poetically chronicles his attachment to her:

> A man within a woman—no, rather a god
> speaks through her mouth;
> and I, having heard her,
> am no longer my own master.
>
> .   .   .   .
>
> Oh lady who leads souls
> through fire and water to bliss,
> make me never return to what I was.
>   (*Rime,* p. 268, no. 235)

> As much as I flee and even hate myself,
> so much, lady, with truest hope,
> I turn to you; and my soul is
> the less afraid, the nearer I am to you.
> In your face and in your beautiful eyes,
> full of every salvation,
> I aspire to all that heaven promises.
>   (*Rime,* p. 224, no. 163)

One of Michelangelo's drawings of a woman is thought to be of Colonna (British Museum, London), and some art historians contend that

Michelangelo included the marchesa in his *Last Judgment*—significantly, at the feet of the Virgin Mary.[13]

Like Michelangelo, Colonna was also deeply interested in church reform, and throughout her mature life she closely allied herself with counterreformational forces. Indeed, several of her closest ecclesiastical friends (Giberti, Sadoleto, Contarini, Pole) were members of that early reform group, founded before 1520, the Oratory of Divine Love. In subsequent years, her interest in the movement intensified. Among other activities, she became a staunch defender of the Capuchins, an order of reformed Franciscans established by Matteo da Bascio and approved in 1528 by Clement VII. When the Capuchins were opposed by other orders, such as the Observants, Colonna used all her influence to defend the group until Paul III confirmed its privileges in 1536, allowing the order to grow and flourish during the decades and centuries ahead.[14]

To her later dismay, Colonna particularly fell under the influence of Bernardino Ochino (1487–1564), the most celebrated Capuchin and, by all accounts, the greatest preacher of his time. Every Italian city clamored to hear him, and whenever he was nearby, Colonna went to listen to his sermons. In 1537, apparently at his request, she traveled to Ferrara to seek permission of Ercole II d'Este for Ochino to found a Capuchin convent in that city. The following year, doubtless due in large part to Colonna's efforts, the illustrious preacher was elected vicar-general of his order.

During the next few years, however, Ochino and his followers were increasingly suspected of having Lutheran tendencies. Accusations of heresy soon followed. In 1542, as the Roman Inquisition was being established, Ochino was summoned to Rome. Fearful of impending imprisonment and possibly even death, he fled Italy to Geneva and spent the remaining years of his life unhappily in the north. He was driven out of England during the reign of Mary Tudor and was exiled from Switzerland as well as Poland before meeting his death in Moravia in 1564.

Before leaving Italy, Ochino wrote to Colonna to explain his decision to flee.[15] He wrote again when he arrived in Geneva, but, on the advice of Cardinal Pole, the marchesa did not open this second letter, immediately forwarding it instead to the Vatican. Although she now disavowed Ochino and broke off all communication with him, the Roman Inquisition nonetheless continued to investigate Colonna's beliefs and kept a watchful eye on her until her death a few years later. In fact, more than one historian has speculated that death saved Colonna from a perilous confrontation with the Inquisition. Roland H. Bainton writes, "Had she lived, she would almost certainly have been suspected of heresy," and, G. K. Brown adds, "There can be little doubt that . . . ecclesiastical authority would have treated her severely."[16]

In the spring and summer of 1543, while staying at the Convent of Santa Caterina in Viterbo, Colonna suffered a long and serious illness. But she slowly recovered enough to return the following year to Rome, taking up residence in the Convent of Sant' Anna de' Funari. She became ill again at the beginning of 1547 and was moved to the Cesarini palace. On February 15 she made out her will; she died ten days later. Michelangelo was at her deathbed. In a sonnet on her death, he wrote,

> Heaven has taken from me the splendor
> of the great fire that burned and nourished me;
> I remain a coal, smoldering under the ash.
>   (*Rime*, p. 302, no. 266)

In a subsequent letter to Giovan Francesco Fattucci, dated August 1, 1550, Michelangelo spoke feelingly of the marchesa, "who was devoted to me, and I no less to her. Death has deprived me of a great friend" (*Lettere*, p. 259). But Michelangelo did find one consolation.

> Although her body is dead,
> we cannot forget
> her sweet, graceful, sacred verses.
>   (*Rime*, p. 301, no. 265)

Vittoria Colonna's contemporaries almost universally acclaimed her poetry. In addition to the previously cited comments of Andrea di Asola, Girolamo Britonio, and Ariosto, are many other notable words of praise from some of the chief figures of the age. Bembo, for example, in a letter to Colonna dated January 20, 1530, remarks that she has "more excellence in the art" than any other woman poet (*Carteggio*, p. 61). A decade later the poet Giovanni Guidiccioni writes to the marchesa of her verse: "You have arrived at the truest perfection of style and thought that one can imagine" (*Carteggio*, p. 212). Likewise, Aretino, writing on February 28, 1540, to Paolo Interiano Genovese about the major women poets of the day, speaks of the "famous" Veronica Gambara but the "eternal" Vittoria Colonna (*Lettere*, p. 643). Although demand for copies of her verses was great, Colonna's modesty prevented their publication for many years. Nonetheless, the poems freely circulated in manuscript, as Colonna often sent individual efforts to friends and, in fact, sent manuscripts of her collected poems to at least three persons: Francesco della Torre (secretary to her close friend Bishop Giberti), Marguerite of Navarre, and Michelangelo.[17]

In 1535 Colonna's first poem appeared in print: her sonnet "Ahi quanto fu al mio sol contrario il fato" (*Rime*, p. 38) was published in a book of Bembo's poetry. The following year three of her poems, including the epistle to her husband at war (excerpts translated below), were printed in the collection *Vocabulario di cinquemila Vocabuli Toschi*. Finally, in 1538 an entire book of Colonna's poetry was published in Parma, and another twenty or so editions of her verse were to appear during the remainder of the century. Her claim to the title "literary queen" of the Italian Renaissance seems thoroughly justified.[18]

The most recent edition of Colonna's poetry by Alan Bullock (1982) contains 390 poems divided into three sections: love poems (141), spiritual poems (217), and epistolary poems (32). Her earliest known poem—and the only one definitely written before her husband's death—is the extraordinary "Epistle to Ferrante Francesco d'Avalos, Her Husband, After the Battle of Ravenna," composed in 1512, following the famous battle in which Ferrante not only first won fame as a soldier but was also briefly taken prisoner along with Fabrizio Colonna, Vittoria's father. The epistle is at once a humanistic exercise and a passionate *cri de coeur*. On the one hand, the poem—written in terza rima (*a b a, b c b,* and so forth) and replete with classical allusions (Hector and Achilles in the excerpts given below; Typhoeus, Aeolus, Pompey, Cato, and Mithridates, among others, in the omitted passages)—is a conscious imitation of Ovid's *Heroides,* a set of imaginary verse epistles by famous women of antiquity, such as Dido, Medea, and Penelope, addressed to their absent husbands and lovers. On the other hand, in marked contrast to the noble and dignified tone of the poems written after Pescara's death, the epistle is unique in the youthful sense of anger and self-pity that pervades it. The young Colonna complains about her lonely life, her separation from her husband, and her fears about his safety. She contrasts his single-minded, insensitive quest for fame on the battlefield with her distress at home, and this leads her to bemoan the plight of all women helplessly awaiting the return of their men from war.

Colonna's *Love Poems,* written in her middle years, and her later *Spiritual Poems* are less personal than the epistle and more reflective of both the artistic and intellectual currents of the age. Natalia Costa-Zalessow has written of the perfect balance in Colonna's verse between humanistic Neoplatonism and Christianity, within the framework of sixteenth-century Petrarchism.[19] Although Petrarchan and Neoplatonic elements suffuse all of Colonna's mature work, the former is more evident in the *Love Poems,* the latter in the *Spiritual Poems.*[20]

The *Love Poems* were written during the years immediately after Pescara's death, the late 1520s and possibly the very early 1530s. As in the subsequent *Spiritual Poems,* the sonnet predominates. Faithfully adhering to the Petrarchan form, each poem contains an octave, composed of two quatrains with the same fixed rhyme scheme (*a b b a a b b a*), and a sestet, comprised of two tercets with varying rhyming patterns (often *c d e c d e*, but sometimes such arrangements as *c d c d c d, c d e c e d, c d e d c e*, and so forth).

Despite superficial similarities, the *Love Poems*, in imagery as well as in theme, are much closer to the Petrarchan model than the later sonnets. *Love Poems* 4 and 5 below, for example, clearly illustrate Colonna's indebtedness to the tradition: the fourth with its apostrophe to Love, ever armed with his fierce arrows, and its typically Petrarchan conceits (for example, Love's "sweet yoke" and "gentle prison"); the fifth with its extended nautical metaphor very obviously recalling Petrarch's famous sonnet 189 ("Full of oblivion, my ship passes through a harsh sea").

Moreover, just as Petrarch devoted his sonnets to celebrating his beloved, so in Colonna's love poems Pescara—by all accounts no more than a mere mortal, morally and spiritually—is transformed into something of a male Laura. As John Addington Symonds wrote, "Death consecrates her husband for Vittoria, as death canonised Laura for Petrarch. He has become divine, and her sole desire is to rejoin him in a world where parting is impossible."[21]

Hence the Colonna of this middle period incessantly refers to her deceased husband as "my beautiful sun" and "my eternal light." In her memory now, he was not only a great warrior who possessed an "invincible heart," "prudent foresight," and "godly judgment," but also an ideal lover whose merest glance chased away her sorrows and made her tears sweet and her sighs pleasant. At the same time, Colonna speaks painfully of her own psychological and physical distress at his loss. She complains of the "bitter weeping" and "melancholy sighs" of her widowhood; she believes that with his death she was "forever cut off from any happiness."

The final three sonnets in this group indicate her desire to remain devoted to his memory, for her only relief in life is in directing her thoughts to him. Indeed, she hopes that his memory will inspire her to reject the vanities of this world and embrace the true joys of the spiritual life.

Written during the 1530s and 1540s, the ten or fifteen years prior to Colonna's death, the *Spiritual Poems* reflect, as Dennis J. McAuliffe cogently suggests, a profound religious conversion within the poet.[22] (This was, after all, the period of her friendships with Michelangelo and Ochino.) Whereas in the *Love Poems* she devoted her life and her verse to Pescara, her "beautiful sun," who was admittedly but "a part of the perfect good," in the *Spiritual Poems* she now devotes her verse and her soul to the "true Sun."

The keynote to these later works is appropriately struck in the very first sonnet in the group. Although her "chaste love" for Pescara and her desire to keep his name alive on earth dominated her earlier poems, Colonna will now write only in praise of the Lord. Her new inspiration will be the example of Jesus Christ. Writing, which for Colonna originally was a cathartic experience (*Love Poem* 1: "I write only to unbosom my inner sorrow"), is now a celebratory act, a religious experience.

In other poems, following her contemplative "light," Colonna exhibits affinities with Ignatian meditation (sonnet 7: "I see the Lord on the cross, stretched naked") and post-Tridentine mysticism, thus anticipating such meditative and mystical poets of the late sixteenth and seventeenth centuries as San Juan de la Cruz, Jean de La Ceppède, Robert Southwell, John Donne, Friedrich von Spee, George Herbert, Jan Luyken, and Sor Juana Inés de la Cruz.[23] Similarly, Neoplatonism, present in some of the *Love Poems* (7 and 8), is a dominant element in the *Spiritual Poems,* perhaps most evidently in the sixth sonnet, which speaks of the "ladder" that leads the soul to heaven.

Indeed, it is possible to view the entire corpus of Colonna's poetry as embodying the Neoplatonic ladder of love, progressing as the poems do from the early declarations of passionate earthly love in the epistle to her husband at war through the Petrarchan delineation of idealized human love in her middle years to the final religious poems that culminate, poetically if perhaps not chronologically, in her *Triumph of Christ's Cross.* Influenced, typically, by Petrarch's *Triumphs* as well as by *The Triumph of the Cross* (1497) by the famous early church reformer Girolamo Savonarola, Colonna's glorious work, written in terza rima (like the Petrarchan *Triumphs*), presents a mystical vision of Christ, the Virgin Mary, and Saint Mary Magdalene.

It is significant that the Magdalene concludes Colonna's vision, for throughout her life the poet felt a strong attachment to the saint, which was demonstrated in numerous ways. In March of 1531, for instance, the marchesa asked Federigo II, duke of Mantua, if he could arrange for her to have a "beautiful picture of Saint Magdalene, from the hand of an excellent painter." The duke turned for such a painting to no less an artist than Titian, whom he called "the most excellent painter of our time." Titian executed the painting at once and sent it to Colonna the following month.[24] In addition to including the Magdalene in the *Triumph of Christ's Cross,* Colonna devoted *Spiritual Poem* 8 to her and toward the end of her life (c. 1545) wrote at great length on the saint in a letter to her husband's aunt Costanza d'Avalos.

> I see the fervent Magdalene listening at the feet of our Lord. . . . I think of how that beloved disciple merited the privilege of being the first of all to see the glorious resurrected Lord, Who, thankful, thus rewarded her ardor, her perseverance, and her dear and faithful love. And to prove further that she was his apostle, He commanded that she be the messenger to bring the disciples the news of His resurrection. . . . I see the converted woman from

the moment she so ardently began to love Him, then everyday growing more passionate, until with new and humble emotions she followed Him to the cross; and when others lost faith at His death, her love burned even more, as she ever followed and served the holy mother, being at one with both the Queen of Heaven and the Holy Spirit. She became the most perfect herald of the Divine Word, and on the high mountain of her penitence she was often visited by her resplendent Sun. (*Carteggio,* pp. 300–301)

Just as Colonna looks ahead to later meditative and mystical poets, so, in her copious writings on the saint, she clearly anticipates the widespread Baroque tradition of lyric poems devoted to the Magdalene, a tradition that included such diverse poets as Giambattista Marino, Robert Southwell, Philippe Desportes, John Donne, Lope de Vega, George Herbert, Joost van den Vondel, Richard Crashaw, Andreas Gryphius, and Andrew Marvell.[25]

Colonna seems to have identified with the saint on many different levels—personal, philosophical, theological. The Magdalene represented for Christian theology the contemplative path to salvation, while her sister Martha symbolized the active path. On the choice between these two "lights," contemplatives like Colonna were fond of quoting Luke 10, verse 42: Christ's judgment that Mary had chosen the good part, which shall not be taken away from her. Moreover, like Colonna in the artistic and political worlds of her day, the Magdalene also moved in a world dominated by men, and yet she was able through her great devotion to become the only woman (excluding the Virgin Mary, of course) to achieve in Christ's eyes status equal to the apostles. Finally, the saint's remarkable "life"—from flagrant prostitute to passionate convert to faithful disciple of Jesus to hermit blessed with mystical visions in a deserted cave—was yet another manifestation, and a powerfully dramatic one, of the Neoplatonic progression from earthly love to divine love.

In the Magdalene legend, Colonna obviously found a spiritual model for life. She doubtless would have wished that her own exemplary existence and poetic art might play a similar role for her readers, no matter how distant in place or time.

The poems below correspond respectively to the following numbered poems in the Bullock edition: *Rime amorose disperse* 1; *Rime amorose* 1, 6, 19, 45, 53, 58; *Rime amorose disperse* 15, 44; *Rime spirituali* 1, 13, 28, 46, 49, 73, 77, 155, 90; *Rime spirituali disperse* 36. I have followed Bullock throughout with two exceptions: for *Love Poems* 1 and 4, I have reverted to the more traditional texts commonly found in other editions of Colonna's poems (compare *Rime amorose* 1 and 72 in, among others, the 1840 and 1910 editions) as well as in all recent anthologies (for example, Baldacci, Costa-Zalessow).

The translations are intended to be literal, not poetic. They have the general appearance of the original poems in that the lines are fairly uniform in length and correspond as closely as possible to the lines and divisions of the actual works. No attempt has been made, however, to reproduce the meter or rhyme scheme of the poems. For a full appreciation of Colonna's poetic achievement, the reader must consult the poems in their original language.

NOTES

1. Maud F. Jerrold, *Vittoria Colonna, with Some Account of Her Friends and Her Times*, p. 3.

2. Vittoria Colonna, *Carteggio*, pp. 399–400.

3. Ibid., pp. 400–403.

4. Vittoria Colonna, *Rime*, ed. Bullock, p. 152.

5. On this episode, see Colonna, *Carteggio*, pp. 23–26 and 47–51, as well as the dedicatory epistle to *The Book of the Courtier*.

6. Colonna, *Carteggio*, pp. 411–13.

7. For example, see Robert J. Clements, ed., *The Poetry of Michelangelo*, p. 197.

8. Galeazzo di Tarsia, *Rime*, p. 14.

9. Colonna, *Carteggio*, pp. 317–21, 432–34.

10. For correspondence with Pietro Aretino, see his *Lettere*, pp. 272–74, 446–47, 449–50, 525–26; and Colonna, *Carteggio*, pp. 89, 150–51, 163. For correspondence with Marguerite of Navarre, see Colonna, *Carteggio*, pp. 185–88, 200–206, 289–92.

11. Jacob Burckhardt, *The Civilization of the Renaissance in Italy*, p. 274.

12. Roland Bainton, "Vittoria Colonna," in *Women of the Reformation in Germany and Italy*, p. 212.

13. For example, see Maria Luisa Rizzatti, *The Life and Times of Michelangelo*, p. 56.

14. See "The Capuchin Constitutions of 1536," in *The Catholic Reformation: Savonarola to Ignatius Loyola*, ed. Olin, pp. 149–81.

15. Colonna, *Carteggio*, pp. 247–49.

16. Bainton, "Vittoria Colonna," p. 214; G. K. Brown, "Vittoria Colonna," in *Italy and the Reformation to 1550*, pp. 235–39. On Vittoria Colonna and the Counter-Reformation, see especially Bainton and Brown as well as, among others, A. G. Dickens, *The Counter-Reformation*; B. J. Kidd, *The Counter Reformation*; and A. D. Wright, *The Counter-Reformation: Catholic Europe and the Non-Christian World*.

17. For an exhaustive account of the diffusion and publication of Colonna's poems, see Alan Bullock's edition of the *Rime*, pp. 223–323.

18. James Cleugh, *The Divine Aretino*, p. 67.

19. Natalia Costa-Zalessow, ed., *Scrittici italiane dal XIII al XX secolo*, p. 64.

20. For background discussions of Petrarchanism and Neoplatonism in Cinquecento poetry, see, respectively, Giorgio Santangelo and Nesca A. Robb; on Colonna and the poetics of her age, see Mila Mazzetti as well as Dennis J. McAuliffe's dissertation. All in the Bibliography.

21. John Addington Symonds, *Renaissance in Italy: Italian Literature*, vol. 2, p. 256.

22. McAuliffe, "Vittoria Colonna: Her Formative Years," pp. 92–98.

23. On the meditative tradition and late Renaissance poetry, see Louis L. Martz, *The*

Poetry of Meditation; for examples of these trends, see the anthologies of Harold B. Segel and Frank J. Warnke listed in the Bibliography.

24. Colonna, *Carteggio,* pp. 64–67, 70–72.

25. Joseph Gibaldi, "Petrarch and the Baroque Magdalene Tradition," *Hebrew University Studies in Literature* 3 (1975): 1–19.

Epistle to Ferrante Francesco d'Avalos, Her Husband, After the Battle of Ravenna

My most noble lord, I write you this
to recount to you how sadly—and amid so many
uncertain desires and harsh torments—I live.
I did not expect pain and sorrow from you.

. . . .

I did not believe a marquis and a Fabrizio,
one a husband, the other a father, would be
the cruel, pitiless beginning of my suffering.
Love of my father and love of you,
like two famished and furious snakes,
have always lived, gnawing, in my heart.
I believed the fates had more kindness.

. . . .

But now in this perilous assault,
in this horrible, pitiless battle
that has so hardened my mind and heart,
your great valor has shown you an equal
to Hector and Achilles. But what good is
this to me, sorrowful, abandoned?
My mind has always been uncertain:
those seeing me sad have thought
me hurt by absence and jealousy.
But I, alas, have always had in mind
your daring courage, your audacious soul,
with which wicked fortune ill accords.
Others called for war, I always for peace,
saying it is enough for me if my marquis
remains quietly at home with me.
Your uncertain enterprises do not hurt you;
but we who wait, mournfully grieving,
are wounded by doubt and by fear.
You men, driven by rage, considering nothing

but your honor, commonly go off, shouting,
with great fury, to confront danger.
We remain, with fear in our heart and
grief on our brow for you; sister longs for
brother, wife for husband, mother for son.

. . . .

You live happily and know no sorrow;
thinking only of your newly acquired fame,
you carelessly keep me hungry for your love.
But I, with anger and sadness in my face,
lie in your bed, abandoned and alone,
feeling hope intermingled with pain,
and with your rejoicing I temper my grief.

Love Poems

1

I write only to unbosom my inner sorrow,
on which my heart feeds, wishing nothing else,
and not to add light to my beautiful sun,
who left on earth a most glorious mark.

And I lament for good reason: just thinking
I might diminish his glory makes me grieve;
another pen and someone with far wiser words
must come to save his great name from dying.

Purest faith, fervor, and intense pain are
my excuse, for my sadness is so profound
that time and reason can never hope to curb it.

A bitter weeping, not a sweet song,
and melancholy sighs, not a clear voice,
make me vaunt not my style but my grief.

2

In your victories, oh my eternal light,
neither time nor season showed you any favor;
your sword, your virtue, your invincible heart
were your allies, both summer and winter.

Your prudent foresight and godly judgment
vanquished the enemy forces so quickly
that the manner, no less than the deed, lent
greater honor to the high enterprise and to you.

Spirited armies and haughty regal souls,
wide rivers, steep mountains, lofty cities—
all were crushed and conquered by your courage.

You attained the richest gifts of this world.
Now you enjoy in heaven other, truer triumphs;
other leaves adorn and encircle your brow.

3

So many sweet thoughts and high desires
were nourished in me by that sun who chased away
every cloud and made each day on earth bright,
just as the sight of him chased away my sorrows.

During his beautiful, brief stay with me,
he made my tears sweet and my sighs pleasant,
with his handsome, serene glance, oh lovely light,
though now all seems dark to me everywhere.

I see his valor extinguished, his lofty virtues
dead and gone, and, by this great loss,
the noblest minds are sad and confused.

Fervent desire for the glory of ancient times
has, with his death, disappeared from the world;
and I am forever cut off from any happiness.

4

You know, Love, that I never turned my foot
from your gentle prison, or freed my neck
from your sweet yoke, or tried to take back
all that my soul gave you from the first day.

Time has not changed my ancient faith;
the bond is still as tight as I tied it then;
nor has the bitter fruit that I ever gather
made the high cause less precious to my heart.

You have seen, in a burning, faithful heart,
how much your dear, sharp arrow can do—
against its strength even Death is powerless.

Make loose, at last, the bond yourself;
for liberty never really mattered to me,
and now, indeed, it seems late to regain it.

5

Amid harsh rocks and violent winds, I test,
in a frail boat, the ocean of this life;
and I have neither art nor skill for steering it;
and every aid to my rescue is delayed.

Bitter death in one moment extinguished
the man who was my star and my bright beacon;
now against troubled seas and stormy weather
I no longer have help, only greater fear:

not of the sweet song of the godless sirens,
not of crashing against these haughty shores,
not of being grounded on shifting sands;

but only of ever sailing on this ocean,
which I have furrowed so long without hope,
for death conceals my true port from me.

6

That flower of every virtue, in a fair field,
with breath of my joyous hope, once offered me
such fragrance that this sweet seed even now
makes the bitter fruit pleasant and desirable.

Whether fate will be kind to us or harsh,
we cannot know until the final hour,
for as one ill disappears, another pursues:
always doubtful is our wretched state.

But change of neither time nor fortune
can change in me the noble intention
of praising the subject, of mourning the loss.

From that old passion is born in my heart
a single faith that will be just as sincere
the last year as it was the first day.

7

I live upon this fearful, lonely rock,
like a sad bird that shuns the green branch
and the clear water; I withdraw from those
I love on earth and from myself as well,

so that my thoughts may hasten to the sun
I adore and worship. And although they do not fly
as high as I wish, still, when I summon them,
they turn their flight from other paths to this one.

And at the instant, happy and fervent, they reach
the place where I direct them, their joy,
though brief, far surpasses any worldly delight.

But if, as my eager mind wishes, they could
recreate his noble features, I would perhaps
have here on earth a part of the perfect good.

8

While I lived here in you, oh blessed light,
and you with me, by your grace, united
you kept our souls, and our life was
dead in ourselves and alive in the beloved.

Although, because of your lofty and divine state,
I now no longer enjoy such good here below,
do not diminish your aid to this faithful heart
against a world that is an armed enemy to us.

Sweep away the thick clouds from all around,
so that on swift wings I may try to fly
on the right path already taken by you.

Let it be to your honor that I close my eyes to
the frail pleasures in this mortal, false life,
and open them in the other life—eternal and true.

Sacred Poems

1

Although my chaste love for a long time held
my soul desirous of fame, living like a serpent
in my breast, now, weeping, my soul languishes,
turned toward the Lord from whom comes its cure.

May those holy nails henceforth be my quills,
may the precious blood be my undiluted ink,
the sacred, bloodless body be my writing paper,
so that I may inscribe, within, what He suffered.

It is useless to invoke Parnassus or Delos here,
for I aspire to other water, to other mountains
tend, where human foot does not climb by itself.

That Sun Who illuminates the elements and sky,
I pray that, when He reveals His clear fountain,
He offers me drink equal to my great thirst.

2

The true Sun offers to man two lights:
one leads to a fleeting and feeble end,
to a brief thought, to fragile and mortal work;
with this we think, discern, understand, desire.

The other, by which God alone is worshiped,
leads us to heaven by paths little used,
and then from there relies more on those wings
that only He, by His great mercy, grants.

With the first, natural light, unworthy desire
conquers the gentle heart that lends spurs to
and checks the strong motives of our every wish.

With the other, we scorn the world and ourselves,
closing our heart to the shadow, opening it
to the pure ray that transforms us in God.

3

I wish that my ears were closed and deaf, so that
I might listen more intently with my thoughts

to the high angelic voices and the sweet accents
that true peace reconciles with true love.

A vital air blows between chord and chord,
divine and pure in those living instruments;
and it moves their melodies toward one end:
that the eternal harmony is never discordant.

Love raises our voices, and love lowers them;
it directs and beats the ample measure equally,
because it never strikes in vain, out of tune.

And ever sweeter is the sound, although it passes
through changes in several, diverse notes,
for the song's Composer is very careful there.

4

Like a hungry little bird that sees and hears
his mother beating her wings about, when
she brings him nourishment, so that he, loving
both the food and her, rejoices and is happy;

and, chafing within his nest and bursting
with a desire to fly himself and follow her,
he thanks her by singing in such a manner
that his tongue seems loosened beyond its power;

so I, whenever the warm and living ray
of the Divine Sun that nourishes my heart
flashes more than its usual brilliance,

I move my pen, impelled by inner love;
and without being fully aware myself of
what I am saying, I write His praises.

5

From to joy to joy, from one to another train
of sweet and lovely thoughts, Divine Love
guides me out of the cold, barren winter
and leads me to His green, warm springtime.

Perhaps the Lord—since He sees my breast
is molten wax, on which the eternal seal
has impressed, deep within the very center
of my heart, a profound and a genuine faith—

perhaps He wishes to lead me to port not by
a steep ascent, with bitter struggle, but by
a smooth path, with gentle yoke and light burden.

Or, then again, perhaps in this brief peace
the wise and generous Father and Master is
arming me and fortifying me for a long war.

6

The great Father draws the soul to heaven,
bound with string of love, and the knot is tied
by His dear Son's hand; and so lovely a manner,
no less than the act itself, contents the heart.

Such is it that I feel a subtle, living ardor
so penetrate within that, burning, I rejoice,
and I listen and hear a clear, high sound
that recalls me to true honor and glory.

Oh steps of faith and charity and hope,
and of the humility that exalts mankind,
make us a ladder leading up to highest heaven,

where the blessed souls, together united,
one after the other, from last to first, all
gaze at themselves in the great eternal mirror.

7

I see the Lord on the cross, stretched naked,
with feet and hands nailed, His right side
opened, His head crowned only with thorns,
and on every side insulted by vile people.

He bears on His shoulders the heavy weight
of the world's sins; and in such a state
He conquers with only a heart aflame with love
both death and the furious, hostile mob.

Patience, humility, and true obedience,
with other divine virtues, were the stars
that ornamented the sun of His charity;

and thus in that bitter struggle all of these,
after His beautiful death, made brighter
the glory of His everlasting generosity.

8. ON MARY MAGDALENE

Seized in her sadness by that great desire
which banishes all fear, this beautiful woman,
all alone, by night, helpless, humble, pure,
and armed only with a living, burning hope.

entered the sepulcher and wept and lamented;
ignoring the angels, caring nothing for herself,
she fell at the feet of the Lord, secure,
for her heart, aflame with love, feared nothing.

And the men, chosen to share so many graces,
though strong, were shut up together in fear;
the true Light seemed to them only a shadow.

If, then, the true is not a friend to the false,
we must give to women all due recognition
for having a more loving and more constant heart.

9

When will the day be, Lord, that my thought,
always fixed on You, may actually see You?
For while it wanders and strays among the clouds,
it will never be able to find the true Light.

Sometimes I perceive a beautiful, lofty image
that foreshadows Your spirit within my heart,
but that intense vision, though brightly shining,
is always unclear and always incomplete.

Oh, let Your wounded hand tear off at last
the veil that has kept me for two decades
among diverse emotions, bound in this blind error;

and let my soul, no longer reined by dark
or spurred by bright rays, but unchained,
see the great Sun in the most blessed Heaven!

The Triumph of Christ's Cross

I saw then a chariot that seemed,
with bright, lovely, joyous splendor,
to encircle the sky, the land, the sea.

Upon it was the Emperor of Heaven,
He Who descended among us to deliver us
from cruel bondage and from evil death.
Many have fed their avarice and their envy
with the goods of others, haughty victors
vilely seeking a greedy, wicked reign.
But He conquered and gave His kingdom,
when in sacrifice He gave Himself,
washing away our sins with His pure blood.
The victory was His, the prize ours:
with his death He let us have life,
we who were the prey of the great enemy.

. . . .

I saw the honored and sacred head,
which usually wears a crown full of stars,
now wearing a crown made of sharp thorns;
and wounded was the hand that guides heaven
and gives light to the sun, life to mortals,
virtue below, and eternal glory above.
On His shoulders, so that Heaven might
welcome our mortal remains, I saw the symbol
that makes me always weep for the first sin:
the Cross, that firm pledge of our joy,
which we should worship with clasped hands,
because it supported our true support.
The weight was not grievous to His shoulders;
the thought of our condition, alas,
must have made the weight seem light.
At His right in the car, on a royal throne,
I saw the Virgin, paradigm of all virtues,
through whom we can flee eternal damnation.
She was, before all other temples, temple
sacred to God; and I saw how with humility
she cast down the proud and the wicked.
At the holy feet I saw that other Mary,
the Magdalene, burning with joyous love,
her radiant golden hair flowing forth.
True piety moved her to weep here;
and thus heaven wills that, with equal measure,
she now reap the seeds of glory, not of sorrow.

. . . .

At the sepulcher she sought her dead Lord,
Who appeared to her alive and gave

her great sea of tears a happy port.
Blessed is she who scorned worldly fruit,
root and all, for now from her Lord
she receives other, everlasting sweetness.
I, who beheld a more beautiful dawn,
illuminated by another Sun, with heat other
than that which opens and colors our flowers,
here held my eyes and thoughts steadfast.

BIBLIOGRAPHY

Primary Works

Aretino, Pietro. *Lettere*. Ed. Francesco Flora. Milan, 1960.
———. *Letters*. Trans. Thomas C. Chubb. Hamden, Conn., 1967.
Ariosto, Ludovico, *Orlando furioso*. Ed. Cesare Segre. Milan, 1976.
———. *Orlando Furioso*. Trans. Guido Waldman. New York, 1974.
Baldacci, Luigi, ed. *Lirici del Cinquecento*. Milan, 1975.
Bembo, Pietro. *Prose e rime*. Ed. Carlo Dionisotti. 2d ed. Turin, 1978.
Castiglione, Baldesar. *The Book of the Courtier*. Trans. Charles Singleton. Garden City, N.Y., 1959.
———. *Il libro del cortegiano*. Ed. Bruno Maier. Turin, 1964.
Clements, Robert J., ed. *Michelangelo: Self-Portrait*. Englewood Cliffs, N.J., 1963.
Colonna, Vittoria. *Carteggio*. Ed. Ermanno Ferrero and Giuseppe Müller. 2d ed. Turin, 1892.
———. *Rime*. Ed. Alan Bullock. Rome, 1982.
———. *Rime*. Florence, 1910.
———. *Rime*. Ed. Pietro Ercole Visconti. Rome, 1840.
Costa-Zalessow, Natalia, ed. *Scrittici italiane dal XIII al XX secolo*. Ravenna, 1982.
Guidiccioni, Giovanni. *Opere*. Ed. Carlo Minutoli. Florence, 1867.
Holanda, Francisco de. *Diálogos de Roma*. Ed. Manuel Mendes. Lisbon, 1955.
———. "Three Dialogues." Trans. Charles Holroyd and A. J. Clift. In *Michael Angelo Buonarroti*, by Holroyd. 2d ed., pp. 229–79. London, 1911.
Machiavelli, Niccolò. *The Art of War*. Trans. Ellis Farneworth. Ed. Neal Wood. Indianapolis, 1965.
———. *Opere*. Ed. Alessandro Montevecchi. Turin, 1971.
Michelangelo Buonarroti. *Complete Poems and Selected Letters*. Trans. Creighton Gilbert. Ed. Robert N. Linscott. 1963. Reprint. New York, 1965.
———. *Lettere*. Ed. Enzo Noè Girardi. Arezzo, 1976.
———. *Rime*. Ed. Ettore Barelli. Milan, 1975.
Olin, John C., ed. *The Catholic Reformation: Savonarola to Ignatius Loyola*. New York, 1969.
Ovid. *Heroides and Amores*. Trans. Grant Showerman. Ed. G. P. Goold. 2d ed. Cambridge, Mass., 1977.
Petrarch, Francesco. *Canzoniere, Trionfi, Rime varie, e una scelta di versi latini*. Ed. Carlo Muscetta and Daniele Ponchiroli. 4th ed. Turin, 1958.
———. *Petrarch's Lyric Poems*. Trans. Robert M. Durling. Cambridge, Mass., 1976.

_____. *The Triumphs*. Trans. Ernest Hatch Wilkins. Chicago, 1962.

Savonarola, Girolamo. *The Triumph of the Cross*. Trans. J. Procter. London, 1901.

_____. *Triumphus crucis*. Ed. Mario Ferrara. Rome, 1961.

Segel, Harold B., ed. *The Baroque Poem*. New York, 1974.

Tarsia, Galeazzo di. *Rime*. Ed. Cesare Bozzetti. Milan, 1980.

Tasso, Bernardo. *Lettere*. Venice, 1597.

_____. *La lirica*. Ed. Giorgio Cerboni Baiardi. Urbino, 1966.

Warnke, Frank J., ed. *European Metaphysical Poetry*. 1961. Reprint. New Haven, Conn., 1974.

Related Works

Bainton, Roland. "Vittoria Colonna." In *Women of the Reformation in Germany and Italy*, pp. 201–18. Minneapolis, 1971.

Brown, G. K. "Vittoria Colonna." In *Italy and the Reformation to 1550*, pp. 235–39. Oxford, 1933.

Bullock, Alan. "Domenico Tordi and Vittoria Colonna: Forty Years On." *Italica* 55 (1978): 20–35.

_____. "Four Unpublished Autographs by Vittoria Colonna in American and European Libraries, Together with New Data for a Critical Edition of Her Correspondence." *Italica* 49 (1972): 202–17.

_____. "Four Unpublished Writings by Vittoria Colonna in Italian and American Libraries." *Italian Studies* 27 (1972): 44–59.

_____. "A Hitherto Unexplored Manuscript of One Hundred Poems by Vittoria Colonna in the Biblioteca Nazionale Centrale, Florence." *Italian Studies* 21 (1966): 42–56.

_____. "Un sonetto inedito di Vittoria Colonna." *Studi e problemi di critica testuale* 2 (1971): 229–35.

_____. "Three New Poems by Vittoria Colonna." *Italian Studies* 24 (1969): 44–54.

_____. "Vittoria Colonna and Francesco Maria Molza: Conflict in Communication." *Italian Studies* 32 (1977): 41–51.

Burckhardt, Jacob. *Die Kultur der Renaissance in Italien*. 2d ed. 1868. *The Civilization of the Renaissance in Italy*, trans. S. G. C. Middlemore. 1878. Ed. Irene Gordon. New York, 1961.

Clements, Robert J., ed. *The Poetry of Michelangelo*. New York, 1966.

Cleugh, James. *The Divine Aretino*. New York, 1966.

De Sanctis, Francesco. *Storia della letteratura italiana*. 1870–71. *History of Italian Literature,* trans. Joan Redfern. 2 vols. 1931. Reprint. New York, 1968.

Dickens, A. G. *The Counter-Reformation*. New York, 1969.

Gibaldi, Joseph. "Petrarch and the Baroque Magdalene Tradition." *Hebrew University Studies in Literature* 3 (1975): 1–19.

Jerrold, Maud F. *Vittoria Colonna, with Some Account of Her Friends and Her Times*. 1906. Reprint. Freeport, N.Y., 1969.

Kidd, B. J. *The Counter-Reformation*. 1933. Reprint. Westport, Conn., 1980.

McAuliffe, Dennis J. "Vittoria Colonna and Renaissance Poetics, Convention, and Society." In *Il Rinascimento: Aspetti e problemi attuali*, ed. Vittore Branca et al., pp. 531–41. Florence, 1982.

_____. "Vittoria Colonna: Her Formative Years, 1492–1525, as a Basis for an Analysis of Her Poetry." Ph.D. diss., New York University, 1978.

Martz, Louis L. *The Poetry of Meditation*. Rev. ed. New Haven, Conn., 1962.

Mazzetti, Mila. "La poesia come vocazione morale: Vittoria Colonna." *Rassegna della letteratura italiana* 77 (1973): 58–99.

Rizzatti, Maria Luisa. *The Life and Times of Michelangelo*. Trans. C. J. Richards. Philadelphia, 1967.

Robb, Nesca A. *Neoplatonism of the Italian Renaissance*. 1935. Reprint. New York, 1968.

Santangelo, Giorgio. *Il petrarchismo del Bembo e di altri poeti del '500*. Rome, 1967.

Symonds, John Addington. *Renaissance in Italy: Italian Literature*. 2 vols. 1881. Reprint. New York, 1964.

Thérault, Suzanne. *Un cénacle humaniste de la Renaissance autour de Vittoria Colonna, châtelaine d'Ischia*. Florence and Paris, 1968.

Wilkins, Ernest Hatch. *A History of Italian Literature*. Cambridge, Mass., 1962.

Wright, A. D. *The Counter-Reformation: Catholic Europe and the Non-Christian World*. London, 1982.

A RENAISSANCE GENTILDONNA

eronica Gambara

RICHARD POSS

The word *Correggio* is widely known as the name of the painter Antonio Allegri, a virtuoso who ranks with Raphael and Titian as one of the best of Italian High Renaissance painters. Correggio is, of course, the small town in which Allegri was born and raised and in which he produced his first works under the discerning patronage of the ruling family. During the first half of the sixteenth century, however, the word *Correggio* would have referred to the town's rulers and especially to Veronica Gambara: poet, patron, administrator, and guiding spirit of a flourishing court. From the early sixteenth century until her death in 1550, Veronica Gambara presided over a court whose luminaries included the leading political and literary figures of the day. Poets, princes, and prelates gathered for discussions of literary and philosophical topics as well as for good food, singing, dancing, storytelling, and dalliance. The Renaissance successors to the medieval "courts of love," Veronica's salon and others like it were important components of the intellectual life of the Renaissance, providing patronage for artists, poets, and musicians, as well as an arena for the testing and permutation of humanistic ideals. Veronica Gambara's writings consist of some 50 poems and over 130 letters.[1] Except for two Latin odes, all are in Italian. The poems are mostly sonnets, but she employs other forms including the madrigal, the ballad, and *stanze* in ottava rima. Her poetry falls into four categories: love poems to her husband in the Bembist Petrarchan manner, poems on political issues of the day, devotional poems, and Virgilian poems in praise of the pastoral countryside of Brescia and Correggio. The letters are mostly to her friends, among them Pietro Bembo, Agostino Ercolani, Lodovico Rosso, Isabella d'Este, and the Marchese del Vasto. Some are familiar and affectionate, others are formal and conventional.

Veronica Gambara was born on November 30, 1485, on her family's feudal estates in Pratalboino, near Brescia. She was the daughter of Count

Gianfrancesco da Gambara and Alda Pia. In an age of hereditary aristocracy she was born into an ancient and noble family and was related to the most illustrious names in nothern Italy, among them the Carraras, the Picos, the Estensi, and the Gonzagas. Her mother, Alda, was the sister of Emilia Pia, whom Castiglione upholds as a model of feminine virtue in *Il Cortegiano*. Of her youth we know very little except that she was inclined toward poetry from an early age and received a thorough humanistic education. As a young woman she studied Greek and Latin, philosophy, Scripture, and theology, especially the early patristic writers. Her heart, however, was in poetry, and she drew her poetic style and her ideals of decorum and harmony from the two dominant figures in Italian Renaissance poetics, Virgil and Petrarch. The greatest influence on her writing, however, was destined to be Pietro Bembo, the reigning literary figure in Italy at the time and leader of a resurgence of Petrarchism. She first wrote to him in 1502 at the age of seventeen and two years later began sending him her sonnets. Bembo became her poetic mentor, teaching her and praising her work, while she became his admirer and disciple. They met and became intimate friends, and their correspondence continued until Bembo's death in 1547.[2]

In 1509, at the age of 24, Veronica Gambara was married to Count Giberto X, lord of Correggio. It was an arranged marriage, and it is quite probable that they had never met before. But if Gambara's poetry is any indication, love grew quickly between them. Many of her poems describe the sweetness of their happy love, often celebrating her lover's eyes, his *occhi lucenti*, in phrases drawn from Petrarch. At the time of their marriage the count had already led a distinguished career as a professional soldier, serving under King Ferdinand of Naples and Popes Sixtus IV, Innocent VIII, Alexander VI, and Julius II. He had also been married, to Violante Pico, niece of the humanist and Neoplatonist Pico della Mirandola. After his marriage to Gambara, he settled down to the more domestic occupation of rural count, giving his time to hunting and administration. Gambara seems to have relished her role as wife, mother, and *Signora* of Correggio. She had two sons, Ippolito and Girolamo. Their small court attracted learned visitors as Gambara's reputation grew, and soon it became a very fashionable salon for the cultured nobility. Their palace was splendidly decorated and had an impressive library, and a circle of intimates began to meet there with some regularity: Ercole d'Este of Ferrara, Isabella d'Este of Mantua, the infamous Pietro Aretino (a favorite of Gambara's),[3] Bernardo Cappello, and, of course, Pietro Bembo.

In 1515 Veronica and Giberto traveled to Bologna and were presented to Pope Leo X and to Francis I, the king of France. Leo X (Giovanni de' Medici) was the second son of Lorenzo the Magnificent and a highly cultivated patron of the arts. When elected to the throne of Saint Peter, he is reported to have said, "Now that God has given us the papacy, let us enjoy it." His lavish patronage of churches, painting, and sculpture included the rebuilding of Saint Peter's in Rome. Francis I for his part was no less the cavalier Renaissance prince, with an engaging and energetic manner and a great love for music, dancing, art, and women. The French monarch was quite taken with Gambara's erudite wit, and the two became friends. Francis later came to the court of Correggio as a guest.

The painter we know as Correggio, Antonio Allegri, was a close friend of Veronica and the Gambara family. In a letter of September 3, 1528, to Isabella d'Este, she refers to him as "our Master Antonio Allegri" and describes a painting of the Magdalene in the desert which he was completing.[4] This does not necessarily mean (as some suggest) that it was Gambara who first introduced Allegri to Isabella, but it is clear that Gambara was promoting his career. Antonio's family had long been established in Correggio, and Gambara quite naturally encouraged the painter's development with commissions. His work in Correggio was so successful that he acquired, through Gambara's friend Scipione Montino della Rosa, commissions in nearby Parma, culminating in the decoration of San Giovanni Evangelista.

Veronica Gambara brought the painter to the attention of Charles V when he visited Correggio. On the occasion of the emperor's second visit, Allegri was in charge of the decorations in the town and painted two rooms of Veronica's *casino* himself. Antonio's career grew rapidly from one commission to another, but more important, he remained in the area all his life, never settling farther than Parma, about twenty miles from Correggio. In the year of his death he was a witness to the marriage settlement of Gambara's son Ippolito.

Veronica Gambara was not a reclusive scholar; she was very much a product of her times, exuberant and flamboyant. We know that she was fond of horses—but spurned physical exercise—and loved good food and beautiful clothes. In a letter to her friend and purchasing agent Lodovico Rossi, she writes, "Monsignore my brother has praised so highly a Florentine cloth, called *peluzzi,* that I have fallen in love with it, and I must have some right away for a dress."[5] Nor was she flirtatious or coquettish. All indications are that she was not beautiful in appearance and was in fact rather unattractive. At the same time she was vivacious, genial, and a brilliant conversationalist. Conventional praise is often suspect, but she was genuinely admired and respected for her intelligence and her charm.

In any case, her happy married life came to an end on August 26, 1518, when Giberto died. Gambara, not yet thirty-three, was plunged into bitter and violent grieving. Even here she appears to have been flamboyant and theatrical.[6] She shut herself away and stayed in bed with a fever for several months. When she emerged, she was dressed as a widow and vowed never

to go out of mourning. She had her rooms draped in black cloth and
would only drive horses that were "blacker than night." She had carved
above the door to her bedchamber these lines spoken by Dido in Virgil's
Aeneid:

Ille meos, primus qui me sibi junxit, amores
Abstulit; ille habeat secum, servetque sepulchro.

He, who first joined me to himself, took my love away;
He will keep it and guard it in the grave.

(4:28–29)

Dido is speaking here of Sychaeus, and she will quickly contradict herself,
breaking faith with the ashes of her dead husband in her passion for
Aeneas. But Veronica Gambara, in spite of the implications of the allusion, does not. She never remarried and seems not to have given her love
to anyone again. The flamboyance of her grieving has been interpreted in
various ways. Some suggest that it reveals the essentially superficial nature
of her character, that she was never stirred by truly "deep" emotions.[7] It
may more aptly be taken as a sign of the age, especially of the courtly
milieu, in which meaning lies in gesture, and in which classical allusion
does not inhibit sincerity.

At Giberto's death Gambara was left in control of the estate. She took
over the duties of governing the territories and applied herself single-
mindedly to the careers of her two sons. Ippolito, being the eldest, pursued a military career and served first the Venetian Republic and then
Charles V. Girolamo entered the Church, was papal nuncio in 1538 with
the king of France, and later with Charles V and Phillip II of Spain. He
was made a cardinal in 1561 and eventually became archbishop of Ta-
ranto. Girolamo was a Renaissance prelate-warrior, a churchman who
commanded armies in the field. Both sons were known to be fierce, passionate, and given to violence.[8]

In 1530 Gambara attended the papal coronation of the Emperor
Charles V in Bologna. After meeting with the countess, the emperor decided to visit her in Correggio. He stayed at the splendid *casino,* which is
reported to have had over 360 rooms. She had a new highway built in his
honor. The *Via dell'Imperatore* was two miles long, and led up to the
casino. A magnificent pageant attended his arrival and extravagant celebrations followed. Charles, then at the height of his glory, granted to the
house of Correggio various privileges, and told Gambara that he loved her
for three reasons: first, for her renowned virtue; second, for the nobility of
her family; and third, because she was the sister of Umberto, governor of
Bologna, whom he greatly loved.

As a ruler Gambara was conscientious and energetic. She promoted literacy among her people, and at a time when wars crisscrossed northern Italy with bewildering frequency, she saw that widows, orphans, and refugees in her territories were cared for. In 1538 Galeotto Pico, lord of Mirandola, attempted an invasion and led an assault upon Correggio. Calling the people together, Gambara organized an inspired defense, repelled the invader, and saved the city. When famine followed close upon war, she wrote to her friend Ludovico de'Rossi in Bologna, and had him buy grain from Romagna and send it to Correggio.[9] It was an exciting age in which to live. In 1512 she traveled to Brescia to attend the funeral of her father. She was still inside the town when it was taken and sacked by the French army under Gaston de Foix. She was in hiding for several days, then escaped to Correggio.

These experiences gave authenticity to Gambara's poems exhorting the political leaders of her day to make peace. Many of these are addressed to her friend Emperor Charles V. As the most prominent and powerful leader in Europe, he was in a position to exert a decisive influence on the course of events. She shared with the emperor a set of values essentially medieval in character. Charles's dream was much like Dante's: a united Europe under the temporal jurisdiction of the Holy Roman Emperor and under spiritual control of a reformed Catholic pope. Sonnet 6 appears at first glance to be the sort of fawning flattery a courtier-poet in search of patronage might use. Certainly lines like "A god is made among us from mortal man" do nothing to dispel that impression—especially since she is speaking of Charles V, not Christ. The line would fit very comfortably in one of Gambara's sonnets on the miracle of the Virgin birth. The resemblance is, however, intended. Here the allusion to Christ helps reinforce a parallel both Gambara and Charles took very seriously: that pope and emperor held offices under divine authority to govern the spiritual and temporal worlds, respectively. Thus the pope descends from Christ who was announced by John the Baptist, and the emperor descends from Augustus who was "announced" by Julius Caesar. This scheme was already obsolete when Dante articulated it in the early fourteenth century, but the ideal held on, and the title of Holy Roman Emperor still recalled the prestige of the ideal if it did not realize it.

In sonnet 6 Gambara compares Charles to Augustus. In my translation I have arranged the first words of each stanza ("That," "That, but more benign," "So that, if," "Then this") to parallel the syntactical structure Veronica gives to the Italian ("Quella," "Quella, ma più benigna," "Che, se," "Questo"). The first quatrain is devoted to Augustus, the second to Charles. The first tercet of the sestet describes Augustus, the second Charles. In each comparison Charles is elevated above Augustus. He is born under the same star "but more benign" because he is a Christian ruler. And although Augustus conquered many tribes (some of those mentioned were not actually subdued by Augustus, though he did reign over them), what Charles had done in modern Europe was more meritorious. To read this as mere flattery is to miss Gambara's intention, which is to align herself with the highly "unrealistic" imperial ideal.[10]

When Charles was elected Holy Roman Emperor in 1519, his chief competitor for the office had been Francis I, king of France. The two were natural antagonists: Charles was quiet and serious; Francis was jovial and impetuous. Charles considered his own dominion as imperial, not national or personal; Francis was alarmed at being nearly surrounded by Charles's territories. When Francis I was captured at the Battle of Pavia in 1525, the emperor was in a position to realize the old dream of world monarchy.[11] He had the French king in prison, and Henry VIII of England was ready to invade Normandy. Instead of pressing his advantage, however, Charles prepared a peace treaty with Francis. Many were surprised at this; Henry was disgusted. The Venetian ambassadors wrote of their admiration for Charles's restraint. Veronica wrote a sonnet in praise of his classical magnanimity. In addition to signing the treaty, Francis married Charles's sister Leonora. But as soon as he was free, he repudiated all sections of the treaty and formed the League of Cognac with the pope, Venice, Florence, Milan, and England to counter Charles in Italy.

In sonnet 9 Gambara praises and flatters Pope Paul III on the occasion of his third meeting with Charles in 1534. But her tone contains virulence and anger at the sufferings of the northern Italian states. She ends the first line with the words *Italia mia* (my Italy), which are the opening words of Petrarch's famous canzone 128 in the *Canzoniere*. Petrarch's poem, commonly called *Italia mia,* is an impassioned plea for peace addressed to the rulers of Italy's city-states. Petrarch's most important political poem, it exhorts the leaders to remember their noble Roman heritage and to throw off the yoke of the "barbarians" (that is, German mercenary armies), which in his time, as in Gambara's, were ravaging the countryside. Petrarch's poem became a monument of Italian "nationalist" feeling. Gambara's allusion aligns her indignation with Petrarch's and points to foreign interference as the root of Italy's suffering.[12] Then in a flattering comparison with the apostle Paul, she calls Paul III the "second vessel, not less perhaps than the first." Thus when Pope Paul III "renews in you the ancient glory," he is bringing back both the sacred glory of the apostles and the imperial glory of Rome.

Francis and Charles came to one of many truces in 1538. For this treaty Pope Paul III, who was seventy years old at the time, traveled from Rome to Nice to mediate.[13] This is the occasion Gambara writes about in sonnet 4. The two were very far apart now, and the negotiations took place in separate headquarters between representatives of each country and the papal nuncios. Thanks to the Pope's persistence, an agreement was finally reached. Only then did Charles and Francis consent to meet each other, with Leonora looking on, at the town of Aiguesmortes. In her sonnet Gambara exhorts the two contenders to join in fighting the common foe of all Christians, the Turks. She mentions only that the Turks "hate Christ, and deny Him," but the seemingly inexorable advance of the armies of Sulieman the Magnificent was a real threat to much of Europe. Vienna had barely escaped the Turkish siege in the autumn of 1529. Francis, however, had made a secret agreement with the Turks to obtain help against Charles. Even though they were brothers-in-law, Francis I and Charles V remained lifelong adversaries and made several treaties of peace, all of which were broken. In Germany, Martin Luther's doctrines led to bloody peasant riots, and the Ottoman threat continued to worry much of Europe. In Spain, the nobles still retained much of their local autonomy and resisted the centralization of authority Charles depended upon. Gambara writes from the sidelines both to ingratiate herself with those in power and to influence their behavior. Desiring most of all an end to the fighting, she cheers them on when they are acting rightly and largely ignores them when they act wrongly.

The poems of Gambara's *Rime* were left uncollected at her death, and it seems unlikely that she worked with the order of the poems to fashion a single work from them. The first poem of this group is a sonnet sent to Vittoria Colonna, marchesa of Pescara, when Vittoria was in Milan in 1525. It is appropriately placed at the beginning because it contains allusions to the first sonnet of Petrarch's *Canzoniere*. Most sonnet sequences begin in this manner, with a sonnet modeled upon and answering to the first poem in Petrarch's collection. The tone of shame and repentance, of guilt for love which was youthful sin, is also in the Petrarchan original. Where she was nourished by "vaghi e giovenil pensieri" (youthful and straying thoughts), Petrarch was nourished by sighs during his "primo giovenile errore" (first youthful error).[14] Thus placing herself in the Petrarchan context, she plays variations on her original, but never to the extent of using deliberately anti-Petrarchan devices. As a disciple of Bembo, she is a "faithful" imitator.

Sonnet 2 was also sent to Vittoria Colonna and is an adoring tribute to the great Neoplatonist writer who inspired Michelangelo. In this and in other of her writings she seems to have had in mind, besides the natural desire of one *poetessa* to communicate with another (this had been part of the sonneteering vogue since the time of Dante), a desire to make contacts and to ingratiate herself with as many influential people as possible. This is a feature of Veronica's life and writings frequently commented upon disparagingly by critics.[15] It can be said in her defense that, unlike many poets who exchanged grandiose praise in the hope of patronage or financial favors, she was mainly concerned with the advancement of her two sons.

The purpose of Petrarch's *Canzoniere* was to praise and immortalize through poetry the beloved lady, and although the ordering of individual poems was the result of careful thought, the literary fiction was that the collection was a casual grouping composed in the order given. Thus there are in Petrarch's work many occasional poems, poems addressed to individuals, poems on political and devotional themes, poems that accompanied gifts. Gambara's poems mirror this diversity. Sonnet 18 describes the pastoral beauty of Correggio and her *casino*. Among the occasional poems is sonnet 21, written to celebrate a marriage. Full of Petrarchan and Virgilian echoes, it is a festive and solemn hymn to Venus and Hymen, and all the "great gods who govern mortals," in hopes that they will grant happiness to the fortunate pair. Her devotional poems range from meditations on the mystery of the incarnation in sonnets 28 and 29 to the intriguing psychomachy of sonnet 25, where "the interior man" tries to bring reason back into the heart, where a war is raging between the thoughts and the desires. The ballad has the rhythm and meter of a merry carnival song, but it is a sweetly melancholy lament for the loss of hope.

Veronica's most vigorous and refreshing poems are undoubtedly the love poems to her husband. Also couched in Petrarchan language, they radiate fervent devotion and warm affection. In madrigal 1 she praises the multifarious depths of her husband's "occhi lucenti e belli," his lovely, shining eyes. This delicate little poem imitates poem 110 of the *Canzoniere,* where Petrarch is overcome by Laura's "begli occhi lucenti." Veronica uses the Petrarchist terminology formalized by Bembo and his school, such as the phrase "in un punto" (all at once) in line 5, which she takes from line 12 of Petrarch's poem. Petrarch has run away from "Amor." He withdraws and prepares to defend himself when his internal questioning begins: "Why are you afraid?" he asks himself. But before he can answer he is struck by the rays that come from her eyes and enter through his. The rays melt him "in un punto," and he is conquered in an instant just as when lightning and thunder strike at once. Gambara adapts the image of the eyes as avenues through which a miraculous and instantaneous transfusion occurs. Whereas Petrarch is devastated and converted by the rays from his lady's eyes, Gambara as a female Petrarchan persona celebrates the variety of emotional states she sees there. Where Petrarch is taken by a single blow, Gambara is filled with a range of effects as diverse as those in her lover's eyes, an experience which she relishes.

We notice also that reversing the roles presents no problem for Gambara. The standard Petrarchan situation has the lady elevated above the lover. She is angelic, virtuous, and perfectly beautiful. But her refusal to return the poet's love makes her hard, cruel, and cold as ice. The poet praises her beauty, complains bitterly of her cruelty, and remains in a miserable state, oscillating between ecstasy in her presence and torture in her absence. Gambara selectively appropriates those conventions that express her situation and leaves the rest. Although hers is a married, consummated love (Petrarchism, like courtly love, was usually adulterous), she avoids mention of those themes that would seem intrusive. By doing this she maintains one of the prerequisites of Petrarchan diction. It is not confessional. The individuality of the speaker is exchanged for an elevating universality. The "I" of the love poems could be anyone; her sonnets could be, like Petrarch's, set to music and sung by others. A good example of this refinement of individuality is madrigal 2, which praises her lover's beauty without giving us any specific information about him or her. She compares her lover to Mars and to Adonis, Venus's lovers in mythology. He is stronger than the warrior god, more lovely than the young hunter. The poem's strength lies in the simplicity and directness of the comparison. The presence of descriptive detail, or of anything factual concerning the speaker or the beloved, would compromise the rich and langorous effect of the classical allusion.

How good is Veronica's poetry? The situation is similar to that of Spenser's *Amoretti*, a work often ignored because it achieved something in which modern critics have limited interest. To begin with, Petrarch's verse was artificial, elegant, refined, and rhetorical. It employed a limited vocabulary within a strictly defined decorum. Gambara's deliberate adherence to Bembo's doctrine of imitation gives her work the same drab appearance that the *Amoretti* are widely supposed to have. One will not find "originality" as long as that word is defined as departure from convention. But we will find artifice, elegance, and refinement. Examined from within the convention, her poems are balanced and delicate, and often have a sweetly poignant musicality. She is generally successful in the formal and rhetorical aspects of imitation, but she largely fails in not achieving the depth of expression called for by her Petrarchan original. The same can be said of Bembo.

Veronica Gambara spent the last years of her life in quiet study and meditation, living at her *casino* and rarely traveling. She died in June 1550 and was buried beside her husband in a tomb decorated with olive and laurel to signify peaceful rule and poetic fame. Both the church and the *casino* were destroyed by the Spanish armies in 1556, one year after the abdication of the emperor who, during his visit, promised protection to the town and on whom Gambara had placed such high hopes.

Many collections of poetry in the sixteenth century included some of

Gambara's poems, but at her death she left no authoritative collection of her writings. No attempt was made to organize a comprehensive collection until Rizzardi's edition in 1759. The nineteenth century saw some renewal of interest in her work, and some commentaries and biographies appeared. Rizzardi's edition was revised and expanded by Pia Mestica Chiappetti in 1879, and since then several other poems and letters have appeared. In the twentieth century there still is not much interest in Gambara; the lion's share of enthusiasm goes to Vittoria Colonna and, more recently, to Gaspara Stampa. Clearly a need exists for a modern critical edition of Veronica Gambara's writings.

One cannot help but notice that Gambara was terribly "traditional." Far from being "oppressed" in any sense, she was born into the highest and most affluent level of society, had the best education that could be provided to anyone, moved in circles that included the most powerful people in Europe, and ruled over a territory for much of her life. Her friend and mentor Pietro Bembo was a virtual dictator of poetics and literary criticism in sixteenth-century Italy.[16] Both in her appealing and in her unappealing aspects, she embodied the values of the Italian High Renaissance. She did many things very well. With considerable acumen she guided her state through a turbulent period. She always recognized and encouraged talent, whether it was the young prodigy Rinaldo Corso or the painter Antonio Allegri. Her poetry combined high seriousness with shameless flattery. Her unabashed worldliness and her religious devotions were both pursued with equal fervor.

Gambara is not in the first rank of poets, and it is doubtful that she though of herself as a writer by vocation. Italian literary historians tend to rank her as one of the top three women poets of the sixteenth century, below Gaspara Stampa and Vittoria Colonna. The comparison is just, for she stands properly between the two, between the mysticism of Colonna and the emotion of Stampa. Both are intensely lyrical compared to the more refined and conventional verse of Veronica. For us, she is the model of the Italian Renaissance *gentildonna*, or virtuous lady, who acted as governor, patron, writer, wife, and mother. She approached her poetry with *sprezzatura*, gracefully and casually, in much the same way that the male courtier was expected to dance, sing, and versify as well as ride horses, wrestle, and wage war and diplomacy. When the poet Ariosto visited Correggio in 1531 on his last diplomatic mission for Duke Alfonso I of Ferrara, he met Gambara and recorded his admiration for her near the end of *Orlando Furioso:*

Veronica da Gambara è con loro
Si grata a Febo e al santo aonio coro.

Veronica Gambara is with them,
So dear to Apollo and the sacred Muses.

The present translation is based on Pia Mestica Chiappetti's edition of the author's works, although use has also been made of more recent manuscript finds by Costa and others. In my translations I have tried to steer a middle course through the two extremes of, on the one hand, transliteration, and on the other, the creation of an entirely different English poem. I hope that when I have veered it has always been on the side of literalness.

NOTES

1. Gambara's work is not readily available. There is no complete edition of her works in Italian, and only a few of her poems and letters have been translated into English. Most of her poems (and all the ones contained here) can be found in Pia Mestica Chiappetti's *Rime e lettere* of 1879, the most recent edition of her collected works. I have numbered the poems according to that edition. Additional writings that have come to light since then are listed in the Bibliography.

2. For Gambara's letters to Bembo, see Chiappetti, ed., pp. 91–110. For Bembo's letters to Gambara see *Opere in volgare di Pietro Bembo*, ed. Marti, pp. 856–62.

3. For Gambara's letters to Aretino, see Chiappetti, ed., pp. 264–86. Among Aretino's letters to Gambara are numbers 78, 129, 180, and 223 of the first book and number 376 of the second book, in Francesco Flora, ed., *Tutte le opere di Pietro Aretino*, vol. 1. Also of interest in this regard are letters 1.158 to Gambara's son Girolamo and 2.158 to Paolo Interiano, in which Aretino praises the women poets Vittoria Colonna, Veronica Gambara, and Maria Spinola.

4. This letter is printed in Adolfo Venturi, *Storia dell'arte italiana: la pittura del cinquecento*, vol. 9, pt. 2, p. 470.

5. See Riccardo Finzi, *Umanità di Veronica Gambara*, p. 12.

6. See Chiappetti, ed., pp. xix–xxi, and Maud F. Jerrold, *Vittoria Colonna*, p. 156.

7. For example, Jerrold writes, "Veronica was not a woman to live in her affections, things did not go deep enough with her for that" (pp. 156–57).

8. See Finzi, pp. 11–12.

9. This letter is in Chiappetti, ed., pp. 180–81.

10. The Renaissance papacy, for example, being both a spiritual authority and a territorial power, was far from subscribing to such a program. For a sympathetic account of Charles's aspirations, see Gertrude von Schwarzenfeld, *Charles V: Father of Europe*.

11. Ibid., pp. 109–116.

12. Machiavelli quotes from *Italia mia* at the close of *Il Principe* in his exhortation to his countrymen to expel the barbarians and restore liberty to Italy.

13. For a description of the meeting, see von Schwarzenfeld, pp. 178–81.

14. All quotations from Petrarch are from Gianfranco Contini, ed., *Canzoniere*. For English translations see Robert Durling, *Petrarch's Lyric Poems*.

15. See Jerrold, p. 157.

16. For a discussion of Bembo's role in Petrarchism and the standardizing of the vernacular language, see chapter 3 of Fiora A. Bassanese's *Gaspara Stampa*.

Madrigal 1

Eyes lovely and shining,
how is it that in one second
you generate so many varied qualities?
Joy, sorrow, pride, humility, and arrogance
you display all at once, whence with hope
and with fear you fill me,
and with all sweet effects, and pungent, and fiery;
in the burnt heart they converge for you
whenever you wish.
Since you are my life and death,
eyes happy, eyes lovely and dear,
be always serene, lively and clear!

Madrigal 2

If, when for Adonis or for Mars
the lovely Venus was pining,
you, my Lord, had been seen by her,
that kindled torch,
only for you who are more worthy than they
would have burned to a blazing radiance;
because in arms you greatly surpass
the bellicose Mars, and in beauty Adonis
surrenders to comparison.
Therefore, if the heavens exalt you
and make you immortal, do not marvel,
for such is justly yours.

Sonnet 1

When by youthful and straying thoughts[1]
I was nourished, now fearing, now hoping,
now crying in pain, now happily singing,
torn by desire now false, now true,

With strains proud and piteous I gave vent
to the heart's conceits, loving his hurt
much more than looking for good,
squandering all the days in sorrow.

Now that with other thoughts and desires
I nourish the mind, I have consigned the pen
and the dear rhymes to eternal silence.

If, in this raving, I tread again
on those first transgressions, now repentance
seizes on the inner grief, proclaiming my guilt.

Sonnet 2

O sole glory of our generation,
Wise Lady,[2] graceful, indeed divine,
to whom all who are worthy of fame
today make reverent homage:

Surely you will be remembered forever!
Nor will withering time be able
to make of your lovely name impious pillage,
but from him you will draw ample victory.

To you our sex should raise a noble and sacred temple
as we have already to Pallas, and to Phoebus,
of richest marbles and of finest gold.

Since you are the example of virtue,
I wish, Lady, that I could praise as much
as I revere, love, and adore you.

Sonnet 4

Conquer your wrath and your ancient hatred,[3]
Charles and Francis, in the holy and blessed name
of Christ, and in His faith, who more than any other
has been your friend: Be at peace.

Let your weapons be ready to tame
his irreverent enemy, not just for Italy
but for all Europe, and for all lands washed by the sea,
where the sun touches upon hills and valleys.

The great Shepherd[4] to whom the keys of Heaven
were given, turns to you and prays that you
be taken with pity for His flock.

Be stronger in piety than in hatred, O royal pair,
and let a single desire ignite you both:
to vanquish those who hate Christ, and deny Him.

Sonnet 6

That happy star is in the fateful heaven
which was companion to the high birth
of great Augustus Caesar, who held the empire
of the world, and was noble, and immortal.

That, but more benign, to the wonderful birth
of the great Charles was guide, so that I hope more
to see him, to say better the truth:
A god is made among us from mortal man.

So that, if in conquering the Indians, the Medes, the Scythians,
the Cantabrians, the Britons, and the ferocious Gauls,
the first one merited having such high honors,

Then this one who has already conquered two worlds
and united so much anxious discord in so much peace
now merits even more praise and greater honor.

Sonnet 9

Behold that already three times, my Italy,
to heal your bitter and heavy wounds,
he who in government holds the celestial keys[5]
has begun happily to negotiate with Charles.

From great knowledge and pious intent
he hopes to bring you peace and pleasant days,
no longer fearing that evil Fortune
may despoil your beautiful lands, as it once did.

This is the second vessel, not less perhaps
than the first, strong and wise, elected to be tested
by Christ to save his beloved flock.

He renews in you the ancient glory
and with the light of his sacred radiance
illuminates the world, and rectifies its errors.

Sonnet 14

Seeing you, O eyes serene and clear,
there rises in the soul such pleasure, such bliss,
that each hurt, each affliction, each great pain
I consider mild, and I call them sweet, and dear.

Not seeing you, O sweet and rare lights,
fatal symbols of my life,
this soul grows into such fiery sorrow
that my days are more bitter than absinthe.

I live only to contemplate you,
my limpid stars, sweet and joyous;
the rest of my life is affliction and tears.

Yet, if I thirst so to see you,
do not marvel. Everyone flees from Death,
from whom you are my shield.

Sonnet 18

Since fortune brings me to see you again,
sweet hills, and you, clear fresh waters,
and you, noble site,[6] whom Nature makes
delightful, lovely, and adorned,

Well can I call the day blessed
and praise always that longing to see you again,
which before was lying dead
in the heart all surrounded with sorrow.

I see you now, and such sweetness feel,
that despite Fortune's torments,
I muse here in sweet forgetfulness.

So may heaven always be generous,
blessed setting, for in me is extinguished
every desire, if it is not of you alone.

Sonnet 21

Loosen your golden tresses! And adorn[7]
your hair with laurel and myrtle,

resplendent Venus! And may the holy loves
have in you a sweet and fertile stay.

And you, sacred Hymen! Singing aloud
of lovely roses and purple flowers
with golden plectrum, in verses high and resonant,
you give honor unto this exalted day.

And you great gods who govern mortals,
spread for us with full hands your joy,[8]
peace, tenderness, love, and faith,

So that the chaste kisses and glad hours
enjoyed by two will be so sweet
that Heaven cannot grant them more reward.

Sonnet 24

Go, lying thoughts and vain hopes,
blind, voracious desires, burning wants;
Go passionate sighs, bitter pains,
constant companions to my endless sorrow.

Go forth, sweet memories, sharp chains
for the heart recovers the bridle of reason
which was lost, and breaks away from you,
recovers its liberty and is free again.

And you, poor Soul! In such affliction bound,
be released henceforth, and to your divine Lord
gracefully turn back your thoughts.

Ferociously conquer proud Fate
and break its snares. Then, free and nimble,
turn back your steps to the safer path.[9]

Sonnet 25

In the heart's secret and most profound place
where stand in battle formation the thoughts
and the desires, where war is waged so fiercely
that reason swiftly takes her leave,

The interior man reasons, and uses every art
to bring her back, and make her know the damage,
but out in the exterior go the senses;
without spirit they take part unaware.

I am made of flesh, am therefore weak and infirm.
They cannot grasp the beautiful high concepts
which spirit sends to those in whom the spirit lives.

Therefore guide, O Lord, my affections,
which without your help are evil, to the sacred shores,
before my soul grows further into error.

Sonnet 28

O great mystery, only through faith understood!
Your beautiful body is made the temple of God,
Sacred Virgin, and in that humble and pious
being lives virtue descended from heaven.

He burned so brightly in your humility,
which He wanted so much to save, that He
closed himself in you, and from you he issued,
without touching or offending the virginal cloister.

He created himself in you, as in the white fleece
the heavenly dew; the parched earth
He alone replenished with water.

This the effect was, that was the sign;
thus we sing with you today, declaring
Glory to God, who is never fully praised.

Sonnet 29

Today through you, Virgin pure,
there is revealed on earth such a miracle
that Nature falls, astonished, and wonders
at your marvelous handiwork.

God is made man, and under human care,
dressed in irksome mortal flesh,

remains what he was, his divinity
hidden in an infant's form.

Of mixed nature he was not, nor ever divided,
but always God and always veritable man,
as powerful on earth as in Heaven.

Then turn toward me, O Virgin, the rays
of your grace, that I may understand
this high and profound mystery.

Ballad

Now hope has passed away
which once kept me burning.
I mourn less since I know
nothing remains the same.
            Now hope has passed away.
    This false one once in fire
held me, keeping hope alive;
mocking my pain,
she has left me crying
and loving and desiring;
she takes me to death each hour
with passion tenacious and strong
and with more perseverance.
            Now hope has passed away.
    I hoped, and that hoping
nurtured me in a sweet flame.
Now I hope no more, and this soul
yearns only for tears
and calls on Death each hour
to relieve her sorrow;
for the heart is hopeless now
where hope once made a sweet home.
            Now hope has passed away.
    While I had him to guide me
every pain seemed light.
Without him, I am lost and dead,
each little hurt seems grave,
long affliction and brief pleasure
I have always felt since then.

To have once served with him
is my only reward.
        Now hope has passed away.
   My soft sweet hope
from me, alas, has flown.
and in leaving stole away with her
my burnt heart, and my weary life.
Being thus dismayed
and of all hope deprived,
I remain alive, not living,
finally, utterly without hope.
        Now hope has passed away.

NOTES TO THE TRANSLATION

  1. Sonnets 1 and 2 were addressed to Vittoria Colonna.
  2. In the Italian *Donna saggia,* a woman of socially exalted position possessed of wisdom.
  3. Addressed to Emperor Charles V and Francis I, king of France.
  4. Pope Paul III.
  5. Again, Paul III.
  6. Gambara's *casino.*
  7. It is not known for whose wedding this poem was written, or even if it was written for a particular couple.
  8. "With full hands" (a man piena) recalls Virgil's *Aeneid* 6.833: "Manibus date lilia plenis," where the ritual scattering of lilies by Anchises honors the doomed Marcellus, Augustus' heir. Dante transforms the phrase into a celebratory gesture in *Purgatorio* 30.21, where it is used by angels welcoming Beatrice (but still preserving a note of pathos for the departing Virgil). Thus the line becomes a tag for ritual celebration with a qualifying sadness at leaving something behind.
  9. This sonnet is influenced by poem 153 of Petrarch's *Canzoniere.*

BIBLIOGRAPHY

Primary Works

Amadduzzi, Luigi, ed. *Undici Lettere inedite di Veronica Gambara e un'ode latina tradotta in volgare.* Guastalla, 1889.
Chiappetti, Pia Mestica, ed. *Rime e lettere.* Florence, 1879.
Costa, E., ed. *Sonetti amorosi inediti e rari.* Parma, 1890.
Rampini, A. L., ed. *Sonetti inediti.* Padua, 1845.
Rizzardi, Felice, ed. *Rime e lettere.* Brescia, 1759.
Salza, A., ed. *Rime inedite e rare di Veronica Gambara.* Ciriè, 1915.

Related Works

Bassanese, Fiora A. *Gaspara Stampa*. Boston, 1982.

Bembo, Pietro. *Opere in volgare*. Ed. Mario Marti. Florence, 1961.

Bullock, Alan. "Veronica o Vittoria? Problemi di attribuzione per alcuni sonetti del cinquecento." *Studi e problemi di critica testuale* 6:115–31.

Chubb, T. C., ed. *The Letters of Pietro Aretino*. New Haven, Conn., 1967.

de Courten, Clementina. *Veronica Gambara: Una Gentildonna del Cinquecento*. Milan, 1934.

Durling, Robert. *Petrarch's Lyric Poems: The "Rime sparse" and Other Lyrics*. Cambridge, Mass., 1976.

Finzi, Riccardo. *Umanità di Veronica Gambara*. Reggio Emilia, 1969.

Flora, Francesco, ed. *Gaspara Stampa e altre poetesse del'500*. Milan, 1962.

————. *Tutte le opere di Pietro Aretino*. Vol. 1, *Lettere*. Verona, 1960.

Gardner, Edmund G. *The King of Court Poets: A Study of the Work, Life, and Times of Lodovico Ariosto*. New York, 1968.

Gould, Cecil. *Paintings of Correggio*. Ithaca, N.Y., 1976.

Jerrold, Maud F. *Vittoria Colonna*. New York, 1969.

Labalme, Patricia H. *Beyond Their Sex: Learned Women of the European Past*. New York, 1980.

Petrarch, Francesco. *Canzoniere*. Ed. Gianfranco Contini. Turin, 1964.

Popham, A. E. *Correggio's Drawings*. London, 1957.

Venturi, Adolfo. *Storia dell'arte italiana: la pittura del cinquecento*. Vol. 9, pt. 2., p. 470. Milan, 1926.

von Schwarzenfeld, Gertrude. *Charles V: Father of Europe*. Chicago, 1957.

aint Catherine of Genoa

DONALD CHRISTOPHER NUGENT

Whether or not because the subject ultimately addresses something ineffable, the student of mysticism is apt to have to acknowledge, eventually, that mysticism is best defined by a mystic. That is, by someone who embodies its particular genius, rather than by the abstractions of genus and specific difference. Such a person is assuredly Saint Catherine of Genoa, for she is a model mystic. She was in fact chosen as the model for Friedrich von Hügel's masterpiece *The Mystical Element of Religion as Studied in Saint Catherine of Genoa and Her Friends,* sometimes characterized as the foremost study of mysticism in the English language in our century.[1] And Von Hügel's work in turn was avowedly in part the model for the monumental work of Louis Massignon, *The Passion of Al-Hallāj: Mystic and Martyr of Islam.*[2] This hints at Catherine's at least potential universality. For example, I have suggested that her doctrine of annihilation has its analogies with the Buddhist doctrine of annattā, of "no-self."[3] For all her universality, Catherine is completely orthodox, and her influence has been incalculable. Her role at the genesis of the Oratory of Divine Love is such that it has been advanced that she "began the effective reform of the Catholic Church" on the eve of the Reformation.[4] All the same, her impact was to be felt within Protestantism as well as Catholicism. To begin, there are "striking" analogies between Saint Catherine and Saint John of the Cross.[5] She was praised by Saint Francis of Sales, who acknowledged that he had "read and re-read" her most original work, the *Treatise of Purgatory,* many times.[6] Her influence extended to such spiritual writers of the Catholic Reformation as Saint Aloysius Gonzaga, Saint Robert Bellarmine, Cardinal de Berulle, Madame Acarie, Fénelon, and Bossuet. Friedrich Von Schlegel translated her *Dialogue,* and Cardinal Newman incorporated her ideas into what may be his finest poem, "The Dream of Gerontius."[7] Protestant interest in Catherine dates from at least the nineteenth century. Thomas C. Upham of Bowdoin College translated her life in 1845. Protestants were correct in detecting kinship between such things as the perfectionism of Catherine and that of John Wesley. Catherine was an example to individuals like Phoebe Palmer, an early leader in both the Perfectionist Movement and in women's rights. That Catherine was a laywoman, not a nun, enhanced Protestant receptivity toward her.[8] And perhaps all the foregoing will enhance that of our own.

For all this, Saint Catherine of Genoa (1447–1510) is not as well known as her earlier Italian compatriat, Saint Catherine of Siena (1342–1380). One reason may be that she was but one of a number of Catherines to rise with the late Renaissance, including Blessed Catherine of Racconigi (1486–1547), Saint Catherine of Ricci (1522–1590), and Saint Catherine Tomas (1533–1574). For another, no astonishing miracles are attributed to her. Finally, strictly speaking, she wrote nothing. Still, the substance of her sayings are considered well preserved in her *opera*, compiled by her disciples in the years following her death, and their impact upon religious literature has hardly been, as has been suggested above, insignificant.

Catherine Fieschi was born in 1447 of an ancient Genovese family that had produced several popes. Her father was Viceroy of Naples. Her natural disposition was to the religious life, but at thirteen her family frustrated her desire to enter the convent. Instead, at sixteen this elegant beauty (as indicated by a portrait of her) was married by the Guelf Fieschi into the Ghibelline Adorno family. Her husband, Giuliano, was as wayward as she was devout, a circumstance that drove the naturally spontaneous and affable Catherine inward, and by turns to worldly distractions and escapism. On March 20, 1473, she suddenly experienced a great second conversion, an experience of being overwhelmed by the enormity of God's love. Thenceforth she was an inspiration even to her dissolute husband, who eventually became a Franciscan tertiary. Contrary to some opinion, however, Catherine did not, and she once matched the reproach of an over-eager Franciscan with this *riposte:* "If I thought that your habit had the power of gaining me one single additional spark of love, I should not hesitate to take it from you by force"![9] Though married, Catherine and her husband agreed to a life of perpetual continence, and living now as brother and sister, they entered the service of the hospital of the Pammatone, within which they eventually moved. Catherine employed herself first as nurse and in time as *rettora* (administrative head) of the hospital. Her life there was marked by heroic service—not least during the deadly plague that decimated Genoa in 1493—long and mysterious fasts, and by periods of ecstatic absorption in worshiping God. Her husband preceded her in death in 1497, and Catherine's own health broke completely in the last years of her life, a matter to which we shall return. She died in 1510, and her remains, still not completely corrupt, were placed in a glass-encased tomb of the Capuchin chapel adjoining the old hospital where she spent the last three decades of her life. She was canonized in 1737.

Thus passed Catherine's quiet and rather hidden life, all but a failure to the world, unknown to most of Italy, much less to Christendom. But for all that, this woman was undoubtedly a spiritual genius, and Von Hügel chose his model well, for she incarnates and illuminates something of most of the issues associated with mysticism perennially, a matter beyond our purview here.

Catherine is first and foremost a mystical theologian. By this is intended, of course, a theology that is infused, rather than acquired or scholastic. As she put it of her great conversion experience: "Love, is it possible that you have called me with such love and made me know in an instant that which language cannot express?"[10] And this can suggest that her theology is one of *affectus* as well as *intellectus,* love as well as illumination. One consequence is that she cannot readily be characterized as a "bridal mystic" (*Brautmystik*), the tradition descended from the *Song of Songs,* rich in loving devotion and replete with bridal imagery, on the one hand; or, on the other, the more abstracted and sapiential "essence-mystic" (*Wesenmystik*), generally associated with the Neoplatonic tradition. Bonzi da Genova relates her to the former, but Von Hügel demurs.[11] In this I think that Von Hügel is more discerning: Catherine sought not "the mystical kiss," but God. Hers is a spirituality of love, but of pure love. She has in fact been acclaimed "the doctor of pure love."[12] Pure love, of course, is disinterested love, a love that seeks nothing for itself, a great theme (and controversy) of mystical literature. Catherine takes this as far as it will go, seeking no sensible consolations, such that Von Hügel at one point will speak of "the stamp of staunch virility" in her piety.[13] For years, she was content to subsist on little more than the Eucharist during Lent and Advent. Her spirituality was also, then, ascetic (for example, she wore a hair shirt and was a vegetarian). Finally, as much of the foregoing might suggest, her theology was that of "the way of negation" (the *via negativa,* apophatic). That is, it is premised of the (I regret to say) "idea" that God is incomparable, as a consequence of which the way to God is through the denial of all created being, including oneself, and certainly one's ideas and images of God. Theoretically, she herself stated it as follows: "All that can be said [about God], is not [God]."[14] Hers is, if you will, a "nothing" (*nulla*) mysticism, that is, it would reduce everything to nothing but, as in Saint John of the Cross, this "nothing" becomes "everything." She can symbolize this in what is probably her most compelling statement: "My *Me* is God."[15]

With this, her theological *naïveté* (in the scholastic sense) has become sublime. For all this, she was by no means totally theologically naïve. She was a woman of the Renaissance, and she was informed by learned forces, including Augustinian and Neoplatonic currents mediated through Liguorian humanists, plus such things as Franciscan voluntarism.[16] This learned tradition may have helped moderate any tendencies to an other-worldly quietism or an exaggerated dualism. Her utterly uncompromising doctrine of "annihilation" can seem at times to approach such things. But both Von Hügel and Bonzi da Genova acquit her of any such taint, with the latter speaking of her doctrine of annihilation as "an absorption of the human in the divine, of a duality that tends to be surpassed, of a dialectic of two poles."[17] In a few words, from apparent contradictions can emerge a larger truth. The thing to bear in mind is that what we have with Catherine is not a theological system, but a theological life.

And, as it would be, a theological death. As we have said, in her last years her health failed completely, and Catherine's disintegration seemed total: physical, psychological, and at times even spiritual. Yet no one has questioned her sanity, much less her sanctity. Attending physicians pronounced her sickness to be supernatural, but there is evidence of a gastric cancer. Of course, even these things are not necessarily mutually exclusive. In any event, this was well before modern analgesics, and Catherine's death was one of the most awesome recorded in spiritual literature, and it is amply recorded in her *Spiritual Dialogue*.

Catherine had prayed that "Your pure love . . . will annihilate me,"[18] and in *her* terms this prayer seemed to have been answered. One of her foremost figures is fire (*fuoco*), and Catherine burned. According to her disciples, her prayers were as "sighs, cries, and inner fire."[19] And in her last days, Catherine asked the attendants "to open the window to see if the world was on fire."[20] Catherine had become, as it were, a holocaust.

In mysticism, life and death, too, are dialectical, not dualistic, and Catherine's death seems anticipated in her life. And anticipated also in what is considered her most original work: *The Treatise on Purgatory*. This is what Bonzi da Genova calls her "ultramundane catharsis."[21] True, and it can also be, with Catherine, intramundane catharsis. Von Hügel speaks of her "insistence upon an unbroken spiritual life, in spite of and right through physical death."[22] In other words, there can be not just survival after death, but purgatory on earth. The latter at least Catherine is open to and, to return to our metaphor, hers is a "loving purgatory of divine fire."[23] This fire is ultimately love. And, to use the great centrality of Saint Augustine, longing. In other words, the conformity of the soul to God, which is the business of purgatory, is something that the soul itself longs for. It takes place spontaneously, instinctively, and "naturally." If you will, Catherine has naturalized purgatory as well as supernaturalized life. And she has put purgatorial purgation and mystical purgation on the same plane.

If some of this seems highly suggestive of structures of Saint John of the Cross after Catherine, some of it can also be suggestive of Nicholas of Cusa before her. Purgatory is, of course, the essential prelude to the Beatific Vision. But, for Catherine, the Beatific Vision is not just the end of purgatory, but part of the process. That is, the souls in purgatory are drawn to God by His own powerful glance, which they sense if not see darkly. This seems like the same glance of Cusa's great *Vision of God* (1453), really "the gaze of God," the transforming gaze of God.[24] Catherine seems logically to represent a link between Cusa and John of the Cross. But her work may be more experiential than either of these great spiritual masters, and that may be why it can often seem to be so self-authenticating.

The sources on Saint Catherine of Genoa are a serious problem, a matter enormously alleviated by the critical edition of Bonzi da Genova (1960–62), but unlikely ever to be resolved. Catherine's "works" are three: The *Biography* or *Life, The Treatise on Purgatory,* and *The Spiritual Dialogue.* None are by Catherine. They represent an archaic and repetitive mosaic of her sayings, with biographical additions and theological accretions and development of her immediate and contemporary disciples. They are considered faithful. The first publication of her works was in 1551, a work that went through many editions with various titles. Moreover, there are inevitably various and divergent manuscripts. Von Hügel and Bonzi da Genova both discuss the textual problem in depth.[25] Bonzi's critical edition features three manuscripts, published parallel, with further variations annotated. There are, as suggested, various nineteenth-century translations in English, all superseded by the critical work of Bonzi da Genova. A recent and valuable discussion of these matters will be found in the Paulist edition (pp. 47–67), translated by Serge Hughes.

I have rendered anew various passages from the *Life,* or to be more precise, *Biography,* plus about 60 percent of the *Purgatory.* In general, my translation prefers fidelity to felicity of expression. If it lacks something of the freedom and literary finesse of other translations, it is hoped that there may be compensation in the effort to recapture the raw, ingenuous quality of Catherine and her first disciples. With reference to the *Purgatory,* one might observe that, with Catherine, the torments of hell *are* mitigated. Hopefully, something of pure love is operative there, too.

NOTES

1. Von Hügel's book was published as two volumes in London in 1908. Both Evelyn Underhill and Morton Kelsey have declared its importance. Underhill states so on the jacket of a Von Hügel volume; Kelsey, in a private conversation some years ago.

2. Louis Massignon, *The Passion of Al-Hallāj: Mystic and Martyr of Islam,* trans. Herbert Mason, 4 vols. (Princeton, N.J., 1982).

3. Donald Nugent, "The Annihilation of Saint Catherine of Genoa," International Medieval Congress, Kalamazoo, Michigan, May 1984.

4. John Olin, *The Catholic Reformation: Savonarola to Ignatius Loyola* (New York, 1969), pp. 16–17.

5. Jean Baruzi, *Saint Jean de la croix et le problème de l'experience mystique,* p. 597.

6. P. Umile Bonzi da Genova, *S. Caterina Fieschi Adorno,* vol. 1, p. 126, note 7.

7. Von Hügel, vol. 1, pp. 88–90.

8. All the above is from *Catherine of Genoa,* trans. Serge Hughes, pp. 39–41.

9. *S. Caterina da Genova* (Genova: Presso Vita Francescana, 1954), see title page for contrary opinion and vol. 2, pp. 191–92 for quotation.

10. *Ibid.,* vol. 2, p. 116.

11. Ibid., vol. 1, pp. 607–10, 111.

12. Pierre Debongnie, *Sainte Catherine de Gênes: La grand dame de pur amour,* p. xix.

13. Von Hügel, vol. 1, p. 116.

14. Bonzi da Genova, vol. 2, p. 288.

15. *Ibid.,* p. 171: "*il mio Mi é Dio.*"

16. Bonzi da Genova, vol. 1, p. 616.

17. *Ibid.,* p. 534. See also Von Hügel, vol. 1, p. 238, on the "*Totum Simul.*"

18. Bonzi da Genova, vol. 2, p. 403.

19. *Ibid.,* p. 407.

20. *Ibid.,* p. 455.

21. Ibid., vol. 1, p. 146.

22. Von Hügel, vol. 2, p. 90.

23. Bonzi da Genova, vol. 2, p. 322.

24. Nicholas of Cusa, *The Vision of God,* trans. Emma Gurney Salter (New York, 1960), p. 14.

25. Von Hügel, vol. 1, pp. 371–466; and Bonzi da Genova, vol. 2, pp. 1–105.

Biography

I have given the keys of the house to Love, with ample authority to do all that was needed, excepting neither soul nor body, property nor parents, friends nor the world, but that not a spark would be wanting of all the law of pure love requires.

And when I saw that Love accepted my cares and went about its work, I turned toward the said Love, occupied with His gracious operations, and He with such love, solicitude, and justice did nothing more or less than was needed, satisfying me inwardly and outwardly. With this I was so contented that had he thrown me soul and body into hell, it would have seemed to me all love and good will. . . .

If I spoke of spiritual things that I felt and understood through the eye of love, of the fire that often besieged me, immediately Love reproved me to the effect that I ought not to speak, but that I ought to allow myself just to burn without any display, neither with word nor with any act that would serve to support the soul or the body.

If I were silent and showed no regard for anything, but only said, "If you die, you die; if you are unable to bear it, let it be, nothing matters to me," still Love reproved me, saying He did not want me to look at what He was doing. And He said, "I want you to close your eyes so that you are unable to see what I am doing. I want you to be as dead and wholly annihilated. I want that nothing be done of your own self. . . ."

After that, I closed my mouth and became as a thing immobile, tightened in the grip of this love, and I felt such peace and interior contentment, that I could no longer support myself. . . .

Pure Love said, "What have you, that you cannot support it? If you still feel anything, it is a sign that you are still alive. I do not want that you sigh or lament, but that you be as the dead and the dying. I do not want to see a sign of life."

I do not want created love, that is, love that can be tasted, that can be understood, that is able to delight, which passes through the intellect, the memory and the will, because the love that I want passes beyond all these things. . . .

When I see that man is lost of himself when he is occupied with self-love, in such a way that he cares neither for God nor dreads hell . . . I say that if self-love has such force, how much more force is there in pure love, which is God Himself? . . .

Within myself I am unable to see anything but God, because I do not allow other things to enter, and my own self less than others, for I am my own enemy.

However, if it is necessary to name this Me, in order to live in a world which cannot speak otherwise, when I give myself a name or when others name me, I say within myself: My *Me* is God. I do not know another Me than my God Himself.

Thus I say of being: Everything that has being has it from the essence of God, by participation. But Pure Love cannot stand to see this. . . . This love cannot endure such a similitude, but exclaims with the great impetuosity of love: My being is God Himself, not by participation, but by transformation and annihilation of its own being.

But because man is created for beatitude, from which he has been alienated by his own being, which is the opposite of his beatitude, therefore we are obliged to submit ourselves to the power of God, which consumes us . . . otherwise the soul would not find stability or contentment, for it is not created to any other end. Therefore, when God attracts the free will with such sweet deception, He does it. And when He has done it, he is able to conduct it to its own annihilation. Therefore, in God is my being, my Me, my strength, my goodness, my delight, my beatitude. . . . I see clearly that the creature in this world is deceived, because it sees and esteems that which is not, and it does not see or esteem that which in truth is.

You see how the soul is imperfect in its own will, and how it becomes perfect as it approaches that of the sweet love of God. And in this way is to be understood the words of Saint Paul: "I live now not I, but Christ lives in me." O blessed is that soul that dies to itself in everything, because it lives to everything in God!

Treatise on Purgatory

I say that the pain of the damned is not infinite in degree, for the sweet goodness [of God] pours out its rays of mercy even in hell. Although the man who dies in mortal sin merits an infinite pain an infinite time, mercy has made only the time infinite, but the pain is mitigated in degree. God could have in justice given greater pain to him than He has.

But the souls in purgatory have their wills in total conformity with that of God. Accordingly, God corresponds to that conformity with His goodness, by which they remain happy, as regards their will, for He purifies them of original and actual sin.

As for guilt, such souls remain as pure as when God created them, for they passed from this life sorrowing for their sins, with the will to commit no more. Because of this sorrow, God pardoned this guilt at once, and thus remains only the rust and deformity of sin, which is then purified in fire, painfully.

And therefore these souls, purified of all guilt and united with God by the will, see God clearly according to the degree that God makes Himself known to them. And seeing how great is the enjoyment of God, for which the soul was created, it is completely conformed to God, a conformity instinctive to the soul, about which one is unable to reason or to exemplify. The mind feels it in its effects and grasps it in an interior sense.

Nevertheless, one example comes to mind. If in all the world were but one bread which could take away the hunger of all creatures, just to see it alone would be satisfying. Thus, man by nature, if he is sound, has the instinct to eat it. And if he does not eat it and is neither sick nor dead, the hunger always increases. Knowing that this bread alone can satisfy him, he remains in intolerable pain.

But this is hell that, the more they feel the proximity of this bread and are not able to see it, the more frustrated is their natural desire. And if they were certain that they would never see this bread, at that point they would have hell complete. The complete hell of the damned is being deprived of all hope of ever seeing this true bread, this true, saving God.

But the souls in purgatory have this hunger: They do not see this bread, but they have hope of seeing it and being entirely satisfied by it.

Beyond this I see clearly that, as the purified spirit finds no other place than God for its repose, being created to that end, the soul that is in mortal sin has no other proper place than hell, because God has ordained that place for it. For in the instant that the spirit is separated from the body, the soul goes to its ordained place, without any other guide than the nature of its sin.

And I say that if the soul is not found in that place which proceeds from the justice of God, it would dwell in an even greater hell, being outside the order of divine mercy, not having the pain that it merits. Not finding itself in its proper place, it would at once hurl itself there.

Thus in purgatory, if the soul separated from the body does not find itself in the purity with which it was created, seeing itself to have impediments which can be taken away only by means of purgatory, it gladly hurls itself there at once.

And if the soul should not find the ordained place enough to remove its impediments, it would be born that instant in a hell worse than purgatory. For purgatory is almost nothing compared to seeing itself separated from God. . . .

I see still that the divine essence is so pure and clear, far more than man can imagine; that the soul knowing itself to have the least imperfection would hurl itself at once into a thousand hells rather than find itself in His presence with the least stain. . . .

Of such import is this that language cannot express nor heart comprehend, except that I see that purgatory is just as painful as hell. But I see that the soul accepts it as a mercy, not making much of it, compared to the stain separating it from His love.

And it seems to me that the pain of those in purgatory is mostly in seeing in themselves something displeasing to God, that they have acted freely against the divine goodness. And this I say because, being in the grace of God, they see the true consequence of what deprives them of God.

Of this I am so certain, from everything I have so far comprehended in this life, that compared to it every word, every sentiment, every image, every conception of justice, every truth, soon seems to me more false than true. And in comparison to what I feel the mind is nothing, and I remain confused in not finding a vocabulary more precise.

I see so great a conformity between God and the soul, that when His Majesty sees it in that purity in which He created it, drawn in a certain manner with flaming love, it would be enough to annihilate it, even though it be immortal. And it is so transformed in God, that it knows no other than He.

And continuously drawing it and enkindling it, He leads it back to its state of origin, that is, to the purity in which it was created.

When the soul with interior vision is seen thus drawn by God with the fire of such love, it feels as though melting in the heat of that flaming love of its sweet God, which feels to superabound in the mind. And seeing that God never fails to draw it to its perfection, with such care and providence, it continues through pure love alone.

What the soul sees, God shows it in His light. And if it is discovered to have any impediments to the attraction, that is, to the unifying glance that God has given it in order to draw it to Himself, the instinct of the soul would be to be without blemish in order to be drawn to Him. This [frustrated instinct] constitutes that pain of the souls in purgatory.

Not that they look to the pain, which is so great for their part, but that they look rather to the opposition that they find against the will of God. Clearly they see the accession of this inestimable and pure love toward them; which draws them powerfully with that unifying glance. It is as if they had nothing other to do than this. . . .

I see also that there proceeds from the divine love toward the soul certain fiery rays and lightning, so penetrating and powerful that they ought to annihilate not only the body but even the soul, if that were possible.

These rays have two operations in the soul: The first to purify it, the second to annihilate it.

As gold becomes better the more it is melted, the soul is melted in Him, and every imperfection is annihilated. And this is the effect that fire has on material things, but the soul as such cannot be annihilated in God: Only its lower part.[1] And the more it is purified, the more it is annihilated. But in God the purified soul rests.

When the gold is purified at last to twenty-four carats, the fire cannot consume it any further. Thus, this divine fire in the soul consumes every imperfection and leads it to the perfection of twenty-four carats, everyone in his own time.

And when it is purified, the soul remains entirely in God, without anything of its own. For the purification of the soul consists in the deprivation of us in us,[2] because our being is God. He has thus led us to Him, that is, purified the soul to twenty-four carats, which then is impassible, because nothing remains to be consumed.

And even if this purified soul were to stay in the fire, it would not be painful, but it would be as the fire of divine love, as eternal life, as the blessed souls themselves. Even in this life one might experience this, while still in the body, but I do not believe that God would keep the said souls on earth, except through special dispensation. . . .

And when the soul is found on the way to returning to its primal state, great is its ardor in being transformed into God. . . . This ultimate state of love is that which is done without man, for the soul is found with hidden imperfections. If man saw them, he would be desperate. But this last state of love is going to consume them all, after which they are shown to him. Thus, the soul sees the product of God, the effects of the fire of love, which consume the imperfections.

And what man judges perfect remains defective with God. For all man's works, which appear to be perfect—as he sees them, feels them, understands them, wants them, as in truth has memory of them—in all these things man is contaminated. If his works must be perfect, said works must be worked in us without us.[3] It must be the work of God, without man.

And this is that operation of God alone, with His pure and cleansing love. This is so penetrating and burning to the soul that the body seems besides itself, as if it were a blazing fire, a fire not to be quenched until death.

Truly it is that the love of God redounds in the soul, as I see it, giving it a happiness that I cannot express. But this happiness of the souls in purgatory does not diminish a spark of pain. However, if the love is attenuated, so is the pain, so great is the perfection of the love with which God has seized them. Thus, the souls in purgatory have the grandest happiness and the greatest pain, and the one does not impede the other.

And if the soul could be purged by an act of contrition, it would see that in an instant it would wipe out all its debts. . . . This is so because of the clarity with which it sees its impediments. But on the part of God, not a whit of the debt is to be pardoned, because of the balance of His justice. On the part of the soul, it no longer has any choice. It can only see what God wants, nor would it want to see anything other.

And if alms were given it in its behalf in the world, which alms would shorten its time, it could not turn with affection to see it, but would leave it to God, who is paid in His own way. For if it could so turn, it would be selfish. It would divert its vision from the divine will, which would be a hell.

The souls in purgatory are indifferent to all that God gives them, whether pleasure or pain. Nor can they concern themselves with their own needs, so intimate with and transformed are they in God's will, which orders their happiness.

And if a soul were presented with the Beatific Vision while still owing one hour of purgatory, it would represent a great injury. It would be a greater suffering than ten purgatories, for pure goodness and justice could not support it, and it would be improper to God.

Wherefore, it would be intolerable for the soul to be liberated prematurely, which would then see that God was not fully satisfied with it, were it lacking only the blinking of an eye. It would rather undergo a thousand hells than be presented to God not yet entirely purified. . . .

I see that souls endure the pains of purgatory in view of two reasons. The first is that they gladly suffer those pains, and it seems to them that God has shown them great mercy as against what they merit, in view of what God has offered to them. For if His goodness did not temper justice with mercy—which justice is satisfied by the blood of Jesus Christ—one sin alone would merit a thousand perpetual hells. And because they see the great mercy done to them, they suffer their pain gladly. And they would not want to increase one carat, unless they seem to merit it justly and it be ordained. The other reason is a certain happiness, which is never lacking to them, and even increases as they come closer to God.

These things are not turned back on themselves, but they see them in God, to whom they are more attentive than to the pain that they suffer. For the least vision that they can have of God exceeds every pain and joy that man can experience. . . .

This concept that I see of the souls in purgatory, I perceive this way in my mind, especially for two years now, and every day I see it and feel it more clearly. For I see my soul in this body as in a purgatory, conformable and similar to that other purgatory. The body does not die to the measure that it can endure [the purgation], and always it [the purgation] increases at the end.[4]

I see my spirit alienated from all spiritual things that could nourish it, such as cheerfulness, delight, or consolation. It is not able to taste anything temporal or spiritual: Neither of the will nor of the intellect, nor even of the memory. I am indifferent to my happiness.

And my interior is found immobilized and besieged, little by little deprived of everything which could support spiritual and bodily life. Once removed, they [the supports] are recognized as *only* supportive, and abhorred, for the soul would be without any support. The spirit has in itself this instinct to strip itself of everything that impedes its perfection. Its impetuosity is such that it would put man in hell in order to obtain its end [perfection].

This is why it shuffles off everything which could nourish the interior man, and is thus subtly besieged. It cannot endure the least imperfection, which it holds in horror.

Wherefore, it is besieged within, and it cannot even bear with those who practice with it the way of perfection. And when it sees nourishment in anything, it leaves that place and especially any person in particular.

As regards its exterior part, it again remains besieged, for the spirit does not correspond to it. It could find no place on earth that it could endure, according to human instincts. In God alone was its comfort, who granted all this through love and with great mercy in order to satisfy His justice, and this gave the soul a great contentment and peace. . . .

And the above things I see, touch, and experience in myself, but I do not have a fitting vocabulary to express what I would say. What I have said seems to transpire within me, spiritually.

The world is the prison in which I seem to live, bound to the body, and the illuminated soul, out of grace, recognizes the significance of what prevents it from following its destiny. Since it is so delicate, it receives from God through grace a certain dignity that makes it similar to God. That is, it makes it the same thing [as God] through participation in His goodness.

And as it is impossible for God to suffer, so as those souls approximate Him, they receive more of His properties. . . .

Not of themselves capable, through grace is shown to them the penalty still remaining between themselves and God. The more they are without sin, the more they recognize this. As the impediments become more abhorrent, the soul remains recollected in God. . . .

And as the man who would die before offending God, yet feels death and its pain, the divine light grants him a certain eager anticipation, making him prefer the honor of God to his own corporeal death. Thus the soul, acknowledging the ordinance of God, esteems more that ordinance than all the torments, terrible though they can be, whether interior or exterior. For God exceeds everything that can be imagined or felt.

The soul neither sees nor speaks of such things, but knows them in an instant, and it does not see them in its lower self, because God occupies it with Himself, keeping it so absorbed that it can think of nothing else. God makes man oblivious of self. Purgatory purifies him.

NOTES TO THE TRANSLATION

1. "Im lei propria" (Bonzi da Genova, vol. 2, p. 339); that is, the equivalence of our distinction between the ego and the ultimate self, the empirical self and the true self.
2. "Di noi in noi" (Ibid., p. 340).
3. "Detta operatione sia operata in noi senza noi" (Ibid., p. 343).
4. This significant paragraph is lacking in the Paulist edition of Saint Catherine.

BIBLIOGRAPHY

Primary Works

Bonzi da Genova, P. Umile. S. Catherine Fieschi Adorno. 2 vols. N.p., 1960–62. Volume 1 is a study; volume 2 is the critical edition of Saint Catherine's work.
Debongnie, Pierre. Sainte Catherine de Gênes. Traite du Purgatoire, Dialogue. Nemur, 1962.

Garvin, Paul. *The Life and Sayings of Saint Catherine of Genoa*. Staten Island, N.Y., 1964.
Hughes, Serge. *Catherine of Genoa*. Paulist edition. New York, 1979.
Libro de la vita mirabile e dottrina santa, de la beata Catherinetta da Genoa. Genoa, 1551.
Upham, Thomas. *Life of Madam Catherina Adorna*. New York, 1858.

Related Works

Baruzi, Jean. *Saint Jean de la croix et le problème de l'experience mystique*. Paris, 1931.
Cistellini, Antonio. *Figure della riforma pretridentina*. Brescia, 1948.
Debongnie, Pierre. *Sainte Catherine de Gênes: La grand dame de pur amour*. Paris, 1960.
Izard, Georges. *Sainte Catherine de Gênes*. Paris, 1969.
Kaye-Smith, Sheila. *Quartet in Heaven*. London, 1952.
Newman, John Henry. *Verses on Various Occasions*. London, 1903.
Toso d'Arenzano, Rodolfo. *L'Ideale di Madonna Catarinetta*. Genova, 1978.
Underhill, Evelyn. *Mystics of the Church*. London, 1925.
Von Hügel, Friedrich. *The Mystical Element of Religion as Studied in Saint Catherine of Genoa and Her Friends*. 2 vols. London, 1908.

Saint Catherine of Bologna

JOSEPH R. BERRIGAN

Some Italian cities feel especially blessed by the living memories of saints who have dwelt there. Milan has feasts for two of its greatest bishops, Ambrose and Charles Borromeo. Padua celebrates its patron, Anthony, as Siena does its remarkable daughter, Catherine. In this grouping of cities and saints, Bologna does not appear the least: like Siena, it honors one of its own; like Padua, it venerates a vessel of Franciscan poverty. Catherine of Bologna in a sense returns the favor, for she provides her city with something missing in those others. After more than five centuries her body remains incorrupt in her beloved convent of Corpus Christi. The years and the damp have discolored her flesh, but there she still sits, intact after half a millennium. In Bologna she is simply "la santa."[1]

She was born in Bologna and died there in her convent of Poor Clares, but another city had some share in developing her sanctity.[2] Her father was from Ferrara and was a diplomat in the service of Nicholas III d'Este. Catherine grew up in the court of Ferrara as the playmate and the eventual lady-in-waiting to Margaret d'Este. There she received her education and training as a calligrapher and miniaturist. There, too, she was won over to the life of a Franciscan, first as a tertiary and then as a Poor Clare.

The attention we pay to these Renaissance courts is usually focused on politics, education, or the fine arts. The Ferrara of Nicholas III provided the context for the work of Guarino da Verona as the Mantua of the Gonzagas welcomed Vittorino da Feltre. Perhaps naturally enough Guarino and Vittorino and their schools have captured our attention. And yet one of Vittorino's own Gonzaga charges, Cecilia, became a nun, and from the inner circle of the Ferrara court Catherine de' Vigri entered the Poor Clares, first at Ferrara and then at Bologna.[3] Somewhat later in the century the same thing happened at the small court of Camerino in the Marches, where the natural daughter of its lord, Giulio Cesare da Varano, became a Poor Clare.[4] Most significantly, the convent she chose to enter

was in Urbino, the city of the Montefeltros. The preaching of the Franciscans was bearing bountiful fruit in these signorial courts throughout
the fifteenth century. Once the women entered the convent, they were
trained in the traditions of Franciscan spirituality, including not only
Francis, Clare, and Bonaventure but also Angela da Foligno and Ubertino
da Casale. The several convents were as interconnected as were the courts
of the Renaissance signori.

Life in these convents was an imitation of Christ—as Angela da Foligno
would have it, a way to the cross.[5] In Ubertino's language, the monastery
was a desert of the spirit.[6] The Poor Clares lived a life of humility and
poverty. Not only did they consciously follow Christ and Francis, but they
also set themselves against the pride and avarice of their own world. Like
their Franciscan forebears, they meditated upon the passion of Christ in
all of its excruciating detail. They did this so powerfully that they saw
visions and endured physical pain. Contemplation, suffering, and visions
were as much a part of their world as poverty and humility. The whole
complex was graced by the presence and conversation of the Virgin Mary
and of angels. But all was not peace and joy, angelic visitations and ineffable sweetness; these women were engaged in mortal combat against the
enemy of the human race and of all that is good and true. Military metaphors and the clangor of spiritual weapons resound throughout the convents of the fifteenth century. Saint Paul has something to do with this
language as do the courts from which many of the Poor Clares came, but
one senses that they had seen with their own eyes that they were being
assailed on all sides by fierce, relentless foes. This is certainly true of
Catherine of Bologna and Battista da Varano.

The common context and the shared experiences of these convents nurtured the private spiritual lives of the Poor Clares. The individual expressions are present in the biographies and the works of these holy wom-
en who could write—for example, *The Seven Weapons of the Spirit*.
Catherine must have been a charming woman.[7] Her amiable disposition
is evident from many of the stories told of her by Illuminata Bembo and
her other biographers. Perhaps the most winning is the vision in which
Mary gives the Infant Jesus to Catherine to hold. Artists have found the
depiction of Catherine and the Infant an almost irresistible subject.
Catherine's charm extended beyond Mary and painters to the most difficult group of all, her fellow nuns in the convents at Ferrara and Bologna.
Her popularity may well have to do with her approach to her fellow Poor
Clares, an approach summarized in three rules she followed in leading her
life as a nun. She always had good things to say about others and practiced the virtue of humility faithfully. She minded her own business and
did not interfere in others' affairs. Whether serving as portress, baker, or
mistress of novices in Ferrara or abbess in Bologna, she lived by these

simple rules and endeared herself to her peers. She made certain that the young nuns were fed properly, even at the risk of being censured herself.

At times, Saint Catherine's spirituality has an Augustinian quality, as when she advises her fellow nuns to exercise the gifts that God had given them. The Father should dwell in their memory, the Son in their intellect, and the Holy Spirit in their will. They should remember all that God the Father had granted them. They should meditate upon the birth and death of Christ. They should rouse their will with the fervor of the Holy Spirit, "since no finer gift has been given men than good will, without which no one can be saved, with which no one can be damned. The growth of good will entails the growth of merit. In heaven good will is crowned, in hell bad will is punished."[8]

Catherine was taught Latin as well as Tuscan and composed works in both languages. She learned to write beautifully and to draw and paint. In her free time in Bologna she devoted herself to the elaboration of a breviary that is still a prized possession of the convent at Corpus Christi. Her abilities as an artist have won her the title of patron of the arts. And these moments of free time were found in the busy life of an abbess who was ill when she returned to Bologna in 1456.

By her own testimony she had composed her *Weapons of the Spirit* in 1438, some eighteen years earlier.[9] This work is the fruit of more than ten years in the religious life, six of them as a Poor Clare. It is based upon her experiences of visions, both celestial and diabolical. She clearly intended the work as a resource for the younger nuns, the novices in her charge. Before she takes up the seven weapons of her title, she recommends the virtue of obedience as the necessary first step toward control of oneself and defeat of the devil. This is a virtue Saint Catherine herself exemplified according to her biographers.

The first weapon she recommends is diligence: zeal for doing good, devotion to self-mastery, and alertness to the wiles of the devil. She advises careful moderation in our practice of virtues, since our enemy may use our very zeal to trip us up. Closely associated with the first weapon is the second, distrust of ourselves. Catherine urges us to remember the dire malevolence of the devil, shun our own devices, and rely upon obedience to our superiors. Persistent obedience will allow the full glory of our humility to shine forth.

Saint Catherine's third weapon is clearly needed: if we are to distrust ourselves, we must trust God. This trust is the third weapon, particularly to be wielded when we are in great tribulation and feel abandoned. God has promised to be with us and we can be sure of His faithfulness. Knowledge of this is our unshakable ground of hope, guaranteed to us by His own sufferings. The memory of Christ's passion is the fourth weapon. From the very beginning Franciscans and Poor Clares meditated on this

theme, and Saint Catherine was particularly devoted to this contemplation. The *Vita Alia* says that she was constantly absorbed in thinking of
the passion: her whole life was a continuous reflection upon Christ's sufferings for us and a constant prayer of thanksgiving.[10]

As our distrust of ourselves is complemented by our trust in God, so the
memory of Christ's passion is set off against the memory of our own
death, the fifth weapon. We do not know when we shall die, but we know
that some day we shall have to render an account to God of our stew-
ardship. Here, too, we should follow the path of obedience and not allow
the devil to use our inevitable mortality against us. The sixth weapon
takes us beyond this time of trial and suffering to the glories of paradise,
the glory of God. Our rewards will be so great that we should desire only
to suffer in this life. Angela da Foligno warned her readers that pleasure in
this life might mean suffering in the next.[11] Saint Catherine does not cite
her explicitly but does introduce both Saint Augustine and Saint Francis.
The story of the dream she sets before her novices has an ancestry that
goes back through Hrotsvitha to the days of early Egyptian monasticism.

The seventh and last weapon is the authority of the Holy Scripture,
which should always be with us. It provides consolation as well as instruction. The Scripture is always present to the sisters through the epistles and gospels at daily Mass and the psalms and other readings in choir.
Saint Catherine recommends that her novices regard these passages as so
many letters sent directly by God to them. They should not only listen to
them carefully, but they should also meditate upon them in their cells.

In conclusion, Saint Catherine turns to some practical advice after dealing with the seven weapons. She tells her readers to evaluate their experiences in the light of the Scripture and never to allow the devil to trick them
through the appearance of good. We should also be careful of how our
thoughts proceed and not allow the devil to lead us into despair. Our
expectation and delight should be this world's opposition and persecution. Our most cherished possession should be the hope with which we
look forward to our triumph and reception into the joys of paradise.[12]

Four years before Saint Catherine left Ferrara for Bologna, Girolamo
Savonarola was born in Ferrara. Like Catherine's father, his father, too,
was associated with the Este court, but as a physician, not a diplomat.
Like Catherine, he, too, left the world, although he became a Dominican
and achieved a different kind of fame in Florence. Among his poetic works
is a fragment of a canzone he composed in honor of his fellow Ferrarese
and mendicant. There is something quite pleasing in reading a poem by
Savonarola in honor of Saint Catherine of Bologna.[13]

> O beautiful soul, who left your holy body
> On earth as you ascended to heaven
> To make us believe in the other life,
> Now that the long war has been supplied,

In which you never were dismayed,
You never turned your back upon your Spouse,
But always went before Him
With honest heart and pure mind,
To celebrate your great victory
In everlasting glory
Beyond this rough, blind, harsh life
There where forever you are safe with Christ.

Your holy body clearly shows
How high God has exalted you in Heaven
And the virtue seen among us now,
Courteous spirit, example to the dire world,
Celestial flame to tepid consciences,
And blessed refreshment to the afflicted.
Should one with devout lament
Bow down before you, Virgin blessed,
He will be released from a thousand feeble thoughts.
How highly you are valued
By Christ, O crowned spouse, is clear to
Both heaven and your native world.

From a thousand directions the people run
To see your body, on the strength of only rumor.
Although you are dead, your body seems alive
And seems to recall your soul.
Everyone who sees it is amazed
And filled with wonder does it homage.
O! Would any heart be so savage
That it would not melt in tears of sweetness,
When it saw the holy deeds, the humble face?
If then there is a paradise
And this body is so prized in this world,
How beautiful to behold would be the soul?

O happy soul, who never turned
Your holy feet from the straight path
And forever scorned what the world desires.

NOTES

1. On Saint Catherine and Bologna, see L.-M. Nuñez, O.F.M., *La Santa nella storia, nelle lettere, e nell'arte.*

2. *Specchio d'Illuminazione* is a vernacular life of Saint Catherine by one of her fellow Poor Clares, Illuminata Bembo, who was both a contemporary and an associate of "la santa." It may be found in *Atti e Memorie degli Uomini illustri in santita nati o morti a Bologna,* ed. G. B. Melloni, pp. 441–79. Two later Latin lives are in *Acta Sanctorum* 2 (March 1865): the first life, shorter and closer in time to Saint Catherine, is by Joannes

Antonius Flaminius (pp. 36–45), while the second is by Jacobus Grassettus, S. J. (pp. 45–89).

3. On Cecilia Gonzaga, see the letter from Gregorio Correr to her, Codex Marcianus Latinus XII 155 (= 3953), folios 80v–89v.

4. See Battista da Varano's *My Spiritual Life*.

5. On Angela of Foligno, see "A Lovely and Useful Instruction." *Vox Benedictina* 2 (1985): 24–41.

6. On the influence of this idea, see *My Spiritual Life*, chapter 12.

7. See the short biography in English in *Butler's Lives of the Saints*.

8. Life by Grassettus, p. 72.

9. She provides this information in her subscript.

10. Grassettus, p. 75.

11. "A Lovely and Useful Instruction," p. 32.

12. The text I have used for the following translation is *Le armi spirituali*, edited by Guido Battelli (Florence, 1922).

13. This poem by Savonarola is quoted by Battelli at the conclusion of his introduction.

The Seven Weapons of the Spirit

JESUS · MARY

With reverence I make this request, by the sweet and gentle love of Jesus Christ, of anyone who learns of this little work. It was composed with divine assistance by me, a little barking puppy under the table of the excellent and most refined servants and brides of the immaculate Lamb, Jesus Christ. I am a sister of the Monastery of Corpus Christi in Ferrara. Beware of the vice of unbelief and do not attribute this work to the vice of presumption or derive any error from this little book. I, the above mentioned little puppy, am writing it with my own hand, only because I fear divine rebuke if I fail to say what may help others. And I also understand, as the sweet memory of past Saints tells us in their books, that each creature should strive to make itself laudable in its Creator, through the manifestation of the Divine Providence accorded to it by this divine Creator. And in this is known the infinite love of our Lord God, since in His clemency He deigns everyday to assist and to preserve His creature and to support it in the constant dangers that assail it. And through this we have an increase in faith in Him, our God and true Creator, since we know that He preserves His handiwork.

Thanks be to God.

1. HERE BEGINS THE TRACT ON SPIRITUAL WEAPONS

In the name of the Eternal Father and of His only begotten Son, Christ Jesus, the splendor of this paternal glory; in my love for Him I exclaim with a joyful heart and say to His most beloved servants and brides: "Every lover who loves the Lord come to the dance singing of love. Come dancing and be utterly ablaze. Yearn only for your Creator, who has freed you from the perilous state of the world and has placed you in the most noble cloister of holy religion. You should purge yourself of every stain of sin and adorn yourself with all the noble and holy virtues. You should recover the beauty of your soul and restore it to its original innocence. In that way the soul may, after this pilgrimage, worthily enter the glorious bridal chamber of its most chaste and virginal spouse, Jesus. From His hands it shall receive the prize of triumphant glory, which He has prepared for those who abandon, out of love for Him, the vain pleasures of this wanton world, who submit themselves to the rule of reason and abandon their own will. They find shelter in the security of holy religion and dedicate themselves fully to another's will, as they follow the way of holy obedience and abandon their own will in everything."

But since one cannot do this without violence to oneself, I shall write here below, after a while, some instructions to comfort those persons who have entered this most noble battle of obedience and find themselves strongly opposed and troubled by their own will, by their desires and opinions. They are deeply saddened, believing that by this they lose all merit of obedience. This is not true, since every virtue is perfected by its opposite. I shall show the truth of this as I proceed further, when I shall speak of the excellent and most elegant virtue of obedience, which is worthily called noble, royal, imperial.

So one who wishes to pass without peril and with blessedness from the way to the fatherland should choose obedience as the most gentle, noble, and refined spouse that can be found. And it, like an impenetrable shield, will give us full victory over our enemies and bring us to the safety of eternal reward, as Christ said, "He who follows me does not walk in the darkness but will have light" (John 8:12). But since at the beginning and even at the end of this battle we must pass through a stormy sea that is along the way of many vexing temptations and very fierce battles, I shall place here at the beginning some weapons to use legitimately against the craftiness of our enemies. But it is necessary for anyone who wants to enter this battle never to lay down his weapons, because our enemies never sleep. Let us then take up our weapons with great fervor and confidence to the praise of Christ Jesus.

Anyone of so refined and gentle a heart that he wishes to take up the cross for Jesus Christ, our Savior, who died on the field of battle to bring us life, should first seize the weapons necessary for such a battle and especially those that now follow in order. The first is diligence. The second is distrust of oneself and the third is trust in God. The fourth is the memory of the passion, the fifth the memory of our own death, and the sixth the memory of the glory of God. The seventh and last is the authority of Holy Scripture, as Christ showed us in the desert.

The soul that is espoused by the inestimable ring of good will, that is, divine love, if it wishes to serve God in the spirit of truth, should first of all cleanse its conscience by a pure and general confession; it should make the most definite commitment never to sin mortally. It should rather die a thousand times, if that were possible. The person who is in mortal sin is not a member of Christ, rather he is of the devil and is deprived of the goods of our holy mother Church. He can do nothing meritorious toward eternal life. So to will to serve God faithfully, the commitment not to sin mortally is necessary, as I mentioned previously.

But note this: should you be in mortal sin, you should never despair of God's goodness and never cease doing good to the utmost, so that through it you may escape sin. And with this hope you always should do good, no matter what state you may be in. Beyond this, the faithful servant of Christ should always be disposed to walking the way of the cross. For all those who serve God must do battle against God's enemies and receive diverse grievous blows from them. So it is necessary to have good and excellent weapons to fight against them vigorously and especially those that now follow.

2. OF THE FIRST WEAPON, DILIGENCE

I say that the first weapon is diligence, that is, care to do good, for Holy Scripture curses those who are tepid and negligent in the way of the Lord. The function of the Holy Spirit is to breathe good inspiration in us but our duty is to accept them and put them into operation. We should do constant violence to our sensuality, which is forever tempting us to the opposite of what the spirit wishes. And so it is necessary to resist sensuality with true diligence and not to allow the time granted us to pass without the fruit of good deeds, as it is written, "He who wishes to climb on high should not rest, but with his thoughts, words, and deeds he should exercise himself in God." But we should act with discretion, so that when our adversary attacks us like a vile traitor from the rear we can defend ourselves.

By "from the rear" you should understand the situation when he wants to slay you under the appearance of good. There is danger in doing too much as in doing too little. So I have told you to act with discretion, since it flavors and makes perfect all the other virtues, according to the words of the glorious doctor of the ancient holy fathers, Saint Anthony of Vienna.

So we must exercise discretion in all of our virtuous activity, both spiritual and temporal. When our enemy sees that he cannot prevent Christ's handmaiden from doing good, he tries to trick her into doing too much.

So every virtue should be practiced with due moderation, so that we may use the weapon of true and diligent discretion for our salvation and the praise of Christ.

3. OF THE SECOND WEAPON, DISTRUST OF ONESELF

The second weapon is distrust of oneself, the sure and unshaken belief that by oneself a person can never do anything good, as Jesus Christ said, "Without me you can do nothing" (John 15:5). Nor can he any longer resist the fury of our enemies, since they are so clever and malevolent. And let no one trust in his own wisdom, for if he does he should realize that he will fall in great ruin, in accord with a just judgment: our enemy is more malicious than we are. He is the very essence of malice. And so I have said that the second weapon to use against him is not trusting in oneself.

And blessed is she who has this most noble trait. The more exalted a religious is, either by virtue or by office, the more need she has of this attitude. I heard this story from an aged and most experienced man of religion. He said that when he had held clerical office and had to decide some issue concerning the conduct of his monastery, this was his experience. If he decided the matter according to his own ideas, God always arranged it that for the most part trouble ensued. If, on the other hand, he acted with the counsel and according to the opinions of the majority of his brethren, everything turned out well and he was greatly consoled. How then can a simple nun, especially one who has just entered the religious life, be arrogant enough to prefer her own thoughts and zeal? She should much rather accept the advice and will of her prioress or mistress. In that way the virtue of holy humility will shine forth in her and the weapon of distrust of oneself will be exercised to the praise of Christ.

4. OF THE THIRD WEAPON, TRUST IN GOD

The third weapon is trust in God. By His love we should have great zeal and courage in not fearing to engage in battle against the devils, the world, and our own flesh, which was given to us to serve the spirit. And so let us place these adversaries under the feet of our affection. Let us trust in God and firmly hope that He will grant us an abundance of His grace, by means of which we shall have full victory over our enemies. We know that God does not abandon one who hopes in Him.

Sometimes the servant and bride of Christ, by God's permission, may find herself in such dreadful and fierce storms that she turns with full heart to heaven and cries out, "My God, do not abandon me!" But even in the depth of her fear and worry that she is abandoned, she is lifted up, by a divine and secret mystery, in utter perfection with God Himself. We have an instance of this in His only Son, when at the very point of his painful and bitter death, He cried out, "Father, why have you abandoned me?" (Matthew 27:46). And yet we truly understand that at that moment Christ, the true Son of God, triumphed in the fullness of perfection, as He totally obeyed His eternal Father, with whom He was perfectly united. But insofar as He was able to suffer and to die, He said, "My God, why have you abandoned me?" This occurred because the divine nature that was inseparably united to Himself really left the human and sensitive element in its own nature. This was the demand of justice: the painful obedience of Christ would erase the delight our first father had taken in his disobedience.

I now return to my subject. The servant of Christ should not fear that she is abandoned, although sometimes this may seem to be true. She should realize that our eternal Father and God would not allow her to suffer what His own Son had not suffered. Rather, precisely when she is in the greatest difficulty and tribulation she should trust in divine assistance and remember the sweet promise He made through the mouth of the prophet, "I am with him in tribulation, I shall save him and glorify him."

So who would not wish to be troubled to have so sweet and faithful a companion, who offers to be with his faithful ones in the time of adversity? Oh how strong the reason we there have to wish to be more troubled than consoled! In this, then, fix your sure hope, so that the third weapon of trust in God will be exercised by us to the praise of Christ.

5. OF THE FOURTH WEAPON, THE MEMORY OF THE PASSION

The fourth weapon is the memory of the most glorious pilgrimage of that immaculate Lamb, Christ Jesus, and especially of His most sacred passion and death, ever bringing the presence of His most chaste and virginal humanity before the eyes of our intellect. And this is the best remedy to conquer every battle. And without it we shall not overcome our enemies; every other weapon will be of little help without this one, which surpasses all the others.

O most glorious passion and remedy for our every wound! O most faithful mother, you bring your children to the heavenly Father! O true and sweet refuge in all adversities! O sustaining power, you guide youthful minds to complete perfection! O radiant mirror, you enlighten those who look upon you and cure their deformities! O impenetrable shield, you most elegantly defend the man who hides behind you! O flavorful manna, full of all sweetness; you preserve your lovers from all deadly poison! O loftiest of steps, you exalt to infinite rewards the man who spreads his wings upon you! O true place of refreshment for pilgrim souls! O never failing fountain, you bring coolness to those who in their thirst are inflamed by you! O most abundant sea for the one who sails straight on you in his ship! O olive most sweet, your branches spread throughout the universe! O lovely bride of the soul, which is always in love with you and never looks at another!

And so, dearest and most beloved sisters, be ceaseless in your cultivation of this subject. You should be reflected in its splendid refulgence and thus preserve the beauty of your own souls. And truly this passion is the wisest of mistresses and will bring you, beloved novices, to the beauty of every virtue. Thereby you will attain the prize of victory to the praise of Christ.

6. OF THE FIFTH WEAPON, THE MEMORY OF OUR OWN DEATH

The fifth weapon is the memory of our own death, which we must die; the intervening time is called the time of mercy, during which God awaits us from day to day, so that we amend our lives from good to better. And if we do not do so, we must render an account not only of our evil deeds but especially of the good deeds omitted by our negligence. How well the glorious apostle Paul expresses it, "While we have time, let us do good" (Galatians 6:10).

Consequently, it is a great help to recall frequently our death and to be constantly prepared for it, since we do not know the day or the hour when that most severe judge will send for us. We shall have to render an account to Him of the talent of good will given to us to use in His praise and for the salvation of our soul and that of our neighbors.

Thus the novices should be very careful, as I mentioned earlier, that they not be too self-assured and transgress the rule imposed upon them by their prioress or mistress. They should rather be intent upon walking along the way that has been set before them concerning the governance of their body and soul. I say this because sometimes the enemy with clever malice makes those who are only slightly instructed in the spiritual battle think that they must soon die and that they will have little to take with themselves unless they perform further penance. And by this the evil one teases and tricks them into breaking the rule of true obedience, which is more meritorious, without any doubt, than any possible penance. So it is necessary that we use prudently this weapon of the memory of our death, so that it can be exercised for the salvation of our soul and the praise of Christ.

7. OF THE SIXTH WEAPON, THE MEMORY OF THE GLORY OF GOD

The sixth weapon is the memory of the joys of Paradise, which are prepared for the one who will properly do battle and abandon all the vain pleasures of the present life. For this reason that most sacred doctor, Saint Augustine, says that it is impossible to enjoy both present and future pleasures. So, most beloved sisters, you should wish not to have any pleasure or delight in this world. You should not be troubled by the difficulty of denying your own will, as you recall the words of our patriarch Saint Francis, that the most excellent gift one can receive from God in this world is for the servant of Christ to know how to conquer himself and to want to do so, by denying his own will. He also said, "So great is the reward I expect that every pain is a delight to me," to show how he gloried in his sufferings because he remembered the blessings of heaven.

And to confirm the joys that are prepared for us there, I will add here this little story. Shortly after I entered this monastery, there came among us a young woman who soon grew tired of doing good and regretted abandoning the way of the world. It happened that while she was feeling this way she went to confession to a most experienced servant of Christ. She told him that she wanted to return to the world. He was stunned and told her, "Daughter, watch what you do, for from your words I realize that you are the one about whom I had a vision last night or rather this morning. It caused me to wonder greatly, since I did not understand its meaning." She said, "Please tell it to me." He answered, "I was brought to a most beautiful celebration, where there were countless young women; they all shone more radiantly than the sun with an ineffable beauty; they were all clothed in marvelous glory and on their heads they wore garlands of the most beautiful flowers. Thus adorned, they came forward to meet another young woman, who apparently wanted to join their company. And so with great festivity, celebration, and glory they were going forth to welcome her. When she was quite close to them, she seemed to regret that she had come and turned back. When that most glorious throng saw her conduct, they all seemed saddened. At that point the vision disappeared but now I understand that God showed it to me because you were coming to me. So I beg you, daughter, do not follow your bad will and temptation. Stand strong and persevere, so that finally you may join that most glorious and festive company that I saw. And you will rest forever among those radiant virgins, who are expecting you." Upon hearing this, more out of shame than anything else, she remained among us, but after a short time she made it clear that her conduct was not religious. She was given back to her people and soon finished her life in the vanity of the world. And thus the vision of the servant of Christ came true. She had lost the crown of her virginity and justly was not allowed to mount to that virginal barony, which the servant of Christ had seen.

Therefore, most beloved sisters, be strong and constant, persevering in doing good solely from the pure love of your Lord God. Hope firmly in the joys of Paradise, so that you may finally attain them, as you say with our seraphic Saint Francis, "the just are expecting me, until you give me recompense," to the praise of Jesus Christ. Amen.

8. OF THE SEVENTH WEAPON, THE AUTHORITY OF THE HOLY SCRIPTURE

The seventh weapon with which we can overcome our enemies is the authority of the Holy Scripture, which we should carry in our heart. From it we should derive counsel, as from a most devoted mother, in all the things that we must do, as we read of that prudent and holy virgin Saint Cecilia, where it reads, "she always carried the gospel of Christ hidden in her breast." And with this weapon our Savior Jesus Christ conquered and confounded the devil in the desert, when He said, "It is written that not by bread alone does man live but by every word that comes forth from the mouth of God" (Matthew 4:4).

So, beloved sisters, do not allow those daily lessons read in choir and at table to be in vain and think that the epistles and gospels you hear every day at Mass are fresh letters sent to you from your heavenly spouse. With intense and fervent love lay them up in your breast and as often as you can reflect upon them, especially when you are in your cell, as that you may better and more securely embrace in sweetness and chastity Him who sends them to you. In doing this, you will find that you are constantly consoled, since you see that you receive so frequently news of Him whom you love with the utmost fervor. Oh, how dear and sweet is the divine conversation of Christ Jesus in the soul that is truly inflamed by Him! Now is not the teaching of the gospel the very word of the honeyed mouth of Christ? Surely it is. How attentively, then, you should understand and savor it!

And here I conclude the aforementioned weapons. But I beg you, dearest sisters, that you learn to use them prudently and never be found without them, so that you can more easily overcome your adversaries. And be careful that you are not tricked by the appearance of what is good. Sometimes, after all, the devil appears in the form of Christ or the Virgin Mary or an Angel or a Saint. In every vision that occurs, take up the weapon of the Holy Scripture, where you see the way the Mother of Christ behaved, when the angel Gabriel appeared to her. She said to him, "What kind of greeting is this?" And this is how you should behave whenever you have an apparition or visitation. You should first of all be sure whether it is a good or bad spirit, before you pay any attention to it. And blessed are those who do so.

No less necessary is it to guard with care the thoughts of your mind. Sometimes the devil puts good and holy thoughts in the mind to trick it under the appearance of the good. Afterward, to show that this is so, he assails the mind with a strong temptation to the vice which is the opposite of the earlier virtue. The enemy behaves in this manner to bring the person into the pit of despair.

The dowry that Christ Jesus wants from you is that you be stalwart in battle, strong and constant combatants; by the virtue of patience you therein exercise you will earn the due reward. For its sake, then, you should wish to bear and sustain many troubles, discomforts, anxieties, disgraces, derisions, and a painful death, however it may come. By reason of these and similar disasters you will be sure to carry with you the nuptial regalia, that is, the insignia of Christ. As you know, He says to His gentle spouse, the Cross of love, "You will bear me, as I have suffered for you, my spouse." He also says, "Whoever wishes to mount unto me, the fount of life, must come by the narrow way."

So then, most beloved sisters, remember to keep your nuptial regalia safe and sound, so that you can safely await the grand and glorious embassy that your spouse will send to you. Thus adorned, you can accept His invitation to mount to such a height. Oh, how happy you will be then! You will taste the fruit of the anguished and bitter pains and toils that you have borne. You will have persevered with true patience in the place where God has called you.

And in doing this, you will not find yourselves in the confusion and falsity that is mine, since I have not delighted in carrying the cross of Christ as I should have. So I can well say that I justly expect nothing but ruin and confusion before God and man. Despite all this, I recall the words of the prophet, "Even if I shall die, I shall hope in His mercy."

I do not want to be parted from that excellent virtue called Hope. Speaking to me, Hope said in her courtesy that I shall truly be able to mount aloft to Heaven, if in this world I have not place to rest my head; that I shall find the greatest pleasure there, if I always have some grief to bear here; that I shall be greatly honored there, if I am despised, afflicted, and troubled here; that I shall be satisfied in Paradise, if I never have what I want here; that I shall sing sweetly in the presence of my God, if I chant psalms humbly in the choir; that He will make me immortal, if here I do not fear death or pain; that I shall be empress of His kingdom, if I live here poor and mendicant; and that, if I persevere in His most chaste and virginal love, without doubt I shall rejoice with Him for eternity.

The peace of Christ, sweet love, be ever in your hearts, dearest Mothers and Sisters, and in those of the entire Christian people. May then ever bless and praise our true and one God, in a perfect Trinity, and the incarnate Word.

MY CHRIST

I, the abovementioned puppy, have, on my own, written by divine inspiration, in my own handwriting, this little book in the monastery of Corpus Christi, in the cell where I lived, covered as it was with mats. This was during the time of the most reverend mother and abbess Sister Taddea, who was the sister of Messer Marco de'Pii, around the year 1438. And during my life I have not shown it to anyone. To the praise of Christ Jesus. Amen.

BIBLIOGRAPHY

Primary Works

Angela of Foligno. "A Lovely and Useful Instruction." *Vox Benedictina* 2 (1985): 24–41.
Battista da Varano. *My Spiritual Life.* Trans. Joseph R. Berrigan. Saskatoon, 1986.
Catherine of Bologna. *Le armi spirituali.* Ed. Guido Battellio. Florence, 1922.

Related Works

Acta Sanctorum, March, 2 (1865): 36–89.
Bembo, Illuminata. *Specchio d'Illuminazione.* In *Atti e Memorie degli Uomini illustri in santita nati o morti a Bologna,* ed. G. B. Melloni. Vol. 3, pp. 441–79. 1818.
Butler's Lives of the Saints. Ed. Herbert Thurston, S.J., and Donald Attwater. Vol. 1, pp. 536–39. 1956.
Nuñez, L.-M., O.F.M. *La Santa nella storia, nelle lettere, e nell'arte.* Bologna, 1912.

PART TWO

rance

THE "HEPTAMERON,"
A SIMULACRUM OF LOVE

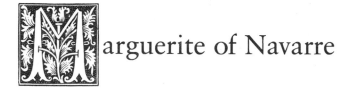 arguerite of Navarre

MARCEL TETEL

Marguerite of Angoulême could not have come from a more privileged background. Since neither of the last two kings of France, Charles VIII (died in 1498) and Louis XII (died in 1515), left any male heir, the Angoulême branch of the Valois were to inherit the throne. Marguerite and her brother, the future Francis I (born in 1494), spent their childhood first in Cognac, Angoulême, and then in the Loire Valley in the chateaux of Blois and Amboise. It is in these settings that she learned Latin, Italian, and Spanish, studied classical philosophy and the Scriptures. Her marriage to Charles, duke of Alençon, from 1509 to his death in 1525, produced no children. Meanwhile, as soon as he acceded to the throne in 1515, Francis I launched a series of military campaigns aimed at conquering northern Italy; after an initial victory at Marignano, he was defeated at Pavia (1525) by his archenemy Charles V, the Holy Roman emperor, and taken prisoner to Madrid. It was his sister Marguerite who went to Madrid and, through her diplomatic skill, arranged his freedom for a high ransom. Until his death in 1547, the French king was to confront the Holy Roman emperor who survived him.

Marguerite, on the other hand, devoted much of her energies to spiritual matters as well. Already beginning in 1521, she entered into a dialogue with Guillaume Briçonnet and Jacques Lefèvre d'Etaples, the two most prominent French figures of Evangelism, the forerunner movement of the Reformation. They formed her religious framework as much as she encouraged them to pursue reforms within the Church and to translate into French and reinterpret the Scriptures. One result of her involvement in religious reform was the publication of her *Miroir de l'âme pécheresse* in 1531, which did not please the theologians of the Sorbonne at all; significantly enough, this work was to be translated into English in 1548 by the future Queen Elizabeth. In 1527, Marguerite married Henri d'Albret, king of Navarre, who survived her by seven years. From this union only one child lived, Jeanne d'Albret, the mother of Henri IV, who converted to Catholicism to gain the throne in 1589 and was supposed to have declared that Paris was well worth a mass.

The world of politics (secular and religious), diplomacy, conflict, checks and balances—Renaissance Realpolitik—as practiced by her brother and his two competitors, Henry VIII and Charles V, left Marguerite more and more disillusioned. And she preferred then to withdraw for longer periods of time to her various chateaux—courts in her lands in southwestern France. There she could achieve some measure of serenity through the writing of her intense spiritual and lyrical poetry and theater, and also draw on her observations to compose the novellas that posterity knows as the *Heptameron*.

When Marguerite of Navarre began writing her novellas, she envisioned a French *Decameron,* or so she says, but since the number published posthumously, seventy-three, could only fill seven days, the editor took the liberty of naming these novellas the *Heptameron*.[1] And following the archetypal model, he provided a liminary synopsis for each novella, thus a first reading of them. Marguerite's modeling of her work after Boccaccio's *Decameron,* first published in French in 1545, shows the overriding influence of Boccaccio in this genre and reveals the high regard that Renaissance *novellieri* felt toward this writer and his work.[2] Marguerite of Navarre, however, is innovative in her use of Boccaccio's form; she develops and animates the frame around the novellas much more than her predecessor does. The expanded frame, in fact, became the trademark of Renaissance novella collections. Through the use of storytellers and their activities, the frame gives cohesion and structure to the succession of tales. Above all, the frame becomes analogous to that other fundamental Renaissance innovation, perspective, in that both animate and give depth to the foreground, that is, both produce and multiply potential meanings.

The frame of the *Heptameron* consists of the general prologue, a short prologue to each of the following days, and the discussions by the storytellers after each tale. In addition to mentioning the influence of Boccaccio, the general prologue introduces the storytellers and establishes the privileged status of their pastime, storytelling—also writing, as a means of dealing with the frailness of the human situation. But above all, this prologue assumes an emblematic, a figurative, function. For example, the flood that dominates the prologue could infer (without excluding any biblical connotations) an ever-menacing cataclysm, the arrival of Fortuna either good or bad, and thus the need for human interdependence and for spiritual comfort (the monastery), thereby suggesting the contrast between the spiritual and the material world—and the needed convergence of the two. The short prologues to each day develop this contrast by focusing on the metaphor of food, spiritual and substantive; at the beginning of each day, the storytellers listen to a reading from the New Testament and then partake of a meal that signifies metaphorically the matter of the tales and the storyteller's judgmental perspectives. Finally, these short prologues blur the difference between fiction and reality; here, just as in the commentaries following the tales, the storytellers take on a life of their own imbued with allusions to their own character and morality, to amorous relationships they may have with one another, and to their knowledge and involvement with contemporary historical figures and events. Thus it becomes purposely difficult to differentiate representational fiction, the tales, from a simulated *lived* fiction, the frame. Then is it a fiction within a fiction? Or a reality simulated to contrast better with a fiction that constantly claims a mimetic veracity?

In recreating a semblance of animated life and acting as narrators' personae, the storytellers also become the first readers of the tales, their first commentators. Each tale, therefore, is subjected to interpretations by several critical voices who produce a kaleidoscopic or anamorphic notion of truth, that is, a meaning of the tale according to the storyteller's viewpoint. This multivocal approach raises the question as to whether or not and to what extent one voice can be privileged over another.

Since the Female Voice and the Male Voice are each composed of five individual voices, this multivocal presence in each gender has the effect of multiplying and suspending meaning. Each gender Voice is represented by a gamut of opinions, ranging from the spiritual and the ideal position to a cynical, practical and earthly stance. Among the women storytellers, Oisille figures at the top of the hierarchy; she reverts to the Scriptures as a basis for most of her opinions and "feeds" her colleagues from them each morning and evening. Her male counterpart is Dagoucin who expresses the Neoplatonic point of view as the model to follow.[3] Parlemente, the principal female frame protagonist and usually considered to be a persona of Marguerite of Navarre, incorporates in her perspective the tenets of Oisille and Dagoucin. She also assigns a very special status to virtue, honor, and marriage, yet as the *Heptameron* progresses, she allows a somewhat jaundiced view of Man to pierce through these other strong beliefs. Longarine and Ennasuite, two other women storytellers, adhere for the most part to the principles of virtue, honor, and marriage, while not shunning the notion of *serviteur*—the courtly lover within or outside of marriage—but still they remain skeptical of woman/man relationships because of their own observations and experiences. A similar diffidence toward human relationships is displayed by Geburon and Simontaut, two of the men storytellers. Nomerfide, the youngest woman in the group, adheres rather constantly to a *carpe diem* view of life; although the other women dismiss her disposition because of her age, she does stand up well to them and makes a good case for herself—or rather offers as convincing a voice as that of the others. Her male counterparts are Hircan, Parlemente's husband, and Saffredent, both of whom stress the concept of woman as an object of sexual gratification and almost always seduceable. The tales of these last three storytellers are essentially comic, often in the fabliau tradition; they offer a relief from the more tragic tales and are used to undermine the goodness of Man/Woman.

The tales of the *Heptameron,* then, represent, for the most part, how men and women are, and the frame proposes discursive models that men and women should emulate. In the discussions that follow each tale, however, the storytellers, now commentators, do not always agree on the meaning of the tale or on the motivations of the characters' actions. Here, too, the persona of the narrator, the storyteller—ultimately Marguerite of Navarre herself—has the choice of manipulating the number and the identity of the commentators involved and thus the meaning of the tale. Indeed, the discussions following the tales pose a fundamental question of how to read the commentaries. Are the viewpoints of the more hedonistic, sardonic, disillusioned storytellers simply used as foils to valorize exclusively the opinions of Parlemente, Oisille, and Dagoucin? Among critics, such a reading has not been unusual. Or, is the reader to regard these discussions more in a symposiac context wherein each opinion retains its validity and contributes to a multivocal and diversified construct? In fact, does not the entity of the archetypal Narrator, the author, disseminate itself among the ten different storytellers? Another question arises in respect to the tales themselves—those that depict the more seamy aspect of human passions and comprise the greater part of the *Heptameron:* greed, deception, masochism and sadism, the game of sexual power and manipulation, eroticism. Are these tales included to represent a significant pattern and code of human behavior, or do they simply function as antiparadigms—that is, evil shown in order to advocate virtue. It is very possible that the two semantic reasons, representation and foil, for the overwhelming presence of this type of tale are not by any means mutually exclusive: indeed, they can serve both a mimetic and a moral purpose.

Ultimately strong and genuine faith offers the only possible solace— after one has experienced the vagaries and pitfalls of man/woman relationships. Ideally one should seek goodness in the other and give one's goodness to the other—this is called perfect love—but in practice, flesh and the senses dominate, given the inherent weakness of human beings and the fallen state of humankind. Yet, man/woman relationships are necessary, if not welcome, for they make one realize the transient nature of these relationships and of life, and then pave the way to a higher spiritual comfort. Marguerite of Navarre assigns this fundamental perspective of the *Heptameron* to Parlemente, the persona that embodies a lived praxis premised on a disillusionment that in turn propels the individual toward a spiritualized life:

> "Those whom I call perfect lovers," replied Parlemente, "are those who seek in what they love some perfection, whether it be beauty, goodness or grace, those whose constant goal is virtue and whose hearts are so lofty and so pure that they would die rather than make their goal that which is low and condemned by honor and conscience. For the soul, which was created solely that it might return to its Sovereign Good, ceaselessly desires to achieve this end while it is still within the body. But the senses, by means of which the soul is able to have intelligence of its Sovereign Good, are dim and carnal because of the sins of our forefather Adam and consequently can reveal to the soul only those things which are visible and have some nearer approximation to perfection. The soul runs after these things, vainly thinking that in some external beauty, in some visible grace and in the moral virtues it will find the sovereign beauty, the sovereign grace and the sovereign virtue. But once the soul has searched out these things and tried and tested them, once it has failed to find in them Him whom it loves, it passes beyond. In the same way children, when they are small, like dolls and all manner of little things that are attractive to the eye and think that the pebbles they collect will make them rich; but then, as they grow up, the dolls they love are living people and the things they collect are the necessities of human life. [Then,] when they learn through experience that in earthly and [transitory] things there is neither perfection nor felicity, they desire to seek the source and maker of these things. Yet, if God does not open the eyes of faith, they will be in danger of leaving ignorance behind only to become infidel philosophers. For only faith can reveal and make the soul receive that Good which carnal and animal man cannot understand."
> (p. 229)

The doctrine of Ficinian Neoplatonism is, of course, easily discernible in this discourse; its underpinning, though, assumes quite a pessimistic view of human nature that prefigures Calvinism and then Jansenism in the next century. The assumption, in this often quoted passage, of an initial idealized goodness of man is soon undermined by his more actual depraved state. Didacticism here is meant to prevail by means of a lofty rhetorical paradigm that is, however, constantly undermined by opposite norms. The resolution lies either in making a choice between the two or in accepting exceptional models, rhetorical or narrative, to counterpoint the norm and thus present the reader with the challenge of a composite picture of human behavior contrasting the ideal with the pragmatics of daily life.

Although the vast majority of the tales, through their depiction of passionate obsessions or excesses, may wish to convey a dim view of man, many are repeatedly said to be true. The storytellers insist on numerous occasions that the tales they are about to narrate really did happen to people they have known and who may be known as well to the others. Nothing leads one to assume that some of the storytellers' claims are not indeed factual; events in Marguerite of Navarre's entourage or gossip among a certain set (the court of Francis I, the court of Navarre) did without a doubt provide the basis, if not the substance, for some of these tales. The question remains, however, whether or not all such claims of veracity are always to be taken literally. Are not some of these assertions to be doubted and considered more as a part of a literary convention quite common to novella narration? In the final analysis, whether or not these claims of veracity are to be taken literally, in part or as a whole, they do create an interplay of fiction and history/reality, since these tales, even if they did occur, still compose a work of fiction.

This osmosis willfully confuses fiction and history/reality in order to shift fiction toward history/reality and thus suffuse the whole *Heptameron* with a rhetoric aimed at convincing the reader that man/woman behave in a fashion, whose motives, often inscrutable, can only be rectified through faith and divine grace. Yet this didactic purpose of the tales coexists with their function as entertainment and pastime. Many of these tales, though some elicit compassion or pity, are narrated in order to avoid or overcome a feeling of isolation (the stranded storytellers can be considered in an emblematic situation of the human condition), of *ennui* (a frequent word in the *Heptameron*), that is, a melancholic anxiety. To do so, many of the tales are intended to elicit laughter: therapeutic, cathartic, mocking, or gratuitous. Protagonists within the tales laugh, and then so do the storytellers upon telling them. Although initially some of this laughter may be mocking or gratuitous, even cruel, much of it is eventually meant to produce a cathartic or therapeutic effect upon the laugher—including the reader, of course.

Like all literature, but particularly in the tradition of the Renaissance novella, the tales of the *Heptameron* are intended to serve both a *utile* and *dulce* purpose. As a matter of fact, Marguerite of Navarre takes great care to orchestrate the sequence of stories; she alternates tragic ones with amusing ones, long ones with short ones. In this regard, she has not lost sight of the Florentine master. Just as the tales are a pastime for the storytellers, they are to have the same function for the reader, hence the conscious arrangement of stories and the interweaving of laughter. Thus a rhetoric of pastime punctuates the *Heptameron,* a pastime that, analogous to the notion of food, connotes a double meaning: not only the *utile* and the *dulce,* but the spiritual and the material, morality and laughter. Although one can undermine the other, depending on the perspective of the characters within the tale, of the storyteller of a particular tale, or of the storytellers in the course of discussing a tale, laughter and didacticism, in the more global frame of the *Heptameron,* are meant to coexist, reinforcing each other.

The confrontation between, on the one hand, a societal moral code bordering sometimes on the romanesque (even in the sixteenth century) and on the other hand, the realities of human behavior (at least from a male perspective) is admirably exemplified in the tenth novella, the longest of the *Heptameron* (thirty-two pages in the edition used here), and significantly enough told by Parlemente. The tale pits Amador against Florida; Amador has pledged, if not deliberately decided, to love Florida. Although each one has been obliged in the course of time to marry another, Amador has consistently renewed his love for Florida, but after many years of faithful *service,* he now seeks, through any number of subterfuges, sexual gratification. Yet Florida "resolved, in short, to go on loving Amador with all her heart, but, in order to obey the dictates of honor, never to let it be known, either to him or to anyone" (p. 144). Later, to protect her honor, Florida disfigures herself (p. 146). In spite of her resistance and disfiguration, Amador persists, and before seeking his death in war, he dramatizes his irrational desire through a transparent rhetorical stance:

> "If I am to die anyway," Amador broke in, "then the agony will be over all the sooner! Nor am I going to be deterred because you've disfigured your face! I'm quite sure you did it yourself, of your own volition. No! If all I could get were your bare bones, still I should want to hold them close!" (p. 148)

When the storytellers take hold of the tale, what transpires is the opposition of a female to a male code in regard to woman/man relationships. Parlemente asks:

> "Don't you think that this woman was tried to the limits of endurance, and that she put up a virtuous resistance in the face of it all?"
>
> "No," replied Hircan. . . . "The example of Florida is not going to make me change my opinion on this matter. I still maintain that no man who loved perfectly, or who was loved by a lady, could fail in his designs, provided he went about things in a proper manner. All the same, I must applaud Amador for at least partly fulfilling his duty."
>
> "What duty?" demanded Oisille. "Do you call it duty when a man who devotes himself to a lady's service tries to take her by force, when what he owes to her is obedience and reverence?"
>
> "Madame," replied Saffredent. . . . "They [women] have honor just as men, who can give it to them or take it away, have honor; and they see the things we patiently endure; but it is therefore only right that our long-suffering should be rewarded when honor cannot be injured."
>
> "But you are not talking about true honor," intervened Longarine, "true

honor which alone gives true contentment in this world. . . . For no one is
truly contented, unless he is contented within himself."

"Well, whatever you all might say," said Geburon, "in my opinion
Amador was the most noble and valiant knight that ever lived. . . . He's a
man who never experienced fear in his life, a man whose heart was never
devoid of love or the desire for courageous action." (pp. 153–54)

Although Geburon has the last word, the reader must remember that he is
the master ironist in the *Heptameron* so that his remarks serve to recall
the confrontation and evolution of the Florida/Amador relationship.

The storytellers only begin to interpret the Florida/Amador relationship. What emerges from their discussion is a possible difference between the female and male psyches. And is that difference irreconcilable?
Can a Platonic relationship endure if there is not at the same time and on
a parallel track a fulfilled conjugal love outside of the relationship? Is the
courtly love code subverted here or valorized? The rhetoric of *fin amors*
was, after all, only a vehicle toward sexual gratification. Does the code of
honor still hold if it overtests the other? Is Parlemente convincing when
she has Florida find her perfect Lover by entering a convent at the end of
the tale? Does Florida's self-defiguration also mark a point in the text, a
self-referential instance, when the mask is taken off the fiction and a
higher meaning is exposed, de-figuring what has preceded that act?

It is not easy nor is it, perhaps, advisable to pinpoint, in a literary
corpus, an authorial voice to only a single one, especially if the author
writes in more than one genre. As a matter of fact, an author can, to a
degree, assume a different persona in each genre in order to manifest more
precisely different preoccupations, or to engage in a discourse that fulfills
certain spiritual needs. Thus Marguerite of Navarre shows a significant
affinity for lyrical poetry that is markedly couched in a religious discourse
often bordering on the mystical. These poems, many of which are collected under the title *Chansons spirituelles,* picture a soul, a spirit, that
wishes to escape the earthly realm and ascend to the ethereal realm, to
rejoin the kingdom of God. For the most part, these poems reproduce the
same vertical movement that must reflect not only a religious fervor but
also a certain disillusion with the queen of Navarre's life observations and
experiences. Such repeated outbursts indicate of course a most personal,
if not intimate, discourse and must have served as well a cathartic purpose. This latter function is all the more evident in some poems written
between the death of her brother, King Francis I, and her own in 1549.
Her poetry certainly reveals a very strong and genuine faith, but one wonders if it does not also reflect a personal sense of crisis resulting from her
involvement in a most contrasting worldly realm of politics, intrigue, deception, and aggressive passions. And in such a context, the *Heptameron*

with its gamut of narrative voices bridges the abyss between the worldly and the spiritual.

Since the *Heptameron* established the dialogic mode as a basis of discourse, it is not surprising that Marguerite of Navarre also wrote a number of plays (about ten). This theater is composed of religious plays, such as *La Nativité de Jésus Christ,* and of secular plays such as the *Comédie du parfait amant* and the *Comédie des quatre femmes* that reelaborate some of the problematics found in the *Heptameron*.[4] Of course, this theater is today considered armchair theater; it is not likely to be staged. The characters are not living individuals but stylized mouthpieces for virtue and vices, with room in a number of plays for some characters in an intermediate gray zone. Some of this theater, then, is a kind of amplified dramatization of a principal function of the *Heptameron* frame. The symposiac nature of the discussions following the tales, however, is replaced in the theater by more dynamic rhetorical stances and didactic discourses. The essential significance of this predominance of the dialogic mode is that it strongly demonstrates Marguerite of Navarre's hold on the dialogue to represent opposite viewpoints, some good, some negative, and thereby to embrace a multivocal epistemology that illustrates the human situation. In this respect, she provides another example of an important element of Renaissance humanism, namely, the representation of an epistemological and ontological complexity by means of a multivocity of opinions.

Just as the voices in the *Heptameron* are multiple and varied, so are those in the other genres practiced by Marguerite of Navarre in order to articulate the dilemmas, the diversity and inscrutability, of the human situation. Although these voices fragment the answer, they reconstitute themselves into a syncretic whole. And if a wide abyss still separates heaven and earth, God and man, the flight toward God always remains the necessary, natural, and most desirable goal. But a side of woman/man in the midst of this consciousness cannot shed earthly strands. And so in the space of this diverging dichotomy remains the deep anxiety of a woman—the sister of a king, the duchess of Alençon by a first marriage, and the queen of Navarre by a second.[5]

NOTES

1. *L'Heptameron des nouvelles de tresillustre et tresexcellente princesse Marguerite de Valois, royne de Navarre, remis en son vray ordre, confus au paravant en sa premiere impression, et dedié à tresillustre et tresvertueuse princesse Jeanne de Foix, royne de Navarre, par Claude Gruget Parisien* (Paris, 1559). A year earlier, the first edition containing only sixty-

seven tales appeared as *Histoires des amans fortunez,* and as the complete title of the second edition indicates, the first one had also been modified by its editor Pierre Boaistuau.

2. "For example, I don't think there's one of us who hasn't read the hundred tales by Boccaccio, which have recently been translated from Italian into French, and which are so highly thought of by the [most Christian] King Francis I, by Monseigneur the Dauphin, Madame the Dauphine and Madame Marguerite. If Boccaccio could have heard how highly these illustrious people praised him, it would have been enough to raise him from the grave. As a matter of fact, the two ladies I've mentioned, along with other people at the court, made up their minds to do the same as Boccaccio" (Marguerite of Navarre, *The Heptameron,* trans. Chilton; this translation will be used in all subsequent citations of this work).

3. Neoplatonism combines an ancient and a Christian reading of Plato, as well as the rhetoric of courtly love, to posit woman as the manifestation on earth of God's perfection and her function as a medium for the human soul to reach this perfection. In a broader perspective, Neoplatonism rests on man's love of God to have his soul reach a state of perfection. Marsilio Ficino, a Florentine philosopher of the fifteenth century, systematized this thinking in his commentaries on Plato's works. Compare Jean Festugière, *La Philosophie de l'amour de Marsile Ficin et son influence sur la littérature française au XVIe siècle* (Paris, 1941); Robert V. Merrill and Robert J. Clements, *Platonism in French Renaissance Poetry* (New York, 1957).

4. The secular theater was published of late as *Théâtre profane,* ed. V. L. Saulnier (Geneva, 1965). The religious theater is to be found in *Les Marguerites,* ed. Frank, and in *Les dernières poésies,* ed. Lefranc. A few plays are also included in Marguerite of Navarre's *Oeuvres choisies,* ed. H. P. Clive, 2 vols. (New York, 1968).

5. The following translation first appeared in *Marguerite de Navarre: The Heptameron,* translated with an introduction by P. A. Chilton. In this edition, I have used American spellings and quotation marks.

From the *Heptameron*

PROLOGUE

. . . They all concurred in this, and Parlamente, seeing that it had fallen to her to make the choice, addressed them all as follows.

"If I felt myself to be as capable as the ancients, by whom the arts were discovered, then I would invent some pastime myself that would meet the requirements you have laid down for me. However, I know what lies within the scope of my own knowledge and ability—I can hardly even remember the clever things other people have invented, let alone invent new things myself. So I shall be quite content to follow closely in the footsteps of other people who have already provided for your needs. For example, I don't think there's one of us who hasn't read the hundred tales by Boccaccio, which have recently been translated from Italian into French,[1] and which are so highly thought of by the [most Christian] King Francis I, by Monseigneur the Dauphin,[2] Madame the Dauphine,[3] and Madame Marguerite.[4] If Boccaccio could have heard how highly these illustrious people praised him, it would have been enough to raise him from the grave. As a matter of fact, the two ladies I've mentioned, along with other people at the court, made up their minds to do the same as Boccaccio. There was to be one difference—that they should not write any story that was not truthful. Together with Monseigneur the Dauphin the ladies promised to produce ten stories each, and to get together a party of ten people who were qualified to contribute something, excluding those who studied and were men of letters. Monseigneur the Dauphin didn't want their art brought in, and he was afraid that rhetorical ornament would in part falsify the truth of the account. A number of things led to the project being completely forgotten—the major affairs of state that subsequently overtook the King, the peace treaty between him and the King of England, the confinement of Madame the Dauphine, and several other events of sufficient importance to keep the court otherwise occupied. However, it can now be completed in the ten days of leisure we have before us, while we wait for our bridge to be finished. If you so wished, we could go each afternoon between midday and four o'clock to the lovely meadow that borders the Gave de Pau, where the leaves on the trees are so thick that the hot sun cannot penetrate the shade and the cool beneath. There we can sit and rest, and each of us will tell a story which he has either witnessed himself, or which he has heard from somebody worthy of belief. At the end of our ten days we will have completed the whole hundred. And if, God willing, the lords and ladies I've mentioned find our endeavors worthy of their attention, we shall make them a present of them when we get back, instead of the usual statuettes and beads. I'm sure they would find that preferable. In spite of all this, if any of you is able to think of something more agreeable, I shall gladly bow to his or her opinion."

But everyone of them replied that it would be impossible to think of anything better, and that they could hardly wait for the morrow. So the day came happily to a close with reminiscences of things they had all experienced in their time.

FIRST DAY. STORY ONE

In the town of Alençon, during the lifetime of the last Duke Charles,[5] there was a procurator by the name of Saint-Aignan. He had married a noblewoman of the region who was more beautiful than she was virtuous, and who, on account of her charms and well-known flightiness, was the object of the attentions of the Bishop of Sées. To achieve his ends the prelate took care to humor the husband. The result was that not only did the husband fail to notice the wicked behavior of his wife and the Bishop, but he even came to forget the affection he had always had for his master and mistress. Indeed, things went so far, that although he had in the past been their most loyal servant, he turned so much against them that he even brought in a sorcerer to procure the Duchess's death. And so the Bishop continued his affair with the wretched woman, who for her part continued to do his bidding more out of greed than love. Besides, the husband had urged her to go on cultivating him. However, in the town of Alençon there also lived a certain young man. He was the son of the Lieutenant-General, and the procurator's wife became half demented with infatuation for him. She frequently made use of the Bishop in order to obtain commissions for her husband that would get him out of the way while she saw the son of the Lieutenant, who was called du Mesnil. This arrangement persisted for quite some time. She had the Bishop for profit, and young du Mesnil for pleasure. Of course she swore to du Mesnil that if she bestowed favors on the Bishiop, it was only so that they themselves would have more freedom to indulge in their pleasures. In any case, she assured him, the Bishop got nothing from her but fair words, and nobody but he, du Mesnil, would get anything else.

One day, when Saint-Aignan had gone to visit the Bishop, his wife asked him if she might go into the country. The town did not agree with her, she said. No sooner had she arrived at her husband's farm in the country than she wrote a note to du Mesnil, telling him to come and see her there around ten o'clock the same evening. This the poor young man duly did. But as he was about to go through the door, the chambermaid, who usually let him in, came out to meet him.

"Go somewhere else, friend," she said. "Your place is already taken!"

Du Mesnil thought the husband must have turned up, and asked her how things stood. The good woman felt sorry for him. There he was, a good-looking, well-bred young man, so much in love, and so badly treated in return! So she told him all about his mistress's wild behavior. That will teach him to fall in love like that, she thought to herself. She told him how the Bishop of Sées had only that moment arrived and was already in bed with Madame, who, as a matter of fact, had been rather taken aback, since she had not expected him till the following day. The Bishop had managed to keep the husband busy back in his residence, and had got away to see her secretly under cover of darkness. Well, you never saw anyone so flabbergasted as du Mesnil was at that moment. He could not believe his ears. What he did was to hide in a nearby house, where he kept watch till three o'clock in the morning, when he saw a figure emerge. And it was a figure that, in spite of the disguise, he recognized only too well as that of the Bishop.

Du Mesnil was in despair as he rode back to Alençon. It was not long before his obnoxious mistress followed on, and went to see him, assuming that she would be able to go on leading him by the nose as usual. However, he told her that as she had been in contact with sacred things she was too holy to speak to a sinner such as himself. He was very penitent, though, he said, and hoped that his sin would soon be forgiven. She realized that the game was up, and that it was no use making excuses, or promising and swearing never to do it again. So she went off and complained to her Bishop. Then, after due deliberation on the matter, she spoke to her husband, saying that she could not bear to stay in Alençon any longer. It was that Lieutenant's son, the man whom he, her husband, had regarded as a friend. He was forever pestering her in a most dishonorable fashion, and in order to raise herself above any possible suspicion, she wanted her husband to take a house in Argentan. The husband, being in the habit of taking orders from his wife, agreed.

They had not been living at Argentan very long before the wretched woman sent word to du Mesnil that in her opinion he was the most despicable man alive, that she knew all about the way he had maligned the Bishop and herself in public, and that she would see to it that he came to regret it. The poor young man had actually never said anything to anybody except her, and was extremely worried lest he find himself in the Bishop's bad books. So he rode over to Argentan with a couple of servants, and eventually found the good lady attending vespers at one of the Dominicans' churches. He went up to her, knelt down at her side, and said:

"Madame, I'm here to swear before God that I've never spoken to anyone except yourself about matters that could affect your honor. You've behaved in an abominable way toward me, and what I've said to you is only half of what you really deserve. If any man or woman dares say to the contrary that I've maligned you in public, then here I am in person to deny the charge!"

There were a lot of people in the church, and du Mesnil had his two sturdy servants with him. So she forced herself to address him as agreeably as she could. She had no doubt, she assured him, that what he said was true. She knew he was far too decent a man to speak ill of anyone, let alone speak ill of her, the woman who was so fond of him. But her husband had heard rumors, and she would be glad if he would go and speak to him personally, in order to make it clear that he had not said the things he was accused of saying, and that he did not believe such tales either. Du Mesnil agreed to this. Thinking she wanted him to go back to her house with her, he took her by the arm. But she said that it would not be a good idea to go back together, because her husband would think that she had primed him on what to say. Grabbing hold of one of his servants by the sleeve, she said: "Leave this man with me, and when the time's ripe, I'll send him to let you know. In the meantime go back to where you're staying and lie low."

Off he went, never dreaming that she was planning to trap him, while she took his servant back to her house and gave him some supper. The man kept asking her when it would be time to go to fetch his master, to which she replied that he would be coming shortly. But when it got dark, she secretly sent one of her own serving-men to bring du Mesnil, who, not suspecting the danger ahead, went back to the house quite fearlessly, accompanied only by the one servant, the other having been detained by Saint-Aignan's wife. As he went in, his guide told him that the mistress would like to speak to him first, before he spoke to her husband, that she was waiting for him in a room with his other servant, and that he ought to send the one he had with him out by the front door. This he did, and went on alone up a dark staircase. But Saint-Aignan had prepared an ambush, and there were men hidden in a closet, waiting for du Mesnil. Hearing the noise on the stairs, Saint-Aignan asked what it was, and [was told] that it was a man trying to get in the house without being seen. At this point, out jumped an individual by the name of Thomas Guérin, who was a professional assassin, and had been hired for the occasion. Defend himself as he might, the poor young man could do nothing against the hail of blows from Guérin's sword, and he fell dead at his assailant's feet. The servant who had been with the lady of the house said: "I can hear my master's voice on the stairs. I'm going to him."

But she held him back, saying, "Don't worry about him. He'll be coming up shortly."

But then he heard his master shouting out: "I'm dying! God have mercy on my soul!"

The servant wanted to run to his aid, but Saint-Aignan's wife still managed to hold him back.

"Don't worry about it," she said. "It's my husband teaching the young rascal a lesson. Let's go and see what's happening."

Leaning over the top of the stairs she called out to her husband: "Well then? Have you done?"

To which came the reply: "Come and have a look. I have just avenged you on the man who has brought so much shame upon you." So saying, he thrust his dagger a dozen or so times into the body of the man on whom he would never have dared lay a finger had he been alive.

Now that the murder had been committed, and the dead man's servants had got away to take the news to his poor father, Saint-Aignan realized that it could not be kept quiet. But he reckoned that du Mesnil's servants would not be regarded as credible witnesses, and that no one in his own household had seen the deed, apart from an elderly chambermaid and a girl of fifteen. The old woman he tried to seize without anyone knowing, but she managed to escape and get safely to the Dominican convent. She turned out to be the most reliable witness to the murder. The young girl stayed in the house for a few days and he managed with the help of one of the murderers to win her round. Then he took her off to Paris, and got her into a brothel, so that no one would take her seriously as a witness. To cover up all traces of the murder he burned the body of the deceased man, and put the bones which had not disappeared in the fire into the mortar he was using at that time to build an extension on his house. Finally, he sent an urgent message to court to ask for a pardon. He maintained that he had on several occasions forbidden entrance to a certain person whom he suspected of having dishonorable intentions with regard to his wife, that this person had, notwithstanding, come under suspicious circumstances to visit his wife and that, in consequence, having discovered the said person outside his wife's bedroom door, he had, being emotionally disturbed and not in a rational state of mind, killed him. However, before he could have the letter dispatched to the chancellory, the distressed father informed the Duke and Duchess of what had happened, and they in turn informed the chancellor, in order to prevent the pardon being granted. Realizing that his request was not going to succeed, Saint-Aignan fled to England, along with his wife, and a number of her relatives. Before he left he told the assassin who had committed the murder on his orders that he had [received] official instructions from the King to arrest him and have him put to death, but that in view of his services, he was prepared to save his life. So he gave him ten écus to get out of the country. The man accepted, and was never seen again.

However, the murder was clearly authenticated by the two servants of the dead man, by the old chambermaid who had taken refuge with the Dominicans, and by the bones that were later discovered in the mortar. The case was brought and tried in the absence of Saint-Aignan and his wife. Judgment was pronounced on the two defaulters, the sentence being death. Their property was to be forfeited to the sovereign, and they were to pay fifteen hundred écus to the father to cover his legal expenses. Saint-Aignan, now safe in England, realized that he was a dead man if he went back to France. He ingratiated himself into the service of one or two eminent noblemen, and, partly through this and partly through the influence of his wife's family, he managed to get the King of England to forward a request to the King of France for a pardon and the restoration of his property and privileges. But the King had heard what an appalling case it was, and merely sent the details of the trial to the King of England, inviting him to see for himself whether a pardon was warranted, and informing him at the same time that the Duke of Alençon alone in the realm had the right to confer pardons within his own duchy. In spite of these protestations the King of England would not rest. Indeed, he was so persistent in the matter that in the end Saint-Aignan got what he had been asking for, and eventually returned to his house in France.

To crown his criminal career, he then fell in with a sorcerer called Gallery, in the hope that the occult arts would enable him to avoid paying the fifteen hundred écus to the deceased man's father. To this end he and his wife traveled, in disguise, to Paris, where he spent a great deal of time closeted in a locked room with his sorcerer friend. He had not told his wife what he was up to, and so one morning she spied on him, and saw Gallery showing him five wooden dolls. Three of the dolls had arms hanging by their sides, and two had their arms up in the air. Gallery was explaining:

"We've got to make dolls like these, but out of wax. The ones with their arms hanging down are the ones we're going to cause to die. The ones with their arms up are the ones whose favors and goodwill we're after."

To which Saint-Aignan replied: "This one here will be the King. He's the one whose good books I want to be in. And this one will be the chancellor of Alençon, Jean Brinon."

"We have to put the dolls underneath the altar," Gallery went on, "so that they can hear mass being said, and when we put them there we have to say certain words, which I'll tell you later."

When they came to the dolls with the arms hanging down, Saint-Aignan said that one of them was Gilles du Mesnil, the father of the dead man, because he knew that for as long as the Lieutenant had breath in him he would never give up trying to track him down. The other two were women. One of them was the Duchess of Alençon, the King's sister, because she was so fond of her old servant du Mesnil, and because she knew so much about Saint-Aignan's other evil doings that if she too did not die, he, Saint-Aignan, could not hope to live. The other doll was his own wife. It was she who was at the bottom of all this trouble, and he was quite certain she would never renounce her wicked ways.

Seeing all this through the keyhole, and realizing that her husband had her marked as a dead woman, the wife decided to beat him to it. So, on the pretext that she had to go to borrow some money, she went off to an uncle of hers, called Néaufle, who was the Duke's *maître des requêtes,* and told him what she had overheard. Néaufle, loyal servant that he was, reported the story to the chancellor of Alençon. As it happened the Duke and Duchess were not at court at the time, so the chancellor took the whole extraordinary affair to Madame la Régente, the mother of the King and of the Duchess herself. She immediately called in the provost of Paris, La Barre, who got to work so efficiently that Saint-Aignan and the sorcerer were both arrested. They both confessed voluntarily, without torture or any other means of coercion having to be employed.

The case was duly brought to law, and laid before the King. There were some people who wanted the lives of the accused spared, and pleaded that the pair had merely sought by their magic practices to obtain the King's good graces. But the King held his sister's life as dear as his own, and ordered them to be sentenced as if they had made an attempt on his own person. His sister, the Duchess of Alençon, however, begged him to spare Saint-Aignan's life, and commute the death sentence into some other form of harsh punishment. Her request was granted, and Saint-Aignan and Gallery were sent to Baron de Saint-Blancard's galleys at Marseilles. In the galleys they ended their days, and with plenty of time to reflect on the seriousness of their crimes. As for the depraved wife, she led a more immoral life than ever, once her husband was out of the way, and died a most miserable death.

"Just consider now, Ladies, the amount of trouble that was caused by one woman. Just think of the whole train of disasters that this one woman's behavior led to. I think you'll agree that ever since Eve made Adam sin, women have taken it upon themselves to torture men, kill them and damn them to Hell. I know. I've experienced feminine cruelty, and I know what will bring *me* to death and damnation—nothing other than the despair that I'm thrown into by a certain lady! And yet, I am mad enough to admit that though I suffer Hell, it's a Hell far more delightful to me than any Paradise that any other woman could offer."

Parlamente, pretending she did not know that it was to herself that he was referring, replied: "Since Hell is as agreeable as you say, you presumably have no fear of the devil who put you there."

"If my devil," retorted Simontaut with some irritation, "were to turn black, as black as it has been cruel to me, then the fright it would give you all would be as great as the pleasure the mere sight of her gives me. But the fire of love makes me forget the fire of this Hell. So, I will say no more, and invite Oisille to tell the next story. I'm sure that if she'll tell us what she knows about women, she'll corroborate my own view."

They all turned toward Oisille, and urged her to start. She accepted, and, with a laugh, began.

"It seems to me, Ladies, that the person who's just asked me to tell the next story has, by telling a true story about *one* wretched woman, succeeded in casting such a slur on *all* women, that I have to think back a very long way to find a story that will belie the low opinion he has of us. But there is one that comes to mind. It's a story that deserves not to be forgotten, so I shall tell it to you."

STORY TWO

In the town of Amboise there was a certain mule-driver in the service of the Queen of Navarre, the sister of King Francis I, and it all happened while the Queen was staying at Blois, around the time when she gave birth to a son. The mule-driver had gone over to collect his quarterly pay, while his wife

stayed behind in their house on the other side of the bridges in Amboise.
Now the husband had a servant, and this man had been desperately in love
with the wife for quite a while. One day, unable to stand it any longer, he
had come out with his declaration. But being a very virtuous woman, she
had given him a very sharp reply, and threatened to get her husband to give
him a beating and throw him out of the house. After that the man had never
dared open his mouth to her in this fashion again, or in any other way
indicate his feelings. However, the flames of passion smoldered secretly
away, until the fateful day when the husband went off to Blois. The lady of
the house had gone to vespers in the church of Saint-Florentin, in the
[castle, and a long way] from the house. Left to himself in the house, the
servant got it into his head that he would take by force what he had failed to
obtain by supplication and service. He broke an opening in the partition
that separated the room where he slept from that of his mistress. The hole
could not be seen, because it was covered by the curtain of his master's bed
on one side, and by the curtain round the servant's bed on the other. So his
foul intentions were not suspected, until the good lady had actually got into
bed, accompanied by a little lass of eleven or twelve years of age. The poor
woman had just fallen asleep, when the servant jumped through the hole
and into bed with her, wearing nothing but his shirt, and clutching his bare
sword in his hand. The moment she felt him by her side, she jumped up, and
told him what she thought of him, like the virtuous woman she was. His
love was no more than animal lust, and he would have understood the
language his mules spoke better than he understood the virtuous appeals to
reason that she now made. Indeed, what he did next proved him even more
bestial than the animals with whom he had spent so much of his life. She
ran too fast round the table for him to catch her, and was in any case so
strong that she had already twice managed to struggle free from his
clutches. He despaired of taking her alive, and stabbed her violently in the
small of the back, thinking no doubt that the pain would make her surrender, where terror and manhandling had failed. However, the very opposite happened. Just as a good soldier will fight back all the more fiercely
if he sees his own blood flowing, so the chaste heart of this lady was only
strengthened in its resolve to run, and escape falling into the hands of this
desperate man. As she struggled to get away, she reasoned with him as well
as she was able, thinking she might somehow bring him to recognize the
wrongness of his acts. But by now he was worked up into a frenzy, and was
in no state to be moved by words of wisdom. He went on lunging at her
with his sword, while she ran as fast as she could to get away. When at last
she had lost so much blood that she felt death approaching, she raised her
eyes to heaven and, joining her hands in prayer, gave thanks to her God.

"Thou art my strength, my virtue, my suffering and my chastity," she
prayed, humbly beseeching that He would receive the blood, which,

according to His commandment, was shed in veneration of the blood of His son. For she truly believed that through Him were all her sins cleansed and washed from the memory of His wrath. And as she sank with her face to the floor, she sighed, "Into thy hands I commend my spirit, my spirit that was redeemed by thy great goodness."

Then the vicious brute stabbed her several times again, and, once she could no longer speak, and all her physical resistance was gone, he took the poor defenseless creature by force. When he had satisifed his lusts he made a speedy getaway, and in spite of all subsequent attempts to track him down, it has proved impossible to find him. The young girl who had been sleeping with the poor woman had been terrified, and had hidden under the bed. Once the man had disappeared she came out and went to her mistress. Finding that she was unable to speak and just lay there motionless, she ran to the window and called out for help from the neighbors. There were plenty of people in the town who were fond of her and thought highly of her, and they now rallied round immediately and fetched doctors to tend her. When they examined her they found twenty-five fatal wounds. They did what they could to help her, but to no avail. She lingered on for another hour, unable to speak, but indicating by movements of her eyes, and gestures of the hands, that her mind was still clear. A man of the church came and questioned her about the faith in which she died, and about her hope for salvation through Christ alone. Although she could only reply by signs, no words could have conveyed her meaning more clearly. And so, with joy on her face, and her eyes turned heavenward, her soul left this chaste body to return to its Creator. No sooner had the corpse been lifted from where it lay, prepared for burial and placed before the door of the house to await the burial party, than the poor husband arrived. There, completely unforewarned, he was confronted with the spectacle of his wife lying dead in front of his own house. When he heard how she had died, his grief was doubled. Indeed, so deep was his sorrow that he too came near to death. His wife, this martyr of chastity, was then laid to rest in the church of Saint-Florentin. All the virtuous women of the town were present, as was their duty, to do all possible honor to her name. For them it was a great blessing to have lived in the same town as one so virtuous. For women of more wanton ways the sight of such respect being paid to her body made them resolve to amend their lives.

"Here we have, Ladies, a true story—a story that should strengthen our resolve to preserve this most glorious virtue, chastity. And we, who are all of good birth, ought to die of shame at the thought that our hearts may be tinged with worldly feelings, when in order to shun those very feelings, even a poor mule-driver's wife does not fear to face what was a most cruel death. Can any woman regard herself as virtuous unless she has, like this woman, resisted till the last? So let us humble ourselves, for God's graces are not given to men for their noble birth and for their riches, but according as it pleases Him in His goodness. He has no regard for persons, but elects whom He will, and those whom He has elected He honors with virtues and [crowns with His glory.] Often does He choose that which is low, that He might confound that which the world places high and considers worthy, even as He himself has said, 'Let us not rejoice in our own virtues, but let us rejoice that we are inscribed in the Book of Life, from which nor Death, nor Hell, nor Sin can erase us.' "

There was not a lady in the company who did not have tears in her eyes, so moved were they all by the tragic and glorious death of the mule-driver's wife. Each and every one vowed that should the same happen to her, she would do all in her power to follow this martyr's example. Then, seeing that they were losing time in praising the dead woman, Madame Oisille turned to Saffredent and said: "If *you* don't tell us something to make us laugh, I don't think there's anyone here who can make up for what I've done in making you all weep! So it's you I choose to tell us the next story."

Saffredent replied that he would be only too happy if he could tell his companions, and a certain lady in particular, something to please them, but that this would be unfair, since there were others older and more experienced than he who ought to be allowed to speak first. However, he finally agreed that since it fell to his lot, he might as well speak now—after all, the longer he delayed, the more competition he would have, and the worse his story would be judged.

STORY THREE

I've often wished, Ladies, that I'd been able to share the good fortune of the man in the story I'm about to tell you. So here it is. In the town of Naples in the time of King Alfonso[6] (whose well-known lasciviousness was, one might say, the very scepter by which he ruled) there lived a nobleman—a handsome, upright and likeable man, a man indeed whose qualities were so excellent that a certain old gentleman granted him the hand of his daughter. In beauty and charm she was in every way her husband's equal, and they lived in deep mutual affection until a carnival, in the course of which the King disguised himself and went round all the houses in the town, where the people vied with one another to give him a good reception. When he came to the house of the gentleman I have referred to, he was entertained more lavishly than in any of the other houses. Preserves, minstrels, music—all were laid before him, but above all there was the presence of the most beautiful lady that the King had ever

seen. At the end of the banquet, the lady sang for the King with her husband, and so sweetly did she sing that her beauty was more than ever
enhanced. Seeing such physical perfection, the King took less delight in
contemplating the gentle harmony that existed between the lady and her
husband, than he did in speculating as to how he might go about spoiling
it. The great obstacle to his desires was the evident deep mutual love between them, and so, for the time being, he kept his passion hidden and as
secret as he could. But in order to obtain at least some relief for his feelings, he held a series of banquets for the lords and ladies of Naples, to
which he did not, of course, omit to invite the gentleman and his fair wife.

As everyone knows, men see and believe just what they want to, and the
King thought he caught something in the lady's eyes which augured
well—if only the husband were not in the way. To find out if his surmise
was correct, therefore, he sent the husband off for two or three weeks to
attend to some business in Rome. Up till then the wife had never had him
out of her sight, and she was heartbroken the moment he walked out of
the door. The King took the opportunity to console her as often as possible, showering blandishments and gifts of all kinds upon her, with the
result that in the end she felt not only consoled, but even content in her
husband's absence. Before the three weeks were up she had fallen so much
in love with the King that she was every bit as upset about her husband's
imminent return as she had been about his departure. So, in order that she
should not be deprived of the King after her husband's return, it was
agreed that she would let her royal lover know whenever her husband was
going to his estates in the country. He could then come to see her without
running any risks, and in complete secrecy, so that her honor and reputation—which gave her more concern than her conscience—could not possibly be damaged in any way.

Dwelling on the prospect of the King's visits with considerable pleasure,
the lady gave her husband such an affectionate reception that, although he
had heard during his absence that the King had been paying her a lot of
attention, he had not the slightest suspicion of how far things had gone.
However, the fire of passion cannot be concealed for long, and as time
went by its flames began to be somewhat obvious. He naturally began to
guess at the truth, and kept a close watch on his wife until there was no
longer any room for doubt. But he decided to keep quiet about it, because he was afraid that if he let on that he knew, he might suffer even
worse things at the hands of the King than he had already. He considered,
in short, that it was better to put up with the affront, than to risk his life
for the sake of a woman who apparently no longer loved him. He was, all
the same, angry and bitter, and determined to get his own back if at all
possible.

Now he was well aware of the fact that bitterness and jealousy can drive women to do things that love alone will never make them do, and that this is particularly true of women with strong feelings and high principles of honor. So one day, while he was conversing with the Queen, he made so bold as to say that he felt very sorry for her when he saw how little the King really loved her. The Queen had heard all about the affair between the King and the gentleman's wife, and merely replied:

"I do not expect to be able to combine both honor and pleasure in my position. I am perfectly well aware that while I receive honor and respect, it is *she* who has all the pleasure. But then, I know too that while she may have the pleasure, she does not receive the honor and respect."

He knew, of course, to whom she was referring, and this was his reply: "Madame, you were born to honor and respect. You are after all of such high birth that, being queen or being empress could scarcely add to your nobility. But you are also beautiful, charming and refined, and you deserve to have your pleasures as well. The woman who is depriving you of those pleasures which are yours by right, is in fact doing herself more harm—because her moment of glory will eventually turn to shame and she will forfeit as much pleasure as she, you or any woman in the Kingdom of Naples could ever have. And if I may say so, Madame, if the King didn't have a crown on his head, he wouldn't have the slightest advantage over me as far as giving pleasure to ladies is concerned. What is more, I'm quite sure that in order to satisfy a refined person such as yourself, he really ought to be wishing he could exchange his constitution for one more like my own!"

The Queen laughed, and said: "The King may have a more delicate constitution than your own. Even so, the love which he bears me gives me so much satisfaction that I prefer it to all else."

"Madame, if that were the case, then I would not feel so sorry for you, because I know that you would derive great happiness from the pure love you feel within you, if it were matched by an equally pure love on the part of the King. But God has denied you this, in order that you should not find in this man the answer to all your wants and so make him your god on earth."

"I admit," said the Queen, "that my love for him is so deep that you will never find its like, wherever you may look."

"Forgive me," said the gentleman, "but there are hearts whose love you've never sounded. May I be so bold as to tell you that there is a certain person who loves you, and loves you so deeply and so desperately, that in comparison your love for the King is as nothing? And his love grows and goes on growing in proportion as he sees the King's love for you diminishing. So, if it were, Madame, to please you, and you were to receive his love, you would be more than compensated for all that you have lost."

The Queen began to realize, both from what he was saying, and from the expression on his face, that he was speaking from the depths of his heart. She remembered that he had some time ago sought to do her service, and that he had felt so deeply about it that he had become quite melancholy. At the time she had assumed the cause of his mood lay with his wife, but she was now quite convinced that the real reason was his love for her. Love is a powerful force, and will make itself felt whenever it is more than mere pretense, and it was this powerful force that now made her certain of what remained hidden from the rest of the world. She looked at him again. He was certainly more attractive than her husband. He had been left by his wife, too, just as she had been left by the King. Tormented by jealousy and bitterness, allured by the gentleman's passion, she sighed, tears came to her eyes, and she began: "Oh God! Must it take the desire for revenge to drive me to do what love alone would never have driven me to?"

Her words were not lost on the gentleman who replied: "Madame, vengeance is sweet indeed, when instead of taking one's enemy's life, one gives life to a lover who is true. It is time, I think, that the truth freed you from this foolish love for a man who certainly has no love for you. It is time that a just and reasonable love banished from you these fears that so ill become one whose spirit is so strong and so virtuous. Why hesitate, Madame? Let us set aside rank and station. Let us look upon ourselves as a man and a woman, as the two most wronged people in the world, as two people who have been betrayed and mocked by those whom we loved with all our hearts. Let us, Madame, take our revenge, not in order to punish them as they deserve, but in order to do justice to our love. My love for you is unbearable. If it is not requited I shall die. Unless your heart is as hard as diamond or as stone, it is impossible that you should not feel some spark from this fire that burns the more fiercely within me the more I try to stifle it. I am dying for love of you! And if that cannot move you to take pity on me and grant me your love, then at least your own love for yourself must surely force you to do so. For you, who are so perfect that you merit the devotion of all the honorable and worthy men in all the world, have been despised and deserted by the very man for whose sake you have disdained all others!"

At this speech the Queen was quite beside herself. Lest her face betray the turmoil of her mind, she took his arm and led him into the garden adjoining her room. For a long time she walked up and down with him saying nothing. But he knew that the conquest was almost complete, and when they reached the end of the path, where no one could see them, he expressed in the clearest possible way the love that for so long he had kept concealed. At last they were of one mind. And so it was, one might say, that together they enacted a Vengeance, having found the Passion too much to bear.

Before they parted they arranged that whenever the husband made his trips to his village, he would, if the King had gone off to the town, go straight to the castle to see the Queen. Thus they would fool the very people who were trying to fool them. Moreover, there would now be four people joining in the fun, instead of just two thinking they had it all to themselves. Once this was settled, the Queen retired to her room and the gentleman went home, both of them now sufficiently cheered up to forget all their previous troubles. No longer did the King's visits to the gentleman's lady distress either of them. Dread had now turned to desire, and the gentleman started to make his trips to his village rather more often than he had in the past. It was, after all, only half a league [out of the town]. Whenever the King heard that the gentleman had gone to the country, he would make his way straight to his lady. Similarly, whenever the gentleman heard that the King had left his castle, he would wait till nightfall and then go straight to the Queen—to act, so to speak, as the King's viceroy. He managed to do this in such secrecy that no one had the slightest inkling of what was going on. They proceeded in this fashion for quite a while, but the King, being a public person, had much greater difficulty concealing his love affair sufficiently to prevent anyone at all getting wind of it. In fact, there were a few unpleasant wags who started to make fun of the gentleman, saying he was a cuckold, and putting up their fingers like cuckold's horns whenever his back was turned. Anyone with any decency felt very sorry for the man. He knew what they were saying, of course, but derived a good deal of amusement from it, and reckoned his horns were surely as good as the King's crown.

One day when the King was visiting the gentleman and his wife at their home, he noticed a set of antlers mounted on the wall. He burst out laughing, and could not resist the temptation to remark that the horns went very well with the house. The gentleman was a match for the King, however. He had an inscription placed on the antlers which read as follows:

Io porto le corna, ciascun lo vede,
Ma tal le porta, che no lo crede.[7]

Next time the King was in the house, he saw the inscription and asked what it meant.

The gentleman simply said: "If the King doesn't tell his secrets to his subjects, then there's no reason why his subjects should tell their secrets to the King. And so far as horns are concerned, you should bear in mind that they don't always stick up and push their wearers' hats off. Sometimes they're so soft that you can wear a hat on top of them, without being troubled by them, and even without knowing they're there at all!"

From these words the King realized that the gentleman knew about his affair with his wife. But he never suspected that the gentleman was having an affair with *his* wife. For her part, the Queen was careful to feign displeasure at her husband's behavior, though secretly she was pleased, and the more she was pleased, the more displeasure she affected. This amicable arrangement permitted the continuation of their amors for many years to come, until at length old age brought them to order.

"Well, Ladies," concluded Saffredent, "let that story be a lesson to you. When your husbands give you little roe-deer horns, make sure that you give them great big stag's antlers!"

"Saffredent," said Ennasuite, laughing, "I'm quite sure that if you were still such an ardent lover as you used to be, you wouldn't mind putting up with horns as big as oaks, as long as you could give a pair back when the fancy took you. But you're starting to go gray, you know, and it really is time you began to give your appetites a rest!"

"Mademoiselle," he replied, "even if the lady I love gives me no hope, and even if age has dampened my ardor somewhat, my desires are as strong as ever. But seeing that you object to my harboring such noble desires, let me invite you to tell the fourth story, and let's see if you can produce an example to refute what I say."

During this exchange one of the ladies had started to laugh. She knew that the lady who had just taken Saffredent's words to be aimed at her was not in fact so much the object of his affections that he would put up with cuckoldry, disgrace, or injury of any kind for her sake. When Saffredent saw that she was laughing and that she had understood him, he was [highly] pleased, and let Ennasuite go on. This is what she said:

"I have a story to tell, Ladies, which will show Saffredent and everyone else here that not *all* women are like the Queen he has told us about, and that not all men who are rash enough to try their tricks get what they want. It's a story that ought not to be kept back, and it tells of a lady in whose eyes failure in love was worse than death itself. I shan't mention the real names of the people involved, because it's not long since it all happened, and I should be afraid of giving offense to their close relatives." . . .

SIXTH DAY. PROLOGUE

The next morning Oisille rose earlier than usual to prepare her reading in the hall. The rest of the company, having been told of this, and anxious to hear her excellent teaching, dressed themselves with such haste that they kept her waiting hardly at all. Oisille knew the fervor in their hearts, and read to them the Epistle of Saint John the Evangelist, an Epistle full only of love, because every morning till then she had been reading the Epistle of Saint Paul to the Romans. The assembled ladies and gentlemen found this such sweet nourishment that although they listened for half an hour longer than usual, it seemed to them that they had been there no more than a quarter of an hour. Afterward they went to the contemplation of the mass, where they commended themselves to the Holy Spirit in order that they might that day satisfy those who would listen to them. After they had eaten, and rested for a while, they went off to spend their day in the accustomed manner. Madame Oisille asked them who should begin the day's stories. Longarine replied: "I call upon Madame Oisille. The lesson she read us this morning was so beautiful that she cannot fail to tell us a story worthy to complete the glory she won this morning."

"I regret" replied Oisille, "that I cannot this afternoon tell you anything as rewarding as what I told you this morning. But at least the intention of the story that I shall tell you will not be out of keeping with the teaching of Holy Scripture, where it is written 'Trust not in princes, nor in the son of man, in whom there is no salvation.' And, so that you will not forget this truth for want of an example, I am going to give you one which is true and so fresh to the memory that those who witnessed the pitiful sight I shall recount have hardly yet dried their tears."

STORY FIFTY-ONE

The Duke of Urbino, called the Prefect, who had married the sister of the first Duke of Mantua, had a son of eighteen to twenty years of age, and this young man was in love with a girl from a good and noble family. She was the sister of the abbé de Farse. Since he did not have the freedom to speak with her as he would have liked (such was the local custom), the young man drew on the help of a gentleman in his service. This gentleman happened to be in love with a beautiful and virtuous young woman in the service of the Duchess, and it was through this young woman that the Duke's son declared his great love to his beloved. The poor young woman saw no wrong in acting as messenger, and was glad to be of help, since she believed the young man's intentions to be so good and noble that he could not possibly have desires which she could not honorably convey. But the Duke himself was more concerned with furthering the interests of his family than with pure and noble love. He was afraid lest his son run the risk of a commitment to marriage. So he had a keen watch put on him, and it was reported to him that the Duchess's lady-in-waiting was involved in the carrying of letters on behalf of his son to the girl with whom he was so much in love. The Duke was so enraged that he resolved at once to put a stop to it. But he could not hide his anger sufficiently to prevent the Duchess's lady-in-waiting hearing about it. She was overcome with terror, for she knew the extent of the Duke's wickedness and that it was as great as his conscience was small. So she approached the Duchess to beg her for permission [to retire to a place away from court until the Duke's fury had

subsided. But the Duchess told her that she would try to discover her husband's mood before giving her permission.] However, the Duchess very
soon discovered how the Duke felt from the malevolent way he spoke of
the affair, so not only did she grant permission to her lady-in-waiting, but
also advised her to withdraw to a convent till the storm had passed. This
the girl did with as much secrecy as possible, but not with sufficient secrecy to prevent the Duke finding out. Putting on a good-humored air, he
approached his wife and asked her where the young woman had gone.
She, thinking that he knew all about it, told him what he wanted. When
he heard, he pretended to be distressed, and said that there was no need to
go to such lengths. He did not mean the girl any harm, and his wife must
call her back, because the gossip would not do them any good. She replied
that since the poor girl was so miserable because she had lost favor, then it
would be better for the moment if she did not appear in his presence. But
he would not listen to any of her objections, and ordered her to have the
girl brought back at once. Accordingly the Duchess made the Duke's
wishes known. But the girl was not reassured and begged her mistress not
to make her take the risk. She knew very well, she said, that the Duke was
less inclined to grant pardons than he pretended. Nevertheless, the Duchess assured her that she would not come to any harm, and vouched for it
on her life and honor. The girl knew that her mistress was very fond of her
and would not readily deceive her, so she took her promise on trust, feeling, moreover, that the Duke would never go against a promise pledged
on his wife's life and honor. Thus it was that she went back with the
Duchess. But immediately the Duke was informed, he came into his wife's
room. No sooner had he set eyes on the girl than he said to his wife,
"How can this creature dare to come back?" Thereupon he turned to his
gentlemen, and ordered them to arrest the girl and throw her into prison.
The poor Duchess, who had persuaded the girl on her word to come out
of her place of refuge, was overcome by despair and threw herself on her
knees in front of him. She besought him for the sake of his own honor and
for the sake of his family not to do such a thing, for it was she herself who,
in order to obey him, had brought the girl back from her safe hiding
place. But none of her pleas, nor any of the arguments she could think of,
were able to soften his hard heart, or overthrow his stubborn desire to
avenge himself upon her. Without so much as a word in reply, he left the
room, and ignoring all legal forms, God and the honor of his house, he
had the girl cruelly put to death by hanging.

I could not begin to describe the distress of the Duchess. I can only say
that it was such as befitted a lady of honor and of noble heart who was
obliged to witness the death of a person whom she had wished only to
save and to whom she had pledged her word. Even less could one express
the grief of the young man who had been her devoted servant. He took it

upon himself to do everything in his power to save his beloved's life, even offering to sacrifice his own in her place. But nothing could move the Duke's heart to pity. His sole pleasure was to wreak vengeance on the people he hated. And so it was that this innocent young woman was put to death by this cruel Duke, against all laws of honor and justice, and to the great sorrow of all who knew her.

"Ladies, observe the effects of wickedness when combined with power."

"I had heard," said Longarine, "that the Italians are subject to three vices above all others, but I wouldn't have thought that cruelty and the spirit of revenge would have gone so far as to put someone to death in such a cruel manner for such a trivial reason."

Saffredent said to her, laughing: "Longarine, you've mentioned one of the three vices. We must be told about the other two."

"If you don't know what they are, then I'll tell you. But I'm sure that you do know what they are, all of them."

"Do you mean by that," said Saffredent, "that you think I'm full of vice myself?"

"Not at all," she replied. "Just that you know all about the ugliness of vice, so you are able to avoid it better than anyone else."

"There's no need to be surprised by this act of cruelty we've just heard of," said Simontaut. "People who've traveled through Italy have seen the most incredible things, things which make this a mere peccadillo by comparison."

"Yes, indeed," said Geburon. "When Rivolta was taken by the French there was an Italian captain whom everybody regarded as a valiant comrade-at-arms and who came across a man lying dead, a man who was only an enemy in the sense that he had been a Guelph, while the captain was a Ghibelline.[8] He tore the dead man's heart out of his chest, roasted it over a charcoal fire, and ate it. When some people asked what it tasted like, he replied that he had never tasted a more delicious or enjoyable morsel. Not content with this fine deed, he killed the dead man's wife, who was pregnant, tore out the fruit of her womb and dashed it against the battlements. He then filled the corpses of both husband and wife with oats and gave them to his horses. So judge for yourselves whether a man like that would be capable of hanging a girl whom he suspected of doing something he didn't like."

"It would seem," said Ennasuite, "that the Duke of Urbino was more worried about his son marrying somebody poor than about finding a wife to his liking."

"One cannot doubt, I think," answered Simontaut, "that it is the nature of Italians to love things created merely for the service of nature more than nature itself."

"It's even worse than that," said Hircan, "because they make their God out of things that are against nature."

"Those are the sins I was referring to," said Longarine. "Everyone knows that to love money, unless one is using it to some end, is idolatry."

Parlamente said that Saint Paul had not been unaware of the Italians' vices, nor indeed of the vices of all those who regard themselves as rising so high above their fellows in honor, wisdom and human reason, upon which they rely so heavily, that they fail to render to God the glory that is His due. Consequently the Almighty, jealous of His honor, makes all those who think themselves better endowed with sense than others more insensate than maddened beasts, causing them to show by acts against nature that they are reprobate.

Longarine interrupted to point out that that was the third sin the Italians were subject to.

"Now that comment gives me a great deal of satisfaction," said Nomerfide, "because it means that the people we usually think of as being the greatest and most subtle speakers are punished by being made more stupid than the beasts. So one must conclude that people like myself who are lowly, humble and of little ability are filled with the wisdom of the angels."

"I can assure you," said Oisille, "that your view is not far removed from my own. For no one is more ignorant than the person who thinks he knows."

"I have never seen," said Geburon, "a mocker who was never mocked, nor a deceiver who was never himself deceived, nor arrogance that was never in the end humiliated."

"That reminds me of a practical joke I once heard of, which I would have been pleased to tell you about, if it were decent," said Simontaut.

"Well, since we're here to tell the truth," said Oisille, "whatever it may be, I nominate you to tell it to us for our next story."

"Then since it is my turn," answered Simontaut, "I will tell you."

STORY FIFTY-TWO

Near to the town of Alençon there lived a gentleman by the name of the Seigneur de Tirelière. One morning he walked from his house into town. It was not far, and as it was freezing extremely hard, he thought the walk would warm him up. So off he went, not forgetting to take with him the heavy coat lined with fox fur which he owned. When he had carried out the business he had to do in town, he met a friend of his, an advocate named Antoine Bacheré. After chatting for a while about business matters, he said that he felt like getting a good dinner—provided that it was at someone else's expense. As they were talking this over, they sat down in front of an apothecary's shop. Now in the shop was a serving lad, who, overhearing what they were saying, thought it would be a splendid idea to give them a dinner they would not forget. So he went out of the shop into a side-street where everyone went to relieve their natural needs, and found a large lump of excrement standing on its end, frozen solid and looking just like a little sugar loaf. He quickly wrapped it up in a nice piece of white paper, just as he did in the shop to attract customers. Then he hid it in his sleeve, and as he was going past the gentleman and his lawyer friend, he pretended to drop it near them. Then he went into a house, as if he had been going to deliver it. The Seigneur de Tirelière lost no time in picking up what he believed to be a nice little sugar loaf. Just as he was doing so, the apothecary's lad came back, looking around to see if anyone had seen his piece of sugar. Our gentleman, thinking he had properly outwitted the lad, hurried off to a nearby inn, saying to his comrade as they went: "We'll pay for our dinner at the lad's expense!" When they got inside he ordered some good meat, some bread, and a good wine, thinking he now had adequate means to pay. As he ate and warmed himself by the fire, his sugar loaf began to thaw out. The stench filled the whole room. The gentleman, from under whose coat the foul smell was issuing, started to get angry with the serving wench: "You are the most disgusting people in this town I've ever seen! You or your children have littered the whole room with shit!"

The wench replied: "By Saint Peter, there's no muck in this house, unless it's you that brought it in!"

At this point, not being able to stand the smell any longer, they got up and went over to the fire. The gentleman got out his handkerchief—now stained with the thawed out sugar loaf! He opened his coat—the one lined with fox fur. It was ruined! All he could say to his companion was: "It's that wretched apothecary's lad! We thought we'd tricked him and he's well and truly got his own back!"

And, after paying the bill, they left somewhat less pleased with themselves than when they had come.

"Well, Ladies, that is the sort of thing that often happens to people who enjoy playing tricks like the Seigneur de Tirelière. If he hadn't wanted to eat at someone else's expense, he wouldn't have ended up having such a disgusting meal at his own. I'm afraid my story wasn't a very clean one! But you did give me leave to tell the truth. And that is what I've done, my aim being to show that when a deceiver is himself deceived, no one is very sorry."

"People generally say that words themselves never stink," said Hircan, "but those about whom they were uttered didn't get off so lightly as far as smell was concerned!"

"It is true," said Oisille, "that words like that do not smell, but there are other words, words referred to as disgusting, which have [such] an evil odor that the soul is far more disturbed than is the body smelling something like the sugar loaf in your story."

"Tell me, I beg you," said Hircan, "what these words are, which you know to be so foul that they make an honest woman sick in her heart and in her soul."

"It would be a fine thing," said Oisille, "if I uttered words which I would advise no other woman to say!"

"By these very words," said Saffredent, "I know what these terms are which women who want to appear modest don't generally use! But I would like to ask everyone here why it is that if they daren't actually speak about such things, they are so ready to laugh when they hear others speaking about them?"

"It isn't that we laugh because we hear these fine words," replied Parlamente. "But the fact is that everyone is inclined to laugh when they see somebody fall over or when somebody says something unintentional, as often happens, even to the most modest and best spoken of ladies, when they make a slip of the tongue and say one word instead of another. But when you men speak amongst one another in a disgusting fashion, out of sheer wickedness and in full knowledge of what you are doing, I know of no decent woman who would not be [so] horrified that not only would she not want to listen, but would want to avoid the very company of such people."

"It's true," said Geburon. "I've seen women make the sign of the cross when they hear [such] words, and go on doing so until the speaker stopped repeating them."

"Yes," said Simontaut, "but how many times do they hide behind their masks, so that they can have the freedom to laugh just as much as they pretend to complain?"

"Even that would be better," said Parlamente, "than letting everyone know that they found such language amusing."

"So you would praise hypocrisy in ladies, just as much as virtue itself?" said Dagoucin.

"Virtue would be better," said Longarine, "but when it is lacking, one must use hypocrisy, just as people wear high shoes to cover up the fact that they are not very tall. If we can hide our imperfections, even that is something worth doing."

"On my oath," said Hircan, "it would be better to show a little imperfection sometimes, rather than to cover it up so carefully under a veil of virtue!"

"True enough," said Ennasuite. "Honor can be put on like a borrowed garment, but the borrower will be dishonored when he has to give it back.

I could mention a certain lady who, precisely because she made too much effort to conceal a trivial fault, ended up falling into a much more serious one."

"I've a good idea who you mean," said Hircan, "but at least don't give her name away."

"Ah! You have permission to speak next," said Geburon, "on condition that after telling us the story you will tell us the names of those involved, and we will swear never to reveal them."

"I give you my word," said Ennasuite, "for there is nothing that cannot be recounted in an honorable fashion."

NOTES TO THE TRANSLATION

1. A reference to the first translation in French of the *Decameron* by Antoine Le Maçon in 1545 dedicated to Marguerite of Navarre herself.

2. The second son of Francis I and the future king Henry II.

3. Catherine de' Medici, who married Henri in 1533.

4. Marguerite of Navarre herself.

5. Charles, duke of Alençon, the first husband of Marguerite.

6. Alfonso V the Learned or the Magnanimous, king of Aragon and of Sicily from 1443 to his death in 1458.

7. I have horns, everyone can see them, / But some have them, who do not believe it.

8. The two opposing political parties in Italy from the twelfth to the fifteenth century; the Guelphs recognized the political power of the popes, whereas the Ghibellines favored the German Holy Roman emperors.

BIBLIOGRAPHY

Primary Works

Allaire, Joseph L., ed. *Le Miroir de l'âme pécheresse. Discord étant en l'homme par contrariété de l'esprit et de la chair. Oraison à nostre seigneur Jésus Christ.* Munich, 1972.

Dottin, Georges, ed. *Chansons spirituelles.* Geneva, 1971.

François, Michel, ed. *L'Heptaméron.* Paris, 1960.

Frank, Felix, ed. *Les Marguerites de la Marguerite des Princesses.* 4 vols. Paris, 1873.

Glasson, Simone, ed. *Les Prisons.* Geneva, 1978.

Lefranc, Abel, ed. *Les dernières poésies de Marguerite de Navarre.* Paris, 1896.

Le Hir, Yves, ed. *Nouvelles.* Paris, 1967.

Le Roux de Lincy and Anatole de Montaiglon, eds. *L'Heptaméron.* 4 vols. Paris, 1880. Reprint. Geneva, 1969.

Marichal, Robert, ed. *La Coche.* Geneva, 1971.

————. *La Navire.* Paris, 1956.

Saulnier, Verdun Louis, ed. *Théâtre profane.* Geneva, 1965.

Translations

The Queene of Navarre's Tales. Containing Verie Pleasant Discourses of Fortunate Lovers. Now Newly Translated out of French into English. London, printed by V.S. for John Oxenbridge, and are to be sold at his shop in Paule's churchyard at the sign of the Parot, 1597.

Codrington, Robert, trans. *Heptameron; or, The History of the Fortunate Lovers. Written by the Most Excellent and Most Virtuous Princess de Valoys, Queen of Navarre.* London, 1654.

Chartres, John Smith, trans. *The Heptameron of the tales of Margaret, Queen of Navarre. Newly translated from the Authentic Text of M. Le Roux de Lincy.* 5 vols. London, 1894.

Chilton, P. A., trans. *The Heptameron.* London and New York, 1984.

Other translations were published in 1750, 1855, 1885, and 1896.

Related Works

Benson, Edward. "Marriage Ancestral and Conjugal in the *Heptaméron*." *Journal of Medieval and Renaissance Studies* 9 (1979): 261–75.

Cazauran, Nicole. *L'Heptaméron de Marguerite de Navarre.* Paris, 1976.

Clements, Robert J., and Joseph Gibaldi. *Anatomy of the Novella: The European Tale Collection from Boccaccio and Chaucer to Cervantes.* New York, 1977.

Clive, H. P. *Marguerite de Navarre: An Annotated Bibliography.* London, 1983.

Dubois, Claude Gilbert. "Fonds mythique et jeu des sens dans le *Prologue* de *L'Heptaméron*." In *Etudes seiziémistes offertes à V. L. Saulnier,* pp. 151–68. Geneva, 1980.

Febvre, Lucien. *Autour de 'L'Heptaméron': Amour sacré, amour profane.* Paris, 1944 and 1971.

Freer, Martha W. *The Life of Marguerite d'Angoulême, Queen of Navarre, Duchesse d'Alençon and de Berry, Sister of Francis I, King of France.* London, 1854. Cleveland, 1895.

Gelernt, Jules. *World of Many Loves: The 'Heptameron' of Marguerite de Navarre.* Chapel Hill, N.C., 1966.

Jourda, Pierre. *Marguerite d'Angoulême, duchesse d'Alençon, reine de Navarre (1492–1549): Etude biographique et littéraire.* 2 vols. Paris, 1930. Reprint. Turin, 1966. Geneva, 1978.

Krailsheimer, A. J. "The *Heptameron* Reconsidered." In *The French Renaissance and Its Heritage,* pp. 75–92. London, 1968.

Norton, Glyn P. "Narrative Function in the *Heptaméron* Frame-Story." In *La Nouvelle française à la Renaissance,* pp. 435–47. Geneva, 1981.

Sckommodau, Hans. *Galanterie und vollkommene Liebe im "Heptameron."* Munich, 1977.

Stone, Donald. *From Tales to Truth: Essays on French Fiction in the Sixteenth Century.* Frankfurt am Main, 1973.

Telle, Emile V. *L'Oeuvre de Marguerite d'Angoulême, reine de Navarre, et la Querelle des Femmes.* Toulouse, 1937. Reprint. Geneva, 1969.

Tetel, Marcel. *Marguerite de Navarre's 'Heptaméron': Themes, Language, and Structure.* Durham, N.C., 1973.

————. "Une Réévaluation de la dixième nouvelle de *L'Heptaméron*." *Neuphilologische Mitteilungen* 72 (1971): 557–65.

Williams, H. Noel. *The Pearl of Princesses: The Life of Marguerite d'Angoulême, Queen of Navarre.* London, 1916.

ouise Labé

JEANNE PRINE

Louise Labé published a single volume during her lifetime, and it contains all that we know of her work: a dedicatory epistle, the prose "Debate Between Folly and Love," three elegies, and twenty-four sonnets.[1]

Like the Latin elegiac poets to whom she owes much, Louise has often been accused of treating a single theme—the agony of passionate unrequited love.[2] Yet her range is considerable. In the dedicatory epistle, she is a courageous defender of her sex and an accomplished prose stylist, capable of alternating rhetorical periods with incisive wit.[3] The "Debate Between Folly and Love" reveals a mind both erudite and playful, but never ponderous. The "Debate" is highly original and displays Louise's considerable knowledge of classical literature and mythology.[4] Along with Marot and Ronsard, Louise successfully adapted the classical elegy to sixteenth-century French.[5] She was among the first to compose a sonnet cycle in France, and her sonnets, like her other works, are characterized by a blend of passion, rhetoric, and wit.[6] Louise Labé has never lacked readers, although at times they have dwindled to a happy few.

On the other hand, Louise has attracted more than her share of inventive biographers.[7] Little is known about her life, but the legends surrounding her name more than make up for the lack of fact. Louise was already a figure of myth in her own time, known to her contemporaries by a series of charming epithets—"la belle Amazon," "Capitaine Louise," "la belle Cordière"—and the less flattering one, "plebeia meretrix," contributed by Calvin.[8] Oddly, not one refers to her work, but in elegy 1 she compares herself to Sappho, singing "de l'Amour Lesbienne."[9] And in elegy 3, perhaps indulging a rhetorical taste for hyperbole, she paints a portrait of herself in her youth: as skilled as the mythical Arachne with her needle and as bold as Ariosto's Bradamante when it came to horsemanship and the arts of war.[10]

In all likelihood, Louise was born between 1515 and 1524 at Parcieu

en Dombes near Lyon, where her father, Pierre Charly (called Labé) pros-
pered as a rope manufacturer.[11] At that time Lyon was the cultural capital
of France, thoroughly Renaissance, that is, Italianate, in character when
Paris was still a medieval town. A flourishing center of banking, trade,
and printing, Lyon stood at the crossroads between France and Italy, with
Germany to the north and Spain to the south. Lyon became a haven for
humanist thinkers who introduced the "new learning" and renewed interest in classicism from Italy.[12]

Louise received an excellent education according to the humanist ideal.
Whether conjecture or fact, she was said to have been her father's favorite
child, and when her mother, Etiennette Deschamps, died in 1524, Pierre
Charly saw to it that his daughter studied music, letters, and the practice
of arms, as well as needlework.[13] She learned Latin, Italian, and perhaps
Spanish and Greek. And she became an elegant, original and highly accomplished writer in her own tongue at a time when the vernacular was
far from being firmly established as the literary language of France.[14]

Dancing, singing, playing the lute, and even composing sonnets were all
accomplishments of which Castiglione might have approved. But Louise
far exceeded the decorative standard prescribed for women in *The Book
of the Courtier* when she became adept at the practice of arms.[15] Legend
has it that she fought against the Spanish at the siege of Perpignan. The
probable truth is only slightly less colorful: she may well have taken part
in a tournament in 1542, the year of the siege, or perhaps later, in 1548.[16]

Elegy 3, in which the poet depicts herself as the bold Bradamante riding
proudly armed and furiously charging her enemy, goes on to describe her
as devastated by love in spite of her skill and strength. This aspect of
Louise's life has attracted the attention of admirers, detractors, and biographers alike rather than her considerable literary achievements. In the
nineteenth century, Prosper Blanchemain suggested that Louise fell in love
with the Dauphin Henry. A likelier candidate is the poet Olivier de
Magny; there is some evidence that Louise was involved in a love affair
with him which ended unhappily. More recently, Dorothy O'Connor has
argued that Louise was a courtesan, a *cortigiana onesta* after the Italian
fashion.[17]

Whether or not that was the case, "la belle Amazon" and "Capitaine
Louise" gave way to "la belle Cordière" when Louise married Ennemond
Perrin, a wealthy rope manufacturer like her father, around 1543. During
this period of her life, Louise seems to have enjoyed the friendship of
Lyon's most notable literary figures, including Maurice Scève, Pernette
Du Guillet, and Pontus de Tyard, along with Olivier de Magny. She made
the acquaintance of many more, including Marot, Ronsard, Du Bellay,
and Baïf. It is not known for certain whether she actually presided over
the brilliant salon or collected the impressive library which legend at-

tributes to her, but it is clear that Louise Labé led a highly cultivated life at Lyon, devoting herself to friends and work.

In 1555 her works were published at Lyon by Jean de Tournes. The first edition was followed by three more in 1556, two at Lyon and one at Rouen.[18] For reasons that are not known, Louise retired to the country after 1556. Sometime during the early 1560s, her husband died, and she herself died in 1566, perhaps of the plague. She was buried at her birthplace, Parcieu en Dombes, but no trace of her grave remains.[19]

After her death, interest in Louise Labé's work declined. No new editions appeared between 1566 and 1762, and it was not until 1887 that the first scholarly edition was published at Paris by Charles Boy. Only recently, another scholarly edition, this one by Enzo Giudici, has appeared.[20]

If scholars have neglected her, Louise has had followers among fellow poets. Robert Greene translated the "Debate Between Folly and Love" in the sixteenth century, vastly altering it in the process and giving no credit to its author, and Rilke translated the sonnets. Louise's works have been translated into many other languages, including Spanish, Italian, Dutch, Polish, Hungarian, and Rumanian. But to date, no complete edition has appeared in English, although various works have been published separately.[21] Critical attention, although growing, remains less than Louise deserves.[22]

The edition of 1555 begins somewhat mysteriously with the letters "A.M.C.D.B.L." (A Mademoiselle Clémence de Bourges Lionnoize).[23] What follows is a letter dedicating the volume to a young Lyonnaise noblewoman named Clémence de Bourges.[24] In this letter, Louise encourages her friend to devote herself to literary study and writing, and she exhorts all women of talent "to raise their minds a little above their distaffs and spindles and to exert themselves to make it clear to the world that, if we are not made to command, we ought not to be disdained as companions in domestic and public affairs by those who command obedience."[25] Louise's characteristic playfulness soon intervenes. She goes on to announce that if women give full rein to their abilities, they will shame men into working much harder to prove their vaunted superiority, thereby rendering a service to society.

Louise's command of language throughout the epistle is very sure. She is a master of the full-blown rhetorical period, and she adopts a tone of excessive modesty in keeping with the Renaissance convention.[26]

Should the dedicatory epistle be regarded as what one modern critic has called it, "a veritable feminist manifesto?"[27] Louise does not challenge the right of men to rule, but she does challenge bourgeois convention by urging women to take up serious artistic and scholarly pursuits rather than restricting themselves to the domestic sphere. Louise is remarkably frank about matters of passion; chastity and reticence do not seem to have been her chief characteristics, although these were the virtues most highly recommended for women during her time. Whether or not she was a courtesan, Louise enjoyed a remarkable degree of freedom in her education and in taking up such "manly" pursuits as the art of war.

According to the elegies and sonnets, Louise's detractors included the upright women of Lyon, staunch defenders of convention. Her replies to them suggest that she was not indifferent to criticism. Sonnet 24 begins apologetically: "Do not blame me, ladies, if I've loved."[28] But it ends on a wry note of warning—they may find themselves in worse condition for less cause. Even the most staunchly virtuous are not immune to the power of love. The speaker of the sonnet has the consolation of having suffered love's assault and endured, winning poetic powers in the bargain.

Like Gaspara Stampa's, Louise Labé's sufferings bore fruit. Rilke praises Louise as one of those blessed lovers "who lament for one alone, but the whole of nature unites with them: it is the lament for one who is eternal."[29]

When she dedicated her works to Clémence de Bourges, she was, says Rilke, "not afraid of frightening this child with the long-suffering of love. She revealed to her the nightly mounting of desire; she promised her pain like a more spacious universe; and she guessed that she herself, with her experienced woe, fell short of that, so darkly expected, because of which this adolescent girl was beautiful."[30] Clémence de Bourges was said to have died of grief after the death of her beloved Jean du Peyrat in 1562.[31]

The image of the woman who falls tragically in love and suffers grief to the point of madness and even to the point of writing poetry takes a humorous turn in the "Debate Between Folly and Love." The "Debate" was highly regarded by Louise's contemporaries, but it is hardly known at all today.[32] Its form is a mixed one, reminiscent of Erasmus's *Praise of Folly* and Lucian's *Dialogues of the Gods,* yet nevertheless quite original. More declamation than drama, it contains long speeches framed by several dramatic "scenes." The "Debate" is at once comic and serious, satirical and poignant; an interesting mixture of tones is one of its chief characteristics.[33]

When the "Debate" opens, Jupiter invites all the gods and goddesses to a festival. Folly and Cupid (or Love) arrive at the palace door at exactly the same time. Cupid is a familiar mythological figure, but Folly is Louise's own creation, a powerful goddess who resembles the young woman who delivers her own eulogy in Erasmus's *Praise of Folly.*

Folly and Cupid quarrel over who should enter the palace first. When he attacks her, Folly becomes invisible, blinding Cupid to punish him, then bandaging his eyes. Louise's charming etiological myth explains why "love is blind." It also raises more serious philosophical issues. There is no proof that Louise knew Plato's *Phaedrus,* yet she links Folly (or madness) to love in much the same way as Plato does in that dialogue. It is no accident that Folly and Cupid arrive at the festival together. As the "Debate" eventually reveals, these two unlikely companions, opposites in sex, age, and temperament, are closely connected, representing two aspects of love.[34]

When Cupid takes his complaint to Jupiter for a fair hearing, his mother Venus chooses Apollo to plead her son's case. Mercury agrees to defend Folly. The two divine pleaders are as different from one another as Cupid and Folly, and so are their speeches.[35]

Apollo delivers the first speech. He begs Jupiter to restore Cupid's sight and keep Folly from coming near him. The speech is a model of decorum, polished, elegant, full of mythological allusions. Apollo's tone verges on pomposity as he stresses the harmonious qualities of love, describing how Cupid's gift to gods and humans gives rise to friendship, marital accord, brotherly love, and various cultural attainments. He claims that music, poetry, and social harmony all have their origin in love.

Needless to say, Apollo's defense of Cupid is thoroughly Apollonian and more than a little Neoplatonic. According to the Neoplatonic dogma fashionable among Lyonnaise poets, true love was controlled not by passion, but by reason.[36] As Castiglione tells us, "if the emotions are properly governed and controlled by reason, then they become virtuous, and if otherwise, then vicious."[37] True love ennobles the soul, and it begins in a curious way, according to the Neoplatonists. At the sight of the beauty of the beloved, the lover's soul leaves his body through his eyes to enter the beloved's body (also through the eyes) and lodge in her heart. Her soul, at least if she reciprocates his love, does the same. A poetic variant describes the eyes of the beloved as dangerous emitters of love's arrows which fly straight to a lover's heart.

The many Neoplatonic references in Apollo's speech to light and vision underscore the irony of Cupid's blindness. In proper Neoplatonic fashion, Apollo connects Folly with illicit passion; she has threatened the rational nature of love by blinding Cupid.[38]

Mercury eschews rhetoric in favor of the facts.[39] He asserts that there has been an alliance of long standing between Cupid and Folly, names Cupid as the aggressor in the quarrel, and flatly denies that Cupid deserves to regain his sight. Mercury claims that Folly is responsible for the world's creativeness, curiosity, invention, and daring. She is the power behind exploration, the development of science, and other kinds of knowledge, crafts, theater, games, and entertainments, and all the human activities that give rise to pleasure and laughter.

Playfully countering the Neoplatonic idea that lovers exchange souls through their eyes, or that vision is the medium of love, Mercury claims that Folly always precedes Cupid to prepare the lover's heart for his arrows. She alone makes Cupid's conquests possible, and he could not exist without her.

Further, Mercury rejects the idea that the lover's soul is controlled by reason. He draws a humorous, yet moving and ultimately serious, portrait of women who love passionately to the point of madness. Without hope of being loved in return, they lose all reason and take up the lute and the pen (here one suspects playful irony) to express themselves.[40]

The kind of passionate unrequited love these women feel comes close to that depicted in the elegies and sonnets. But its nature is not entirely tragic; in the "Debate," as in the poems, the lover's despair gives rise to music and poetry. By connecting madness with both love and art, Louise echoes the *Phaedrus*, although similar ideas may be found in Augustan elegiac poetry. Louise never makes any serious claims for the redemptive nature of love, except insofar as it finds expression in art. Plato, on the other hand, makes the highest possible claim for love: it can raise the lover to the level of divine truth, permitting glimpses of reality.[41]

Folly and Cupid enter into a relationship at the end of the "Debate" that is emblematic of the true nature of love. They must remain together with Folly leading blind Cupid. In a sense, these antagonists have become one, just as Neoplatonic lovers are supposed to do. Jupiter orders them to live together harmoniously and wisely postpones any decision on the debate for three times seven times nine centuries.[42] Still, it would appear that Mercury has made his point: Love and Folly are inseparable.

Scholars have regarded either the "Débat" or the sonnets as Louise's crowning achievement. The elegies, however, are beginning to receive more attention, an excellent example of which is Gertrude Hanisch's recent study. As she argues, the sixteenth-century French elegy had its origin in Latin elegiac poetry.[43]

The elegy has had a curious history in European literature. Even in classical times, its beginnings were obscure. According to Horace, "the elegiac couplet was first used as the vehicle of lament,"[44] and some modern scholars believe its name was derived from a Greek cry of woe.[45] The earliest elegies were songs of mourning sung to the accompaniment of a flute, and their meter was most likely a combination of hexameter and pentameter lines. Later, *elegy* came to mean any Greek poem written in couplets of a hexameter followed by a pentameter line. Elegies were written about any number of subjects, and only in the seventh century B.C. does the form become associated with love, when Mimnermus of Colophon wrote *Nanno,* a book of love elegies, to a girl who was a flute player like himself.[46]

The Roman elegiac poets took Mimnermus, along with the more learned Alexandrian erotic elegists like Callimachus, as their model.[47]

Elegiac meter became firmly associated with love in Latin poetry, but it was a kind of love not far removed in its passionate intensity and hopelessness from the original tone of Greek elegy. Elegy remained largely the vehicle for the lover's lament until the eighteenth century, when once again it was associated entirely with death and mourning.[48]

Who were the Latin elegists? Tibullus, Propertius, Catullus, and Ovid were the major figures who perfected the Latin elegy and shaped a new lexicon for generations of love poets to come.[49] For the Augustan elegists, love was a kind of madness rather than a blessing, and they constantly described it as a terrible disease of divine origin. The suffering lover languishes, grows thin and pale, endures insomnia, and weeps incessantly. His favorite word for his condition is *furor,* madness, although he also talks about flames, poison, and fatal sickness. As Hanisch explains, "he suffers more tortures than Tantalus and Sisyphus; love is a wound, an illness for which there is no cure."[50] As Propertius himself puts it, "omnes humanos sanat medicina dolores: / solus amor morbi non amat artificem" ("Medicine cures all human pains; only love does not love a cure for sickness").[51]

The elegiac poet's mistress, whose company he once enjoyed, is either faithless or absent. Luck notes that he "seems to be haunted by an ever-present sense of loss, of having been robbed of some irretrievable happiness."[52] Whether she has betrayed him or is simply absent, he must remain where he is, in a passive state of deep suffering, crying, like Catullus, "odi et amo."[53]

As often as he laments, the poet praises his beloved's beauty. Catullus says of Lesbia: "Lesbia formosa est, quae cum pulcherrima totast, / tum omnibus una omnes surripuit Veneres" ("While Lesbia, Lesbia is loveliness indeed. Herself of particular beauty, has she not plundered womanhood of all its graces, flaunting them as her adornment?").[54] In a similar mood, Propertius cries about his beloved Cynthia:

> Haec sed forma mei pars est extrema furoris; sunt maiora, quibus, Basse, perire iuvat: ingenuus color et multis decus artibus, et quae gaudia sub tacita dicere veste libet. (I.iv.11–14)

> Even her shapely form is but the least part of that which frenzies me. Yet greater charms are there, for which, Bassus, to die with passion is my joy. A natural color, grace sprung from skill in many an art, and joys whereof her couch keeps the secret.[55]

The god responsible for such passion is Eros, or Love, himself, a boy whose formidable weapons are his bow and arrows and whose target is the lover's heart.[56] The lover may also be snared by his mistress's eyes, as Propertius swears: "Cynthia prima suis miserum me cepit ocellis / contactum nullis ante cupidinibus" (Cynthia first snared me, miserable, with her eyes. Before that I was never touched by desire).[57] If Love is a warlike god, constantly attacking the lover, at times the victim joins forces with him to become a soldier in Love's or Venus's wars.[58]

Whether he pursues love actively in this way or suffers passively, the lover's affair is an unhappy one, so painful at times that he longs for death, another of the Latin elegy's major themes. Release through death is a favorite subject of Propertius's, and Tibullus also elaborates upon it:

Ergo cum tenuem fuero mutatus in umbram candidaque
ossa super nigra favilla teget, ante meum veniat
longos incompta capillos et fleat ante meum maesta
Neaera rogum.

(III.ii.9–12)

When I shall journey to the shadowy land,
And over my white bones black ashes be,
Beside my pyre let fair Neaera stand,
With long, loose locks unbound, lamenting me.[59]

Hanisch points out that the lover's thought of impending death is related both to the *carpe diem* theme, another frequently encountered component of the Latin elegy, and to the idea that poetry offers the lover some consolation because it is immortal. This latter benefit extends as well to the beloved whose name and beauty live forever in the lover's works.[60]

From time to time, however, the lover tires of his agony and decides to renounce his faithless mistress forever. Catullus is a well-known example of complete renunciation; he repudiates Lesbia in poems that combine pathos with obscenity.[61] Propertius also ends by renouncing Cynthia after five years: "quinque tibi potui servire fideliter annos."[62]

There is one other characteristic of Latin elegy of importance to students of Louise Labé's poetry, and that is its mythological content. Latin elegiac poetry is highly learned at times as well as deeply personal. Gilbert Highet writes that Propertius "cannot record his own emotions without at the same time recalling the mythic parallels which intensify his experience."[63] Catullus, Tibullus, and Ovid make similar use of mythic material, although at times it becomes either very obstruse or merely decorative in the Alexandrian manner.

Louise's elegies are all long poems (the shortest contains one hundred lines) in decasyllabic couplets, and all three take up the typical theme of passionate unrequited love, although the treatment varies from poem to poem. Each elegy is addressed to someone in the manner of an epistle: elegy 1 and elegy 3 to the ladies of Lyon and elegy 2 to an unnamed absent lover.[64]

The first elegy announced Louise's debt to the Latin poets:

Au tems qu'Amour, d'hommes et Dieus Vanqueur,
Faisoit bruler de sa flamme mon coeur,
En embrasant de sa cruelle rage
Mon sang, mes os, mon esprit et courage:
Encore lors je n'avois la puissance
De lamenter ma peine et ma souffrance.[65]

When Love, conquerer of gods and men,
Made my heart burn with his fire,
Inflaming my blood, my bones, my mind and soul
With his cruel rage
Once again I lacked the power
To sing my pain and suffering.

The love described here is Propertian, as Hanisch stresses.[66] The speaker has been so robbed of strength by love that she cannot write; she has been deprived of the poet's only consolation for pain. Able to write verse again, she announces her theme: she will avoid the subject matter of epic and concentrate on love. Thus, her scope is thoroughly elegiac; she goes on to compare herself to the lyric poet Sappho who also sang of love (obviously Louise had no female elegiac models from which to choose).

In elegy 1, Louise addresses a female audience: "Dames, qui les lirez, / Des mes regrets avec moy soupirez" (Ladies who read these lines, sigh with me over my regrets).[67] Here Louise touches on an opposition that finds full expression in elegy 3 and sonnet 24. On one hand, the poem's speaker represents the victim of intense passion; on the other hand, the ladies she addresses appear to have been untouched by love. Her purpose is to teach them to pity, not censure, love's victims. The implied comparison between the speaker and the ladies of Lyon serves to heighten the effect of love's devastating power.[68]

The idea that love has robbed the poet of her strength is further extended to the legendary queen Semiramis, once a warrior, now laid low by the god.[69] Semiramis's decline is revealed by a series of rhetorical questions: "Where is the sword, where is that cuirass with which you crushed the audacity of the enemy?"[70] Numerous references to her former warlike character offer a sharp contrast to Semiramis languishing in love. Critics have noted a possible resemblance here to Louise's own legendary exploits in arms, and the elegy undoubtedly also contains a play on the ancient lover/soldier topos frequently found in Latin elegy.

Finally, elegy 3 ends on another note reminiscent of the Augustan poets—the *carpe diem* theme. Prevalent in sixteenth-century French poetry, this theme finds its finest expression in poems like Ronsard's "Quand vous serez bien vieille, au soir, a la chandelle," where it is combined with the notion that poetry confers immortality. In Louise's first elegy, those who scorn love (that is, the ladies to whom the poem is addressed) are given a grim warning. In old age they may find themselves burning with desire, pathetically trying to become beautiful again.

Elegy 2 turns from the universal power of love to a more personal lament for the speaker's absent lover. The "ami" to whom this poem is addressed has been identified by many scholars as Olivier de Magny, but his precise identity is of less importance than the fact that he represents the type of the absent (and possibly faithless) lover found in Augustan elegy.[71]

The second elegy is truly an epistle, perhaps even modeled on Ovid's *Heroides*.[72] In it, the speaker refers to her lover's "premiere lettre," in which he promised to return. The tone of elegy 2 suggests that the speaker has been betrayed and fears her lover will never come back—even that he may have fallen in love with someone else. These circumstances coincide with what is known of Louise's association with Magny, and at the same time they are typical of elegiac poetry in general. Louise's elegies are firmly grounded in classical tradition, as one might expect of sixteenth-century French poetry, yet she is not merely imitative or conventional. Her awareness of genre and rhetoric is combined with deeply felt experience, giving rise to the blend of passion and artifice characteristic of successful lyric poetry.

Elegy 2 ends on a sombre note worthy of Propertius. The speaker describes what her lover will read on her white marble tombstone if she dies of love before his return. With Petrarchan extravagance, she describes herself as entirely consumed by love's fire because her beloved was not there to extinguish the flames with his tears.[73]

Hanisch notes that Louise varies the rhetorical effects of the second elegy from the formal rhetorical question to the intimate conversational tone of "Tu es tout seul, tout mon mal et mon bien: / Avec toy tout, et sans toy je n'ay rien" (You alone are everything to me—all my evil and my good. With you I have everything, without you nothing).[74]

Like Tibullus, whose elegies oscillate between imagined happiness and real despair, Louise's speaker moves between "tout" and "rien." She recalls the past, hopes passionately for her lover's return, and despairs at his absence and the fear that he will never come back.[75]

Elegy 3 has been a rich source of information about Louise's early education, since it contains the charming portrait of its speaker as a needle-woman, scholar, and soldier. The poet's technique in the third elegy is more dramatic than in the other two.[76]

Rather than presenting a monologue, the speaker recalls a conversation she had with Love. The god delivers a warning:

Tu penses donq, O Lionnoise Dame,
Pouvoir fuir par ce moyen ma flame:
Mais non feras, j'ai subjugue les Dieus
Es bas Enfers, en la Mer et es Cieus.[77]

Do you think, O Lyonnaise lady,
that this way you can escape my flame?
You won't do it—I have conquered
the gods and the infernal regions,
the sea and the sky.

The topos of Love as a warring god is particularly vivid as the elegy continues:

Ainsi parloit, et tout eschaufe d'ire
Hors de sa trousse une sagette il tire,
Et decochant de son extreme force
Droit la tira contre ma tendre escorce:
Foible harnois, pour bien couvrir le coeur,
Contre l'Archer qui tousjours est vainqueur.[78]

Thus he spoke. And hot with rage
He took an arrow from his quiver
And let it fly with mighty force
Straight it hit against my tender skin—
A flimsy armor to protect the heart—
Against the Archer who is always the victor.

Equally vivid is the description of Love's suffering in the elegiac fashion: "Et de travail qui me donne sans cesse, / Boire, manger, et dormir ne me laisse" (And the pain he gives me without cease / Will not allow me to drink, to eat, or sleep).

The speaker reveals that she has been under Love's power from the age of sixteen to her present twenty-nine, lamenting that the emotion, which is normally fleeting, is only augmented by time in her case. Mythological examples bolster the argument, and the elegy ends with a prayer to Love to end her pain before she resorts to death or else allow her to be loved in return with "an equal or a greater flame."

Louise's elegies are typical of the Renaissance in their classicism and original in their tone of frank passion conveyed with rhetorical precision. As Hanisch expresses it, Louise's achievement in the elegies "freed the [form], allowing it to become the vehicle for lyrical expression which it had been for the Roman elegists and would eventually become for Ronsard."[79]

As mentioned earlier, Louise was one of the first poets in France to publish a sonnet cycle. Hers contains twenty-four sonnets on the subject of love. Bound together by the underlying theme of passionate unrequited love, the sonnets vary markedly in content, tone, and rhetorical effects. They range from more formal treatment of mythological subjects to rhetorical display in the Petrarchan manner to intimate and frankly passionate conversation. In Louise's hands the sonnet form never becomes rigid or overly artificial; each poem's structure illuminates its meaning.

The first sonnet, written in Italian, reveals several things of importance to the entire sequence. First, Louise's debt to Italian poetry, more specifically to Petrarch, the great master of the sonnet form, is indicated by her choice of language for sonnet 1. Second, the sonnet mentions Ulysses in its first line, raising the possibility that the cycle will attempt to echo Homer's epic in some way. Indeed, many of the recurring themes of the sonnets are those of the *Odyssey:* the loneliness and longing endured by Odysseus (Ulysses) and Penelope, the absent hero's travels, his wife's abandonment, and his eventually triumphant return. By providing a link to the *Odyssey* in sonnet 1, Louise introduces a note of initial hope: the speaker's lover may, like the Greek hero, return at last, even after an absence of many years. She, too, is like Ulysses since she must endure terrible torments and feel endless desire—all at the hands of a cruel god. The cycle also contains a formal reference to Homer's epic in its twenty-four separate poems. Finally, the first sonnet depends not only on a reference to epic and on the imagery of the Latin love elegy for its effect, but also on Petrarchan antithesis, a device which Louise employs throughout the sequence.

Although it is difficult to find much direct influence of Petrarch on Louise's work, she does seem particularly fond of certain Petrarchan conceits: antithesis and oxymoron, extreme heat and cold (burning and freezing), torrents of tears, love as warfare, the beloved as sun or star, the beloved's musical gifts, the exchange of lovers' souls, and love's physical symptoms.[80] Obviously, there is much overlap here with elegiac *topoi*, and it remains an open question how much Petrarch himself borrowed from the Augustan elegists. That he knew their work, or at least Ovid's and Catullus's, is certain, but scholars have not yet thoroughly investigated the matter.[81]

What there is of Petrarchanism and Platonism in the sonnets may indicate the influence of her friend Maurice Scève on Louise. For the most part, however, the sonnets are characterized by her own blend of playfulness, passion, carefully controlled rhetoric, and what Henri Peyre has called "directness of tone and . . . pathetic intensity of feeling."[82]

Louise's apparent "sincerity" and powerful expression of emotion may account for the enduring popularity of the sonnets, but there is no reason to confuse her poetic achievement in the sequence with simplicity or spontaneity. Even O'Connor diminishes Louise's stature as an artist when she writes that Louise used her poetry as a sort of base to contain the overflow of emotion from her aching heart.[83]

Sonnets 2, 3, and 4 contain respectively a *blason,* or praise of the lover's various attributes; imagery of fire and fountains; and the familiar idea that Love is a cruel warlike god. Louise employs the sonnet form with surprising variety and firm control. For the most part, she follows the usual division into octave and sestet but may include subtle variations to enhance a poem's meaning.[84]

Among the most popular of the poems are 5, addressed to Venus, 7, an example of playful Platonism, and 9, which takes up the Petrarchan theme of the beloved's visit in a dream. Sonnets 12 and 14 are companion pieces on the theme of the consolation of poetry and music; both are lute poems, a minor genre in the Renaissance. Sonnet 17 is a deliberate echo of a Petrarchan topos—the lover's flight into nature and solitude. Several other sonnets, including 15, 16, and 19 combine images of nature with mythological references in the elegiac manner. Sonnet 18 is another charming example of a poem with classical antecedents; it is a *basium,* or kiss poem, in the Catullan manner.

The twenty-second poem is vital to an understanding of the sequence as a whole. Here, Louise makes explicit an idea that runs through the sonnets: love is not only personal emotion, not only a *furor* caused by a god, but also a force woven into the very fabric of the cosmos. In one of her most positive characterizations of love, Louise calls it "la puissante harmonie" (line 9), explaining that discord in matters of love among the gods would cause terrible chaos in the universe.

Sonnet 23 reverses the typical renunciation poem of the Latin elegists. Rather than denouncing her faithless lover, the speaker checks her anger and begs his forgiveness. The concluding lines, "Mais je m'assure, quelque part que tu sois, / Qu'autant que moy tu soufres de martire" (But I am assured, wherever you may be, that you suffer a martyrdom as great as mine), indicate that the lover's absence may have been against his inclination, like that of Ulysses.

Sonnet 24 is Louise's final word to the ladies of Lyon, reminiscent of both the first and third elegies in its note of apology and warning to the prudish Lyonnaises. It provides a poignant conclusion to the sequence and has been one of the most widely read of the sonnets.

The following translations are based on Enzo Giudici's edition (in turn based on the edition of 1556) of the complete works. I have tried to keep them as straightforward and close to the original as possible. The rich rhymes and musicality of the sonnets and elegies have been sacrificed to accuracy, a loss which is practically unavoidable in translating from French to English. Many readers will find Louise's French in the poems easily accessible, particularly in the Giudici edition with its modern spelling.

NOTES

1. To date, the best complete editions are by Boy (1887) and Giudici (1981). All page numbers refer to Giudici.

2. For example, see Dorothy O'Connor, *Louise Labé: Sa vie et son oeuvre*, p. 137: "La poesie de Louise Labé traite exclusivement de l'amour." Helmut Hatzfeld refers likewise to Louise's "amorous tragedy" ("The Role of Mythology in Poetry During the French Renaissance," p. 393). The general tendency has been to regard her as the author of the sonnets, while the other works are ignored for the most part, and to regard the sonnets as passionately sincere, practically spontaneous utterances. Harvey and others argue to the contrary, as I attempt to do. The Latin elegiac poets have also been accused of sincerity (Catullus), narrow range (Propertius), simplicity (Tibullus), and utter artlessness (Sulpicia). See, for instance, the mention of Propertius's protest in Gertrude S. Hanisch, *Love Elegies of the Renaissance*, p. 11; Gilbert Highet, *Poets in a Landscape*, p. 103, for the notion that Propertius treated a single theme—obsessive love; Georg Luck, *The Latin Love Elegy*, pp. 107–9 for what amounts to a denial that Sulpicia *was* a poet; also see Kirby Flower Smith on Tibullus's simplicity (*The Elegies of Albius Tibullus*, p. 68) and Michael Putnam (*Tibullus: A Commentary*, p. 12) for the counter-argument.

Catullus, whose range was astonishing, is described by Karl Pomeroy Harrington as noteworthy for "the intensely personal character of many of his subjects and the directness and simplicity with which he expresses his mood" (*Catullus and His Influence*, p. 51). Louise, then, is in good company. It remains for scholars to describe the rhetorical or other means by which all these poets achieve their effects.

3. See I. D. McFarlane, *A Literary History of France: Renaissance France, 1470–1589*, p. 163.

4. On the originality of the *Débat*, see Fernand Zamaron, *Louise Labé: Dame de franchise*, pp. 62–63; O'Connor, p. 94, and especially Gerard Guillot, ed., *Louise Labé*, pp. 60–61.

5. See Gertrude Hanisch's invaluable study of the elegies in *Love Elegies of the Renaissance*, pp. 53–72. She is one of the few scholars to examine Louise's debt to Latin elegiac poetry.

6. Other sonneteers include du Bellay, Marot, Pontus de Tyard, Baïf, and Ronsard. On the subject of Louise's blend of passion and rhetoric, see McFarlane, p. 165.

7. Louise's early biographers include Pernetti in the eighteenth century and Breghot du Lut, Turquéty, and Prosper Blanchemain in the nineteenth. The foremost biography is Dorothy O'Connor's *Louise Labé: Sa vie et son oeuvre* (1926). For statements about Louise by her contemporaries, see Charles Boy, ed., *Oeuvres*, vol. 2, pp. 89–114.

8. Edwin Marion Cox dismisses the charge: "We may be certain that this description is unjustified, and is only the savage epithet which his narrow and sour intellect led him to apply to one who was the exponent of something beyond his comprehension and appreciation" (*The Debate Between Folly and Cupid*, p. xix).

9. Line 15, Enzo Giudici, ed., *Oeuvres complètes*, p. 130.

10. See lines 33–42, Giudici, ed., p. 138.

11. See Boy, ed., vol. 2, p. 30 for Louise's date of birth, and for the place, p. 31.

12. O'Connor takes up the importance of Lyon in detail on pages 9–41. Cox describes

the contrast between a medieval Paris and Renaissance Lyon on pages xvi–xviii. Also mentioned in an unpublished essay on Louise Labé by Frank J. Warnke.

13. Zamaron argues that Louise was her father's favorite child (p. 16).

14. See McFarlane, pp. 135–142 and 151–52.

15. See Castiglione's *The Book of the Courtier*, trans. Bull, pp. 214 ff., and Ruth Kelso's *Doctrine for the Lady of the Renaissance*.

16. The legend that Louise fought at Perpignan has been traced to Blanchemain (Hanisch, p. 55). For an alternative explanation, see Boy, ed., vol. 2, pp. 38–42.

17. See O'Connor, pp. 82 ff.

18. Giudici, ed., pp. 9–10.

19. Boy, ed., vol. 2, pp. 71–75, and Cox, trans., p. xxvii.

20. For a list of editions and translations, see Giudici, ed., pp. 237–48. More detailed descriptions of early editions may be found in Cox, trans., pp. xxiii–xxvii.

21. Giudici, ed., pp. 245–48.

22. A partial bibliography may be found in Giudici, ed., pp. 248–56.

23. Ibid., pp. 94–95.

24. See Boy, ed., vol. 2, pp. 121–25, for the history of the family of Clémence de Bourges.

25. The translation is mine. For original, see Giudici, ed., p. 18.

26. For topos of affected modesty, see Ernst R. Curtius, *European Literature and the Latin Middle Ages*, pp. 83–85.

27. Hanisch, p. 53. Also see "Louise Labé's 'Débat de Folie et d'Amour': Feminism and the Defense of Learning" by Anne R. Larsen.

28. "Ne reprenez, Dames, si j'ay ayme," Giudici, ed., p. 164.

29. Rainer Maria Rilke, *The Notebooks of Malte Laurids Brigge*, trans. Norton, p. 198.

30. Ibid., p. 200.

31. Giudici, ed., p. 94.

32. Boy, ed., vol. 2, pp. 5–6, and O'Connor, p. 93. Some scholars regard the medieval debat as Labé's model for this work. See McFarlane, p. 162, and Hanisch's note on p. 55.

33. The *Débat* is divided into five "discourses," of which the last is taken up by Mercury's and Apollo's long declamations. For discussion of tone, see Larsen, p. 43, and McFarlane, p. 162.

34. Socrates argues that love and poetry are forms of divinely inspired madness. See Plato's *Phaedrus*, trans. Helmbold and Rabinowitz, pp. 25–42.

35. The *Débat* is characterized by both balance and antithesis. Its six characters form three pairs, each embodying a contrast: Folly/Cupid, Jupiter/Venus, Mercury/Apollo.

36. Larsen argues that "according to standard Neoplatonic ideology, as outlined by Leone Ebreo in his *Dialoghi d'amore* (1535), true love is engendered and controlled by Reason." She goes on to say that Mercury "devalues Neoplatonic idealism" in the *Débat* (p. 51).

37. Castiglione, p. 293.

38. Apollo links Folly to Phaedra, Myrrha, and other women whose unnatural or excessive desires are legendary. In her presence, he says, "honte se perdra du tout." See Giudici, ed., pp. 61–62. Likewise, Venus calls Folly "femme abandance" (p. 36). Needless to say, the ideal Neoplatonic love extolled by Apollo was chaste.

39. Larsen, p. 47.

40. "Plus elles ont resiste a Amour, et plus s'en treuvent prises. Elles ferment la porte a raison. Tout ce qu'elles creingnoient, ne le doutent plus. Elles laissent leur ocupacions muliebres. . . . Elles prennent la plume et le lut en main: escrivent et chantent leurs passions" (Giudici, ed., p. 85).

41. Louise does have Mercury say of the fool: "il sera mis jusques au ciel," however (Giudici, ed., p. 74). For Plato, see *Phaedrus*, pp. 25–42.

42. These are mystical numbers as Giudici (p. 125) and others have noted.

43. O'Connor, *Love Elegies of the Renaissance*, pp. 2–21 and 53–72. O'Connor also mentions the Augustan elegists as Louise's source for the form. Hanisch argues for Marot and possibly Petrarch as intermediaries but grants that Louise knew the Latin poets in the original (see p. 56). For the impact of Latin poets on Louise's contemporaries, see McFarlane, pp. 261 and 103–4. Also see Harrington, *Catullus and His Influence*, pp. 109–14.

44. Aristotle, "On the Art of Poetry," in *Classical Literary Criticism*, p. 81.

45. Harrington, ed., *The Roman Elegiac Poets*, p. 16. The Greek literally means "cry oh, cry oh," etc., but Suidas renders it more elegantly as "woe! woe! cry woe!" I am indebted throughout to Harrington's section on the early history of elegy, pp. 15–24.

46. See Ibid., p. 17.

47. Ibid., p. 18.

48. See *The Princeton Encyclopedia of Poetry and Poetics*, pp. 215–217, for a brief history of the elegy.

49. See Luck, *The Latin Love Elegy*, which takes up minor as well as major figures on pages 49–57 and 100–117. Sulpicia is of particular interest as a woman writing about a beloved man, although Luck's discussion of her is too biased to be very helpful. Instead, see Kirby Flower Smith, ed., *The Elegies of Albius Tibullus*, pp. 77–78, and H. J. Rose's *Handbook of Latin Literature*, pp. 288–89. For the Latin elegists in general, see not only Luck and Smith but also Harrington, ed., *The Roman Elegiac Poets*, pp. 15–67.

50. Hanisch, p. 16. Also see pp. 11–19 for characteristics of elegiac poet/lover.

51. II.i.57–58, in H. E. Butler, ed. and trans., p. 66. Translation is not Butler's but mine.

52. Luck, p. 72 (speaking of Tibullus).

53. Catullus, LXXXV, in Harrington, *Catullus and His Influence*, p. 107. The entire poem consists of two lines: "Odi et amo. quare id faciam, fortasse requiris. / Nescio, sed fieri sentio et excrucior" (I hate and I love. Why this is perhaps you ask. I don't know, but I feel it and I'm tortured). The translation is mine as are all others not otherwise noted.

54. Catullus, LXXXVI.5–6, in Harrington, *Catullus and His Influence*, p. 107. Translated by Peter Whigham on page 198 of *The Poems of Catullus*.

55. In Butler, ed. and trans., p. 12. Butler's translation, p. 13.

56. As in Propertius, II.xii.13–16: "In me tela manent, manet et puerilis imago: sed certe pennas perdidit ille suas; evolat ei nostro quoniam de pectore nusquam assiduusque meo sanguine bella gerit" (Butler, p. 94) (In me his weapons remain, and he remains in the image of a boy, but surely he has lost his wings, since he flies nowhere from my heart but, always in the same place, wages war in my blood).

57. Propertius, I.i.1–2, in Butler, p. 3.

58. See Tibullus, I.i, in Smith, ed., pp. 107–9, and II.vi, pp. 146–48, for two variations on the lover-soldier topos. Also see Hanisch, p. 12. The military language of love is characteristic of Latin elegiac poetry, ranging from the tormented in Propertius, to the often humorous in Ovid.

59. Translated by Williams, trans., p. 97. Original in Smith, ed., p. 150.

60. See Hanisch, p. 13.

61. Catullus's LVIII is a good example. See Whigham, trans., p. 279, for the text, and p. 118 for the translation.

62. "I was able to serve you faithfully for five years" (Propertius, III.xxv.3. This and III.xxiv are entirely poems of renunciation. In Butler, ed. and trans., pp. 256–59.

63. Highet, p. 81. For the use of Greco-Roman mythology in sixteenth-century lyric poetry, see Helmut Hatzfeld's "The Role of Mythology in Poetry During the French Renaissance."

64. A similar device is often used in the Latin elegy. The identity of the person to whom

the poem is addressed may strongly affect the tone of the whole, as in Propertius, I.v, addressed simply to "invide" ("envious one"). The device ranges from the true epistolary address to conversation to prayer and contributes much to the personal, impassioned, seemingly uncalculated tone of elegiac poetry. It is used with equal frequency and success in lyric meters. Hanisch shows that Louise employs the device both subtly and effectively (p. 57). However, she argues that Marot and others confused the elegy with the verse epistle and that Louise specifically follows the Ovidian *heroide,* especially in elegy 2 (see p. 29). Although I do not necessarily agree with her on this point, I am indebted to Hanisch's analysis of the elegies on the whole.

65. Giudici, ed., p. 129.

66. See Hanisch, p. 59.

67. Giudici, ed., p. 130.

68. See Hanisch, p. 57.

69. Dante depicts Semiramis as so overcome by lust that she made all forms of it legal to avoid censure. See canto 5, lines 54–60, of the *Inferno.*

70. See lines 61–90 in Giudici, ed., p. 131.

71. Some critics have found Italian influence in the poem, including traces of Gaspara Stampa, whose work Louise may have read. See Giudici's lengthy note on pages 167–68.

72. See Hanisch, p. 67. The *Heroides* were long epistolary poems from mythological women to their absent lovers. For a more complete description, see Rose, pp. 328–29. However, the amatory epistle was a popular form with other elegists, including Propertius; see Harrington's *Roman Elegiac Poets,* pp. 49–50. The major difference between Louise's elegy 2 and Ovid's *Heroides* (and imitations) is that in the latter, the poet does not express himself directly. Instead, he chooses a female mythological figure as the speaker of the poem. The *Heroides* are among the least "personal" of Latin amatory epistles for this reason. They also tend to be highly learned, full of decorative rhetoric, and even precious. As Rose puts it, "the ladies plead their cases with the arts of the rhetoricians . . . a little cloying if the reader goes through too many at a sitting" (p. 328). Nothing could be further from the directness of Louise's poetry.

73. Hanisch finds this touch precious (pp. 61–62). Also see Tibullus, III.ii, in Smith, ed., pp. 150–51 which also ends with an epitaph.

74. Lines 81–82, Giudici, ed., p. 135. See Hanisch, p. 68.

75. See Hanisch, p. 67, and Putnam, p. 11, on Tibullus's tendency to juxtapose an ideal world of past or future fulfillment to present despair.

76. Elegy 3 was probably composed first, according to O'Connor, pp. 135–37.

77. Giudici, ed., p. 138.

78. Ibid., p. 139.

79. Hanisch, p. 72.

80. See Leonard Forster, *The Icy Fire: Five Studies in European Petrarchism,* pp. 1–60, esp. pp. 6–23.

81. Petrarch had a manuscript of Catullus in his possession. See Harrington, *Catullus and His Influence,* pp. 97–98. Also see page 105 for a discussion of early editions of Catullus, Tibullus, and Propertius. Hanisch mentions the likely connection between Petrarch and the Latin elegists on page 61.

82. Henri Peyre, *Literature and Sincerity,* p. 21. I am indebted to an unpublished essay by Frank J. Warnke for the influence of Scève on Louise Labé. Also see Odette de Morgues, *Metaphysical, Baroque, and Precieux Poetry* (Oxford, 1953), p. 26.

83. O'Connor, p. 134: "Elle usait plûtot de la poesie comme d'un vase ou elle put verser le trop-plein de son coeur endolori."

84. Examples abound in Lawrence E. Harvey's *The Aesthetics of the Renaissance Love Sonnet.*

From the *Works of Louise Labé of Lyon*

TO MADEMOISELLE CLÉMENCE DE BOURGES OF LYON

The time having come, Mademoiselle,[1] when the stern laws of men no longer bar women from devoting themselves to the sciences and disciplines, it seems to me that those who are able ought to employ this honorable liberty, which our sex formerly desired so much, in studying these things and show men the wrong they have done us in depriving us of the benefit and the honor which might have come to us. And if anyone reaches the stage at which she is able to put her ideas into writing, she should do it with much thought and should not scorn the glory, but adorn herself with this rather than with chains, rings, and sumptuous clothes, which we are not really able to regard as ours except by custom. But the honor which knowledge will bring us cannot be taken from us—not by the cunning of a thief, not by the violence of enemies, not by the duration of time.

If I had been so blessed by Heaven as to have a mind great enough to understand whatever it desired, I would furnish an example in this regard rather than an admonition.[2] But having spent part of my youth in the practice of music and having found the time remaining to me too brief for the rude nature of my understanding, not being able myself to do justice to the goodwill I bear for our sex—to see it not only in beauty but in knowledge and eminence surpass or equal men—I cannot do otherwise than beg excellent Ladies to raise their minds a little above their distaffs and spindles and to exert themselves to make it clear to the world that, if we are not made to command, we ought not to be disdained as companions in domestic and public affairs by those who govern and command obedience.

And in addition to the recognition that our sex will gain by this, we will have furnished the public with a reason for men to devote more study and labor to the humanities lest they might be ashamed to see us surpass them when they have always pretended to be superior in nearly everything.[3]

For this reason, we must inspire one another in so worthy an undertaking from which you should not spare your intellect, already accompanied by many different graces, nor your youth and other favors of fortune, to acquire the honor which literature and the sciences are accustomed to bring those persons who follow them.

If there is something worthy of respect after glory and honor, the pleasure which literary study usually gives us ought to move everyone of us to action. This pleasure is distinct from other diversions. When one has indulged in them for as long as one wants, one cannot boast of anything except having passed the time. But study rewards us with a pleasure all its own which remains with us longer. For the past delights us and serves us better than the present, but the pleasures of the senses[4] are immediately lost and never return, and sometimes the memory of them is as disagreeable as the acts were delectable.

Moreover, the other sensual pleasures are such that whatever memory of them comes to us cannot put us back in the frame of mind we were in. And however strong the impression of them we have fixed in our minds, we know well that it is nothing but a shadow of the past which deceives and betrays us. But when we put our thoughts into writing, even if afterward our minds race through no end of distractions and are constantly agitated, nevertheless, returning much later to what we have written, we find ourselves at the same point and in the same state of mind we were in before. Then we redouble our happiness, because we regain the past pleasure we had in what we were writing, or in understanding the sciences to which we were devoting ourselves. Furthermore, the judgment which our second impression makes of the first gives us a singular satisfaction.

These two advantages which come from writing ought to spur you on, assured as you are that the first will not fail to accompany what you write, as it does all your other actions and your way of life. The second will be yours to take or refuse, depending on whether your writings please you.

As for me, in writing these works of my youth to begin with, and after reviewing them later, I did not seek anything but an honorable pastime and a way to escape idleness, and I did not intend that anyone other than myself should ever see them. But since some of my friends found a way to read them without my knowing anything about it, and (thus we easily believe those who praise us) since they have persuaded me that I should bring them to light, I was not so bold as to refuse them. But I did threaten to make them drink half the measure of shame which would be the result.

And because women do not willingly appear alone in public, I have chosen you to serve as my guide, dedicating this little work to you. I do not send it to you for any purpose other than to assure you of the goodwill I have borne you for a long time and to make you, seeing this rough and badly written work of mine, long to create another which might be more polished and more elegant.

God keep you in good health.

From Lyon, July 24, 1555.

Your humble friend,

LOUISE LABÉ

2

O beautiful dark eyes, O glances turned away,
O burning sighs, O scattered tears,

O black nights in vain awaited,
O bright days in vain returning.

O sad laments, O obstinate desires,
O lost time, O wasted pain,
O thousand deaths, held out in a thousand nets,
O worst evils destined against me.

O smile, O face, hair, arms, hands, fingers;
O mournful lute, viol, bow, and voice:
So many flames to burn a maiden![5]

Of you I complain, bearing so many torches
Into my heart in so many places,
Yet not one spark has lit on you.[6]

3

O endless desires, O empty hopes,
Sad sighs and customary tears,
Engendering in me many streams,
Of which my eyes are the fountains and springs.

O cruelty, O inhuman severity,
The pitying gaze of the heavenly stars,
O former passions of a frozen heart,
Do you think to increase my pains again?

Let love take aim at me again,
Fling new fires and new darts at me;
Let him be vexed and do his worst:

For I am so torn in every part
That he can no longer find a place
To make me worse by wounding me once more.[7]

4

Since cruel Love first poisoned
My heart with his fire,
Always burning with his divine madness,
He has not left my breast for a single day.

Whatever pain he has given me,
Whatever threat of impending ruin,[8]
Whatever thought of death that ends it all,
Nothing can shake my passionate heart.

The more Love comes to assault us hard,
The more he makes us gather our forces,
Forever fresh in his battles.

But he never gives us assistance at all,
He who despises gods and men;
The stronger they are, the stronger he appears against them.

5

Bright Venus,[9] who wanders through the sky,
Hear my voice that rich in pain shall sing,
To you as long as you appear to shine,
Above, of love's long strain and tired care.

My watchful eye will be more moved,
And seeing you more tears will shed;
The tears will bathe my soft bed better,
With your eyes bearing witness to my pain.

Now human spirits grow fatigued,
And by sweet rest and sleep are seized.
But I bear pain while daylight shines:

And when I am completely broken,
Arranged exhausted on my bed,
I must cry out my agony all night long.

6

Twice or thrice blessed the return
Of that clear star and happier still
That which he honors with his gaze.
She who would receive the happy day,

She who could boast of fortune's favor,
Who could kiss the most beautiful gift of Flora,[10]
The finest that Aurora ever saw,
And then could stay upon his lips!

To me alone this bliss is due,
For so many tears and so much time I have lost;
But, seeing him, I'll entertain him so,

So employ the power of my eyes,
To have more influence over him,
That in a little time I shall make a great conquest.

7

One sees all living things die,
Because the subtle soul and body part;
I am the body; you are the better part:
Where are you, then, O best-beloved soul?

Don't leave me so long faint with suffering,
If you wait too long, you'll come too late to save me;
Alas! Don't put your body at such risk:
Return to it the other half it loves.

Do nothing, love, that might endanger
This loving union and encounter;
Don't come to it with severity,

Not with harshness—but sweet grace,
That gently gives to me your beauty,
Once cruel, now kind.[11]

8

I live, I die: I'm drowned and burned.
Enduring freezing cold, I feel excessive heat.
For me, life is too hard, too soft;
My melancholy mixes with my joy.[12]

Suddenly I laugh at the same time I cry,
And in delight feel deep pain of grief;
My good disappears and forever remains;
All at once—I wither and bloom.

So love leads me inconstantly on,
And just when I think that I'm lost in great grief,
With no thought at all, the sorrow is gone.

Then when I believe my joy is secure,
And longed-for happiness at hand,
He puts me back in misery again.

9

As soon as I begin to find
Desired rest in my soft bed,
My sad spirit, drawn out of me,
Turns straight[13] to you, surrenders there.

Then it seems within my tender breast
I have the good which I have so desired,
For which I have so loudly sighed,
That from the sobs I thought my heart would break.

O sweet sleep, O happy night for me!
Pleasant rest, full of peace,
Continue every night my dream.

And if my poor loving spirit
Must never have its bliss in truth
See that it has at least a lie.[14]

10

When I see your fair head crowned
With green laurel; when you make your lute lament
So well you could force
Trees and rocks to follow you;[15] When I see you splendid

And surrounded by ten thousand virtues,
At honor's peak, so high no one can reach,
And from the highest stealing praises,
Then says my passionate heart to itself:

"So many virtues which make you loved
Which make you esteemed by everyone,
Could they not likewise make you love?

And add to your praiseworthy virtue
The name of being kind to me once more?
Sweetly inflame you with my love?"

12

Lute, companion of my misfortune,
Faultless witness of my sighs,
True recorder of my sorrow,
You have often grieved with me.

And the pitiful weeping has troubled you so,
That beginning some delightful song,
You make it suddenly sorrowful,
Changing your joyful tone to grief.[16]

And if I force you to sound joyful,
You slacken your strings and silence me;
But seeing me sighing tenderly,

Then you approve my sad lament;
In my sorrow you compel me,
And I hope for a sweet conclusion from sweet pain.

13

Oh, if I were ravished on that beautiful chest
Of him for whom I'm dying,
If envy did not prevent me[17]
From living out the brief course
of my days with him.

If, holding me, he'd say, "dear love,
Let us be satisfied with one another, sure
That neither storm, Euripus,[18] nor the sea
Could separate our lives";

If, while I circled my arms around his neck,
Like the ivy circles the tree,
Death came, envious of my ease,

Then, when he sweetly kissed me again,
And my spirit fled upon his lips,
I would die blessed,
Happier than when I was alive.

NOTES TO THE TRANSLATION

1. In the edition of 1555, the dedicatory epistle was addressed only to "A.M.C.D.B.L." ("A Mademoiselle Clémence de Bourges Lionnoize"). Clémence de Bourges was of noble birth, the daughter of Claude de Bourges and Francoise de Mornay. She was probably born around 1532 and died in 1562. The degree of friendship between her and Labé is not known. See Boy, vol. 2, pp. 121–25.

2. Here Louise's use of the topos of affected modesty begins.

3. A playful allusion to the so-called "querelle des femmes," an ongoing literary argument over the relative merits of the sexes. The quarrel was largely among men; along with Christine de Pizan (1365–1430), Louise is one of the few women who took up the issue.

4. The French is "les plaisirs des sentimens."

5. As Giudici and others have noted, the language of the original is very ambiguous, blurring the catalog of the beloved's characteristics with the lover's suffering. It is as though his features and her pain have become intertwined.

6. E. Turquéty first noted the similarity between this sonnet and Olivier de Magny's "Sonnet 55" in *Soupirs*. The enumeration of the beloved's characteristics, or blazon, is a device often found in medieval and Renaissance lyrics.

7. An adaptation of "interditte speranze" by Sannazaro, also translated by Olivier de Magny. See O'Connor, pp. 143–45. Louise's images are both classical and Petrarchan. From the Petrarchan tradition she borrows tears and sighs; the Augustan elegists provide (perhaps by way of Petrarch) the notion of Love as a fierce god waging war.

8. "Quelque menasse et procheine ruine," an example of hendiadys.

9. "Clere Venus" is both the planet, or morning star, and the goddess of love.

10. "Le plus beau don de Flore," or the beloved's lips; the allusion, probably to the rose, follows Petrarchan convention, as does the comparison of the beloved to "ce cler Astre" in line 2.

11. Unlike that of Maurice Scève, Louise's Platonism is entirely playful in this sonnet.

12. Sonnet 8 begins with a series of Petrarchan antitheses that continue through the second quatrain.

13. "Incontinent," which also suggests, as an adjective, "incontinent esprit," or "wanton spirit," a paradox blending the spiritual and sensual in a fashion typical of Louise.

14. The final rhyme "songe/mensonge" neatly juxtaposes the ideas of the dream and the lie.

15. The reference is to Orpheus, who could charm animals, stones, and trees with his lyre.

16. Giudici suggests that major and minor keys are being contrasted here: "le *ton plein* c'est le ton majeur, tandis que le *ton par feints* . . . c'est le mineur, et *mode lamentable* signifie mode plaintif, élegiaque" (p. 181).

17. The destructive effect of envy on love was a theme of Catullus's, whose poetry was almost certainly known to Louise in the original.

18. The Euripus is a strait between Euboea and the Greek mainland.

BIBLIOGRAPHY

Primary Works

Antal, Paul J., trans. *Louise Labé's Dedicatory Epistle to Her Complete Works. Allegorica* 1 (1976): 151–55.
Boy, Charles, ed. *Oeuvres*. 2 vols. Paris, 1887. Reprint. Geneva, 1968.
Cook, Alta Lind, trans. *Sonnets of Louise Labé*. Toronto, 1950.
Cox, Edwin Marion, trans. *The Debate Between Folly and Cupid*. London, 1925.
Knapp, Bettina L., trans. *Louise Labé: The Sonnets*. Paris, 1964.
Giudici, Enzo, ed. *Oeuvres complètes*. Geneva, 1981.
Guillot, Gerard, ed. *Louise Labé*. Paris, 1962.

Related Works

Aristotle. "On the Art of Poetry." Trans. T. S. Dorsch. In *Classical Literary Criticism,* pp. 29–75. 1965. Reprint. New York, 1977.
Baker, M. J. "The Sonnets of Louise Labé: A Reappraisal." *Neophilologus* (January 1976): 20–30.
Butler, H. E., ed. and trans. *Propertius*. New York, 1912.
Castiglione. *The Book of the Courtier*. Trans. George Bull. 1967. Reprint. New York, 1978.

Curtius, Ernst R. *European Literature and the Latin Middle Ages.* Trans. Willard R. Trask. Bollingen Series 36. Princeton, 1953.

Forster, Leonard. *The Icy Fire: Five Studies in European Petrarchism.* Cambridge, Mass., 1969.

Girault, Yvonne. *Louise Labé: Nymphe ardente du Rhone.* Lausanne, 1966.

Hanisch, Gertrude S. *Love Elegies of the Renaissance: Marot, Louise Labé and Ronsard.* Saratoga, 1979.

Harrington, Karl Pomeroy. *Catullus and His Influence.* Boston, 1923.

———, ed. *The Roman Elegiac Poets.* Norman, Okla., 1968.

Harvey, Lawrence E. *The Aesthetics of the Renaissance Love Sonnet.* Geneva, 1962.

Hatzfeld, Helmut. "The Role of Mythology in Poetry During the French Renaissance." *Modern Language Quarterly* 13 (1952): 392–404.

Highet, Gilbert. *Poets in a Landscape.* New York: Knopf, 1957.

Kelly, Joan. "Did Women Have a Renaissance?" In *Becoming Visible: Women in European History.* Ed. Renate Bridenthal and Claudia Koonz. Boston, 1977.

Kelso, Ruth. *Doctrine for the Lady of the Renaissance.* Urbana, Ill., 1956.

Larsen, Anne R. "Louise Labé's 'Débat de Folie et d'Amour': Feminism and the Defense of Learning." *Tulsa Studies,* pp. 43–55.

Luck, Georg. *The Latin Love Elegy.* London, 1959. 2d ed. London, 1969.

McFarlane, I. D. *A Literary History of France: Renaissance France, 1470–1589.* New York, 1974.

O'Connor, Dorothy. *Louise Labé: Sa vie et son oeuvre.* Paris, 1926.

Peyre, Henri. *Literature and Sincerity.* New Haven, Conn., 1963.

Plato. *Phaedrus.* Trans. W. C. Helmbold and W. G. Rabinowitz. Indianapolis, 1956.

Preminger, Alex, Frank J. Warnke, and O. B. Hardism, Jr., eds. *The Princeton Encyclopedia of Poetry and Poetics.* Princeton, 1974.

Putnam, Michael C. J. *Tibullus: A Commentary.* Norman, Okla., 1973.

Rilke, Rainer Maria. *The Notebooks of Malte Laurids Brigge.* Trans. M. D. Herter Norton. New York, 1964.

Rose, H. J. *A Handbook of Latin Literature.* New York, 1960.

Smith, Kirby Flower, ed. *The Elegies of Albius Tibullus.* Darmstadt, 1964.

Varty, Kenneth. "Louise Labé's Theory of Transformation." *French Studies* 12 (1958): 5–13.

Whigham, Peter, trans. *The Poems of Catullus.* Berkeley and Los Angeles, 1969.

Williams, Theodore C., trans. *The Elegies of Tibullus.* Boston, 1908.

Zamaron, Fernand. *Louise Labé: Dame de franchise.* Paris, 1968.

THE WOMAN BEHIND THE LEGEND

ianne de Poitiers

SANDRA SIDER

For more than four centuries the legend of Dianne de Poitiers[1] has fascinated poets, historians, and students of the Renaissance. Most studies of her life have concentrated on isolated aspects of her complex personality—notably Dianne's ability to influence court politics during the years when her lover Henry II was king of France (1547–1559).

Dianne's letters and her two extant poems reveal the woman behind the mask of "cold beauty." This woman interests us today because she intertwines the chivalric romance of medieval France with the clarity and harmony of the Renaissance.

Dianne was born at the close of the fifteenth century,[2] in Saint Vallier on the Rhone, into a family that enjoyed several connections with royalty. Imbert de Batarnay,[3] her maternal grandfather, was held in esteem by the Bourbons for his diplomatic talents and close friendship with Anne of France,[4] daughter of Louis XI. Aymar de Poitiers, Dianne's paternal grandfather, had married the illegitimate daughter of the Dauphin Louis. Although his wife died without issue, Aymar had been showered with honors that were later inherited by Dianne's father. From as early as she could remember, Dianne fit quite naturally into the world of dukes, duchesses, and royal favor.

Located on the road between Lyon and Valence, Saint Vallier was one of the resting places for pilgrims, merchants, and aristocratic travelers on their way to and from Italy. Jehan de Poitiers, Dianne's father and count of Saint Vallier, entertained the most prestigious visitors in his chateau. His passion for hunting and his dauphiné estates filled with wild game made him the perfect host for his sporting guests. By the age of six Dianne had learned to manage her own horse and was welcomed into the hunt. Many years later her reputation as a huntress helped propagate the myth of the goddess Diana that distinguished her from other women at court and encouraged the Dauphin Henry to worship her as a goddess.[5]

When Dianne was around ten years old, her father placed her in the cultured court of Anne of France, whose reputation as a huntress was later exceeded only by that of Dianne. Dianne's formal education was accomplished in Anne's "courtesy school" in palaces such as Chantelle and Moulins, quietly resplendent with beautiful objects and fine works of art. The gracious yet severe Anne instructed Dianne and other girls in the Latin classics and the church fathers, and even more important, in the principles of diplomatic strategy and the practical virtues of stability, fortitude, and strength of will.[6]

It was Anne of France who arranged Dianne's marriage to the Senechal of Normandy, Louis de Brézé, grandson of Charles VII and Agnes Sorel. In 1515 Dianne became Louis's wife in the magnificent Paris residence of Charles of Bourbon. She was fifteen and Louis was fifty-six, but the marriage evidently pleased them both until Louis's death in 1521, which left Dianne a wealthy, desirable young widow. Like Louise of Savoy (also raised by Anne of France), Margaret of Austria, Mary of Hungary, and other competent and ambitious young women, Dianne chose not to remarry.[7]

With income from the skillful managing of her Norman estates, Dianne was able to return to court in the 1530s as one of the honor matrons of François I. She thoroughly enjoyed the life at court and concerned herself with advising the court tutors and governesses on the welfare of the royal children, and with arranging the marriages of her two daughters by Louis. In 1537 she probably gave birth to a third daughter, Diane of France, whose father was the Dauphin Henry.

Dianne's behavior epitomized the secular virtues praised by Christine de Pizan. Dianne had her faults and biases, but her letters reveal economic and political talents, common sense, kindliness, and love of harmony and tranquility.

Along with hundreds of other aristocratic girls, Dianne knew the works of Christine. Dianne's library[8] at her chateau of Anet included almost all the "feminist" literary texts of her day, such as Guillaume Postel's *Most Marvelous Victories of Women of the New World,* Martin Le Franc's *The Champions of Ladies,* and Symphorien Champier's *Ship of Virtuous Ladies* (dedicated to Anne of France).[9]

Besides excelling in the domains of finance and diplomacy, Dianne was also knowledgeable in practical medicine. Her library contained some important texts, such as: Ambroise Paré's *The Method of Treating Wounds Made by Arquebuses and Arrows,* Andreas Vesalius's *On the Human Body,* Jean Fernel's *Medicina,* Charles Estienne's *Dissection,* and Jacques Dubois's text on menstruation and female maladies translated by the royal physician Guillaume Chrestien and dedicated to Dianne. Chrestien testified to Dianne's reputation as a medical consultant in obstetrics,

gynecology, and pediatrics. The royal physicians repeatedly complimented Dianne's competence and patience in the treatment of members of
the royal household.

If we try to visualize Dianne's library, we must remember that the art of
printing was barely a century old by the time she died in 1566. Approx-
imately half of Dianne's books were written by hand. Most of these handsome volumes were written on parchment and ornamented with miniature paintings highlighted in gold. Dianne's library boasted a fair share
of classical literature—Ovid translated into French, Boethius, Cicero (including his *Letters*), Aristotle, Aesop, and Seneca (the *Letters*). She also
owned many tales of chivalric romance, as well as chivalric treatments of
ancient history such as "The Life and Deeds of Mark Antony and his
friend Cleopatra." Several versions of the Tristan story, plus manuscripts
of Lancelot's adventures and the *Romance of the Rose,* were among the
most beautifully illustrated in her collection.

Dianne was honored by the authors of books who either dedicated their
works to her or addressed her in a prefatory epistle. Probably the most
famous romance dedicated to Dianne was part of the *Amadis of Gaul*
translated into French. Books of poetry were dedicated to Dianne by
Pierre de Ronsard, Joachim Du Bellay, and Henry's court poet Olivier de
Magny.

Ronsard and Du Bellay were contemporaries a few years younger than
Dianne's daughters. Verses written to Dianne by leading poets such as
these were widely read and helped perpetuate the legend of Diana. Du
Bellay celebrated Dianne's patronage of the arts, and Ronsard styled her
as the sister of Phoebus Apollo. As other writers have pointed out, Dianne's cultivation of her own legend as the goddess Diana gave birth to a
parallel legend of her lover as Apollo. Henry became the sun whose reflected brilliance was spread throughout France by the charity and patronage of Diana, the moon goddess.

Dianne's greatest patronage concerned the architects and artists selected to renovate the chateau of Anet. In Gabriel Symeoni's dedication to
his *Life and Metamorphoses of Ovid,* he closed with a tribute to Anet,
Dianne's "royal and divine palace . . . [on which have labored] the best
and rarest spirits of the world." The chief artists commissioned by Dianne
were Benvenuto Cellini, Jean Goujon, Jean Cousin, and the architect Philibert Delorme.[10]

Jean Goujon, whose other projects include the Hotel Carnavelet in
Paris, worked on many of the ornamental details at Anet. His masterpiece
was the massive yet sensuous fountain of Diana sculpted for one of the
courtyards. This piece equals the expressiveness of Goujon's Fountain of
the Innocents in Paris; today it can be seen in the Louvre. Jean Cousin
touched Dianne's life in several ways. Besides his stained glass paintings at

Anet, he had designed part of the facade on the funeral monument in Rouen for Dianne's husband, and he later chiseled the mausoleum built for Dianne next to her chapel at Anet. He also may have been the designer for Dianne's set of tapestries depicting variations in the Diana legend.[11] Benvenuto Cellini's contribution to the chateau was a bronze bas-relief of the goddess Diana placed beneath the arch that graced the main entrance.

Dianet (as the locals called Anet) was the masterpiece of Philibert Delorme, court architect of François I, Henry II, and Catherine de' Medici as regent. As Delorme and Dianne envisioned the chateau, its renovations would epitomize classical architecture in France. Delorme's basic reference work was the groundbreaking treatise *On Architecture* by Leon Battista Alberti, of which Dianne owned a lavishly illustrated copy. Delorme closely followed the classical laws of proportion and harmony in his designs for modernizing the chateau. The lines of Anet contained in their restraint and formal harmony the attributes in Dianne's own personality that proved most useful in her diplomatic functions at the chateau.

During Henry's reign, Dianne's power in diplomatic negotiations equaled that of Louise of Savoy forty years earlier. At Anet the king and Dianne held official audiences enthroned on a black velvet dias decorated in Dianne's colors of black and white. Ambassadors were instructed to consult with Dianne, a fact resented by the emperor's representative. The Venetians, on the other hand, expressed their approval of the improvements Dianne had made in Henry's appearance and personality. Dianne's letters show her thorough understanding of political matters and her total confidence in wielding her "power behind the throne."

The many masquerades, state dinners, and other festivities at Anet and elsewhere contributed to Dianne's power, especially since Henry—as dauphin and later as king—dressed himself in her colors and styled himself as her knight.

As a boy, Henry had spent many months as a hostage locked away in a Spanish prison. There he and his brother spent much of their time retelling the tales of chivalry that Henry and Dianne later collected in finely bound volumes. Henry's letters to Dianne are those of a knight to his lady in one of the medieval Courts of Love. She played Guinevere to his Lancelot, Iseult to his Tristan, Oriana to his Amadis. Even at his official entry into Paris, Henry's costume sported his *H* interlaced with Dianne's *D*; the same insignia decorated the arch carried over his head.

When the royal progress of 1548 reached Lyon, the city closest to Dianne's childhood home, Henry and Dianne were delighted with a marvelous forest erected in the town square. In it danced a company of girls with silver crescents in their hair and costumed in Dianne's colors. At the official dinner, the city's mayor addressed Dianne, and Lyon's chief poet Maurice Scève recited verses in praise of Dianne and the king.

Part of Dianne's hold on Henry—part of the secret of her power, in general—was that she somehow led others to enter a world of experience in which they felt a bit of profundity in their own lives. No matter how banal some of Dianne's mythological festivities may appear to today's readers, members of the French court and foreign guests were often awe-struck during the celebrations directed by Dianne and her entourage. The world of classical humanism with its "purity" and "nobility" of thought permeated the everyday lives of the Renaissance aristocracy. The king was honored to be included in a masque where he played Apollo to Dianne's Artemis.

From what we can surmise from the two extant poems by Dianne, this mythological imagery did not inspire her lyrics. These were private verses meant for Henry's eyes only. Her style recalls the chansons of the late fifteenth century and the simple charm of poets such as Clement Marot.

Henry died in 1559 after a hideous accident at a Paris tournament. Dianne spent the remainder of her life away from Paris, usually at Anet. She enjoyed walking through her gardens, spent hours riding across her estates, read in her library, and labored many hours each week for local charities. She built a hospital at the edge of one of her forests, staffing it with widows from the nearby village. Dianne had been known for her skill as a midwife; now she trained others to practice the profession. Always concerned with children, Dianne established a sort of day-care center for neighborhood children. Next to it she founded a home for unwed mothers. Dianne supported them until their children were born, then provided each of them with a sizable dowry.

Dianne traveled to her native dauphiné toward the end of 1565, visiting friends and attending to business interests. Upon Dianne's return to Anet, the historian Brantôme recorded his impressions of her beauty and kindliness. This is the last public record of Dianne de Poitiers, for she died in the spring of the following year.

Dianne's lengthy will records for posterity the immense wealth that she inherited and earned through her service to the crown.[12] This document, an almost paradoxical combination of grandiosity and piety, illustrates the dominant elements in her strong personality. Dianne's bequests to her two legitimate daughters give a rare glimpse into her attitude as a mother, and possibly into the relationship between the two girls. Dianne assigned the lion's share to Françoise, her firstborn, then warned both girls to rest content with their portions. At the same time Dianne showed a sense of fairness, charging Françoise to reimburse her sister should Louise lose any property then in litigation. But Dianne's piety overrode her love for her children. She demanded that they raise their children in the Catholic faith and cautioned that if either girl or her descendents should abjure the faith, then the other would be able to seize all inherited property.

Dianne's will is a microcosm of forces at work during her lifetime. Her grandiose, sweeping sense of purpose accomplished improvements in medical care, greatly expanded the royal library, encouraged a new spirit in French architecture, and pushed Henry on to military triumphs that enlarged the realm considerably. But her best trait became her worst when she allowed piety to influence her pragmatic sense of politics.

Dianne's own words in her more than one hundred extant letters vividly bring these forces to life. They are written in the crisp, direct style often used by French letter writers in the mid-sixteenth century, almost to the extent of aridity.[13] Dianne's words go right to the point with precision and logic.[14] She displays no formal rhetorical training beyond the usual courteous closings—the type of epistolary formula that she would have learned as a girl at the court of Anne of France.[15] What her letters do demonstrate is a sense of decorum and Dianne's uncanny ability to temper frank words of advice with delicacy and tact.[16]

Dianne's extant letters were written for a variety of purposes, public as well as personal. The most public letters are those in which she wrote in the king's name for diplomatic or financial reasons, and the few letters that Henry and Dianne actually penned together, passing the pen between sentences. Many of her letters to personal friends—the royal governess, for example—relate to public concerns such as the health of the princes and princesses. Many of her letters about very private affairs, such as the management of her inherited property, became subjects of public discussion during her lifetime.

Since Henry apparently destroyed all of Dianne's letters to him and almost all of her love poetry, we have very few private letters from Dianne. This is a disappointment for the modern reader, who would be fascinated to study the tender side of such a powerful Renaissance woman. But the letters we do have are rich enough. They evoke the atmosphere of French courtly life at a time when the entire Western world looked to France, and from the point of view of the one woman who fit that life most perfectly.

NOTES

1. This is the spelling of Dianne as she signed it.

2. September 3 seems the most probable date for her birth. Erlanger lists the other dates proposed, p. 13.

3. See Bernard de Mandrot's biography of Imbert de Batarnay.

4. See Jehanne d'Orliac's biography of Anne of France.

5. Françoise Bardon's excellent book on Dianne and the myth of Diana focuses on the iconographical evidence.

6. Anne of France wrote a handbook teaching these virtues for her daughter Suzanne.

7. For detailed studies of Louise of Savoy as regent, see Paul Henry Bordeaux and Dorothy Moulton Mayer; for biographies of Margaret of Austria, see Ghislaine de Boom and Jane de Iongh, who also wrote an interesting biography of Mary of Hungary.

8. Dianne's library is extensively cataloged by Ernest Quentin Bauchart, vol. 1. The library, augmented by subsequent owners, was broken up and sold in 1723.

9. Secondary works on women in the Renaissance include those by Mary Agnes Cannon, Natalie Z. Davis, Ruth Kelso, Ian Maclean, René de Maulde La Clavière (somewhat dated), Hannelore Sachs, and Foster Watson.

10. P. D. Roussel relates the history of the chateau. Anthony Blunt includes many photographs of architectural details at Anet.

11. Bardon presents an analysis of the Anet tapestries; also see the articles by J. Goldsmith Phillips and Edith A. Standen.

12. Georges Guiffrey prints Dianne's will as an appendix to her letters, pp. 199–214.

13. Maulde La Clavière faults female French letter writers in the sixteenth century, Dianne included, for their lack of "Italianate seductive charm" (p. 308).

14. See Guiffrey's evaluation of her style, p. lxxxviii.

15. Dianne's letters show what Fumaroli would call "an interiorized rhetoric" of personal style and taste (p. 900).

16. K. T. Butler praises the epistolary talents of women in the sixteenth century, p. 23.

Poems

1

In truth it was Love one lovely morning
Who arrived with a blossom genteel:
He adorned himself in your very image;
Marjoram and jonquils quickly
Overwhelmed me until my mantilla
Overflowed, and my trembling heart as well.
For you see, this blossom so noble
Was a young man, courtly and kind.
Trembling and turning away, I said
"No!" . . . "Do not be deceived," said
Love, and suddenly before me appeared
A marvelous wreath of laurel.
"It is better," I said, "to be wise than queen."
Thus I trembled and hesitated . . .
Diane was finished, and you know full well
What morning it was that I recall.[1]

2

Farewell delights of my heart,
Farewell my master and lord,
Farewell true noble knight!

Farewell royal banquets,
Farewell epicurean feasts,
Farewell grand festivities!
Farewell sweet, dovelike kisses,
Farewell our secret joy!
Farewell, farewell, my heart's true love,
Farewell supreme delight![2]

March 28, [1545/1546],[3] Fontainebleau[4]

To Monsieur My Ally, Monsieur de Humières[5]

Monsieur my ally, after hearing of the remarks that you have made against the order that the queen has made to Monsignor[6] about persuading you to soften the hatred that you have for your son because of his marriage,[7] this letter again begs you to consider what the queen might think of your having done something on her behalf, instead of worrying yourself about this shameful affair. For when a thing is done, one must approach it with virtue and patience. In desiring to place blame on your son, you place it on yourself; as for me, you may believe that wherever I might have the means to be of service to you, I would employ myself with as good a heart as I commend myself to your good grace. May God, my ally, grant you a good, long life. From Fontainebleau, this 28th day of March.

    Your most obedient ally and friend,

DIANNE DE POYTIERS

October 20, [1548], Moulins[8]

To Monsieur My Ally, Monsieur de Humières

Monsieur my ally, I advise you that the king[9] has been marvelously pleased with the good reception that the Dauphin[10] has made for the Queen of Scotland.[11] I know well that this is because of your teaching. If you want to please the king, then continue to teach the Dauphin these little courtesies, for that will make the king very happy. You know what he wants done for the dwellings at St. Germain, concerning which you do not have to be told twice. Until I might see you, I will conclude, after commending myself to your good grace, God willing, monsieur my ally, to grant you that which you most desire. From Moulins, the 20th day of October.

Your perfectly good ally and friend,

DIANNE DE POYTIERS

October 2, [1549], Compiègne¹²

To Madame, Madame the Duchess d'Aumale¹³

Madame, I cannot tell you what pleasure it has been to hear your news. In that you are doing so well in your pregnancy, I am so pleased that it is not possible to be more so, and pray our Lord that you remain in this good condition, assuring you, madame, that I greatly desire to be near you because of the envy that I have of seeing you, which does not seem to be possible however much I might desire it. And, awaiting what I would well have, I beseech you, madame, to send me your news as often as you can. You may believe that you will find me all my life of as good a heart ready to do you service, in whatever you would want to command me, as humbly to your good grace I commend myself, praying our Savior to give you, madame, a good, long life. At Compiègne, this 11th day of October.

Yours most humbly to obey you,

DIANNE DE POYTIERS

May 20, [1551], Oiron¹⁴

To Madame My Ally, Madame de Humières

Madame my ally, I am well pleased about what has happened at Blois, and that you are in good health; as to that which I am overseeing, you would do well to do what is necessary there. The King and Queen are writing you concerning the health of monsieur d'Orléans,¹⁵ and also to see whether the wetnurse has milk as good as required. For here they say that it is not good and that it upsets him, on account of which it seems to me that you would do well to investigate the situation, and if she is not good, to hire another for him. And I believe that if her milk has worsened since I saw her, it is because she has not conducted herself as she should have. It seems to me that if you make her drink cider or beer, that should refresh her thoroughly. I think that the doctors would agree with me on this. I trust you to put all this in good order. As for madame Claude,¹⁶ the King and Queen are very grieved at her discomfort, on account of which I beseech you to inform them about her condition. Moreover, when you see there is need of anything, have it done and without asking their advice. Before you were sent here, it was necessary to foresee many things, about which the King and Queen bothered themselves as much as possible. I have wanted to tell you that you have set everything in such good order that no fault can be found. And now I pray our Savior to grant you, madame my ally, a good, long life. At Orion, this 20th day of May.

Your entirely good ally and friend,

DIANNE DE POYTIERS

October 17, [1551?], Anet[17]

To Monsieur, Monsieur the Constable[18]

Monsieur, I have received the letters that you sent me from the Queen and also your own, for which I thank you very much, being well pleased about what you write—that the King was indeed happy with the entertainment that I gave him here. You also write that you found him stouter; I think that he will not grow any thinner in your hands, given the good cheer that they say you are making for him. May our Savior have it last as long as possible. If I had any news I would tell you, but I will not mention my building program, where I am not wasting any time. I hope that when you come here you will find something new that will please you. Now I humbly commend myself to your good grace, praying the creator to give you, monsieur, a very good, long life. At Anet, this 17th day of October.

Your humble good friend,

DIANNE DE POYTIERS

April 12, [1551/1552], Joinville[19]

To Madame de Humières

Madame my ally, I have received the letters that you wrote, and through them I learned about the good health of the Princes and Princesses, about which I am very pleased. They say that there may be some danger of plague at Blois—I beseech you to be very careful, and when you know that there is any danger, immediately move away from Blois to avoid it.[20] As for the rest, madame my ally, I can assure you that the Queen is doing well at this time, thank God, and is out of danger.[21] But I can tell you that no one has ever been so ill, without dying, as she has been, so much so that we did not expect her to live. You can believe that the news that we heard this morning will complete her cure: that is, the taking of Metz, which happened two days ago.[22] Our forces are inside, which is one of the greatest blessings that could have befallen, for if it had been necessary to take the city by force, that would not have been possible without losing many valued men. It seems that we have trusted in our Savior and ought to offer unto Him thanks for the blessing that he has wrought for us. I pray that He grant the King success in his enterprises and a good end to his trip. And now I commend myself well to your good grace, praying our Savior to give you, madame my ally, a good, long life. At Joinville, this 12th day of April.

Your entirely good ally and friend,

DIANNE DE POYTIERS

August 30, [1552], Villers-Cotterets[23]

To Monsieur, Monsieur the Duke de Guise

Monsieur, I received the letters that it pleased you to send me, and through which you thank me for that which I have done for you. I assure you, monsieur, that when it comes to your affairs, I am always eager to be useful to you,[24] as the Marshal de St. André[25] will be able to testify, and about which I will not make a long discourse because for three or four days I have been a little ill with catarrh. Please excuse the fact that I have not written in my own hand. Now I am somewhat better, which is all I want to say about it. On this I humbly commend myself to your good grace, and beseech the creator, monsieur, to give you a good, long life. From Villers-Cotterets, this last day of August.

Yours humble to obey you,

DIANNE DE POYTIERS

January 13, [1552/1553], Paris[26]

To Monsieur, Monsieur the Marshal de Brissac[27]

Monsieur the Marshal, I received the letter that you sent me by messenger on the 27th past, and through which I heard about the state of affairs over there, and even how Don Ferrand[28] raised his camp at Albe to lay siege to St. Amiens, about which I am very pleased, hoping that he will accomplish there no more than he did at Albe. May he receive, thanks to your good help and conduct, as great a defeat as the emperor experienced at Metz.[29] Concerning that, this company is so consoled that it is not possible to be more so, and not without cause, for that was one of the grandest hours for the reputation and grandeur of the King, for which we well ought to thank our Savior, seeing the favor and blessing that he grants us. As for that which you write about needing more funds, I can assure you that the King does not want to leave you destitute. I hope that he will remedy this so well that you will be content, as you will better be able to learn through the dispatch that he is sending you, and in which he will discuss other matters. For the rest, monsieur the marshal, I thank you very much for the remembrance that you have of my son d'Aumale,[30] about whom I can say nothing more, having had no news about him for a long time. If I find out anything more about him, I will let you know, as you are one whom I esteem among my best friends. If meanwhile you need my services, please believe that you will always find me of as good a heart toward your command as I commend myself very affectionately to your good grace. Praying our Savior to grant you, monsieur the marshal, a good, long life. At Paris, this 13th day of January.

Your more than entirely good friend,

DIANNE DE POYTIERS

June 30, [1553?], St. Germain-en-Laye[31]

To My Cousin, Monsieur the Count du Bouchage[32]

My cousin, I heard that you have been feeling poorly on account of the death of one of your sons whom it has pleased our Savior to take, about which I am indeed sad. But since God's will has been thus, it seems to me that you ought not to torture yourself, seeing that you have another son and the means of having even more. Also, you might injure your health, which would make me unhappy. For these reasons, my cousin, I beseech you not to worry yourself any more about this, for that would do you no good. Send me all your news, and believe that if you need anything from me, you will find me of as good a heart at your command as I commend myself well to your good grace and to that of madame du Bouchage, my cousin, to whom I will write no more at this time as this letter is for you both. Praying our Savior to give you, my cousin, a good, long life. At St. Germain-en-Laye, this last day of June.

Your entirely good cousin and friend,

DIANNE DE POYTIERS

Date and place unknown[33]

To Madame de Montagu[34]

Madame my good friend, I saw yesterday, as you desired, your poor sister, with whom I had a long and prudent conversation on the subject of her proposed marriage. I made her consider the dangers and what poor opinion there would be of a man who frequented loose women. But, however much I talked with her about it, I fear that ultimately all my words were only smoke, and I think that even the worst that I had to say failed to impress her. She seemed so afflicted that I did not persist for long, and I do not think that we can hope for any change in a heart so taken. Though I advise you that I see nothing more to do but to let her follow her inclination which will persuade her only too well and push her toward the said marriage, I nevertheless will not forget to discuss this with her again, wishing to give you every proof of my good devotion to serve you, which always is augmented with the affection of your good friend wishing to obey you,

DIANNE

[?September 1555, St. Germain-en-Laye][35]

To Monsieur, Monsieur the Cardinal de Tournon[36]

Monsieur, once again not much time has passed since I wrote you, when I sent you the dispatch about the benefice that you gave my nephew de Polignac.[37] Since then I saw that the King had changed his mind, seeing the dispatches that have arrived from Rome, where I understand that things are well prepared for a successful outcome. I know that the said lord desires your return only because of the affection that you hold in His Majesty's service. I hope that you will have a good trip there, our Savior willing. I beseech you to believe that wherever I can do you service, I will do it with as good a heart as you will always find in me.

 Yours humble to obey you,

DIANNE DE POYTIERS

March 3, [1557/1558?], Fontainebleau[38]

To Monsieur La Vigne,[39] Ambassador for the King to the Grand Seigneur

Monsieur de La Vigne, I have received the letters that you sent me and am well pleased with the good work that you are doing in the service of His Majesty, in which you are held in such esteem that there is no need to remind you. Nevertheless, I beg you that in the Codignac[40] affair, proceed as discreetly as possible, for love of me, assuring you that such would please me well, and also bring honor to yourself. In as much as I would be able to please you, be assured that I will employ myself in your service with as good a heart as I pray God, monsieur de La Vigne, that you could desire. At Fontainebleau, this third day of March.

Your entirely good friend,

DIANNE DE POYTIERS

July 29, [1558], Rheims[41]

To Madame, Madame the Duchess de Nevers[42]

Madame, I have today received the hams from Mayence that it pleased you to send me, for which I humbly thank you very much, with assurance that they are very welcome, being a meat that I heartily like. I am sorry that I have nothing that would be pleasing to you, with which I might serve you as all my life I have desired. But that will be in whatever it will please you to command me, with as good a heart as very humbly I commend myself to your good grace. Praying God, madame, to give you good health and a good, long life. At Rheims, this 29th day of July.

Your humble and obedient,

DIANNE DE POYTIERS

[?March 1558/1559, Villers-Cotterets][43]

To Monsieur, Monsieur the Constable

Monsieur, I have received the letters that you sent me, for which I thank you humbly for the trouble that you have taken, as I think indeed that *your work[44] is so great that you do not have time to write me from your own hand, which is sufficient to remind me of you. Yet the secretary who finishes the rest of my letter and I commend you to our good grace,* praying God to give you that which we desire for you. . . .

Your old and best friends,

HENRI, DIANNE

August 20, [1559], Bayne[45]

To Monsieur de Limoges,[46] at Court

Monsieur de Limoges, I heard through my son monsieur d'Aumale and monsieur d'Avanson[47] the goodwill that you have for me and the desire that you have to help me in my affairs concerning the Marquisate of Cotrone,[48] for which I thank you as much as is possible. I beseech you to continue always in this good opinion, and see to the expedition of this matter, in which, to these ends, I am sending you memoranda and instructions. At the same time, my said son and the said lord d'Avanson will explain the matter to you more fully, and will talk with you at length about it. I assure you well that in all matters where I can employ myself to please you, you will find me of as good a heart at your command as indeed I commend myself to your good grace. Praying God to give you, monsieur de Limoges, that which you most desire. At Bayne, this 20th day of August.

Your more than entirely good friend,

DIANNE DE POYTIERS

June 17, 1562, Anet[49]

Monsieur, Monsieur the Constable

Monsieur, I want to keep my promise to tell you how the partition of my property for my children has been made and completed today, in as much good peace and tranquility as I could have desired. My daughter d'Aumale will have Anet. You might think that this might have caused a few bad feelings in those who will not have such property. Yet they are conducting themselves in such good accord and such good friendship that, thank God, they are continuing to be fast friends, which puts me more at ease. My daughter de Bouillon responded so courteously that monsieur d'Aumale, being quite content, made a grand occasion of it all, seeing that everyone was satisfied with the outcome. This is all that you will have from me this time. Now I commend myself most humbly to your good grace, praying God, monsieur, to give you a happy, long life. From Anet, today the 17th day of June 1562.

Your humble and obedient,

DIANNE DE POYTIERS

NOTES TO THE TRANSLATION

1. Text printed in Quentin Bauchart, vol. 1, pp. 63–64, where he notes that the verses in manuscript are in the Bibliothèque Nationale.

2. Text printed in Guiffrey, note on p. 228; also in Seely, p. 203, who gives another translation on p. 204.

3. In many parts of Europe until the eighteenth century, the New Year began with Easter

or Christmas. This custom confuses modern readers, for an event in January, February, March, and sometimes April usually would have been dated in the year preceding an event in the remaining months. In this essay all letters written between January 1 and Easter of a given year are dated with two years: the year as it would have been recorded in France at the time, followed by the "real" year according to our modern usage. Dates and locations in brackets indicate that the information is based on textual and historical evidence.

4. Guiffrey, pp. 6–7, from Bibliothèque Impériale, manuscript 3128, folio 1.

5. Much of the information in these notes to the translation has been supplied by Guiffrey. He identifies most of the principles, such as the present Jean III de Humières, governor (along with his wife) of the royal children until his death in 1550.

6. The Dauphin Henry.

7. His eldest son Jean, who secretly married a maid of honor of Queen Eleanor. The Dauphin Henry also advised de Humières to accept the situation; he subsequently reconciled with his son. (In 1556 Henry, as king, issued an edict against clandestine marriage.)

8. Guiffrey, pp. 45–46, from Bibliothèque Impériale, manuscript 3128, folio 14.

9. Henry II.

10. The Dauphin François (later François II).

11. Mary Stuart, betrothed as a child to the Dauphin François.

12. Guiffrey, pp. 51–52, from Bibliothèque Impériale, Collection Clérambault, vol. 58, f. 579.

13. Guiffrey, p. 51, note 1, explains why the addressee most likely was Anne d'Este. If he is correct, then the child she was carrying would have been François-Henri of Lorraine, who was killed at the chateau of Blois in 1588.

14. Guiffrey, pp. 84–86, from Bibliothèque Impériale, manuscript 3208, folio 127.

15. Prince Charles-Maximilian, who became the duke d'Orléans after his elder brother died. At this writing the infant was eleven months old.

16. Princess Claude.

17. Guiffrey, pp. 93–94, from Bibliothèque Impériale, manuscript 3038, folio 50.

18. Anne de Montmorency, grand master (1525–1538) and constable (1538–1558). At this writing he was with the king at Chantilly, where they had been hunting.

19. Guiffrey, pp. 97–98, from Bibliothèque Impériale, manuscript 3124, folio 53.

20. The children were moved to Amboise shortly afterward.

21. Catherine's illness was the "purple," similar to scarlet fever.

22. The constable and his forces took Metz peaceably on April 10.

23. Guiffrey, pp. 106–7, from Bibliothèque Impériale, Gaignières manuscript 403, folio 122.

24. The duke de Guise, in charge of the defense of Metz, needed more money for purchasing provisions. Shortly after this letter was written, Henry ordered that the duke be sent all the funds he requested.

25. Jacques d'Albon, marquis of Fronsac, was an old friend of the king.

26. Guiffrey 118–21, from Bibliothèque Impériale, Gaignières manuscript 325, folio 179.

27. Charles de Cossé, count de Brissac, was named marshal of France and governor of Piedmont in 1550. At this writing he was in charge of the defense of Metz.

28. Ferdinand of Gonzaga, vice-roy of Sicily and governor of Milan, was an avowed enemy of the French.

29. She speaks of the terrible retreat of New Year's Day, ordered by the emperor after forty-five days of futile siege in cold and icy weather. Of his sixty thousand men, the emperor lost more than forty-five thousand.

30. Dianne's son-in-law, held prisoner by the marquis of Brandenburg from 1552 until 1554. He was married to her daughter Louise.

31. Guiffrey, pp. 121–22, from Bibliothèque Impériale, manuscript 3036, folio 2.

32. Réné de Batarnay, whose father was the brother of Dianne's mother, Jeanne de Batarnay.

33. Guiffrey, p. 128, from an autograph in the Lajarriette sale catalog of November 15, 1860.

34. Probably Guillemette de Sarrebruche, whose son Robert de la Marc was married to Dianne's daughter Françoise.

35. Guiffrey, pp. 136–37, from a private collection.

36. François de Tournon, bishop of Bourges and governor of Lyon, was Henry II's representative at the Holy See. This letter refers to the cardinal's successful trip to arrange the treaty of December 1555. Under the treaty's terms, the pope and his papal states were protected from the Spanish by the king of France, and Henry's two sons received the realm of Naples and the duchy of Milan.

37. François Armand, viscount de Polignac, who had recently married Dianne's niece.

38. Guiffrey, pp. 150–51, from Bibliothèque Impériale, manuscript 4129, folio 46.

39. Jean de La Vigne, who also served as ambassador to Poland, was at this writing ambassador to Soliman II.

40. Codignac, formerly the French ambassador to Turkey, had fallen into disrepute for neglecting French affairs while attending to private business in the Orient. As Guiffrey points out Dianne perhaps had some private interest in protecting Codignac (p. 151).

41. Guiffrey, pp. 151–52, from Bibliothèque Impériale, manuscript 4711, folio 31.

42. Marguerite de Bourbon, wife of François de Clèves.

43. Guiffrey, pp. 161–62, from Bibliothèque Impériale, manuscript 3139, folio 26.

44. Anne de Montmorency was in the final stages of negotiation for the Treaty of Câteau-Cambresis. The italicized section of this letter is in Henry's handwriting, the remainder in Dianne's.

45. Guiffrey, pp. 175–76, from a private collection.

46. Sébastien de l'Aubespine, brother of Henry's secretary of state Claude de l'Aubespine. He was made bishop of Limoges in 1559. Dianne wrote this letter a few weeks after Henry's death, when she was no longer "at court."

47. Jean de St.-Marcel, whose career in the royal service had been advanced by Dianne's influence. His offices included those of counselor of state and superintendent of the king's finances.

48. Located in Calabria (Italy). Dianne claimed this kingdom through marriage of the Ruffi of Cotrone into the Poitiers family in the early fifteenth century.

49. Guiffrey, pp. 183–85, from Bibliothèque Impériale, manuscript 3122, folio 60.

BIBLIOGRAPHY

Primary Works

Guiffrey, Georges. *Lettres inédites de Dianne de Poytiers*. Paris, 1866.
Quentin Bauchart, Ernest. *Les femmes bibliophiles de France*. Vol. 1. Paris, 1886. See especially the poem on pages 63–64.

Related Works

Anne de France. *Les enseignements . . . à sa fille Suzanne de Bourbon*. Ed. A. M. Chazaud. Moulins, 1878.

Antonibon, Francesca. *Le Relazioni a stampa di ambasciatori Veneti.* Padua, 1939.

Bardon, Françoise. *Diane de Poitiers et le mythe de Diane.* Paris, 1963.

Blunt, Anthony. *Philibert de l'Orme.* London, 1958.

Boom, Ghislaine de. *Marguerite d'Autriche-Savoie et la Renaissance.* Paris and Brussels, 1935.

———. "Un projet d'alliance entre Charles-Quint et François Ier, negocié par Louise de Savoie et Marguerite d'Autriche." *Revue d'histoire moderne* 9 (1936): 197–211.

Bordeaux, Paule Henry. *Louise de Savoie, "roi" de France.* Paris, 1971.

Bushnell, George. "Diane de Poitiers and Her Books." *The Library,* 4th ser., 7 (1927): 283–302.

Butler, K. T., ed. *"The Gentlest Art" in Renaissance Italy: An Anthology of Italian Letters, 1459–1600.* Cambridge, Mass., 1954.

Cannon, Mary Agnes. *The Education of Women During the Renaissance.* Washington, 1916.

Capefigue, J. B. *Diane de Poitiers.* Paris, 1860.

Catherine de' Medici. *Lettres.* Vol. 1, *1553–1563,* ed. Hector de la Ferrière. Paris, 1880.

Chastel, André. "Diane de Poitiers: L'éros de la beauté froide." In *Fables, Formes, Figures,* vol. 1, pp. 263–72. Paris, 1978.

Chevalier, l'Abbé Casimire. *Diane de Poitiers au Conseil du roi. Archives du château de Chenonceau.* Paris, 1866.

Courde de Montaiglon, Anatole de. *Diane de Poitiers et son goût dans les arts.* Paris, 1879.

Davis, Natalie Z. *Society and Culture in Early Modern France.* Stanford, 1975.

Dimier, Louis. "An idealized portrait of Diane de Poitiers." *Burlington Magazine* (1913): 89–93.

d'Orliac, Jehanne. *Anne de Beaujeu, roi de France.* Paris, 1925.

———. *The Moon Mistress.* Philadelphia, 1930.

Erlanger, Philippe. *Diane de Poitiers.* Paris, 1955.

Fahy, C. "Early Renaissance Treatises on Women." *Italian Studies* 11 (1956): 30–35.

Forneron, H. *Les ducs de Guise et leur époque.* Paris, 1877.

Fumaroli, Marc. "Genèse de l'épistographie classique: Rhétorique humaniste de la lettre, de Pétrarque à Juste Lipsius." *Revue d'Histoire littéraire de la France* 78 (1978): 886–900.

Graham, Victor E., and W. McAllister Johnson. *Estienne Jodelle: Le Recueil des inscriptions 1558.* Toronto, 1972.

Hay, Marie. *Madame . . . Diane de Poitiers.* London, 1900.

Henderson, Helen Watson. *The Enchantress: Dianne de Poytiers.* London, 1928.

Hevezy, André de. "l'Histoire véridique de la Joconde." *Gazette des Beaux-Arts* (1952): 6–26.

Iongh, Jane de. *Margaret of Austria: Regent of the Netherlands.* Trans. M. D. Herter Norton. New York, 1953.

———. *Mary of Hungary, Second Regent of the Netherlands.* Trans. M. D. Herter Norton. New York, 1958.

Kelso, Ruth. *Doctrine for the Lady in the Renaissance.* Urbana, Ill., 1956.

Le Roux de Lincy. "Catalogue de la bibliothèque des ducs de Bourbon." In *Mélanges de littérature et d'histoire recueillis et publiées par la Société des bibliophiles françois,* pp. 43–144. Paris, 1850.

McHenry, Bannon. "Gift from a King . . . the Superb Chateau d'Anet." *Connoisseur* (October 1984): 81–88.

Maclean, Ian. *The Renaissance Notion of Woman.* Cambridge, Mass., 1980.

Mahoney, Irene. *Madame Catherine.* New York, 1975.

Mandrot, Bernard de. *Ymbert de Batarnay . . . .* Paris, 1886.

Maulde La Clavière, René de. *Les femmes de la Renaissance.* Trans. George Herbert Ely. London, 1905.

Mayer, Dorothy Moulton. *The Great Regent, Louise of Savoy, 1476–1531*. London, 1966.

Phillips, J. Goldsmith. "Diane de Poitiers and Jean Cousin." *Metropolitan Museum of Art Bulletin*, n.s., 2 (1943): 109–17.

Porcher, Jean. "Les livres de Diane de Poitiers." In *Les Trésors des Bibliothèques de France*, vol. 26, pp. 78–89. Paris, 1942.

Reinach, Salomon. "Diane de Poitiers et Gabrielle d'Estrées." *Gazette des Beaux-Arts* (1920): 181–89.

Roussel, P. D. *Histoire et description du château d'Anet*. Paris, 1875.

Sachs, Hannelore. *The Renaissance Woman*. New York, 1971.

Saint-Armand, Imbert de. *Les femmes de la cour des Valois*. London, 1905.

Salmon, J. H. M. "Diana of Poitiers and the Reign of Henry II." *History Today* (February 1962): 77–85.

Seely, Grace Hart. *Diane the Huntress: The Life and Times of Diane de Poitiers*. New York and London, 1936.

Standen, Edith A. "The Tapestries of Diane de Poitiers." In *Actes du Colloque international sur l'art de Fontainebleau*, pp. 87–98. Paris, 1975.

Stone, Donald. *France in the Sixteenth Century*. Englewood Cliffs, N.J., 1969.

Taylor, Francis Henry. "La belle Diane." *Worchester Art Museum Annual* 3 (1940).

Thierry, Adrien. *Diane de Poitiers*. Paris and Geneva, 1955.

Vilbert, l'Abbé. "Les premières années de Diane de Poitiers." In *Société archéologique d'Eure-et-Loire, Mém. Chartres* 7 (1882).

Watson, Foster. *Vives and the Renascence Education of Women*. New York, 1912.

Yates, Frances A. *The French Academies of the Sixteenth Century*. London, 1947.

Zeller, G. *Les institutions de la France au XVIe siècle*. Paris, 1940.

CHAMPION OF WOMEN'S RIGHTS

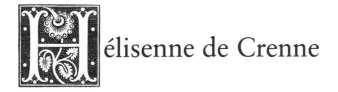

Hélisenne de Crenne

KITTYE DELLE ROBBINS-HERRING

Hélisenne de Crenne, the name that Marguerite Briet chose to use for herself as the author-heroine of *Les Angoysses douloureuses qui procedent d'amours,* is more than a mask to protect an aristocratic lady from scandal. Revealing as much as concealing, it is a double metaphor for her relation to her book, wherein the romanesque *prénom* of Hélisenne, appropriate to epic and romance, is associated with the actual estate of Crenne or Crasnes, her husband's lands near Coucy. Her story itself likewise joins *histoire vécue* with literary reminiscence to recount the phases of an obsessive passion that even today has the power to shock the reader. Hélisenne's fictive autobiography seems to be based in large part on Marguerite's own experiences, shaped and colored in the telling (and quite probably in the original living) by prior literary tradition—art imitates life that imitates art.

Hélisenne/Marguerite must have fascinated sixteenth-century readers—as she continues to fascinate us—with this play of mirrors. She invites her public to guess her identity by planting a myriad of clues in the text of her pseudo-autobiography. She herself explores in her writing many of the contradictions involved in self-expression, both literary and amatory. Like that other, more famous Marguerite, the queen of Navarre (whom she knew at least by reputation), she is paradoxically typical and unique.

Her work is typical in that it incarnates much of characteristic Renaissance thought: the cult of antiquity with its enthusiasm for ornate discourse full of rare words and esoteric mythological references, the taste for melodrama often oddly mingled with philosophical debate, the contrast between colorful realistic details and austere moral maxims in the same narrative. Helen Waldstein and Suzanne Loriente, in their respective dissertations, find in Hélisenne the true spirit of a Renaissance feminist, champion of her sex in the *Querelle des Femmes,* eager to prove herself in the Republic of Letters.[1]

And yet, as Paule Demats points out, Hélisenne's story is unique and exemplary in the intensity of its feeling and in the living paradigm it provides of courtly love as erotic obsession in sixteenth-century France.[2] Marguerite Briet, transforming her intimate journal into a novel of passion, creates herself as love's artist. She simultaneously illustrates the perils of immoderate desire—like one of Marguerite of Navarre's hapless heroines—and transcends those perils through her art. If, as she warns her lady readers, the price she has paid is great, she still has the satisfaction of getting her money's worth in emotion.

Research by Louise Loviot, Abel Lefranc, and more recently, V.-L. Saulnier has established the outline of Marguerite Briet's life from contemporary documents that supplement her own writings.[3] The key passage identifying Marguerite with her pen name occurs in a Latin chronicle *De Abbavilla.* In translation, it reads as follows: "In May 1540 a very learned lady, born in Abbeville, named Marguerite Briet but known to the public as Hélisenne de Crenne, gained fame in French poetry in the noble city of Paris." Hélisenne's works (a novel, a collection of letters, an allegorical treatise, and a translation of the first four books of the Aeneid) were all published in Paris in the years from 1538 to 1541, with editions of her collected *Oeuvres* appearing five times from 1543 through 1560. We may reasonably assume that she frequently visited the capital during these periods, especially as she possessed properties near the city and showed in her writing a lively appreciation for Paris as an intellectual center.

Marguerite and her husband, Philippe Fournel, seigneur de Crasnes, had a son, Pierre Fournel, who was a student at the University of Paris in 1548, when his father arranged for him to receive an allowance of fifty pounds *tournois.* Paule Demats concludes from this information that Marguerite was at least thirty-four years old in 1548 (assuming that she was no less than sixteen at her son's birth), but that she was probably a good bit older, as her sizable literary production implies "un assez long travail" during the 1530s and 1540s.[4] Hélisenne, however, states that she herself was married to her husband at a very early age (shortly after her eleventh birthday); if Marguerite's experience parallels her heroine's here, she may have been younger than Demats thinks in 1548. At any rate, Marguerite Briet was probably born between 1500 and 1515, and the events of her extramarital love affair must have occurred in the half-dozen years preceding the 1538 publication of *Les Angoysses,* so that she would have been in her twenties or early thirties when she first met the handsome young man who was to inspire her passion. Still young enough to burn with *appetit sensuel,* yet a mature woman by Renaissance standards, with at least one child, and after years of reasonably contented married life (her husband, Hélisenne writes, had known how to win the affection of his child bride), Marguerite was suddenly struck by a blinding erotic obsession.

Hélisenne's story aligns her with a series of romantic heroines from Guinevere and Boccaccio's Fiammetta to Anna Karenina and beyond; like her real-life contemporary Louise Labé, she risks marriage, wealth, and social status, the loss of family and friends, for a fickle lover. The *jouvenceau* or adolescent whom she calls Guenelic is scarcely worth her sacrifices—his only merit, Demats notes acidly, is his physical beauty.[5] In part 1 of the three-part novel, the most autobiographical section (parts 2 and 3 are more complimentary but less historical), Hélisenne paints a frequently unflattering portrait of her beloved; he is self-centered, tactless, even cruel, and his thoughtless boasting of his conquest endangers his mistress's reputation and her very life.

At the end of part 1 the author-heroine has been imprisoned by her jealously angry husband; in her isolation she turns to writing her life story in order to console herself, while hoping for eventual rescue by her lover. There is no evidence that the historical Guenelic ever saw his lady again, but it is likely that Marguerite Briet was indeed incarcerated by her husband for a time and that she began to write in prison (as did such celebrated writers as Malory and Charles d'Orléans). By 1552, if not earlier, she was living apart from Philippe Fournel and legally *de luy sepparee quant aux biens*—that is, separated from him and in control of her own property—as the text of a grant she made in that year specifies. She does not seem to have actually ended her marriage, perhaps because of social and economic pressures against such disunion. Marguerite, who belonged to a rich and important family in Picardy, was probably wealthier than her husband: in *Les Angoysses,* Hélisenne's husband threatens to leave her, adding scornfully that he does not want any of her property because he does not wish to profit from the possessions of "a lascivious woman." In *Le Songe* (her allegorical dream dialogue), however, La Dame Amoureuse plans to purchase her husband's consent to a separation by dividing equally with him the lands which are by inheritance hers alone.

Saulnier believes that Marguerite and her husband must often have been on bad terms and informally parted, even before the legal separation.[6] The bitter rancor against her husband and his sister that is evident in her works, particularly in *Les Angoysses,* suggests that publication must have occurred while she was away from him. For there are so many clues in the text to the identity of the pseudonymous heroine (including anagrams such as Icuoc for Coucy, Eliveba for Abbeville, Hennerc for Crenne) that family and friends could hardly have doubted how to read this *roman à clef*. Indeed, *Les Angoysses* places the first definitive break between the spouses at the point where a servant betrays Hélisenne by revealing her secret diary to her long suspicious husband. Nonetheless, there may have been efforts at reconciliation: in 1550 both Fournel and "damoiselle Marguerite de Briet sa femme" are the losers in a court case they had with a Parisian baker over money they owed him. Two years later, as the grant mentioned above makes clear, she was living on her own and able to reward one Christophe Le Manyer rather handsomely for unspecified "good and agreeable services."

Hélisenne/Marguerite's literary success during these years, as shown by the rapid succession of editions, was a source of considerable satisfaction for her (see the Fourth Invective Letter below). Certain of the reasons for her popularity may be easily discerned: to begin with, *Les Angoysses* was the first novel of passion in French in the fashionable manner of Boccaccio and Juan de Flores. A public that enjoyed these authors' works in translation was already prepared to savor a French example of the genre.

By its tone and content, furthermore, Hélisenne's story renewed an older tradition long favored in France, the tragic love tale familiar from prose romances (much in vogue in the sixteenth century), contes, and poetry. The love complaint, on which Boccaccio also drew in writing the story of Fiammetta (in French, *Flammette*), appeared often in poetry that Marguerite Briet would probably have known, from Petrarch to Clément Marot and Maurice Scève. It furnishes the central, unifying theme in Jean Bouchet's book of poetry *L'Amoureux transi sans espoir* (1500) (*The Bashful, Hopeless Lover*) and Anthoine Prevost's romance in verse *L'Amant desconforté* (1530) (*The Discomfited Lover*). When the *Elegia di madonna Fiammetta* came out in French in 1532, its anonymous translator gave it the title *Complainte des tristes amours de Flammette à son amy Pamphile* (*The Complaint of the Sad Loves of Flammette to Her Friend Pamphile*).

Such predecessors provided models for Hélisenne when she decided to write her painful account, even though her own experiences required her to make many changes in plot and characterization and symbolic significance of the love story. Her real-life passion did not altogether fit the mold provided by fictional heroines, nor was her sorrow the same as that expressed by male lover-poets in their works. There are significant parallels, however, not entirely fortuitous, with a woman whose work Marguerite may not have known directly, but whose influence colored sixteenth-century debate over women's roles: Christine de Pizan.[7] I am not thinking here of Christine's poems about her own life with her beloved husband, but rather of her portrayal of extramarital love as a trap which women should avoid if they value freedom and honor, and especially of the way she views the situation of the lady vis-à-vis the courtly lover: if the lady does not yield to her importunate lover she will lose him, yet if she does yield to him she loses her self-esteem and still loses his love in the end. Hélisenne/Marguerite seems to have been well aware of this no-win aspect of woman's position in the love triangle of lover, lady, and society. It is not so much her conventional morality or respect for social rules—despite Richard Berrong's thoughtful analysis of this side of her personality[8]—that makes Marguerite equate lovelessness with liberty and love with lack of reason, but rather her acute feeling that there is no sure way out of her dilemma except death or renunciation.

Through her writing Marguerite experiments with both of these alternatives (the latter especially in the conclusion to *Le Songe*), as well as searching for other solutions. In the process she enters the on-going debate on love and the proper relations between the sexes so essential to French thought at the time. After the ambiguous condemnation of her lover in part 1 of *Les Angoysses*, parts 2 and 3 may be seen as her effort to elevate Guenelic and initiate him into the mysteries of Platonic love, in preparation for his mystical union with the dying Hélisenne. She finds a piquant if somewhat awkward way to recount her death as Hélisenne: writing as Guenelic, she narrates his eventual return to her side and her death in his arms, followed by his own grieving death, as recounted by their mutual friend Quezinstra.

The wish fulfillment quality of this episode, its operatic tone, shows in the archetypal details—a hermit's funereal predictions, a forest setting, Hélisenne's lengthy dying speech to her repentant *ami*, his subsequent fit of melancholy, Quezinstra's "melliflues paroles" about fate, free will, and the lovers' sad ends. We as readers are listening to a Medieval romance or a libretto for Monteverdi, and the transparently fictive nature of this death keeps us from being surprised that Marguerite continued to publish as Hélisenne for years after the appearance of her death scene in print. Demats suggests that only through her imagined death could Marguerite reconcile literature and life, her idealized view of what love should be with her actual experience of what it had been.[9] There is serious question as to how satisfactory this bizarre solution proved to be, for her and her readers alike, but its very melodramatic exaggeration and the ornate language she uses to tell about it are important factors in the early success of the book.

To sum up, the popularity of *Les Angoysses* was based on fashion (in genre, style, and sentiment), tradition (in theme and denouement), and, the third indispensable factor, reflection—the combination of introspection and observation that led Hélisenne to personalize her story, to examine with a critical eye both society's expectations and lovers' aspirations. Her critique is not as thoroughgoing as twentieth-century feminists might like, and she often gets tangled up in inconsistencies and contradictions, yet the attempt she makes is still intriguing, and we must admire the courage (along with a desire for revenge and a taste for notoriety!) that led her to bring her case as wronged wife and unhappy mistress before the jury of her peers, the lady readers to whom she dedicates her work.

A.-M. Schmidt attributes both the *succès de sentiment* and the *succès de scandale* of her book to her boldness in daring to derive a novel from her personal marital misfortunes.[10] We are touched as well as scandalized by her candor. Demats adds that the most important element in Hélisenne's achievement is her ability to use literature for her own purposes—to serve her resentments and her intimate hopes and, most of all, to savor the bitter pleasure of reliving and completing the drama of her love affair.[11] The unique "irritating charm" that many readers find in *Les Angoysses* springs from a weakness that becomes a strength, a confession that becomes an accusation. And from a voyeurism that we are invited to share: Hélisenne's husband's vigilant jealousy—in her letters she calls him Argus, after the hundred-eyed giant of Greek mythology—is a motivating force to equal her own obsession. The lover himself, without quite being reduced to a Bel Indifférent, is less significant than the desire he arouses. We might almost call him a sex object in the modern sense of the term, were it not for Hélisenne's repeated attempts to invest their experience with transcendent meaning.

The conventional goal Marguerite sets for her work—to exhort others not to follow *folle Amour,* that is, Mad Love—should not be considered pure hypocrisy. It is true that the tellers of tales of doubtful morality traditionally claim to be moralists, yet in creating Hélisenne she is indeed presenting us with a cautionary fable, whatever else she is doing at the same time. For the effect on the reader of this woman's story of suffering differs in kind from that of more glamorous figures like Guinevere, Francesca da Rimini, or Juliet: we are moved to question the validity of romantic love as an intellectual concept and as a life-enhancing experience, even if we secretly envy the intensity of Hélisenne's desires. The unglamorous aspect of her obsession is not concealed by silence, nor is it as a rule transfigured by lyric beauty. Whereas many readers of Petrarch's or Louise Labé's poems would gladly embrace their pains if the poetry came with it, Hélisenne's literary skill is sufficient to serve her story but not to overwhelm it.

We cannot justly conclude, however, that Marguerite's writing questions courtly love simply because she lacks the literary power to create her own Vita Nuova. It might be fairer as well as more useful to see her concern with truth and illusion, appearance and reality, as deriving from an awareness of the décalage, the split, which frequently occurs between what she has read and what she has seen—a break that she sometimes explores and sometimes obscures. Her text oscillates between the petty and the poetic—and one irony is that she often writes best, with the most convincing vision and eloquence, when she is least involved with being eloquent.

Another, less expected irony is present as well: many a telling detail, many a gesture or image that strikes a twentieth-century reader as especially colorful or realistic can be traced to one of the stories she took as models. What she has read influences what she sees as well as what she says. Often it is impossible to tell whether a particular incident is based on her life or her model or both, so much do the literary and the literal intertwine. Does her first glimpse of Guenelic follow the pattern of Fiammetta's initial encounter with Pamfilo because Marguerite is adapting her account to her memory of Boccaccio's story, or did that memory perhaps lead her to experience the actual encounter in those terms? Such a question, though unanswerable, is worth posing: it reminds us to keep an eye out for both convergence and divergence when we compare Hélisenne's narrative with preceding ones. Her originality arises from a combination of imitation and innovation.

The convoluted high style that Marguerite prefers for certain episodes has its own irritating charm; even in her day critics disagreed about its worth. Hélisenne did not invent the rhetorical extravagance she calls the *delectable stile poeticque*—her schoolmasters are Jean Lemaire de Belges, Jacobo Caviceo, and Diego de San Pedro, among others—but she has been both praised and blamed for using it. In 1555 François de Billon published a book in defense of women called *Le Fort inexpugnable de l'honneur du sexe féminin;* one feature of his "fortress" is a listing of notable female authors. While not at the top of the list, Hélisenne figures there in an honorable position: "After that noble city of Lyon, Picardie receives no little honor from its daughter Hélisenne. Her compositions are so often in the hands of those French who delight in [*se delectans de*] prose that there is no need to say more about it."[12] Not everyone found her equally delightful.

Claude Colet, in his prefatory letter to the 1550 edition of Hélisenne's collected works, recalls a conversation with the two "gracieuses Damoyselles" who asked him to take on the project.[13] The ladies were discussing with him the merits of various authors, and they included several *vertueuses Dames* among the French writers, putting in first place, naturally enough, "la tresillustre et incomparable Marguerite de France." Hélisenne de Crenne was then mentioned. Her *Angoysses* and other works were too hard for the demoiselles to understand because there were so many obscure Latinate words in them; they asked the scholar to revise the texts for them and translate the rare words into more familiar terms. It is interesting to note that Colet expresses no qualms about the content of the books. Hélisenne's subject matter, especially in *Le Songe,* is "bien

belle et d'edification à toutes gens qui ayment la Vertu" ("very beautiful
and edifying to all who love Virtue"), but he is hesitant to redo the texts of
a living author whose style may be deliberately chosen, he says, to be
understood only by the learned. Nonetheless he is soon convinced that he
should undertake the task, since the young ladies promise to arrange matters with Hélisenne for him. The 1551 edition of Hélisenne's *Oeuvres*
carries the notation that it was revised by the author herself; this claim is
probably incorrect, but Marguerite may well have given her permission to
Colet to do the revisions for her.

Colet's insistence that Hélisenne's intentions in writing are "good, holy
and praiseworthy if well understood" strikes a modern reader as rather
disingenuous—but he had never heard of Freud, after all, and even the
Calvinists of the day believed in the value of the cautionary tale. One of
Hélisenne's own constant concerns is to present her story as edifying and
herself as more victim than villainess. *Amour excessif* and reason or re-
spectability battle for her psyche as, in religious terms, sin and salvation
war for her soul. The latter conflict matters much less to her than the
former: she fears social damnation more than spiritual. The same concern
is shown in her *Familiar and Invective Letters,* when she allows her husband to accuse her of feigning virtue in order to avoid being "expelled
from the society of ladies." And the advice she gives in her "familiar
letters" is almost always designed to show herself as a paragon of piety,
filial devotion, and marital fidelity.[14] Much of her curious appeal comes
from this juxtaposition of cant and sincerity, her open revelation of her
occasional duplicity—like a female Rousseau *avant la lettre,* she seems to
expect us to forgive her because she has so frankly admitted her failings.

Her confession nonetheless failed to impress favorably some of her contemporaries, in style or content.[15] The humanist Étienne Pasquier mistakenly believed that Rabelais had her in mind when the great satirist
ridiculed the Latin jargon of the *écolier Limousin,* and Pasquier's error
has inspired numerous pages of futile scholarly commentary over the
years. Bernier's uncomplimentary assessment, however, has a certain
truth to its sting: in his opinion "Elizaine de Crene, a Picarde, wrote
various very extravagant works." Pasquier, Bernier, and Colet all seem to
think that Hélisenne's text is verbose and pretentiously pedantic, that her
"redundance latinicome" is too much for readers to endure. Before passing judgment on her style, however, let us examine it in more detail.

Both Demats and Secor have analyzed the differences between the original and the revised versions of *Les Angoysses.*[16] Their conclusions are
similar: the newer edition simplifies the language of the text, not only
replacing a number of Old French words (such as *curre, engin*) with more
modern terms, but also and especially—as the young ladies had wished—
substituting synonyms in common use for much of Hélisenne's erudite

Latinate vocabulary. A few of these latter terms are neologisms, either invented by Hélisenne or borrowed from fellow authors of the time. Secor gives several examples of words unattested before Hélisenne: *jubarité* (joy), *letification* (enjoyment), and *tediation* (irritation, boredom, or fatigue).

Most of her learned language, however, is drawn from the traditional vocabulary of Medieval schools and courts, words she had learned from the works of the fifteenth-century poets known as the Grands Rhétoriqueurs as well as from treatises by early humanists and authors of manuals on writing.[17] These words were current in scholarly circles when Hélisenne began to write; they may never have been widely known among the laity, particularly among those French who knew how to read in the vernacular but had little or no training in Latin. When Hélisenne employs a rare Latinate word, she often pairs it with a homelier term, easily understood by every reader—such as "joye et hilarité" (joy and jubilation), "exoculé ny aveuglé" (neither exoculated nor blinded), "scelerité et maulvaistié" (evil and wickedness). This doubling of synonyms from different registers is a stylistic trait frequently found in the French "high style" from the twelfth or thirteenth century on, but Hélisenne is perhaps excessively fond of the technique. She sometimes extends the list of synonyms to three, four, even five terms of varying degrees of familiarity.

Given the choice between a common and a learned term, Hélisenne prefers the learned: for "high-thundering" she uses "altitonant" rather than the ordinary "hault tonant"; for Creator she likes to use "Plasmateur." Her tendency to go to extremes leads her at times to replace a fairly simple phrase in one of her sources with a string of abstruse words that shows off her own learning and seems designed to impress (and more, to intimidate?) her principal readers—the ladies and gentlemen of the gentry.[18] Thus, in a description of the deeds of Hercules drawn from *Le Grand Olympe* she transforms "*surmonté* (tamed, has overcome) Cerberus, chien *à trois testes* (dog with three heads)" into "*suppedité* Cerberus, le chien *tricipite*," where the basic meaning is unchanged but the tone is rendered perceptibly more abstract and difficult.

Some of Hélisenne's excesses may be attributed to the Renaissance spirit—like Rabelais or Marot she is intoxicated by the joys of sheer verbalization—and her desire to demonstrate her knowledge has many parallels among the poets and humanist scholars of the period. Like Maurice Scève, too, Hélisenne treasures the recondite term in itself, as if words were jewels. Hence her pleasure in using *ociosité* ("idleness," related to "otiose"), *caligineux* ("caliginous, dark"), *scaturie* ("source"), *aurigateur* ("charioteer"), and other arcane words.

When Hélisenne began to compose *Les Angoysses*, literary discourse in France used Middle French, a specialized language or, in J. P. Houston's terms, a "stylistic complex . . . made of erudite vocabulary, complicated sentence structure, and varied forms, now medieval, now modern."[19] Hélisenne and her contemporaries wrote—with their individual variations—in Middle French's typical prose style, as had such respected predecessors as Christine de Pizan and Alain Chartier. This ceremonial, intricate, Latinizing eloquence, with paragraphs made up of long sentences arranged into short chapters like traditional philosophical treatises, with an emphasis on analysis and legal or scholastic terminology, yet full of striking images, conforms to the humanist ideal of the late Medieval and early Renaissance authors. It is a type of poetic prose René Sturel finds characteristic of the sixteenth century.[20]

Many of Hélisenne's readers must have enjoyed this fancy writing as much as she did, judging by the laudatory comments of François de Billon and the Abbeville chronicler cited above, as well as by the frequent republication of her words. Even Colet, in his revisions, spares many words and phrases that belong, he says, to the poetic style. So why was Hélisenne singled out for criticism by Pasquier and other similarly minded men?

Many modern scholars assert that she carries the verbal extravagance too far, indulges too much in "the bombast of amorous anguish," is too diffuse, confused, contradictory, repetitious, and uneven.[21] Thus they concur with the harsher critics of her day. Yet, if we carefully compare her prose with the writing of her peers, we find that she writes as well or better than many others. The occasional awkwardness and obscurity of her writing, the magpie fondness for rare words and rhetorical razzle-dazzle, the danger of getting lost in a maze of tangled or at least deeply embedded clauses—all of these seeming faults (familiar also in her contemporaries) are in Hélisenne's case redeemed and often transformed by the intensity of her expressed feeling and the close attention to changing mental and emotional states. Perhaps she gets into trouble because she is a woman writing with a unique combination of passion, erudition, and deliberate confrontation; because she is a well-schooled and frankly partisan champion of women's rights; because she openly expresses her desire for a fulfilled intellectual and erotic life.

Christine de Pizan's learned challenge to the male order is less explosive, defused by her stress on traditional female virtues like chastity and marital fidelity, as by the coolly dispassionate tone that characterizes much of her writing. Pernette du Guillet is herself both passionate and erudite, but her poetry, published only after her death, asserts her transcendence of the physical and poses little challenge to patriarchal society. Louise Labé comes closer to Hélisenne's position, but La Belle Cordelière, as her friends in Lyon called her, considers herself a special case, like the legendary heroine Bradamanta, not so much an advocate for all women's rights. Her vocabulary is also, in the main, simpler, less florid, less provocatively scholastic than Hélisenne's.

Hélisenne's conscious, even conspicuous, display of learning in a work of popular appeal directed (at least in large part) to a readership of women (who were usually less schooled than she) appears to have disconcerted a number of men and women, but for different reasons. The demoiselles who ask Colet's help do not so much criticize Hélisenne's style as they express genuine regret at not being able to understand it. Colet and other detractors show no inability to comprehend Hélisenne's texts—they simply dislike her use of Latinisms and archaic terms on aesthetic or misogynistic grounds. I speculate that, as these same learned men did not criticize their brother writers so severely for similar stylistic features, their anger may have largely sprung from consternation that a mere woman would so aggressively display her arcane learning. What would pass unnoticed in the work of Jean Lemaire de Belges is considered unforgivable in her texts. Perhaps the highly charged and personal nature of much of her writing further exasperated her male readers, especially what we would call today her emerging feminist consciousness.

Hélisenne herself seems to have feared a severe reception of her works, at least in certain quarters, and defends her content and style on several occasions, most notably in the Fourth Invective Letter and in the final chapter of part 1 of *Les Angoysses,* a letter addressed to her lady readers. In the latter instance she first of all counters the opinion of "certain timid ladies" that "immodest love" should be passed over in silence, then expresses her assurance that all ladies who read her book will forgive her candor: "If you know well with what force Love has constrained me, I will be blamed by none [feminine plural]." Her book, she asserts (as ever), will help others avoid the same failings she describes. Then, Hélisenne touches on her style and the book's reception: "I am quite sure that this little work of mine will seem crude and obscure in comparison to those you may have read, composed by orators and historians, who by the sublimity of their intellect write books no less jocund than difficult and arduous; but in this it must serve me as an excuse that our feminine nature is not as apt for learning as men naturally are." She completes her modesty formula by stating that she is not even so presumptuous as to believe herself capable of equaling, much less bettering, the literary achievements of certain unnamed ladies—those who are gifted with such lofty minds that their compositions are most elegant in language. But whatever faults there are in her writing, she says, must be due to defects in her knowledge and not in her will, aspiration, and desire.

This lengthy apology, in which she eschews rivalry not only with learned men but also with other talented women, is an especially insistent development of a traditional opening or closing theme, the author's humble plea for the reader's benevolence. It shows the curious mixture of self-assurance and self-doubt we find elsewhere in her writing, intensified at the moment by her awareness of risking criticism by the publication of her "little work." A learned woman was considered a fascinating anomaly by the men and women of the Renaissance and had to contend with possible attacks from her own sex as well as from the opposite sex. It was quite rare for women of the Middle Ages and Renaissance to be both wives and scholars (though this combination was somewhat more likely to occur in France than elsewhere): Margaret King has analyzed the situation of learned women in Renaissance Italy and found that they were forced to choose "marriage and full participation in social life [relinquishing their studies] . . . or abstention from marriage and withdrawal from the world."[22] Even a circumscribed life of chastity could not disarm all of their critics, and such celebrated women humanists as Costanza Varano, Cassandra Fedele, and Isotta Nogarola feel that they must apologize for being women with pretensions to learning—and sometimes for being women at all. Male humanists, on the other hand, praise these women lavishly or else condemn them bitterly. One anonymous pamphleteer, writing in Latin, goes so far as to assert that "an eloquent woman is never chaste; and the behavior of many learned women also confirms [this] truth."[23] Hélisenne must have encountered many men with attitudes like this Italian's, many who attacked her ability and her integrity. Such opposition seems to have first spurred her to further writing, in her letters and Le Songe, in order to defend herself and to express the views of a woman who could speak with unusual authority in both emotional and intellectual domains. It may also explain the relative brevity of her publishing career and the repeated denials that she ever reached the "fifth and ultimate degree" of love in her relationship with Guenelic. She may have decided that the public notice she once craved had begun to cost too much.

The male establishment's verdict on her is summed up by Bernier: she was a "precieuse et sçavante que son sçavoir avoit rendue folle," that is, a "precious" or overly refined woman whose learning had made her mad.[24] A century before Molière's satires against Les Précieuses ridicules and Les Femmes savantes, censorious male critics were mocking women who had a strong sense of self and refused to let men have all the words. Hélisenne herself never ceases to identify learning with sanity and self-worth; implicitly rejecting Bernier's condescending sarcasms, she finds her folly in love, not learning.

Les Angoysses, as the first native novel of passion in France, had many imitators. It points the way toward L'Astrée, the elegant pastoral novel so popular at the end of the sixteenth century, and Madame de Lafayette's classic psychological novel, *La Princesse de Clèves,* in the seventeenth century. Several scholars have found suggestive parallels between *Les Angoysses* and *La Princesse,* though there is no proof that Madame de Lafayette knew the work of her predecessor (she *was* familiar with the contes of Marguerite of Navarre).

The general reading public seems to have forgotten Hélisenne after the sixteenth century, and the scholars themselves reduced her to a hoax or a legend: La Monnoye, summing up the opinions of seventeenth- and eighteenth-century scholarship, says that she never existed, that her romanesque name conceals some capricious author—in that he is correct!— who wrote a wholly made-up story in over-Latinate language.[25] Apart from what Demats calls the "astonishing divagations" of misguided Rabelais specialists, the most intriguing development in early Hélisenne studies is the appearance in the nineteenth century of a romanticized biography by Hyacinthe Dusevel: he relies on vague reminiscences and active imaginations discovered in Hélisenne's home region of Picardy, where her memory seems to have survived into the eighteenth century, to elaborate a tale of Hélisenne's reception at court by Louise of Savoy.[26] There, according to Dusevel, Hélisenne meets a handsome young knight whose death inspires her novel. Dusevel adds that the ladies of the gallant and frivolous court of François Premier never read *Les Angoysses* without shedding tears.

Along with such charming, though undocumented, romantic fantasies, the nineteenth century sees a rebirth of serious interest in the historical Hélisenne and an effort to place her achievements in context. In 1840, in the first significant scholarly study of her writing, J. M. Guichard sees Hélisenne as the link between Christine de Pizan in the fourteenth century and Madame de Staël in the eighteenth. The author of *Les Angoysses* deserves to take her place among "the courageous and inspired women, worthy of our respect, who have in every era given luster to French literature."[27] Guichard appreciates the poetry and drama of Hélisenne's account of her violent and disordered passion. He sees her as the most complete practitioner of the intimate novel.

At the turn of the twentieth century several scholars, most notably Gustave Reynier and Henriette Charasson, begin to trace Hélisenne's role as creator of the sentimental novel or novel of passion, as well as her contribution to the development of modern psychology and the literary analysis of feelings.[28] In 1929 L. M. Richardson, in *The Forerunners of Feminism in French Literature of the Renaissance from Christine de Pisan to Marie de Gournay,* accords an honorable place to Hélisenne.[29] Richardson takes special note of Hélisenne's *Familiar and Invective Letters* and considers her the only Frenchwoman to champion her sex in the early sixteenth century. These concerns will predominate in subsequent scholarship, along with an increasing interest in her style and the exciting rediscovery of the historical Marguerite Briet behind Hélisenne de Crenne.

In recent years Hélisenne has benefited from the new vogue of the Renaissance among many scholars and general readers, as from the continuing growth of feminist criticism, with its reassessing of the literary canon. Since the 1950s there have been at least five doctoral dissertations devoted to her work, a dozen or more articles and other studies treating her books, and a series of new editions. Part 1 of *Les Angoysses* has attracted the most attention, with two critical editions published in France, but there is also Secor's critical edition of the whole novel (available from University Microfilms) and a Slatkine reprint of the 1551 complete *Oeuvres,* as well as the translation of her letters by Mustacchi and Archambault.

In choosing selections to translate for this volume I have favored part 1, the most famous and most striking example of her writing, and within part 1 itself I thought best to concentrate on the initial half-dozen chapters, as they recount her early life and the beginnings of her tragic love affair. Almost all of Hélisenne's key themes and concerns are introduced in these six chapters, and the obsessive quality of her passion is already made abundantly clear, as are the reactions of her husband and her new love interest to her predicament. While it is painful to have to omit some wonderful episodes that occur later in the story, the summary that I provide of the rest of the novel should give a quick overview of the text as a whole and place the excerpted chapters in context. I have also translated the prefatory poem "Hélisenne aux Lisantes" ("Hélisenne to Her Lady Readers"), the only verse we have by her—which is interesting both as a succinct statement of her views and as a proof of her skill at handling the fashionable *dizain* or ten-line form, plus the dedicatory letter she addresses to "all honorable ladies," setting forth in more detail her intentions in composing her book. In addition to these selections from *Les Angoysses* I have translated major portions of the Fourth Invective Letter from Hélisenne's collected letters, an essay in epistolary form in which she offers a spirited defense of women's right to write literature. This essay is one of a series in which she attacks the misogynistic attitudes shown by, among others, her husband and a self-appointed censor named Elenot. It is to Elenot, at least ostensibly, that she writes the Fourth Letter, though the text makes clear that she expects a wider audience as well. The letter reiterates many of the concerns of *Les Angoysses* in a different framework and allows us to see a new dimension of Hélisenne's role as champion of women's causes.

In all the passages I have translated I have sought to preserve as much as possible of the period flavor of Hélisenne's style, without trying to outdo

John Lyly's Euphues. Where feasible I have used words of the same or similar registers as the originals, that is, words of the same level and category, from concrete to abstract, familiar to abstruse, simple to complex. I have also reproduced, in many cases, the loose, meandering construction she uses in most of her sentences, for I believe its very diffuseness is an essential aspect of her thought patterns. Where she is not systematic, I have not tried to regularize her—thus, for example, as she refers to the classical gods sometimes by their Greek names, sometimes by the Roman equivalents, and elsewhere merely by an allusion to a myth about them, so does my translation. I have added a word in brackets or a note to the translation where needed for comprehension, but I did not want to otherwise disturb the guessing game she likes to play with her readers. I have, however, abbreviated the text in a few places where her tendency to diffuseness and repetition seemed likely to tire a modern reader—though I have certainly left in enough repetition to give a good idea of that element of her style! It is in part by the recurrence of phrases such as "a singular pleasure," "shameless glances," "true possessor of my heart," or "amorous folly" that her story gains its enigmatic power. The repetition of terms, images, and situations, together with the frequent lists of synonyms, translates the lady's obsession and her unending but largely fruitless efforts to deal with it.

Les Angoysses douloureuses is a long and elaborate novel, though not so long or complicated as some of the chivalric romances popular in Hélisenne's day. Demats's edition of part 1 alone runs nearly one hundred pages, while Secor's edition of the whole text in his dissertation takes more than four hundred typed pages. The three parts are roughly equivalent in size, with part 2 somewhat longer than part 1, and part 3 somewhat shorter. They vary considerably, however, in focus, and there is evidence in the text that the three sections were written and may well have been published or at least circulated in manuscript separately (though no such partial editions have been found).

The dedicatory epistle or letter that precedes part 1 is paralleled by similar prefaces within the other two parts—another letter in part 2 and a preamble in part 3. While the three prefaces share many themes, they differ in tone and even intended audience, shifting from an exclusively female to a male or mixed audience. The character of Guenelic also alters for the better, as we have said, and Hélisenne even reminds the readers in part 2 of episodes in part 1, so that she can reinterpret them in less disparaging ways. Scholars speculate as to why she did not go back and change the earlier version, whatever her composition methods, before the novel was published in full form. It might be that this repetition with variation allowed her to have her literary cake and eat it too—she presents both views and leaves it up to us to make sense of them.

Part 1 has twenty-eight chapters, more than either of the others, but its chapters are usually briefer; several are only one or two pages long and treat a single episode. In tone part 1 often resembles a diary or journal—this intimacy is largely lost in the later, less autobiographical sections, yet they too offer fresh insights into Hélisenne's ideas and interests, as filtered through her male narrators. Part 2, chapter 12, "The state and liberality of a reigning princess," is especially intriguing in this regard. It has a double purpose, to portray Hélisenne's ideal female monarch and to pay a playfully exaggerated compliment to her relative Jeanne Briet.[30] The "very beautiful city" of Eliveba where the magnificent princess holds her court is none other than Hélisenne's own beloved Abbeville, transported by the author into exotic Asia Minor, near Troy. The mock-heroic tone that frequently colors the tales of chivalric derring-do in parts 2 and 3 sets *Les Angoysses* off from its conventional models and tempers our reading of Guenelic's slow evolution from selfish boy to perfect lover.

Hélisenne's ironies and sly mockeries do not keep her, nonetheless, from showing a genuine interest in Neoplatonism and Stoicism and the potential these philosophies might have for resolving the conflicts between appearance and reality, reason and sensuality, law and liberty, that trouble her. Throughout *Les Angoysses* she vacillates between two idealized self-images, Hélisenne the inamorata and Hélisenne the lady of honor and wisdom. In part 3 she manages to fuse them into a single, splendid, if equivocal, image in her death scene. It is the crowning irony of the work that Quezinstra, perfect knight and ideal friend, who consistently urges Guenelic to renounce his immoderate desires, becomes a hermit near the lovers' tomb. Thus he finally honors them as saints, martyrs to the very love he has disdained. And the apotheosis of Hélisenne's "little book," which both Pallas Athena and Venus wish to claim, asserts the enduring value of her work in an amusing fashion. Demats points out that her book serves as a new apple of discord similar to the one that led to the Trojan War.[31] Here the outcome is peaceful—the publication of Hélisenne's book, by Jupiter's order, in Paris, the city favored by both goddesses.

Les Angoysses begins with the prefatory poem and letter already mentioned. In part 1 Hélisenne tells the story of her life and all the suffering she has endured for Guenelic. Chapter 1 recounts her noble birth, childhood, and the early years of her marriage. Chapters 2–6 show her sudden surprise by love, her young suitor's attentions, and her husband's growing jealousy. Chapters 7–10 tell of the first exchanges of words and then letters between the lovers. Hélisenne advises Guenelic to give up his dangerous passion, yet she also encourages him. In chapter 11 her husband discovers and reads the love letters (she has kept a copy of her own missive). In fury he slaps her and orders her to remain in her chamber. Later, when Hélisenne once more gazes too ardently at Guenelic in church, her husband beats her brutally as soon as they return home. In chapter 12 Hélisenne tries unsuccessfully to kill herself with a knife. Chapters 13–15 recount her reluctant visit to a monk and the preacher's failure to reform her. As these chapter headings show, the result is a foregone conclusion: "Holy admonitions do not make a woman stung by love wish to desist," "The heart of a woman obstinate in love is impossible to change." Chapters 16–18 tell of the strategems the lovers employ to arrange meetings, their "amorous colloquies," and the husband's continuing abuse of his rebellious wife. Chapters 19–20 center on the lover's reproaches—he is angry that Hélisenne has not rewarded his love service. She calls him by name for the first time and finally admits to him that she would like to gratify his desire. Yet concern for her reputation and doubts of his constancy deter her. He grows more and more insolent and demanding. She dreams of his embraces, but the dream turns into a nightmare. Chapters 21–22 deal with gossip, Hélisenne's declining health, and her "piteous exclamation" against Guenelic and the love from which she cannot free herself. A servant informs her husband that Hélisenne has written down an account of her love affair. In a rage the husband kicks down the door to her room, reads the tale of her (in his words) "unbridled lasciviousness," and decides to kill her before she can consummate her sinful desires and dishonor them both. But the servants intervene. He decides to send her away instead. Chapters 23–27 describe her sad departure, her regrets, her imprisonment in a tower with only two demoiselles for company, and her bittersweet reflections on her fate. The last chapter of part 1 is a final plea for understanding from the "very dear and honored ladies" who will read her book. She excuses herself for speaking without reserve and defends her style as well as her subject matter, closing with a prayer that God will grant the ladies all the virtues necessary to live free of inconvenient passions.

Part 2 recounts the adventures of Guenelic and Quezinstra searching for Hélisenne. Her introductory letter asserts two goals, to warn young men of the perils of passion and to stimulate them to knightly deeds. In chapters 1–2 Guenelic himself says he wishes to teach other young men the virtues of true love, and admits his own past indiscretions, before retelling the story of the love affair from his point of view, emphasizing *his* anguishes. Hélisenne seems to invite us to enjoy the spectacle of Guenelic's suffering—as a fitting counterpart to her own miseries—even as we are expected to sympathize with him. In chapter 3, having learned that Hélisenne has been imprisoned, but not where, he leaves with Quezinstra to find and rescue her. The two young men pretend to be going on a pilgrimage—throughout parts 2 and 3 Guenelic will show a discretion as extreme as his earlier indiscretions. The two friends encounter and defeat brigands on their way to Sirap (Paris), where they spend some time, in chapter 4, before a visit to Gorenflos, the rich duchy that is Hélisenne's fantasy version of a family property with the same name. The next chapters describe the travelers' experiences in Gorenflos: long discussions about love, a terrifying dream in which Guenelic sees Hélisenne dying, a consultation with an astrologer who predicts that Guenelic will see her again in two years, the knighting of the two companions, a series of tournaments where Quezinstra in particular shines (and outshines Guenelic), and, in chapter 11, an aristocratic wedding ceremony they witness that intensifies Guenelic's longing for his lady love. After a rapid tour of the Mediterranean in which they visit the island of Cythera, North Africa, Cyprus, Syria, and other famous spots, most notably Troy, they arrive in Eliveba.

Chapters 12–14 tell of the princess of Eliveba, her elegant court, and the besieging of her city by a suitor whose proposal of marriage she has rejected. As we might expect, both young visitors take her side in the ensuing war, and once again Quezinstra's prowess is extraordinary—he eventually wins a single combat that decides the conflict. Guenelic, meanwhile, is brave but unlucky—captured in battle he narrowly escapes death. In chapter 15 the two companion knights receive the grateful princess's gifts and depart on a new round of visits, to Rhodes, Athens, Thebes, and other distant localities. They assist a prince in putting down a rebellion among his subjects. Though he would like to keep them at his court they insist on leaving—to the prince's admonitions against love Guenelic responds with praise of loyal love service.

Part 3, chapters 1–2, continues their voyages and eventually brings them to Italy, where Guenelic falls ill but recovers. They visit a hermit who advises them to resist sensuality. Guenelic maintains that love makes us virtuous (here Hélisenne repeats at length the well-known doctrine of courtly love that the true lover is ennobled by his love and thus avoids all the deadly sins).[32] The hermit predicts that Guenelic will find his lady, yet will not have the good fortune to enjoy her love in peace. In chapter 3 Guenelic at last discovers her whereabouts, and chapters 4–7 describe his efforts to contact Hélisenne, the lovers' nocturnal conversation through a barred window of her tower, and the plan for her escape that she devises and the two young men carry out—with disastrous results, for Hélisenne is soon struck with a mysterious and fatal malady. Before leaving the castle, however, she has had the satisfaction of sending word to her husband that, if he wants a wife, he should get himself one (since she is his no longer). Chapters 8–12 present a lovingly detailed account of Hélisenne's repentance, her final advice to her lover to purify his passion of all carnal taint and prepare for the reunion of their souls in the next world, her death, Guenelic's grief and his death, and the appearance of the god Mercury who not only conducts the lovers' souls to Minos (who sends them to the Elysian Fields) but takes Quezinstra on a guided tour of the infernal regions. With a touch of malice Hélisenne has Mercury specify that Venus is sending one of the Furies to torment the cruel sister-in-law who had been her jailer. Quezinstra arranges honorable burial for the lovers' bodies and has written on their tombs their sad history, then builds a small chapel and a hermitage nearby, where he will finish out his days in solitude. Mercury carries to heaven the small white-silk package containing Hélisenne's book—there Venus and Pallas Athena dispute possession of the book, until Jupiter sends it down to Paris to be published and thereby perpetuate the memory of these two and their amorous anguishes.

Les Angoysses was indeed published in Paris, as Jupiter and Hélisenne wished, and it has secured her—despite periods of eclipse—a place in literature, the perpetual memory of humanity, as she so ardently desired. Together with her letters, Le Songe, and the translation from the Aeneid, Les Angoysses preserves the record of a lively, energetic, and amazingly determined woman whose voice reaches us clearly across the centuries. Her work has for us the double appeal of gossip and philosophy, diary and poetry, autobiographical realism in emotion, gesture, and concrete detail along with bold theorizing on morality and the nature of women and men. Often conventional or even conservative, yet equally often avant-garde, passionate in her loving and her learning, advocate of more fulfilled lives for all women, starting with herself, Hélisenne is a woman of the Renaissance who speaks powerfully to our times.

NOTES

1. Helen Waldstein, "Hélisenne de Crenne: A Woman of the Renaissance"; Suzanne Marie-Marguerite Loriente, "L'Esthétique des Angoysses Douloureuses Qui Procedent d'Amours d'Hélisenne de Crenne."

2. Paule Demats, ed., Les Angoysses douloureuses qui procedent d'amours (1538), p. xxxvi.

3. Louis Loviot, "Hélisenne de Crenne"; Abel Lefranc, "A propos d'Hélisenne de Crenne"; V.-L. Saulnier, "Quelques nouveautés sur Hélisenne de Crenne."

4. Demats, ed., p. viii.

5. Ibid., p. x.

6. Saulnier, p. 461, n. 1.

7. On Christine de Pizan's attitudes to courtly love, see Liliane Dulac, "Christine de Pisan et le Malheur des Vrais Amans"; Charity Cannon Willard, "A New Look at Christine de Pizan's Epistre au Dieu d'Amours"; and Willard, Christine de Pizan: Her Life and Works, pp. 87–89, 150–53.

8. Richard M. Berrong, "Hélisenne de Crenne's Les Angoisses Douleureuses Qui Procèdent D'Amours."

9. Demats, ed., p. xxxiii.

10. A.-M. Schmidt, in *Histoire des Littératures,* 3:201–2, cited in Demats, ed., p. xxxv.

11. Demats, ed., pp. xxxv–xxxvi.

12. François de Billon, *Le fort inexpugnable de l'honneur du sexe féminin.*

13. "Lettre de Claude Colet," included in Hélisenne de Crenne's *Oeuvres* (Paris, 1550); reprinted in Demats, ed., pp. 102–3.

14. For a translation of Hélisenne's letters into colloquial English, plus an interesting analysis of the development of her ideas and writing style, see Marianna M. Mustacchi and Paul J. Archambault, trans. and eds., *A Renaissance Woman: Hélisenne's Personal and Invective Letters.*

15. Étienne Pasquier, *Lettres;* on Bernier, see Demats, ed., p. vi.

16. Harry R. Secor, Jr., ed., "Hélisenne de Crenne: *Les Angoysses Douloureuses Qui Procedent D'Amours* (1538): A Critical Edition Based on the Original Text with Introduction, Notes, and Glossary," pp. c–cii; Demats, ed., p. xxxv.

17. John Porter Houston, *The Traditions of French Prose Style: A Rhetorical Study,* pp. 3–32, 34–44; Mustacchi, pp. 8–13.

18. On Hélisenne's use of Latinisms, see Secor, ed., pp. lxxx–lxxxiv, xc.

19. Houston, p. 3.

20. René Sturel, "La Prose poétique au XVIe siècle."

21. See especially Houston, pp. 146–47.

22. Margaret L. King, "Book-Lined Cells: Women and Humanism in the Early Italian Renaissance."

23. Ibid., p. 77.

24. Demats, ed., p. vi.

25. La Monnoye, cited by La Croix du Maine.

26. Hyacinthe Dusevel, *Biographie des hommes célèbres du département de la Somme.*

27. J.-M. Guichard, "Hélisenne de Crenne."

28. Gustave Reynier, *Le roman sentimental avant l'Astrée;* Henriette Charasson, "Les origines de la sentimentalité moderne: d'Hélisenne de Crenne à Jean de Tinan."

29. L. M. Richardson, *The Forerunners of Feminism in French Literature of the Renaissance from Christine de Pisan to Marie de Gournay,* pp. 75–76.

30. On Jeanne Briet, see Demats, ed., p. vii.

31. Ibid., p. xxiii.

32. Hélisenne borrows mainly from chapter 5 of Anthoine de La Sale's *Petit Jehan de Saintré,* in which the lady teaches Saintré "many good things and salutary doctrines, touching on how one should flee the seven deadly sins." Compare Secor, ed., p. 459.

The Sorrowful Anguishes Which Proceed from Love

Containing Three Parts, Composed by Lady Hélisenne: Who Exhorts All Persons Not to Follow Mad Love

HÉLISENNE TO HER LADY READERS

Honorable ladies and beautiful nymphs,
Full of virtue and sweet arts,
You who contemplate the paranymphs[1]
With a look to ravish their hearts,
The dangerous blind archer[2]

Will shoot you. Be on guard!
Always take care to watch and ward,
For one who wishes to take is often taken!
I shall serve you as advance-guard:
At my own cost I have damage taken.[3]

*Lady Hélisenne's dedicatory epistle to all honorable ladies, offering them her
humble salutations. And she exhorts them by this letter to love well and
honorably, avoiding all vain and shameless love.*

The anxieties and sadness of the wretched (so I conjecture) are diminished
when one can declare them to a faithful friend.[4] Because I know, from
myself, that ladies are naturally inclined to have compassion, it is to you,
my noble ladies, that I wish to communicate my extreme sorrows. For I
believe that my misfortune will draw from you pitying tears which will be
a cooling medication to me. Alas! when I come to remember the afflictions with which my sad heart has been and is continually agitated, by
infinite desires and love's sharp spurring, I feel a sorrow which exceeds all
others, so that my trembling hand is stopped [that is, I cannot write]. O
very dear ladies, when I consider that, seeing how I was surprised, you
will be able to avoid the dangerous snares of love, by resisting it from the
beginning, without persisting in amorous thoughts, I pray you to avoid
idleness, to occupy yourselves with honorable exercises. In these considerations I have regathered my forces, imploring her who is mother and
daughter of the high-thundering Creator to aid my sad memory and
strengthen my weak hand, so that I may know how to write my story well
for you.

CHAPTER I

*The beginning of the amorous anguish of Lady Hélisenne, endured for her
friend Guenelic.*

At the season when the goddess Cybele throws off her cold and icy garment, and puts on her green robe embroidered with many colors, I was
born to a noble family; my birth caused great joy and happiness to my
parents, because they had lost hope of ever having children.[5] O how justly
I should curse the hour of my birth! Alas! I was born under an evil star!
Neither God in heaven nor Fortune on earth favored me. How happy I
would have been had my mother's milk been poison to me, so that my
soul might have passed on to the next world without suffering such great
anxiety and sadness! But since it pleased the Creator that I was procreated
and born into the world, I must try to mitigate my great and extreme

sorrows, though that seems impossible to me. The first of my misfortunes came when I was one year old; cruel Atropos did me an outrage, depriving me of a person whose loss would have caused me great grief had I not been so young a child: it was my father, whose death caused my mother such great sadness and bitterness that, had it not been for her ardent love for me, her sorrowing soul would have been separated from her body.[6]

Because I was an only daughter my mother took a singular pleasure in having me instructed in good morals and honorable customs of living. And when I reached eleven years old I was sought in marriage by several noblemen. But without delay I was married to a young noble, a stranger to me because his land was far distant from my own; despite our lack of previous acquaintance he was so very agreeable to me that I felt myself quite fortunate and considered myself happy, and also I was the sole pleasure of my husband, and our love was mutual and reciprocal. My felicity was so great that only one thing was missing, to wit health, which eluded me because I had been married too young; but that did not keep me from loving my husband ardently, and when he had to go away to serve his prince I was inexpressibly sad, even though his absence was good for my health.

Continuing in such love I grew up, and, when I first reached thirteen years old, I was so elegantly formed and so well proportioned that I exceeded all other women in beauty of body; and if I had been as beautiful of face I could have boldly named myself one of the most beautiful in France. Whenever I appeared in public many people gathered around to admire me, all saying: "There is the most beautiful body I ever saw," then, regarding my face, "She is beautiful, but it does not compare with the body."

[Hélisenne's beauty attracted the attention of numerous great lords who sought her love, even a king (presumably François Premier) who came to her chateau to see her.] But my husband, as if foreseeing the future, had sent me away, knowing how impossible it would have been for me to resist such a prince. But for a time the rumor ran that I was one of his *amyes* (mistresses). Then the truth became known, so that I shone resplendent in my fame for praiseworthy chastity. Never, for any man I had seen, however gifted by grace and nature, had my heart wavered, and it was my firm intent to live always thus, scorning and abominating those women called inconstant [literally, *flexible*] and subject to such crime.

CHAPTER 2

The origin of Hélisenne's turning to shameful love.

Meanwhile, O my noble ladies, I lived thus constant and with good reason, for there was nothing I desired that was not promptly given me, and I believe that if my husband had known my secret thoughts he would have immediately carried them out. And if changeable Fortune had not been envious of my felicity I would have been much obliged to her. But now justly I must complain of her cruelty to me.

[The way to Hélisenne's misfortunes was opened by a court case over a piece of land which brought her and her husband to a certain town.] I was not at all disquieted, unaware of the misadventure to which I should shortly succumb; but following the natural tendency of the feminine sex, which is never sated with seeing and being seen, I thought I would never see the day of our departure, and continually urged my husband to make it soon. . . . Had it pleased God that I had the wisdom of Cassandra who prophesied the destruction of the most illustrious and noble Trojan blood, alas, I would have spared myself the infinite regrets which daily multiply in my sad heart, but I believe that it was divine predestination, for I know that I will serve as example to others.

Once arrived at our lodging I came immediately to lean on the window sill and look out, exchanging joyful words with my husband, paying no heed to the important business which had brought us there. The day passed in recreation and voluptuous pleasures. The next morning I rose earlier than usual, dressed, opened the window, and, looking across the street, I saw a young man who was also looking out of his window, and I examined him attentively. His form seemed to me very beautiful, and, judging by his physiognomy, I thought him gracious and amiable: he had a smiling face, curly blonde hair, and no beard (a sign of his noble youth). He was quite honorable in garb, without excess. Because of the great heat he wore only a black satin doublet. After looking only too long at him I turned my eyes away but was forced to look back. He was also looking at me, which pleased me very much, but I was amazed to find myself compelled to look at this young man, a thing which had never happened to me before. I had been accustomed to take and captivate men, just to laugh at them; but now myself I was miserably taken. I could not withdraw my eyes, and I desired no other pleasure than the sight of him. O my ladies, I exhort and beg you to contemplate the great power of love, considering that I had never seen him before. You may find that very strange, for most often love comes by frequent encounters. Alas, I tried to resist, wanting to expel love from my heart, for that evening when I was in bed next to my husband I thought about the great affection I had always borne him, and my clear reputation, with nothing to denigrate my honor. In these considerations Reason counseled me to stand firm and not let myself be conquered, and said to me: "How can you take the filthy and fetid path and leave the beautiful lane filled with fragrant flowers? You are bound to a husband; you can take your pleasure in marriage, that's the right road, following it you can save yourself. Poor woman, do you want to prefer lascivious love to matrimonial love which is chaste and modest, which you have so carefully preserved?" In considering all these things, how I was wounded, and my judgment much injured by the ardent love by which I was possessed, Reason still predominated in me, for one good thought brought another, and I began to think over and cogitate many stories, as much from antiquity as modern times, about the misfortunes that came about through breaking and corrupting chastity, exceeding the limits of reason: I remembered the Greek Helen who caused the total destruction of Troy. Then I remembered the seduction of Medea who—as a reward for saving Jason's life—was expelled by him from his country and forced to beg mercy and help from others; thus it came about that the poor unfortunate woman in despair killed her children with her own hands.[7] Afterward I remembered Eurial and the beautiful Lucretia who were very happy and joyous for a while, until Eurial was forced to go away following the emperor and thus caused the untimely death of his lady. Many others came to my sad thoughts, like Lancelot du Lac and Queen Guinevere, who annihilated the good reputation of the magnanimous King Arthur and consequently of the noble knights of the Round Table. And in the same times Tristan de Cornouaille and Queen Yseult suffered most grievous fatigues because their damnable love came to the notice of King Mark.

After having in my imagination considered all these things I was determined to desist from love, when Sensual Appetite attacked me very fiercely, seeking to persuade me to follow him by accumulating in my sad memory innumerable thoughts completely contrary to the first ones, so that I began to feel chills and was in such extremity that my suffering could not be expressed by voice, understood by mind, or imagined by fancy. The image, effigy, or similitude of the young adolescent was painted and inscribed in my thoughts. That gave aid and comfort to love, so that in thinking to mitigate it love grew and augmented, and I said to myself: "It is only silliness to be so timid; I must leave off the sad apprehension of past ills and pay attention to the present. I know many young dames and demoiselles who are said to have lovers, who live in joy and pleasure. Perforce I must follow their example, for I have no more strength to resist. One thing which comforts me is that a person who sins along with many others does not deserve any very great reprobation. And, for my final resolution, I want at least to have the pleasure of the delectable sight of my friend. I will nourish love secretly in my heart, without divulging it to anyone, however faithful a friend." Thus I began to drive out reason, because sensuality remained supreme.

CHAPTERS 3–6

In chapter 3 what Hélisenne calls her "surprise by love" is perceived by her husband, who observes the odd behavior of his wife and her suitor (though the

*pair have not yet exchanged a word). In chapter 4 Hélisenne is forced to change
lodgings, but does not change her heart. In the next chapters her passion and
her husband's jealousy both increase rapidly.*

In such a variety of thoughts I passed the whole night. I was weak and ill
disposed in body and mind; in the morning, when I wished to rise, I found
myself in a bad state because of the harsh suffering caused by my vain and
fruitless thoughts. Nonetheless, moved by a great and fervent desire, I
dressed as hastily as I could in order to go to the window where I expected
such singular pleasure: as soon as I came there I saw the man who was the
true possessor and lord of my heart. Then I began to use shameless
glances, forgetting all fear and modesty, I who till this time had used
simple and honest looks. He, too, had his eyes inseparably on me, which
caused my husband, considering both of us, to suspect something. . . .
[Hélisenne's husband, addressing her familiarly as "mamye" (my friend)
asked her if anything were wrong, noted her melancholy, and offered to
do anything he could to help her, stressing that his affection for her was so
great that he would even give his life for her. She replied with an artful lie,
pretending to be concerned about their court case.] And then, my husband, making a show of believing my words, responded with a joyous
expression: "*Mamye,* I pray you, do not fear that we may be forestalled or
surprised, for I promise you to take such care that you will have no cause
to be irritated; do not worry about anything except living well and having
a good time." And in saying this he showed me my friend, as if he had not
noticed our continual glances, and said to me: "Look there at the hand-
somest youth I have seen in a long time. She would be very happy who
had such a friend."

While he was offering such words, my amorous heart was struggling
within my breast; changing color, I first grew pale and cold, then afterward a vehement heat drove from me the pallor, and I became hot and
red, and I was forced to withdraw because of the multitude of sighs which
agitated me, as I showed by evident signs, gestures, and trembling.[8] And
when I wished to utter laments and exclamations, the extreme distress of
my sorrow stopped my voice. I lost my appetite, and sleep was impossible
for me.

It would be long and difficult to recount the thoughts I had, for I truly
believe that never was a loving woman so cruelly treated in love. . . . [My
husband] showed me greater affection than ever, though I valued his feeling very little, for all the love I formerly bore him had departed from him,
and my young friend was the true possessor of it. I had so much pleasure
in looking at him that I thought no joy could surpass my own, and I was
continually thinking and imagining how I could speak to him. Often I
was so distracted that when my husband spoke to me I made him repeat
his words several times, because my disordered appetite had completely

transported my mind with my futile thoughts. Sometimes I saw my friend play a flute or a lute. I took a singular pleasure in listening to him, and, in short, all his deeds were marvelously agreeable to me.

[On the sixth day of her "sweet delectation" her husband, leaning on the window sill next to her, stated that the young man must be in love with her—she denied this with feigned laughter and withdrew, "outrageously irritated."]

New and various thoughts rushed through my fancy; I was incessantly spurred on by the beauty imagined and painted in my memory of the pleasing youth. But when I had well considered, I began to mitigate and temper my fury, saying to myself: "I ought not to be without hope of having enjoyment of my friend, for my husband does not suspect me, but doubtless thinks me firm and constant.[9] If he has noted my friend's customary glances I will certainly find an excuse. I must learn to suffer patiently, for there is no pain so great that prudence cannot moderate it, no sorrow so sharp that patience cannot break it. Besides, what is deferred is not abolished."[10] [For four more days she continued to gaze at the young man from her window whenever her husband was absent, though she no longer dared to do so in his presence. She thought that seeing her suitor might cool her ardor, but it only inflamed her.] One day I saw my friend going about the street and the desire took me to inquire about his estate and manner of living, which was shown me. He was of low condition, a fact which pained me extremely; but the great fury of love by which I was possessed and overmastered dazzled my mind and blotted out my knowledge so that, however much I was displeased about it, my love did not diminish.[11]

While I lived thus destitute of my liberty, my husband was melancholy and irritated by my behavior and countenance. And therefore he wanted to move to another house, which somewhat vexed me; but considering that my friend would surely be able to find the place, and that love would press and stimulate him to investigate and search, I made no show of discontent, and thus we departed and went to live rather near the temple where one makes the divine oracles, which came at once to my friend's notice.[12] [The next day he showed up, lounging in the doorway of the neighboring house. Her first reaction was to go to her mirror to check her appearance.] Then afterward I began to gaze at him affectionately, and because of the intrinsic sorrow which I felt at the sight of him I began to talk to myself as if I were speaking with him: "Certainly, my friend, you are very diligent, and no negligence could be attributed to you. Therefore you are worthy and deserve reward; at the least you should be given a private audience." While thus I was taking a singular pleasure in my amorous thoughts my husband came to lean on the sill next to me, and he could not keep from unburdening his heart. He spoke in a great fury: "I see there your friend whom you gaze at marvelously; truly I know that you are surprised [by love], which displeases me. I see you using dissolute and shameless glances, and you are so perturbed that reason no longer dominates in you. But I assure you, if you continue in such regards I will show you that you have most grievously offended me." [Hélisenne was at first unable to reply to his accusations, but, "like a woman deeply afflicted by langorous infirmity," had to sit down to keep from falling. She answered his allegations by pointing to her good conduct and reputation, and accusing him of believing slander. Her husband replied:] "Ha, false woman, such excuses will find no entry into my heart, for however much you may have been chaste and modest, I know clearly that your heart has been subverted and heated with libidinous ardor, and you have spoiled your modesty by following lascivious love; therefore I have reason to curse the hour when I first saw you, for such dissolute behavior will denigrate and annihilate your honor and my own. And if the thing comes to my knowledge be sure that I shall take cruel vengeance." [After those words her husband left; Hélisenne was weighed down with sadness and bitterness but later regained enough strength to sob out the following:] "O my very dear friend, unique hope of my afflicted heart, how can I now temper the great ardor which daily grows and multiplies in my heart, so that I burn and am consumed? I see no way to cool my passion, and even if it were possible for me to stop [loving you] I would not want to, because of the delectable pleasure I have in your regard. Alas, Fortune, you drive me to despair; for if I am deprived of the sight of my friend I desire nothing else but that the outrageous Atropos prematurely use her cruelty on me, which will seem sweet kindness to me, however much others fear her." [While Hélisenne was in a state of "vain and superfluous care" her husband returned and, seeing her sadness, thought she was ashamed because of his recriminations and could thus be made to give up her excessive love—in this he was far from the truth, as Hélisenne observes, for death alone could separate her from her love.]

Nonetheless, my husband had moderated his fury, and he said to me: "I pray you, tell me whence proceeds your sadness: is it because you have no opportunity to accomplish your lustful and incestuous will?[13] Or, if that displeases you, are you contrite because you have so long persisted in your continual gazes, unwilling to desist from your folly? Do you repent of having allowed your heart to be surprised, desiring to begin a detestable and abominable life? If I thought that your will was to annul and chase love from your heart, and to overcome yourself and return to more honorable customs of living, I would not hold you in lesser esteem, for I know that the first movements [of emotion or desire] are not in our power to control."

[Hélisenne boldly denied any stain on her heart and, out of resentment, withdrew to another chamber; because it was bedtime she deliberately delayed her return until her husband had gone to sleep.] And around midnight I went to bed in great melancholy, for everything was to me disagreeable, sad, and hateful. But the next morning I went to hear divine services in a small temple. And when I wished to return home, I saw my friend, who threw at me a very piercing glance which penetrated me to the heart; I had so perfect a joy that I forgot all the torments and heavy sorrows I had sustained because of him. I gazed shamelessly at him, careless of his companion, who could observe my immodest and artful glances. And, when I thought of returning home, it seemed to me that I felt more sadness than his sight had given me pleasure. But fearing that my husband might come by, against my will I had to retire.

Thus you have heard, very dear ladies, how I was treated in love, sometimes by extreme pain constrained to groan and lament, and sometimes receiving great joy and consolation from the pleasing sight of my friend. I went ordinarily to hear divine services at the main temple where everyone went; so did my friend, always with several companions. I clearly saw his inconstancy and imprudence by the fact that he was pointing me out [to his friends]. And, as I could infer or presuppose from the obvious signs, he was making public and divulging our love. Moreover, I was certain about it, for one of my demoiselles overheard him saying to one of his companions: "That lady is marvelously amorous of me. See her inviting glances; I suppose that by continuing to pursue her I may easily have enjoyment of her." When this speech was recited to me, the vigor of my heart suddenly failed, and because of my passionate anger I bowed my head to the earth like a purple violet beaten down by the strong wind Boreas. I remained a long time very pensive, then lifting my head I looked plaintively at my friend, and I said to myself: "Alas, Fortune, how harsh, adverse, ferocious, and cruel you are to me! Now I think that it is only simulation and pretense on the part of the one who I thought loved me from the heart, but alas, he has no other goal but to deprive me of honor so he can talk about and deride me. But however well I know him to be such, my heart belongs so much to him that I cannot withdraw it. Nonetheless I will henceforth no longer look at him, at least in public, for a good reputation is easily destroyed, especially when it concerns gentlewomen who are not as modest as their honesty requires." [In these deliberations Hélisenne went home to spend the day alone in her room. That night, lying painfully awake next to her husband, she heard music outside.]

Thus tormented and agitated, I heard several instruments playing in great harmony and melodious resounding. I suspected that it could be my friend, and to know the truth I wanted to get up. Although I had always been fearful of the nocturnal shadows, I became bold and assured. But as I was thinking of jumping out of my bed to go to the window my husband said to me: "Where do you want to go? Truly I think that it is your friend," and without another word he went back to sleep. O how grieved I was, and sadder than those who are detained in a caliginous prison, for fear held me back, so that I did not dare to go to look out the window, and that filled me with ire and anger which I could not restrain! Thus the night passed. But my friend kept coming back, and one time among the others my husband awoke and, turning to me, spoke: "O accursed woman, you have always denied to me what I could have known by obvious signs if I had not been out of my right mind. I am certain and know without a doubt that it is your friend who brings musicians here to entertain you and induce you to condescend to his iniquitous desire. But if he knew your heart as well as I do he would not put himself to so much trouble. For your unbridled lasciviousness has sufficient power to make you provoke him yourself, and if he were an expert in love he would have been able to recognize from your behavior the great ardor which incessantly dominates you. Venus's appetite has envenomed your heart, which used to be pure and chaste; you are so deluded by his love that you have changed all your moods, ways, gestures, desires, and honest manners into the opposite sort. But be assured that I will no longer suffer this, for your disordered life causes me so many troubles and passions that I shall be constrained to use cruelty and ignominy against your person." And when he had said that, he fell silent. And I arose like a mad woman, and without knowing how to pronounce the first word to respond to him, I began to pull out my hair and bloody my face with my nails, and with my trenchant female cry I penetrated the ears of those within hearing. When I could speak, like a woman completely alienated from reason I said to him: "Certainly I believe that some familiar spirit is revealing to you the secret of my thoughts, a thing which I thought was reserved to divine prescience! And truly I love him, effusively and from the heart, and with so great a firmness that only death could separate me from his love. Come then with your sword. Make my soul transmigrate from this infelicitous bodily prison, and I will thank you; for I prefer to die a violent death rather than to languish continually, for it is better to be strangled than to be always hanging. And therefore wait no longer, pierce through my fickle heart, and pull back your sword stained and dripping with my blood. Have no more pity on me than Pyrrhus on Polixene, immolated on the tomb of Achilles. And if you do not do it, the fury and rage which hold me will press me and force me to throw myself off [to my death]." And in so saying my eyes sparkled with hot fury and I struck my chest with my fist, so much that I was so exhausted that I fell unconscious and seemed like a dead woman. And when I returned to my senses I saw my husband

and my demoiselles and other domestics who were astounded at such fainting and swooning. And when I could speak, I asked why we had gotten up, and my husband responded: "As soon as you are abed I will tell you," and without further conversation had me carried to bed by one of my servant girls. And he began to say to me: "O my God, I would never have thought, however sternly I spoke to you of your shame, that the fire of love would be in you so fierce and inextinguishable; for I see that you are on the point of death, which grieves me. For although you have greatly erred, and have confessed to me from your own lips that you are occupied with a new love, I love you so much that it would be difficult and (I believe) even impossible for me to turn away from loving you. But I assure you that I will take cruel vengeance on your friend, who has caused so much sadness in my heart. If you take a fancy to kiss him, within three days I will make you kiss his dead body." When I heard these words my heart was as much oppressed as are those who receive a death sentence, and I could not keep from responding to him: "I prefer that you take vengeance on me, as I have merited it, without harming this young man who has done nothing to offend. Even if he is in love has he deserved death? Being in love is the proper and true nature of young men." I proffered these words with sighs that turned to tears, so that my sorrowful husband was forced to pacify me, swearing to me that, as I was so bitterly upset, he would do him no harm. But he begged me to abandon the mad desire I felt for my young friend, saying that I could do so easily by myself, and that, even if it were difficult, it was still possible. And in making such remonstrations he approached me to achieve the pleasure of Venus, but very promptly I withdrew far from him, and I said to him: "My friend, I beg you to let me rest, for because of the sadness and anguishes by which my poor heart is continually agitated I am weak in all my members, so that I no longer expect to live except in languishing and infirmity." And in so saying, I sat down on my bed, pretending to be grievously afflicted with illness, which greatly distressed my husband. And he tried to calm my tears, sorrows, and sighs; and when he thought he had consoled me a little, he slept until daybreak.

[The next morning Hélisenne's husband took her into his arms and wished to regain her love, but he was no longer able to please her, and it was reluctantly that she slept with him. She covered up her "iniquitous desire" with a show of reasonableness. That same day her husband asked the neighbors about the serenades in front of their house; he was told that it was not the custom unless there was a marriageable girl present. He jokingly told the landlord, an elderly rustic, that someone was in love with either his or the landlord's wife. The old man defended his wife's reputation with a passion that amused Hélisenne, since his spouse was not only seventy-two years old but also ugly and deformed. Meanwhile Hélisenne's husband decided to take her to church on the following day, to see how she would act when she encountered her suitor. The intervening night seemed very long to her.]

But when Proserpina [the moon] began to descend into the realm of the three-headed dog and Phoebus in his chariot mounted the zodiac, wearing on his head his diadem of clear and resplendent rays to light up and illuminate the whole world, I rose suddenly and began to array myself. I wore a gown of crimson satin and an overskirt of white satin, I adorned my head with beautiful embroideries and rich precious stones; and when I was ready I began to stroll, admiring myself in my sumptuous garments like a peacock in its beautiful plumes, thinking to please others as I pleased myself. Meanwhile my husband was dressing, who took a singular pleasure in seeing me, and he said to me that it was time to go. With these words we came out of our chamber. In the company of my demoiselles I walked slowly along the street, maintaining an honorable gravity of manner; everyone looked at me, saying to each other: "See there the creature exceeding and surpassing all others in beauty of body." And after they had looked at me they went to call the rest, making them come out of their homes to see me. It was amazing to see the people gathering around me; and when I reached the temple many young men formed a circle around me, making amorous show of sweet and attractive glances from the corners of their eyes to try to deceive me, but I took no heed of them, for all my thoughts were concentrated on one alone. I looked everywhere but did not see the one who was the single pleasure of my sight, nor did he come until the divine service had begun; when he came he did not make his accustomed glances but only passed before me. I imagined that it was because my husband was present, to keep from making him suspicious, so I was content. . . . When we returned to hear vespers my friend was indiscreet, because in the presence of my husband he showed his affection for me with sweet amorous looks, and pointed me out to his friends even though he had not yet spoken to me. Seeing his inconstancy I gazed at him with soft and simple looks, to show him that he was causing me much heartache, but he did not therefore cease his importunities, for he passed so close to me that he stepped on my white satin skirt. I was very particular about my clothes. It was the thing in which I took a singular pleasure. Yet nonetheless he did not displease me, but on the contrary I would willingly and with a good heart have kissed the spot where his foot had touched. My husband saw it all, who was forced by anger to leave, whence I, against my will and to avoid scandal, had to follow him. Once we reached home he said to me: "I am astounded by your friend, who did not know how to hide his amorous folly in my presence. He showed great presumption to come walk on your skirt. It seems by that that he must have great intimacy and familiarity with you." [Then her husband forbade her to ever be in the same place with the young man again, making her promise to leave immediately, even at the elevation of the host during mass, if the suitor came in, and threatening to leave her if she disobeyed him.] And when [the next day] I was dressed we went to the temple where I found my friend, who continued to importune me, so that I had to change places three times; but he always followed me, talking to his friends about me. And I think he talked about my husband, who was continually with me, for I heard one of his friends say to him that my anxious face showed that I was under suspicion. And, hearing those words, my friend began to laugh. Seeing that, and remembering my husband's command, I left, thinking that I would sometime find a more convenient place for us to share our secret thoughts.

The Invective Letters of My Lady Hélisenne de Crenne

THE FOURTH INVECTIVE LETTER

Epistle sent by my lady Hélisenne to Elenot, who, moved by temerarious presumption, assiduously condemned ladies who wish to occupy themselves with the solace of literary exercises. But, to divert him from his folly, herein are commemorated the splendid and noble minds of certain illustrious ladies.[14]

Since I have carefully considered the arrogant and audacious words you spoke to me it has been easy for me to conjecture that you have reached the heights of temerarious folly: for (according to your account) you believe yourself to be more knowledgeable than mouth could express, intellect comprehend, or fancy imagine. I pray you, tell me if your presumption is not dazzling and blinding you, so that in your mind you think yourself sprung from the brain of great Jupiter like Pallas the goddess of fortitude and prudence.[15] Doubtless you esteem yourself more learned than those who in ancient times resided at the fountain which sprang up beneath the hoof of Pegasus.[16] Certainly, if you wished to divulge the truth of your mad imaginings, you would proclaim publicly that you glory in outdoing in the recital of history Clio the commemorator. In the narration of tragedy you would surpass Melpomene; in comedies, Thalia; in well-modulated sound [music], Euterpe; in melody [dancing to music?], Terpsichore; in geometry, Erato; in literature, Calliope; in knowledge of the heavenly movements, Urania, and in rhetoric, Polyhymnia.[17]

Certainly I believe that you often think it would have been a great glory to Homer, the prince of poets, and the historian Herodotus if they had spoken and written of you.[18] But you judge that the sovereign Creator did not wish to adorn the first ages with something worthy of extreme praise, for fear of impoverishing posterity; and yet you are sad just because you (in your esteem the Phoenix of wisdom) cannot discover among the modern poets and historiographers anyone who would suffice to be your praisewriter. Therefore we may assume that you would much desire that the son of Phoebus and Coronis return to this world and at your request resuscitate the most experienced in learning of the ancients, who could serve you as your dignity deserves.[19] Such presumptions would surely make me laugh, were it not that, in laboring to exalt yourself, you totally abase the others: and you especially blame and disparage the female condition. And speaking in general terms you state that women's minds are uncultivated and obscured [incapable of coherent thought], wherefore you conclude that their only occupation should be spinning.[20] It amazes me how quickly you reach that conclusion. I am convinced that (if you had the power) you would prohibit to the feminine sex the benefice of literary activity, claiming that women are incapable of producing good literature. If you had been more studious and had examined more diverse texts your opinion would be otherwise. At least it would if your inveterate malice did not stimulate you to persist in the enmity you bear ladies, which could explain why you pass over in silence the praise of women with which the noble orators decorated their writings. Quintilian was not ashamed to write that the daughters of Laelius and Hortensius (very famous orators) by their learning made the elegance of their fathers' works singularly praiseworthy or desirable. Damas the daughter of Pythagoras was so very learned in philosophy that, after the Three Sisters had cut the thread of her father's life, she explained the difficult points of his maxims.[21] Queen Zenobia was so well instructed by the philosopher Longinus that because of the abundance and shining wisdom of her writing she was named Ephinisa; Nichomachus translated her sacred works. Deborah was so prudent and discreet and expert in Greek that, as we read in the Book of Judges, for some time she exercised the office of judge over the people of Israel. Moreover, we read in Kings that Athaliah reigned and judged seven years in Jerusalem. Cornelia, the mother of the two Gracchi, formed in them the most eloquent language. Valeria, a Roman virgin, was so expert in Greek and Latin literature that she explained the verses and meters of Virgil according to the faith and the mysteries of the Christian religion. Aspasia was so filled with extreme learning that Socrates, the greatly esteemed philosopher, was not ashamed to learn something from her: Apollo Pythius testifies to this.[22] Alpaides, virgin and nun, was so illuminated by divine grace that she comprehended the sense of the books

of the holy Bible. Arete, a very learned woman, was the mother of Aristippus the philosopher, whom from the beginning she instructed in philosophy. . . . Sosipatra was so illustrious in poetic knowledge that the Ethics
said she had been nourished by the gods.[23] Also there were excellent poet-
esses and female orators, Capiola, Lucera, Sappho, and Armisia sur-
named Androginea. Certainly I believe without doubt that whoever
would wish to wander the sea of learned ladies [*dames scavantes*], making
the effort to point out their praiseworthy works, would spend more time
than did Ulysses in his painful and fatiguing peregrinations. But if you,
wretched fellow, want to keep saying that I mention only ancient examples and that there are none at present equal to those I have listed above,
to that I reply that your words are far from the truth: for I think that there
never was in the past nor can be in the future a more excellent and high-
minded person than the most illustrious and magnanimous princess, my
lady the Queen of Navarre. It is well known that in her excellent and
sublime royal person reside the divine wisdom of Plato, the prudence of
Cato, the eloquence of Cicero, and the reason [that is, wisdom] of Socrates.[24] To speak briefly, her sincerity is so filled with accomplishments
that her own splendor gives luster to the feminine condition, and at the
moment it suffices me to mention her alone, without thinking of other
examples, to confound your vain and useless propositions, to which it is
time for your pestiferous tongue to put an end.

[In the next section, which follows without a break in the text of the
letter, Hélisenne goes on to reproach Elenot for making unjustifed crit-
icisms of men, as well. His "detestable vice of detraction" has impelled
him, after satisfying his appetite for condemning the ladies, to turn to his
own sex.] [You criticize] the very ones who are so well esteemed that, even
if your life equaled that of ancient Nestor, and that you set yourself to
studying assiduously, it would not be in your power to reach the dignity
you would need just to carry their books for them.[25] O how much it
saddens me to remember your superfluous words, nonetheless I feel a
great urgency to recount them, otherwise I could not unburden my afflicted heart. I am sure that you remember that your venomous tongue,
source of iniquities, set itself to disprize the high sweet style of the very
eloquent poet Marot, whose works are so excellent and elegant that kings
and princes sovereignly delight in them.[26] [Hélisenne concludes that Elenot's disparaging words flow from him like water or other liquid (a distilled poison, she suggests) overflowing a too-full cup. His behavior is
therefore only natural and not something to be amazed at.] But alas, how
I am agitated by painful anxiety when I recall how I heard your abominable mouth declare your "amiable" desire to busy yourself with reading
the *Angoysses,* my little composition: certainly your words are completely contrary to my desires, for I would prefer that my books were

always shown to knowledgeable persons; I know that people of exceptional wit have a natural inclination to extol willingly the works of others, therefore, though my works were of small merit, their kindness would condescend to excuse the weakness of my small style. They would understand that I was stimulated to write by the fear of succumbing and being submerged by the perilous sea of idleness. Thus I am without doubt assured that, in their delight in the reading of my little works, they would find them acceptable. Oh, what an inestimable felicity it is to me when I think that my books are circulating in that noble city of Paris: the city which is inhabited by a numberless multitude of marvelously learned people, lovers of the amenity, sweetness, and sauvity which are found in the delectable acquaintance of Minerva. Certainly there is nothing in that enjoyable prospect to disturb me, except when I am displeased at the thought that my cruel misfortune permits—if there is one sole ignorant and malicious person in that aforesaid very erudite city—my books to come before his blind eyes. I am sure that he will make no good account of them, for, though my works are nothing in comparison to the arduous compositions which daily multiply, you will not be able to understand them.[27] I have long recognized the incapacity of your mind, and, because I know that what one does not understand is easily disprized, I do not hope to be able to avoid your dangerous bite. [Hélisenne warns Elenot that he risks the fate of Midas, to be burdened with ass's ears, by his "fol jugement."] This example should make you fearful so that, closing your shameful mouth and restraining your serpent's tongue, you would beg mercy of those you have so grievously offended, for even now, if you wished to extirpate the perversity which resides in you, I would persuade the ladies to pardon you; at my request you would surely find no refusal, since women are naturally filled with honor, sweetness, and clemency.[28] Clear testimony of this is given us by the philosopher Aristotle, who writes that woman is merciful, quick to pity and pardon, and, also, women know that there is nothing more likely to favor achieving a happy life than forgetting injuries suffered: this corroborates their natural goodness, which I wanted to tell you about in order to keep you from despairing of a reconciliation with them. Now think of confessing the offense you have perpetrated against this gracious female sex, that the Church calls devout; if you can do as I ask, it will be well for you, for reason wishes it, honor consents to it, and conscience commands it. I would like for you to communicate this letter of mine to people of excellent and clear minds, because I am sure that, after considering it, they would make you understand that this remonstration was made for your salvation and utility; but if you hide it I fear that, lacking good counsel, you may persist in your old folly, which would arouse the fury of my pen—and that would stimulate me to write you again and to say things that are more distressing than you could predict. On that conclusion I will end this present epistle, praying Heaven's Sovereign that He, as a special grace, illuminate your obscured understanding.

NOTES TO THE TRANSLATION

1. In ancient Greece a paranymph was best man or bridesmaid at a wedding; here Hélisenne uses the term freely to mean the ladies' companions or suitors, that is, their potential lovers. It is interesting that Hélisenne warns other ladies of the dangers of teasing and flirtation, advising them that such efforts to win men's hearts may backfire, and then offers herself as a cautionary example, even though she maintains in her subsequent narrative that she never sought any extramarital involvement, that her efforts to captivate men were just a game. Her playful mockeries, however, led by fate or accident to a disastrous infatuation. The traditional idea that falling in love is a misfortune to be avoided strikes the right melancholy note to introduce *Les Angoysses*. And yet the evident pleasure in her own wit, which Hélisenne's prefatory poem expresses, and the hint of satisfaction in her martyrdom place her in the equally ancient tradition of the heroic poet-lover, from Ovid to Petrarch and Scève, and suggest the fundamental ambivalence that characterizes *Les Angoysses douloureuses* as a whole. The question the text provokes is not so much "does she or doesn't she consummate her love affair with Guenelic?" as it is "does she or doesn't she regret what she calls her folly?" As a woman and as an artist Hélisenne seems to want to have it both ways, and it is her particular blend of self-recrimination and self-aggrandizement (or self-indulgence) that gives piquancy to her writing. While she certainly does not equal her near-contemporary Louise Labé—as lover or poet—her passions are as troubled and troubling in their darkly bitter ambiguity as Labé's more incandescent ardors.

2. My translation cannot reproduce in English verse the full chain of associations set in motion by the simple but effective rhyme words Hélisenne has chosen to lead up to the sting of line 6: "doulceur—ravisseur—mal seur," with feminine *sweetness* metamorphosing into a predatory *ravishing* or seductive attitude that paradoxically makes women vulnerable to Cupid, the blind boy who is dangerously unpredictable and *unsure* or fickle. The image of woman as huntress appears frequently in Renaissance love poetry, but here she suddenly and to her dismay turns into prey (as indeed she would be in the bawdy verse of the period, anyway).

3. Lines 8 and 10 in the original end in a punning rhyme word *pris* (rhyming puns were favored by the court poets such as Marot and the Grands Rhétoriqueurs); *pris* means *taken* in the first instance, and I have translated it literally, but in the second instance it means *price* or *cost:* in order to preserve the repetition of the rhyme word I have given a free version of the last line in its entirety—"A mes despens, dommage et pris" is literally "At my expense, damage, and cost."

4. In making my translations from *Les Angoysses* I have used both the Demats and Secor editions of the text as bases for my English version. In this dedicatory letter, as frequently throughout *Les Angoysses,* Hélisenne borrows freely from her favorite sources, adapting phrases, images, and ideas to suit her own purposes. Though this short letter includes a number of such borrowings from the opening of Boccaccio's *Fiammetta,* the overall effect is quite different. Hélisenne is seeking relief and consolation from her confession: Fiammetta wishes to intensify her sorrows. Hélisenne, moreover, insists on the didactic and morally improving nature of her story. For detailed information on Hélisenne's use of sources, see Demats, appendix 2 and notes, pp. 104–37, and Secor, notes, pp. 424–72.

5. Hélisenne probably acquired a taste for flowery mythological allusions from reading Jean Lemaire de Belges, but the spring goddess he usually refers to is Flora. Perhaps Hélisenne prefers Cybele here because the latter is a mother goddess and hence appropriate to a birth scene. It is curious that Hélisenne, who never mentions her son (or, according to some scholars, stepson), nonetheless shows a predilection for references to famous mothers. See, for example, her citations of celebrated women in the Fourth Invective Letter below.

6. Atropos, one of the Three Sisters or Moirai (Fates) in Greek mythology, cuts the thread of life that Clotho spins and Lachesis measures.

7. Medea's tragic story underwent considerable evolution in late medieval times. Demats, pp. 125–26, n. 4, traces the rehabilitation of Medea in works by Jean de Meun, Jean Le Fèvre, and Christine de Pizan, wherein she becomes emblematic of loyalty and wisdom, in contrast to Jason's ingratitude. But Hélisenne goes further than any of the rest when she changes Medea's act of infanticide from a revenge murder into a deed of poverty and despair. The other unfortunate lovers in Hélisenne's list are still familiar to us today, with the possible exception of Eurialus and Lucretia, hero and heroine of a romance by Aeneas Silvius.

8. Here, as often elsewhere in *Les Angoysses*, Hélisenne manifests the symptoms of love-sickness so well known in Western literature from the days of Ovid on.

9. The verb phrase Hélisenne uses here, *avoir jouyssance de mon amy*, clearly implies sexual union. It recurs later in the text when the lover asks for his reward and also when he boasts to his friends of how easily he could seduce Hélisenne. The story seems to say that Hélisenne continually wants and hopes to consummate her passion but never actually does.

10. Hélisenne juxtaposes here two different proverbs or maxims she found many pages apart in Caviceo's *Libro del Peregrino*. Such a technique shows her attitude toward her sources: they serve as encyclopedia, thesaurus, and even Bartlett's *Familiar Quotations*.

11. The reference to Guenelic's "low condition" has led many readers to conclude that he was a commoner, but his dress, behavior, and social situation suggest to me that he was simply of the lower nobility or gentry—Hélisenne would not have been likely to be struck with a sudden passion for a peasant, artisan, servant, or merchant. In the prefatory letter to part 2 Hélisenne herself appears anxious to dispel any misunderstandings that may have arisen, and there she says that Guenelic is a gentleman, though poor. She goes on to have him made knight, but that is probably sheer romancing.

12. The word that Hélisenne uses for a house of worship is always *temple*, even though the context makes clear that the temples in question are Catholic churches—one hears Mass, attends vespers, and so forth. The preference for *temple* may be only a classicizing affectation or may translate some genuine fusion of religious spheres in Hélisenne's mind. Like many other Renaissance humanists, she tends to mingle Christian and pagan allusions in the same passages—or else to use classical phrases like "the divine oracles" in referring to Christian services.

13. The word *inceste*, "incestuous," hardly seems appropriate here, because there is no family tie between Hélisenne and Guenelic. Probably it conveys the husband's intense disgust at his wife's all-too-evident adulterous desires.

14. Elenot has not been identified. His name may well be an anagram for some censorious person who had dared to contest Hélisenne's views on women's right to practice literature. In the Fifth Invective Letter, for example, she attacks the inhabitants of Icuoc (Coucy) for making slanderous remarks about her and her abilities. At any rate, Hélisenne seems to have known Elenot personally, judging by the references she makes in the body of the letter to speaking with him and having mutual friends; her letter may be motivated as much by fear of his probable disparaging comments on *Les Angoysses* as by anger at his arrogance and his criticism of other women authors (and of one of her favorite poets, Clément Marot). Hélisenne portrays Elenot not just as a typical misogynist but as a vain and

conceited man who puts everyone else down, both women and men. My translation follows
the 1551 edition of the text in Hélisenne's *Oeuvres*.

15. Pallas Athena is the original brainchild (of Zeus, but Hélisenne prefers to use the
Roman name of Jupiter)—Hélisenne is teasing her opponent by comparing him with the
goddess of wisdom and then with each of the Muses in turn—a series of sly digs at the
exponent of masculine superiority.

16. The fountain Hippocrene that Pegasus created by striking Mount Helicon with his
hoof is traditionally sacred to the Muses, who live nearby.

17. Hélisenne follows the usual listing of the Muses with their specialties, except for the
oddly phrased reference to Terpsichore (associated with the dance) and the attribution of
geometry to Erato (patroness of lyric and love poetry) and rhetoric to Polyhymnia (Muse of
sacred song). Hélisenne may have been influenced in the cases of the latter two by the trivium
and quadrivium of medieval universities, for each of the liberal arts, including geometry and
rhetoric, is frequently depicted as a Muselike female figure in art and architecture.

18. Here Hélisenne ironically inverts a familiar classical topos on the misfortune of those
who lived before Homer and thus lacked anyone worthy of singing their deeds. Compare
Horace's *Ode*, book 4, section 9, "In Praise of Lollius," especially lines 13–28: "Not Spar-
tan Helen only became inflamed with love, marvelling at a paramour's trim locks, his gold-
bespangled raiment, his princely pomp and followers; nor was Teucer first to speed the shaft
from Cretan bow. Not once alone has Ilium been beset; nor has great Idomeneus or
Sthenelus alone fought battles worthy to be sung by the Muses. Nor were doughty Hector
and keen Deiphobus the first to encounter heavy blows for chaste wife and children. Many
heroes lived before Agamemnon; but all are overwhelmed in unending night, unwept, unknown, because they lack a sacred bard" (C. E. Bennett, ed. and trans., *The Odes and
Epodes* [New York, 1924], pp. 318–23). I thank my colleague Robert Babcock for his kind
assistance with this and several other classical references in Hélisenne's letter.

19. The son of Phoebus Apollo and Coronis is Aesculapius (or Asclepius), honored as the
god of medicine, an expert healer who could even revive the dead. It would be overweening
pride, indeed, on Elenot's part, if he expected the god to revive Homer or Herodotus in
order for them to praise him! Hélisenne mischievously exaggerates her opponent's vanity to
a kind of cosmic (and comic!) hubris.

20. The advice to women to stick to their spinning (derived perhaps from Proverbs
31:19) is a commonplace of the debate over women's roles, and counterarguments appear
frequently in Renaissance women's writing, especially when the topic is women's ability to
write and perform other "manly" deeds. Labé's autobiographical elegy addressed to the
ladies of Lyon uses the related motif of the needle to assert her superiority in women's arts
that matches her skill in men's arts, while in the preface to her collected works Louise, like
Jeanne Flore, exhorts women to elevate their minds above their distaffs and spindles. Most
interesting is Catherine des Roches's "To My Distaff," where the poet proclaims her intent to
hold onto both pen and spindle, new and traditional roles—and where the very awkwardness of the image of a woman holding and using both implements at once may translate
Catherine's ambivalent feelings about her situation. Hélisenne has no qualms about drop-
ping the distaff in favor of the pen.

21. Quintilian, at the beginning of his *Institutio Oratoria*, a handbook on rhetoric, mentions several Roman women celebrated for their learning and eloquence (*Inst. Or.* 1.1.6):
Cornelia, the mother of the Gracchi, whom Hélisenne herself praises a few sentences further
on in her letter, and the daughters of the noted orators Laelius and Hortensius, whom
Hélisenne cites here. Hélisenne's sentence about the daughters is rather vague: she may mean
that the daughters assisted their famous fathers in the composition of their speeches or that
they presented recitations or explications of the aforesaid speeches, or even, perhaps, that

they wrote themselves in their fathers' elegant styles. Whatever, their function as hand-maidens to their fathers links them to the next person in Hélisenne's catalog of literary women, Damas, the daughter of the Greek philosopher Pythagoras.

22. Zenobia (or Septimia), wife of Odenatus, and after his death reigning queen of Palmyra (ca. A.D. 269), was highly praised by classical authors for her beauty, intelligence, and virtue, despite her ruthless personal ambition. A warrior queen, she won many victories in Asia Minor but was eventually defeated by the troops of the Roman Emperor Aurelianus. Legend identifies her Greek secretary with the Longinus who wrote the famous treatise *On the Sublime;* she herself had a reputation for wit and elegance in her literary accomplishments. Deborah is a familiar biblical figure, famous as a judge in Israel. It is peculiar, however, that Hélisenne says she was able to speak Greek. Athaliah, wife of Jehoram, king of Judah, and daughter of Ahab and Jezebel, reigned over Judah for six years (before being deposed in favor of her grandson Joash). Athaliah, who determined to rule in her own right by destroying all surviving male heirs (except for Joash, who was hidden by the priests), is hardly presented in the Bible as a paragon of the female monarch (see 2 Kings 11 and 2 Chronicles 22–23), yet Hélisenne admires her for her power and astuteness. Hélisenne may say that Athaliah ruled for seven years because she counts also the year in which the queen was deposed.

23. All but three of the wise and erudite women listed by Hélisenne are also cited by her major source for this passage, Cornelius Agrippa's *De nobilitate et praecellentia foeminei sexus* (1529): see the translation of Agrippa's essay, *De l'excellence et de la supériorité de la femme* . . . (Paris, 1801), chapters 21–23, pp. 73–82. See also Mustacchi, p. 120, n. 74. It is significant that Alpaides, Arete, and Sosipatra, the three women added by Hélisenne, are all associated with teaching and explicating religious or philosophical texts. Hélisenne herself frequently asserts a desire and even an implicit duty to guide the young, as in her prefaces to parts 2 and 3 of *Les Angoysses.* This assertion may be simply a nod to the tradition of counsel books for princes and other young people, or it may indirectly reflect Hélisenne's own experiences. Arete, daughter of Aristippus and mother of Aristippus the Younger, both philosophers of the Cyrenaic school of philosophy, is presented by Hélisenne as the instructress of her famous son, thus, presumably, the intellectual as well as physical link between the two men. Like the daughters of Laelius, Hortensius, and Pythagoras, Arete inherits her learning; like Cornelia she is an exemplary mother and passes on her education to the next generation.

24. Hélissene's extravagant praise for Marguerite of Navarre may derive from a hope of notice or patronage rather than any real acquaintance with the royal princess, but there is a persistent rumor recorded by the more romantic biographers of Hélisenne's life, such as Hyacinthe Dusevel, that she was received at the court of François Premier. Her laudatory assessment of Marguerite as the equal or superior of the great men and women of classical antiquity is an early blow struck in the Quarrel of the Ancients and the Moderns that would occupy so much literary attention in France over the next two centuries.

25. Nestor is a character in the Iliad, known both for his great age and for his habit of giving a great deal of (sometimes unwanted) advice. Hélisenne seems to be fond of him—in the preamble to her *Invective Letters* she calls Nestor "the master of eloquence" and prays that her "dear friends and readers" may enjoy lives as long, happy, and prosperous as his. In the Fourth Letter the reference is intended to emphasize the hopelessness of Elenot's pretensions—however long he might live and study he could never improve enough to be worthy even of carrying the books (as servants or slaves traditionally did) of a Marot or a Marguerite of Navarre.

26. Clément Marot (1496–1544) was a favorite court poet and a protégé of Marguerite of Navarre. Hélisenne may be referring here not only to Marot's poetry but also to a transla-

tion into French he made of Erasmus's work in favor of educated women, published by Hélisenne's own publisher Denys Janot under the title of the *Colloque de l'abbé et la femme savante* (see Mustacchi, p. 120, n. 76).

27. Note that Hélisenne drops the third-person mask halfway through the sentence and reveals that the hypothetical ignorant and malicious person she refers to is actually Elenot himself.

28. At the close of her letter Hélisenne returns to a favorite theme, the natural kindness and goodness of women. As in *Les Angoysses*, she is inclined to believe all women merciful and quick to pardon offenses. To turn the tables on men who condemn women as weak, evil, or stupid she uses their own frequently cited authorities against them: Aristotle, Nature, Reason, and even the Catholic Church.

BIBLIOGRAPHY

Primary Works

Crenne, Hélisenne de. *Les Angoysses douloureuses qui procedent d'amours: Contenantz troys parties, Composees par Dame Hélisenne: Laquelle exhorte toutes personnes a ne suyvre folle Amour.* Paris, 1538. Reprint, with the addition of "Hélisenne aux lisantes." Lyon, 1539? Reprint of Lyon edition. Paris, 1541.

————. *Les epistres Familieres & invectives de ma dame Hélisenne, composees par icelle dame, De Crenne.* Paris, 1539.

————. *Les Epistres familieres de ma dame Hélisenne, de nouveau veues, corrigees oultre les precedentes Impressions. Les Epistres Invectives, de Madame Hélisenne, reveuës & corrigees de nouveau. Le Songe.* Paris, 1550.

————. *Les oeuvres de ma dame Hélisenne qu'elle a puis nagueres recogneues & mises en leur entier. Cest ascavoir les angoisses douloureuses qui procedent d'amours, Les Epistres familieres & invectives. Le songe de ladicte dame, le tout mieulx que par cy devant redigees au vray, & imprimees nouvellemet par le commandement de ladicte Dame De Crenne.* Paris, 1543. Reprint. Paris, 1544.

————. *Les oeuvres de ma dame Hélisenne de Crenne. A sçavoir, Les angoisses douloureuses qui procedent d'amours. Les Epistres familieres & Invectives. Le songe de ladicte dame. Le tout reveu et corrigé de nouveau par elle.* Paris, 1551. Reprints. Paris, 1553 and 1560. Geneva, 1977.

————. *Les quatre premiers livres des Eneydes du treselegant poete Virgile, traduictz de latin en prose Françoyse par ma dame Helisenne, à la traduction desquelz y a pluralité de propos qui par maniere de phrase y sont adjoustez: ce que beaucoup sert à l'elucidation et decoration desdictz livres, dirigez à tresillustre et tresauguste Prince Françoys, premier de ce nom invictissime Roy de France.* Paris, 1541.

————. *Le Songe de madame Hélisenne, composé par ladicte Dame, la consideration duquel est apte à instiguer toutes personnes de s'aliener de vice et s'approcher de vertu.* Paris, 1540. Reprint. Paris, 1541.

Demats, Paule, ed. *Les Angoysses douloureuses qui procedent d'amours (1538), Première partie.* Paris, 1968.

Mustacchi, Marianna M., and Paul J. Archambault, trans. and eds. *A Renaissance Woman: Hélisenne's Personal and Invective Letters.* Syracuse, New York, 1986.

Secor, Harry R., Jr., ed., "Hélisenne de Crenne: *Les Angoysses Douloureuses Qui Procedent D'Amours* (1538): A Critical Edition Based on the Original Text with Introduction, Notes, and Glossary." Ph.D. diss., Yale University, 1957.

Vercruysse, Jérôme, ed., *Les Angoysses douloureuses qui procedent d'amours, Première partie*. Paris, 1968.

Related Works

Agrippa, H. Cornelius. *De l'excellence et de la supériorité de la femme*. Trans. Roétitg. Paris, 1801.

———. *De nobilitate et praecellentia foeminei sexus*. Antwerp, 1529.

Baker, M. J. "Fiammetta and the *Angoysses douloureuses qui procedent d'amours*." *Symposium* 27, no. 4 (Winter 1973): 303–8.

———. "France's First Sentimental Novel and Novels of Chivalry." *Bibliothèque d'Humanisme et Renaissance* 36 (1974): 33–45.

Bergal, Irene May. "Hélisenne de Crenne: A Sixteenth-Century French Novelist." Ph.D. diss., University of Minnesota, 1966.

Berrong, Richard M. "Hélisenne de Crenne's *Les Angoisses Douleureuses Qui Procèdent D'Amours:* The Secularization of Reason." *The USF Language Quarterly* 22, nos. 1–2 (Fall–Winter 1983): 20–22.

Billon, François de. *Le fort inexpugnable de l'honneur du sexe feminin*, folios 35b–36a. Paris, 1555.

Charasson, Henriette. "Les origines de la sentimentalité moderne: d'Hélisenne de Crenne à Jean de Tinan." *Mercure de France* 86 (1910), 193–216.

Conley, Tom. "Feminism, *Écriture*, and the Closed Room: The *Angoysses douloureuses qui procedent d'amours*." *Symposium* 27, no. 4 (Winter 1973): 322–31.

Coulet, Henri. *Le roman jusqu'à la Révolution*. Vol. 1, pp. 104–6. Paris, 1967.

Dulac, Liliane. "Christine de Pisan et le Malheur des *Vrais Amans*." In *Mélanges de Langue et de Littérature Médiévales Offerts à Pierre Le Gentil*, pp. 223–33. Paris, 1973.

Dusevel, Hyacinthe. *Biographie des hommes célèbres du département de la Somme*. Vol. 1, pp. 209–11. Amiens, 1837.

———. *Lettres sur le département de la Somme*. Amiens, 1827.

Gosselin, Abbé J. *Mailly et ses seigneurs*, p. 305ff. Péronne, 1876.

Goujet, Abbé Cl.-P. *Bibliothèque Françoise*. Vol. 9, pp. 33–34. Paris, 1740–1756.

Guichard, J.-M. "Hélisenne de Crenne." *Revue du XIXe siècle* 2d ser., 8 (1840): 276–84.

Houston, John Porter. *The Traditions of French Prose Style: A Rhetorical Study*. Baton Rouge, 1981.

Johanneau, E., and E. Johanneau. *Rabelais: Oeuvres*. Variorum edition. Vol. 3, pp. 140–48. Paris, 1823.

Jordan, Mary Farr. "The *Angoysses Douloureuses* of Hélisenne de Crenne." Ph.D. diss., Harvard University, 1969.

King, Margaret L. "Book-Lined Cells: Women and Humanism in the Early Italian Renaissance." In *Beyond Their Sex: Learned Women of the European Past*, ed. Patricia H. Labalme, pp. 66–90, esp. pp. 68–69. New York, 1984.

La Monnoye. Cited by François La Croix du Maine, in *Bibliothèque Françoise*. Vol. 1, p. 362. Paris, 1772.

Le Duchat et La Monnoye. *Rabelais: Oeuvres*. Vol. 2, pp. 41–43. Amsterdam, 1711.

Lafranc, Abel. "A propos d'Hélisenne de Crenne." *Revue des Livres Anciens* 2 (1917): 376–77.

Loriente, Suzanne Marie-Marguerite. "L'Esthétique des *Angoysses Douloureuses Qui Procedent d'Amours* d'Hélisenne de Crenne." Ph.D. diss., University of Southern California, 1982.

Loviot, Louis. "Hélisenne de Crenne." *Revue des Livres Anciens* 2 (1917): 137–45.

Neubert, Fritz. "Antike und Christentum bei den ersten französischen Epistoliers der Renaissance, Hélisenne de Crenne und Estienne du Tronchet (1539 und 1569)." *Romanische Forschungen* 77 (1965): 1–41.

————. "Die französischen Briefschreiber der Renaissance und ihre Verleger." *Germanisch-Romanische Monatasschrift* 49, no. 18 (1968): 349–60.

————. "Hélisenne de Crenne (ca. 1500–ca. 1560) und ihr Werk. Nach den neuesten Forschungen." *Zeitschrift für Französische Sprache und Literatur* 80 (1970): 291–322.

Pasquier, Étienne. *Lettres,* folios 52b–53a. Paris, 1586.

Possenti, Antonio. "Hélisenne de Crenne nel secolo dei romantici e la prima conquista della critica." *Francia* 13 (January–March 1975): 27–40.

Reynier, Gustave. *Le roman sentimental avant l'Astrée,* pp. 99–122, 205–6. Paris, 1908.

Richardson, L. M. *The Forerunners of Feminism in French Literature of the Renaissance from Christine de Pisan to Marie de Gournay.* Baltimore, 1929.

Rumet, N., and F. Rumet. *De Abbavilla . . . .* In *N. and F. Rumet historiens d'Abbeville,* ed. E. Prarond, p. 37. Paris, 1902.

Saulnier, V.-L. "Quelques nouveautés sur Hélisenne de Crenne." *Bulletin de l'Association Guillaume Budé,* 4th ser., no. 4 (1964): 459–63.

Schmidt, A.-M. In *Histoire des Littératures.* Vol. 3, pp. 201–2. Paris, 1963.

Sturel, René. "La Prose poétique au XVIe siècle." In *Mélanges offerts par ses amis et ses élèves à M. Gustave Lanson,* pp. 47–60. Paris, 1922.

Vercruysse, Jérôme. "Hélisenne de Crenne: Notes biographiques." *Studi Francesi* 31 (January–April 1967): 77–81.

Waldstein, Helen. "Hélisenne de Crenne: A Woman of the Renaissance." Ph.D. diss., Wayne State University, 1965.

Willard, Charity Cannon. *Christine de Pizan: Her Life and Works.* New York, 1984.

————. "A New Look at Christine de Pizan's *Epistre au Dieu d'Amours.*" In *Secunda Miscellanea di Studi e Ricerche sul Quattrocento Francese,* comp. Franco Simone and ed. Jonathan Beck and Gianni Mombello, pp. 73–92. Chambéry-Torino, 1981.

THE LYONNAIS NEOPLATONIST

ernette Du Guillet

ANN ROSALIND JONES

Pernette Du Guillet was widely known before and after her early death at twenty-five in 1545, although she is now read less often than her fellow poets of Lyon Louise Labé and Maurice Scève. The seventy poems collected in her *Rymes* (1545) were obviously popular in their day. Well before their publication as an entire collection, two of her shorter poems had been printed, with music, in the Lyon songbook of Jaques Moderne, *Parangon des chansons, neufvième livre contenant xxxi chansons nouvelles* (1541). Her tenth chanson, "Conde claros de Adonis," figured in the debate stirred up by Joachim Du Bellay's *Deffence et illustration de la langue françoyse* (1549); Barthélemy Aneau and Guillaume Des Autelz wrote responses defending Pernette's use of a native French version of the form against Du Bellay's pro-classical critique.[1] *Les Rymes,* first published by Jean de Tournes in Lyon, was rapidly republished with expansions, twice in Paris (1546, 1547) and again in Lyon in 1552.

Antoine Du Moulin, the editor of the first edition of Pernette's poems, dedicated it to "the Ladies of Lyon," whom he addresses as admiring friends of Pernette's. It is quite possible that she did, in fact, have a feminine audience; it is also possible that Du Moulin was working to create one, as suggested by his complimentary remark that "the climate of Lyon" has always produced "a lively skill in the arts, in both sexes."[2] The remark is more than flattery. Pernette's training and fame as a poet were made possible by a combination of social and literary advantages which Lyon provided to women: its many publishers' willingness to experiment with both learned and popular texts; its geographic centrality as a crossroads for humanist and belletristic travelers on their way to and from Italy, Switzerland, and Germany; and above all, its concentration of intellectual life in informal private coteries in which women were apparently welcomed, rather than in the exclusively masculine terrain of universities (as in Paris). Like Louise Labé in her dedication to Clémence de Bourges,

Du Moulin appeals to a growing sense of civic pride as support for the literary work of women in Lyon.

Little is known of Pernette's short life (she was born about 1520 and died, probably of the plague, in 1545). But she must have been a daughter of the nobility or high bourgeoisie. Du Moulin praises her for her musical performances (she was "perfectly skilled on the lute, the spinet, and other instruments") and her linguistic virtuosity: she knew Italian and Spanish (more specifically, he mentions Tuscan and Castilian); she had mastered Latin and was studying Greek as well. The classical languages were unusual accomplishments for a woman, even an educated woman, and Pernette's family must have encouraged such study.[3] Little is known of the Monsieur Du Guillet whom she married in 1538; she had no children.

Pernette's career as a poet was deeply marked by her encounter, in the spring of 1536, with the Lyonnais poet Maurice Scève, whose collection of love poems, *Dèlie,* was published in the city in 1544. She would have been about sixteen, he in his early thirties. The two exchanged poems in an idealizing Neoplatonic dialogue: Scève praises her beauty and musicality; she praises his learning and eloquence. They compose poems on the same events: the exchange of a ring, a meeting by a fountain, an attack by gossips. Pernette identifies Scève explicitly in the wordplay of several poems, in epigram 5, for example, in which the line "ce vice mueras" (you will transform this vice) is also an anagram of Maurice Scève. And her name for him, "Mon Jour" (my day, daylight, sun), corresponds to the mythological scheme he establishes by calling the beloved of his sequence Délie: the goddess of Delos, Diana, the moon. The publication of Scève's 449 dizains may have prompted Du Moulin to collect Pernette's poems, which she had left, he says, in "rough drafts, in great disorder." He also claims that Pernette's "grieving husband" insisted that her poems be made public—a gesture that combined an implicit guarantee of the purity of the love she wrote about with an enactment of husbandly approval of her participation in Lyon's literary salons.

In spite of her editor's warning that the *Rymes* were left in an unadorned state, Pernette's poems are carefully finished and highly polished. One of her best modern critics, Verdun Saulnier, calculates that she wrote an average of a dozen poems a year (seventy, from 1537 to 1545), far fewer than she would have composed if she were offering them as light society entertainment;[4] and the variety of meters and genres in the collection, as well as its precision of language, contributes to the impression they give of leisurely, careful composition and revision. She often produces an effect of naive spontaneity, but it is a deliberate effect, depending on a knowing use of rhythm and often on a twist or reversal of earlier poets' themes.

Pernette uses a wide range of contemporary and traditional poetic modes. In contrast to Scève, whose unvarying ten-line epigrams establish and recycle an elaborate amorous vocabulary that combines Petrarchism and Neoplatonism with philosophy and science, Pernette purifies the mixture of love theories in the poetry of her time. She deemphasizes the suffering of the frustrated Petrarchan lover and insists on love as *amytié*, in analogy with Platonic *philia*, as the enlightened companionship, spiritual unity and mutual tranquility of two similar lovers (they are *pareils* and *semblables*), each of whom finds her/his own best self in the other.[5] She adds to this ideal of intellectual self-perfection the joking riddles and virtuoso wordplay of courtly poets, *rhétoriqueurs* such as Clément Marot (see her *épigrammes*). She takes themes and figures from the Alexandrian Greeks for a series of mythological narratives *(élégies)*. She returns to a variety of medieval verse forms for a dazzling set of metrically diverse songs *(chansons)*, in which she combines sophisticated classical imagery with popular refrains. She experiments with earlier satiric genres such as the *coq-à-l'âne* (a free-associative, obliquely phrased letter-poem) and the *mommerie* (a dialogue among allegorical figures), but she also follows the lead of the Lyonnais poets in their international project of studying and translating love theory; she writes verse paraphrases of such central Italian texts as Pietro Bembo's *Dialoghi d'amore* and of the translation by her fellow Lyonnais, Bonaventure des Périers, of Plato's *Lysis*.[6] It is difficult to know how many of the poems assembled in *Les Rymes* Pernette herself would have chosen for publication, but the collection as it stands suggests that she was widely read and flexible, and that she saw her poetic career not only as a dialogue with Scève but as an exploration of multiple forms and conventions.

In the poems she addresses to Scève as her mentor, nonetheless, she takes on the role of a meek disciple. This position fits smoothly into Neoplatonic love theory, which posits the spiritual refinement of both lovers as a process of mutual admiration and emulation. Pernette adds literary imitation to her courtship of Scève. She uses his verse form, the *dizain*, to praise his fluency and erudition (epigram 4); she vows to replace her ignorance with a new self modeled upon his (epigram 5); and she begs him to train her to write praise poems exactly like his (epigram 6). However humble these poems are, they nonetheless represent an appeal for education, for self-fashioning in a mode that will win fame and praise for the woman poet as well as the man.

And a pair of poems written by the two partners in this exchange suggests that Pernette's view of love is actually very different from that of her mentor. Where Scève's dizain 136 suggests erotic fusion and ineffable bliss, Pernette's eight-line epigram 13 emphasizes mutual duty and long-lasting spiritual satisfaction. Throughout her poems, she foregrounds the intellectual pleasure and the contented commitment she attributes to love, in contrast to Scève's dramas of sexual frustration and psychic torment. Pernette's version of Neoplatonism is imaged in metaphors of luminosity and brilliance, as a triumph over emotional and intellectual deprivation (epigram 2); its symptoms are serenity (epigram 8) and security (epigram 17). For Pernette, love represents access to knowledge, to public recognition, and to a position of equilibrium shared with her lover (chanson 9).

But *Les Rymes* contains many poems that make it a more complex and less stable sequence than its underlying love theory might promise. Pernette is often wittily irreverent; indeed, theoretical solemnity is one of her targets. She parodies the logic-chopping of courtly love puzzles by concluding one with her own commonsensical solution (epigram 24); she sets up ideal *amytié* as the premise for a quasi-legal problem, which she solves neatly in her own favor (epigram 26). In a series of elegantly spiteful jealousy poems, aimed as sharply at her lover as at her rival (who has been identified, thanks to Pernette's transparent puns, as Clémence de Bourges, Louise Labé's dedicatee),[7] she argues—disingenuously—that her own reticent loyalty deserves more recompense than the calculated outpourings of her rival (epigram 31); and there is far more wit than woe in her appeal to women in general to give erring lovers a taste of their own mistreatment (chanson 5). She enters swiftly into a contemporary debate about ideal mistresses by writing an airy self-defense against the kind of charges leveled at venal court ladies by Bertrand de La Borderie in his *Amye de Court* (Paris, 1542): the lilting refrain of her chanson 7 sets up a convincing counterpoint to outsiders' suspicions of an eloquent woman love poet. And in a long poem which impresses her recent commentator, Françoise Charpentier, as the most intriguing, double-voiced balance of sexuality and propriety in the collection,[8] she reworks classical mythology to write a long erotic fantasy in which she plays the role of a teasing, all-powerful Diana to Scève's Actaeon (elegy 2). Only in the final lines of this poem does she return to her posture of chaste obedience and poetic self-sacrifice, in a conventional mode that also appears at work in the resolution of the sequence as a whole. *Les Rymes* ends with two translations from Italian, a poem on despair and a recantation called "Confort." But such farewells to love were conventional concessions to Renaissance readers' sense of an ending rather than confessions of genuine disillusionment, and it is important to remember that Pernette never had the time to organize or conclude her sequence in her own terms.

In spite of her popularity during her lifetime, Pernette fell into relative obscurity during the centuries that followed. The poets of the Pléiade eclipsed those of the Lyonnais school, and the exclamatory Ovidian energy of Labé's sonnets outshone Pernette's more restrained lyrics and her reputation for modest propriety. During the nineteenth-century rediscovery of Renaissance poetry, Labé was taken up by Sainte-Beuve and Scève by Brunetière, but Pernette remained uncelebrated except for three small editions of her *Rymes* published in Lyon in 1830, 1856, and 1864. Again, during the twentieth-century reinterpretation of Scève as a proto-Mallarméan symbolist and of Labé as an early explorer of feminine passion, Pernette received little attention. Verdun Saulnier was the first to give her sustained critical attention, in his monograph published in *Bibliothèque d'humanisme et Renaissance* in 1944. Saulnier shifted from the usual emphasis on Pernette as adjunct to Scève to a thoughtful examination of her particular thematic concerns and stylistic invention. He attributes to her an active role in the interchange with Scève, arguing (contrary to other critics) that Pernette's epigram 13 was written as a correction of Scève's dizain 136.

Pernette has also benefited from recent structuralist interest in the Lyonnais coterie as a significant pre-Pléiade phenomenon, whose members emphasized collaborative work rather than the individualist reputation-building of later poets such as Ronsard (Risset). Comparative studies of the influence of Italian love theory on lyric in France have centered on her reinterpretations of the love philosophy of Leone Ebreo and Sperone Speroni (Perry, Soderstrom). Most recently, the feminist project of restoring women to literary history has led to a popular edition of Pernette's poems by Françoise Charpentier, who argues for a new appreciation of the interplay in *Les Rymes:* "Her songs bring into the rectilinear course of the epigram a space for free play and for the unexpected, the witty malice of the refrain, and even an overflow, startling in such highly abstract poetry, of a natural, direct freshness."[9]

Even in translation (though most pleasurably in the original), *Les Rymes* suggests that Pernette Du Guillet is a nuanced and unpredictably variable poet. Perhaps her early death prevented her from censoring or revising poems that did not conform to Renaissance ideologies of the meek and obedient private woman; perhaps, had she lived longer, she might have deepened her interrogations of the various love languages of her time. But her poems, as they stand, are evidence of a quick lyric receptivity, a restless, experimental mind-set, and a refusal—sometimes implicit, sometimes explicit, often gay, and sometimes acerbic—to be captured or frozen in any single poetic or intellectual system.

NOTES

1. Joachim Du Bellay, *Deffence et illustration de la langue françoyse*, ed. Chamard, p. 114. Chamard identifies Pernette's song as one of Du Bellay's targets, p. 114, n. 3; he cites the defenses by Aneau and Des Autelz, pp. 115–16, n. 1.

2. "Antoine Du Moulin aux Dames Lyonnoizes," in *Pernette Du Guillet: Rymes*, ed. Victor Graham (Geneva, 1968), p. 3.

3. Natalie Davis, in an overview of the educational opportunities of women of various classes in Lyon at this time, cites Guillaume Paradin's remark, in his *Mémoires de l'histoire*

de Lyon, that Pernette's knowledge of Latin set her "above and beyond the capacity of her sex." "City Women and Religious Change," in *Society and Culture in Early Modern France* (Palo Alto, 1975), p. 72, n. 18.

4. Verdun Saulnier, "Étude sur Pernette Du Guillet et ses *Rymes," Bibliothèque d'humanisme et Renaissance,* 4 (1944): 20.

5. For an argument that Neoplatonism satisfied ideological demands for women's chastity at the same time that it allowed women writers to represent more egalitarian relationships than those of Renaissance marriage, see my "Assimilation with a Difference: Renaissance Women Poets and Literary Influence," *Yale French Studies,* no. 62 (1981): 139–40. For a detailed study of Pernette's use of Italian love theory, see T. A. Perry, "Pernette Du Guillet's Poetry of Love and Desire," *Bibliothèque d'humanisme et Renaissance,* 35 (1973): 259–71, and Richard Alan Soderstrom, "The Poetry of Pernette du Guillet and Its Italian Sources and Inspirations," Ph.D. diss., Vanderbilt University, 1981.

6. Jacqueline Risset, focusing on Scève, argues that translation was a privileged genre among Lyonnais poets, in *L'Anagramme du désir,* pp. 80–82. Saulnier discusses Leone Ebreo and Plato's *Lysis* as sources for Pernette (p. 54).

7. Victor Graham sums up the evidence that Pernette's rival was Clémence de Bourges in his introduction to the *Rymes,* p. xv, and in his notes to epigram 36, p. 66.

8. Françoise Charpentier, preface to *Louise Labé, Oeuvres poétiques et Pernette du Guillet, Rymes* p. 23.

9. Ibid., p. 20.

From *Les Rymes*

EPIGRAM 4

Heavenly spirit, transformed by the gods
Into a mortal body sent to this world below,
You can be justly compared to Apollo
For the skillful force that flows forth from you.
Your eloquence and your elegant speech
And the high learning you devote yourself to
Show forth love's height, summed up in you.
For, in its sweetness, your free-flowing pen
Has rightly won you the world's praise and esteem,
Proof of your fluency and uplifting style.

EPIGRAM 5

Since you have deigned to make me renowned,
And through your writing, to force vice to reform,[1]
I shall try to increase the goodness in myself
That can alone transform me into you;
I shall discover how to make myself succeed
In making you see, through an even exchange,
That I will flee far from the vice of ignorance,
Since you have the desire to transform me

From black to white; and through such devotion,
Even when I wander, you will transmute this vice.[2]

EPIGRAM 6

In this ten-line verse, I openly declare
That I am unable to honor your virtues,
Except in my wishes, a feeble excuse;
But who, in writing, could do justice in full
To a man who can make the whole world adore him?
I do not say that if I had your skill,
I would not do my duty, as I ought;
At the least, I'd return the love you vow to me.
Lend me, then, your expert eloquence,
So that I can praise you as you now praise me.

EPIGRAM 13

The bliss of my pain, enflaming desire,
Distilled two hearts into one single duty,
So that one of us lives for the sweet suffering
That allows Death to hold the other in his power.
Blind god, you have given to us
The suffering in pleasure that leads on to honor;
Make us, as well, able to preserve
Long-lasting contentment, shared in our souls.[3]

EPIGRAM 2

The night was so dark, and so fearful to me
That it blotted out both earth and sky,
So that even at noon, I could not see
A single soul, which alarmed me very much.
But then, when I saw the dawn appear,
In a thousand colors, diverse and serene,
I felt so full of joy and ease
That I started to praise, in upraised voice,
The man who brought this light to the world.

EPIGRAM 8

It no longer matters to me
Whether daylight fades or night-time arrives;—
Wintry night, dark without a moon;

For none of that can harm me at all,
Because my Day, through loving, bright light,
Enlightens my whole soul; even at midnight
He makes me perceive, in my spirit-sense,
Things that my eyes could never have seen.

EPIGRAM 17

I am so happy, I cannot describe it,
For I've sounded the depth of his affection,
Through his skillful power, which makes me love him
More than beauty alone; for his grace and fluency
Make me believe that I am the first woman in the world.

CHANSON 9

I am the daytime,
    You, my love, the day,
That's turned me aside
    From every dreary way.
Loving the night is impossible for me.
She comes too ready for vice and venery:
But to be entirely yours,
    There lies my well-being,
For the goodness that is yours
    Supplies all true well-being.
There in darkest gloom,
Where nothing meets the eye
But death and doom,
Which terrify,
Souls still can revel in night,
For it brings lovers to delight.
But the wild bliss
    Of loose dalliance
Comes amiss
    In our alliance.
Our love is braced,
By good luck graced,
On virtue based,—
Equals enlaced.
Night-time cannot reveal a crime,
As daylight does, the forthright time
When sin's exposed,
Its harm outrun,

Its power deposed,
Its craft undone.
Sloth feeds on night,
   Which weakens men
But morning light
   Brings work again.
O blessed day, I praise your light,
I to whom you've brought clear sight,
The careful guide
Who's shown the ways,
Still bright and wide,
To night-time's strays.
Brightly lighted
   By this blessed day,
I'll be delighted
   Through my earthly stay.

EPIGRAM 24

To whom is a lover more deeply obliged,
To love itself, or rather to his lady?
For they together raise his devotion
To a height that is worthy of praise and fame.
To Love he owes his heart, to her his soul;
The soul, which constitutes life for them both.
One invites him to esteem, the other to delight.
And yet here is a most important point,
Which clarifies and solves this problem in my mind:
To wit: without a lady, Love would not exist at all.

EPIGRAM 26

Take as your premise that, because I belong to you
(And want to do so), you belong entirely to me:
Certainly because of this, our common bliss,
You would owe me the same rights I owe you.
And if Love should decide to break his law,
He still could not release us from our bond
Unless he were willing to perjure himself
And to commit assault on you, me and the gods.

EPIGRAM 31

I do not believe a word of what you said:
That you could feel as much desire for me

As you do for that woman, who, instead,
Is served by you, as you (and I) should be.

CHANSON 5

Ladies, if love's allowed
To wander and take wing
Away from what lovers vowed,
Let us try the same thing.
Then fickle hearts
Will learn faith's arts.

If they say we wander too free,
To convince us to return,
Let's keep on, courageously,
Their pleading let us spurn,
For their oaths of devotion
Belie true emotion.

If they try to claim
They were first forsaken,
So they're not to blame
Till vengeance is taken,
Remember, Love's our song,
And it puts them in the wrong.

If I had known at first
That love could play these games,
I'd not have felt the worst
Of passion's hottest flames.
I could have cooled them down
Had I known how I might drown.

It's no wonder at all
That our loves are unsure,
Since men are in thrall
To every new lure.
Their wandering ways permit us
As many lovers fit us.

But given our chance
To lead the dance,
Let us return
If true hearts can learn.
Love will relieve us,
Once lovers believe us.

CHANSON 7

If someone says I line my gown
With the golden rain that showered down
Inside Danaë's tower wall,
    I don't acknowledge that at all.

If someone says my loves are many,
That I don't say no to any,
Taking my pleasures where they fall,
    I don't acknowledge that at all.

If someone says my songs are sung
To the passionate rhythms that drive the young,
And that my love for you will pall,
    I don't acknowledge that at all.

But if it's said that Virtue's worth,
Which has clothed you since your birth,
Sparks your power to enthrall,
    That's the truth on which I call.

But if it's said my heart is charmed
By a pure love that never harmed
My honor or my soul at all,
    That's the truth on which I call.

ELEGY 2

How many times have I hoped, secretly,
to find myself, in summer's heat
as close as can be to the bright fountain
where my desire walks beside
the man who, in philosophy, trains
his noble spirit, in which I have such faith
that I wouldn't fear, without any companion,
to be alone in his company?
What am I saying? Alone? Rather, richly paired
with honor, which his virtue has won for him
from Apollo, the Muses, and a myriad nymphs,
who dedicate themselves to sacred works alone.
Then, when I had watched his gradual arrival,
I would let him speak to me in private;
little by little, I would draw away from him,
and, entirely nude, I would dive into the water.
But at the same time, I would like,

having properly tuned my little lute,
to sing a song to him,
to see a bit what response he would make.
But if he came directly toward me,
I would frankly allow him to approach,
and if he wanted, however slightly, to touch me,
I would throw at least a handful
of the pure water from the bright fountain
straight into his eyes, or at his face.
Oh, then might the water have the power
to change him into Actaeon,
not, however, so that he would be killed
and devoured by his dogs, like a deer
but so that he would feel he was my slave,
and so transformed into a servant
might he think and understand himself to be,
that Diana herself would envy me,
for having taken her power away from her.
How fortunate and splendid I should say I was!
Certainly, I would esteem myself a goddess.
But finally, to satisfy my desire,
would I really want to cause displeasure
to Apollo and also to his Muses,
by depriving them and leaving them bereft
of a man who can serve them exactly to their taste
and bring glory to their lofty, holy chorus?
Away, my hopes!—away with such
a high ambition; it does not belong to me.
Let him go, to serve the nine Muses,
l must not insist on enslaving him to me,
to me, who lacks both grace and merit.
Let him go; let me not anger Apollo,
filling him with powerful divinity
so that he stirs up the whole world against me,
which, one day, expects through my love's writing
to be, along with me, blessed and content.

NOTES TO THE TRANSLATION

1. The French line ends with an anagram of Scève's name, in capital letters: "VICE A SE MUER."

2. The concluding line in French offers another anagram of Maurice Scève: "CE VICE MUERAS."

3. Compare Scève's dizain 136, from *Délie* (my translation):

The bliss of our bliss, enflaming desire,
Unites a double soul into one joined power:
One soul, dying, lives in the sweet pain
That has brought the other, living, to death.
Blind god, you have given to us
Without any other agreement or consent,
And let us possess, without any regret,
The joy of suffering that leads to desire.
Preserve our sensation of such sweet death
As long as we share the breath of life.

BIBLIOGRAPHY

Primary Works

Du Bellay, Joachim. *Deffense et illustration de la langue françoyse.* Ed. Henri Chamard. Paris, 1948. Reprint. Paris, 1966.
Du Guillet, Pernette. *Poésies.* Lyon, 1830. Reprint. Geneva, 1970.
————. *Rymes.* Ed. Victor Graham. Geneva, 1968.
————. *Rymes.* In *Louise Labé, Oeuvres poétiques, et Pernette Du Guillet, Rymes,* ed. Françoise Charpentier. Paris, 1983.
Scève, Maurice. *La Délie.* Ed. I. D. McFarlane. London, 1965.

Related Works

Aynard, Joseph. *Les Poetes lyonnais, précurseurs de la Pléiade.* Paris, 1929.
Baur, Albert. *Maurice Scève et la Renaissance lyonnaise.* Paris, 1906.
Charpentier, Françoise. Preface to *Louise Labé, Oeuvres poétiques, et Pernette Du Guillet, Rymes.* Paris, 1983.
Giudice, Enzo. *Le Opére minori di Maurice Scève.* Parma, 1958.
————. *Scève, poeta de la "Délie."* Rome, 1965.
Jondorf, Gillian. "Petrarchan Variations in Pernette du Guillet and Louise Labé." *Modern Language Review,* 71 (October 1976).
Jones, Ann Rosalind. "Assimilation with a Difference: Renaissance Women Poets and Literary Influence." *Yale French Studies,* no. 62 (1981).
Miller, Joyce. *Convention and Form in the "Rymes" of Pernette du Guillet.* Ph.D. diss., University of Pennsylvania, 1977.
Perry, T. A. "Pernette Du Guillet's Poetry of Love and Desire." *Bibliothèque d'humanisme et Renaissance,* 35 (1973).
Risset, Jacqueline. *L'Anagramme du désir: essai sur la "Délie" de Maurice Scève.* Rome, 1971.
Saulnier, V.-L. *Maurice Scève.* Paris, 1948.
————. "Etude sur Pernette Du Guillet et ses *Rymes.*" *Bibliothèque d'humanisme et Renaissance* 4 (1944).
Schmidt, A. M. "Poètes lyonnais du seizième siècle." *Information littéraire* 4 (1952).
Soderstrom, Richard Alan. "The Poetry of Pernette du Guillet and Its Italian Sources and Inspirations." Ph.D. diss., Vanderbilt University, 1981.
Wéber, Henri. *La Création poëtique au seizième siècle en France.* Paris, 1956.

es Dames des Roches

ANNE R. LARSEN

"It seemed to me the very hallmark of the Renaissance that middle class and aristocratic males began to feel that they possessed such shaping power over their lives, and I saw this power and the freedom it implied as an important element in my own sense of myself. But as my work progressed, I perceived that fashioning oneself and being fashioned by cultural institutions—family, religion, state—were inseparably intertwined." Stephen Greenblatt, in his conclusion to *Renaissance Self-Fashioning*,[1] could have said these words equally well of certain middle-class and aristocratic women during the Renaissance. To none are they more aptly fitting than to the Dames des Roches, "mere et fille." Celebrated by their contemporaries,[2] but mentioned only in passing by later historians of literature and cultural history, their writings have yet to be brought out of the shadows. These include *Les Oeuvres* (1578, with additions in 1579), *Les Secondes Oeuvres* (1583), and *Les Missives* (1586).[3] As upper middle-class educated women, they seized the opportunity that their bourgeois predecessor Louise Labé had proclaimed was their due: "It seems to me," said Labé, "that those women who have the opportunity ought to use that honorable freedom which our sex desired so much in former times to learn the arts and sciences."[4] They realized that owing to circumstances, to their milieu, and to the advantages of their social and financial position, they had a choice. Catherine des Roches chose not to marry so as to pursue a leisurely life of learning with her mother. Madeleine des Roches, in the face of numerous difficulties, chose to reject a fatalistic bent and affirm her ability to shape her existence. In words of comfort to a friend, she asserts: "I believe that happiness depends only on us / Madam, and that each of us can forge his own destiny" (1583, folio Bi).

Both Dames des Roches lived their entire lives in and around the city of Poitiers. Madeleine Neveu (ca. 1520–1587), in 1539 married André Fradonnet, a lawyer active in local politics, who died eight years later. A son and daughter also died in early infancy. Catherine Fradonnet (1542–1587) remained the sole surviving daughter. Madeleine was remarried in 1550 to François Eboissard, seigneur de la Villée and des Roches, a lawyer and one of seventy-five bourgeois elected to the municipal governing board of Poitiers. We know little of Madeleine's life during the 1540s and 1550s except what she reveals in ode 1 translated here. She refers briefly to youthful aspirations cut short by marriage and household concerns. She may have participated in Poitiers's first period of literary renewal from 1545 to 1555 when humanists such as Jacques Pelletier, Jacques Tahureau, Jean-Antoine de Baïf and others brought even greater fame to Poitiers's already solid reputation as a humanist center. One of her primary concerns during these years must have been her daughter's education, which was unique both for the times and for her milieu. It was customary for daughters of the upper bourgeoisie to be sent to convents or, more rarely, to be instructed by male parents and tutors. Catherine des Roches, while probably tutored by some of the leading humanists of Poitiers,[5] was guided and inspired primarily by her mother to the awe of her contemporaries. Both their works and their partnership in presiding over the *salon* that would bring them national fame testify to the dialogue in which they continuously exchanged ideas. Many *elogia* after their death convey the unusual nature of their intellectual bond. Scévole de Sainte-Marthe writes of his admiration on seeing "the mother instruct the daughter and speak to her of all the sciences with as much authority as ease."[6] In an elegy on the death of the Dames des Roches, Lois le Grand relates how in *salon* debates:

> The mother would let her dearest daughter
> Show to a listener how well-versed she was.
> On the pretense that she [the mother] had forgotten a point
> Her daughter would instantly in fluent speech
> Recount the lines of the forgotten passage
> Which her mother knew as well as she.[7]

It is clear from her "Epistle to My Daughter" that Madeleine Neveu was devoted to humanist educators' views on the mother's crucial role in the upbringing of children. As Vives wrote, women should "study . . . if nat for her own sake, at the least wyse for her chyldren, that she maye teache them and make them good."[8] But she deliberately disregarded the strictly utilitarian goals of female education. Nowhere does she enjoin her daughter to aspire to the traditional feminine virtues of humility, silence, and obedience to husband. Her motto could have been the obverse of Vives's injunction: Study for your own sake, she would have said. She frequently admonishes her daughter to seek out fame and immortality through her writings, both rewards of disciplined study. Madeleine Neveu sought no less than to have her daughter be known for herself.[9]

During the 1560s the religious wars exacerbated the legal difficulties that the Dames des Roches experienced until their death.[10] The Protestants of Poitiers destroyed half the city in an uprising in 1562 and, in the siege of the city against the troups of Colligny in 1569, Madeleine Neveu lost two town houses, a loss great enough for her to request a decade later an indemnity from the royal treasury. These were the years, however, when their friendships with local humanists, legists, and poets led them to establish a *salon*. The first evidence of their literary activities appeared in 1571 with the publication of Caye-Jules de Guersens's *Panthée,* to which Madeleine wrote a liminary poem and which Guersens gallantly claimed was originally the work of Catherine. As her suitor, he may have wished, with such an attribution, to sway her toward marriage. In 1574, Catherine circulated an ode to Henry III, newly crowned king. Scévole de Sainte-Marthe translated it into Latin and Joseph-Juste Scaliger into Greek.

Catherine des Roches attracted not only scholars to the *salon* but suitors as well. After Guersens, Claude Pellejay dedicated to her an unpublished volume of amorous sonnets and stanzas. George Diller argues that the Sincero of Catherine's "Sonnets de Sincero et Charite" and "Dialogue de Sincero et Charite" (1579) was in fact Claude Pellejay and that, more important, the sonnets addressed to Charite—a pseudonym for Catherine[11]—were probably written by Pellejay.[12] That Pellejay could have been the lover des Roches had in mind is possible in spite of her several remonstrances to the contrary.[13] That the sonnets of Sincero were written by Pellejay and that the "Dialogue de Sincero et Charite" represents a collaboration between the two lovers (Diller, p. 46) is unlikely. The evidence Diller offers is shortsighted: according to this critic, Catherine could not possibly have sung her own praises "unless she had incredible pride" (p. 41), and Sincero's poems depict a less than perfect lover contrary to des Roches's intention in her dedicatory epistle of depicting a perfect suitor. Diller does not consider that des Roches's concerns in her sonnet sequence and dialogue are largely rhetorical and thematic: rhetorical in that she is reworking a conventional structure combining the dynamics of the virtuously aloof mistress of the Neoplatonic tradition with the plot of the unfaithful lover; thematic in that the heroine as chaste learned woman is a staple of des Roches's works. Charite's adamant plea that her lover be above all sincere and faithful, coupled with her fear of abandonment, make her a forerunner of the Princess of Clèves.

In 1577 the ambulatory court resided at Poitiers for three months and brought along the learned gathering of the Palace Academy. The Dames des Roches could have been introduced at court and may have composed at that time several poems in honor of Queen Louise of Lorraine, the Queen Mother Catherine of Medicis, and the King. These were among the many pieces included the following year in their first volume of collected works published by Abel l'Angelier in Paris.[14] This edition was soon followed in 1579 by a second edition containing additional pieces. Madeleine Neveu's dedicatory epistle to this edition is addressed enigmatically "aux dames" (to the ladies). Who were these ladies? It is tempting to think that they constituted primarily Parisian bourgeois and court "doctes dames" in whose capital the Poitevines ladies were testing their mettle for the first time. Two reasons could have impelled the Dames des Roches to address them so. They published their works the year after they were likely introduced to members of the King's entourage. Publishing in the capital would have been a reminder of that fortunate occurrence. Secondly, as Diller suggests (p. 77), they would have found a larger and more sympathetic audience in an environment where the phenomenon of the learned woman and women's participation in the *salons* and Palace Academy were not exceptional occurrences.[15] Madeleine des Roches's epistle, however, is addressed to two different audiences. She first addresses ladies whom she depicts as possibly contemptuous of her "lowly" verse and to whom she is indebted in friendship: "[I] assure you of the true friendship which I have always borne you (my ladies), that is if some of you deign to read my humble verse." It is possible to identify these ladies as superior in status and even erudition and as part of the Parisian audience whose criticism des Roches forestalls. It was indeed unusual for provincial learned women coming from a city in which there was a thriving printing industry to publish their works in Paris.[16] But des Roches's ensuing portrait indicates female readers of yet a different sort. This second group objects that she should not be writing at all for "silence, the ornament of women, can cover over the errors of the tongue and the understanding." It adopts the moralizing stance of opponents in the *querelle des femmes*. These readers differ substantially from the Parisian "ideal reader" whose patronage des Roches hopes to interest. A clue as to the identity of this audience can be found in ode 3, also addressed "aux dames." There Madeleine criticizes those women who disparage their learned counterparts:

> Some having the tongue of a Satyr,
> Who spend their time in slander
> Will always say: It suffices
> For a *woman* who is wise to spin and do her housework.
> One gets more profit from that.

Others derive importance from quarrels and fine clothes. Des Roches summons these ladies to more worthy occupations:

But far more worthy
Of the Poitevine lady
Than handsome accouterment
Is her custom now
Of choosing ink and pen
For learned use.

In such a manner, she continues, these ladies can avenge themselves of calumny "sans mendier l'écrivain" (without begging a writer to do it for them). Des Roches's inclusion of provincial female readers who are inferior in aspiration to Parisian learned women is a tactical ploy to assure herself the esteem of the latter and to herald those among the Poitevines who like her are part of a new "docte echole" (ode 3).

This "school" of learning or "academy of honor," as the *salon* of the Dames des Roches was so frequently called, acquired further prestige when, soon after the publication of the second edition of their works in 1579, the assizes or "grands jours" brought to Poitiers for three months Parisian humanists and legists accompanied by their wives and children. Henry III commissioned these influential legists, known as the "érudits du roi," to relieve the congestion of the local courts as a result of the property damages caused by the civil wars. On their arrival at Poitiers, two of the lawyers, Estienne Pasquier and Antoine Loisel, headed for the home of the Dames de Roches whose reputation had reached educated circles in Paris. In Pasquier's words: "We had hardly reached Poitiers, Monsieur Loisel and I, that I told him so as not to be idle (our 'grand jours' had not yet opened) that we should visit Mesdames des Roches, mother and daughter, truly an honor both of the city of Poitiers and of our century."[17] Their ensuing conversation with the ladies produced, as Clark Keating aptly puts it, "one of the most famous episodes in sixteenth-century social history" (p. 55). Pasquier chanced to see a flea parked on the bosom of the spirited Catherine. As he was beginning to run out of *propos,* he suggested that they immortalize the flea in poetic exchange. The idea caught on with the habitués of the *salon* who soon produced innumerable *blasons* punning in Latin, Greek, Spanish, and French, on the peregrinations of the "puce" (flea) over the body of the fair "pucelle" (maiden). Catherine readily joined this context of wit and *gauloiserie,* but even in such a context her thematic concerns remain consistent. In the first poem she wrote as repartee to Pasquier, she embroiders on the Ovidian tale of the metamorphosis of the nymph Syrinx into a reed to escape the pursuit of Pan. Similarly her flea, once a nymph, eluded marriage through metamorphosis and now seeks refuge with Catherine.[18]

Social historians have commented on the lack of distinction between "academy" and "salon" in regard to the group of the Dames des Roches, which accounted for its mixture of frivolity and seriousness, gallic humor and moralism.[19] Keating emphasizes, however, that the household of the Poitevine scholars resembled much more that of the Parisian humanist Jean de Morel and the learned court of Marguerite of France than the brilliant court salons of the reign of Charles IX and Henry III (p. 141). The frequent serious discussions that occurred likely inspired some of the works of the hostesses (p. 59). The feminist dialogues of Catherine des Roches, "Dialogue de Placide et Severe" and "Dialogue d'Iris et Pasithee" (1583), could have emanated from lively debates over the role of women in society and the goals of female education. These dialogues are striking for two reasons. First, they synthesize three prevailing views in the formal controversy of the *querelle des femmes:* the age-old traditionalism of the misogynist (Severe), the well-intentioned paternalism of the humanist (Placide), and the independence of the feminist (Pasithee). The last category is not exclusive to women, as Linda Woodbridge has pointed out in her perceptive analysis of the defenses of Cornelius Agrippa and Castiglione, "the only two [major Renaissance theorists] to embrace beliefs fundamental to modern feminism."[20] Second, these dialogues defend the single woman who pursues a life of learning. The arguments of Placide and Severe on the social function of women are summed up early in the dialogue: Severe says, "For all [women] to men are adversary." Placide replies, "But all to men are necessary" (folio 35v). Placide defends primarily the usefulness of education for women. When asked how his daughter Pasithee has benefited from learning, he praises above all her obedience to him and to her duty. She behaves "as I want her to, and as it seems to me she should" (folio 35v). Unlike Severe's promiscuous daughter Iris who is always outdoors and refuses to attend to the *ménage,* Pasithee remains in her room, alone, with her "lutes and violas" and her "beautiful maxims from Plutarch and Seneca flying about on the wings of her thoughts and words" (p. 36). In nature she is like her deceased mother, who was to Placide an ideal wife. Keating assumes that Placide advances the point of view of des Roches in the *querelle.*[21] This leads him, however, to argue erroneously that des Roches "pretends" that the aim of female education is to make of women better housewives, more obedient to their husbands, when throughout her lifetime she was devoted to learning for its own sake. (p. 63). Des Roches presents here not so much her own perspective as the educational views of humanists such as Erasmus, Vives, and More who valorize marriage more than the ideal of celibacy. This dialogue between two fathers is a conventional piece typical of the pro and con positions on women's role in society. That Placide presents humanist educational views is clear from the books he advises women to read, Plutarch's *Precepts of Marriage* and Xenophon's *Economicus,* the two most influential ancient texts in the sixteenth century on women's domestic roles. Echoing Plutarch he proclaims the wife must be a mirror reflecting the thoughts, words, and actions of her husband (folio 38r). He follows this with advice on how Severe can transform his wife into a sweet-tempered companion. His views are reminiscent of Erasmus's colloquy *Coniugium* (Marriage), in which two wives discuss ways to win back the respect of a husband. The dialogue ends with Placide's traditional Boccaccian catalog of ancient virtuous wives, mothers, daughters, and learned women. However, Placide's even longer catalog of contemporary scholarly women directly reveals Catherine des Roches's pride in women who overcame, for the most part, marital and social obstacles to win renown for themselves.[22]

> It suffices that I present to her [Pasithee] names and examples of which our century has many: the erudite Sigea, whose beautiful poem entitled "La Ceintre" should encompass the agreeable abode of the Muses; and Laura Terracina, whose name known to the ends of the earth will never die. But what shall I say of Morata, who worthily received from heaven the name of Olympia? And how can I express the reverence I bear for the memory of the beautiful, noble and virtuous Hippolyta Taurella, whose plaintive elegies gave so much pleasure and sorrow to her absent husband? In what fashion can I worthily speak of sincere Proba, who appropriating the verse of that excellent poet suited the most striking lines to divine mysteries? She thus displayed her own good judgment and the wealth of the poet. I must not forget Clémence Isore, whose generosity endowed Toulouse each year with the beautiful flower of the eglantine awarded to the poet who composed the best Christian hymn. (folio 42v)

He then praises the talents of the learned Diane de Morel who had died in 1581.[23]

The "Dialogue d'Iris et Pasithee," translated here almost in its entirety, contains des Roches's most personal statement on the status of the chaste learned woman. Pasithee is a poet and musician with no interest in marriage. She is acutely aware of the isolation her vocation has brought her. She thus joyfully welcomes Iris's company but has to contend with the latter's naive prejudice and the criticism that Iris has heard around her concerning the "femme sçavante." If Catherine des Roches was ever criticized, it could have been over her refusal to marry and her wish to remain with her mother. It is difficult to assess just what her contemporaries thought because their comments generally occur in *elogia*. Sainte-Marthes refers to the "incredible consensus of character" between mother and daughter that caused them not to want even death to separate them.[24] I have found only one critical statement from the pen of Pasquier who, in his second private letter to Pierre Pithou on the *salon* of the Dames des Roches, remarks that he is displeased by the fact that Catherine, though assiduously courted, "is resolved to live and to die with her mother" (letter 8, p. 20). His displeasure lies primarily in his concern that she will remain childless and the last of her clan. Post-Freudian critics have read into the filial relationship the notion of abnormality (Diller, p. 52). Gabriel Pérouse speculates about a "troublante identification" between them and queries: "Could a certain fear of man have been sublimated (which would explain a good portion of the work?" (p. 219). It is more likely that Catherine rejected marriage because she did not wish to renounce her literary aspirations.

Catherine des Roches was well aware, as a learned woman, of the ambivalence of her age toward women scholars. One prevalent image was that of the learned woman as "armed maiden," a synthesis of Pallas Athena, virgin goddess of war and wisdom, and of the Amazons, mythical female warriors hostile to patriarchal structures. This image reflected the male humanist's ambivalence to the anomalous erudite woman, much as today some professional women in all-male organizations are attributed the role of the militant and unapproachable "iron maiden."[25] Both the Amazons and Pallas Athena are dramatized in Catherine des Roches's work. Two poems, "Pour une mascarade d'Amazones" and "Chanson d'Amazones," project warrior women who, like male rulers, aggressively invoke fame, glory, and absolute governance. In the first poem, des Roches singles out for praise the Amazon Orithya for her traditional identification with her mother and her vow to perpetual virginity. Des Roches may have transposed herself in this triumphant virgin warrior whose mother founded the earliest and most famous of matriarchal societies. In the second, the warriors sing their sexual inviolability that enables them to exchange customary female practices such as spinning for weapons of war. But these Amazons are anomalous in des Roches's work. She may have considered the notion of gynocracy, a highly controversial subject at the time, only to reject it for a more moderate position. She explores such a position in the story of Agnodice and in her sonnet "To My Distaff."

Des Roches's source for "L'Agnodice" is a myth of Hyginus (*Fabula*, p. 274) in which Agnodice's medical skill convinces the Athenians to change the law forbidding women to study obstetrics. Des Roches expands this brief account into a lengthy poem in which Agnodice, having defied the law, reinscribes norms acceptable to her culture. Unlike the fiery Amazons, she reinstates peace and harmony between the sexes. And most important, she veils her rebellion with signs of womanly modesty. Her feminism is a "muted text,"[26] a veiled subversive strategy in the struggle for female learning. In "To My Distaff," des Roches likens the distaff to the pen. Rather than relegate the spindle to an inferior status as was so frequently done by Renaissance male and female writers, she elevates it to a privileged position. She bestows the honor hitherto applied only to letters upon the underrated realm of feminine work.

The Dames des Roches's conciliatory feminism, the fact that they were praised for both their writings and their *ménage,*[27] parallels their conservative political and religious beliefs. They reciprocated the views of the humanists who attended their salon. Donald Kelley describes the latter aptly: "They were philologists as well as patriots, as devoted to the muses as they were to the monarchy."[28] As part of the new emerging class of the "noblesse de robe," they aimed primarily at strengthening national consciousness and the glory of the weak monarchy. Their motto was the old Gallican formula: "To live under one God, one King, one faith, one law" (Kelley, p. 254). They belonged to the party of the moderns who defended the superiority of French culture. They were staunch Catholics, outspoken enemies of the reform movement, and pacifists. The Dames des Roches reflect these ideas in their works. Madeleine's nationalistic zeal led her to protest the prospective marriage of the duke of Alençon, younger brother of Henry III, to Queen Elizabeth (folio 31r). She affirms the divine right of kings (1579, first sonnet, p. 33), and expounds on the progress of the sciences as well as France's superiority over all nations (1579, folios 30v, 39v). Both denounce the Protestant movement and the ravages of the civil wars. Like Pasquier, however, who was uniformly polite in his letters to numerous Protestant scholars, they were on friendly terms with the Protestant humanists Joseph-Juste Scaliger, François de Saint-Vertunien, and Agrippa d'Aubigné.

The Dames des Roches were fully integrated and highly appreciated by a community of humanists, scholars, and poets. Strongly nationalistic, their colleagues prized learned women who could spread the fame of Poitiers and of France beyond its borders. These Poitevine worthies were thus unusual in comparison to other Renaissance learned women. Unlike their earlier Italian counterparts, they were not isolated or pressured to renounce their vocation. Unlike later scholarly women such as Charlotte de Bracchart, Anna Maria van Shurman, or Marie de Gournay[29] who encountered great opposition to their pursuit of learning they were admired at court and encouraged by fellow humanists to write and publish. Their works provide a fascinating glimpse into the development of early modern feminism and evidence of the great vitality of humanist learning among members of the provincial upper bourgeoisie and "noblesse de robe."

NOTES

1. Stephen Greenblatt, *Renaissance Self-Fashioning,* p. 256.

2. Contemporaries such as Estienne Pasquier, Caye Jules de Guersens, Joseph-Juste Scaliger, Scévole de Sainte-Marthe, Peletier Du Mans, Agrippa d'Aubigné, and Marie de Romieu lauded the Dames des Roches in their writings. See George Diller, *Les Dames des Roches,* pp. 1–54.

3. *Les Oeuvres* (1578, 1579) and *Les Missives* (1586) were published in Paris by Abel l'Angelier, and *Les Secondes Oeuvres* (or *Nouvelles Oeuvres*) (1583) in Poitiers by Nicolas Courtoys. References to poems, dialogues, and epistles within these works will include parenthetically the date of the work in which they appear (1579, 1583, or 1586). All translations are mine. The collection of *La Puce* (1582) contains several poems by the Dames des Roches which likewise appear in *Les Secondes Oeuvres*. Luce Guillerm has included several excerpts from their works in his *La Femme dans la littérature française et les traductions en français au XVIe siècle* (pp. 263–83). These excerpts, however, contain errors of transcription.

4. Dedicatory epistle to Melle Clémence de Bourges, *Oeuvres complètes*, p. 48. The Dames des Roches knew Labé's works. Madeleine's first publication included poetry printed at the end of a volume containing Labé's *Débat de Folie et d'Amour* and published in Paris in 1578. This volume has since been lost.

5. Catherine was probably tutored in Latin by someone other than her mother, for Scaliger notes that even though the latter, in his opinion, was more learned than her daughter, she knew only French (cited by Diller, p. 13). Catherine became an excellent Latinist, for she published first translations of two works: Pythagoras's *Symbola* translated as *Les Enigmes de Pythagore* (1583, folios 14v–18v) and Claudian's *De raptu Proserpinae* translated as *Le Ravissement de Proserpine* (1586, folios 41–66).

6. Scévole de Sainte-Marthe, *Eloges des hommes illustres*, p. 339.

7. Lois Le Grand, *Elégie sur le trespas de Mesdames des Roches de Poitiers mere et fille*, p. 6.

8. Juan Luis Vives, *Instruction of a Christen Woman* (1529), cited by Betty Travitsky, "The New Mother of the English Renaissance: Her Writings on Motherhood," in *The Lost Tradition: Mothers and Daughters in Literature*, ed. C. Davidson and E. M. Brown (Ungar, 1980), p. 34.

9. Knowing how much her daughter loved her studies, Madeleine des Roches may in fact have encouraged her not to marry. In a sonnet to a bereaved friend, she lauds the happiness that all women, single, married, or widowed can find for "happiness depends on one's state of mind," not on one's marital status (1583, folio Biv).

10. Madeleine des Roches refers in four instances ("Epistle to My Daughter," second sonnet on page 28, first sonnet on page 38, and sonnet on page 53, all in the edition of 1579) to an unspecified law suit that lasted for thirteen years.

11. It was fashionable for *salon* women to adopt pseudonyms. The learned Maréchale de Retz, whose courtly *salon* flowered for several decades (ca. 1567–1603), was addressed sometimes as Dictynne or as Pasithee. It was to her that Pontus de Tyard dedicated the 1575 edition of his philosophical prose dialogue *Solitaire premier,* in which Solitaire is enamored of Pasithee, the leader of the Muses and representative of the Graces. Catherine des Roches may have been influenced by this work while writing her "Dialogue d'Iris et Pasithee"— Tyard was the main lecturer at the sessions of the Palace Academy in Poitiers (Sealy, pp. 87, 92). Just as Tyard's Pasithee represents the union of poetry and music, so des Roches's heroine is a musician and a poet. *Pasithee* was also the title of a play that Guersens was thought to have composed and to which Madeleine refers in her *Missives* (folio 14r). Charite was the other name for the Graces and was frequently used by poets in an address to the beloved. Ronsard calls Marie "ma Charite" (*Oeuvres,* vol. 1, p. 127) and addresses Marguerite of France, whose patronage was widely sought out by the poets of the Brigade, as Charite and Pasithee ("Chant Pastoral a Madame Marguerite de France," *Oeuvres,* vol. 1, p. 968).

12. Diller, p. 45. Marcel Raymond argues the same point in *L'Influence de Ronsard,* p. 209, note 3.

13. In two instances, des Roches forcefully contends that Sincero is pure invention. In her "Epistle to Her Mother" (1579), she addresses critics who argue that it is not proper for women to write love poetry: "If [she] is in love," they assert, "[she] should not say so," to

which des Roches replies, "I am not in love nor do I pretend to be, for I wrote what I thought and not what I saw in Syncero whom I know only in my imagination" (see my "Catherine des Roches' 'Epistre a sa mere' [1579]"). Elsewhere she claims that Sincero is "my creature" and that she should not envy Ronsard's praise of Sincero nor Charite's happiness in having such a friend (Missives, letter 4, folio 31v).

14. All were included except Madeleine's ode to the king, which was first printed in the 1579 edition of the Oeuvres.

15. Five illustrious salons flourished in Paris throughout the second half of the sixteenth century. See Clark Keating's Studies on the Literary Salon in France. On the women who participated in the sessions of the Palace Academy (1576–1579), see Robert Sealy, The Palace Academy of Henry III, pp. 12–21, and Frances Yates, The French Academies, p. 32.

16. See Hope Glidden, The Storyteller as Humanist, chapter 1 on the printing industry and readerships in Poitiers under Henry III.

17. "Lettre a M. Pithou," in Choix de lettres sur la littérature, la langue et la traduction, ed. Dorothy Thickett (Geneva, 1966), book 6, letter 7, 13.

18. La Puce, pp. 9–13.

19. Alexander H. Schutz, "The Group of the Dames des Roches in Sixteenth-Century Poitiers," PMLA 48 (1933):651; Diller, p. 74.

20. Linda Woodbridge, Women and the English Renaissance, p. 59.

21. Critics have hitherto placed far more emphasis on the "Dialogue of Placide and Severe" than on its sequel, the "Dialogue of Iris and Pasithee," on the assumption that it presents the fullest expression of des Roches's feminist viewpoint. See Diller, pp. 134–37; Lula Richardson, The Forerunners of Feminism, p. 135; and Gabriel Pérouse, Les Nouvelles françaises du seizième siècle, p. 223. Luce Guillerm includes an excerpt from the "Dialogue de Placide and Severe" but does not even mention the women's dialogue.

22. In three other instances, Placide expresses views peculiar to des Roches's oeuvre. To Severe's outburst that a "femme sçavante" is a "monstre," Placide paradoxically lauds such "monstrous" women for their vow to perpetual virginity and their desire to "get along without men" (folio 37r). He asserts that women should be allowed to use the spindle and the pen for "one of these tasks aids the other. Pallas practiced both" (folio 37v). Finally, he argues that truly learned women do not chase after men: "rather, if they remain single, they behave honorably, or if they marry, they live in peace with their husbands" (folio 42r).

23. Catherine des Roches's compilation thus includes two French érudites, Diane de Morel, the youngest daughter of the Parisian humanist Jean de Morel (whose salon was popular with the Pléiade poets), and Clémence Isore, who instituted the Academie des jeux floraux of Toulouse (Du Verdier, Bibliothèque, p. 219); Luisa Sigea, the Spanish Latin tutor at the court of Portugal, whose Latin poem Sintra was published by Jean Nicot in 1566; and four Italian humanists, Laura Terracina, known for her commentary on Orlando Furioso (1551), Olympia Morata (see Margaret King "Book-Lined Cells," p. 82), Cassandra Fedele, whom Catherine mentions later in the dialogue and lauds in letter 24 of the Missives (folio 26r) in connection with Angelo Poliziano's famous éloge, and Hyppolita Taurella, whose Epistola ad maritum suum Baltasarem Castillionem (1525) des Roches could have read in an edition of Morata's Opera Omnia (Basle, 1562, 1570). Interestingly, the central theme of Torella's elegy is a wife's unrequited love for an absent and possibly unfaithful Castiglione. As to Proba, the anonymous annotator of the copy of des Roches's Oeuvres (1579) at the Bibliothèque de l'Arsenal identifies her as Falconia Proba, author of the Fourth century Cento Vergilianus. See also Patricia Wilson-Kastner, A Lost Tradition: Women Writers of the Early Church, pp. 33–69.

24. Sainte-Marthe's portrait of the Dames des Roches in his Latin compendium of worthies (cited in full in Sealy's Palace Academy, p. 130) includes details missing in his French portrait (Eloges des hommes illustres, p. 339). The following is a translation from the Latin

(I am grateful to my colleague Thomas Benediktson for his help). The portrait is entitled "The Poitevine Roches": "The most pleasant memory of that time was when the daughter, who was as erudite, helped her mother, a woman most learned concerning all the disciplines, and able to debate with an incredible facility and copiousness: [this daughter] used to recite the most charming poems written by her mother and herself, and she did so with such great charm that she converted into admiration the minds of all those present. Moreover, daily, very many men loving literature and elegance used to be present, gathering most desirously at the house of these ladies just as at some academy; nor was there any man who did not return more polished. There used to appear in the mother traces of a notable beauty, in the daughter a flowering [beauty] used to shine most whole and most brilliant; in each there was such an incredible consensus of character and thence so great a conspiracy of mutual love that not even death itself could lead them to openly profess that they would ever endure to be separated. Hence it has happened that although innumerable suitors passionately courted the daughter, nevertheless she did not wish to be torn away from the bosom of her mother. Until in the year 1587, the plague arriving at Augustoritus, bitter death extinguished that twin light of the city, having approached them both together on the very same day. For it ought not to surprise one if while they lived, having thoroughly moved the minds and wills of men, death itself had not refused to obey their most honorable desires."

25. On the roles attributed to the lone woman in an all-male organization, see Rosabeth Moss-Kanter, "Women and the Structure of Organization," in *Another Voice: Perspectives on Social Life and Social Science* (New York, 1976), p. 56. Margaret M. King has explored the image of the "armed maiden" in relation to Italian learned women ("Book-Lined Cells").

26. On the notion of the "muted text," see Elaine Showalter, "Feminist Criticism in the Wilderness," *Critical Inquiry* 8 (1981):200.

27. The second "Lettre a M. Pithou,".letter 8, p. 20.

28. Donald Kelley, *Foundations of Modern Historical Scholarship*, p. 242.

29. Charlotte de Bracchart wrote an inflammatory *Harengue . . . Which Addresses Itself to Men Who Prohibit Learning to Women* (Chalon sur Saone, 1604); on Anna Maria van Schurman, see Joyce Irwin, "Anna Maria van Schurman: The Star of Utrecht (1607–1678)," in *Female Scholars*, ed. J. R. Brink (Montreal, 1980), pp. 68–85. Marie de Gournay fought throughout her lifetime against calumny from courtiers and the "school" of Malherbe.

The Works of Mesdames des Roches of Poitiers (1579)

EPISTLE TO THE LADIES

If the well-chiseled marble, or the colors of a paintbrush employed by a skilled hand, acquaint us not only with the corporeal beauty but the manners and traits of those they depict, I thought that the word, true image of the soul, and the fleeting voice recorded by the pen onto paper, gave a certain indication not only of the wealth of the mind and of its acquired or natural capacities but of the native[1] integrity of those who speak or write. For this reason, I sought in this small tableau wherein I have depicted myself to lay hold of my words in order to assure you of the true friendship which I have always borne you (my ladies), that is if some of you deign to read my humble verse. And if, out of greater charity for me, you advise me that silence, the ornament of woman, can cover over the mistakes of the tongue and the understanding, I shall answer that it may well prevent shame, but it cannot increase honor since speech distinguishes us from animals without reason.[2] At least I count on your courtesy, that if you do not judge me worthy of esteem, you will not think that I should be greatly reprehended, for if the value of my writings is not great, nor is their length. Therefore you will find me somewhat worthy of excuse; but I had better end my letter near its beginning for fear that, boring you on account of its length, I contradict myself and your wishes and must then apologize for my excuse. Adieu, my ladies.

EPISTLE TO MY DAUGHTER

Ancient lovers of learning,
Said that to God one must do one's duty,
Then to one's country, and a third to one's lineage,
Leading them through courage,
Either to endure at times suffering,
Or to overcome strong emotions.
I revere the Lord God; as for my country, I lack all power,
Men have full authority,
Contrary to reason and to justice.[3]
But as concerns you, my daughter, who are so dear to me,
I would be liable to great blame and reproach
If I were to lead you on the beaten path,
Seeing that your heart is born unto virtue.
It is not sufficient, however, to be well born,
Acquired sense[4] makes us well-mannered.
And the flame, burning in our soul,
Is soon consumed without learning.
The letter serves as a holy source
For one's diet as well as for medicinal use:
The letter can alter vice,
The letter strengthens the heart of the virtuous,
The letter is that art which fashions matter
Into a more complete form.
May this brief discourse on such a topic
Be welcomed by you,
My only daughter, so precious to me,
Not so much because you have come to be such
And that in you I see my own portrait
In hair, tan, build, and trait,
Manner, bearing, word, countenance,
And age only distinguishes us.

Neither the sight of so great a physical resemblance,
Nor the gracious compatibility of our minds,
Nor this sweet amiable affection
That makes us love another like us,
Can fully account for the extent
Of my perfect love for you,
Nor the effort given me by Nature [to raise you],
Nor so much that it [this effort] is my sustenance.
But to think that in the midst of so many calamities,
Ills, troubles, sorrows, pains,
Subjection, torment, work, sadness,
Which for thirteen years have given me no respite,
You have, child, shown a strong heart
To resist the violent travail
Which overwhelmed me, and you offered me since childhood
Love, advice, support, and obedience.
The Almighty to whom I turned for refuge
Had you provide me my only succor.
To reward you for your worthy services,
I cannot grant you a greater gift
Than to urge you to do your duty
Toward the Muse and divine learning.
"The true center and function of study
Is to accustom oneself to virtue.
To seek to insinuate oneself in her [virtue]
Makes it difficult to change the garment."[5]
Well born and living at a propitious time for learning,
You seem inclined toward the Muses.
May Heaven grant you such a desire
For holy living, the only just [source of] pleasure,
And the Daemon, who began the work,
Guide so well the issue of your thought,
That as a witness to posterity
Of how much honor you will have merited,
You may become immortal some day through your virtue,
It is thus that I have always wished you to be.

ODE I

If my writings do not have engraved on their cover
The sacred name of immortality,
I have neither acquired nor earned it,
Unless it were by favor or grace.

I do not depict Neptune in his fury,
I do not speak of angry Jupiter,
Of the open vase, the flight of justice
Of which our earth rightly laments.

The child of Resource and Poverty
Who is said to burn up the coldest ice,
Delights in hearing lofty songs.
I am content with a more humble harmony.

But who could, weighed down with so much sorrow,
One's spirit racked by a hundred thousand misfortunes,
Behold Apollo, revere the nine Sisters,
And worthily draw from their fountain?

Heaven has indeed infused within our Soul
Small sparks, principles of virtue:
But heat is vanquished by cold
If well-stocked wood does not nourish the flame.

Nature requires that letters and the practice thereof
Go into the perfecting of a chef-d'oeuvre.
She, wise in all things, knows:
Her first forms were shaped through craftsmanship.[6]

Our parents have some "worthy" customs.
To take away from us the use of reason,
They lock us up at home
And give us the spindle instead of the pen.

Conforming our steps to our [female] destiny,
They promise us freedom and pleasure:
And we reap constant displeasure
As we bring our dowry under the laws of Marriage.

Soon after [the wedding] appears a misery
Born within us of a mutual desire,
Accompanied by continuous cares
Which always burden the mother's womb.

We must suddenly change duties
Which somewhat fashioned our lives
For our husbands will sound only
Obedience, hard labor, and avarice.

One husband, having closed the door
To Virtue, mother of learning,

On seeing us fear to receive Virtue
Because she wears a female garb.[7]

Another is inhabited by the spirit of jealousy,
In possessing so chaste a beauty.
In the nest of Love he lets cruelty dwell,
Tormenting his own fantasy.

Pyrrha chose a light seed
To repopulate the earth
Deucalion sowed black stones
Which Heaven itself well endured.[8]

My God, My God, how much tolerance
That I do not care to remember here!
It suffices that I show men
How much their laws do us violence.

The most beautiful days of our youth
Seem but flowers of a gracious spring,
Pressed in by storms and rainy winds
Which halt their ending course.

In the happy moments of my yesteryears,
I bore my wings close by my side:
But in losing my youthful freedom
Before even flying, my wing [pen] was broken.[9]

I so long to spend time with books
And cast my sorrows onto paper.
But some trouble always diverts me
Claiming I should my profession follow.

The Agrigentum [tyrant] worthily honored
The learning of the daughters of Stesichorus.
He who toward us would do the same
Would bring about a similar miracle.[10]

Ladies, let us live as the Amaranth
Who through the winter does not lose its beautiful flower:
The spirit infused with a divine sap
Renders more brilliant its strength through labor.

To help us bear the misfortunes of our lives
God made us share in a mighty intellect
Which we are to turn into an active mind
In spite of death, fortune, and envy.

The Works of M. Des Roches of Poitiers the Daughter (1579)

FOR A MASCARADE OF AMAZONS

After acquiring so much honor and glory,
After winning a double victory,
After binding these haughty warriors:
After showing so much valiance,
Through our flashing eyes and powerful lances,
We carry home the Myrtle and the Laurel.

Audacious Love, desiring that its flames
Utterly enfeeble the virtue of our spirit,
Hurled at our hearts a thousand blazing torches.
But our chastity, defending its hold,
Transformed forthwith the ardent flames into ice,
And thus prevented Love from dwelling within.

Upon seeing chastity mightily repulse him,
Love, scornful, vexed, and angry,
Having been expelled from our heart,
Turned toward our eyes:
But the wretch, alas, had pledged away
His arc and arrows, as if to avow
That our gaze had vanquished him.

Despoiled of his fiercest weapons,
Love sought Mars in the midst of the fray,
Pleading humbly for his help:
Mars, moved by pity, raised from the land
An army of soldiers to fight us,
But was no more successful than the God of Love.

May a heart that refuses sensual pleasure,
And nobility of thought as well as mighty power,
Preserve us always from Love and Mars:
Hence everywhere woman sings
Of the proud rule of the Queen of the Amazons
Who orders the very Gods beneath her standards.

Her name is Otrera, daughter of Martesia,
Who commands this chosen army to serve her,
For she wants through her prowess to immortalize her name:
She holds complete sovereignty

Over the great city of Themyscira
Which is encircled by the famous river Thermodon.[11]

SONG OF THE AMAZONS

We make war
On the Kings of the earth
Braving the most glorious
Through our prudence
And our valiance.
We rule in myriad places
Vanquishing the efforts
Of the most daring and strong
With our victorious arm.

We chase away the vices,
Through practices
Which virtue teaches us:
We flee like the plague
The grievous flame
Which burns the heart:
For the purity
Of our chastity
Forever protects us.

We hold men prisoners
In the places where we rule
And force them to spin:
Their cowardly spirit
Of a greater endeavor [war]
Is unworthy to assume:
If any among you
Wish to quarrel with us
Let him come forward.

TO MY DISTAFF

Distaff, my care, I promise you and swear
To love you always and never exchange
Your domestic honor for a foreign attraction
Which, inconstant, wanders and does not endure.
Having you at my side, I am even more secure
Than if ink and paper were to line up
All around me, for to avenge me

You are well able to ward off an attack.
But distaff, my friend, it is not necessary,
In order to esteem and love you all the more,
That I abandon that honorable custom
Of writing sometimes, of writing in fact
About your worth, Distaff my care,
As I hold in my hand the spindle and the pen.

L'AGNODICE

(In the first fifty-two lines of *L'Agnodice,* des Roches tells of the ravages of Envy in
the lives of the virtuous. From all other ills one profits, she claims, but from Envy
one reaps cruelty, misery, and death. Drawing on Plutarch's *Lives,* she cites the
example of Phocion's unjust death at the hands of the Athenians. Phocion's cre-
mated body was left unburied until his wife gathered up the bones and buried
them by the hearth. Des Roches substitutes "une dame estrangere" (a foreign
lady) for Phocion's wife to fit the story of Agnodice.)

Envy, gazing on this merciful lady,
Felt a poisonous anger well up within.
Rolling her bulging eyes full of horror and terror,
Ah! I shall avenge myself on you (she spoke),
Ha! You seek to help, (foolish woman), to defend
Phocion whose dead ashes I still hate,
Know that soon I shall make you feel
Over your rash assistance a tardy repentance:
For to spite you, I will incite
Husbands to become tyrants of their wives
By prohibiting them books and learning
Thus depriving them of the desire even to live.
Having spoken, she penetrated the hearts
Of the men who, on seeing their lovely erudite wives,
Sought to eradicate from their minds
That most worthy ornament of Beauty, Learning, itself
For they did not wish to leave them anything
That would please them and bring solace to their spirit.
What cruelty Envy sought
In tormenting such gentle comeliness!
The ladies instantly became prey
To fever, languor, and other diseases.
[Envy] made them suffer incredible pain
And they preferred death to the shame
Of telling the doctors of their lingering ills.

The women (O pity!) no longer dared
To help each other, they were made to spin.
Their husbands, seeing their cruel martyrdom,
Did not refrain from mocking and jeering them.
Hoping perhaps to marry again,
They no longer cared to save them.
At that time there lived a noble lady
Whom Heaven had made comely, wise, and subtle.
Moved by compassion for such beauteous countenances
About to be engulfed by the covetous tomb,
And wishing to help them, she disguised herself
In manly accouterment in order to study,
Since it was forbidden then for women
To practice the arts or see them in written form.
This lady hid her golden blond tresses,
Learned medecine and became a most skilled practitioner.
Then, recalling her first intention,
She sought to accomplish her worthy purpose
And cure the ills of her suffering neighbors
Through the [healing] virtues of flowers, leaves, and roots:
[She used] the very herb picked on the spot
Where Glaucus on eating it from man became a god.
Having prepared all, noble Agnodice
Humbly offered the ladies her services.
But thinking her a man,
They refused harshly her help.
One could readily see from their timorous faces
That they feared her hands had a lascivious intent.
Agnodice, seeing their great chastity,
Esteemed them all the more for their integrity.
Revealing then the white round apples of her bosom,
And the beautiful blond tresses of her golden head,
She shows them that she is a maid, and that her noble heart
Desired their deliverance from their sad languor.
The ladies, admiring her native goodness,
And the sparkling whiteness of her soft complexion,
The small twin mounds of her bosom,
The golden curls of her sacred head,
The ravishing flames of her divine gaze,
And the engaging grace of her soft-spoken words,
The engaging grace of her soft-spoken words,
Kissed a thousand times her lips and bosom,
And received succor from her blessed hand.

Soon one saw the wives and daughters
Recover their fresh looks and become more beautiful.
But Envy, present at this scene of human assistance,
Vouched she would soon prevent its course:
She ate out her heart, miserable sustenance,
A meal fit for those over whose lives she rules;
She held in one hand a raging serpent
Whose cruel venom to all places spreads.
Her other hand held a thorny branch,
Her body was leaden, her face full of spleen,
Her bald head surrounded by several crowns of
Hideous vipers which bit her continually.
Dragging her mad rage about her
She brings turmoil to chaste marriages
For another's peace is to her a misfortune.
In the men then she raised doubt as to the worth
And noble virtues of beautiful Agnodice,
Saying that her gaze at their wives and daughters
Held more sway than was decent
For women who would not want their honor to suffer.
Filled with fury, they seized Agnodice
To make of her a woeful sacrifice to Envy.
Alas, not finding her guilty in the least,
They unjustly condemned her to death.
Agnodice, when she realized her misfortune,
Uncovered promptly her golden hair
And showing her fair bosom, graceful abode
Of the Muses, the virtues, the graces, and love,
She lowered her eyes filled with honor and shame,
A virgin blush spread over her features.
She explained that the reason for her disguise
Was not to deceive but rather to honor
Learning whose student she was in her service to the ladies:
That to suspect her of criminal conduct
Was to offend nature and its divine laws.
After she spoke, not a single voice
Was raised against her; rather the entire audience
Marveled at such rare excellence.
All stood in awe without sound or movement,
Attentive only to hearing and seeing her.
Likewise one sometimes sees after a long storm
The winds calm down and the seashore at rest
As when the twin brothers who looked out to sea

Beheld afar a ship in danger of sinking.
Saving it from peril the waves
Cast it forth on the longed-for coast.
The men, vanquished by pity,
Quietly put away their hostile furor,
And kneeling down before the maiden
They asked pardon for their offenses.
Agnodice, experiencing a singular pleasure,
Pleaded ardently that they allow
The ladies of the land to study, and that they not envy the glory
That comes from serving the daughters of Memory.
Envy, knowing she had lost the battle
Through the deeds and rare virtues of Agnodice,
Has pursued ever since with an immortal hate
Ladies who were as virtuous as she.

New Works by Mesdames des Roches of Poitiers (1583)

TO MY DAUGHTER

My dearest, I know that out of reverence, love, and an honorable modesty, you will not send anything to the publishers without me and that you would rather I follow my duty, my desire, and my custom. Let us walk therefore together in this union which has always sustained us, and let us pray that the Divine Power guide us in our work, our thoughts, and our words, protecting us (if it pleases Him) from all calumny and from the venom of ungrateful Envy.

The Works of M. des Roches the Daughter (1583)

EPISTLE TO HER MOTHER

Mother, you quickened me as Prometheus the earth which he himself formed, but you did so without stealing fire: for it was given to you by Heaven. Now, knowing that I hold from you not only this mortal life but yet the life of my life, I follow you everywhere as the shadow does the body. And just as the body in all its proportions, and the shadow in its width cannot be seen without light, so the brilliant luminosity of your mind illumines for us the narrow path where I pray, my mother, that we may find more olive trees than holly. The peaceable branch from the tree of Pallas is as necessary to us as was to Aeneas the golden bough divulged to him by Deiphobus.[12] I know that gold, the son of Earth, brings great credit to its mother, but we have the golden verse of the wise Samian[13] who demonstrates in his writings and recommends what your admirable virtues make clear to all those who know you. Since he [the Samian] wishes to speak, I will be silent, Mother, after humbly beseeching Divine Mercy that it please Him lengthen and prosper your days so that you may live a long life as example of the graces of Heaven.

DIALOGUE OF IRIS AND PASITHEE

(Iris complains of the unfaithfulness of her lovers and of her wearisome family life. Pasithee seeks to help her.)

Pas. Iris, do you want to do the right thing? Rid yourself instantly of the rigors of love and of your parents. *Iris.* How can I, Pasithee? *Pas.* There lived in Argos a lady by the name of Telesilla who, for having vowed herself to the Muses, was healed of a disease.[14] Make a similar vow: they [the Muses] would then heal you of the passions of your spirit. *Iris.* I do not understand you. *Pas.* You must study, turn to books, and seek pleasure from reading: in this way learning, finding root in your soul, would chase away all these vain and frivolous thoughts. *Iris.* Once I read a book of luck which my father had bought. *Pas.* Do you know its title? *Iris.* There wasn't any. *Pas.* Who wrote it? *Iris.* I think it was an Almanac. I took great pleasure in it but I got a headache and had to stop reading it. *Pas.* Ha, I should think so. Now the books I'm referring to do not cause headaches but rather take away all discomfort. *Iris.* Are you speaking of that attractive golden book Eole was looking at the other day? *Pas.* I don't know. What is its name? *Iris.* I can't remember. *Pas.* What is it about? *Iris.* I can't remember that either. *Pas.* Is it in prose or in verse? *Iris.* I didn't look. *Pas.* When was it published? *Iris.* I don't know, but it was really nice looking. *Pas.* You must have surely looked at it, Iris, without profiting at all from it. *Iris.* That's true. *Pas.* You would have pleased your Eole if you had read it a little. And surely he must have shown it to you thinking that you would have liked to read it. *Iris.* I would have been very pleased to read it. But my father doesn't want me to. *Pas.* Oh, if you really wanted to, how easily you could find books to study without his knowing it! When he forbids you from going out so often, you should listen to him. It's too bad that your beauty is not accompanied by some nobility of spirit which lasts far longer. *Iris.* That's what Niree says, that my beauty will pass away like a flower. The other day he wrote that down on a paper which I have in my purse and he told one of my servants to come and present it to me. Look at it. Would you care to read it.

(Iris then asks whom she should love, Eole or a certain foreigner called Lord Felix who spoke to her at length in a language she could not understand. Pasithee enjoins the following.)

Pas. I advise you then to delay loving someone. Wait until a discreet man presents himself in your service and is led to love you on account of some resemblance [between you]. *Iris.* When will that happen to me, Pasithee? Would you please read my palm? Do you know how to? *Pas.* The discretion of a young girl, which leads to the fulfillment of her love, does not simply appear on her palm, Iris, but in her spirit, which reveals her to be wise in all her actions. Such spirits are sought out only by those like them; and what they find is well safeguarded as I have heard it said in these lines:
Fair lady, do not fear contempt
Even though several winters have tarnished your beauty,
Furnish your mind with Virtues and Grace,
For Virtue retains what the eyes have taken.
Iris. I don't see, however, why one thinks learned women are more virtuous; on the contrary, men mock them thoroughly. *Pas.* Yes, the ignorant ones do. But the learned and well taught bear toward them a friendship filled with honorable reverence. Think of what Angelo Poliziano said as he admired

That Cassandra Fidele
Divine honor of Italy.

Following thus the example of the noble Virgin live modestly, speak advisedly, so that if your beauty attracts men, your graces may retain them in a relation of goodwill for which they may justly say: Amorous servitude frees one from all vice. *Iris.* And what must I do for that, Pasithee? *Pas.* Iris, you must read. *Iris.* My father forbids it, claiming it's useless. *Pas.* Learn to write well. *Iris.* My mother does not want me to. She claims that she is astute enough without it. *Pas.* Play the lyre. *Iris.* My brother laughs at that; he says it's a waste of money. *Pas.* Learn to speak well. *Iris.* What? You think I don't speak well enough? *Pas.* Ha, I have been very pleased, Iris. What I am telling you is to prevent you from complaining about the inconstancy of your lovers. If you follow my advice and are not courted by a suitor, you will live a good life; if, on the other hand, you are loved, it will be by an honest man who will be faithful to you. Each seeks to love what resembles him.[15] Men of heart and learning can love more fully for they have greater imagination: Love is formed through images transferred to the lover by the loved one. The eye and the ear are windows through which love reaches the heart. The love of corporeal beauty is perceived through the gaze, and that of beautiful souls enters through the hearing. Embellish, therefore, your soul, if you wish to be uniquely loved by a wise, compatible, and learned friend. Otherwise, live without love to avoid the miseries which come from love: How many poor mistresses have become desolate for having lost their suitors in this unfortunate trip to Portugal! Ha! Our Chariclee cried so much when her favorite [lover] left that it was piteous to see her, for she feared that the daughter of Necessity would wound the heart of him whom she had so softly touched. I remember it said that she [Chariclee] retired to the country to flee social life and that there, while on a walk alone, she sang a song which I have since learned. *Iris.* Sing it, Pasithee, I pray, for now I am in the mood to dance. *Pas.* Iris, your request is so persuasive that since I cannot refuse what pleases you I will tell it. Adapt it as best you can to the dance. . . . The sweet song of Alcyone adorned this tune with much grace. Forgive me, Iris, if I have not presented it well enough to you. *Iris.* It was beautiful, Pasithee, but I would not have wanted it to be any longer for I wished to hear it all and I must be leaving soon. *Pas.* Why are you in such a hurry? *Iris.* As I looked out the window, I saw Eole, who was waiting for me in the street. *Pas.* Wait for him to come here so that he can bring you back home. *Iris.* Oh, he would never come here. He doesn't want to speak to you because you are a learned woman. *Pas.* Ha, ha, I readily excuse him from coming, he and all those like him. I don't think women study in vain since it helps them chase away gallant men of this sort. *Iris.* He asked me, though, that I request your opinion of the song he wrote for me. *Pas.* The song is agreeable enough because you are its subject. But it's not Eole's invention, for he simply transcribed what he saw in your visage. *Iris.* My God, how well you speak, Pasithee! I would come daily to your school if I had the leisure! I take great pleasure in conversing with you. I must, however, take my leave, for Eole is calling me and it's late. I kiss your hands, Pasithee. *Pas.* I commend myself to your grace, Iris.

NOTES TO THE TRANSLATION

1. "Naisve" has the sense of native, or natural, and indicates what is connate with its possessor, with the added notion of rightness or appropriateness free of affectation. See Castor, p. 79.

2. Des Roches expresses a humanist commonplace. In Louis le Roy's words: "God in creating man gave him for the sake of great excellence reason and the word and through these two prerogatives separated him from other animals." From *De la Vicissitude ou variete des choses en l'univers* (1579), cited by Castor, p. 135.

3. Des Roches takes issue with the Salic law, which excluded women from succession to the throne. The topic of gynocracy may have been debated at the salon in Poitiers, for most of the lawyers there defended the law as the "lex regia," the life-principle of the French monarchy (Kelley, p. 199).

4. Cotgrave's synonyms for "sens" include understanding, judgment, reason, and knowledge. Des Roches refers throughout not to the typical domestically oriented education for women but to concepts inherent in education for men.

5. These last four lines, apparently a quotation, express the commonplace that Art (study) perfects Nature, and that virtue is a primordial condition for right living and especially fruitful learning. The last two lines are a play on the proverb "L'habit ne fait pas le moine" ('Tis not the habit [but the heart] that makes a man religious; Cotgrave).

6. Des Roches reworks within a feminist context the Pléiade theory that poetic inspiration dies out if it is not sustained through creative practice. She denounces the "loix d'Hymenee" as the major obstacle to women seeking to become poets.

7. Catherine des Roches's *L'Agnodice* dramatizes the thought of this quatrain.

8. Des Roches uses the myth of Deucalion and Pyrrha for polemical ends. Pyrrha represents the creative acts of women while Deucalion, son of Prometheus, brings destruction in his wake.

9. There is a play here on the word *plume,* meaning wing and pen.

10. Phalaris of Agrigentum in Sicily was proverbially known for his cruelty. In the spurious epistles attributed to him (*Les Epistres de Phalaris,* translated by Claude Gruget in 1550), however, he appears as an enlightened patron of the arts. Des Roches ironically states that it would be a miracle if men imitated Phalaris, who was partially redeemed for his admiration of learned women.

11. These Amazons are depicted in a semiserious vein due to the type of poem in which they appear (the "mascarade" was a popular amusement at the court of the Valois kings) and to the mock-heroic nature of the episode of the Amazons in Ariosto's *Orlando Furioso* (XIX), which probably served as source material.

12. The golden bough was divulged to Aeneas not by Deiphobus but by the Cumean Sybil (*Aeneid,* VI).

13. The Samian is Pythagoras, whose *Golden Verse* and *Symbols* immediately follow this prefatory letter.

14. Catherine des Roches read the story of Telesilla in Plutarch's *Virtuous Deeds of Women* (*Oeuvres,* 1575, XXXV, 231C).

15. What follows is an account of Ficinian Neoplatonic theory. The first translation of Ficino's commentary on the banquet was published at Poitiers in 1546.

BIBLIOGRAPHY

Primary Works

Des Roches, Dames. *Les Missives de Mes-dames des Roches de Poitiers mère et fille, avec le Ravissement de Proserpine prins du Latin de Clodian. Et autres Imitations et meslanges poëtiques.* Paris, 1586.
———. *Les Oeuvres de Mes-dames des Roches de Poitiers mère et fille.* Paris, 1578.
———. *Les Oeuvres . . . seconde edition, corrigee et augmentée de la Tragi-comédie de Tobie et autres oeuvres poëtiques.* Paris, 1579.
———. *Les Premières Oeuvres . . . Les Secondes Oeuvres . . . troisième edition.* Rouen, 1604.

————. *La Puce de Madame des Roches. Qui est un receuil de divers poemes Grecs, Latins et François, composez par plusieurs doctes personnages aux Grands Jours tenus à Poitiers l'an 1579.* Ed. D. Jouaust. 1582, 1583, and 1610. Reprint. Paris, 1868.

————. *Les Secondes Oeuvres de Mes-dames des Roches de Poitiers mère et fille.* Poitiers, 1583.

Du Verdier, Antoine. *Bibliothèque.* Lyon, 1585.

La Croix du Maine. *La Bibliothèque.* Paris, 1584.

Le Grand, Lois. *Elégie sur le trespas de Mesdames des Roches de Poitiers mère et fille.* Paris, 1587.

Plutarque. *Les Oeuvres morales et meslees.* Paris, 1575.

Sainte-Marthe, Scévole de. *Eloges des hommes illustres, mis en français par Guillaume Colletet.* Paris, 1644.

Related Works

Brink, J. R. *Female Scholars: A Tradition of Learned Women Before 1800.* Montreal, 1980.

Castor, Graham. *Pléiade Poetics.* Cambridge, Mass., 1964.

Davidson, Cathy, and E. M. Brown, eds. *The Lost Tradition: Mothers and Daughters in Literature.* New York, 1980.

Diller, George. *Les Dames des Roches. Étude sur la vie littéraire à Poitiers dans la deuxième moitié du XVIe siècle.* Paris, 1936.

Erasmus, Desiderius. *The Colloquies of Erasmus.* Trans. Craig R. Thompson. Chicago, 1965.

Glidden, Hope. *The Storyteller as Humanist: The "Serées" of Guillaume Bouchet.* Lexington, 1981.

Greenblatt, Stephen. *Renaissance Self-Fashioning: From More to Shakespeare.* Chicago, 1980.

Guillerm, Luce, ed. *La Femme dans la littérature française et les traductions en français au XVIe siècle.* Lille, 1971.

Hyginus. *The Myths of Hyginus.* Trans. Mary Grant. Lawrence, Kans., 1960.

Keating, Clark. *Studies on the Literary Salon in France, 1550–1615.* Cambridge, Mass., 1941.

Kelley, Donald R. *Foundations of Modern Historical Scholarship. Language, Law, and History in the French Renaissance.* New York, 1970.

King, Margaret L. "Book-Lined Cells: Women and Humanism in the Early Italian Renaissance." In *Beyond Their Sex: Learned Women of the European Past,* ed. P. Labalme, pp. 66–90. New York, 1980.

Labé, Louise. *Oeuvres complètes.* Ed. Enzo Giudici. Geneva, 1981.

Larsen, Anne R. "Catherine des Roches' 'Epistre à sa mère' (1579)." *Allegorica* 7 (1982): 58–64.

Moss-Kanter, Rosabeth, and Marcia Millman, eds. *Another Voice: Perspectives on Social Life and Social Science,* New York, 1976.

Pasquier, Estienne. "Lettres à M. Pithou." In *Choix de lettres sur la littérature, la langue et la traduction,* ed. Dorothy Thickett. Geneva, 1966.

Pérouse, Gabriel. *Les Nouvelles françaises du seizième siècle: Images de la vie du temps.* Geneva, 1976.

Raymond, Marcel. *L'Influence de Ronsard sur la poésie française (1550–1585).* Paris, 1927.

Richardson, Lula McDowell. *The Forerunners of Feminism in French Literature of the Renaissance from Christine of Pisa to Marie de Gournay.* Baltimore, 1929.

Ronsard, Pierre de. *Oeuvres complètes.* Ed. Gustave Cohen. 2 vols. Paris, 1950.

Schutz, Alexander H. "The Group of the Dames des Roches in Sixteenth-Century Poitiers." *PMLA* 48 (1933):648–54.

Sealy, Robert. *The Palace Academy of Henry III*. Geneva, 1981.

Showalter, Elaine. "Feminist Criticism in the Wilderness." *Critical Inquiry* 8 (1981):179–205.

Wilson-Kastner, Patricia. *A Lost Tradition: Women Writers of the Early Church*. Washington, D.C., 1981.

Woodbridge, Linda. *Women and the English Renaissance: Literature and the Nature of Womanhood, 1540–1620*. Urbana, Ill., 1984.

Yates, Frances. *The French Academies of the Sixteenth Century*. London, 1947.

A PROPAGANDIST FOR THE REFORM

arie Dentière

THOMAS HEAD

One of the central themes of the reform movement of the sixteenth century was the ability of the laity, as well as the clergy, to interpret and preach the Gospel message of salvation. In 1539, Marie Dentière wrote Queen Marguerite de Navarre; her defense of certain reformers exiled from Geneva included a radical understanding of the universality of that message:

> I ask, didn't Jesus die just as much for the poor illiterates and the idiots as for the shaven, tonsured and mitred lords? Did he only say, "Go, preach my Gospel to the wise lords and grand doctors?" Did he not say, "To all?" Do we have two Gospels, one for men and the other for women? One for the educated and the other for the multitude? Are we not all one in our Savior? In whose name are we baptised, in that of Paul or of Apollo, in that of the Pope or of Luther? Is it not in the name of Christ?[1]

For Dentière the priesthood of all believers clearly included women: "For we ought not, any more than men, hide and bury within the earth that which God has . . . revealed to us women. Although we are not permitted to preach in assemblies and public churches, nevertheless we are not prohibited from writing and giving advice in all charity one to the other."[2]

The abbess of the convent of Augustinians in Tournai, Dentière left her monastery in the 1520s and came at length to Geneva during the heady early days of the reform movement led by Guillaume Farel. There Dentière, active as a preacher and polemicist, published two works: *The War for and Deliverance of the City of Geneva, Faithfully Prepared and Written Down by a Merchant Living in That City* (1536), a history of the events of 1526–1536 through which the reform came to power in Geneva;[3] and *A Most Beneficial Letter, Prepared and Written Down by a Christian Woman of Tournai, and Sent to the Queen of Navarre, Sister of the King of France, Against the Turks, the Jews, the Infidels, the False*

Christians, the Anabaptists and the Lutherans (1539), a defense of evangelical theology and the role of women in theological discourse, addressed to Marguerite of Navarre as a prominent noblewoman sympathetic to the evangelical cause.[4]

Other than her two works, only a fragmentary record remains of Dentière's life. After leaving the convent in the mid-1520s, she married Simon Robert, a former priest of that city. Robert and Dentière left Tournai (she later said that she had been "chased out" of her native land) for Strasbourg.[5] In 1526 Robert was introduced to Guillaume Farel, a prominent evangelical reformer.[6] The couple moved to Aigle with Farel, although they returned to Strasbourg during a severe illness suffered by Dentière.[7] Two years later, Robert was named a reform pastor in Bex.[8] Dentière married Antoine Froment, an acquaintance of her husband, presumably after Robert's death in March or April of 1533.[9] She had five children.[10]

The Reformation in Geneva, which Robert Kingdon has characterized as a revolution of the city against its clergy, began in earnest in 1532 with the arrival of Farel from nearby Bern.[11] Farel and his cohorts, including Froment, joined the political revolt of Geneva's citizens against her prince-bishop to the Protestant religious cause, which until then had only scattered support in the city. Both a shouting war in the assemblies and a shooting war in the streets followed between Reformers and Catholics. These culminated in the deposition of the prince-bishop by the Council of Two Hundred; the investment of the city by a mercenary force raised by the bishop and the duke of Savoy, the city's overlord; and the defeat of that force by a Protestant army from Bern in February 1536, guaranteeing the independence of the city. In May, by vote of the male populace, the city dedicated itself to live by the Gospel and the Word of God, suspending the usages of the Roman church; in short, Geneva became a Protestant city-state.[12]

Dentière considered the dramatic events of these years in *The War for and Deliverance of Geneva*. Since the last event she described was the raising of the siege by the Bernese army, the pamphlet was probably written and printed between February and May as election propaganda. Dentière's work was not a descriptive chronicle of events, but an interpretation of those events in terms of sacred history: the victory of the Protestants recalled the victories of God over the forces of Pharaoh and the city of Jericho. For her, it was the shouting war, rather than the shooting war, which was important: a brief, heavily metaphorical description of the actual revolt of the city merchants against the duke and his supporters, up to the first lifting of the Savoyard blockade in 1530, served as a prologue to a much longer discussion of the struggle for the "hearts and minds" of the Genevan populace among several different religious factions between 1533 (the arrival of Farel and Froment in the city) and 1535.

The great heroes of the victory were the preachers Farel, Froment, and Pierre Viret; the villain was the Dominican priest Guy Furbiti, who debated against the reformers on various public stages. The battleground was not the city, but the souls of its inhabitants, where evangelical preachers and priests battled over control of the Gospel. Dentière's prose style is simple, yet forceful, colored with biblical allusions and fervent moral indignation. She is also good at turning coarser phrases. In the midst of her extended metaphor comparing God's deliverance of the Genevans from the duke of Savoy to the deliverance of the Israelites from the Pharaoh, she inserts an equally complex metaphorical pun based on the French word *duc*'s double meaning of duke and horned owl. The duke who once had eaten the chickens hatched by Genevan mothers was now being plucked of his plumage by those same mothers.[13] Dentière emerged as a fine rhetorician, preaching a sermon brimming with both biblical and popular allusions.

Dentière also emerged in the guise of a man. The title page of *The War for and Deliverance of Geneva* attributes the work to "a merchant living in that city." Most likely Dentière felt that the Council of Two Hundred, representatives of the city's monied classes, whose religious sentiments ranged from conservative to moderate Protestantism, would react more favorably toward the rhetoric of a man. Dentière was certainly aware of the polemic stance and tone of her "sermon": the title page bears the advice "Read and then judge."[14] The work almost disappeared after its publication: no printed copies have survived, and it was not attributed to Dentière until the nineteenth century.[15]

For descriptive detail about these events, it is necessary to turn to the two other memoirs of those same years: *The Marvelous Acts and Deeds of the City of Geneva* by her husband, Antoine Froment, and *The Germ of Calvinism, or the Beginning of the Reform in Geneva* by Sister Jeanne de Jussie, a member of the order of Poor Clares.[16] Both works are rich in references to women; a picture emerges from them of active female involvement in the reform of Geneva. Both Natalie Davis and Miriam Chrisman have shown that no broad generalizations are possible about the response of urban women to the reform.[17] As Chrisman concludes, "There was, quite clearly, no pattern of behaviour which a large group of women followed. Reaction to the Reform was an individual matter. . . . The Reformation did not make any fundamental change in the position of women in urban society—their role continued to be within the family and the household. The significant change was the overthrow of the celibate ethic."[18] Some, like Dentière, actively rejected and preached against that ethic, while others, like de Jussie, stood fast not only in their traditional Catholicism, but also in the practice of the celibate religious life.

The attempted reform of de Jussie's convent of Poor Clares provided the opportunity for Protestant women to preach their religious message to their Catholic sisters. As early as 1534, a female Protestant relative of a member of the community had visited and poured forth "venom" into the nun's ears.[19] When, during the next year, Farel and Viret preached at the convent, the prioress was so loud in her denunciation of the reformers that she was led from the room. Locked outside, she began to beat on the walls, and the nuns responded by crying so loudly that the two men eventually abandoned their task, never to return.[20]

Shortly thereafter, Marie Dentière visited the convent with a deputation of male Protestant leaders. The visit is described in de Jussie's colorful account:

> In that company was one false abbess, wrinkled and of diabolical language, possessing a husband and child, named Marie d'Entière of Picardy, who mixed herself up in preaching and in perverting the people from devotion. She placed herself among the sisters. . . . But because of the desire she had of perverting someone, she did not take note of these reproaches and said, "Alas, poor creatures! if only you knew how good it was to be next to a handsome husband, and how God considers it pleasing. For a long time I lived in those shadows and hypocrisy where you are, but God alone made me recognize the abuse of my pitiful life, and I was brought to the light of truth. Considering with regret how I lived, for in these orders there is nothing but sanctimoniousness, mental corruption and idleness, . . . I took about five hundred ducats from the treasury of the abbey, and I left that unhappiness. Thanks to God I have five handsome children and I live wholesomely."[21]

Two issues particularly separated these two women: the changed ideal of chastity and the right of women to preach. The former was part of the general reform program, the latter, a particular concern of Dentière. De Jussie, vowed to a life of celibacy, quoted the words of her abbess in another context, "It is not the trade (*métier*) of women to dispute, since such is not ordained for them. You will find that they ought not to dispute, seeing that it is forbidden for unlettered people to meddle in speaking about Holy Scripture."[22]

Dentière fought hard alongside the male reformers in the struggles described in *The War for and Deliverance of Geneva* to institute the Protestant program, including the abolition of the celibate monastic ideal. In her second work she pushed for more radical parts of the evangelical program, particularly the acceptance of the right of women to preach and to interpret Scripture. In the years 1536–1540 the question of who was to shape and govern the fledgling reformed state of Geneva remained unanswered. In August 1536 Farel invited the brilliant young theologian

John Calvin to come to Geneva to aid in its religious government, and Farel's reform movement eventually underwent a process of "Calvinization."[23] As Calvin himself later recalled in his Farewell Address:

> When I first arrived in this church there was almost nothing. They were preaching and that's all. They were good at seeking out idols and burning them, but there was no Reformation. Everything was in turmoil. To be sure, there was good master William [Farel] and also blind Courault. Moreover, there was Master Antoine Saulnier and that fine preacher Froment, who, having put aside his apron, mounted the pulpit and then climbed back down to his store where he would gab, thus preaching a double sermon.[24]

Together Farel and Calvin made a bold bid for power the next year, when they submitted twenty-one "Articles on the Organization of Church and Worship" to the magistrates for approval and later requested the power of excommunication. Suddenly the Council was faced with a decision between the path of reform envisioned by Calvin and the more moderate ways of Luther or Zwingli. In April of 1538 both Farel and Calvin were exiled; Calvin did not return until 1541, and did not win control of the city for some years.

Marie Dentière published *The Letter to the Queen of Navarre* in April of 1539, in the midst of this fragmentation of Protestantism in Geneva. The full title condemned Lutherans and Anabaptists as strongly as Catholics and non-Christians. Unlike *The War for and Deliverance of Geneva*, this work was published under Dentière's own initials, and thus she fully confesses her female identity. In the opening parts of the work, the dedicatory epistle to Queen Marguerite and a brief "Defense of Women," Dentière sounds a strikingly feminist message, defending the right of women to interpret Scripture and to teach that interpretation to one another privately, even if they were prohibited from preaching publicly. By means of the conceit of addressing her letter to another woman, Dentière defends the publication of her own work. Like her preaching, her writing, at least those copies that were not destroyed, reached an audience that was in part female.[25] In this work she lays a theoretical justification for what she herself had done at the convent of Poor Clares and, presumably, elsewhere. She attacks traditional claims of the inherent weakness of women with a host of biblical examples, taken mostly from the Old Testament. She implicitly counters the argument that Eve's treachery permanently sullied her sex with the simple observation that Judas, the New Testament equivalent, was male. These sections exhibit not only the knowledge of Scripture one would expect from a street-corner reformer, but also an impressive grasp of the theological purposes that Scripture served.

The main body of the work is an exposition and defense of the position of the exiled evangelical reformers, exhibiting the full rhetorical force of

Dentière's simple, but effective style. It is clear that for her, Farel, not
Calvin, was still the leader of the evangelical party. (It is important to
realize that Dentière was an evangelical reformer, not a "Calvinist.") The
war that had once raged between the citizens of Geneva and their Catholic
lords had become a struggle between the true reformers and the faint of
heart now in control of the city. Dentière now applied to the Council of
Two Hundred the same biblical allusions once used to villify the duke of
Savoy, the bishop, and their party. She depicts the current religious rulers
of her city as schemers and "cockroaches" (cafards) who spread dissension and look out for their own economic interests while exiling the true
preachers of the Gospel.

Dentière's language is strong and the object of her criticism clear. Jean
Gerard published 1,500 copies of the work under the false imprint Anvers, chez Martin Lempereur, designed to circumvent the recently tightened regulations on printing in Geneva; of these, 450 were immediately
sent to Thonon, where Froment was pastor.[26] The ruse fooled no one. Six
weeks later the pastors of Geneva seized the remaining copies of the work
and threw Gerard into jail. Shortly thereafter, Froment, on the part of his
wife, and Gerard pleaded their cases before the council. Asked if the work
were "Lutheran," Gerard responded that it was not, but that it was Christian, and since Luther was a member of the church of God, Gerard had no
quarrel with him. The printer was released on payment of a fine, but the
books were not.[27] Soon after, the council passed legislation prohibiting
publication of any books in Geneva without their prior approval. Froment
later remarked that the greatest regret of the council members about the
work was that they had been so "wounded, piqued and dishonored by a
woman."[28] Litigation over the book continued for several years. In 1540
and again in 1542 Froment unsuccessfully attempted to secure the release
of the sequestered copies.[29]

The suppression of the work by the council of Geneva, done as much
for its general religious content as for its feminism, was successful. In June
1539 the council of Bern wrote to Béat Comte asking his advice on
whether to translate the work (which they attributed to Froment) into
Latin.[30] Comte replied that, while the work contained nothing contrary
to Scripture, it was inopportune. Furthermore, since the title proclaimed it
to be the work of a woman, and women were prohibited by Scripture
from the office of prophesying (the exact argument rejected by Dentière
herself), Comte concluded that the work should be suppressed.[31]

Over the next several years Froment got into several lawsuits with other
reform pastors and was accused of using his post as pastor in Thonon as a
base for commercial speculation in oil.[32] As early as 1538, Farel, who
had long known the couple, denounced Froment to Calvin and suggested
his wife's complicity; by 1540 he wrote Calvin that Dentière had caused

Froment's fall into moral turpitude.[33] The couple, once friendly with Farel and the other exiled reformers, had fallen out of favor, even as Dentière was busily defending those exiles in her writing. Froment later remarried, but it is unsure whether he did so on Dentière's death or on separation from her.[34]

Ironically Dentière's success as a polemicist has caused her omission from the literary canon. While de Jussie has been studied as an example of a conservative female response to the reform, Dentière and her suppressed works have been almost forgotten.[35] Marie Dentière fought not only for the success of the evangelical reform in her adopted city, but also for the place of women in that movement. One of the chief attractions that the evangelical reform held for the marginal people of sixteenth-century French society was the message of universal access to religious truth. Groups who had long been the recipients of authoritative teaching—such as the printers of Lyon—rallied to the promise of the ability to test the clerical interpretation of Scripture against what they read in the vernacular.[36] Dentière clearly states the aspirations of women to preach and interpret that Gospel message for themselves. The mere fact that Marie Dentière preached to the Poor Clares shows how much the Reform altered for a time the social and religious situation of women.

That change, however, was limited. Such varied groups as de Jussie and her sisters, on one side, and the Council of Two Hundred, on the other, resisted it. As Jane Douglass remarks, "The only 'women's liberation' of interest to the sixteenth-century Reformation was the elimination of the monastic view of women, sex and marriage which had flourished both in the monastery and among the laymen."[37] Thus the system against which Dentière preached in de Jussie's convent was overthrown, but the right of Dentière and women like her to preach, to write, and to interpret Scripture, exercised during the period of reform struggle itself, was sharply curtailed as the Reformation consolidated its power. The institutionalization of reform government led to the suppression not only of her *Letter to Queen Marguerite,* but of the exile of much of the evangelical party, including Farel and Calvin. Even the return of Calvin in the 1540s and his "marriage of convenience" with the Genevan government did not free the strictures on female religious discourse. For, while Calvin was sympathetic to certain forms of female spirituality, he held a view of the "qualified but definite subordination" of women to men.[38] The victory of the Reformation, won in a city like Geneva partially through the work of women like Dentière and many others discussed by Froment and de Jussie in their chronicles of the years of reform, led to only limited changes in the religious life and status of those women.[39]

The following translation includes three selections: the opening section of *The War for and Deliverance of Geneva* in which Dentière compares

God's deliverance of the Israelites to the reform in Geneva and thus lays the ideological background for her main narrative;[40] the dedicatory epistle and "Defense of Women" from *The Letter to the Queen of Navarre;*[41] and the concluding peroration of that work.[42]

NOTES

1. Marie Dentière, *Epistre très utile,* as published in Albert Rilliet, "Restitution de *La guerre de délivrance,* p. 383.

2. *Epistre très utile,* dedicatory epistle. Published in Aimé-Louis Herminjard, ed., *Correspondance des réformateurs dans les pays de langue française,* vol. 5, p. 297.

3. *La guerre et délivrance de la ville de Genesve.* The first modern edition of the work was published from a faulty manuscript copy by Gustave Revilliod in "La chronique du Marchand de Genève." It was later reedited from a better manuscript copy by Albert Rilliet for "Restitution de *La guerre et délivrance,*" pp. 337–76. Dentière was identified as the author of the work by Rilliet, pp. 319–35. Théophile Dufour provided corrections for Rilliet's text (*Notice bibliographique,* pp. 135–36). Dufour also accepted Rilliet's identification of Dentière as the work's author. Only manuscript copies of the work are known to survive: the faulty second- or third-generation copies in Zurich and Basle, used by Revilliod, and the Geneva copy made by Pierre Bourrit in 1754 directly from a printed exemplar, used by Rilliet. The work was first noticed in the eighteenth century by Jean Senebier, *Histoire littéraire de Genève,* 3 vols. (Geneva, 1786), vol. 1, p. 75; and by Emmanuel Haller, *Bibliothek der Schweizer-Geschichte* (1787), vol. 5, p. 142. Senebier, who incorrectly identified the printer as Jean Belot, had not seen a printed copy; Haller may have used one. On these notices and the various known manuscript copies, see Rilliet, pp. 309–14. For a full notice on its publication history, see Dufour, pp. 134–36.

4. *Epistre très utile.* Excerpts from this work have been published by Herminjard, ed., vol. 5, pp. 295–304, and by Rilliet, "Restitution de *La guerre et délivrance,*" pp. 377–84. For a full notice on its publication history, see Dufour, pp. 155–59. The original edition is extremely rare. The only extant exemplar of the work is presently in the Musée historique de la Réformation in Geneva, where it bears the number D. Den. 1; Gabrielle Berthoud, *Antoine Marcourt, réformateur et pamphlétaire,* vol. 129, p. 66, n. 185. In 1540 it had belonged to Jean Devantier, a notary at Montheys in the Valais and, in the nineteenth century, to Ernest Chavannes of Lausanne, (Herminjard, ed., vol. 5, p. 295, n. 1, and 297–98, n. 5; Rilliet, "Restitution de *La guerre et délivrance,*" p. 325; Dufour, p. 155). Unfortunately, this essay has been prepared without benefit of having consulted the entire work.

5. Herminjard, ed., vol. 5, p. 298.

6. Ibid., vol. 2, p. 450.

7. Ibid., pp. 127 and 134.

8. Ibid., pp. 139–44.

9. A letter of Antoine Sauliner to Farel dated November 5, 1532, indicates that Robert and Froment knew one another (ibid., pp. 453–54). On Simon Robert's death, see vol. 6, pp. 173–74, n. 28.

10. On the records of Dentière's movements, marriages, and children, see Dufour, pp. 158–59. Two daughters by Robert and one daughter by Froment are found in the public records of Geneva. The full number of her children is provided by Jeanne de Jussie, *Le Levain du Calvinisme, ou Commencement de l'heresie de Genève,* ed. Grivel, p. 174.

11. Robert Kingdon, "Was the Protestant Reformation a Revolution? The Case of Geneva," in *Transition and Revolution: Problems and Issues of European Renaissance and*

Reformation History, ed. Kingdon, pp. 53–107. Froment first appeared in Geneva in November 1532 (Froment, *Les actes et gestes merveilleux de la cité de Genève,* ed. Revilliod, p. 13, and de Jussie, p. 51.

12. For general accounts of the Reformation in Geneva, see E. William Monter, *Calvin's Geneva,* and Henri Naef, *Les origines de la réforme à Genève.*

13. Rilliet, ed., "Restitution de *La guerre de délivrance,* p. 346. This passage is translated below.

14. Ibid., p. 337.

15. See above, note 3.

16. Froment, *Les actes et gestes merveilleux de la cité de Geneve,* ed. Revilliod, and de Jussie, *Le Levain du Calvinisme, ou Commencement de l'heresie de Genève,* ed. Grivel. Like Dentière, these authors, writing from the opposing sides of the reform, had trouble publishing their works, although they wrote some years after Dentière. Froment finished his account in 1554 but was unable to obtain permission for its publication. (The edition of Revilliod only prints part of Froment's text.) On its suppression, see *Guillaume Farel, 1489–1565. Biographie nouvelle écrite d'après les documents originaux* (Neuchâtel, 1930), pp. 50–52. De Jussie composed most of her work in 1532, the year of her exile, and completed it in 1546 while residing in Annecy, where she had become the abbess of her exiled community; it was not published until 1611 in Chambéry, a Catholic city. On the publishing history of the work, see Albert Rilliet, *Notice sur Jeanne de Jussie et le livre intitulé Le Levain du Calvinisme,* pp. 1–12.

17. Natalie Davis, "City Women and Religious Change," in *Society and Culture in Early Modern France,* pp. 65–95. Miriam Chrisman, "Women and the Reformation in Strasbourg, 1490–1530," *Archiv für Reformationsgeschichte* 63 (1972): 143–67. Compare studies of French noblewomen: Nancy Roelker, *Queen of Navarre, Jeanne d'Albret* (Cambridge, Mass., 1968), "The Appeal of Calvinism to French Noblewomen in the Sixteenth Century," *Journal of Interdisciplinary History* 2 (1972): 391–418, and "The Role of the Noblewomen in the French Reformation," *Archiv für Reformationsgeschichte* 63 (1972): 168–194; and Charmarie Blaisdell, "Renée de France Between Reform and Counter-Reform," *Archiv für Reformationsgeschichte* 63 (1972): 196–225. As Steven Ozment has pointed out, the school of scholarship represented in these studies, which derives from the work of Lucien Febvre, tends to understate the importance which religious ideas, rather than emotion and moral sentiment, played in the religious practices of the Reformation (*The Reformation in the Cities: The Appeal of Protestantism to Sixteenth-Century Germany and Switzerland,* p. 13).

18. Chrisman, "Women and the Reformation in Strasbourg," p. 166. For a good introduction to the new Protestant ideal of a married clergy, see Steven Ozment, *The Age of Reform, 1250–1550: An Intellectual and Religious History of Late Medieval and Reformation Europe* (New Haven, 1980), chapter 12, "Marriage and the Ministry in the Protestant Churches."

19. De Jussie, pp. 91–93.

20. Ibid., pp. 135–40.

21. Ibid., pp. 173–74. Perhaps Dentière was brought to preach to the nuns specifically because of the previous failure by the men Farel and Viret to win them over.

22. Ibid., p. 125.

23. The phrase was coined by Sebastian Castellio, who remarked, "Farel himself, alas what a pity, was now Calvinized." *Contra libellum Calvini* (1562), as cited by Ozment, p. 361.

24. Calvin's words come from the eyewitness account of Pastor Jean Pinault, as translated in Monter, p. 95.

25. See Miriam Chrisman's *Lay Culture, Learned Culture. Books and Social Change in*

Strasbourg, 1480–1599 (New Haven, 1982) on women as book owners and readers (pp. 70–73) and as writers of Protestant polemic (pp. 159–60).

26. On the publication of the *Epistre très utile,* see Dufour, pp. 155–58, and Berthoud, pp. 65–70. On its relationship to the legal regulation of printing in Geneva, see Paul Chaix, *Recherches sur l'imprimerie à Genève de 1550 à 1564,* vol. 16, pp. 15–17. About the same time Gerard also reprinted selections from Marguerite of Navarre's *Mirror of the Sinful Soul* (Herminjard, ed., vol. 5, pp. 295–96, n. 3; Dufour, pp. 190–91).

27. The legal cases took place between May 1 and May 13. Extracts from the minutes of the legal proceedings have been printed by Herminjard, ed., vol. 5, pp. 302–3, n. 18; Alfred Cartier, "Arrêts du Conseil de Genève sur le fait de l'imprimerie et de la librairie de 1541 à 1550," *Mémoires et documents publiés par la Société d'histoire et d'archéologie de Genève* 23 (1888–1894): 533–35; and Berthoud, p. 68. Many of the court's questions related directly to statements in Dentière's text. Later in the month, too late for the trial, the Council of Bern sent a letter to the Pastors of Geneva supporting Froment and Gerard (Herminjard, ed., vol. 5, pp. 321–23.

28. An unpublished passage from the *Actes et gestes* cited by Herminjard, ed., vol. 5, pp. 456–57.

29. On January 2, 1540, and again on August 16, 1542, Froment unsuccessfully sought their release. (Minutes of the Council of Geneva as cited in Berthoud, p. 66, n. 188).

30. Herminjard, ed., vol. 5, pp. 332–33. The Council of Bern thought that Froment himself was the author of the work. This confusion probably stemmed from Froment's representation of his wife before the Council of Geneva, where Dentière would have been prohibited from arguing her case. There was no conscious attempt to hide the identity of the author: the title page bore her initials, the dedicatory epistle clearly stated that the book was the work of a woman, and Froment, both in his *Actes et gestes* (which was itself suppressed) and in his deposition in court, stated that his wife was the author (Herminjard, ed., vol. 5, pp. 302–3, n. 18).

31. Berne, *Ratsmanuale,* entry for August 26, 1539, cited by Berthoud, p. 69, n. 204. The same passage was translated into French by Herminjard, ed., vol. 5, pp. 332–33, n. 2.

32. On Froment's legal battle with Christophe Fabri in 1540, see Herminjard, ed., vol. 6, pp. 176–78. On the accusation of speculation in oil made by the congregation of Thonon in 1541, see vol. 6, pp. 401–4 and vol. 7, pp. 381–83.

33. Letters of Farel to Calvin, dated October 14, 1538, in Herminjard, ed., vol. 5, p. 151; and February 6, 1540, in vol. 6, p. 173.

34. On Froment's remarriage, see Dufour, pp. 158–59. Froment discussed Dentière's publication of *The Letter to the Queen of Navarre* in a chapter of *The Marvelous Acts and Deeds,* which was never published. He did not indicate whether she was still alive (Rilliet, "Restitution de *La guerre,*" pp. 326–27). There is some suggestion in Genevan sources after 1540 of infidelity on the part of Froment's wife: this could refer either to Dentière or to his later wife.

35. Besides the editions of Dentière's works and the notices of them in Dufour, she received brief notices in Henri Hauser, *Manuel de bibliographie historique, Souces de l'histoire de France. XVI siècle (1494–1610),* 4 vols. (Paris, 1906–1915), vol. 2, p. 113, n. 983, and in Alexandre Cioranesco, *Bibliographie de la littérature française du seizième siècle* (Paris, 1959), nn. 9450 and 9451. She is omitted from other standard reference works. Davis cited her work several times in "City Women and Religious Change" (pp. 82, 89, and 95). In contrast, Jane Douglass used Jeanne de Jussie as the counterexample of a woman who remained Catholic ("Women and the Continental Reformation," in *Religion and Sexism: Images of Woman in the Jewish and Christian Traditions,* ed. Ruether, pp. 309–14). Robert Kingdon used *The Germ of Calvinism* as a source to answer the question "Was the Protestant Reformation a Revolution? The Case of Geneva," passim (which includes translated

passages from *The Germ of Calvinism* on pp. 87–95). Also see Rilliet, *Notice sur Jeanne de Jussie et sur le livre intitulé Le Levain du Calvinisme*.

36. Natalie Davis, "Strike and Salvation at Lyon," in *Society and Culture in Early Modern France* (Stanford, 1965), p. 6.

37. Douglass, "Women and the Continental Reformation," pp. 313–14.

38. Jane Douglass has treated Calvin's ideas on the right of women to preach, including Dentière's role in the Geneva reform, in "Christian Freedom: What Calvin Learned at the School of Women," *Church History* 53 (1984): 155–73. Douglass has expanded her analysis of Calvin's ideas on Christian freedom and its application to women in *Women, Freedom, and Calvin* (Philadelphia, 1986). For other treatments of Calvin's views on women, see Willis De Boer, "Calvin on the Role of Women," in *Exploring the Heritage of John Calvin*, ed. David Holwerda (Grand Rapids, Mich., 1976), pp. 236–72; and John Bratt, "The Role and Status of Women in the Writings of John Calvin," with a response by Charmarie Blaisdell, in *Renaissance, Reformation, Resurgence. Papers and Responses Presented at the Colloquium on Calvin and Calvin Studies*, ed. Peter de Klerk (Grand Rapids, Mich., 1976), pp. 1–17 and 19–32. The quotation is taken from Bratt, p. 1.

39. Douglass discusses de Jussie's *Le Levain du Calvinisme* primarily as a witness of direct female involvement, on both Catholic and Protestant sides, in the battles of the reform ("Women and the Continental Reformation," pp. 309–14).

40. Rilliet, ed., "Restitution de *La guerre de délivrance*, pp. 339–53.

41. Herminjard, ed., vol. 5, pp. 295–98; and Rilliet, ed., pp. 378–80.

42. Herminjard, ed., vol. 5, pp. 300–304; augmented by Rilliet, ed., p. 384.

The Fight for and Deliverance of the City of Geneva, Faithfully Told and Written Down by a Merchant Living in That City

TO ALL THOSE WHO DESIRE TO KNOW AND UNDERSTAND THE WAR FOR AND DELIVERANCE OF THE CITY OF GENEVA, GREETINGS IN OUR LORD JESUS CHRIST

For the reason that many people are astounded by the wars, divisions, and debates which have occurred, principally in the last three years, here in the city of Geneva, I have wished to collect and put into writing all these things, manifest and public, to each one in the city, in order that all those who know it will understand how the citizens, bourgeoisie, and inhabitants of that city lived and conducted themselves, and how God always protected, assured, and defended them in the face of all and against all their mortal enemies. This is a very eloquent thing to all those who love God and His Word, and it is for them a great consolation to uncover, to open, to see, to tell, and to speak, but for all their enemies, traitors, and adversaries of God and of this city, it is a great desolation, ignominy, and confusion.

One ought not be astounded that God has so miraculously delivered us from our enemies for free and without our having either merited or deserved it. For it is always God's work to show his virtue and power in things considered hopeless by men, so that that honor and glory is provided by Him for all, although it belongs to Him. For He has no regard for the force or the number of His adversaries, but only for the faith and the confidence that one has in Him. For He is as powerful, or even more so, in the weakness, smallness, scorn, and contempt of his own people, than in the highness, wisdom, and prudence of others, and He is as able to give victory to a small number as to a great multitude, as He has done for us and for many others in times passed.

For He is the God of hope, the God of strength, the God of battles and victories, and, if He is not subject to men, then it is necessary that all obey Him. Behold the kings, princes, and lords of the earth, whose hearts He holds in His hand. He does no more than speak a word, and the thing is done. He worked for His people and by his people as much as it pleased Him, against all odds. Who is there, I ask you, who would have thought that He would have been so prompt to give aid in things so hopeless? Behold Abraham and his sterile wife Sarah, two old people, without hope of ever having a child.[1] Nevertheless, against all odds, He helped them and provided a lineage for them in their old age. For God is so powerful that He can give and provide that which He has promised, as much at one time as at another. He takes regard neither for the difficulty of time, nor for old age, nor for anything else, but only for the faith that one has in His promises. Similarly Zechariah and his wife Elizabeth had that which they did not expect, to have John in their old age.[2]

Jesus Christ himself, the true Son of God, came and was born of the Virgin Mary in a most difficult time, fuller of tyranny than one would know how to describe, when Herod reigned, the one who, in order to destroy and annihilate the fame of Jesus, had little infants killed. Notwithstanding this, it was necessary that all of his enemies be ground under the soles of his feet; and so, it was necessary that the grand Goliath, proud, haughty, conceited, well armed, and equipped, be pulled down, ruined and destroyed, killed and put to death by his own knife, by this little David, sweet and benign. What would we now say of Herod's force, of his power so easily overthrown? That Jesus was found stronger and more powerful than him. Multitude, prudence, and force did not cause victory here, but only the faith and the full trust that one had in God.

That great town Jericho was completely shut up, well munitioned, well fed, and fortified against Joshua. But simply at the sound of his trumpet circling the city for seven days, the walls fell down and the city was sacked and put to fire.[3] And what more could I say of the great victories of past times obtained through the faith of those who were strong in battle against the Assyrians, who reversed the arms of those strangers who had conquered the royal lands?[4] Their God, is He not also ours? Yes, certainly! Is He less powerful than He was? No! The God of Abraham, of Isaac, of Jacob, and of the other patriarchs and prophets, is He not ours? Ha! This is not the god of idolators, made by the hand of man, deadened or drunk at the tavern, like the god Baal, for it is the living God, who consumed the sacrifice of Elijah by fire, showing Himself to be the God of the children of Israel.[5]

Those who are in the service of the Pharaoh are miraculously put to flight against all odds. See how, even in affairs of utter hopelessness and in those times when one would not expect it, the hope of men is undone. For God, having pity on His people, did not wish His name to be blasphemed, and sent His servant Moses to Pharaoh, saying. "Let my brothers go and they will come to the land which has been promised them."[6] But the Pharaoh persisted in wishing to do nothing, notwithstanding all the things which Moses did in his presence. As Pharaoh was enraged against them, he wished to kill and murder them with a great army and to abolish their name without which they would never be remembered, so that he pursued them beyond the point of endurance, with the result that they lost all hope. The sea on one side, the mountain on the other, and their enemies at their back with a great army, with the result that there was no longer a way of evading their enemies' hands. Their path lacked direction, there was no longer anything to eat, they were beset and surrounded on all sides, and what is more, they were few in number. But God, who never forgets His own, came to deliver them by a means which they did not expect, dividing the sea one side from the other for them so that they passed dry shod. But their enemies persisted; not knowing the work of God, they followed after and all died in the sea. Behold what deliverance was provided the Israelites, what grace, what mercy was granted them!

But that granted to us is greater, if we were not so blind. It is not granted for men, or by men, but by God and against the wishes of men. The result is that each one knows that God is our God, powerful in granting grace, deliverance, and greater things, when and to whom He wishes, without one having gained, merited, or deserved it. For if ever mercy was granted to a people, it is granted to us; behold, if I dared to say it, even greater. For each enemy which the Israelites had, we have two; for each tyranny and cruelty, we have a thousand; for each Pharaoh, one hundred; for each malice, envy and stubbornness, one hundred thousand; in short, it is an impossible task for a merchant like me to know how to describe it fully. But if God touched the heart of some good person more powerful than me, who had more inventive language, more exquisite words, that man would announce it. Please do not examine the style or the rudeness of my language. For the nation and the state of my merchandise must excuse for it.

If, as in all things, it is necessary in the beginning to know and hear how this last (if it is necessary so to call it) war started and proceeded, it is necessary first to know and hear its origin and beginning, to what end, for what reason, and by whom that war was made and waged. You will find that the common proverb "If you wake a sleeping dog, it's not the dog's fault if he bites" applies to those who would bring it to mind. Those who wished to battle against God and His Word have battled against themselves; thinking to pillage, they have, in the words of the prophet, been pillaged; in setting fire, they have been burned; in wishing to kill, to hang, and to murder, they have died; in embracing much, they have retained nothing; in seeking to win all, they have lost all; in sitting on two saddles, they have fallen on their backsides. What more need I say? Is it not a great folly to bare one's claws against an eagle, or to wish to stop the sun from rising? Yes, certainly! Even more is it so to seek to stop the Word of God from taking its course, for in making it withdraw, you advance it. Just as he who seeks ill and finds it has not wasted his time, so, too, these tyrants, brigands, and murderers who, under the shadow of war, have maintained the faith and the law of the Pope and have exercised their brigandries to root out and annihilate the truth and the living Word of God, His Holy Gospel, and the freedoms and immunities of the city, they will find that these things are impossible for them.

For it is true that, for all time, since the city of Geneva was built and constructed, she has had and still has great freedom and immunity, without any subjugation, and so it is established undeniably in writing within the town hall. The city has the right to elect syndics for judging and regulating cases in all justice and fairness, as is presently done; it holds forth good and correct justice to each one, without excepting anyone, just as the Word of God teaches; it punishes the wicked and defends the good; it does not permit any idolatries, blasphemies, thefts, or public drunkenness to reign, nothing which would be against the commandment of God; it punishes all who contravene that commandment, all the time allowing everyone to speak in all sweetness and benevolence. The result is that all who wish to speak against their manner of living are permitted, and if there is any one who can show a different way of living according to the Word of God, and that what they hold is done of God and according to the Gospel of Jesus, that person would be welcomed and given permission, requested to render justice to our preachers, such that each one might follow the example.

By force of tyranny the duke (once upon a time called "of Savoy"), with his nobles, bishops, and priests, has wished many times to usurp and abolish this justice, as well as everything which pertains to it. Behold the life he imposed: wives and the daughters of good merchants, who do not reside with their fathers, mothers, and kinsfolk, are violated and raped by force before their own husbands without any one speaking against it, for anyone who grumbled would be persecuted. This state of affairs endured no little time, but for the space of thirty years.[7] Seeing that these things were insupportable to a people of honor and heart, and that they were no longer able to endure and suffer it, some people declared to this good prince of peace (if I do not lie) that there would be justice, thinking that he as well was a friend of the city, given the services and pleasures which they had done for him, even more so since he was their prince and lord. But in place of giving justice and reason (in as much as he was accustomed), he secretly permitted the worst to be done. Those who wished to maintain these freedoms and liberties of the city, they were put to death miserably: he fetched them from the Piedmont in faith and trust, and then put them to death and chopped them up, and what is more, returned them dirtied in beer barrels in all derision and mockery.[8] He has never ceased to persecute this poor city in such ways, searching by all means known to him to find a way to destroy and ruin it, not only by famines and war, but by other things as well.

But God, who takes pity on His own, did not wish to permit such injuries to be done, and inspired the citizens of Geneva to recognize the good and venerable prince for what he was, and gave them heart to make a pact with the citizens of Bern and Fribourg, with the goal of maintaining their freedoms and immunities, in all justice and fairness, just as has since been done.[9] But the duke, realizing that he would lose his feathers, just as has happened in recent times, acted and plotted on one side and on the other to make great alliances with many princes and lords. But it all served no purpose, except to make the duke a prophet, in as much as that which he feared, losing his own country, did indeed come to pass. For that which a man dreads comes upon his head.[10] That fear did not come to pass without injury, for each one took a feather from him and he was left plucked, fully naked and without feathers. It is fitting that he who wished to pluck and be plucked, that he was left without them.[11] Women boldly sat to hatch their chicks, for the dukes would no longer eat them.[12]

This first alliance caused the begetting of great treasons against the city and great discord of people against one another. Those who took the side of the enemies suffered much loss of goods, and as traitors they were exiled, taking the name of Mammellus, causing the Aydguenos great pains and labors in resisting their enemies and their dealings.[13] For those who were not first destroyed by the sword of God have never since ceased plotting treason against the city with the bishops, priests, monks, and nuns.

Not content with all the innumerable injuries and outrages they caused (which I will omit, in order to avoid prolixity), after five years had passed they began a war against the city where the poor merchants lived.[14] But, so they say, from an old policeman comes a new rascal, and from too much investigation there comes no good. Their homes were burned, the poor people destroyed, the duke condemned to pay a fine of twenty-one thousand *écus* and his lands were to be confiscated if he ever again broke his promise to the city, as he had just done. Pharaoh, seeing the great works which Moses did in his presence, was only more obstinant. So, too, the duke, seeing his loss and the evils and outrages which had been done, did not wish to desist, making it necessary that he be destroyed and wasted. It was as difficult for Moureau to change his skin, as for a leopard his color, for a brigand to be a merchant, for an infidel to keep faith and loyalty, but his loss and tribulation would be good, if it led him to God.

Our good God, having pity on His poor people, and seeing them so pillaged, consumed, vexed, and tormented, had wished to deliver them at a most difficult time, at a time filled with tyranny, at a time one would not expect, and even at a time when the traitors controlled the government offices, syndics did according to their pleasure, wishing to deliver the city by many plots to its enemies. Sixteen principals conspired in treason, of whom some lost their lives, others were exiled, and the rest dishonored. The least of their plots would have sufficed, according to the ways of men, to deliver and waste not only a city, but even a kingdom, if God, by His grace, had not brought about what followed.

Firstly, three years later syndics were elected who were pleasing to the bishop, canons, and priests, to the great prejudice and detriment of the city. At that time it happened that Guillaume Farel, the preacher of the Gospel, came visiting some Christian churches with various companions and brothers. And passing through Geneva, he wished to preach Jesus, and Him crucified, publicly. . . .

A Most Beneficial Letter, Prepared and Written Down by a Christian Woman of Tournai, and Sent to the Queen of Navarre, Sister of the King of France, Against the Turks, the Jews, the Infidels, the False Christians, the Anabaptists and the Lutherans

TO THE VERY CHRISTIAN PRINCESS MARGUERITE OF
FRANCE, QUEEN OF NAVARRE, DUCHESS OF ALENÇON AND
OF BERRY: M.D. WISHES SALVATION AND INCREASE OF
GRACE THROUGH JESUS CHRIST

Everyone, my very honored lady, especially the true lovers of truth, desire to know and hear how they ought to live in these most dangerous times; so, too, we women ought to know how to flee and avoid all errors, heresies, and false doctrines, just as much those of the false Christians, Turks, and Infidels, as those of others suspect in doctrine, as has already been shown in your writing.[15] Although many good and faithful servants of God were inspired, in times past, to write down, preach, and announce the Law of God, the coming of His Son Jesus Christ, his works, death, and resurrection; nevertheless they were rejected and reproved, principally by the wise men of the people. And not only were these people rejected, but also God's own Son, Jesus Christ the just. Therefore it should not amaze you if, in our time, we see similar things happen to those to whom God has given the grace of wishing to write down, speak, preach, and announce the same things that Jesus and his Apostles said and preached. We see that the whole world is full of malediction, and its inhabitants troubled, because they see the great tumults, debates, dissension, and divisions of one against the other, greater than have ever happened on earth: gross envy, quarrel, rancor, malevolence, greed, wantonness, theft, pillage, drawing of blood, murder, tumult, rape, fire, poisoning, war, kingdom against kingdom, nation against nation. In short, every abomination reigns. Father against son, and son against father, mother against daughter, and daughter against mother, each wishing to sell the other: the mother to deliver her own daughter up to every misfortune. So that surely there are few, in terms of the people who are on the earth, who truly seek how they ought to live, given that such things happen among those who call themselves Christians. And one does not venture to say a word about those people: for one wishes that this thing be done, the other that; the one lives well (or so he says), the other badly; the one is wise, the other foolish; the one has knowledge, the other knows nothing; the one holds this thing dear, the other that. In short, there is nothing but division. Either one or the other must necessarily live badly. For there is only one God, one Faith, one Law, and one baptism.

Yet still, my very honored lady, I have wished to write you, not in order to teach you yourself, but in order that you may take care with the king your brother, to heal all these divisions, which reign in those places, towns, and peoples over which God has commissioned him to reign and govern, and also to take care for your lands, which God has given you, for the purpose of watching over and giving order. For we ought not, any more than men, hide and bury within the earth that which God has given you and revealed to us women. Although we are not permitted to preach in assemblies and public churches, nevertheless we are not prohibited from writing and advising one another, in all charity. I have wished to write this letter not only for you, my lady, but also to give courage to other women held in captivity, so that they will no longer fear being exiled, like me, from their countries, parents, and friends for the Word of God. And principally for those poor little women who desire to know and hear the truth; they do not know which road, which path they ought to follow. And henceforth they will not themselves be so tormented and afflicted, but now rejoice, consoled and moved to follow the truth, which is the Gospel of Jesus Christ. Even to the present day this has been so hidden that one would not dare say a word and it seemed that women ought not read anything or listen to the Holy Scripture. This is my principal cause, my lady, that which has moved me to write to you, hoping in God, that henceforth women will no longer be scorned as in the past. For day to day God changes the hearts of His own people for the good. I pray that this will shortly be so through all the world. Amen.

A DEFENSE OF WOMEN

Not only do we wish to accuse any defamers and adversaries of the truth of very great audacity and temerity, but also any of the faithful who say that women are very impudent in interpreting Scripture for one another. To them, one is lawfully able to respond that all those who are described and named in the Holy Scripture are not to be judged too temerarious. Note that many women are named and praised in the Holy Scripture, not only for their good morals, deeds. bearing, and example, but for their faith and doctrine, like Sarah and Rebecca, and principally among all the others of the Old Testament, the mother of Moses, who, notwithstanding the edict of the king, protected her son from death and caused him to be reared in the house of the Pharaoh, as is fully described in Exodus 2. Deborah, who judged the people of Israel in the time of the Judges, is not to be scorned.[16] I ask, would it be necessary to condemn Ruth, given the fact that she is of the feminine sex, because of the story that is written about her in her book? I do not think so; she is rightly numbered in the genealogy of Jesus Christ.[17] The Queen of Sheba had such wisdom that she is not only named in the Old Tesament, but Jesus also named her among other sages.[18]

If it is a question of speaking of the graces which have been given to women, what greater grace was given to any creature on the earth than that given to the Virgin Mary, mother of Jesus, to have born the Son of God? She did not have less than Elizabeth, mother of John the Baptist, who had a son miraculously, as she was sterile.[19] What preacheress has done more than the Samaritan woman, who was not ashamed to preach Jesus and his word, confessing it openly before all the world, as soon as she heard from Jesus that one must adore God in spirit and in truth?[20] Or is anyone other than Mary Magdalene, from whom Jesus had driven seven devils, able to boast of having had the first revelation of the great mystery of Jesus' resurrection? And were not the other women, to whom, instead of to men, his resurrection was announced by his angel, commanded to speak, preach, and declare it to others? Just as much as there is imperfection in all women, nevertheless, the men are not exempt from it.

Why then is it necessary to gossip about women? Seeing that it was not a woman who sold and betrayed Jesus, but a man, named Judas. Who are they, I ask you, who have invented and contrived the ceremonies, heresies, and false doctrines on the earth, if not the men? And the poor women have been seduced by them. Never has a woman been found to be a false prophet, just fooled by them. Nevertheless, I do not wish to excuse by this the overly great malice of some women, which outstrips the bounds of measure. But there is no longer reason to make of that malice a general rule, without any exception, as some do daily, particularly Faustus, that scoffer, in his *Bucolics*. Seeing that work, surely I am unable to fall silent, given that it is more recommended and used by men than the Gospel of Jesus, which is defended by us, and given that this fable teller is in good repute in the schools.[21] If God has given graces to some good women, revealing to them something holy and good through His Holy Scripture, should they, for the sake of the defamers of the truth, refrain from writing down, speaking, or declaring it to each other? Ah! It would be too impudent to hide the talent which God has given to us, we who ought to have the grace to persevere to the end. Amen!

THE CONCLUDING SECTION

If according to one or two witnesses, those who acted contrary to Moses died, what of those who are contemptuous of Jesus, who is much greater than Moses? Particularly of those who call themselves leaders of the people, like bishops, priests, monks, preachers, and others calling themselves the light of the world? Such types only set store by their belly, having great bishoprics, great prebends; they have no regard for anything other than themselves. They recognize full well that they are not suited to such offices, but in order to provide for their dogs, their horses, their ribaldries, and their mistresses, and in order to nourish their bellies, which are their God, they hold and occupy the place of pastors. Since they are nothing but wolves and spendthrifts, wishing to have dominion over the people, they say: "It is mine, it is my town, it is my bishopric, my parish! Who would dare [take] it from me?" They retire to worldly arms in order to be better at their ease in bodily comfort; they do not at all consider the ordinance of God to be true, but think to diminish it through human power, through condemnations and the ordinances of man. Such that if anyone contradicts, preaches, or writes against them, that person would be suddenly judged heretical, a seducer of the people, an inventor of new sects. They ought to resist such people through correct doctrine and to confound them powerfully through the Word of God, as the holy apostle Paul would have done, and not by sword, banishment, exile, fire, and injury. All preachers and ministers of the Word of God ought to proceed in imitation of that apostle, giving no heed to anything except that God be glorified and honored throughout the world and that one be joined in the next to our Savior. But it was necessary that Judas be with Christ. Asses pass under the chimney; indolent bellies reign over the people; the prophets are also confused with the false apostles, truth with falsity, the light with the shadows, and the black with the white. Such people are in great number, if they are not already equal to or more numerous than they ever were in the time of Saint Paul, and are now even more dangerous. That apostle complained strongly about those things which had already seduced and confused the Galatians: their return to circumcision and Mosaic ceremonies previously abolished by the Word of God. And if now one complained about our false apostles throughout the land, it would not be without legitimate cause, given that they have acted like cowardly soldiers in battle. For when it is a question of doing battle against the enemy, they are good in striking, chewing, and hitting at table. But can you find them in assaults, skirmishes, and ambuscades against the enemies of Truth? They do not want to chew there, since there are cuts, injuries, and outrages there. There they are as bold as slugs. If it were not so, they would not be such good mercenaries and so suited for holding good cities in garrison. Along with that, they are very knowledgeable and learned in all manners of things for knowing how to please their bellies, and in falsely marking and accusing both those whom they had exiled and repulsed by force and those dead in battle.

But, virtuous lady, for all this, you should not be amazed if we see some punishment of God come; for those who make these troubles are nothing other than hypocritical monks. Since there are such asses, wolves, and impudent hypocritical libertines among the sheep, they ought to be made to flee and driven away by all, like chimeras, so that they no longer seduce the poor people by their false doctrine and lying conversation. They would be a strong and dangerous thing to fear, if God by His grace were not able to do what He has done. For He has struck those of this sort, so that they are put to flight; and daily they flee, without anyone giving chase, for they well know that the judgment of God will come on their heads. And principally that poor miserable man, upon whom God looks mercifully, who has given sufficient scandal to the poor people not only by his false doctrine, but like an impudent, has left (if one dares to say it) his own wife besieged in Neuchâtel. Not content with that, this man has returned to his own vomit; the mortarboard of a doctor of the Sorbonne always reeks of garlic.[22] Notwithstanding this, some of his party, who are not worth even as much as he, search and seek for a reason to canonize him.

In conclusion, few people are present who do not look out for themselves, rather than for the people of God; they give power to men, and not to the church of Jesus; nearly all are mute dogs, each gnawing a bone. It is the best policy in the world; they have nothing to fear. Everything is well put together, cockroaches are welcome, and all who well know how to please "My Lord" and "My Lady" are well nourished and treated. For one is silent and the other says nothing, seeking and plotting to crush his brothers. Surely this is what the prophet Isaiah said would happen: "They have returned in their way, each to the avarice of his side." Such that one intrigues for a bishopric, the other petitions for a priory; the first makes a complaint, the other fights a duel with him; the first has nothing, the other is full; the first goes hungry, the other is satisfied; the first wished for something, and nevertheless has less than nothing. In short, there is nothing but avarice, ambition, and confusion. Surely, as someone leaves, someone else comes; each without being sent by God; each making divisions in the church of Jesus. Each destroys, both the one who is pleasing and the one who wishes to please. For one is not able to be pleasing both to God and to man; it is necessary to love one and to hate the other. The good servant pleases his master, and gives no care to anything except that his master be served and honored. The true pastors and ministers of Jesus are persecuted, banished, and exiled, since they have no care and give no thought of pleasure to anything other than serving, honoring, and praying to their Savior and Master. Please send no one except those who demand nothing but His honor and glory and the edification of all. So it shall be!

NOTES TO THE TRANSLATION

1. Genesis 16:1–2.
2. Luke 1:5–14.
3. Joshua 6:1–21.
4. 1 Kings 20:16–30. Judith 14:11–15:11.
5. 1 Kings 18:30–40.
6. Exodus 5:1.
7. In 1504 the duke of Savoy took over complete control of the state; the rebellion of the city against him began in 1526 but was not fully successful until 1536.
8. Dentière refers to the case of two young Genevans named Navis and Blanchet who were executed in 1518.
9. This pact was made on February 23, 1526.
10. Proverbs 10:24.
11. Rilliet suggests that Dentière is punning here on the similarity of *elles* (a pronoun standing here for feathers) and *ailes* (wings) (*La guerre et délivrance,* ed. Rilliet, p. 346, n. 10).
12. In this paragraph Dentière used an extended metaphor based on a pun. The French word *duc* can mean a horned owl as well as a duke. Through the revolt of the citizens the duke or owl of Savoy lost his plumage and was no longer able to prey on the offspring of the

women of the city. Dentière's husband, Antoine Froment, used the same pun to describe the defeat of the duke by the French in 1536 (*Actes et gestes*, p. 218).

13. The name Mamelli was given to the members of the Savoyard party loyal to the duke, while the name Aydguenos, or Eidguenots, was used to signify the Genevan merchants' party. These two factions appear in the minutes of Geneva's Council as early as May 1520. The duke's party fled the city in August 1527. On the development of factional rivalry and more generally on the events discussed in this passage, consult Monter, pp. 35–59. According to Jeanne de Jussie, the merchant party took their name from a German word meaning "good ally" (*Le Levain du calvinisme*, p. 7).

14. In 1530 the merchant party of Geneva led by Besançon Hugues overcame a counterattack by the Savoyards and finally broke their blockade of the city with the aid of Bern and Fribourg. The Savoyards attempted similar blockades of the city at several points over the next six years, until their final defeat in 1536.

15. Dentière refers to Marguerite of Navarre's *Mirror of the Sinful Soul*. See the chapter in this volume on Marguerite and her works.

16. Judges 4:4–10.

17. Matthew 1:5.

18. 1 Kings 10:1–13; 2 Chronicles 9:1–12; Matthew 12:42; Luke 11:31.

19. Luke 1:36–56.

20. John 4:7–30.

21. Publius Faustus Andrelinus (1462–1518) published the *Bucolica* c. 1496, and it became one of the most popular works of Renaissance pastoral poetry. The best edition is Wilfred Mustard, ed., *The Eclogues of Faustus Andrelinus and Ioannes Arnolletus* (Baltimore, 1918). For a brief biography of Andrelinus, see pp. 11–19. The Genevan notary Guillaume Messiez noted that Faustus's works were used as texts in the public schools of the city in 1534. Ironically, he also described how he studied Scripture under Farel, Viret, and Froment. Théophile Heyer, "Petit mémorial du notaire Messiez," *Mémoires et documents publiées par la Société d'histoire et d'archéologie de Genève* 9 (1855):23.

22. Pierre Caroli, a professor at the Sorbonne and canon of the church of Sens, came to Geneva in the 1530s as a reformer and was an associate of Farel and Froment in the Affair of the Placards in 1535. Already at that time Farel disliked this more moderate and ecclesiastically oriented reformer. By 1539 Caroli was in Lausanne, where he was to become chief pastor for a time. In 1543–1544 Caroli and Farel carried on a vitriolic debate in print, and Caroli's career later stagnated. The best overall treatment of Caroli is still Eduard Baehler, *Petrus Caroli und Johann Calvin, Jahrbuch für schweizerisch Geschichte*, vol. 29 (1904). The costume of professors at the Sorbonne, including mortarboards, had become antiquated by the sixteenth century and was made the butt of jokes by Erasmus and others.

BIBLIOGRAPHY

Primary Works

Dentière, Marie. *Epistre très utile, faicte et composée par une femme chrestienne de Tornay, envoyée à la Royne de Navarre, seur du Roy de France, contre les Turcz, Juifz, Infideles, Faulx chrestiens, Anabaptistes et Lutheriens*. Geneva, 1539.

———. *La guerre et délivrance de la ville de Genesve, fidèlement faicte et composée par un Marchant demourant en icelle*. Geneva, 1536.

Herminjard, Aimé-Louis, ed. *Correspondance des réformateurs dans les pays de langue française*. 9 vols. vol. 5, pp. 295–304. Geneva, 1866–1897.

Revilliod, Gustave, ed. "La chronique du Marchand de Genève." *Mémoires et documents publiées par la société d'histoire et d'archéologie de Genève* 13 (1863): 27–39.

Rilliet, Albert, ed. "Restitution de l'écrit intitulé: *La guerre de deslivrance de la ville de Genesve* (1536)." *Mémoires et documents publiées par la société d'histoire et d'archéologie de Genève* 20 (1881): 309–84.

Related Works

Berthoud, Gabrielle. *Antoine Marcourt, réformateur et pamphlétaire.* Geneva, 1973.

Blaisdell, Charmarie. "Response to the Role and Status of Women in the Writings of John Calvin." In *Renaissance, Reformation, Resurgence: Papers and Responses Presented at the Colloquium on Calvin and Calvin Studies,* ed. Peter De Klerk, pp. 19–32. Grand Rapids, Mich., 1976.

Bratt, John. "The Role and Status of Women in the Writings of John Calvin." In *Renaissance, Reformation, Resurgence: Papers and Responses Presented at the Colloquium on Calvin and Calvin Studies,* ed. Peter De Klerk, pp. 1–17. Grand Rapids, Mich., 1976.

Chaix, Paul. *Recherches sur l'imprimerie à Genève de 1550 à 1564. Etude bibliographique, économique et littéraire, Travaux de l'humanisme et renaissance.* Vol. 16. Geneva, 1954.

Chrisman, Miriam. "Women and the Reformation in Strasbourg, 1490–1530." *Archiv für Reformationsgeschichte* 63 (1972): 143–67.

Davis, Natalie. "City Women and Religious Change." In *Society and Culture in Early Modern France,* pp. 65–95. Stanford, 1965.

De Boer, Willis. "Calvin on the Role of Women." In *Exploring the Heritage of John Calvin,* ed. David Holwerda, pp. 236–72. Grand Rapids, Mich., 1976.

De Jussie, Jeanne. *Le Levain du Calvinisme, ou Commencement de l'heresie de Genève.* Ed. Ad.-C. Grivel. Geneva, 1865.

Douglass, Jane. "Christian Freedom: What Calvin Learned at the School of Women." *Church History* 53 (1984): 155–73.

————. "Women and the Continental Reformation." In *Religion and Sexism: Images of Woman in the Jewish and Christian Traditions,* ed. Rosemary Ruether, pp. 292–318. New York, 1974.

————. *Women, Freedom, and Calvin.* Philadelphia. 1986.

Dufour, Théophile. *Notice bibliographique sur le Catéchisme et la Confession de Foi de Calvin (1537) et sur les autres livres imprimés à Genève et à Neuchatel dans les premiers temps de la réforme (1533–1540),* pp. 134–36. Geneva, 1878.

Dupont, Louis. *Antoine Froment, ou les commencements de la réforme à Genève.* Strasbourg, 1857.

Froment, Antoine. *Les actes et gestes merveilleux de la cité de Genève.* Ed. Gustave Revilliod. Geneva, 1854.

Kingdon, Robert. "Was the Protestant Reformation a Revolution? The Case of Geneva." In *Transition and Revolution: Problems and Issues of European Renaissance and Reformation History,* ed. Robert Kingdon, pp. 53–107. Minneapolis, 1974.

Monter, E. William. *Calvin's Geneva.* New York, 1967.

Naef, Henri. *Les origines de la réforme à Genève.* 2 vols. Vol. 100, parts 1 and 2, of *Travaux d'humanisme et renaissance.* Geneva, 1968.

Ozment, Steven. *The Reformation in the Cities: The Appeal of Protestantism to Sixteenth-Century Germany and Switzerland.* New Haven, 1975.

Rilliet, Albert. *Notice sur Jeanne de Jussie et sur le livre intitulé Le Levain du Calvinisme.* Geneva, 1866.

Roelker, Nancy. "The Appeal of Calvinism to French Noblewomen in the Sixteenth Century." *Journal of Interdisciplinary History* 2 (1972): 391–418.

———. "The Role of the Noblewomen in the French Reformation." *Archiv für Reformationsgeschichte* 63 (1972): 168–94.

PART THREE

erman Principalities/
Hapsburg Empire

THE NUREMBERG ABBESS

aritas Pirckheimer

GWENDOLYN BRYANT

Barbara Pirckheimer was born in Eichstätt, Bavaria on March 21, 1467. She was the eldest of Dr. Johannes Pirckheimer and Barbara Löffelholz's twelve children, three of whom died at an early age. Their fourth child, Willibald, the only one of Barbara's brothers to live to adulthood, distinguished himself as a humanist and diplomat.[1] At the age of twelve Barbara was sent to study in the Klarakloster in Nuremberg, where the family had settled and where her father served as a legal advisor to the city council.[2] The convent of the sisters of Saint Clare was a wealthy institution that received many of the daughters of Nuremberg's patrician families and enjoyed an excellent reputation for both its piety and learning.[3] Barbara took the veil probably around 1483, thereby dedicating herself to a life of poverty, celibacy, asceticism, and seclusion.[4] Sometime before 1485 she began calling herself "Caritas," a name whose appropriateness she later humbly denies in a letter to Conrad Celtis.[5]

Like their elder sister, all but two of the Pirckheimer girls also became nuns, with three of their nieces, Willibald's daughters, following suit. Giving only a small percentage of the female children in marriage seems to reflect a family preference: as members of one of the richest and most powerful patrician families of the city the Pirckheimer daughters were especially vulnerable to unfavorable matches.[6] This is not to suggest that Caritas and her sisters did not prove themselves well suited for the conventual life; on the contrary, Caritas was chosen to become abbess of the Klarakloster in 1503, and her younger sisters Klara, Sabina, and Eufemia all eventually served their respective convents in this same capacity.[7]

In a letter dated December 20, 1503, Willibald Pirckheimer expresses his ambivalence toward the news of Caritas's election: "Public opinion pressed me to congratulate you, while reason not without force and power moved me to console you."[8] In spite of this initial concern over the weight of the burden that would rest on his sister's shoulders, he nevertheless goes on to encourage her to fulfill valiantly her duties—"Qui certat, coronatur"—although at this time he could not have known the extent to which she would have to fight to preserve the Klarakloster and its way of life.

In becoming abbess Caritas assumed responsibility not only for the spiritual and corporeal welfare of about sixty members of her order, but also for the direction of a complicated organization within a large and prosperous city. She served as the sisters' mouthpiece in political, financial, and social dealings with the outside world, and in particular in her relations with the curator, the official designated to protect the interests of the Klarakloster vis-à-vis the city council.[9] Since the council provided considerable aid to the convent, the sisters found themselves dependent on this governing body.[10] As abbess, Caritas was accountable for the maintenance of the abbey's buildings and new building projects, and she gave much energy to the enlargement of the sisters' library.[11] Besides the cloister buildings and gardens within the walls of the city of Nuremberg, the abbey owned considerable property in the area around Nuremberg that was acquired for the most part through donation by wealthy Nuremberg families. Although these lands were not cultivated by the sisters of Saint Clare, Caritas was indirectly responsible for their profitability.[12]

Since the Klarakloster was also an educational institution serving the function of a Latin school for girls in the city of Nuremberg, its abbess provided, in a sense, intellectual leadership as well. As a learned woman from a family with a tradition of scholarship,[13] Caritas was able to maintain contact with several of the great scholars of her day and to keep abreast of developments in the humanist milieu in which her brother played so great a role. However, unlike Willibald, who could use Jupiter as a synonym for God and who had a reputation as a philanderer,[14] she never allowed herself to be seduced by the humanist fashion for pagan texts or a love of earthly pleasures. And although her intellectual curiosity embraced the church fathers, Latin moralists, contemporary theological questions, and the Bible, it did not extend into the realm of pagan fables explored by Willibald or his friend Albrecht Dürer.[15]

But rather than preventing admiration on the part of Willibald's humanist circle, Caritas's very orthodoxy—in addition to her saintliness and learning—attracted the praise and literary attentions of celebrated scholars such as Conrad Celtis.[16] Crowned *poeta laureatus* in Nuremberg by Emperor Frederick III in 1487, Celtis visited Willibald in Nuremberg in 1501. There he must have heard Caritas spoken of very favorably, because at Easter in 1502 he sent her a copy of his edition of Hrotsvit of Gandersheim's recently discovered manuscripts, which he had dedicated to Caritas.[17] In a letter of March 1502 she thanked him for the "scripta amabilia Rosuitae virginis doctissimae" and for not neglecting to share his wisdom with the weaker sex, and consoled him for having been recently attacked by robbers.[18]

In April of 1502 Celtis sent a copy of his *Norimberga* along with a dedicatory ode to Caritas that praises her as a "Virgo Romana benedocta lingua."[19] The *Norimberga* was not a religious work, rather it was an elegiac description of the city of Nuremberg that was to have been part of a larger project, the *Germania Illustrata,* a vast poetical, historical, and geographical glorification of the fatherland. Caritas's letter of thanks written on April 25, 1502, is particularly revealing of her convictions, for although it begins with modest protestations of her unworthiness as a recipient of such an honor—she, a "stupid, ignorant, and simple girl"— the main body of the letter is a warning against the vanity of secular learning. In no uncertain terms Caritas urges the renowned professor to turn his attentions from the writings of the pagans to the Holy Scripture, so that he may gather "immortal riches" and not be caught empty-handed on the Day of Judgment. She quotes Saint Gregory to convince Celtis that the very subtlety of his knowledge exposes him to be judged more harshly for his sins.[20] Not surprisingly, this letter seems to mark the end of their correspondence; it appears Caritas half-expected to provoke Celtis's displeasure, for when she wrote to Willibald to ask him to correct any Latin errors and afterward transmit her letter to Celtis, she felt it necessary to explain again that her intention was not to hurt Celtis, but to do him a service.[21]

Celtis and Willibald are not the only humanists with whom Caritas corresponded: during the first two decades of the sixteenth century Christoph Scheurl addressed many letters to the abbess of Saint Clare, dedicating his first book, *Die Früchte der Messe,* to her in 1506. Nine years later he published his translation of forty letters his uncle, Sixtus Tucher, had written to Caritas and her friend and prioress Apollonia Tucher during the years 1498–1506.[22] The *Viertzig Sendbriefe* treat moral and religious questions, and it is unfortunate that neither Caritas's portion of the Tucher nor the Scheurl correspondence has survived. However, over twenty of her letters to Anton Tucher and Kaspar Nutzel are extant, along with many others to various city and ecclesiastical authorities.[23]

While her exchanges of letters with some of the most important men of her epoch doubtless earned Caritas a measure of fame, she is perhaps most remarkable for her steadfast defense of the Klarakloster during the Reformation years. This battle is recorded in the "Denkwürdigkeiten" of 1524–1528, which were first published in 1852 by Constantin Höfler.[24] The first twenty-nine chapters of these memoirs tell of Caritas's growing problems with Lutheran sympathizers: parents of her nuns, preachers and confessors who serve the convent, the hostile populace, and the city council pressure and harass the sisters of Saint Clare who choose to protect their traditional beliefs and remain faithful to the pope and the Roman Catholic Church.

In 1524 and 1525 Caritas trembled for the future of her convent when the city council of Nuremberg closed many monasteries and convents and, with the Reformist *Religionsgespräch* of 1525, presented an ultimatum on June 7, 1525 demanding that she and the sisters comply with the following five points, which Caritas recorded herself in chapter thirty of the "Denkwürdigkeiten":

1. The abbess should free the sisters of their vows.
2. Each sister should be free to leave the cloister, or her parents should have the right to remove her from it. The council will then provide for her material needs.
3. The sisters should wear secular dress.
4. Small windows should be installed, so that the relatives of the sisters can see them when they visit, even if they are alone during the conversation.
5. The sisters should draw up an inventory of all they possess. These things should be accomplished within four weeks' time.[25]

Caritas explains her stand on these five points in the chapter that follows, stating first of all that since the sisters are bound by vows to the Almighty, rather than to any mortal creature, it is not in her power to free them, nor does she need the sins of others on her conscience: "ich het genung zu tragen an meinen eygen sunden, wollt frembder sund nit mer auf mich laden" (I have enough to bear with my own sins, I do not want to be burdened any longer with foreign sins).[26]

As to the nuns' freedom, she tells the council's envoys that she could not have run the abbey had not her "dear children" obeyed her willingly during the twenty-two years in which she was in charge. Furthermore, she does not want the nuns' mothers attempting to convince them that they are wrong to obey their abbess and to be faithful to their vows. She points out with respect to the sisters' upkeep that it would be less costly to the city government were it to leave the convent as before.

In response to point number three, Caritas replies that though the habit does not the monk make, it is not physically possible to reclothe such a large convent in four weeks, especially considering that the sisters of Saint Clare have always sewn their own clothes. The council's worry, that a glimpse of them in their garden wearing their traditional cowled habits will incite the people to riot, is nonsense: she tells them she is far more afraid that the incendiary sermons of the preachers, to which the convent has also been exposed, will provoke the populace to violence.[27]

Caritas broaches the subject of the small window, "geschichtfenster," with vehemence, for she in no way wants a reformed or open cloister ("offens closter"), and if this is what the city wishes, let them say so at once so she can leave.[28]

Because the abbess's position on the five points is recorded as a conversation between her and the council's messengers, she seems not to answer every point with equal thoroughness or directness, nor is her refusal to comply with each point always unambiguous. She replies to the council for the most part in their own language, presenting purely *practical* obstacles to the ordered changes, and even her argument concerning the vows presents a kind of practical dilemma: logically, how can she free her sisters of promises made to someone else?

Chapter thirty-two of the "Denkwürdigkeiten" gives an account of the meeting of the entire convent called by Caritas so that each sister might have her say concerning each of the five points, and in which they all agree to remain true to their vows and to obey their abbess. However, to prevent worse measures, they decide that a small window is to be installed, but that no one will be allowed to converse there alone, since her interlocutors could then accuse her of conversations that had not taken place. It is also decided to contact a certain influential Christoph Kress, who had been able to intervene for other orders so that they were allowed to continue wearing their habits.

The episode recounted in the following chapter serves as a preliminary to the drama of chapter thirty-four: four of the nuns' mothers demand to enter the convent, pretending that this is by order of the council. Ignoring their threats to use force, Caritas offers only to let them speak to their daughters through the "redefenster," the little window through which they are normally allowed to converse in the chapel. Furious, the women return to slander Caritas before the city council, which then sends two representatives to speak with the abbess. After hearing her out, the men pronounce the nuns' mothers to be liars.[29]

These unpleasant, but essentially peaceful, encounters lead up to the forcible removal of three sisters, Margaret Tetzel, Katharina Ebner, and Klara Nützel from the Klarakloster, an action detailed in chapter thirty-four of the "Denkwürdigkeiten." When the young women refuse repeatedly to leave with members of their families who have come to take them home, they are physically pushed and pulled out of the convent. During these events Caritas showed strength and clear-headedness: although she could not prevent the mothers of the nuns from carrying them away, since the council might have retaliated by closing the convent, she nevertheless did not make it easy for them. Caritas refuses adamantly to take it upon herself to free the nuns of their vows, or to order them to leave, or even to let their relatives slip them through the back garden gate. Instead she insists that the act of forcing them to leave against their wills be as public as possible, telling the abductors that if they are in the right, there is no reason for them to be ashamed of their action.[30]

Subsequent exchanges of letters between the curator, Kaspar Nützel, and Wenzel Linck, an Augustine preacher, and Caritas failed utterly to win Caritas over to Lutheran thinking. It was not until after the Reformation leader Philipp Melanchthon visited the Klarakloster that the sisters of Saint Clare were afforded a measure of peace. Already informed of the predicament of the Clares by Willibald Pirckheimer, Melanchthon, accompanied by Nützel and others, visited the Klarakloster in November of 1525. Caritas joyfully records the content of her interview with Melanchthon in chapter fifty of the "Denkwürdigkeiten." It appears that after an initial exposition of the new doctrine ("der saget vil dings auf die newe lere"), the Reformer listened to Caritas, who explained that to her and her sisters grace was more important than works, but that a holy life could be led within convent walls. With this, Melanchthon agreed. In fact, they seem to have been at odds only on the binding nature of conventual vows, for Melanchthon maintained that the sisters were not held by them. In contrast to the other men who told passionately of having forbidden the Franciscans to preach[31] and having forcibly taken the nuns from the convent, Melanchthon criticized all violence of this type as sinful and declared that though the Clares should not be given much, neither should anything be taken from them ("wolt man in nit vil geben, solt man in auch nichcz nemen"), nor should the convents be destroyed.[32]

Thus the Klarakloster was allowed to survive, but only for the lifetime of those who had already been admitted into the order, for the city council forbade acceptance of new members. Nor could the nuns attend Roman mass, receive the Catholic sacraments, or be confessed by priests. In spite of these reforms and the tremendous pressure exerted on the sisters to renounce their cloistered life and Catholic beliefs, only one of them chose voluntarily to become a Protestant and to leave the convent of Saint Clare.[33] What greater testimony to the satisfactory functioning, both spiritual and material, of an institution could one wish?

At Easter in 1529 Caritas Pirckheimer and the sisters of Saint Clare celebrated her twenty-fifth anniversary as abbess of the Klarakloster. Two letters written by Willibald's daughter Katharina describe it as a rather elaborate and quite joyous celebration: Willibald provided wine and silver vessels, there was much music-making, and young and old alike sang and danced.[34] Caritas gave each of the sisters a small ring and she received many presents from them. Three years later on August 19, 1532, Caritas died at the age of sixty-six.

NOTES

1. Willibald Pirckheimer was a wealthy patrician humanist who corresponded with Spalatin, Zwingli, Pico della Mirandola, Erasmus, and other Reformers and men of letters. He was a close friend of Albrecht Dürer and, like Dürer, had also traveled in Italy. In fact, he has been called "the German humanist who more than any other incorporated the Italian Renaissance into his way of life" (Lewis W. Spitz, *The Religious Renaissance of the German Humanists*, p. 159). An indefatigable translator of both Greek and Latin texts, Pirckheimer could not hide his epicurean tastes for food, wine, women, and even men.

2. Johannes Pirckheimer had received his doctoral degree in Padua in 1465, and as a doctor could not be elected to the council of Nuremberg. Instead he served Wilhelm of Reichenau, bishop of Eichstätt, as a legal expert, and later Dukes Albrecht IV of Bavaria and Sigmund of Tirol, which meant that he divided his time between the cities of Munich and Innsbruck. After 1488 he returned to Nuremberg to work for the city council.

3. Compare Johannes Kist, *Das Klarissenkloster in Nürnberg bis zum Beginn des 16. Jahrhunderts*, pp. 124–25.

4. As followers of Saint Clare, the Clares were sworn to the same ideal of poverty as were the Franciscan monks. Saint Clare left her noble family in 1212 to become a follower of Saint Francis and to found her own order.

5. Josef Pfanner, *Briefe von, an und über Caritas Pirckheimer*, letter 47, p. 105. See the following translation for the text of this letter.

6. Compare Jean Wirth's review of the exhibition catalog *Caritas Pirckheimer, 1467– 1532: Eine Ausstellung der Katholischen Stadtkirche Nürnberg* in *Bibliothèque d'Humanisme et Renaissance* 46 (1984): 513–14.

7. *Caritas Pirckheimer, 1467–1532: Eine Ausstellung der Katholischen Stadtkirche Nürnberg*, p. 14.

8. "Ad congratulandum enim me tibi vulgi hortabatur opinio, ad consolandum vero non inanis aut inepta me inpellebat ratio." Pfanner, *Briefe von, an und über Caritas Pirckheimer*, letter 36, p. 83.

9. In German, the *Pfleger*.

10. Kist, *Klarissenkloster*, pp. 10–15.

11. Walther von Loewenich, "Charitas Pirckheimer," *Jahrbuch für Fränkische Landesforschung* 31 (1971): 37.

12. *Caritas Pirckheimer, 1467–1532. Eine Ausstellung*, p. 103.

13. The Pirckheimers were merchants and scholars. Not only did Caritas's father and brother hold doctoral degrees, but her grandfather Hans Pirckheimer had also obtained this degree after studying in Italy, and even her great-aunt had a reputation as a highly cultivated lady.

14. Spitz, *The Religious Renaissance of the German Humanists*, p. 160.

15. Compare the following translations for letter number 47 in which Caritas denounces such studies.

16. For Celtis's biography, see Michael Seidlmayer, "Konrad Celtis," *Jahrbuch für Fränkische Landesforschung* 19 (1959): 395–416, or Lewis W. Spitz, *Conrad Celtis: The German Arch-Humanist*.

17. Compare Josef von Aschbach, "Rosvitha und Conrad Celtis," *Sitzungsberichte der Kaiserlichen Akademie der Wissenschaften* 56 (1867): 3–62.

18. Pfanner, *Briefe von, an und über Caritas Pirckheimer*, letter 45, p. 101.

19. Compare ibid., pp. 103–4, for this ode and its modern German translation.

20. Ibid., p. 106.

21. Ibid., letter 35, p. 82.

22. Sixtus Tucher (1459–1507) was a professor of law and rector at the University of Ingolstadt before becoming prior of Saint Lorenz in Nuremberg.

23. Compare letters 45 through 65 in Pfanner, *Briefe*.

24. The title "Denkwürdigkeiten" seems to have first been used by Höfler, who was the first to publish the four manuscripts conserved in the Staatsarchiv in Nuremberg.

25. Josef Pfanner, *Die "Denkwürdigkeiten" der Caritas Pirckheimer*, vol. 2, p. 69.

26. Ibid., p. 71.

27. Caritas requested on numerous occasions that the convent not be sent preachers sympathetic to the Reformation. Even after the Franciscans had been formally forbidden by the council on March 17, 1525, to preach and perform the sacraments at Saint Clare, Caritas tried to have them reinstated.

28. Pfanner, *Die "Denkwürdigkeiten,"* vol. 2, p. 72.

29. Ibid., p. 78.

30. For an English translation of this chapter of the "Denkwürdigkeiten," see the translations that follow. The original text appears in Pfanner, *Die "Denkwürdigkeiten,"* vol. 2, chapter 34, pp. 79–84.

31. See above note 27.

32. Pfanner, *Die "Denkwürdigkeiten,"* vol. 2, p. 132.

33. Loewenich, p. 45.

34. Pfanner, *Briefe*, letters 150 and 151, pp. 239–42.

Letter 47

Caritas Pirckheimer to Conrad Celtis

To the very honorable professor, Master Conrad Celtis, from the humble praying sister Caritas of the order of Saint Clare of Nuremberg.

I wish you bodily and spiritual health in Jesus Christ the Supreme Savior. Remarkable master, doctor and most erudite in philosophy, I received with indebted respect and the greatest thanks once again a little book dedicated by your Excellence to me, an insignificant woman, along with your sweetest letter, which pleased me beyond measure. But since I, a pauper, can never repay so great a gift, I invoke Him from whom the best is given and from whom every perfect gift comes, that He in His usual clemency may replace me with respect to your kindness, illuminating and inflaming your ardent mind with the splendor and love of true wisdom which descends here below from the Father of All Light,[1] so that not only the visible and earthly things begin to be known by you, but also the invisible and eternal things, according to the cry of the Apostle who says, "Set your affection on things above, not on things on the earth."[2] Certainly, I cannot help but confess that though the description and praise of my earthly fatherland, which is contained in this little book, pleases me very much, how much more attractive and sweeter the description and glorification of the heavenly fatherland Jerusalem would be for me, that superior one above, from which we in this vale of tears, misery, and ignorance are exiled, and toward which we must strive with all our strength.

In truth, your Dignity knows me as your unworthy little pupil, as your enthusiastic disciple, and I even add, as the lover of your spiritual health; and for this reason I ask you with my spirit most urgently not to give up worldly philosophy, but rather to exchange it for something better, that is, to turn from the writings of the pagans to the Holy Pages, from earthly things to heavenly ones, from creatures to the Creator. After all, what is the use of all creatures, if we are neglected by the Creator? This could easily happen, if we prefer creatures to the Founder—may this never be.

Thus although one should not blame the science or any knowledge of a thing, which is good, especially if it is contemplated and ordered by God, one should always prefer mystical theology and a good and virtuous life. For human reason is weak and can err, whereas faith is true and a healthy conscience cannot err.

I beg you, excellent Doctor, to weigh well in your heart what the wisest of men, after having investigated everything under the sun, admits: "Vanity of vanities, he says, and all is vanity and spiritual vexation!" However, the plenitude of wisdom is the fear of God.[3] Therefore, if all things are vain except to fear, honor, and love God, whom to serve is to reign, then we must certainly not cling to vanity, but must in the greatest hurry return to the most certain truth which lies hidden in the Holy Scripture. For it is there that we find the most precious pearls, because from every field of the Lord the mystical theology takes the kernel from the shell, the spirit[4] from the letter, sucking the oil from the stone, and picking the flower from the thorns.

I invite you with the greatest friendship to this saintly occupation, that is, to meditate on the law of the Lord and the Holy Scripture, you my very special Lord and Teacher, whom I wish to be great in the Lord's eyes, and I pray you not to put this off further until tomorrow. Do now, very dear one, everything that you can do. For you ignore when you will die and what will happen to you after your death is also hidden from your eyes. Tomorrow is an uncertain day and you know not whether you will have a tomorrow. Thus, while you have time, gather for yourself immortal riches; for we do not have a lasting situation here, rather we seek the future one. And certainly it is not revealed to us when we must depart from this mud, bereft of sediment, and not carrying any of our possessions except our virtues and our sins, for which we are prepared to receive reward or punishment at the strict trial of the Just Judge, because he requires of us not words but works. Then as Saint Gregory said, what will

seem right will be revealed as certain, because the greater and more profound is our knowledge, the more severely we will be judged, unless we
have lived a more saintly life.

This is why I exhort your Lordship, in the name of our special friendship, to lay aside the depraved fables of Diana, Jupiter, Venus, and the
other damned whose souls burn at this moment in the flames of hell.
Hence their names and memory should be completely rejected, detested,
and surrendered to oblivion by orthodox men professing the Christian
faith. Make friends of God for yourself now by venerating the saints and
imitating their acts, so that when you have departed from this life they
may receive you in the eternal tabernacle, fiat, fiat.

I have written you these things more with the intention of conversing
with you in a friendly way, than of instructing you. If, however, I have
gone too far, or have not shown enough respect for your dignity, doubtless punishment and blame is due to Him who ordered me, an ignorant
little girl without experience, to answer you under pain of disobedience.[5]
And therefore I beg that my humble obedience excuse my error.

It remains to say something about the power of the name Caritas,
which, to tell the truth, I bear only in name, not in reality, because as
Johannes Gerson, doctor in Paris, testifies, mystical theology is nothing
other than the art of love or charity as the science of loving God.[6] But
science without charity is recognized as more damnable than praiseworthy, according to the Apostle's words: "Knowledge puffeth up, but charity
edifieth, the letter killeth, but the spirit giveth life."[7]

My sister Klara, a girl of undeniably good nature, joins me in wishing
you good and enduring health now and for eternity. From the house of the
servants of the King of Ages in the year 1502 of the Virgin's parturition
the twenty-fifth of April.

From the *Denkwürdigkeiten*

On Wednesday on the eve of Saint Vitus,[8] which is also the eve of our
beloved Lord's Corpus Christi, holiest of days which was neither observed
nor celebrated, day on which there was no demonstration of the slightest
reverence to the Most Blessed Sacrament, the wicked wives sent to me one
hour before the meal to say that they would come in during the meal to
get the children, and that they would bring other people with them to
show me that they were sufficiently strong. Right away I sent to the city
hall to bid them send me two witnesses to be present at this affair—since
the women were bringing others with them—in order that there be a few
people on our side to prevent the wives from making unjust accusations as

before.[9] But the children did not yet know exactly when this would happen; they had many plans and still hoped that even though the encounter took place, they would yet save themselves, for no one would use any such violence against their wills. But when I called them in and told them that their mothers wanted to take them away this very hour, they all three fell to the floor screaming, weeping, and howling and exhibited such woeful behavior, that may God in heaven have pity. They would gladly have fled and hidden themselves, which I would not permit, because we feared they would force their way in and search for the children everywhere, and the harm would be even greater. Likewise, the entire convent wept and wailed, because these were pious and clever children who remained with us willingly and in heart and soul did not want to leave us.

The sister Margaret Tetzel was twenty-three years old and had been in the Holy Order for nine years; Katharina Ebner and Klara Nützel both joined the order on the same day and took their vows on the Day of the Discovery of the True Cross, the third of May. Six years had passed since they had entered the cloister. Katharina Ebner was twenty years old, Klara Nützel nineteen, when they were taken out. Then with many tears, we took off their veils and belts and the white skirts, and put little shirts on them and worldly belts, and headdresses on their heads. I led them with a few sisters[10] into the chapel, where we waited probably an entire hour before the wild she-wolves[11] rode up in two carriages. Meanwhile, cries came from among the common folk who gathered in a large crowd as when a wretched man is led to execution. All the streets and the churchyard were so full that the wives could scarcely enter the churchyard with their carriages. There, they were ashamed that so many of the people were present: they would have liked to have seen us come through the back gate into the garden. They sent the two men to me, Sebald Pfinzing and Endres Imhoff, who had been ordered by a councillor as I had bid to serve as witnesses. I did not want to do it; I did not want to treat the matter secretly. I said that if they were in the right, then they should not be ashamed. I would not give the sisters back at any other spot than where I had taken them in, that was, through the chapel door.

So around eleven o'clock the wild wolves and she-wolves came among my beloved little sheep, entered the church, pushed all the people outside, and bolted the church shut, and I unfortunately had to open up the convent door to the chapel. They still wanted me to go out into the church with the children, which I refused to do. Then they wanted me to forcefully order the children to come out on their own, which I also refused to do. If it was left up to them, not one of them would in any way cross the threshold of the door. They asked the men to make an end of it immediately, because the people were still gathering; they feared a riot. I said to the men, "So you go in and talk with them so they do it willingly. I cannot and do not want to force them to do what goes against their heart and soul."

Therefore the two men went inside. I said, "I place my poor little orphans with you, as the council ordered me yesterday, and commend them to the Highest Shepherd, who has saved them with His precious blood." Taking leave of one another with countless hot tears,[12] all three children fell around me howling and screaming and begging me not to abandon them, but unfortunately I could not help them. I went out with the sisters, leaving the wretched children alone in the chapel, and locked the door of the chapel that opens into the churchyard so that no one could enter the cloister.

Then the wicked wives ran inside like wild she-wolves, Fritz Tetzel's wife with one of her daughters, Hieronymus Ebner's wife and Sigmund Fürer's and our curator's,[13] Kaspar Nützel's wife with her brother Linhart Held, who was there in place of the curator, and also Sebald Pfinzing's little son and others. The wives then bade the children come out with kind words, saying that if they would not do so willingly, they would pull them out forcibly. Then the bold Christian knights defended themselves with words and acts as much as they could, and with great weeping, crying, entreating, and imploring, but there was less pity for them than in hell.

The mothers told the children that it was their duty according to God's commandment to obey them,[14] that they wanted them out because they wanted to save their souls from hell, that their daughters were sitting in the maul of the devil, and that they could not suffer this on their consciences. The children cried that they did not want to leave the pious, holy convent, that they were absolutely not in hell, but if they broke out of it they would descend into the abyss of hell, and that they would demand from them their souls on the Day of Judgment before the Strict Judge.[15] Although they were their mothers, they certainly were not obliged to obey them in matters that went against their souls.

Katharina Ebner said to her mother, "You are a mother of my flesh, but not of my spirit, because you did not give me my soul. For this reason it is not my duty to obey in these matters which go against my soul." They made a great mockery of this and other things, saying they would answer to God for the children and take all the sin upon themselves. Held extended his hands so that Clara Nützel could strike them, saying that he would take all the sins she committed in the world on his soul, and he would take responsibility for them on Judgment Day.

Each mother argued with her daughter, for a while promising her much and for a while threatening her. But the children wept and screamed incessantly; the battle lasted a long time, and Katharina Ebner spoke so courageously and steadfastly, proved all her words with the Holy Scripture, captured them all with her words, and told them how much they acted against the Holy Gospel. The men outside might have said after this that they never in all their living days had heard anything like it: she had talked without interruption for absolutely an entire hour, and without a wasted word—rather so very meaningfully that each word weighed a pound.

Now neither side wanted to give in to the other: the children did not want to go and the secular did not want it said that they had seized them by force; so Held and also the wives threatened them, saying that if they would not come with them right now, and they had to leave them, then the children must nonetheless know that they would not leave them inside, in short, sooner or later they had to come out, it was this and nothing else, for they would certainly send people who were strong enough, need they tie their hands and feet together and pull them out like dogs. But this did not help at all; the children did not want to surrender themselves.

Then the men sent again to me complaining how anxious they were, and that they did not know how to handle the whole matter, neither side would give in to the other; Katharina Ebner was so especially defiant and fierce, they had fought with them until they had not a dry thread.[16] If they had known beforehand, they would not have taken thirty guilders[17] to end up like this, with the help of God no one would ever again bring them to such a disgrace in their lifetimes. They said that even if they abandoned the matter now, it would certainly result in great catastrophe for me and the convent, that we would be attacked with violence and that this was bound to happen in the end after all, that I should talk the children into going. On this I stood firm. They asked me to dissolve the children's vows, since they were probably bound by obedience to them not to go. I said, "You have heard from me several times before that I do not have the authority to free them from what has been vowed to God." The men bade me go back into the chapel to the children again so that the women would see that the fault did not lie with me; they would protect me so that the women showed me no arrogance. So I went back again inside the chapel with a few sisters. There among the wild she-wolves stood my poor little orphans struggling with all their might. I greeted the women and said that in accordance with the council's order I had freed their children, and they could see how willingly they came out. They bade me dissolve the children's vows. I said to them among other things, "Dear children, you know that what you vowed to God I cannot undo, that I do not in the least want to make this decision, rather I commend you to the Almighty God who will in His time carry it out, but what you until now owed to me, I will free you from as much as I can and should, as I also did today when I was alone with you." With this the secular were well satisfied and told me that

I had done my part, that they did not ask any more, that what had been vowed to God was not valid, that the vows were already void, and that the children had not the right to take any vows except in baptism.

The three children screamed in a single voice, "We don't want to be freed of our vows, rather we want to keep our vows to God with His help. Even if the honorable mother were to set us free and all the convent were there, we would nevertheless not want to leave, for we do not have any duty contrary to our vows." Margaret Tetzel cried, "O dear Mother, do not push us from you!" I said, "Dear children, you see that unfortunately I cannot help you, their force is too great. If more harm should come to the convent, you would not see this favorably either. I hope we will not be separated because of this, rather that we will be reunited and dwell eternally beside our true Shepherd, I commend you to Him, He who saved you with His precious blood."

Katharina said, "Here I stay and I do not want to give in, no one should have the power to pull me out, but if I am pulled out by force, this will be forever against my will, and I will bewail it to God in heaven and to all the earthly world." As soon as she had said this, Held took her under the arms and began to tug and pull her. Then I ran away from this with the sisters, I did not want to see this wretchedness. A few sisters remained in front of the chapel door. They heard the great fighting, tugging, and dragging accompanied by the loud crying and weeping of the children. Each of them was pulled by four people—two in front pulling, two behind pushing—so that the little Ebner and Tetzel fell on one another in a heap on the threshold, and the poor little Tetzel had her foot almost worn away. The wicked wives stood there and conjured their daughters out in the name of all the devils.

Ebner's wife threatened her daughter, telling her that if she did not advance, she would throw her down the pulpit stairs. She had scarcely thrown her down, when she threatened her again, wanting to throw her to the ground so that she must bounce back again. Then she brought her with much scolding and cursing into the church. Then there arose an unbelievable crying, wailing, and weeping before they ripped off the clothing of the Holy Order and dressed them in secular clothes.[18] The children, however, carried their cowls home with them. The sisters in the choir heard the cries and fighting as did the laymen who stood in front of the church. They had gathered in a crowd such as when a poor man is led to be put to death. When they wanted to set them up on the wagons in front of the church, there arose once again a great lamentation. The wretched children called in loud voices to the people and complained to them that they had suffered violence and injustice, that they had been pulled out of the cloister forcibly. Klara Nützel said loudly, "Oh, beautiful Mother of God, you know that this is not my will." As they were being driven away, several carriages, a few hundred youths, and other people ran after them. Our children were still crying out and weeping. Ebner's wife had hit little Kathy in the mouth, so that it had begun to bleed and bled the whole way. When one of the wagons arrived in front of her father's home, the children raised new cries and wept loudly, causing the people to feel very sorry for them. The lansquenets who ran with them also said that if they had not feared a riot and the city soldiers[19] who were also there, they would have struck out with their swords and helped the wretched children. Little Kathy got out in front of the Ebners' door at the fruitmarket; she clapped her hands together on her head and with great weeping complained to the people how it had taken place against their wills with violence and injustice, until almost all the fruithandlers wept with her.

What later happened to the children among the wild she-wolves we cannot know, for four days later we were told that Klara Nützel had not yet eaten a bite in the world, and that the others wept without ceasing. They had done everything they could, I give witness to this before God and men. Afterward they never spoke ill of the convent, rather, on the contrary, when given the occasion, they said the best of us, and bore within them a great yearning and desire to return to the cloister. God help us to be reunited in joy! Each of us parted with great pain in our hearts. We truly had a sorrowful eve of Corpus Christi; it was afternoon before the convent went in to the midday meal.

NOTES TO THE TRANSLATION

1. James 1:18 may have served as Caritas's source of inspiration for this passage: "Every good gift and every perfect gift is from above, and cometh down from the Father of Lights, with whom is no variableness, neither shadow of turning."

2. Colossians 3:2. "The Apostle" is, of course, Paul.

3. Caritas gives a somewhat shorter version of Solomon's declaration that begins Ecclesiastes (Eccles. 1:2): "Vanity of vanities, saith the Preacher, vanity of vanities; all is vanity." She combines it with the conclusion of the chapter, which reads: "Let us hear the conclusion of the whole matter: Fear God, and keep his commandments: for this *is* the whole *duty* of man" (Eccles. 12:13).

4. "Saporem," the taste or savor of the letter.

5. Here Caritas puts the responsibility for any possible offense to Celtis on her brother Willibald, since it was at his request that she wrote Celtis.

6. Compare James L. Connolly, *John Gerson, Reformer and Mystic*, pp. 288–304, for a summary of Gerson's theory of mystical theology. Gerson (1363–1429) opposes his mystical theology, in which the soul unites with God through loving desire and charity, to the scholastics' speculative theology, which proceeds by reason. Mystical theology is studied in the school of the affections by exercising the moral virtues and requires no great learning, whereas speculative theology is attained only through the training of the intellect.

7. Once again Caritas unites two biblical verses, both of them from Paul's letters to the

Corinthians: "Now as touching things offered unto idols, we know that we all have knowledge. Knowledge puffeth up, but charity edifieth" (1 Cor. 8:1). And: "Who also hath made us able ministers of the new testament; not of the letter, but of the spirit: for the letter killeth, but the spirit giveth life" (2 Cor. 3:6).

8. June 12, 1525.

9. The girls' mothers had previously demanded they be released from the convent and had brought slanderous charges against Caritas before the city council when she refused.

10. In the German, "rotswestern."

11. In the German, "grimigen wolfin."

12. In the German, "mit unzelligen hayssen zechern."

13. Kaspar Nützel (ca. 1471–1529) became the *Pfleger* or (Pro)curator of the Klarakloster in 1514, and as a member of the city council served as a mediator between Caritas and the city government. Despite his Reformist sympathies, he did prove a source of aid and support to the cloister, which probably explains his absence at the forced removal of his daughter, Klara Nützel.

14. The mothers are of course referring here to the Fifth Commandment: "Honor thy father and thy mother: that thy days may be long upon the land which the Lord thy God giveth thee."

15. In the German, "sie wolten ir sel an dem jungsten tag vordem strengen richter von in fodern."

16. In the German, "das sie keinen trucken faden an in heten," that is, their clothes were soaked with perspiration.

17. Perhaps we can here assume that the witnesses sent by the council were paid thirty guilders or florin for their services.

18. Here Caritas seems to contradict herself, for she mentions earlier that the girls' veils, belts, and white skirts had already been removed and replaced by "Hemdlein" (little shirts), worldly belts, and headdresses ("auflegerleyn auf das haubt"). Perhaps these concessions to secular fashion were not considered sufficient by the girls' mothers.

19. "Die statknecht," the lansquenets or "landsknecht," were mercenaries.

BIBLIOGRAPHY

Primary Works

Höfler, Constantin. "Der hochberühmten Charitas Pirckheimer, Abtissin von S. Clara zu Nürnberg, Denkwürdigkeiten aus dem Reformationszeitalter." In *15. Bericht über das Wirken des historischen Vereins zu Bamberg*. Bamberg, 1852.
Pfanner, Josef. *Briefe von, an und über Caritas Pirckheimer*. Landshut, 1966.
———. *Das "Gebetbuch" der Caritas Pirckheimer*. Landshut, 1962.
———. *Die "Denkwürdigkeiten" der Caritas Pirckheimer*. Landshut, 1962.

Related Works

Aschbach, Joseph von. "Rosvitha und Conrad Celtis." *Sitzungsberichte der Kaiserlichen Akademie der Wissenschaften* 56 (1867): 3–62.
Caritas Pirckheimer, 1467–1532: Eine Ausstellung der Katholischen Stadtkirche Nürnberg, Kaiserburg Nürnberg, 26. Juni–8. August 1982 (exhibition catalog). Munich, 1982.

Caritas Pirckheimer. Ordensfrau und Humanistin—ein Vorbild für die Okumene. Festschrift zum 450. Todestag. Ed. Georg Deichstetter. Cologne, 1982.

Connolly, James L. *John Gerson, Reformer and Mystic.* London, 1928.

Eckert, W. P., and Christoph von Imhoff. *Willibald Pirckheimer.* Cologne, 1971.

Graf, Wilhelm. *Doktor Christoph Scheurl von Nürnberg.* Leipzig and Berlin, 1930.

Kist, Johannes. *Charitas Pirckheimer: Ein Frauenleben im Zeitalter des Humanismus und der Reformation.* Bamberg, 1948.

————. *Das Klarissenkloster in Nürnberg bis zum Beginn des 16. Jahrhunderts.* Nürnberg, 1929.

Krabbel, Gerta. *Caritas Pirckheimer: Ein Lebensbild aus der Zeit der Reformation.* Münster, 1947.

Loewenich, Walther von. "Charitas Pirckheimer." *Jahrbuch für fränkische Landesforschung* 31 (1971): 35–51.

Loose, Wilhelm. *Aus dem Leben der Charitas Pirckheimer, Abtissin zu St. Clara in Nürnberg.* Dresden, 1870.

Rupprich, Hans. *Der Briefwechsel des Konrad Celtis.* Munich, 1934.

Schlemmer, Karl. *Gottesdienst und Frömmigkeit in der Reichsstadt Nürnberg am Vorabend der Reformation.* Würzburg, 1980.

Seidlmayer, Michael. "Konrad Celtis." *Jahrbuch für fränkische Landesforschung* 19 (1959): 395–416.

Spitz, Lewis W. *Conrad Celtis: The German Arch-Humanist.* Cambridge, Mass., 1957.

————. *The Religious Renaissance of the German Humanists.* Cambridge, Mass., 1963.

Strauss, Gerald. *Nuremberg in the Sixteenth Century.* New York, 1966.

Wirth, Jean. Review of *Caritas Pirckheimer, 1467–1532: Eine Ausstellung der Katholischen Stadtkirche Nürnberg. Bibliothèque d'Humanisme et Renaissance* 46 (1984): 513–14.

Wuttke, Dieter. "Dürer und Celtis. Von der Bedeutung des Jahres 1500 für den deutschen Humanismus. 'Jahrhundertfeier als symbolische Form.'" *Journal of Medieval and Renaissance Studies* 10 (1980): 73–129.

A VIEW OF PRACTICAL LIVING

nna Owena Hoyers

BRIGITTE EDITH ARCHIBALD

The Renaissance, originating in Italy and spreading throughout Europe, assumed a unique form in Germany. Yet in Germany its secular, anticlerical aspect, though still present, was not as pronounced as in other countries. The German humanists and reformers with whom the Renaissance was inexorably linked studied the classics, but they did not accept the humanistic ideal of pure humanity and remained true to the medieval doctrine of the church. They concerned themselves primarily with the quality of personal life. Profoundly Christian, they saw Christ as the ideal moral personality and blended this ideal with the ideal of self-reliance they found in antiquity.[1]

Anna Owena Hoyers[2] was just such a Renaissance person in both her life and her writing. The ideal of Christ was ever present, and she compared everything else to this ideal. Like the humanists and reformers, Anna studied the classics and was knowledgeable in the fields of astronomy and mathematics. She was born in 1584 to Hans Owens, a well-known astronomer, and his wife née Wennecke Hunnens, daughter of an alderman and councilor in Oldensworth, North Germany.[3]

At the age of fifteen Anna married a wealthy public official, Hermann Hoyer, who was related to the royal house in Denmark and who had been employed in important diplomatic missions.[4] Although her poetry does not convey any ill feelings toward her own marriage, one wonders what she thought of marriage,[5] for she never remarried after being widowed at age thirty-eight and strongly urged widows to remain single in her poem "Advice to Widows."

After her husband's death, she was named the guardian of their children and executrix of her husband's large estate. She seems to have enjoyed complete freedom in the running of his estate, for after his death, Anna made Hoyersworth a gathering place for the Anabaptists, fanatics, and sectarians who had been driven out of other provinces. Of course this angered the local residents and clergy. Especially the established orthodox clergy were incensed at the heresy of some of Anna's friends and demanded investigations into the activities on her estates. As the result of these investigations the heretics were banished from the Hoyersworth estate, leaving Anna bitter and defiant toward the orthodox clergy.[6] She wrote a biting satire against the "Learned Men of Higher Education," directing her invective especially against the clergy of Flensburg:

> O you false slave parsons,
> Fritz Hansen and Fritz Dame.[7]
> O serpents and vipers,
> You, Satan's own brood,
> How can you so boldly
> The Truth oppose?
> And with your erudition
> Many a soul offend?

She suffered financial embarrassment because of her extravagant beneficence toward her friends. She also became involved in endless lawsuits over debts that her husband had left unsettled. Toward the end of her life she was forced to sell most of her possessions to clear these debts. She went to court with the mayor of Husum to settle a quarrel over a house there and lost her case. On March 17, 1625, she requested the appointment of trustees for her children's inheritance and divided the property among her children so that she no longer was burdened by the duties of the executorship.

Toward the end of her life, she traveled extensively throughout the northern countries. Having alienated herself from the local populace, she probably felt the need to cultivate powerful friends and relatives who would be useful to her.

Finally, almost impoverished, she sold the Hoyersworth estate and permanently moved her residence to Sweden. She wrote a poem to commemorate her safe arrival and her welcome by the queen of Sweden, to whom she looked for protection. Throughout the poem "A Song of Praise to the Kingdom of Sweden"[8] there are glimpses of homesickness:

> Yes, God be praised.
> He has shown me great mercy,
> Led me with His hand
> Out of Holstein without harm.
> To her serene Highness
> I have been commended.
>
> . . . .
>
> Although I have been sitting many years
> Poor and in want as though forgotten,
> I have lived here some and there some,

In the city and in the country,
In the sorrowful state of widowhood,
Here in this foreign place.

From her adopted land, she took as active an interest in English political affairs as she had taken in the local Schleswig-Holstein affairs. She wrote the poem "A Writing Sent over the Sea to the Believers in England by the Hand of an Old Woman, Who Though Unnamed, Is Known to God." In the poem she accuses the English of high treason in their execution of Charles I:

You English perjurers,
Opposers of God's order,
How have you thrown yourselves
Into the scorn for all near and far
Since you have shortened the life's goal
Of the King your Lord?
Did Satan blind you completely
That you have thus desecrated yourselves?

In 1655 at the age of seventy-one, Hoyers's health began to fail and on September 27 she died. Hoyers's humanism was not divorced from the main concerns of public life. In her book of twenty-three poems, *Annae Ovenae Hoijers Geistliche und Weltliche Poemata,* published in 1650 by Ludwig Elzevieren, Amsterdam, she attacked all those practices and beliefs that were hostile to a truly religious and moral life.[9] She is a Renaissance woman because she devoted herself to her family without being dominated by them, because she was an independent thinker who had the courage to express her own views, although contrary to the majority. She is a Renaissance woman also in the extent of her education,[10] and in the measure of her magnanimity.

Glimpses of the Renaissance woman are seen in Anna's writings, too. Although replete with Latin words and phrases, her stanzas also contain local dialect. Her topics cover a wide range of subjects, though the Scriptures do dominate.

Education was extremely important for Anna. Almost all of her poems can be considered "Erbauungs Literatur," or educational/devotional literature. She wanted to educate herself, her people, her family, and her children. In the poem "A Conversation Between Mother and Child," the education of her child is paramount.[11] What is unique about the poem is that the child appears, not as an echo of the mother, but as an independent thinker who often initiates the learning situation:

The child speaks:
Mother, I have often heard you say
One should divest oneself of the world

And not request vain things
But seek out virtue.
Mother: That's right, my child, take care
And observe my words.
Child: Yes, dear mother, I yearn
To follow your good teachings,
But tell me where to find virtue.

The mother continues to answer the child's varied questions and responds to his confidence and confession with concern and understanding.

Several of her poems were specifically dedicated to her adopted country of Sweden. Her "Loblied" or "Song of Praise" declares the purpose of the poem:

To honor the Swedish Crown
And all who live under it,
Written on the 7th of September 1644
In the Royal City of Stockholm.
May God keep the honorable Queen
And also the noble Lords.

A paraphrase of the book of Ruth was dedicated to the Swedish Queen Marie Eleonore. Six of the fifty-one pages are devoted to praising the Swedish queen.

Contrarily, Hoyers denounced the excesses and hypocrisy of the clergy. Her bitterest indictment against the clergy is found in her satirical poem "De Dänische Dorp Pape" (The Danish Village Parsons). Written in low German dialect, it describes the debauchery, drunkenness, and lechery of two village parsons, Herr Hans and Herr Hack, who spend their time, especially Saturday evenings, not preparing themselves for their ministry or working on sermons, but in drinking with the peasants, whom they secretly despise. Not only is the poem written in low German dialect, but the debauchery is realistically detailed to the point of including bodily processes. One of the peasants, Trüloss Bahr, for example, says:

I have laid something under the table;
The maid must sweep it away
Or you will all be sick.

Herr Hans chides him that he should have spoken sooner, but Trüloss answers:

It came before I noticed it;
I drank a little too much.

Instead of blessings, curses are a part of the ministers' conversations. Such expressions as "The Devil take you!" are constantly on the parsons' lips, and brawls seem commonplace occurrences. At the end of the poem, the parsons commend themselves for having chosen such an easy and lucrative profession. Herr Hack states:

> We have good days,
> Live in peace and without complaint;
> Better than the soldiers.
> The offering brings us large gain;
> Our babble brings us yearly income.

One of the most interesting poems Anna wrote is her "Advice to Widows," in which she strongly urges women who are older widows not to remarry. The reasons she gives are simple: the men who would marry older widows are solely interested in the widow's monetary value. Her views are undoubtedly garnered from her own experience as a young, wealthy widow who undoubtedly was sought after for her wealth. But Anna demonstrated her independence and rejected the protection of a man, choosing to formulate her own life style.

Though some critics may want to place Anna with the Baroque poets, she shows none of their style. She maintains a rather simple, unadorned realistic style with very few descriptive passages. Her style is that of the humanist intent on getting an idea expressed. One does, however, find a departure from the seriousness in her playful use of her own name. She rearranges the letters to form Johannae Osnavari, or she signs her name at the end of a poem as Hermann Hoyer's Witwe (widow) Anna Ovenna, or Hans Ovens Thochter (daughter) Anna. Quite often she uses the Latin form Annam Ovenam Hoyers to introduce poems.

In her poem "Deutsche Wahrheit" (German Truth), Anna employs four letter crosses in a variety of ways. They are interjected after she states her name as the author of the poem. The format of that poem is also very interesting. The poem is divided into two parts. The first part consists of a conversation between Truth and Pious Heart. Truth as a characteristic of God is God's representative in the poem, and Pious Heart is the human representative. The second half of the poem consists of a series of questions and answers. Eight lines from the end line, which is in Latin, Anna inserts a letter cross.[12] The German line reads:

S.
D.
S.D.B.D.S.
D.
S.

Sing Deinem Breutgam Davids Sohn.
(Sing to your bridegroom, David's son.)

Anna scattered letter crosses throughout her poetry to go along with either the German lines or in some cases with the Latin lines. Two such examples are:

C.	C.
C.R.C.	C.V.C.
C.	C.
Christus Rex Crucis	Christus Vita Christianorum

Anna Owena Hoyers is an interesting poet who has been too long neglected by the literary critics—perhaps because she was such an independent and unusual woman. Her poetry is noteworthy for it gives us insight into the heart, life, and mind of a German Renaissance woman.

NOTES

1. See Roy Pascal, *German Literature in the Sixteenth and Seventeenth Centuries,* for a detailed account of the German Renaissance and its ties to the Reformation.

2. The name Hoyers has various spellings. In her book of poetry, Anna herself spells it Hoyers at times, Hoijers at other times.

3. Little biographical data is available on Anna Owena Hoyers. The best sources are the *Allgemeine Deutsche Biographie,* vol. 13; Eduard Emil Koch's *Geschichte des Kirchenliedes und Kirchengesangs,* vol. 3, and a 1915 dissertation by Adah Blanche Roe entitled "Anna Owena Hoyers," Bryn Mawr College, Penn.

4. Roe points out that Hermann Hoyer was engaged to another lady before he chose to marry Anna. No one knows what caused him to make the change, but there is speculation that Anna was wealthier than the other woman as Anna had a dowry of 100,000 Lubeck marks, a sum which was worth more at that time than it would be today. Anna Owena brought her husband a fortune, and he himself was not poor, so that the family was very wealthy. See *Allgemeine Deutsche Biographie,* vol. 13, p. 217.

5. Some feel that although Anna bore her husband seven children, there was really very little deep affection between husband and wife. *Allgemeine Deutsche Biographie,* vol. 13, p. 217.

6. On May 24, 1623, the duke of Schleswig-Holstein ordered an investigation into the private church services that Dr. Nicholas Teting held on the Hoyersworth estate. Those conducting the investigation declared that Teting held some very unorthodox views: that in 1625 the kingdoms of this world would come to an end and that the millennium would then begin; that Christ received the human part of his person from the Holy Spirit and that the conception took place through faith; that Christ dwells bodily in the hearts of believers.

7. Friedrich Dame was the *propst* (prior or provost) and pastor of Saint John's Church in Flensburg, and Friedrich Hanssen was a colleague. These two were responsible for inciting the duke to investigate the Hoyersworth estate and ultimately for exiling Anna's friend Teting from the province.

8. All translations are my own and are taken from the 1650 edition published in Amsterdam by Elzevieren Verlag. This is the only complete volume of Anna Owena Hoyers's published works. In addition, various parchment manuscripts are in the Royal Library of Stockholm and in the Library of Breitenburg Castle near Itzehol. The title page of the Breitenburg

manuscript reads, "Lieder von Anna Hoyers eines Stallers Wittwe" (Songs by Anna Hoyers, the widow of a province official), and then in a different script, "ein Manuscript welches bei ihre gedruckte Bücher eingebunden war worin sie sich diesen Namen gegeben Anero Hireijo" (a manuscript in which she names herself Anero Hireijo and in which she bound her works).

It is not insignificant that her poetry was published by Elzevieren. F. A. Egbert in *Allgemeines Bibliographisches Lexicon* (Leipzig, 1821), appendix 2, pp. 1111–15, explains that Ludwig Elzevier Junior established his publishing house in Amsterdam in 1640 and until 1655 conducted it alone. From that time on, until his death in 1662, he worked in partnership with his cousin Daniel. He was the last of the distinguished Elzevier family and with him ended the glory of their publications. Elzevier Junior and Senior published mainly Greek and Latin classics and writings on the church fathers.

9. See Pascal, p. 13, for a description of Renaissance writers and thinkers among which Anna can be counted.

10. Roe, p. 20, points out that Helene Höhnk in the article "Anna Owena Hoyers," *Niedersachsen* vol. 9, no. 8, 128–29, describes Anna as highly esteemed by her contemporaries and that she is addressed as "die Hochgelehrte und Wohlweise." The many Latin words and phrases in her poems show that this was not merely a courteous formality. That she was also acquainted with astrology, an interest probably inherited from her astronomer father, is demonstrated in the following lines:

> Do all diligently
> To His Praise
> To conquer the moon.

> Let not your mind
> As hitherto
> Be ruled by Scorpion.

> The way of the Solar System
> Is somewhat troublesome,
> Hot-tempered and proud.

> Fling the star of Mars
> Far from thyself.

11. For a critical analysis of this poem, see Cornelia Niekus Moore, "'Mein Kindt, Nimm disz in auct': Anna Hoyers' Gespräch eines Kindes mi seiner Mutter als Beispiel der Erbauungsliteratur für die Jugend im 17. Jahrhundert," in *Jahrbuch zur Geschichte des Neueren Protestantismus* (Göttingen, 1980), pp. 164–85.

12. The letter cross is a variation of the acrostic and seems to have been used extensively in Latin during the Middle Ages. A Latin verse which Hoyers probably knew and which may have served as a model is the following:

Inter cuncta micans	I	gniti sidera coelI
Expellit tenebras	E	toto Phoebus ut orbE
Sic caecas removet	J E S U S	caliginis umbraS
Vivificansque simul	V	ero praecordia notU
Solem justitiae	S	ese probat esse beatiS

To the Christian Reader

This book written by a woman[1]
Will undoubtedly be enjoyed
Because such has never been seen
Coming from a woman:
One should read it and observe it
And not take notice of the scoffers
Who say: it is not right
That a woman should write:[2]
Christ praises Mary most,
Even though Martha cooks and feeds him,
Because she has chosen the better portion.
In seeking for her soul's salvation:
As this woman has done
May this book be a testimony
That wisdom is not to be gotten
From the worldly wise and Higher-Schools
But from the Holy Ghost
Must be requested and taught.
May no one be ashamed
To take a woman as an example:[3]
May you, dear reader, read through
And judge[4] it afterward.
May the Holy Ghost illumine[5] you
And lead you to God's Kingdom.

AMEN

German Truth

You pious hearts in the fellowship[6]
Let, I pray you, this small book
Be dear for the sake of Truth.
Take it from me, so that as I here
Present it and offer it to you:[7]
Read and judge rightly.
In it is simply shown
The type of clever letter knight.[8]
What kind of people are Babel's lovers
Which today rule the world.
Be warned about their doings.

"*Cavete vobis*,"[9] speaks the Lord.
Be obedient to his true teaching;
Love Truth, Honor God,
And do not let yourselves be misled;
Or you will sorely rue it
And punishment will fall upon you.[10]
. . . .
Pious Heart and German Truth
Here together speak.
Pious Heart full of sorrow bewails, inquires, and says,
Because Truth has been expelled:
        Pious heart:
O God what is keeping Truth?
Who is hindering her course?
We yearn for her with our hearts.
Won't she simply return?
But as far as I can see
And understand with my intellect,
I notice that she feels particularly
Hindered by the Parsons:
Who are highly esteemed in the World,
Upon whom the majority lay stress.
The Lords of the pulpit from higher education
Are Babel's dearest paramours;
The titled ones—pious trouble makers,
Accusers and expellers of the truth,
Avaricious bloodsucking porcupines—
Lie as crossbars against the Truth,
Rule the entire Roman Empire;
No one can compare to their power:
They devour fastidiously, sleep effeminately,
And desire men's honor.
They mislead many by their teachings.
Sal Diaboli[11] has obviously
Salted them; that is clear:
The arrogance, the greed, the incontinence;
The tree is known by its fruit;
Their hearts are full of cunning;
In them is the Anti-Christ.
I would thoroughly grind them
Were I permitted to do so to evil people;
But truth is hidden

And must remain covered for a while;
Because she awakens nothing but hatred
And is not to everyone's taste.
The sunshine's splendor chills the night owl;
If the wolf hears a sheep bleating,
He quickly stretches out his claws,
Tears the flesh, licks the blood:
The same happens to Truth
When she lets her brightness be seen;
And also those who stand with her:
The same happens to them.
Veritas parit odium[12]—
One hears this daily, therefore
I must act as though I were mute.
O eternal Truth, come,
Let yourself soon be seen again
Make clever the dull, the evil pious,
And straighten out that which is crooked.
Come please, O dear Truth, come.
      Veritas speaks:
Tarry yet a little.
I am coming quickly—
In due time—
I am not far off.
No liar
Shall, as heretofore
Has happened,
Oppose me,
Neither delay
My progress.
Only have patience
In God's grace
And wait for me,
Thereupon I will
Cheer you with my presence.
      Pious heart:
Dear Truth, no longer delay.
I am very frightened, I am constrained,
I would like to know if it will take long.
And I ask again, please tell,
Why God in the earth
Poses himself so angrily.

And encourages punishment
Because, as the Scripture announces,
He purposes to do good?
  Veritas:
God wants to do good for you as for all his children,
But your sins which hinder him are great,
There are godless companions among you
Who maltreat the people and pretend
To catch them as fowlers with billets!
Your judges and priests, who are not praiseworthy,
Are rich, fat, satiated, have no mercy,
Do not help widows, orphans, and the poor.
Just like a bird cage are their houses:
That's how you want it and desire no wisdom.
How should all this end?
Do you think God will suffer it any longer?
Don't believe it. Believe He will curse your doings,
Afflict you in anger with more calamity,
If you will not repent,
Do penance, and honor him with your life.
But what good does it to speak about it?
Who will hear it? And who inquires about it?
A great evil—tyranny, sin and ignominy—
Daily increases and grows in your land;
Indeed, overflows like a fountain from a spring of water;
Therefore God's anger cannot be assuaged.
A lion comes from the forest terribly roaring,
Thus says the Scripture, which must yet be fulfilled.
Jeremiah 5 verse 25, chapter 6 verse 7 etc., etc.
 Look there for answers to your questions
 Why the vexations do not end
 And what will occur in the future.
 If one will wager, I will dare
 What do you bet in a few days
 Babylon's fall will be mourned
 And one person will ask another:

Question: Where is Babylon the great city
 In which each found refuge?
Answer: She is destroyed by God's hand;
 His terrible wrath has burned her.
Question: Where have her riches gone?
Answer: The warriors have taken them.

Question: Where are the tradesmen and merchants?
Answer: They will no longer fetch spoil.
Question: Where are the aldermen and chancellor?
Answer: They are no longer of importance.
Question: Where have the squires gone?
Answer: They have been exterminated.
Question: Where is the beautiful lady?
Answer: Gone! She will nevermore be found.
   Along her streets one no longer sees
   As heretofore people strutting
   In velvet shoes and with pearl garlands;
   She is no longer recognized by her own.
Question: Where now are all her bachelors,
   Buffoons, troubadours, and musicians?
Answer: Also gone the way of the others;
   Some slain, many deserted.
   No one is seen joyfully leaping;
   No one is heard playing or singing.
Question: What are the citizens and peasants doing?
Answer: One hears them do nothing but sorrowing,
   Fields and vineyards are rotting,
   Many people have died of hunger.
Question: What kind of work is left for
   The public officials, bishops and parsons,
   The titled gentlemen from the universities,
   Expellers of truth, tormentors of the pious,
   The barons and prelates?
Answer: Their attacks did not succeed.
   They no longer flourish
   They bewail their loss;
   Their grandeur and great splendor
   Have faded, no longer esteemed,
   And blunt their sharpened sword,
   Their power not worth three farthing,
   Their great houses, high fortresses,
   Have been turned into owl's nests
   Wherein wild animals and ravens
   Have found housing and shelter.
   Their great courage is small;
   They have fallen from a great height.
   It is as the prophet has written;
   The Lord does as He has spoken
   Nought, nought, nought is the crown,

Babylon is completely gone.
One does not hear anymore of it
Therefore rejoice, O Zion;
Sing to the Bridegroom David's Son
The Lord of Hosts a song,
Hosianna in a sweet voice.
Praise be to God in the Highest.
Hallelujah, Hallelujah,
Help is nigh.
Hallelujah.
Deo Triune Gloria.

AMEN

Anna Owena Hoyers's Advice, Which She Has Given to All Old Widows to Live Thereafter

You widows over fifty years
Keep quiet, be very honorable,
Love the life of being alone:
Remain where God has placed you,
Give him your heart:
And don't go dancing
With Heinz, Kunz, Hans, Fritz, or Franz.
They are not as reliable
As many a woman may imagine—
They only love your money;
Without it you are loathsome.
I know it; take note of what I say.
You are only a bother for the men;
They do not love you.
If they pose as friendly
Their heart is far from it;
They deceive themselves.
They go to bed with sighing,
Get up with lamenting;
Look at you askance with grieving.
The old blood kills the spirit;
Nothing that you do is pleasant,
No jesting goes to their heart.
Trust me, I am showing you the truth;

An old woman with a man
Can never ever flourish.
I have seen many examples
Of what strange things happen
When old women wed.
One has learned from the neighbors
How they were dragged by their hair
In their old age:
So that I thought: O poor woman,
How your old body is being abused;
You may speak of unhappiness,
You have made a bad deal
Because you have taken
This blow from your husband.
Truly, there is no prospering
When old women wed;
Regrets will come.
How many a man falls into adultery
And into God's wrath and destruction,
Into the hand of the judge?
Dear old woman, please tell,
Where does this come from? One asks:
Have you not been the cause?
Yes, certainly you have been guilty
That the man cannot love you:
For there is nothing to see
In your body and face
Which may move them to love—
He may look in front or in back;
With an old woman no man can become vigorous
Be he in bed or at the table;
Think about this you old ones.
Wedlock is not suitable for you;
No man will be revived by you;
Who can hold it with an old one?
They are a purgatory for men.
Many a one who has gotten his money at a price
Would soon be free of it again:
They say: O that I had a young wife
With whom in the marriage bed
I can stretch out my limbs.
I have acted very foolishly
Since I have let myself be bound thusly

For the sake of mere money.
O phew the disgrace, who will loosen the band?
Is there no one in the whole land
Who can soften my sorrow?
May God condemn that parson to Hell
Who united me with the old post;
He acted treacherously:
May the plague overtake him.
He spoke: grow and multiply
But knew that it was impossible.
Alas! Alas! It has happened;
Things that have happened cannot be changed;
Gone is my joy and laughter:
My heart is stirred to groaning
As often as I see her move about;
Oh, oh, how am I to live?
Who will help me? Who will stand by me?
Who will loose me from her again?
Who can end my suffering?
No one without God: He helps in trouble.
I will pray that he will death
Send to my old one.
This kind of talk one hears, and lots more.
O dear old one, that's how it is;
Daily he wishes you dead;
Curses both time and hour
In which you he did wed;
Nothing about you is agreeable:
And this is the saddest
Which takes away all pleasure and joy—
He cannot become a father;
He cannot beget children from you.
As long as you live, he must be
On earth a barren tree.
Your magnetism has lost its power.
No child will be born from you.
That brings pain into the heart
And hurts him when he sees
In the neighbor's house children
Having fun with their father:
When they, as tender plants young and fresh,
Sit with their mother at the table
By his side,

When looks at them the husband
Of the old woman and says then:
What shall bring me delight?
In my house I have no amusement;
Lonely am I with the old woman
Who cannot cheer me!
Oh, that I have been thusly wed!
How my precious time is wasted;
I rue my days:
Thus you old women see
What happens in your marriage.
Stop his complaining
By remaining unwed in purity,
Then you will not suffer grief
Nor vexation for the men.
If you want to be well,
Then leave marriage
For the young women;
For there is hope yet;
A young woman can help
Her husband build a world.
An old woman can serve
Only to sit quietly
Or attend to her children's children
And be helpful—
To cradle them, diaper them, keep them clean,
And to wash their behinds:
That's because God gives you strength
And other things you can do at home
With sewing or spinning.
Trust God and pray in times of trouble,
Then you will win your bread
Without a man.
God receives the needy;
He is the man for all pious widows,
A father to their children:
Who knows what each needs,
Who gives necessities and provisions;
His treasure never decreases.
Look only to him, to no one else;
Take everything from his hand;
Be thankful for his gifts;
Willingly and gladly be poor as rich;

May it be alike to you if God
Feeds you by angels or by ravens.
Have you leftovers, give to him who asks
In a pious Christian way;
Have you not much, give a little.
Teach the young people
To fear God and to honor their elders,
To live with their neighbors in peace.
In humility, breeding, and piety
Be an example to the young women;
Lead them in virtue;
Teach them to honor their husbands,
To rule the house, to better the welfare,
And to raise the children well.
May each one learn his lesson,
Then everything will be well at home;
It is fitting to praise it.
Therefore as widows it is fitting
To walk in a Christian manner
With teachings and instructions.
Be patient in poverty,
Joyful in adversity,
And do not be afraid.
Hope for the best and trust truly
That God will not leave in need
Those who trust his promise.
Then riches and money will fall to your share.
On the world do not be dependent
To delight yourself in it:
But as true Christians
Do not set your heart, mind, and spirit
On fleeting, worldly goods.
In the joy of God spend your time,
Read and pray, sing and write;
Set a good example for all:
If you cannot read, listen,
And meditate in quiet;
God is well pleased with this.
Thus his praise will be spread abroad
And the majesty of his name
Cultivated in every place;
Always help where you can
And with diligence that you will gain much

With works and words.
In the good life continue on,
Do your deeds according to God's Word,
Go to the Temple diligently;
Listen to what is said
And continue to pray;
Follow Hannah's example:
Who spent her time chastely,
Served the Lord day and night,
Put her trust in him:
Therefore salvation was granted to her.
This is the true manner of widows.
God will see to their welfare;
They will see him
In a green pasture.
Blessed are such women.

Anna Owena Hoyers's Brief Reflections on the Marriage of Old Women, Since God Has Nothing to Do with It

THESE MY BRIEF REFLECTIONS I HAVE WANTED TO SHARE
WITH CASPARO, CHRISTIANO, AND FEDERICO-HERMANO
HOYERS. MY DEAR SONS, AND ALL YOUNG FELLOWS AND
YOUNG AND OLD MEN, WHO STRIVE FOR HONOR AND
WANT TO BE WED, I COMMEND THEM TO GOD'S GRACE.

A man who desires to be wed
Should first of all ask God for grace:
And afterward follow through
With Anna Owena Hoyers's advice:
He who doesn't will suffer misfortune.
It is painful for me to see
An old woman stand before a parson,
To let herself be wed to a man.
No pleasure, joy, or amusement
Can be had with an old woman;
Her appearance brings an aversion.
Whom can that not hurt?
O poor man who has pledged

To thus spend his time
Without fruit, joy, and pleasure!
All his work is lost;
It is courting misery.
There is no sweetness!
No matter how one adorns her,
Let the pope, bishop, father, lord, and servant
Chatter, talk intimately, or rage;
Even if they declare it suitable,
I do not like it.
I consider the marriage of old women
A form of honest harlotry,
To tell the truth:
But no one will listen to me;
My advice finds no lodging, so to speak,
But yet I must attempt
To say: It is an abomination
That such should be in wedlock
Who no longer can be fit for it.
Look at the end of such a marriage,
I pray you all once again,
Look with your own eyes.
"Grow and multiply," said the Lord;
No old woman can do that;
Is not such a marriage abominable?
O dear men, young and old,
Stay away from old women;
I warn you conscientiously:
For in such a marriage
God's blessing cannot flourish.
Such a marriage belongs
To the horror of destruction;
The spirit of life is choked,
Many goods are demolished,
The Lord's anger and judgment incurred,
And the conscience is seared;
Think well about this:
Do not give your noble freedom,
Masculine strength, and charm
To old women.
It is fitting, though,
That one honors old women,
Because the Scripture teaches to do so,

When they conduct themselves nobly,
Teaching the young women to be
Chaste, submissive, and economical.
If they are honorable old ones,
Their hope is in the Lord;
He is the one whom they desire.
And to know none other
In their widowhood one should
Stretch out a helping hand to them,
Name them dear mother:
But WIFE, that is too much
And too far afield of the goal;
Therefore, let such remain
In their retirement and unanimity,
Then without remorse and pain
Beguile time with joy.
If a man is already old,
He is no longer able to grow and reproduce
Or build up his house
And place new joists,
Namely dear little children,
With a young woman;
But a young man in the house
With an old woman
Accomplishes nothing;
Nothing can be done with her.
Her breasts are empty;
There is nothing left in them.
The old body is full of complaints;
Nothing good can be born from it.
Therefore, you suitors, I advise you,
Choose a young, virtuous woman,
Then your pedigree will sprout;
She can increase your generation
And wait upon you in love,
Serve you in all things.
Those who do this, O weal to them!
Let old women be untouched,
Unmolested, and undisturbed;
Bring a young virgin into the house
And thus honor your marriage.
Whoever doesn't do this is vexed;
He will suffer disgrace.

NOTES TO THE TRANSLATION

1. Anna introduces the Elzevieren edition of *Geistliche und Weltliche Poemata* with this address to the Christian reader. I have kept my translation as close to the original as possible. For this reason, I have retained the original Latin phrases in my translation, but I have not retained single Latin words.

Hoyers's published collection of poems shows irregular punctuation with a predominance of slashes at the end of lines. It was common for published poets in Germany at this time to use the slashes in place of commas, semicolons, and colons because there was no standard for orthography or punctuation.

2. Anna uses the Latin word *Scribent.*

3. Anna simply uses the Latin derivative *Exempel.*

4. Anna wrote *Iudicirn,* again a Latin derivative.

5. Anna uses *illustrir.*

6. These introductory remarks are preceded by two letter crosses:

D.
K.
D.K.VV.K.D.
K.
D.
Du Klare VVarheit Komb Doch.
(Thou clear Truth, do come.)

K.
L.
D.
VV.
K.L.D.VV.B.VV.D.L.K.
VV.
D.
L.
K.
Komb Liebe Deutsche VVarheit
Bring VVieder Dein's Liechts Klarheit.
(Come, dear German Truth
Bring the light of thy clarity.)

Although acrostics and their variations are now considered elementary, they were looked upon with high reverence in the Middle Ages. The acrostic traces its origins back to the Scriptures—e.g., in twelve of the psalms, called abecedarian psalms, one finds this device. Psalm 119 for example is composed of twenty-two divisions corresponding to the twenty-two letters of the Hebrew alphabet. Each stanza consists of eight couplets. The first line of each couplet in the first division begins with aleph (a), the first line of each couplet in the second division with beth (b), and so on to the end. This peculiarity is not retained in the translation; however, Hoyers was probably aware of this device in her Vulgate and in the German translations of the Bible since the initial letter was prefixed to each division. Hoyers probably used the letter crosses to break the monotony of the long verse and also to give a visual device which would help the reader to retain the main thought of the text.

7. In the original Anna wrote *praesentir* and *offerir.*

8. Anna wrote *Letter-Knecht* in the original and probably meant those educated by the universities, especially the orthodox clergy.

9. Be on your guard.

10. After these introductory remarks, Anna again inserts two letter crosses:

F .
H.
VV.
F.H.VV.H.VV.H.F.
VV.
H.
F .
Fromme Hertzen VVerden Heut
VVarheit Herzlich Finden.
(Pious hearts will today
Find affectionate Truth.)

In the second letter cross, Anna states that German Truth has been sent out by a woman and prays that she may not fall into the hands of the scoffers:

K .
D.
D.
L .
D.
VV.
K.D.D.L.D.VV.T.VV.D.L.D.D.K.
VV.
D.
L .
D.
D.
K .
Komb Doch Du Liebe Deutsche VVarheit
Treib VVeg Die Lügen Durch Dein Klarheit.
(Do come, thou dear German Truth
Drive away all lies through thy clarity.)

11. The salt of the devil.
12. Truth is offensive.

BIBLIOGRAPHY

Primary Works

Allgemeine Deutsche Biographie. Edited by the Historical Commission of the Bavarian Academy of Sciences. Published by R. von Liliencron and F. X. von Wegele. Vol. 13. 1884. Reprint. Berlin, 1967.

Hoyers, Anna Owena. *Geistliche und Weltliche Poemata.* Amsterdam, 1650.

Koch, Eduard Emil. *Geschichte des Kirchenliedes und Kirchengesangs.* Vol. 3. Stuttgart, 1868.

Roe, Adah Blanche. "Anna Owena Hoyers." Ph.D. dissertation, Bryn Mawr College, Penn., 1915.

Related Works

De Boor, Helmut, and Richard Newald, eds. *Geschichte der deutschen Literatur.* Vol. 5. Munich, 1951.

Frels, Wilhelm. *Deutsche Dichterhandschriften von 1400 bis 1900.* 1934. Reprint. Stuttgart, 1970.

Gabriel, Paul. *Das deutsche evangelische Kirchenlied von Martin Luther bis zur Gegenwart.* Berlin, 1951.

Goedeke, Karl. *Grundriss zur Geschichte der deutschen Dichtung.* Vol. 3. Dresden, 1887.

Jöchers, Christian Gottlieb. *Allgemeines Gelehrten-Lexikon.* Hildesheim, 1961.

Milch, Werner. *Deutsche Gedichte des 16. und 17. Jahrhunderts: Renaissance und Barock.* Heidelberg, 1954.

Müller, Günther. *Deutsche Literatur von der Renaissance bis zum Ausgang des Barock.* Potsdam, 1957.

Pascal, Roy. *German Literature in the Sixteenth and Seventeenth Centuries: Renaissance, Reformation, Baroque.* New York, 1968.

Schöne, Albrecht, ed. *Die deutsche Literatur: Texte und Zeugnisse.* Vol. 3. Munich, 1963.

Wackernagel, Philip. *Das deutsche Kirchenlied von der ältesten Zeit bis zum Anfang des 17. Jahrhunderts.* Stuttgart, 1841.

THE AUSTRIAN CHAMBERMAID

elene Kottanner

MAYA C. BIJVOET

During the night of February 20, 1440, Helene Kottanner, chambermaid of Queen Elizabeth of Hungary,[1] and an unnamed Hungarian collaborator broke into a closely guarded vault in the royal stronghold at Plintenburg[2] and secretly removed from its heavily sealed casing the Holy Crown of Saint Stephen.[3] The next day, they smuggled it out of the castle in a pillow and on a sled rushed their precious booty to the queen, who within a few hours of the crown's arrival at her castle in Komorn[4] bore a son.

These events, their historical context, and immediate political consequences are related with remarkable vividness and poignancy in a brief manuscript preserved in the National Library at Vienna.[5] Known as *Die Denkwürdigkeiten der Helene Kottanner,* it contains the personal recollections of Elizabeth's adventurous chambermaid and is the oldest memoir by a woman in the German language. With a sharp eye for detail, an acute understanding of human nature, and a sure sense of the principles of characterization and narrative development, Helene Kottanner paints an absorbing picture of the period and tells of individual destinies caught in the movement of history.

The little prince born on February 21, 1440, was named Ladislaus[6] and was crowned king of Hungary in Stuhlweissenburg at the age of three months.[7] Without Helene Kottanner's secret mission to Plintenburg his coronation may not have taken place. After the death of Elizabeth's husband, Albrecht II,[8] on October 27 of the previous year, Hungary's leading noblemen demanded a king capable to ward off invasions threatened by the Turks. They urged Albrecht's widow, thirty-one years old and five months pregnant, to marry Wladislaus III, king of Poland, who was then sixteen.[9] But Elizabeth, strong-willed and ambitious and raised for the throne by her father, King Siegmund, had no desire to yield her power to a foreign ruler.[10] She and Albrecht had no male successor at the time, but all her hope was focused on her unborn child, for her physicians had predicted that it would be a boy. Since she could not openly oppose the wishes of the Hungarian magnates whose support she needed, she nominally agreed to marry "the Pole," as Helene Kottanner invariably calls him, while secretly plotting to get in her possession the Holy Crown, which Albrecht, along with her own crown and all the royal insignia, had brought to the Plintenburg stronghold in the beginning of July 1439. The sudden death of the bishop of Gran, keeper of the crowns, had necessitated their removal to a safe place.[11] Helene Kottanner, with Albrecht's young daughter Elizabeth[12] on her arm, stood by and looked on as the crowns and insignia, in the presence of Albrecht, Elizabeth, and all the leading nobles of the country, were placed in the vault and entrusted to the care of the new guardian, Count Georg von Sankt Georgen und Bösing.

Albrecht's funeral in Stuhlweissenburg is not mentioned in Helene's *Memoirs*. She briefly describes the circumstances surrounding the king's illness and death, and then concentrates on the Holy Crown and on her own role as a devoted servant and accomplice of her mistress. Early in November 1439 she was again an eyewitness when the queen, alarmed by rumors that Albrecht may have taken advantage of one of her numerous absences shortly before his death to recover the crown and hide it elsewhere, personally ascertained the falseness of these allegations and, reluctant to let the treasure out of her sight, moved the crowns into her own bedchamber. That night, a fire broke out in the room and almost destroyed the crowns. The following day, they were returned to the vault, and the doors and locks were covered with multiple seals. Elizabeth appointed her cousin Ladislaus von Gara both guardian of the crowns and commander of the Plintenburg.[13] Then she moved her court to Komorn, and after secret deliberations with her most loyal advisors ordered Helene Kottanner to go back to the stronghold and abduct the Holy Crown. Helene did this with courage and intelligence, though aware of the unlawfulness of the undertaking, as her fearful thoughts and fervid prayers during the night of the theft suggest. Why Queen Elizabeth singled out this simple woman to execute her dangerous plan is not difficult to understand. From the *Memoirs* she emerges as bright, trustworthy, and endowed with a good measure of common sense. A mother herself, she felt protective and maternal toward the young widow and understood her predicament. As a chambermaid, she was frequently sent on errands for the queen so that her sudden arrival at the Plintenburg, under the pretext of fetching the ladies-in-waiting who had stayed behind, raised no suspicion. Moreover, she was intimately familiar with the situation and had seen with her own eyes where and how the crown was hidden.

With the Holy Crown safely in her possession, Elizabeth, to secure the legitimate rights of her son, wanted Ladislaus crowned at the earliest op-

portunity.[14] The royal household celebrated the boy's birth with bonfires
and a ride at night in lighted boats on the Danube, and on February 22 he
was baptized in the chapel at Komorn. The Polish faction, however, remained firm in its wish to see Wladislaus III as king of Hungary and
insisted that Elizabeth remarry as soon as possible. Lords and nobles
flocked to Komorn to pay their respects to the queen and her young son,
but many of them were two-faced and in reality unwilling to acknowledge
the child's claims to the throne. Of this Elizabeth was well aware. Together
with her confidante, she watched from the battlements of the castle as on
her command the leaders of the opposition were surprised and arrested in
a hamlet across the river, where they had gathered for secret pourparlers.
Hasty preparations for the coronation got under way, and behind the
locked doors of the chapel Helene Kottanner quickly sewed the future
king's tiny ceremonial dress. On May 12, Elizabeth and a large train of
state and church dignitaries summoned for the occasion set out for Stuhlweissenburg, where they arrived two days later. On May 15, the day of
Pentecost, the twelve-week-old child was confirmed, knighted, and
anointed king. Upon her lengthy description of the coronation ceremony
follows a passage of particular significance to the narrator; she discusses
the legal traditions of Hungary, shows that the three "laws" ruling the
legality of a sovereign's claims have been respected here, and then, to advance further evidence of the lawfulness of Ladislaus's kingship, commits
a deliberate lie—the only historical inaccuracy of importance in her otherwise faithful account. Illustrious nobles, she reports, mentioning the full
name and title of some, carried the orb, scepter, and staff symbolic of
regal authority during the procession through the city. In fact, these royal
insignia were still in the treasure chamber at the Plintenburg.[15]

   In the last part of her story, broadening the political perspective, Helene
Kottanner expands on the opposition and hatred between the queen's
German-Bohemian associates and the Hungarian lords who supported
the Polish king. She describes the fear of the Hungarian people for Elizabeth's regiments, peasants fleeing their villages as the queen's retinue
approaches, conflict and strife between her Hungarian and German soldiers, and citizens refusing the royal family entrance into their towns. The
queen, receiving word of conspiracies aiming to end the life of her son, in
great anguish and fear moved her family from Stuhlweissenburg to
Raab.[16] There it was decided to send the little king to Ödenburg under
the military protection of Ulrich Einziger. Helene Kottanner was asked to
accompany the child, which she did, reluctantly, leaving her own husband
and children behind. Upon their arrival in Ödenburg, Ladislaus's attendants learned that the Polish king had captured Elizabeth's most loyal
partisan, Count Ulrich von Cilly, as well as her cousin, Ladislaus von
Gara, and the bishop of Gran. With their help, Wladislaus hoped to effect

his own crowning as king of Hungary.[17] Kottanner's secret was carefully kept, and these men, suspecting the queen of imposture, believed that the true Holy Crown was still in the vault, for all the locks and seals were intact. With this last observation, Helene Kottanner's account breaks off in the middle of a sentence. Whether she voluntarily stopped here or was forced to discontinue the narrative for political or other reasons, we do not know.[18]

Sparse indeed is the information we possess about the author herself. In all likelihood, Helene Kottanner was born in 1400 in the Austrian town of Ödenburg.[19] Her father, Peter Wolfram, belonged to the local gentry and was an official in the service of West Hungarian lords. She first married the Hungarian patrician Peter Székeles (1402–1431), mayor of Ödenburg, and about a year after his death she married Johann Kottanner, chamberlain of the provost of the Viennese cathedral. Helene and Peter had several children, one of which, Katharina, is mentioned in the *Memoirs*. How and why Helene Kottanner became Queen Elizabeth's chambermaid is unknown, but already in 1436 she was at Albrecht's court in Vienna. Together with her husband and children she followed her lord when he came to Hungary in April 1439.[20]

The *Memoirs* present her as an energetic, enterprising, and quick-witted woman. She obviously knew her way around the intrigue of the court and was not easily deceived. Despite the fact that her first husband was Hungarian, she did not speak the language, although she could understand it. Like her father, Elizabeth, who did know Hungarian, surrounded herself exclusively with German speakers. About her personal life and private concerns, Helene Kottanner tells us practically nothing, but her relationship with the queen—their understanding of one another and complicity in the face of adversity, a shared sense of purpose in which differences of class and rank are almost forgotten—is her supreme interest. She and the queen appear as two allies who, through simple feminine cunning, outwit the lords of the land.

From our modern perspective, Helene Kottanner's active participation in the related events adequately explain why she wanted to commit it all to paper. Yet the idea that a fifteenth-century bourgeois matron like Helene, neither particularly learned nor particularly sophisticated, should tell this story primarily to immortalize her own achievements seems unlikely. That her intentions were purely historical or literary is equally improbable. Before the eighteenth century, female historians were curiosities and those women who did try their hand at chronicles and historical writings, like the versatile and highly talented Christine de Pizan, for example, were scholars, well read, and usually accomplished in other genres. There is no evidence that Helene Kottanner had much formal education, or that she cared for intellectual pursuits, although she must have read a number of chronicles. Speculating about the difficulties facing a would-be female historian in the past, Natalie Zemon Davis postulates as primary requirements that the woman have access to archives and materials and could familiarize herself with the accepted modes of historical discourse, with the rules for ordering and expressing historical data; she should also have a sense of connection with the areas of public life considered suitable for treatment in writing, and have an audience which would take her seriously.[21] For most women, confined to the duties and delights of the domestic sphere, this was impossible. Only convents occasionally produced small-scale religious histories written by nuns about an admired mother superior of their own order. In the case of Helene Kottanner, however, all these basic requirements were met. She needed no access to records or documents, for she herself played a pivotal part in the historical process and saw with her own eyes most of what she describes; she obviously knew the modes of contemporary history writing, was herself involved, be it indirectly, in several areas of public life, and meant to be taken seriously by her readers, although not as a historian, but as a faithful servant deserving of compensation. To remind Ladislaus Posthumous of the precarious circumstances of his coronation, to convince him and his entourage of the importance of her own role in the events, and to persuade him to impart the rewards promised by the queen, his mother, are the main purposes of her *Memoirs*. Every element of the text, including her conspicuous lie, serves those goals. This is why she emphasizes throughout Elizabeth's unfailing confidence in her intelligence and wisdom, her selfless devotion to the queen and her son, her fear of detection and punishment, her grief when forced to leave her husband and children, the little king's emotional dependence on her, and above all, the legality of Ladislaus's regency presented as dictated and effected by the Almighty.

Though she never mentions her addressee by name, his identity can be derived from the text. Having relocked and sealed the door of the vault and then making her way back to the women's quarters, Kottanner passed through the chapel. There she vowed to donate a chasuble and an altar cloth, "which my gracious lord, King Ladislaus, must pay for." Later, after the birth of Ladislaus, she reminds Elizabeth of the services rendered, and the queen replies that if everything turns out well and God wills it, she will elevate Helene and her family, which sounds like an admonishment to Ladislaus to keep his mother's promises. It seems more than likely that Ladislaus's guardian, Friedrich III, soon separated the boy from the most loyal followers of his family, so that Helene Kottanner had to use the written word to inform Ladislaus of the events during his mother's rule.[22] Elizabeth died on December 19, 1442, and, according to the *Memoirs*, never learned the details of what happened on the night of the theft, for the two women never again had the opportunity to talk in private. Her son died on November 23, 1457. Hence, the text must have been written between these dates, probably around 1450. Helene Kottanner eventually received the hoped for reward in 1452.[23]

On paleographical and linguistic grounds, the manuscript can certainly date from that time. Much conjecture revolves around the rationale of the spaces left blank throughout the manuscript for the narrator's name. Five times her first initial is written in by a first hand, and three times both initials appear by the same hand; her whole name is written in by a second hand in five other places. Probably for reasons of security, the names of her Hungarian collaborator and his servant have also been left out. There are many spelling mistakes, words missing, unnecessary repetitions, and corrections by a second hand, which leads some critics to believe that what we have is a copy rather than the original. Whether the one or the other was written by Helene Kottanner herself, or dictated by her to a scribe, cannot be verified. The handwriting is regular and practiced. Karl Mollay, who assumes dictation, finds it difficult to imagine that a common fifteenth-century woman, even one as quick-witted and experienced as Helene Kottanner, could have composed the *Memoirs* from beginning to end without the help of a scholarly pen and mind.[24] Her account indeed has all the features of an oral narration and was most likely dictated, but it also has an unmistakable feminine focus and bespeaks the observing eye and sensibility of a woman, which suggests that the writer recorded the spoken word with fidelity. As opposed to her contemporary Ulrich von Lapiz, for instance, whose autobiography stresses activities and ambitions of concern to men—tournaments, campaigns, hunting— Helene Kottanner focuses on simple joy and grief, shows compassion for pillaged peasants, understands the horror and fear provoked by Elizabeth's army, and confines her observations mostly to her own domain, the women's quarters.[25]

From a historical point of view, Kottanner's eyewitness report is an invaluable source of information on this episode in Hungarian history; it is more accurate than any other contemporary chronicle dealing with the period. She also provides interesting details on the inner arrangement of the Visegrád stronghold, sheds new light on contemporary medical practice and theory, explains some legal and cultural traditions, describes how the royal family traveled and lived—their vestments, ornaments, toys, and utensils, rituals and ceremonies—and imparts a sense of the tremendous importance of royal crowns and insignia in this society, which challenged the divine sanction of hereditary kingship yet was by no means free of feudalism. In comparison with other historical writings produced at the time in Latin as well as in German, her vocabulary is rich, her language vivid and varied, her spelling exceptionally uniform. As a work of literature, the *Memoirs* is superior to the writings of the humanists Aeneas Sylvius Piccolomini (1405–1461) and Johann Dlugósz (1415–1480), and much more expressive and lively than the comparable *Leben König Sieg-munds* by the merchant Eberhard Windecke.[26]

Particularly delightful is Kottanner's use of certain events as symbolic of the fate of the future king. When one of the queen's ladies inadvertently knocks over a burning candle and the fire almost reaches the royal crowns, the narrator observes that though the Holy Crown and the future king were but two cords away from another and both in close proximity of the flames, the devil was powerless and could not harm them. Later, while the Hungarian and his helper labor with files and hammer to break open seals and locks in the vault, Kottanner, who in an adjacent room lies prostrate begging God for mercy, suddenly hears the din of armored men at the door. She interrupts her prayers to see who is there but finds the place deserted. This happens several times. Clearly, these noises were the product of her own feverish and guilty conscience, but she attributes them to evil forces and turns the incident into symbolic evidence that the devil sides with the queen's opponents, while God protects and helps Elizabeth. Mysteriously, the commander of the castle and his men fail to hear the sounds of hammering and filing coming from the vault, nor do they notice the smell of burned wood the next morning. God's helping hand is felt throughout the first half of the narrative, from the fire in the queen's bedroom up until Ladislaus's glorious coronation. Thus Kottanner also justifies her unlawful deed from a spiritual and religious point of view.

Helene Kottanner's *Memoirs* is a unique and new phenomenon in German literature of the time. The memoir form, in which the narrator is at the center of the related events, did not flourish in Germany until many centuries later, when the genre had already reached a high level of sophistication in France, where female authors, usually connected with a court, mastered much earlier the art of merging the history of their own person with contemporary political events. Helene Kottanner, the simple, thoroughly German and bourgeois matron, was a modest predecessor of the pompous and frivolous chambermaids who later became famous for their literary confessions: Madame de Motteville, Madame de Hausset, Madame de Pompadour, Mademoiselle d'Avrillon, chambermaid of Joséphine de Bauharnais, and so many others. Kottanner is an early representative of a particular group of women employed at the European courts, women of humble or patrician origin who left the narrow existence of their home and family to live and work in the households of sovereigns and nobles. Often these communities were large and highly diversified. Their position at such a court gave them privileges and superiority over the women of their own class. Their direct confrontation with leading figures and the machinations of power, their active share, sometimes, in crucial political dealings, gave these women self-confidence and the conviction of the importance of their own person and function. Because she was in close contact with her mistress, became her representative and confidante, and was informed of many secret arrangements, the chambermaid often was the most influential personality in the variegated servant regiment of the court. At the largest courts in Europe this responsible function was habitually held by ladies of noble birth, but commoners could also rise to leading positions. At the court of Albrecht of Hungary, Helene Kottanner occupied such an important post. As Elizabeth's chambermaid, she was not only in charge of the queen's wardrobe and the material well-being of her ladies-in-waiting, but she was also entrusted with the education of the king's children, gave council and was listened to, and had a considerable impact on Elizabeth's decisions.[27]

Throughout the *Memoirs* she remains a loyal, but utterly sensible, champion of the queen's cause. When she disagrees with Elizabeth and finds her instructions ill advised, she is not afraid to say so. She relates how the queen once loses heart and, regretting the theft, orders her chambermaid to return the crown to its appointed place. The latter angrily accuses her mistress of cowardice and refuses to obey, explaining that if the crown were back at the Plintenburg, it would surely fall into the hands of the Polish faction. The queen abandons the project. Despite her deep affection and admiration for Elizabeth, Helene Kottanner is free from obsequiousness. Unlike the majority of her literary successors, Elizabeth's chambermaid is also far from an indiscrete gossip; not a word of frivolous prattle disfigures her factual account. She stands in the foreground of the narration, yet with noteworthy authorial impersonality she views herself mostly as an agent, rarely as an individual in her own right. In Elizabeth she portrays a shrewd sovereign and conscientious mother, but her personal habits and idiosyncrasies, even her physical features, she refuses to reveal. Elizabeth, as we know from other testimonies, was not only bright but also particularly well educated. Her chambermaid was not; yet she had a highly developed sense of the relevant, of decorum and decency, balance and measure, both in regard to the selection of material and its presentation. She had the good taste and inner refinement of a thoughtful and pious woman. Given her background and circumstances, the literary talents she displays in the *Memoirs* are considerable. In Helene Kottanner the history-writing nun finds a gifted secular counterpart.

Kottanner's account caused a stir among her immediate contemporaries. It also caught the imagination of later generations. Echoes of the story resound in *De Monarchia et Sacra Corona Regni Hungariae* (Frankfurt, 1659) by the Hungarian nobleman Peter von Réva. Before its discovery in the Royal Library at Vienna in 1834, however, the history of the manuscript itself is shrouded in darkness. Its subsequent publication by an unknown editor in 1846 brought Kottanner's work to the attention of scholars and a wider circle of readers interested in the late medieval and early Renaissance past. Gustav Freytag included a section of her story in his famous *Bilder aus der deutschen Vergangenheit* (1866). The modern Austrian novelist Heimito von Doderer has taken a special interest in his talented female compatriot; a segment of her *Memoirs* appears in his novel *Die Dämonen* (1956); he translated the text into modern German, and devoted an essay to Helene Kottanner.[28] There is also a historical novel for children by the Hungarian novelist Maria Kilényi that is based on the *Memoirs*.[29] Outside Austria and Hungary, however, Helene Kottanner is virtually unknown. No complete rendering of her *Memoirs* into modern German has yet appeared, nor has the work ever been translated into English.

Kottanner's graphic descriptions and her conscious preparation and development of culminating points reveal the skill of an expert stylist. She also mastered the art of composition. Structurally, the narrative consists of five chronologically ordered and thematically focused blocks that flow logically one out of the other and build up to a climax, then follow a descending line. The opening section, a summary of the general historical background, leads up to King Albrecht's sudden death, which leaves Elizabeth a widow responsible for the future of the state. The second part concentrates on the theft of the Holy Crown and ends with Ladislaus's birth and baptism. The atmosphere of fear and foreboding expressed in her impressionistic evocation of evil forces operative during the night of the theft contrasts sharply with the mood of triumph pervading the description of the coronation in the third, climactic, part. The flight of the queen and the little king to Raab marks a reversal of fortune that seems complete when it is decided to separate the royal family in the last part. The journey from Stuhlweissenburg to Raab took only two or three days, but as presented by Helene Kottanner, it seems to last much longer. Her dramatic portrayal of this exodus beset by dangers and troubled by miraculously extreme and constantly changing weather conditions leaves a lasting impression of mental anguish and physical suffering borne bravely for a crown and everything it stood for.

Though brief, Helene Kottanner's *Memoirs* could not be reproduced in its entirety here. What follows is a selection of key passages, which, it is hoped, will give the reader an idea of her style, descriptive talent, and narrative technique. In the translations I have attempted to remain faithful to the atmosphere and rhythm of the original, preserving the verbal and phrasal repetitions characteristic of the period. If willing to adjust to this deliberate slow motion, which we impatient moderns often find difficult to appreciate, the reader will discover in the *Memoirs* of Helene Kottanner a delightful and moving ancestor of the historical novel.

NOTES

1. Elizabeth (1409–1442) was the daughter of Siegmund of Luxemburg, the king of Hungary and German emperor. In 1442, she married Albrecht V, duke of Austria, who upon Siegmund's death became king (Albrecht II) of Hungary. He and Elizabeth were crowned in Stuhlweissenburg, the coronation city, on January 1, 1438. On May 18 of the same year, Albrecht was elected king of the Holy Roman Empire.

2. Hungarian Visegrád, forty-two kilometers north of Pest on the Danube. The stronghold belonged to Queen Elizabeth.

3. The king's crown, named after the Holy King Saint Stephen (1001–1038).

4. Hungarian Komárom, west of Visegrád on the Danube.

5. Codex 2920. It consists of sixteen heavily damaged leaves, written on both sides.

6. Ladislaus Posthumous, born on February 21, 1440, son of Elizabeth and her husband King Albrecht II, who had died on October 27, 1439. Ladislaus died in 1457.

7. Hungarian Székesfehérvar, south of Budapest. All Hungarian kings were traditionally crowned here.

8. Born in 1397. He married Elizabeth in 1422, succeeded her father as king of Hungary in January 1438, and became German emperor a few months later. He died of dysentery.

9. Wladislaus III, born in 1424, was crowned king of Poland upon the death of his father, Wladislaus II, in 1434 but was not allowed to rule until 1439.

10. Siegmund's only child and natural heir to the Hungarian throne, Elizabeth steered her own course and displayed considerable political ambition even during Albrecht's lifetime.

11. Archbishop Georg von Pálocz crowned Albrecht on January 1, 1438, and since then kept the Holy Crown as well as the queen's crown and the royal insignia in his castle at Gran. It is understandable that as soon as Albrecht heard of the bishop's death, he went to Gran to take possession of the treasure.

12. Elizabeth (1436–1505), daughter of Albrecht and Elizabeth, later married King Kasimir IV (1447–1492) and was the mother of King Ladislaus II (1490–1516) and grandmother of King Ludwig II (1516–1526) of Hungary.

13. Ladislaus von Gara was lord of Machovia (south of Syrmia, in between Bosnia and Serbia). His mother, wife of Count Palatine von Gara, and Elizabeth's mother, Barbara, were sisters, both daughters of Count Hermann von Cilly.

14. As Helene Kottanner explains, Hungarian tradition dictated that coronations be held on major holidays. Elizabeth chose the earliest possible date, May 15, Pentecost, the day on which Ladislaus is crowned.

15. See Karl Mollay, ed., *Die Denkwürdigkeiten der Helene Kottannerin*, p. 82.

16. Hungarian Györ.

17. The Polish Wladislaus was indeed crowned king of Hungary on July 17, 1440, though not with the Holy Crown, for Elizabeth had taken it with her to Vienna and pawned it to Friedrich III. See Mollay, p. 60, n. 125.

18. Alice Wengraf doubts that Helene Kottanner voluntarily left her story unfinished. "Aus den Denkwürdigkeiten der Helene Kottannerin," *Ungarische Rundschau* 3, no. 8 (1970): 435–36.

19. For a long time scholars believed that Kottanner came originally from Siebenburg in Saxonia. The question is elucidated by Mollay, pp. 76–77.

20. See Mollay, pp. 77–78.

21. Natalie Zemon Davis, "Gender and Genre: Women as Historical Writers, 1400–1820," in *Beyond Their Sex*, ed. Labalme, pp. 154–56.

22. Wengraf, pp. 438–39.

23. See Mollay, pp. 90–91.

24. Mollay, p. 92. Herbert Zeman postulates an *arrangeur*, who rewrote and consider-

ably modified the account dictated by the simple burgher woman but preserved her expressive language in many descriptive passages. "Österreichische Literatur: Zwei Studien," *Jahrbuch der Grillparzer-Gesellschaft* 3, no 8 (1970): 17–18.

25. Kottanner's characteristically feminine focus is discussed in greater detail by Wengraf, p. 441.

26. See Mollay, p. 83; Wengraf, p. 438.

27. On Helene Kottanner as an early and unique representative of the "literary chambermaid," see Wengraf, pp. 438–41.

28. Heimito von Doderer's translation of Helene Kottanner's *Memoirs* has not been published.

29. Maria Kilényi, *Könnyek és Korona* (Tears and crown), Budapest, 1947.

From Helene Kottanner's *Memoirs*

THE THEFT OF THE HOLY CROWN

When the noble queen had answered her vassals' queries concerning the Polish king in the manner you have heard,[1] and she had written a letter, and the Hungarian nobles who would take it to Poland were ready to depart, the delegation left and went from Plintenburg to Ofen.[2] Then the queen herself and her young daughter Princess Elizabeth also left the stronghold and rode to Komorn. There Count Ulrich von Cilly, her loyal friend, joined her, and together they deliberated and thought of a way to get the Holy Crown secretly out of the Plintenburg. Then my gracious lady came to me, and she said that I should do it, because no one she could trust was as familiar with the circumstances there as I was. This troubled me deeply, for it would be a hazardous undertaking involving great danger for me and my little children. I weighed the matter and wondered what to do, and there was no one to whom I could turn for advice, except God alone. Then I realized that if I did not do it, and something evil happened, it would be my fault, a sin against God and the world. Hence, I agreed to undertake the perilous journey and risk my life, but I did ask for a helper. When they wanted to know who I thought might be suitable for the task, I proposed a man whom I considered most devoted and loyal to my lady. He was Croatian. They informed him of the secret plan and told him what was desired of him. He became so afraid, however, that he turned pale as if he were half dead, and he did not accept but went out to his horses in the stable. I do not know whether it was the will of God or whether this man also behaved foolishly at other times, but shortly thereafter the news reached the castle that he had fallen off his horse and was seriously wounded. When his injuries were better, he left the castle and made off to Croatia. This delayed the execution of our secret plan. My gracious lady was much distressed because the coward knew about her plan, and I too, was very worried, but it was all the will of God. For if we had been able to carry out our plan at that time, my gracious lady would have gone to Pressburg[3] with the Holy Crown, and then the noble child which she was still carrying in her body might not have been crowned king; indeed, she might not have had the assistance and power which, as it turned out, she had later.

But when the time came when God the Almighty wished to perform His miraculous deeds, He sent us a man who was prepared to abduct the Holy Crown. He was Hungarian and his name was ———, a loyal man, wise and practical. Then we assembled and made ready the things we needed for the enterprise, and we acquired some locks and two files. And he who was willing to risk his life with me donned a black velvet night shift and felt shoes. He put a file in each shoe and hid the locks underneath his shift. I took my lady's signet and also the keys, three of them, to the first door; because near the door-hinge there was a chain and a bolt, and before our departure from the castle we had attached a lock there. When we were ready, my lady sent a messenger ahead of us to the Plintenburg to inform the castellan and the lords who were in charge of the protection of the queen's ladies-in-waiting that they should pack and be ready to ride to my lady in Komorn when the carriage came, for she needed to go to Pressburg. This message was communicated to all the members of the royal household there. When the carriage meant for the ladies-in-waiting was ready, and the sled on which he who shared my worries and I were to travel, the queen appointed two Hungarians to accompany me to her ladies. Then we set out on our journey. When the castellan learned who had been sent for the ladies, it surprised him and all the other vassals of the queen as well, that they had allowed me to go so far away from my young mistress, who was still a child and who did not like me to leave her, as they all knew very well. Since the castellan was indisposed and forced to keep to his bed, he wanted to lie near the door which formed the first entrance to the Holy Crown. But then God caused his illness to become worse, and because that door was in the room of the ladies, he was reluctant to have his servant sleep with him there. Then he wrapped a piece of linen cloth around the lock we had placed there and pressed on it a seal.

When we arrived at the Plintenburg, the ladies were glad to be going to my noble mistress, and they made everything ready and had a trunk made for their wardrobe. This took a long time, and the hammering went on until after eight o'clock. To while away the time, my companion joined us in the room and conversed with the ladies. Now in front of the hearth there was some firewood, used to heat the room, and he hid the files underneath the wood. The men who served the ladies, however, had seen something under the logs and they started whispering among themselves.

I noticed this and warned him immediately. My words frightened him so much that all the color was drained from his face, and he quickly retrieved the files and hid them somewhere else. Then he said to me: "Woman, see to it that we have light." So I asked an old woman to give me a few candles, explaining that I must pray because it was Saturday night (February 20, 1440), the first Saturday after carnival. I took the candles and concealed them carefully. When all the ladies and everybody else had retired and gone to sleep, only I and the old woman I had brought with me remained in the little room (adjoining the treasure vault).[4] This old woman was not German; she did not speak or understand the language and knew nothing of our plan, nor was she familiar with the place or the people. She lay there and was fast asleep.

At the appointed time, he who shared my concerns came through the chapel and knocked on the door. I let him in and again locked the door behind him. To assist him with the work he had brought along a servant whose Christian name was the same as his, a man most devoted and loyal to him. I went to them and wanted to give them the candles, but then the candles were gone. I was desperate and did not know what to do. The entire plan almost failed, only for lack of light. But then I came to my senses, regained my composure, and quietly awakened the woman who had given me the candles. I told her that I had lost them and that I still needed to pray for a long time. To my great relief, she gave me others, which I gave to him, and I also gave him the locks which he was to place there later and my lady's signet with which he was to replace the seals. I also gave him the three keys to the first door. Then he removed the linen cloth which the castellan had wrapped around the lock, and he opened the door and entered with his servant. They set to work on the other locks, and the sounds of their hammer and files could be heard distinctly. But even if the guards and the castellan's men had been on the alert that night and actively watching the treasure entrusted to their care, God the Almighty surely would have stopped their ears to prevent them from hearing anything. Only I heard it all very well and kept watch, all the while invaded by many fears and cares. I kneeled down in deep devotion and prayed to God and to the Holy Virgin that they might assist me and my helpers. Yet I was more in anguish about my soul than about my life, and I begged God that if the undertaking were against His will, I should be damned for it; and if misery should come of it for the land and the people, that He may have mercy on my soul and let me die here on the spot. While I was praying in this manner, I suddenly heard loud noises and a rumble, as if a great many armored men were at the door through which I had admitted the man who was my helper; and it seemed to me that they were about to force open the door. This frightened me, and I stood up, intending to warn the men that they should stop the work. But then it occurred to me that I should go to the door first, which I did. When I reached the door, the noises were gone and I heard no one. I said to myself that it must have been a ghost, and I went back to my prayers and promised Our Dear Lady to make a barefoot pilgrimage to Zell,[5] and I vowed that as long as I had not done that I would not sleep on feathers on Saturday nights. And on every Saturday night as long as I live I say a special prayer to the Holy Virgin out of gratitude for the mercy she has bestowed on me, and I beg her to thank for me her Son, Our Dear Lord Jesus Christ, for His great mercy and compassion. While I was still at my prayers like this, I again seemed to hear loud noises and the din of armor at the door that led to the apartment of the ladies. This frightened me so much that my whole body trembled and I broke into a cold sweat for fear. I realized now that it was not a ghost after all and that, while I stood at the chapel door, they had gone around to the other side in the meantime. Not knowing what to do, I strained my ears to see if I could hear the women, but I heard nothing. Then I went softly down the stairs through the room of the queen's ladies to the door that led to the treasure chamber, but when I arrived there I heard no one. Relieved, I thanked God and resumed my prayers, and I said to myself that it must be the devil who tried to foil our plan. When I had said all my prayers, I stood up and wanted to go into the vault to see what they were doing. But he came to meet me and said that I could be pleased, for everything had gone well.

They had filed off the locks on the door, but the locks on the crown's casing were so tight that it had been impossible for them to file them off and they had burnt them open. There was so much smoke that I worried that some people might notice the smell and wonder where it came from, but God prevented that and protected us. Since the Holy Crown was now free, we again closed the doors everywhere, replaced the locks that they had broken off, pressed my lady's seals on them once more, locked the outer door, and left the piece of cloth with the seal as we had found it and as the castellan had put it there. I threw the files in the ladies' privy where you can find them, if you break it open, as evidence that I am speaking the truth. They carried the Holy Crown away through the chapel of Saint Elizabeth,[6] where I, Helene Kottanner, still owe a chasuble and an altar cloth for which my gracious lord King Ladislaus must pay. Then my helper took a red velvet bolster, opened it up, removed part of the feathers, put the Holy Crown into the pillow, and sewed it back up. It was now almost morning, and the ladies and all the men were getting up and preparing themselves for the journey.

Now these ladies had in their service an old woman who worked for them. My lady the queen had given orders to pay this woman for her services and then leave her behind so that she could return home to Ofen. But when the woman had received her pay, she came to me and said that she had seen something unusual in the hearth and wondered what it was. This worried me, for I understood immediately that it was something related to the casing in which the crown had been kept. I talked the idea out of her head as well as I could and then went secretly to the hearth and threw into the fire whatever remnants I could find, hoping that they would burn completely. Then, to the surprise of everybody, I took the old woman with me on the journey. They all wondered why I did that. I told them that I planned to obtain for her from the queen a prebend at Saint Martin's in Vienna, as indeed I did.

When the queen's ladies and all the servants were ready to depart, my companion took the bolster in which the Holy Crown was hidden and ordered the man who had helped him to carry the pillow out of the castle to the sled on which he and I were to travel. The good fellow took the pillow on his shoulder and then put over it an old cowhide with a long tail which dangled behind him. All those who saw him go laughed about it. We left the castle and arrived at the market, where we wanted to eat. All we could find, however, was some herring, of which we ate a little. Then we sang a mass. It was already late now, and we still had to go from Plintenburg to Komorn on that same day, which is a distance of about twelve miles. As we were about to ride off and were seating ourselves, I quickly felt with my hand on which side of the pillow the Holy Crown was, so I would not sit on it. On the way, I thanked God the Almighty for his mercy, but I kept looking back for fear that anyone might be following us.

There was indeed no end to my worries; I thought about it all the time and marveled at what God had done and wondered what He still might do. While at the castle, I had not had one single night of undisturbed sleep because of the important task entrusted to me, and I had had many bad dreams. One night in particular, I dreamed that a woman had penetrated through the wall into the vault and taken away the Holy Crown. Afraid, I got up immediately and, taking with me a maid of honor, went to the vault. There I found everything as I had left it. The maid of honor then said to me: "It is no wonder that you cannot sleep well. Important business has been confided to your care."

We stopped at the inn where we intended to eat, and the good servant took the pillow and carried it to the place where we wanted to sit. He put it down on a table across from me, so that I could watch it while we were eating. When the meal was over, the good fellow again picked up the pillow and put it on the sled as before, and so we drove on until the darkness of night.

Then we reached the Danube. It was still frozen, but in some places the ice was very thin. When we were in the middle of the river, the carriage with the ladies proved too heavy; it broke the ice and fell over. The women all screamed, and there was much chaos and confusion. I was frightened and feared that we and the Holy Crown would perish in the Danube. But God came to our rescue; none of our people went through the ice, and of the things that were on the carriage only a few fell into the water and disappeared into the deep. Then I took the duchess of Silesia and the highest-ranking ladies with me on the sled, and with the help of God we all made it safely across the ice.

Upon our arrival at the queen's castle in Komorn he who shared my worries took the pillow with the Holy Crown and carried it inside to a place where it would be safe. I myself went directly to the apartments of the women to see my mistress and was received immediately by the noble queen, who knew now that I had carried out my mission successfully with the help of God. But of the miraculous and truly wondrous assistance of God which I had witnessed there, her grace knows nothing; she died without ever learning of it. She and I were not to be together much longer, and I never had the chance to be alone with her long enough to tell her the whole story from beginning to end. I also never had the opportunity to ask the one who shared my secret whether he, while working in the vault, had experienced the same miracle as I had; for he could not speak German, and there was no one I could trust to translate his words for me.

THE ROYAL BIRTH

The queen lay on a couch, resting a little, when she received me. She told me what had happened to her that day. Two honorable ladies from Ofen, both widows, had come to her grace . . . and they had brought with them two nurses, a midwife, and a wet-nurse to suckle the baby. The wet-nurse had come with her own child, a boy, for the wise maintain that the milk of a woman who has given birth to a son is better than the milk of a woman who has brought forth a daughter. These women were to accompany the queen to Pressburg to assist with her delivery there. According to the predictions, the child was due in only a week. It may be that the predictions were wrong, it may also be that God intervened. If the queen had not gone into labor that night, she would have left early the next morning, for all the carriages had been packed and the royal household was ready for departure.

As I was talking to the noble queen, her grace told me that the ladies from Ofen had bathed her in a tub and that she had felt unwell after that. Then I lifted up her shift, and I saw several signs that told me clearly that the birth of the child was not far off. The ladies from Ofen were now far away in their lodgings on the other side of the market, but we still had another midwife with us, whose name was Margret. She had been sent to my grace by the wife of Count Hans von Schaunberg and was supposed to be very good, as turned out to be true. So I said: "Gracious lady, get up. In my opinion you will not be going to Pressburg tomorrow." Her grace rose from the bed and went and began to prepare herself for the hard work, while I sent for the steward's Hungarian wife Margit, who came right away. A lady named Fronacher also happened to be present. These two I left with my gracious lady while I went quickly to the midwife sent by the Lady von Schaunberg. She was asleep in the room of the little princess. I said to her: "Margret, wake up immediately. Her grace is going to have the child." Heavy with sleep, the woman answered: "Holy Cross, if we have the child today there's little chance we will go to Pressburg tomorrow." She refused to get up, and since this was taking too long, I rushed back to my noble lady to make sure that nothing went wrong, because the two women with her knew nothing about such matters. The queen asked: "Where is Margret?" And I repeated to her the foolish answer the woman had given me. Then her grace said: "Hurry back to her and tell her to come; this is no joke." So I went back to the woman and with angry words chased her out of bed. And when she came to my noble lady, it did not even take half an hour before God the Almighty sent us a young king; in the same hour in which the Holy Crown arrived from the Plintenburg at Komorn, within that very hour King Lassla was born.

The midwife was shrewd. She said: "Noble lady, if you promise to grant me whatever I ask for, I will tell you what I hold here in my hands." The noble queen answered, "Yes, dear mother," and then the midwife said: "Gracious lady, I have in my hands a young king." The noble queen was happy, and she lifted her hands to God and thanked God for His mercy.

CELEBRATIONS AND BAPTISM

The noble Count von Cilly ordered a bonfire, and the members of the queen's household went with torches on the water and made merry until after midnight. The next morning a message was sent to the bishop of Gran, that he should come and baptize the young king. He came, and the pastor of Ofen named master Franz was there, too. My noble lady wanted me to be the child's godmother, but I told her: "Gracious lady, I owe you obedience in everything else, but I beg you, please, take the lady Margit." And that she did. As we were about to baptize the young king, we undressed the young queen, Princess Elizabeth, and removed the black gown she had worn to mourn the death of the noble and most precious King Albrecht, and dressed her in a golden gown with red woven into it. And all the queen's ladies-in-waiting were also told to dress elegantly in honor of God, Who had given to the people and the land a rightful lord and heir. Then the most honorable prelate Lord Dionysos, archbishop of Gran, took the young king and administered to him the sacrament of baptism and lifted him out of the font. And Count Bartholomeus of Croatia, the pastor of Ofen, and the lady Margit lifted the noble king out of the font. And they named him King Ladislaus, which provoked the anger of some who were of the opinion that he should be called King Peter, because that was the name he had brought with him.[7] Others thought he should have been named Albrecht after his father, who had been a truly pious king. But my noble lady had promised it to God and to the Holy King Saint Ladislaus, and she had sent offerings to Grosswardein and a silver image of a child to the Holy Blood at Wilsnack, and had begged God for an heir, so that she was bound by the will of God.[8]

LADISLAUS'S CORONATION IN STUHLWEISSENBURG

On the day of Pentecost [May 15, 1440], I got up early, bathed the noble king, and dressed him as nicely as I could. Then they took him to the church where all kings are crowned. Many good people were there, ecclesiastics as well as laymen, as you have heard before. We walked into the church, and they carried the young king up to the choir. But the door to the choir was closed, and the city elders were inside. The queen and her son the noble king stood without. The queen addressed the citizens in Hungarian, and they likewise answered back in Hungarian, and they required her to take the oath in place of her son, since on that day the noble king was exactly twelve weeks old. When this had been done according to their old custom, they unlocked the door and admitted their natural liege and lady as well as the others, clerics and laymen, who had been summoned to attend. But the young queen, the lady Elizabeth, stood above near the organ so she would not get hurt in the crowd, for she was only four years old. The mass was about to begin, and I had to lift up the young king and hold his grace while he was confirmed. Nikolaus von Uljak, from Freistadtl, had been appointed to invest the young king with knighthood and thus make him properly one of the nobles of the realm. The noble Count von Cilly had a sword all mounted with silver and gold, on which was written the motto: "Intrepid." This sword he presented to the young king, and with it he would be dubbed a knight. Then I, Helene Kottanner, took the king on my arm, and the lord from Freistadtl took the sword in his hand and knighted the king. But the blow was so forceful that I could feel it in my arms. The queen, who stood next to me, did not fail to notice this, and she said to the man: "Az Istenert, meg ne sertsd!" which means "For God's sake, don't cause him pain." He answered "Nem," which means "No," and he laughed. Then the Right Reverend Prelate, Archbishop of Gran, took the holy oil and anointed the child king. They dressed him in the golden gown that is always worn during coronation ceremonies, and then the archbishop took the Holy Crown and placed it on the head of the noblest king that ever lived in holy Christendom, King Ladislaus, son of King Albrecht, grandson of Emperor Siegmund. He was crowned with the Holy Crown on the holy day of Pentecost by the archbishop of Gran in Stuhlweissenburg. There are three laws in the kingdom of Hungary, and whoever fails to observe them shall not be acknowledged by the people as their rightful king. The first law requires that a Hungarian king be crowned with the Holy Crown; the second that he be crowned by the archbishop of Gran; and the third that the coronation take place in Stuhlweissenburg. All three laws were observed in the case of the noble King Ladislaus.[9] And on the day on which they crowned him he was exactly twelve weeks old. I ought to tell you, though, that as the archbishop placed the crown on the child's head and kept it there, Ladislaus held up his head with the strength of a one year old, and that is rarely witnessed in children of twelve weeks.

When the noble king had been crowned on my arm at the altar of Saint Stephen, I carried him up a small flight of stairs to a platform, as is their tradition. There they would read the official coronation document, which is part of the ceremony. But we needed a golden cloth for the king to sit on, as is the custom there. So, to comply with the rule, I took from the cradle a cover red and golden and banded with white ermine. Notice now that the colors red and white again came together by accident.[10] The noble king was placed on the golden cloth, and Count Ulrich von Cilly held the crown above his head until the high mass was finished. The noble young king himself, however, had little joy of his coronation, for he wept so loud that it could be heard throughout the entire church; and the common people marveled and said it was not the voice of a twelve-week-old baby, but rather of a one-year-old child, which of course it was not. Then Nikolaus von Uljak bestowed knighthood in the name of the noble King Ladislaus.

After the mass I carried the noble king down from the platform and put him in his cradle; he was very tired from being held for so long. They then carried him to Saint Peter's Church, where I had to take him out of the cradle once more and set him on a chair, as is the custom; for every king who is crowned there must sit on it. Then I lifted him up and put him in the cradle again. From Saint Peter's Church they carried the noble king to the inn while the royal family followed on foot. Only the noble Count von Cilly rode on his horse, because he had to carry the Holy Crown and hold it over the noble king's head so that all could see that it was the Holy Crown with which the holy King Stephen and the other kings had also been crowned. And Count Bartholomeus carried the orb, while a duke from Lindbach named Thomas von Szecs held the scepter, and another nobleman walked in front of the king with the staff of legate to show that no part of Hungary is a fief of the Holy Roman Empire. They also displayed the sword with which his grace had been knighted, and the dignitaries and nobles threw coins among the people. The noble queen herself had such high respect for her son and was so meek that I, humble woman, had precedence over her grace that day and had to stay closest to the noble king, because I had carried him on my arm to the anointing and the coronation. . . .

. . . When the noble king arrived in the inn, exhausted after all this commotion, they finally allowed him to rest. The lords and everyone else went out of the room, and the noble queen was left alone with her son. Then I kneeled down before the noble queen and reminded her grace of the services I had rendered to the royal family, to her and to the noble king as well as to her other children. The noble queen offered me her hand and said: "Stand up. If it be the will of God that everything turns out well, I will elevate you and your family, which you have well deserved, since you have done for me and my children what I could not have done myself."

THE YOUNG KING LEAVES STUHLWEISSENBURG

When all this had come to pass, we received the news that the Polish king was in the vicinity of Ofen and about to cross the Danube with the intention to enter the capital, as indeed he did. When the Pole arrived at the capital, the townspeople refused to let him into their city, but the Great Count allowed him to enter through the castle. This demonstrated the duplicity of the Great Count, Lord Lawrence von Haidenreich, who had been double-dealing for a long time. When the noble queen heard this, she consulted with the friends and lords who were with her at that time. They recommended that she send her soldiers to Ofen, and if they found the Pole and his men unprepared for an attack, which was in fact the case, they should capture the city. Count Ulrich von Cilly and other members of the royal household gathered their troops and set out thither. Then someone among the people said: "If the ones in front attack the king of Poland, we will attack the ones in the back." This came to the ears of von Cilly, who then refused to go on further, turned around, and went back to Stuhlweissenburg. Whether those words had been meant as a warning, or rather to deceive, God surely must know, for He knows our hearts. But if von Cilly had continued on his way, he would have found the one from Poland unaware of any danger. When he was told later that they had planned to attack him, the Polish king spoke as follows: "I have not come out here to fight; I have come to dance and make merry because if I did not, Duke Albrecht would do it for me."[11] He said that because the noble Duke Albrecht had come out to be with my noble lady and the noble King Ladislaus, his cousin, and assisted them well. But the Pole had not

come to dance and celebrate; he had come in case he needed to fight and
risk his life for the sake of his friends, and he certainly would have done so
if he had seen the necessity for it.

They now wanted to take the king away from Stuhlweissenburg to a
place not far off, but because of the enemy they did not know where. In the
queen's company there happened to be two bishops, one was the bishop
of Raab and the other was the bishop of Wesprim.[12] The lords resolved to
take the noble king to Wesprim because it was closest. Instantly, a message was sent to Wesprim, but the vassals who occupied the town would
receive neither the king nor the queen. The bishop himself was probably
partly responsible for that. But it must have been God's will, because if
they had accepted to take us in and we had gone on our way thither, the
enemy would have encircled us as David in the town of Ceila.[13] Then the
lords advised that the king be taken to Raab, and they consulted with the
bishop. The bishop declared himself willing to take in his natural liege
and lady, and he said that even if the devil sat at God's right-hand side he
could do nothing but accept that King Ladislaus is the rightful successor
to the throne of Hungary. Then we prepared ourselves for the journey
through the country to Raab. When evening had come and all were in
bed, my gracious lady sent to me the noble lady Margret with the message
that I should go to her grace right away. This frightened me, for I understood it concerned some reverse. The noble queen was alone and, absorbed in thought, walked back and forth in the room. She spoke to me:
"Well, what would you advise me. Our situation is very delicate; they
want to decide for us where to hide the Holy Crown, but if it falls in the
hands of the enemy nothing good can come of it." We weighed the matter
together for a long time. Since we were staying at the Brobsthof[14] and
there was a little walled-in garden there, I said: "Gracious lady, let us bury
the crown in the garden; for even if the town is lost to the enemy, we will
find a way to get into the garden over the wall." But the wise queen replied: "I have thought of that myself but rejected the idea, because someone might conclude that the crown had been lost." Then I retreated for a
while and meditated, and appealed to the Mother of Mercy that she might
intercede for us and obtain pity for us from her Son, so that we would
decide wisely, and no evil would ensue. Then I returned to the noble
queen and said: "Gracious lady, unsurpassed indeed is your wisdom. The
following solution seems best to me: Her grace knows that the king is
worth more than the Holy Crown; therefore, let us place the Holy Crown
in the cradle beneath the king, and wherever God takes the king the crown
will go, too." Her grace liked the idea, and she said: "This we shall do and
I leave it to your own care."

The next morning, I took the Holy Crown, wrapped it well in a cloth,
and then put it on the bottom of the cradle in the straw; for his grace did

not sleep on feathers yet. Beside it I placed a long spoon of the kind that is used to make mash for babies. I did that in case someone were to reach into the cradle—they would think that what lay there was the bowl in which the king's food is prepared—and no one knew of this at the time, except my noble lady and I. When we were ready for our journey through the country, a large number of mounted knights and also many foot soldiers took up position around us; and so we went on our way, much troubled and worried, because the peasants had deserted their villages and fled to the forest of the Schild mountains, and most of them belonged to lords who were against us. When we approached the mountains, I dismounted and took the noble king out of the cradle and laid him down in the carriage in which the noble queen and her young daughter Elizabeth traveled. We maids and ladies-in-waiting formed a circle around the royal family so that, in case anyone wanted to shoot into the carriage, we could keep the shots at bay. Large numbers of foot soldiers marched on either side of the carriage and looked in the bushes to see if one of the enemy was hidden among the trees and wanted to harm us. But with the help of God we crossed the mountains unharmed. Then I took the noble king out of the carriage and put him in the cradle and rode next to it myself. They had not carried him very far, however, when he began to weep; he was content neither in the cradle nor in the carriage, and the wet-nurse could not get him to calm down either. So I took him on my arm and carried him thus a good part of the way until we both grew tired; then I put him back into the cradle. As we traveled through the country, the weather changed constantly. Several times it rained so hard that the noble king got thoroughly wet. We were equipped only for a short journey and not for a long and difficult one, but I had taken along a fur coat in case we might need it in an emergency. I used it to cover the cradle when the rain was very heavy, and when it was completely soaked I let it be rubbed dry and then spread it again over the cradle as long as it kept raining. Sometimes a nasty wind blew into the cradle so that the noble king could barely open his eyes. At other times it was again so hot that he perspired all over and drops of sweat appeared on his brow from the heat and little bubbles on his skin. All this the noble king had to endure while we traveled through the country.

NOTES TO THE TRANSLATION

1. Elizabeth had agreed to marry the young Wladislaus III of Poland, but stipulated several conditions which she did not think he and his followers would fulfill.

2. Ofen (Hungarian Buda) on the Danube is now the eastern part of the Hungarian capital.

3. Now Bratislava.

4. One could also get there via the castle chapel, but the normal entrance was through the women's apartments and up a small flight of stairs.

5. Mariazell in Steiermark.

6. Elizabeth of Thüringen (1207–1231), daughter of King Andreas II of Hungary. She was canonized in the year 1235. Until 1539 her remains rested in Marburg an der Lahn. What her reliquary in the chapel at the Plintenburg contained is unknown. See Mollay p. 55, n. 68.

7. February 22, the date of Ladislaus's baptism, is Saint Peter's Day.

8. Saint Ladislaus (1077–1095) and Elizabeth's father, King Siegmund, had been buried in Grosswardein (Hungarian Nagyvárad). Wilsnack was a popular pilgrimage place in Mark Brandenburg, where the cult of the Holy Blood flourished from 1383 to 1532.

9. The "laws" described here were really unwritten rules, legal traditions which—with the exception of the first one—were observed uninterruptedly from 1001 to 1526. The only Hungarian king not crowned with the Holy Crown was Elizabeth's opponent Wladislaus, king of Poland, who was crowned in Stuhlweissenburg on July 17, 1440, by the archbishop of Gran, the same person who had crowned Elizabeth's son two months earlier.

10. Red and white were the colors of Albrecht's and Elizabeth's families. They "accidentally" occur together several times in the course of the story, which Helene Kottanner interprets as a sign of divine providence.

11. Albrecht VI (1418–1463), duke of Austria and second cousin of Elizabeth's late husband, Albrecht, was known for his love of pleasure and his excessive life style. Upon hearing the news of Ladislaus's birth, he left Austria and rode to Plintenburg in record time to attend the coronation and partake in the festivities.

12. Hungarian Veszprém.

13. Ceila, now Kîla, a village on the way to Hebron. David had to flee from there to escape encirclement by Saul.

14. An inn.

BIBLIOGRAPHY

Primary Works

Mollay, Karl, ed. Die Denkwürdigkeiten der Helene Kottannerin (1439–1440). Vienna, 1972.

Secondary Works

Davis, Natalie Zemon. "Gender and Genre: Women as Historical Writers, 1400–1820." In Beyond Their Sex: Learned Women of the European Past, ed. Patricia H. Labalme, pp. 153–83. New York, 1980.
Doderer, Heimito von. Die Dämonen. Munich, 1956.
———. "Helene Kottanner. Denkwürdigkeiten einer Wienerin von 1440." In Die Wiederkehr der Drachen, pp. 221–26. Munich, 1970.
Freytag, Gustav. Bilder aus der deutschen Vergangenheit. Vol. 2, pp. 370–82. Leipzig, 1924.
Rupprich, Hans. "Das Wiener Schrifttum des ausgehenden Mittelalters." Österreichische Akademie der Wissenschaften 228, no. 5 (1954).
Wengraf, Alice. "Aus den Denkwürdigkeiten der Helene Kottannerin." Ungarische Rundschau 3 (1914): 434–41.
Zeman, Herbert. "Österreichische Literatur: Zwei Studien." Jahrbuch der Grillparzer-Gesellschaft 3, no. 8 (1970): 11–65.

argaret of Austria

CHARITY CANNON WILLARD

In *The Book of the City of Ladies,* written around 1405, Christine de Pizan raises the question of the abilities of women to fulfill roles in public life. Her mentor, Dame Reason, reassures her: "In case anyone says that women do not have a natural sense for politics and government, I will give you examples of several great women rulers who have lived in past times. And so that you will better know my truth, I will remind you of some women of your own time who remained widows and whose skill governing—both past and present—in all their affairs following the deaths of their husbands provides obvious demonstration that a woman with a mind is fit for all tasks."[1] Although Christine had great confidence that her works would be read and remembered by future generations, few could have fulfilled her words as well as one of her sixteenth-century readers, Margaret of Austria, the widowed aunt of Emperor Charles V who was his regent in the Netherlands for more than two decades.

If her role in society was seemingly glorious—stateswoman, patron of the arts, musician, builder, as well as guardian and educator of several royal children with important destinies—the misfortunes of her early years would have been more than sufficient to ruin the life of a less sturdy character. As it was, she suffered, but rose above her suffering, adopting as her motto: *Fortune Infortune Fort Une,* which can be interpreted to mean that the variations of Fortune can torment one sorely.[2] The concerns and triumphs of her public life are recorded in her extensive correspondence, whereas an echo of her inner sorrow is to be found in her poetic albums.

Margaret, the daughter of Maximilian, an Austrian prince, and Mary, a Burgundian duchess, was born in Brussels in 1480, two years after her brother Philip. Although her parents' marriage had been arranged for political considerations, the heiress of the extensive Burgundian realms had fallen very much in love with her chivalrous, and somewhat quixotic, prince, son of the Holy Roman Emperor Frederick III. Unfortunately, their marriage, intended to insure a union between two great European powers, was of brief duration. In 1482 Mary, expecting the birth of a third child, was thrown from the horse she was riding and did not recover from her accident. Her tomb in the Church of Our Lady in Bruges is one of the masterpieces of Burgundian art, but her death marked the beginning of her daughter's misfortunes. Duchess Mary's Flemish subjects, especially the spirited citizens of Ghent, were not pleased to be ruled by Maximilian, a foreigner. Conniving with the French king, Louis XI, they rose up against Maximilian and forced him to sign a treaty at Arras, the conditions of which were dictated by Louis. One of them was the marriage of the two-year-old Margaret to the French dauphin, ten years older than she. Louis had earlier tried to obtain the hand of Margaret's mother for his heir, and having failed to bring off that extraordinarily unsuitable match, he was determined to have the daughter, along with the provinces of Artois and Burgundy as part of her dowry. It was further agreed that the young princess should be sent at once to the French court to be reared under the direction of Louis XI's daughter, Anne de Beaujeu, duchess of Bourbon, who soon became regent of France for her brother after the king's death in 1483.

Anne de Beaujeu, an intelligent and able, if relentlessly ambitious, woman, insisted on a completely French education for the young princess from the north, but fortunately for Margaret, Anne's ideas on education were quite advanced for the day, strongly influenced by Christine de Pizan's concept of the place of women, especially princesses, in society. Christine's *Livre des Trois Vertus* (Book of the three virtues), where many of her educational ideas are set forth, was not only to be found in duplicate in the Bourbon library at Moulins, but it served as the model for Anne de Beaujeu's book of advice to her own daughter, Suzanne de Bourbon.[3] Margaret was later joined under Anne de Beaujeu's tutelage by two children from the house of Savoy orphaned by the death of their mother, Margaret of Bourbon. These were Philibert, who was about her own age, and Louise, who was four years their senior. Fate would link their fortunes for many years to come.

Unfortunately, in spite of all this preparation, Margaret was not to be queen of France. A better match for the young king presented itself to Anne de Beaujeu's mind: Anne de Bretagne, sole heiress to the one province that had so far escaped the clutches of the French crown. Although she had already been married by proxy to the widower Maximilian, the adroit French regent managed to have that marriage annulled and to force her brother to repudiate his still unconsummated marriage to Margaret, an insult that the princess was quite old enough to feel keenly and never to forget. Furthermore, because of French reluctance to give back the two provinces that had formed part of her dowry, she was not allowed to leave the country for another two years. It was only when Charles VIII was preparing his first expedition into Italy that, fearing the menace of an attack on his northern border, he agreed to the Treaty of Senlis (1493), which restored Margaret to her father.

Plans were soon in the making for another marriage, however, one which would unite the house of Hapsburg with Spain. Margaret and her brother Philip were to marry two children of the Catholic rulers, Ferdinand and Isabella. Thus, in November 1495, Margaret was married by proxy in Malines to Juan, heir to the throne of Castille, a marriage that was solemnized in Burgos in April 1497. In the meantime Philip was wed in Antwerp to the Spanish princess, Juana. The Spanish prince was charming, so that Margaret found him enchanting, but his health was so delicate that after only five months of what had turned out to be an extremely happy marriage, he died. His charm is still apparent from the effigy on his tomb in Avila. His seventeen-year-old widow was expecting a child, but the daughter who was born to her did not long survive. Once more Margaret was an unhappy captive in a foreign land. It was not until the fall of 1499 that she was allowed to return to her home in the north, a journey that was finally hastened by the prospect of her serving as godmother to her brother's firstborn son, Charles. It was in Spain, however, that Margaret learned her first lessons in diplomacy.

In Flanders, more matrimonial maneuvers were already taking place. There was talk of a marriage between Margaret and Louis XII of France, but he, too, eventually married the widowed Anne of Brittany; there was also the possibility of a match with Arthur, prince of Wales (Henry VIII's older brother), but he married Margaret's sister-in-law, Catherine of Aragon. Finally, her brother Philip, apparently quite insensitive to Margaret's anti-French feelings, which were perhaps forgotten in his eagerness to maintain peace with France, determined to marry her off to her childhood companion, Philibert, now duke of Savoy. However, when Philip expected her to sign a document declaring that she had not been subjected to any pressure in agreeing to this marriage, she refused to sign.[4] In spite of this resistance, the marriage took place in the fall of 1501.

The Duchy of Savoy stretched from Macon, the south of the Burgundian vineyards, to Nice on the Mediterranean coast. To the east it was bounded by the Swiss confederacy and the dukedom of Milan, and to the west by France and Provence. In view of its strategic importance, it is not surprising that Maximilian and Louis XII, as well as Philip, were interested in promoting peaceful relations with this buffer state. Margaret was a useful pawn in their calculations.

Philibert, like Margaret twenty-one years old, was known as "the Handsome." Graceful, energetic, and athletic, he was the complete opposite of the pale, intellectual, and spiritual Juan of Castille, whom she had truly loved. However, she had no choice but to become his dutiful wife, and indeed, she became much interested in the government of his realm, which he was all too willing to delegate. It was by this marriage that she was fated to become the aunt of two rival monarchs whose conflict was inevitable and perpetual; Philibert's sister, Louise, was the mother of the future Francis I, as her brother was the father of the future Charles V.

As duchess of Savoy, Margaret lived habitually in the Château of Pont d'Ain, near Bourg-en-Bresse, and not far from the city of Lyon, which was then an intellectual center scarcely less important than Paris. The associations she formed there were undoubtedly significant in her intellectual development, just as Philibert's lack of interest in governing his realm encouraged her taste for diplomacy. But once more her marriage was marked for disaster. Philibert, chilled after too much violent exercise, died unexpectedly on September 10, 1504, at the age of twenty-four. This third marriage had lasted just three years.

Inevitably, Margaret was in need of consolation, and she may well have found it in the book that had been influential in her early education, Christine de Pizan's *Livre des Trois Vertus,* for it has much to say about the trials and responsibilities of widowhood, based on the author's own experiences. It says, for instance, that it is the widow's first duty to honor her husband's memory and look to his soul's salvation.[5] Margaret soon determined to carry out this obligation, and at the same time fulfill a vow once made by her mother-in-law, Margaret of Bourbon, by building a church and monastery at Brou. So it was there, in a magnificent monument of late Flamboyant architecture, that Margaret's mortal remains were eventually to join those of her husband and his mother.

She also determined not to marry again but, as Christine suggested as a suitable alternative, to live on her lands.[6] In this way she could oversee the building of the church at nearby Brou. But in order to do this, Margaret needed considerable amounts of money. To make use of her dowry for this purpose, she was obliged to visit her father, Maximilian, in Austria, and on the way back to Savoy, to pass by Strasbourg, where she was able to conclude an arrangement with her brother-in-law, the new duke, to retain control of Bresse, Faucigny, and Vaud, although this did not entirely end her problems with the young Duke Charles. Christine had, indeed, warned that widows were often subject to efforts to despoil them of what was rightfully theirs. Echoing Christine's admonition to widows to take on the heart of a man, Margaret wrote, "Even though we may be a woman, our heart is of a different nature."[7]

It was during this absence from Pont d'Ain that the poet and early humanist Jean Lemaire de Belges, who had entered her service only the year before, wrote the first of his two delightful *Epîtres de l'Amant Vert*

(Letters from the green lover),[8] recording the death of Margaret's pet parrot, a souvenir of her days in Spain, who had fallen prey to one of her dogs. The poet invented the charming fiction that the bird had committed suicide, throwing itself into the dog's path in despair, because of her absence. Margaret's collection of dogs and birds was one of her sources of consolation for many years.

For the church at Brou, Margaret first made use of the talents of Jean Perréal, who had been her drawing master at the French court, and of Michael Colombe, who had designed Duke Francis II of Brittany's tomb in Nantes Cathedral, but due apparently to quarrels with the monks of Brou and perhaps other disagreements, some involving Jean Lemaire, who had been Margaret's overseer for the undertaking, all three departed and further work was directed by a Fleming, Van Boghem. Thus it turned out that the church, which might have been a monument of French Renaissance architecture, represents instead the culmination of Gothic Flamboyant.

Even though she thought she had made a satisfactory plan for her life, this was not in accord with her father's and her brother's intentions. They had devised a plan for marrying her to Henry VII of England, but this time she resolutely refused, insisting that three matrimonial misadventures were quite enough. For the rest of her life she was to wear the widow's weeds she assumed on the death of Philibert.

Nevertheless, misfortune still pursued her. In September 1506, her brother died in the Spanish city of Burgos. He was eulogized by Erasmus and Margaret dedicated to him a Latin epitaph, but his widow, Juana, was so inconsolable that her none too stable mind was affected to the point where, although she was heiress to the Castilian crown, she was incapable of being queen in more than name. Maximilian, who was not always noted for his practicality, did not at this moment underestimate his daughter's political capacities. He lost no time in appointing her regent for her nephew Charles in the Netherlands, along with giving over to her the task of rearing her brother's children, not only the seven-year-old Charles, but also his older sister Eleanor, now eight, and two younger sisters, Isabel, aged five, and one-year-old Marie. So it was that only one month after Philip's death she was obliged to leave the tranquility of the Château in Pont d'Ain forever, traveling by way of Germany to confer with her father in Rothenburg, and eventually to the Netherlands, where she established her court in Malines, midway between Brussels and Antwerp.

In that quiet provincial town she settled herself in a small hotel, scarcely a palace, opposite the old palace where her foster children already lived. There she would live for the rest of her life, assembling an art collection, a library, and surrounding herself with artists and men of letters. There she and her courtiers made music and wrote poetry as a respite from the arduous political administration that now became the center of her life. This public life is recorded in her letters, first a long exchange with her father, in which she offered advice as well as received it, and then other series with her ambassadors, her rivals, and eventually her nephew. Many of these have been published, but others are still in manuscript. Their number is astounding and their contents revealing of her nature and vitality. Fortunately she shared her subjects' industry and practicality. To these she added the feminine virtues of tact, flexibility, and adaptability. She had need of them all to deal with the war that still raged in Gelderland, the heritage of her grandfather, Charles the Bold, and eventually with the jealous rivalry of her nephew's tutor then chancellor, William of Croy, lord of Chièvres, who chose to follow a policy of conciliation with the French that Margaret refused to accept. Beyond their personal animosity, however, was the traditional conflict between French and English interests that had divided the country since the late fourteenth century.

Margaret's albums of poetry and many of her books still remain, along with inventories of her works of art. Two of the albums include musical scores and handsome painted decorations. There is also her copy of Christine de Pizan's *Cité des Dames* and *Livre des Trois Vertus* in a large, illustrated volume, where one can still see traces of candle wax on some of the folios.[9] It is curious that Margaret, whose ideas of government were far from medieval, who was the patroness of modern painters such as Bernard van Orley, Jacopo de' Barbari, and Jan Gossaert (Mabuse), and who attracted humanists to her court, admiring Erasmus and lending him one of her most precious manuscripts for his translation of the New Testament, should at the same time have preferred the poetic forms of the late Middle Ages and indulged in the sort of poetic games or contests that provided courtly entertainment at least a century earlier. The contradiction between the public and the private woman is evident and altogether fascinating.

Margaret's attachment for her foster children created an atmosphere of affection that remained with them throughout their lives, in spite of the demands made on them because of their station in life and the relentless determination of Charles to follow the family tradition of marriages for political advantage. The day would come when they would divide among themselves most of the crowns of Europe, Eleanor as queen of Portugal and then of France, Isabel the queen of Denmark, Sweden, and Norway, and Marie, briefly the queen of Hungary and eventually Margaret's successor as governor of the Netherlands for her brother. In the end, two of them would follow him to Spain to be near him during his final retreat at the monastery of Yuste.[10]

Margaret was the governor of what is now Holland, Belgium, and the

most northern region of France along the modern Belgian border from
1507 until her death in November 1530. There was a brief period of
respite—and perhaps of disillusionment—when Charles was declared of
age at the beginning of 1515 and Chièvres's influence was at its height. All
was changed again two years later when, on the death of his grandfather
Ferdinand of Aragon, the young prince inherited the crown of a united
Spain. In 1517 he set out for the country that would henceforth be the
center of his life. This event was followed at the beginning of 1519 by the
death of Maximilian. Margaret was once more the governor of the
Netherlands in her nephew's name.

The first period of this renewed activity was devoted, in concert with
her formal rival, Chièvres, to ensuring the election of Charles as emperor
of the Holy Roman Empire, filling the heritage, and also fulfilling the
ambition, of his grandfather Maximilian. The coronation took place in
Charlemagne's Cathedral of Aachen on October 20, 1520.

Margaret's own greatest triumph took place nearly ten years later
when, in 1529, she negotiated with her former sister-in-law Louise of
Savoy the Treaty of Cambrai, known as the Ladies' Peace. Once more,
both of them might have recalled Christine's advice on the proper role of
queens and princesses, who having less vanity and egotism than their
men, were better suited to making peace. Indeed, Christine's sentiment is
once more echoed in a letter Margaret wrote to her ambassador, Rosim-
bos, on January 3, where she says: "First the bitterness of the reproaches
written and spoken on either side were such that ill-will and hatred were
the inevitable consequences. The hostilities also which ensued were so
fierce that neither of the two sovereigns could compromise his dignity by
being the first to talk of reconciliation. . . . On the other hand, how easy
for ladies to make the first advances in such an undertaking."[11] The animosity between Charles V and Francis I, sharpened by competition for
the Imperial crown, had indeed been great, especially since the capture of
Francis I at Pavia in 1525 and his subsequent imprisonment by Emperor
Charles in Madrid. Although he was released by the Treaty of Madrid in
January 1526, he had no sooner crossed the mountains into France than
he broke his agreements with Charles, even though his two sons were still
replacing him as hostages. His mother, who had served as regent during
his absence, had suffered greatly at his captivity as well as that of her
grandsons, and was all too willing to try to meet with her sister-in-law to
discuss something better. Thus the two ladies, and Louise's daughter,
Margaret of Navarre, met in the city of Cambrai on July 5, 1529. Galler-
ies had thoughtfully been erected between the residences of the two regents so that they could pass from one to the other without being observed. Thus, after the inevitable ceremonies that accompanied such
events, they were able to talk freely and in private. Here Margaret was

intelligent and adept enough to exploit every personal and practical advantage, showing a knowledge of facts and a power of decision that once more marked her as a woman of extraordinary ability. The treaty signed on August 3, 1529, was almost entirely favorable to her nephew Charles.

In essence, the Peace of Cambrai was a confirmation of the Treaty of Madrid. It is recorded in a bulky document that deals with innumerable territorial questions and the respective rights of the two monarchs and of their subjects. Especially significant, however, were the agreements that Charles should be recognized as sovereign over Artois and Flanders and that Francis should renounce all claims to Milan, Genoa, and Naples in Italy. The two French princes, Francis's sons, were to be released on the payment of a large ransom, but Francis also had to agree to pay Charles's debts to England, a particular advantage to the emperor financially. Finally, Francis was to marry at once Charles's sister, the widowed Eleanor, whose betrothal to Francis several months earlier as part of his release had left her in a most unenviable position. However unhappy this marriage may have been for Eleanor, it was a brilliant political triumph for Charles. On the pillars of the Hall of Justice in Bruges, which was just nearing completion, medallions of Eleanor and Francis, supported by cupids, were added to the figures of other principal members of the triumphant Hapsburg-Burgundian-Spanish dynasty.[12]

The years of struggle to support her nephew's enormous ambitions had, however, taken their toll on Margaret in both body and mind. Though not yet fifty, she felt old and weary. A leg ailment that had bothered her for some time, even during the negotiations at Cambrai, grew worse the following year. The doctors mistakenly treated her for gout, but in November 1430 she developed a high fever and unmistakable signs of infection appeared. Margaret herself was the first to realize that she would not recover. On the last day of the month, having received her confessor and then her notary, she dictated to her secretary her final letter to Charles, one in which the formal language cannot disguise her devotion to him and to his welfare and her sorrow at taking leave of him. On the first day of December she died, and so was free at last to make her final journey back to Brou to Philibert de Savoy in the memorial church she had never seen. Once more, however, she was obliged to wait for two years until the church was finished and consecrated on March 22, 1532. There she now lies in a double representation, in her robes of state on a magnificently carved tomb, but underneath this grandeur is another simply clad recumbent figure, Margaret prepared to meet her Maker, a fitting symbol of this singular personage whose whole life was lived on two planes, the princess, duchess, and regent, but also the tender human being, the often suffering woman.

NOTES

1. *The Book of the City of Ladies,* trans. E. J. Richards (New York, 1982), p. 32.

2. The Old French verb *infortuner* can mean to torment or render unhappy.

3. *Les Enseignements d'Anne de France à sa fille Suzanne de Bourbon,* ed. A.-M. Chazaud (Moulins, 1878). See also H. de Chabannes and I. de Linarès, *Anne de Beaujeu* (Paris, 1955), and Ruth Kelso, *Doctrine for the Lady of the Renaissance* (Champaign, Ill., 1956), esp. p. 330.

4. Jane De Iongh, *Margaret of Austria, Regent of the Netherlands,* trans. Herter Norton, pp. 111–12.

5. *Le Livre des Trois Vertus* (based on Boston Public Library ms. 1528), chapter 1, folio xxii (translations are my own): "If it should happen that the wise princess should become a widow, she will grieve and weep for her spouse as good faith dictates, she will withdraw for a time after the burial service, in a dim light, in pitiful and mournful costume and headdress, according to the requirements of custom. She will not be unmindful of the welfare of her lord's soul, but will pray and have prayers said very devoutly in masses, services, offerings, and oblations, and she will recommend his memory to devout people. Neither these recollections nor her good deeds will be limited to a brief period, but will continue as long as she lives."

6. *Le Livre des Trois Vertus,* I, xxiii: "If the princess is a widow without children, or if she chooses to live more comfortably and peacefully, after she has claimed what is due her in addition to her assigned dowry, she will go to live on her lands, and there she will give thought to how she can conduct herself wisely and live well within her means."

7. De Iongh, *Margaret of Austria,* pp. 127–28. *Le Livre des Trois Vertus,* III, iv: "If she is to bring her case to a successful conclusion, she must take on the heart of a man, which is to say that she must be constant, strong, and wise in judging and pursuing her advantage, not crouching in tears like a simple woman, or like a poor dog who retreats into a corner while all the other dogs jump on him."

8. *Les Epîtres de l'Amant Vert,* ed. J. Frappier (Lille and Geneva, 1948), introduction and pp. 5–17.

9. Margaret's illustrated albums of poetry are to be found in Brussels, Bibliothèque Royale mss. 11239 and 228. See Marcel Françon, ed., *Albums Poétiques de Marguerite d'Autriche.* Her copy of Christine de Pizan is ms. 9236-37. This writer has had occasion to observe the traces of wax on the folios of the *Livre des Trois Vertus.*

10. Jane De Iongh, *Mary of Hungary, Second Regent of the Netherlands,* trans. Herter Norton, esp. pp. 273–89, and Ghislaine De Boom, *Eleanore, Reine de France,* pp. 220–25.

11. Quoted by Eleanor Tremayne, *The First Governess of the Netherlands, Margaret of Austria,* p. 253. The unpublished original, in Margaret's own hand, is to be found in Lille, Archives du Nord, document B 19034.

12. Karl Brandi, *The Emperor Charles V,* trans. Wedgewood, pp. 279–80.

Chanson

Forever lies this sorrow in my heart,
Which endlessly, both day and night, does smart,
Tormenting me till I would gladly die,
My life is nothing more than one long sigh
And thus inevitably I must depart.

I thought that of misfortune I'd my part
When this accursed sorrow's sharpest dart
Had pierced me through and sought to make me die,
So that my life is nothing but a sigh,
And thus inevitably I must depart
Forever with this sorrow in my heart.[1]

To Margaret's Father, Maximilian of Austria

My Lord,
I recommend myself most humbly to your good graces. My Lord, having considered the affairs in which you are involved at present, which are in no way insignificant, and knowing that you must make the right decision about them, which, I beg God, will be according to your true desire for your own good and the future tranquility of your family, which is indeed the result which I most desire to see, I have therefore made bold to send you a document which I believe, my Lord, will be useful, if it pleases you to trouble to read it or have it read to you by Marnix, and none other. After having seen it, my Lord, may it please you to return it to me. I believe, my Lord, that you will find therein more truths than I would wish, and several other things of which you may already be aware. But, my Lord, as one who night and day thinks only of being of service to you, I would not want to fail to warn you of anything I thought might be of use to you. I beg of you, my Lord, to take this in good part and to forgive me if I have been too bold in sending you my aforesaid document. I pray God, my Lord, to give you a long and prosperous life. From Malines, the 13th day of March.
Your most humble and obedient daughter,

MARGARET[2]

Brussels, September 8, 1529

To Louise of Savoy

Madame,
The gentleman whom it has pleased the king and you to send to me has presented your letters to me and, with no fault whatsoever, I have found him just as you have said in your letters and so, aware of this, I have revealed to him at his leisure (so that he may retain it all the better) the matter I had begged you to send him to hear. Because I am sure of him,

Madame, and as he has promised me that he will tell you everything, I shall not attempt to say more, except that you must believe that in this as well as in any other way whatsoever that I can render agreeable service to the said king and you, that I will do it with such good heart as to merit Heaven, begging you at the same time to be so good as to spare me for, in view of the fact that the sight of you and your presence is so distant, they nevertheless remain present and in communion with such good and desired company.

With the hope, Madame, that you will grant him a good reception, according to your wishes and in order to have more frequent news of this much desired companionship, I am sending you this messenger, my *Maître d'hôtel* Lalaing,[3] who is the one about whom I have already spoken to you, and because he is his father's son, I hope, Madame, that you will place more trust in him than in any other, and I assure you that you can have such confidence, for he is both discreet and trustworthy, so that the king and you can send me by him whatever you may wish, and I will do the same with your envoy. It will give me great comfort to have news of you frequently, as one who will remain, until death

Your more than good sister,[4]

MARGARET[5]

To Margaret's Nephew, Emperor Charles V

My Lord,

The time has come when I can no longer write to you with my own hand, for I am so greatly indisposed that I fear that what remains of my life will be brief.[6] I am prepared for whatever may come, and my conscience is at peace, entirely resolved to accept whatever it may please God to send me. I have no regrets whatsoever, save only the lack of your presence so that it is impossible for me to see you or speak with you once more before my death, but for this I shall compensate in part (because of the misgiving I have already mentioned) with this letter of mine, which I fear will be the last you will have from me. I have appointed you my sole and universal heir in all matters, and also the executor of my will, the carrying out of which I commend to you. I leave to you your Netherlands which, during your absence, I have not only preserved as you left them to me on your departure, but I have considerably augmented them. I return to you the government of them, which I believe I have acquitted loyally and in such a manner that I expect divine recompense for my efforts, along with your satisfaction, my Lord, and the goodwill of your subjects. Above all things I recommend peace to you, especially with the kings of

France and England.[7] And finally, I beg of you, my Lord, that the love it has pleased you to bear for this poor body may be a reminder of the soul's salvation and a recommendation of my poor servants and serving women,[8] and in the end commending you to God, whom I pray, my Lord, to grant you prosperity and long life. From Malines, the last day of November, 1530.[9]

Your ever humble aunt,

MARGARET

NOTES TO THE TRANSLATION

1. Françon, *Albums Poétiques*, p. 131. According to Françon, this is the only poem that can be attributed without question to Margaret, for it alone is written in her own hand. Other editors have been less rigorous.

2. Autograph letter, published by A. Le Glay in *Correspondance de l'Empereur Maximilian Ier et de Marguerite d'Autriche sa fille, gouvernante des Pays-Bas,* vol. 1, p. 386.

3. Margaret's envoy in this case was Philippe de Lalaing, son of Antoine de Lalaing, count of Hoogstraten, a close associate and great friend of the duchess. The Lalaings represented a long line of Burgundian courtiers and diplomats, of whom the best known is undoubtedly Jacques de Lalaing, the valiant knight of Duke Philip the Good's day.

4. In an attached letter Margaret acknowledges the receipt of a gift from Louise of Savoy, a daisy (*marguerite*) which was the work of her own hand, and Margaret sends her a gift in return.

5. Published by Ghislaine De Boom in *Correspondance de Marguerite d'Autriche et de ses ambassadeurs à la cour de France concernant l'exécution du Traité de Cambrai, 1529–1530* (Brussels, 1935), pp. 9–10.

6. This letter was dictated by Margaret to her secretary from what was indeed her deathbed. It is to be found in a "Recueil de documents relatifs à l'époque de Charles Quint," Brussels, Bibliothèque Royale, ms. 14.828, fol. 26. It was first published by L. P. Gachard, *Analectes belgiques* I, Paris, 1830, pp. 378–79.

7. This is undoubtedly a reference to the Peace of Cambrai.

8. The day she wrote this letter she also dictated to her notary bequests for the members of her household.

9. Margaret died the following day, December 1, 1530.

BIBLIOGRAPHY

Primary Works

De Boom, Ghislaine, ed. *Correspondance de Marguerite d'Autriche et de ses ambassadeurs à la cour de France concernant l'exécution du Traité de Cambrai, 1529–1530.* Brussels, 1935.

Françon, Marcel, ed. *Albums Poétiques de Marguerite d'Autriche.* Cambridge, Mass., and Paris, 1934.

Le Glay, A., ed. *Correspondance de l'Empereur Maximilian Ier et de Marguerite d'Autriche sa fille, gouvernante des Pays Bas.* 2 vols. Paris, 1845.

Strelka, Josef. *Gedichte Margarethes von Osterreich*. Vienna, 1954.

Van den Bergh, L. P. C., ed. *Correspondance de Marguerite d'Autriche, gouvernante des Pays-Bas, avec ses amis sur les affaires des Pays-Bas de 1506 à 1528*. 2 vols. The Hague, 1842–1847.

Related Works

Brandi, Karl. *The Emperor Charles V*. Trans. C. V. Wedgewood. London, 1939.

Bruchet, Max. *Marguerite d'Autriche, Duchesse de Savoie*. Lille, 1927.

Bruchet, Max, and E. Lancien. *L'Itinéraire de Marguerite d'Autriche, gouvernante des Pays-Bas*. Lille, 1934.

De Boom, Ghislaine. *Eleanore, Reine de France*. Brussels, 1934.

————. *Marguerite d'Autriche-Savoie et la Pré-Renaissance*. Brussels and Paris, 1935.

De Iongh, Jane. *Margaret of Austria, Regent of the Netherlands*. Trans. M. D. Herter Norton. New York, 1953.

————. *Mary of Hungary, Second Regent of the Netherlands*. Trans. M. D. Herter Norton. New York, 1958.

Margareta Van Oostenrijk en Haar Hof. Catalog of an exhibition organized by the city of Malines, July 26–September 15, 1958. Malines, 1958.

Marguerite d'Autriche, Fondatrice de Brou. Catalog of an exhibition organized by the city of Bourg-en-Bresse, June 1–July 15, 1958. Brou, 1958.

Strelka, Josef. *Der Burgundische Renaissance Margarethes von Österreich und seine Literarhistorische Bedeutung*. Vienna, 1957.

Tremayne, Eleanor. *The First Governess of the Netherlands, Margaret of Austria*. London, 1908.

PART FOUR

he Low Countries

GERMANIC SAPPHO

nna Bijns

KRISTIAAN P. G. AERCKE

The tiny contemporaneous caricature of Anna Bijns, drawn in an initial capital *O* in one of her own printed refrains,[1] stands as a perfect emblem of the poet's life and work. The low-browed face with the beady eyes, frightful nose, and sharp tongue does indeed not seem to belie the lifelong motto of this sixteenth-century Antwerp schoolmistress: "Sour rather than sweet." This portrait is the only known attempt to preserve her likeness in a city of portrait painters. As arcanely concealed within the book as the facts of her life in her poetry, this instant caricatural *vituperatio* mirrors her own spontaneous shouting that "Lutherans stink like goats" and deserve "a full dozen of faggots under the arse."

Traditional criticism and biography designates Luther, "the wolf in sheep's garb" of her refrains, as the pain of her life and his early successes in Antwerp as her main stimulus and target. In this sense it was a strange quirk of fate that toward the close of the fifteenth century master tailor Jan Bijns acquired the house "The She-Wolf" on the Great Market and named his second child Martin. Jan Bijns held important religious functions in his guild and named his firstborn after its patron saint. Thus Anna was reared in the almost superstitiously pious atmosphere of the lower middle class in the cosmopolitan town. Except for some dates, the names of a few relatives, and some paltry notary's data, her life passed unrecorded. Anna Bijns's first biographer,[2] out of necessity relying on much conjectural skill, dogmatized that in the first decade of the new century the "meek but ardently religious maiden of the people"[3] was tutored by Franciscan Minorites and spent most of her time attending services in the nearby Cathedral of Our Lady. Her literary gift resulted in an early production of rhetorical refrains on Paradise, the Virgin, or the spiritual New Year. It is not unlikely that the Franciscans developed the talent of which she was well aware:

> Please read this ode from four angles with care,
> Start at the tail, in front—or wherever you want,
> For it'll make sense, it'll be poetry still.

Any association with the flourishing Antwerp Chambers of Rhetoric is uncertain, but she probably contributed refrains in the "foolish," the "amorous," and the "serious" modes to their contests. In general, her appreciation of these bourgeois poets and their semiprofessional institutions was very slight (as her refrain " 'Tis a waste to cast pearls before swine" makes clear). Insufficiently argued attempts have been made to ascribe the remarkable production of prose novels in Antwerp between 1510 and 1520 at least in part to Bijns's talent and spare time.[4] The delicate analyses of young women in *Marieken van Nieumeghen* and in *Floris ende Blanchefloer* might indeed point toward a female author, and some linguistic and poetic idiosyncrasies agree with Anna Bijns's.

When Jan Bijns died in 1516 he left behind some real estate to support an ailing wife and three children. Whether Anna, his oldest daughter, ever abandoned any matrimonial plans out of inclination, frustrating experience, necessity, or a growing misandric tendency due to her younger sister's fast and unhappy marriage cannot be traced. Mother Bijns, Anna, and Maarten moved to a less fashionable neighborhood, where the latter opened one of the small private schools that provided most of the primary education at the time. Very likely Anna assisted both in the household and in the school, writing poetry after working hours.

Bijns's refrains are the sole indicators of her reaction to the first reformational phenomena in Antwerp. Her biographer enthusiastically claims that she ordained herself as the "avenging angel of the insulted Faith" when she learned about Luther's Theses, the "revolting insults flung in the face of Heaven."[5] She was still a burgher's daughter, and it was unusual for the bourgeoisie in the Netherlandic Provinces to take a firm stand in defense of Catholicism. Also, the conservative rhetoricians of the Chambers kept a careful distance between art and life. Despite the absence of a native heretical substratum, Antwerp Lutheranism[6] found a favorable subsoil in the combination of important foreign communities, the humanist tradition, and the fame of the city as a center of learning and book printing. Gradually, however, local heretics such as Loyken Pruystinck contributed with local issues to the general confusion between the subsequent Lutheran (1515–1526), Anabaptist (1534–1539), and Calvinist movements (after 1526). This complex background is essential to an understanding of Bijns's counterreformational poetry, which has been decried as oversimplified. One wonders whether it was always easy or possible to distinguish between the intricate nuances of Catholic orthodoxy and the many guises of "heresy." If she coined the term "Lutherie" as a summary of the entire complex reformational process,[7] it was in an attempt to guard herself with the unsophisticated shield of polemical stubbornness against the no less fanatical attacks of literary "anti-Papists." Both parties availed themselves of cheaply printed pamphlets to disseminate their ideas and vilify one another. Bijns's argument "Answer a fool according to his foolishness" (Proverbs 26:5) and the endnote "Written against a Lutheran refrain brimming with venom," added to a no less militant poem of her own, suggest such a logomachy characterized by a retaliative repetition of familiar arguments and ready images. Hers was the only powerful Catholic voice in print against anonymous Protestant authors whose billets (collected in the *Dordtsche Bundel*) were written and printed, sold and read, at great personal danger. Some printers would publish official and heretical material at the same time; Jacob van Lieshout, who printed Bijns's first collection of refrains, was executed for this reason.

Bijns's zeal did not free her from financial care. When her brother Maarten married in 1536, she opened a one-classroom school of her own. Tuition fees depended on the curriculum, but in general, prayer and writing brought in most. As a member of the reactionary Schoolmasters' Guild, she must have seen enrollment and income dwindling as new schools responded to the more moderate and liberal tastes of an increasing number of parents. Ever harsher "Plakkaten" (decrees) from Madrid against heresy,[8] and even the institution of the Spanish Inquisition itself (1550), could not prevent the Catholic party from becoming the virtual underdog in the relatively free religious climate of the 1560s. The following lines express Bijns's disappointment with the success of the reformed schools and her own poverty:

> What ought I give for kin or riches
> When my earthly skin I'd gladly wager
> To keep unharmed the Bride of Christ.

Earlier in her career she had already testified to her unmercenary attitude toward art by exprobating the "noble students of Mercury" for using rhetoric "where filthy dung belongs" and for fawning on the philistines who "hold Grand Rhetoric and music sweet no dearer than vile terrestrial mud." Whereas most rhetoricians practiced poetry as a craft and for its own sake,[9] Bijns's idea was quite different. She considered the Holy Spirit the head of the Church, as in "Return, return, roving herd," and also as the dispenser of the gift of poetry. Hence the poet's mission is dual but indivisible: as an artist he must let pure devotion yield blossoms of artistic beauty, and as a crusading Christian his task is to apply this art anew in defense of his Church.

Though Anna Bijns was the most important and most widely read woman writer of the age in her language, she profusely apologized for this. She feared that her womanhood might interfere with the martial aspect of this poetic program. To her, failing as a *miles* implied failing as a *clericus* and vice versa, the former as the result of an inability to command or convince an audience. In the following powerful lament this ambidextrous argument is taken up apologetically as topos and as metaphor:

> I'd engage in battle till stained with blood
> If, by God, heresy could surely be crushed
> Which now with harpy's claws rents the Church asunder.
> But alas! Frailty forces me to flee.
> If God's spirit would reinforce my mind
> And spark off my thought with Solomon's wit,
> My brain wouldn't get a moment's rest
> Ere its might had crushed the spiders
> That from Scripture suck their poison
> And revealed to dark malice its reeking bed of dull senselessness.

As she saw "Lutherie" and consequently the Counterreformation gathering momentum, with ever more ordinary people entangled in the ugly web of suspicion and persecution, criticism of secular and monastic clergy entered her religious poetry—a theme not unfamiliar in the earlier literature of the Southern Netherlands.[10] Some priests and monastics might have created despair and confusion in the minds of the humble through their dissolute life-style, but as Bijns's supplication suggests, these were only a minority.[11]

> Return—for God's wrath needs little time to cool—
> To your Mother's roof, choose a shortcut home.
> It's compassion that thus moves my tongue.
> Think how banished and under heretics' banner
> You'll stumbling be making your woeful way.
> Throw off these fetters, these dreary shackles
> And while leaving Babylon head for Jacob's tabernacle,
> For guides are standing by to lead you back.

And although she had occasionally defended the clergy against hypocritical and vulgar hypercriticism,[12] she must have felt that the clergy in general was not adequately helping her conducting the Counterreformation in Antwerp. The idea that the success of "Lutherie" was perhaps largely due to its skilled preachers and inspired libelists came naturally to her rhetorician's mind. If the Word was indeed the gift of the Holy Spirit, then the ordinary parish priests had obviously and sadly been deprived. Having remained virtually unchallenged for many centuries, they were losing the ideological battle partly because of their inability to manipulate sermons and more popular exhortations toward *convincing* rather than confirming. Thus Bijns wrote,

> Alas! They're mostly just dumb dogs.
> They cannot bark—and that is why God's law
> Is now neglected and brushed aside!

The most militant and intellectual of the Catholic party were Anna's former tutors, the Franciscan Minorites. It was again with them that her literary production and fortunes became affiliated. Considering the virtually insolvent poet's impossibility to offer financial guarantees and the reactionary orthodoxy of her refrains, one might wonder who else but the Franciscans would have assisted her in editing her work at a time when so many people in Antwerp were risking their lives by producing and reading anti-Papist and anti-Spanish material. In 1528, twenty-three of Bijns's most polemical counterreformational refrains were released under a title as outspoken as its contents:[13]

> This is a delightful and pure booklet which contains many beautifully artistic refrains, full of references to the Scriptures and teachings of diverse matters which can be looked up by the lines in the added index; all made very well by the honorable and ingenious maiden Anna Bijns, who refutes with truly subtle and rhetorical skill all the errors and great abuses originating in the damnable sect of Luther. The latter has been condemned not only by all doctors and universities but even by His Imperial Majesty—and not without good reason.[14]

This title presents the poet as a *miles gloriosus* rather than as a *miles Christi,* but very likely she did not write it herself. The pert statement clashes remarkably with the editor's complaint in de Castelein's *De Const van Rhetorike* (The art of rhetoric, 1555)[15] that the Flemish authors of the era were too shy about seeing their work printed. De Castelein's remark is also contradicted by the exceptionally fast and faithful translation of the collection into Latin by the humanist and priest Eucharius (Ghent, 1529).[16] The Dutch text was reprinted in 1541 and again in 1548, but for none of its several editions contemporary data concerning reception, sales, or circulation are available. All this suggests that the publication was aimed at a limited, essentially clerical, audience, and the contents and the internal organization of the volume strengthen the impression. The latter is too tight for an accidental collection. A general complaint about moral and social decay precedes allegorical refrains that introduce Luther as the *radix malorum.* This point is then taken up and elaborated in the next refrains, which are really inductive catalogs of ethical and social problems in the provinces of the Netherlands during the sixteenth century. This organization and especially the abundance of biblical and scriptural source references and allusions to the patristic authors[17] in the margins make the volume a useful tool for the writing of sermons.

A much thicker volume of counterreformational refrains was published exactly around the time that Anabaptism and Calvinism were gaining many supporters in Antwerp.[18] *The Second Book Containing Many Beautifully Artistic Refrains* (Antwerp, 1548; reprinted in 1553, in 1564 together with the fourth edition of the first volume, and in 1565) was clearly intended as a sequel for the same audience, for it has the same format, layout, and internal organization. This time, however, the Franciscans unambiguously claimed responsibility for the edition in an exuberant—Latin!—preface by Brechtanus, who was himself a reputed tragedian and author of sermons. As in the first collection, only counterreformational refrains were included, but Brechtanus introduced a new note:

> Ne parcas igitur numis pietatis amator. Hic tibi non magno venditur aere liber.

> So don't be too thrifty, you who love piety, for this book is sold quite cheaply.

Greed enters the catalog of Lutheran sins in this volume, though in the refrain "The will I've got . . ." I find significant this casual but bitter remark,

> I'll fight the Lutherans till I breathe my last,
> Avoiding nothing—though I work for scanty thanks.

The general tone in this volume is coarser, less poetic, and it is surprising that the selection does not suggest that Bijns was aware of the changed fortunes of Lutheranism and the reorientation within the reformational movement. The poet's involvement in the editing work must be doubted. The printer's mark, for example, contains a naked Venus and Cupid, the very same "modernist indecency" that Anna had condemned in a refrain as the wicked outcome of Lutheran dissoluteness:

> But that Cupid with his barbs,
> Lucretia, Venus, or her associates
> Are represented in their rooms stark naked,
> Which must surely lead to impure things—
> If only 't would give people wrong ideas—
> That they don't care about. What perversity!

There is also no obvious reason why the long "Yet, when compared, Martin Rossom comes out best" (1542) was excluded. In this refrain she compared, on the basis of name and action, Martin Luther and Martin Rossom—the infamous Gelderland condottiere[19] who had only a few years earlier ransacked and horrified the Netherlands before finally breaking his teeth on the walls of Antwerp. In 1548, his name must still have caused shudders of horror and awe. Thus the exclusion of the refrain is even harder to understand because it illustrates best her basic polemical technique of presenting "Lutherie" as an utterly nauseous and repugnant misapprehension through the *vituperatio* of Luther as a person. Bijns suggested that Luther (like Rossom) was responsible for the actual murder of two hundred thousand German peasants[20] and (unlike Rossom) of many more souls as well. Murder, theft, sacrilege, countless abandoned children, and gangs of hungry runaway monks and nuns in the country— such evils could all be traced back to Luther's odious life and doctrine, according to Bijns. She believed that the doctrine was merely intended as an apologetic justification of the life.[21] Revocations of former heretics, fragments of the texts of the Diet of Worms (1521), accusations printed in Imperial "Plakkaten" (ordinances), pamphlets, and the like—these were her sources of "information" on the life under "Lutherie." Her metaphorical arsenal suggests that she tried to create disgust for the Reformation through the presentation of the heretical life as disgusting and disease-ridden on the material and the spiritual level. The antithetical paradigms of light versus darkness and health versus corruption run throughout her entire counterreformational corpus, the positive terms referring to the Catholic "flock," the negative to Luther—"the wolf in sheep's garb"—and his retinue. Antonomasia on the three levels of comparison— simile, metaphor, and metonym—presents the opponents as "poisoned seed," "blind guides," "Turks or Huns," "pus and corruption," "madness," "vermin and worms," "putrid graves and cesspools," "children of darkness, and stupidity," "foul airs," and "Goliath or Pilate-like." Antithetical values apply to the Catholic party, which is praised as a "healthy crop," "trusty flock," "healthy body, mind or orchard," "light, Solomon's wit," "frail vessels," "children of the sun," and "David or Christ-like." The *fons et origo* of the corruption is easy to indicate in the following two passages:

> Had not Luther spoken out so loudly,
> We would not have Anabaptism around.

> If Luther had kept his tongue behind his teeth,
> For such cruel action there'd surely be no need.
> And now he plans to wash it off his hands
> As Pilate did with our Savior's death.

For the misogamic Bijns, the monk's marriage was the ultimate symbol of his hypocrisy and bad faith toward pope and emperor. Summarized, her anti-Lutheranism consists of the following personal charges.[22] Luther denies free will and doubts hell. He condemns prayer, indulgences, services for the dead, church ornamentation—even the churches themselves. Since everybody, and especially Luther himself, can comment on and discuss the Scripture, and since the sacraments of marriage, confession, and communion are to be abolished, neither priests nor pope ought to be retained. Holy days will no longer be observed, the Virgin and the saints no longer adored, and fasts, confession and spirituality likewise abolished. Bijns's solution was drastic: "Cut off the rotten limbs ere the whole body decays" for "They are spared still far too much." The refrains "Lord, have You forgotten Your Church entirely" and "The Holy Church's Council is scorned" clearly reveal the lack of confidence of an impetuous *miles Christi* in the slow efficiency of the Council of Trent (1545–1564).

Probably because of her lower middle-class background, she admonished and chided the mass of newly converted rather than the trained leaders, for the former might still be saved. Executions, crowd scenes, little or major daily annoyances were the sources of the imagery and satire that she preferred to abstract theological argumentation. "Facts" amassed in mostly inductive arguments set out to prove that the life of those who succumbed is wicked, inferior, and soon deplored. With constant apostrophes—direct questions, repetitions and exclamatory remarks— and a careful choice of hyperbolic imagery she played on the audience's emotions.

In 1567 reformed militants, enflamed by the Franciscan prior's philippic sermons, set fire to his monastery. Later in the same year, Anna's third and most voluminous collection (over 250 pages) was published—with a ponderous preface by Henrick Pippinck, the same prior. Pippinck blandly but unambiguously announced the book as a fundraiser for the restoration of his monastery. While eulogizing the noble patroness who financed the edition, he minimalized the role of the by now seventy-four-year-old poet: "You see, this third book was not written by a woman but by the true Spirit who has wrought this through her, and is still doing so." He also took up Bijns's own qualms: "Even if this is a maiden's work, don't reject it for that reason, for learned men have read and approved it." The volume carried a lengthy title:

A very pretty and pure book, explaining God's power and Christ's grace toward sinful Mankind. Moreover, also the veritable cause of the great plague that harms us in these times; with plenty of sound moral advice, proving that a sincere faith is the right way to a new life in Christ. Artistically made in order to stave off God's wrath and to receive peace in this world and in the eternal life of the next, by the honorable and pious, Catholic and very renowned maiden Anna Bijns in the true spirit of Christ, whose great wit dwells in Antwerp and there instructs the young in the true Faith. Published only now by B. Henrick Pippinck, minister provincial of the Netherlandic Provinces, to the glory of Christ and for the salvation of all mankind.[23]

The "sound moral advice" emerges in themes which show that the polemical crusader of ere had turned from accusation to self-accusation and contemplative meditation. She complains ("Is it not a thing to wonder at, if all the world is plagued?"), indulges in purely medieval literary flagellation, rejoices in the beauty of nature,[24] expresses something like pity for the lost souls, and urges the living heretics to return to the orthodox creed: "Offer new fruits to the new King." An exceptional refrain of Bijns's ultimate creative phase is the long "Lord, if all deserts me, will Thou stand by me?"—an *in articulo mortis* poem unusual because of the simple but poignant physical analysis of the last agony itself rather than of its moral implications.

This selection of prayer and piety, pity and regret, matched the contemporaneous *mea culpa* attitude of some in the Catholic camp, who interpreted the apparent success of the Reformation despite harsh opposition as a divine affliction. It would be uncautious, however, to infer from this third volume that only at the close of her life Anna Bijns had begun to respond to the changing situation. As the phrase "Published only now" in the title of the book suggests, Pippinck had selected to a great extent from her still unpublished refrains. Some of those dated back as far as 1527–1529, but the emphasis was on the 1542–1545 period. This indicates that she had never quite been the blind fanatic her earlier editors, Brechtanus especially, had made her out to be. Only in the late nineteenth century did some scholarly editions[25] of recently discovered refrains reveal an Anna Bijns rather different from the "honorable and pious, Catholic and very renowned maiden." Since the beginning of her literary career till at least 1533 she had been active in the "wise" (nonpolemical), "amorous," and "foolish" refrain modes, accumulating an oeuvre twice the bulk of her religious work that was published in the sixteenth century. Her "foolish" refrains are not numerous and either coarsely scatological (for example, "Better to fart than to be harmed" is about a peculiar contest in a nunnery) or "wise" refrains in disguise ("Make merry and leap the scythe," for instance, is a critique of hypocritical criticism and a plea for common sense). It is not known whether her amorous refrains were based on personal experiences or were merely intended as entries to refrain contests organized by the Chambers. In some of these she assumes a male, in others a female, persona. As whimsical is her treatment of Eros: vile *vituperatio* and sweet love, misandry and misogyny alternate insconsequently. The amorous theme and imagery are unimaginatively conventional in the laudatory lover's poems but more like the "real" Anna Bijns of the polemical refrains in the bellicose poems of amorous frustration.

The male acrostics in many amorous refrains probably refer to friends mainly among the Franciscans. The name Bonaventura appears often: twenty times, sixteen of which in conjunction with the name "Anna."[26] This does not necessarily refer to a real affair with a lover, for the prominent Franciscan Bonaventura—a staunch advocate of celibacy and ascetism—obviously fitted her theme of misandry and misogyny. The fact that this theme in her love poetry has received little attention is all the more remarkable because of its unquestionable correlation with her counterreformational subject—as for example, in "These covet happy nights and lose their happy days." "Man" equals Luther, a faithless hypocrite, a wolf in sheep's garb. "Woman" is like the innocent Catholic: good-natured, trustworthy, an easily ensnared member of the flock. Intimacy between the sexes: "nasty stains in a clean sheet." In "To refuse becomes a girl well" she warns girls to keep their heads cool in courtship and advises them to treat their suitors with utter cruelty. A grotesque view of marriage underlies some satirical refrains. "Unyoked is best! Happy the woman without a man" summarizes her misandric arguments, but for harmony's sake she complemented it with a refrain "Unyoked is best! Happy the man without a woman!" Self-reliance, freedom of an inferior creature's domination, and social independence rank higher than "what a man is good for." Marriage is the result of temporary insanity, and her persona would like to see the possibility of divorce—éven if it would cost his last nickel in bribes to the priest.

Remarkable mixtures of classical topoi (for example, Jason or Aeneas as archetypes of unfaithful lovers), conventional patterns of fifteenth-century courtly love poetry,[27] and popular satire, these refrains introduce a new note in Netherlandic love poetry. Jealousy and bitter complaints, a yearning for solace and tenderness, unexpectedly tender diminutives alternated with utterly uncourtly sarcastic realism, are found together in the same poem. And who else but Anna Bijns would invent such similes to describe the winsome effects of coquetry as "I walk as ponderously as if I were a cow" or "My face just turned red with spots all over."

Following iconoclastic riots in 1566, the Spanish king's special envoy Alva succeeded in ruthlessly "cutting off the rotten limbs." By 1573 the Calvinist northern Netherlands had won a factual independence, whereas in the still dominantly Catholic south orthodoxy had been firmly re-established. Only the cosmopolitan Antwerp of Anna Bijns had known very strong Protestant contention, personified in Mayor Marnix van Sint-Aldegonde, whose *Biëncorf* (Beehive, 1569) was the flagrant counterpart of Anna's counterreformational collections.

But for the Reformation in the southern Netherlands all was over by the time of the poet's death in 1575. She was buried with a pauper's service in the Cathedral of Our Lady. Her three counterreformational collections were published eight times during her life and five times in the early seventeenth century, obviously for devotional rather than polemic reasons. The first collection was translated into Latin within one year—a very rare occurrence. Her third book was anthologized and adapted as a reader for use in schools.[28] Seventeen manuscript codices of the sixteenth and seventeenth centuries contain refrains attributed to her.[29] She was attributed thrice the epithet "Brabantian Sappho," and some sources considered her one of the most famous women of her age.[30] Brabantian and Dutch rhetoricians honored her with odes. But the question remains whether she was appreciated by some contemporaries for purely poetical or for ideological reasons. For the fact is that her friend Matthys de Castelein did not even mention her among the Flemish rhetoricians who did insist on seeing their work in print (1555), and neither does her name appear in the fairly extensive list of rhetoricians in the *Nederduytsche Helicon* (1610).

It was not until the publication of the Protestant anthology *Geuzen Liedboeck* (Gueux song book, 1574 or 1581) in the northern Netherlands that new Catholic authors continued Bijns's work—but without her raciness or straightforward inspiration. Katharina Boudewijns is considered the best of her successors, with her book *Prieelken der Gheestelijcken Wellusten* (Bower of spiritual voluptuousness, Brussels, 1587). Bijns's mastery of the difficult rhetorical refrain was a major factor of her supremacy as early Renaissance poet in Dutch; it is also quoted as her greatest achievement. The refrain form that fitted her like a natural skin had been more like a straitjacket to many Chamber poets with its inflexible lacings of rhyme schemes, imported *mots recherchés*, and *nugae difficiles*. Bijns's refrains usually consist of four or more stanzas, preferably of fifteen lines each. The last stanza is introduced by the envoy "Prince," or occasionally, "Princess." A tag line or aphorism ("stock") indicates the theme and concludes each stanza epigrammatically. Anna Bijns, a contemporary of Ronsard (1525–1585), was the first rhetorician who challenged the received notion that rhyme skill was the primordial concern of the refrain: she introduced a variant of the French alexandrine into Dutch poetry, emphasizing rhythm without rigid syllabic count. Enjambment occurs often, as in the reproduction of natural speech; similarly, caesura serves as a natural breathing pause rather than as a syntactic gap—in order to produce a naturally dramatic union of passion in theme and expression.

Apart from a few scraps and fragments into French, German, and English, Bijns's works have not been translated into any modern language. I have not tried to imitate the complicated and perfect rhyme schemes; instead, in order to preserve the natural flow of the original, I have opted for a free verse that tries to represent something of the rhythm of Anna's lines.

NOTES

1. "Oh God, what rumors reach our ears" is the opening line of refrain 13 in Anna's second collection. The copy with the little drawing is in the Koninklijke Akademie voor Wetenschappen, Amsterdam.

2. F. Jos Van den Branden, *Anna Bijns: Haar leven, hare werken, haar tijd 1493–1575.* Van den Branden was keeper of the city records.

3. Van den Branden, p. 20. This translation, as well as all the following translations from primary and secondary sources, is my own. Refrains will be indicated by my title.

4. The idea was suggested by Jos Van Mierlo, "Anna Bijns en de volksliteratuur in haar jeugd te Antwerpen," *Verslagen en Mededelingen van de Koninklijke Vlaamse Akademie* (1955): 329–72, and by L. Debaene, "Rederijkers en Prozaromans," *De Gulden Passer* 27 (1949): 1–23. Lode Roose presented interesting counterarguments in *Anna Bijns, een rederijkster uit de hervormingstijd,* p. 150ff. Some of the novels, besides the two mentioned in the text, include *Margareta van Lymborch; Jonker Jan; Tgevecht van Minnen; Alexander van Mets; Van den Tien Esels; Broeder Russche.*

5. Van den Branden, p. 20.

6. Prior to May 1518, Luther had sent his German translation of the New Testament and other texts to Antwerp for translation and publication. In 1519 the Augustine community heard Prior Praepositus preach Lutheran doctrine for the first time. An imperial ordinance of 1521 ordered all heretical publications to be burned, and until 1526 razzias, executions, and book burnings could temporarily suppress heretical outbursts.

7. Loyken Pruystinck's call for social reforms coupled with religious renewal was successful especially among the lower classes, but Loyken did incur criticism from Luther himself. In fact, it has been suggested that Loyken rather than Luther was the main butt of Anna's polemical refrains.

8. Some ordinances went to such extremes that the city magistrature refused to announce them in their original form. Often fostering reformational or progressive sympathies themselves, the magistrates were of course mainly concerned with the economic survival of Antwerp as a center of international trade and business. The Spanish Inquisition was instituted in 1550 partly because of the renewed efforts of the Marans to turn Antwerp into a distribution center of heretical literature for export. Initially most of the Inquisition's victims were foreigners.

9. A few of the most outstanding rhetoricians, like Cornelis Crul and Jan vanden Berghe, did voice their personal, reformed sympathies.

10. Conrad Busken Huet, *Het Land van Rembrandt* (The Hague, 1974), pp. 107–29, discusses the authors Boendale, Maerlant, and Geert Groote and dwells at length on the famous Middle Dutch version of the *Roman de Renart,* the highly anticlerical beast-epic *Reynaert de Vos.*

11. According to city historian Floris Prims (*Geschiedenis van Antwerpen,* VI–VII, 1938–1946), most of the secular and monastic clergy were even quite ascetic and exemplary in their lifestyle.

12. "They're not angels, but faulty humans. / Contemplate yourselves, you scurvy sheep," in "Priests are folks just like anybody else"; and "Even if monastics seem a little foolish now and then . . . ," in "Make Merry and leap the scythe."

13. The only officially surviving copy was acquired in 1872 by the Bibliothèque royale, Brussels.

14. The University of Louvain condemned the Lutheran Theses on November 7, 1519. Emperor Charles V ordered on March 20, 1521, that all books condemned by Louvain be confiscated and burned. The careful investigation into the orthodoxy or heretical tendencies of the Augustine community probably began in its library.

15. *Bibliotheca Belgica* (1979), vol. 1, p. 458. Matthys de Castelein's *De Const van Rhetorike* (Ghent, 1555) was the first manual for rhetoric in Dutch.

16. Eucharius (1488–1544, Ph.D. 1504 Paris) was rector of the Latin school in Ghent. A fragment from the preface: "*Vade Retro,* Evil One, a virgin has smashed your barbs with the sword of Reason. Be miserably damned. Anna Bijns of Antwerp first made it for all who read Dutch. Now disseminate it among the peoples so that Luther shall go unheeded; for with pitch and pitchblack handshake did he engage in crooked deals."

17. J. Verest, *Manuel de littérature* (Bruges, 1926).

18. Calvinism, which reached Antwerp via France, appealed strongly to the commercial bourgeoisie and the local nobility through its theory of predestination; its theocratic aspects would strongly influence the nationalistic party of the northern provinces in the next decades.

19. Maarten van Rossom ("Zwarte Marte," "Black Martin") played a short but intensive part in the struggle of the European powers over the southern Netherlands. While Emperor Charles V—legal ruler of the territories—was detained in Algiers, trying to end Barbarossa's piracies, the French king, François I, had his ally Willem, duke of Kleef and Gulik, move an army into the southern Netherlands. This force was commanded by Maarten van Rossom. In June 1542, his sixteen thousand Gelderlanders sacked, burned, and looted their way through the entire duchy of Brabant. Maarten's reputation was such that the news of his approach created a panic in Antwerp. All able bodies, women included, were mustered to the defense of the city. The walls were reinforced with rubble from the demolished Chartreuse— a reference to this is found in Anna's refrain "Oh Lord, Have you forgotten your Church altogether": "With stones of cloisters, of churches torn down / We think to fortify our cities." Rossom laid siege to Antwerp but was driven back. Anna's refrain "Yet, when compared, Martin Rossom comes out best" was thus clearly intended to present Luther as worse than the vilest scoundrel on the face of the earth.

20. The reference is to the German peasants' revolt of 1525.

21. Roose, ed., *Anna Bijns, een rederijkster uit de hervormingstijd,* p. 233.

22. Ibid., p. 237ff.

23. Van den Branden (p. 136) thinks that Anna took her unpublished refrains to Pippinck with the request to publish some, but Roose (*Anna Bijns, een rederijkster uit de hervormingstijd,* pp. 55–60) thinks that Pippinck found a set of refrains in manuscript form among the remnants of the burned library. This seems the more likely hypothesis.

24. Roose (ibid., p. 287) interprets the consideration of nature metaphysically (Bonaventura's *vestigium Dei* idea that Nature must lead Man to the Creator), but it is perfectly legitimate to read "He must be beautiful who created all this" as a hymn to nature itself.

25. W. Van Helten, ed., *Refereinen van Anna Bijns, naar de nalatenschap van Mr. A. Bogaers,* with glossary, variants, and dating (Rotterdam, 1875); E. Soens, "Onuitgegeven gedichten van Anna Bijns," *Leuvense Bijdragen* (1900), and "Verspreide refereinen van Anna Bijns," *Leuvense Bijdragen* 11 (1910): 37–103; *Nieuwe Refereinen van Anna Bijns benevens enkele andere Rederijkersgedichten uit de XVIde eeuw,* ed. W. Jonckbloet and W. Van Helten (Ghent, 1886); *Refereinen en andere gedichten uit de XVIde eeuw, verzameld en afgeschreven door Jan de Bruyne,* ed. K. Ruelens (Antwerp, 1879–1881).

26. Van den Branden (p. 82), mentions that a certain Brother Engelbert, who transcribed many refrains from the manuscript, altered the original letters or words of one refrain in order to replace the original acrostic BONAVENTURA ANNA with his own BROEDER ENGELBERT. Jonckbloet was mainly responsible for the Victorian theory that Anna was leading a double life with Bonaventura as her passionate lover (*Geschiedenis van de Nederlandsche Letterkunde* [Groningen, 1873], vol. 1, p. 366). The theme still surfaces occasionally, as in L. Willems, "Het Bonaventura-raadsel in het leven van Anna Bijns," *Verslagen en Mededelingen van de Koninklijke Vlaamse Akademie* (1920): 415–45.

27. Roose, ed., *Anna Bijns, een rederijkster uit de hervormingstijd*, pp. 190–95. Also in Jos Van Mierlo, *Studiën over Anna Bijns* (Ghent, 1950).

28. *Den Gheestelijcke Nachtegael* (The spiritual nightingale, 1623) contains a selection of fifty-one refrains from the third collection.

29. The codices are now in Belgium: Dendermonde, Ghent (University Library), Brussels (Royal Library), Bruges (Bisschoppelijk Seminarie), and abroad: Haarlem (Bisschoppelijk Museum), The Hague (Royal Library), Berlin (Prussian State Library), and London (British Museum). Roose attributes refrains to Anna Bijns on the basis of recurring expressions and imagery, acrostics, dates, and mainly technical elements, such as length of verse line and of stanza (*Anna Bijns, een rederijkster uit de hervormingstijd*, p. 71ff.).

30. Van den Branden says that the Latin translation carried her fame to southern France, where she was considered one of the three most prominent women of her age (p. 55). The first to call her "Sappho, Lesbia teutonicis" was Brechtanus. Jonckbloet says that the French considered her as one of the seven most important women of the time (vol. 1, p. 187).

Dedication

Artistic tempers, with art on your minds
Nothing here but what in good faith was done.
Now knowing this, relish its affection even more.[1]
And in case of a fault, well, 'tis a woman's work!

Bright spirits, to learn from you what's right
I am prepared to do; let your wisdom join mine.
In technique my skill, I know, is poor,
Not masterly yet; hence my teachers I praise highly.
So, eagerly, by artists I'll be taught.

For love of Truth, for an ever stronger Faith
I have blithely worked and shed no tears.[2]

[January 11, 1528]

'Tis a Waste to Cast Pearls Before Swine

Crafty spirits, noble Mercurists,
Rhetoricians, subtle artists,
Economize on sterling words.
Hold in reserve ingenious conceits.
Men of letters: your cheap artistic claims
Apply Rhetoric where filthy dung belongs.
Noble Rhetoric, I weep for the affront

That you bear such verbal disrespects
From whomever and whenever. Shame!
Many a conceited fool you'll find
To whom Rhetoric seems naught but trite.
No need to perform our art soigné
Before vain windbags, tongue-tied themselves.
'Tis a waste to cast pearls before swine.

As the sweetest of fruits I sing your praise,
A gift directly from the Holy Ghost,
Respected by most, oh noble Rhetoric.
Joy with joyous occasion you join.
But where dense pigs convene in feast
Art is not invited at all.
Artist to philistine will yield
And shy away frustrated, for boors aplenty
Hold Grand Rhetoric and music sweet
No dearer than vile terrestrial mud.
Try to declaim—a play or pretty refrain,[3]
Always one will chat or eat or quaff.
Nobody's giving a hoot! So, indeed,
'Tis a waste to cast pearls before swine.

If you're inclined to art beware,
Take care: avoid all spivvish churls
Who despise our refined ideas.
In hailing yokels of art unaware
Refuse your art—be grudging,
And don't spend it till they beg for it.
If they don't listen then be silent.
Where uncouth peasants have assembled
Art is held in low esteem,
And trod under foot, an artist demeaned,
Called a ranter, a fool, a goon—
His name acquired, and lost his honor.
Save your art for a more suitable cause.
'Tis a waste to cast pearls before swine.

Prince, I'm ill content with some confrères[4]
Who quack their Art at any revel.
These fill their belly but don't pay off.
Famous artists cry out and rightly so:
The former shouldn't have been initiated at all

Or been given the lofty honor's name
Or been inscribed in nobler artists' lists.
Scratch them out, who like vulgar jinglers
Break down art and so forfeit their life.
My limbs tremble, my heart fails a beat
When Rhetoric I see on sale for money.
Like snow for sun my joy melts away,
And thus I repeat my initial remark:
'Tis a waste to cast pearls before swine.

[1524]

Make Merry and Leap the Scythe

Many sisters in their shed convened
For sure were having a lot of fun.
But one of them, in piety foremost,
Put on a very edifying mien.
Well, you damper, the others said,
Why not make merry and join our sport?
No need for such sourpusses here.
Get up and join in, we'll all have more fun.
Mother Superior won't scold us today,
Not if we sing, or laugh, or play.
She said "nil obstat," believe it or not,[5]
Only rarely such blessing occurs.
Make merry and leap the scythe.

Indeed, spoke the nun, to join in such folly,
I hope, will not enter my mind.
Even though we're quite among our own
'Twere a scandal should anyone know.
No sisters dear, it doesn't attract me at all.
Imagine the others' sniggers should they learn.
If so rudely we put ourselves down
We'd be a laughingstock till the end of time.
Not for two fire-pans as a reward,
The prettiest around, would I do it.
Jump, the others said, you'll do fine;
Also, just you try give us all the slip.
Make merry and leap the scythe.

For no mean reason I delay to jump,
Spoke the nun. I clearly see what can go wrong.
Suppose I slipped and fell—the idea!
And the scythe's edge would kiss my bum!
No, dear sisters, even for the highest bid
I forgo the jump. So forbear a little.
Not with tons of sins as heavy burden
I would incur such penance hard.
Please! Now this should be enough.
If I fell I'd be sorely afflicted
And for a month rather wouldn't speak.
No, they said, don't butter us up like that!
Make merry and leap the scythe.

Thus they strafed our dear little nun.
Jump, jump, all the sisters encouraged.
Well, she thought, won't they ever refrain?
I fear I'll just have to jump.
Still, I'd reward with both of my clogs
Who's willing to jump instead of me.
Fear and joy don't blend together.
Joy they say? I'd rather be spinning.
Still, these acrobatics I better now perform
'Cause methinks, these nuns they really mean it.
And lo! Undaunted, she made it.
Then all of that circle agreed:
Make merry and leap the scythe.

Prince,
This our sister hadn't quite foreseen,
Thinking she'd really get a scar somewhere.
Sometimes things end better than surmised.
For proof, take this sister's case.
Even if monastics seem a little foolish now and then
Don't take offense, don't complain
As gossips do, who slander no matter whom.
They should first look at their own.
How else to bear the strain of the Orders?
You too would spice it with a touch of joy.
Melancholy thoughts need be dispelled, or not?
Make merry and leap the scythe.

Unyoked Is Best! Happy the Woman Without a Man

How good to be a woman, how much better to be a man!
Maidens and wenches, remember the lesson you're about to hear.
Don't hurtle yourself into marriage far too soon.
The saying goes: "Where's your spouse? Where's your honor?"
But one who earns her board and clothes
Shouldn't scurry to suffer a man's rod.
So much for my advice, because I suspect—
Nay, see it sadly proven day by day—
'T happens all the time!
However rich in goods a girl might be,
Her marriage ring will shackle her for life.
If however she stays single
With purity and spotlessness foremost,
Then she is lord as well as lady. Fantastic, not?
Though wedlock I do not decry:
Unyoked is best! Happy the woman without a man.

Fine girls turning into loathly hags—
'Tis true! Poor sluts! Poor tramps! Cruel marriage!
Which makes me deaf to wedding bells.
Huh! First they marry the guy, luckless dears,
Thinking their love just too hot to cool.
Well, they're sorry and sad within a single year.
Wedlock's burden is far too heavy.
They know best whom it harnessed.
So often is a wife distressed, afraid.
When after troubles hither and thither he goes
In search of dice and liquor, night and day,
She'll curse herself for that initial "yes."
So, beware ere you begin.
Just listen, don't get yourself into it.
Unyoked is best! Happy the woman without a man.

A man oft comes home all drunk and pissed
Just when his wife had worked her fingers to the bone
(So many chores to keep a decent house!),
But if she wants to get in a word or two,
She gets to taste his fist—no more.

And that besotted keg she is supposed to obey?
Why, yelling and scolding is all she gets,
Such are his ways—and hapless his victim.
And if the nymphs of Venus he chooses to frequent,[6]
What hearty welcome will await him home.
Maidens, young ladies: learn from another's doom,
Ere you, too, end up in fetters and chains.
Please don't argue with me on this,
No matter who contradicts, I stick to it:
Unyoked is best! Happy the woman without a man.

A single lady has a single income,
But likewise, isn't bothered by another's whims.
And I think: that freedom is worth a lot.
Who'll scoff at her, regardless what she does,
And though every penny she makes herself,
Just think of how much less she spends!
An independent lady is an extraordinary prize—
All right, of a man's boon she is deprived,
But she's lord and lady of her very own hearth.
To do one's business and no explaining sure is lots of fun!
Go to bed when she list, rise when she list, all as she will,[7]
And no one to comment! Grab tight your independence then.
Freedom is such a blessed thing.
To all girls: though the right Guy might come along:
Unyoked is best! Happy the woman without a man.

Prince,
Regardless of the fortune a woman might bring,
Many men consider her a slave, that's all.
Don't let a honeyed tongue catch you off guard,
Refrain from gulping it all down. Let them rave,
For, I guess, decent men resemble white ravens.
Abandon the airy castles they will build for you.
Once their tongue has limed a bird:
Bye bye love—and love just flies away.
To women marriage comes to mean betrayal
And the condemnation to a very awful fate.
All her own is spent, her lord impossible to bear.
It's *peine forte et dure* instead of fun and games.
Oft it was the money, and not the man
Which goaded so many into their fate.
Unyoked is best! Happy the woman without a man.

[1542]

Yet, When Compared, Martin Rossom Comes Out Best

Lately, melancholy's weight was hard to bear,
Made sore my mind, chased phantoms throbbing through my head,
Kept me brooding over oh so many things.
Just considering the world's present course,
What was there to brighten up my mood
With nothing but sorrow to spare—and I was sad.
And then my weary fancy in its rambling
Called forth a pair of men
With names the same but not much else.
One, Martin Luther, whose error spawns and spreads;
The other, Martin Rossom, whose cruel sword
Proved far too sharp for many far and near.
Rossom racks the body, Luther lays waste the soul,
So what's up! "Evil creature" fits them both.
To choose between these two? Waste of time.
Still, since Luther through his error kills your soul,
When compared, Martin Rossom comes out best.

.   .   .   .

Martin Rossom, nobleman by birth,
As Emperor's renegade also his honor forsook;
But Luther betrayed the Lord Supreme
To whom his allegiance he had pledged
And put a nun's coif above his own.[8]
A nun who had promised God the same!
Why, Rossom spurns Emperor, but Luther's evil tongue
Wags at Pope and Emperor alike,
Teaches subjects' revolt against their betters,
Spreads defamatory libel of kings and princes,
Flings filth at church lords just the same.
Rossom wrought havoc fierce in Brabant's land
But his flaming fury did most often
Leave the Church alone, at least.
And blessed maidens he didn't even touch
(Though 'tis rumored that he did, here and there).
Martin Rossom: model of the tyrant harsh?
When compared, Martin Rossom comes out best.

Where Martin Rossom's crime was treason,
Martin Luther's was double so foul,
For many a Christian soul his evil kiss
Slammed heaven's gate forever shut. Thus,
The Desecrator of Our Lord must have sent
This double plague to infect the Christian world.
Rossom a killer? Luther through his actions
Sent two hundred thousand peasants to their graves.
Blood of men and women freely flowed, with
Water and fire curbing his heretic's views.
So, he has butchered both the soul and body.
Martin Rossom merely racked the latter.
Now, he's just as cruel to the meek and lowly,
But through his hand, if they're patient, they'll soon be placed in God's.
Not that this would make his guilt seem less—
I'm not excusing him, I'm not washing him white!
Yet, though both be venomous vipers,
When compared, Martin Rossom comes out best.

. . . .

Martin Rossom and Martin Luther,
The best of both still a mutineer.
'Tis not strange that Rossom knows no fear,
For he's a soldier, a worldly cavalier.
But Martin Luther, that braggart, claims, he dares,
To comprehend Scripture down to its least detail,
With the Holy Ghost leading him on the way.
If supposedly he knows the way, his erring sure looks weird
But of course the ghostly spirit that guides him most
Has firmly wrapped its tail round Dymphna's painted feet.[9]
Martin Rossom sacked Brabant for tons of loot,
A sad affair which many still deplore,
But Luther himself has hands none too clean.
Monasteries were emptied by apostates on his command
Of their treasure and holy vessels. God will find out
If he didn't get a share himself. How about that?
Satan clasps both Martins in a tight embrace,
Yet, when compared, Martin Rossom comes out best.

Martin Rossom, Freebooters' Prince,
Mastermind in stealing and plunder;
Luther, all false prophets' Prince,
If your histories I'd set out in full,
The reader would be much distressed, I guess—

'Twould also be a loss of time and paper.
Thus for now I hold my duty excellently done.
Allow me to defer the sequel to some other time.
Luther, Rossom, and Lucifer (for he fits in real well),
I wonder who's worthiest of the three.
Rossom piles much gruesome plunder in his lair,
Luther is conniving night and day,
Intent on poisoning our Christian lands.
So, this couple is wicked, very clearly so.
But Luther's venom most of all I fear,
For eternal damnation follows in its rear.
Even though the choice of either isn't worth a rotten fig,
When compared, Martin Rossom comes out best.[10]

[*1548 collection*]

These Covet Happy Nights and Lose Their Happy Days

Nuns, beguines, professed in various orders
(Though after Luther they esteem them little)
Now roam about the world and breathe its air.
Spending lonely nights is off their mind,
To carnal lust instead they're now inclined.
Though their days be happy it's happy nights they want.
Nun marries man, friar is joined to lady.
But what's in store for them—let me tell you:
Shreds and tatters will soon be on their back.
Bummer's flesh—that's all each has got to bring.
For labor their limbs are far too stiff.
How could they ever hope to manage?
Look and see how they spend their days:
They scold, they fight, what else, I ask?
Sometimes that's just as far as they'll go
When it's belly-filling time, habits still set
To the lazy dainties of their cloisters.
Thus, I make so bold as to confirm:
These covet happy nights and lose their happy days.

Wining and dining well and free of care
These monks and nuns they know well how to!

Alas! How will they fare
With nil to sink their teeth in, pour down their throat,
Or when the convent's refectory bell of old
Rings, but for them no more? But worst of all:
Settling down in peace is not their lot.
Whether in Antwerp, Bruges, or Ghent,
Decent folks bide their distance, don't come close.
So now and then Luther's gang doles out a meal,
If not, they pass their beggar's hat.
These former abbey lords,
These former damsels, insolvent sluts,
They're held in general contempt
Whom with respect were neared before.
Solace they seek but cannot find,
Cast out by friends and kin and all.
I'll say it yet again: experience proves best:
These covet happy nights and lose their happy days.

Unused to care, this rabble yet must eat—
Do they know where to go for it?
Hunger will clasp them by the throat, they fear.
People aren't wont and won't give credit
For fear they'll never get what's due.
There monastic wheat for them was ground,
All was ready brewed and ready baked
And when the refectory's bell was rung—it never failed!—
All went in to take their seat. That history is past.
What wasn't dainty enough back then
Their mouth waters for right now.
And though they're hungry for monastic bread
It can't be so! Pitiful, what?
And then, when they've spawned their brats
And one yells: Feed! Another has to shit!
Crying all night till the head would burst—
Well, to such a hectic life are doomed
Who found former wealth too hard to bear.
So, I'd like to get this off my chest:
These covet happy nights and lose their happy days.

The abbey served them buffet free of charge
But when now their belly asks for food, it's paid in cash.
Warm they were, well fed and decked out fine:
With greatcoats, habits, trimmed with fox and fur.

Now often their limbs go bare.
And though the Lutherans might give them things at first
Soon they give no more.
Shoes, stockings, clothes—it all begins to wear.
Friends and kin pretend they weren't close
Though they might be next of blood—but not of good.
What dowry they brought, 't has stayed behind.
Under no one's rod they chose to live,
Now lost they roam without a shepherd's staff,
At random, unsure how to struggle through.
From brothers nor sisters, nephews nor nieces
Help is forthcoming. And if they dare complain
A tough scolding is their beggar's gift.
So this is what I write:
These covet happy nights and lose their happy days.

Then their kid insists on being fed,
And it's porridge they need to get, light and heating.
Alas! Poor brother—wasn't your hood then snug enough?
For methinks, sour beer—homemade, not ready bought—
Is what your grouchy tapster often serves you instead.[11]
Tsj—that's a fine domestic mess you've got.
Why, what not do these wanton nuns have to face!
With kiddies yelling all over the place—
One shouts here, another sobs there.
Clothes, shoes, clogs, there's always things they need,
Underwear and shifts, woollens and linen—nothing is there.
A house with empty corners and nothing in there to see,
Except for snotty brats, in a batch of six at least.
What not! They wither fast, our lazy nuns,
With all these shitty diapers to wash.
And our worldly brother, too, needs to work some more:
How 'bout a wheelbarrow to make his muscles tight?
Weren't books then nicer to handle?
These covet happy nights and lose their happy days.

Prince,
If thus in dire straits they end up lost,
Abandoned, 'tis sad, by all,
They'll surely get caught in Satan's web
Shacking up like that, heedless of the rule:
A lowly fallen nun, a friar apostolate.
Unclean love with paupers must swiftly fade,

Lack of money teaches them a different song.
Then, they start hating one another
And then the devil's sin, despair,
Destroys their fear of foul and shameful deeds.
One goes whoring, another robs and murders.
Children they abandon: leave them to the dogs,
Or do you think that's not the way it goes?
And at last their head settles all accounts
When they're tied to the rack or hung by the neck.
Most of them are smothered by their sins,
Those whom the abbeys couldn't keep in.
I say it once again, 't has oft come true:
These covet happy nights and lose their happy days.

[1548 collection]

The Will I've Got, but No Force to See It Through

The nations I surveyed, one by one,[12]
Yield a curiously wondrous fact
Namely that so many learned people around
Resist but little Luther's shocking creed.
Hence to you, Sir, I direct my plea.
Prove anew your allegiance to our cause
In this wicked sightless world.
Will you strengthen Christ's hopes in the faith?
I strive to give my most and yet I know
That little from my unbacked skill comes forth.
And if heretics ever heed the things I write
It's in mock, mistaken for a woman's trifle.
So, Sir, for faith's assistance whet your wit.
Take up your pen, you champion clerk,
In times auspicious as never before.
If sentinel be your title, sound your trumpet loud
For you note enemy host all around God's people.
The will I've got, but no force to see it through.

Even with exile perhaps as my future fate,
Or mockery, derision, even beating in store,
I'd suffer all this and yet thank the Lord.
What ought I give for kin or riches

When my earthly skin I'd gladly wager
To keep unharmed the bride of Christ.
I'd engage in battle till stained with blood
If, by God, heresy could surely be crushed
Which now with harpy's claws rents the Church apart.
But alas! Frailty forces me to flee.
If God's spirit would reinforce my mind
And spark off my thought with Solomon's wit,
My brain wouldn't get a moment's rest
Ere its might had crushed the spiders
That from Scripture suck their poison,
And revealed to dark malice its reeking bed of dull senselessness.
Like a lamb from a hungry wolf, my heart will leap away.
The will I've got, but no force to see it through.

Where I can't go further you have to proceed.
Show your wit ablaze so mine flares up too,
And then put it on high for all of us to see.
Let pure devotion engender artistic beauty
For Christian lands are drenched in pus and corruption.
Teeth are whetted against holy altars,
Saints held in contempt at foolish carousals,
Purgatory's souls insulted in public,
The web woven under guise of virtue:
Satan's songbirds are active and rounding up sinners
Who must sink deep in the marsh of laments.
Great discord these raise among the peoples,
Turn sweet into sour, God's word into curse
To suit their own case with zeal near unending.
I wish I could sink my teeth into them
Instead of letting their wickedness occur.
The will I've got, but no force to see it through.

The Lord has showered you with His bounty;
Don't hide this largesse, don't bury your treasure
But liberally enlighten those that can see.
Great your reward! Undaunted, you'll succeed.
Help me wield the sword as heresy's scourge—
For so Paul has said. Write then your verses
And do not succumb. Let's call out these caitiffs
Who spoil healthy crops with poisonous seed,
Who strike at Truth with energy unbounded
And lay waste without shame-marked cheeks

The rules of religion, bent on own advantage.
And who thus wallow in evil I should convert?
Sooner I get the moon as reward for my crying.
Me they would heckle, insult, laugh off the stage
Who rail at the Lord after Turks and Huns,
Who bitterly speak of pope and prelate, of monk and nun.
But try, perhaps you can cap and kick back.
The will I've got, but no force to see it through.

Prince,
Artistic soul (even with art not really involved right here),
Still with love in mind I conclude, as I set out.
Imbibe my words with eager care.
Don't think I've presumed too much.
Goodwill's blossom will never fade in your heart.
I beseech you: let's torture these nitwits together.
Yea, these devil's swains who spare church nor crop.
Let their undoing be our concern forever.
Skullduggery for sure is their favorite game:
So avoid them—to disturb them is to raise them.
They're wolves, though as sheep decked out,
And blind guides, to the pit directing the blind.
In your metrical web, you noble, most excellent, man,
This vermin ensnare ere they spoil the orchard whole.
I'll fight them till I breathe my last
Avoiding nothing—though I work for scanty thanks.
For giving me such counsel I'll think you a friend.
The will I've got, but no force to see it through.

Agreeably	Noteworthy	Natural	Able spirit
Act	Now and ever	Nimbly	As metrist proud
All	New doctrine	Naught but	Absurdity
Artists	Now rejoice	Nearly	Although I erred here.

Sour rather than sweet

Though here I wrote some rather reproaching stuff
Against the Lutherans, 'tis nothing to wonder at,
For they will do it as well, and twice as spitefully,
Against the Holy Church, to undermine the faith.
But most of all my argument is based
On what the Wise Man Without Mockery has said:[13]
Thou shall repay the raving fool in his own coin!

[*1567 collection*]

He Must Be Beautiful Who Created All This

Please wake up, dear folks, wake up and rise,
Abandon your grief, for May has come home.
Perk up yourselves with pure spiritual beauty.
Cast off your sorrows, no matter where you're hurt.
And when you're impressed by the forces of life
Then in jubilant hymn profess the Creator's might
And rejoice in Him from whom every being is being received.
Green meadows smile, rich harvests of fruit in bud;
Herbs, good for healing, longing for pluckster's hands;
Trees, with luscious verdant foliage cloak; 'tis joyous to behold;
Fertile made the earth with showers of dew;
Gaily painted birds, celebrating in song—
If you, too, have eyes to see, be sure to say:
He must be beautiful who created all this.

Flowers, whom winter had chased underground,
With pure blossoms adorned sure make a pretty sight!
Barren shrubs beget green twigs;
To enjoy our usufruct of these real well
We should sing His praises, don't you think?
It's all in reason, for He alone bestows all growth.
When wandering into a field all green,
And your heart opens up in blossoms of joy,
Then think: how splendid His beauty in the life to come
If He bejewels the world in such style.
Ever—if never, the default is yours—
Let the Creation raise up your heart to the Creator.[14]
If a well-made person or wondrous being catches your eye,
Birds in the sky, fish in the brook,
Plenty of pure little flowers in the field,
Exalt Him whose clemency shines forth; repeat:
He must be beautiful who created all this.

When you go take in the country airs,
Which delight you so much, then give some thought
To the Land up there, with sweeter fruits in plenty,
Where summer reigns eternal and no sighs are heard.
There pluck the flowers to ease your desires,
There make a home to settle your heart.
There think how lavishly He is praised

Who so gorgeously paints flowers down here,
So that never such colors served on emperor's crown.
Cease your moaning, jubilate instead,
Sing paeans, hymns of praise, and joy:[15]
For hoar frost and snow have made their adieus.
Now the garlands of May are twined once more;
And if in the greens an air you hear, a reed in song,
Reflect, and in your innermost exult:
He must be beautiful who created all this.

If you behold sun and moon, luminous bodies,
And the stars that dot the sky:
Mere reflections these of the light eternal.
So, gaze upward, to the highest stars
And behold the light that fathers all theirs,
The divine powers of which beam forth in the sun
So that all things in growth grope for the sky,
So that flowers in clusters cover mountains and vales
Like no painter could do with so many colors.
So, reasonable folks, let my argument not go unheeded.
Unless an error you want to pursue, then seek the Creator
In every of His creatures, applying your rational sense.
Because, for anything of beauty, in wet or on dry,
The Creator's gorgeous beauty is really no match at all.
So let your love's fiery passion urge you on to say:
He must be beautiful who created all this.

Prince!
Princes and princesses, laymen and clerics, too,
Feel free to gaze on the things of this our earth.
But in praising the labor the laborer should come first:
He who in the world's garden arranges for flowers
To engender rich choice of fruits, who gives birds their song,
Each in different tune according to its kind,
Who endows with colors, with perfumes all flowers, all fruits,
And all sweet herbs with distinct taste,
With distinct virtue, to our advantage.
And note, how from soil so coarse
Spring wheat and grain, just to feed us—
From one grain come many—thanks to Him.
Is not then this Lord a wonderful ruler,
Whose divine power was never understood?
So, when you're thinking of this, also think:
He must be beautiful who created all this.

[1567 collection]

Lord, If It All Deserts Me, Will You Stand by Me?

Death, I think of thee, and freeze.
I set myself going, but forth nor back
I can escape, so I quail.
I needs depart, final goal unknown:
Low in hell, or raised to heaven's loft.
No doubt: all endowed with the gift of life
Must also die—a verdict fixed,
And no appeal forthcoming.
My days are numbered, my years recorded,
Hour by hour I'm closer to death.
How and where, time and place are hidden.
Many my sins, beyond compare,
With Satan's tempting hard upon me.
For Grace, poor sinner, I want to plead
'Cause if on my merit I'll be judged,
Down to hellish rogues I needs be sent.
So merciful Jesus, I call unto Thee:
Lord, if it all deserts me, will You stand by me?

When infirmity's pain is too much to bear,
When my nose sheds its flesh, my rosy cheeks pale,
My lips turning blue;
When confession, when cross are yearned for,
When pains of sorts my body torment,
When my pulse beats weaker
And the sweat of death my skin bedews,
When rotting flesh an evil stink exhales,
When my skin a clayish hue assumes
And lower every hour my spirits sink;
When "grave" and "low'ring" are talked about,
And friends, who covet my goods and not myself,
Toward the money unite their thoughts;
When tintinnabulum God's host precedes[16]
And my limbs are oiled, then rubbed;
When my stomach refuses to digest
Oh, Jesus Christ, then look at me.
Lord, if it all deserts me, will You stand by me?

When memory falters, strength succumbs
And ghostly envoys press their way;

When my kinsmen who'll inherit
Don't look at me but at what's mine;
When my heart is hugged by deathly pangs
And my limbs already die a little;
When deprived of earthly succor
To God's presence I am called, alone,
To account for my misdeeds complete,
Where I did it and how oft,
And when my conscience poor and loaded
Small mischief holds for much
Which in health oft was forgot;
When hourly God's stern justice I expect,
When day is past and night is nigh
And anew I ponder: doom or free, then,
Lord, if it all deserts me, will You stand by me?

When most have run away from me,
One tired of nursing, or of waking,
And all wish my pains behind me;
When bitter is the mouth and the battled heart thirsty,
When naked of virtue this poor soul
Doubts the comfort of God's justice;
When body quakes with terror
And tongue for speech is lamed;
When lustral water is sprinkled
And frail the vessel fights to enter port;
When bless'd candles should be lit,—
Heart about to burst, eyes growing dim—
When all hope of relief is lost
And I'll be asked of all this time, these years
Back to when I first began to be;
Ah—when lips are moved to prayer,
When soon, Fie! the world will scold,
Lord, if it all deserts me, will You stand by me?

Prince, princes and princesses, with your incandescent love,
Your loving heart, torn asunder on the cross,
The crimson blood of your five bleeding wounds,
Stand by me in that hidden hour.
Let mercy trickle with your bloody sweat,
Sweat of terror mortal in the little garden.[17]
When agitated I lay, supremely in need
And only with my deeds to take,[18]
Be Thou then my guide, my Prince, my Hope.

With a morsel of the living bread, I pray,.
My pilgrimage please further.
Grant me truly as daughter of the Church
Confession complete, and all the sacraments.
And wrap your wings around me in shelter
Against the hellish monsters' claws.
Let your own grim death temper my heart
And wash pure my evil, corrupted soul.
Lord, if it all deserts me, will You stand by me?

NOTES TO THE TRANSLATION

1. The affection with which she wrote the poems.

2. This dedication (with acrostic) opened Anna's first book (1528).

3. The reference is to the meetings of the Chambers of Rhetoric. Also, the habit of selling occasional bits of poetry made on demand is criticized.

4. The Prince (occasionally Princess) was the protector and patron of the Chamber, so not necessarily a royal noble. Sometimes the reference is to Christ. When the rhetorician read his refrain aloud at the meeting of the Chamber, he addressed himself to the "Prince" if this dignitary was present.

5. "Cleared, permission granted." The game has no particular significance.

6. Prostitutes.

7. Compare Shakespeare, *The Merry Wives of Windsor*, II.2: "Never a wife in Windsor leads a better life than [Mrs. Page] does. Do what she will, say what she will, take all, pay all, go to bed when she list, rise when she list, all is as she will. And truly she deserves it; for if there be a kind woman in Windsor, she is one."

8. Viz. Katharina von Bora's, whom he married on July 13, 1525.

9. The devil, who in paintings of Saint Dymphna crouches at her feet.

10. I have deleted stanzas 2, 3, and 6.

11. Meaning "the spouse will often pick up a quarrel with you" or "you often behave like a sourpuss at home."

12. This poem is Anna's answer to an ode sent to her by a Flemish colleague rhetorician.

13. Solomon.

14. According to Bonaventura's "vestigium Dei" theory, the Creator should be worshiped through His Creation.

15. Greek hymn of praise, thanksgiving, or triumph, especially in warfare.

16. The little bell carried by an acolyte in front of the priest who brings the Last Sacraments to the dying.

17. Garden of Gethsemane.

18. Compare the plot of *Elckerlijck* (*Everyman*).

BIBLIOGRAPHY

Primary Works

Bijns, Anna. *Konstighe Refereyne vol schoone Schrifturen ende Leeringen, Begrepen in drye verscheyde Boecken, Waer van de twee eerste wederlegghen de dolinghen comende uyt de

Luthersche secte, ende alwysen deser tijden, het derde toont d'oorsaecke der plaghen, met veel seer stichtighe vermaninghen tot de deught. Antwerp, 1646. (This is the first single volume edition of the three collections. I am grateful to the Museum Plantin-Moretus, Antwerp, for the use of their copy of this rare edition.)

Roose, Lode, ed. *Anna Bijns, Refreinen.* Antwerp, 1949.

————. *Meer Zuurs Dan Zoets.* Hasselt, 1975.

Secondary Works

Basse, Maurits. *Het aandeel der vrouw in de Nederlandsche Letterkunde.* Ghent, 1920.

Branden, F. Jos Van den. *Anna Bijns: Haar Leven, Hare Werken, Haar Tijd 1493–1575.* Antwerp, 1911.

Busken Huet, Conrad. *Het Land van Rembrandt; Studiën over de Noordnederlandsche Beschaving in de Zeventiende Eeuw.* The Hague, 1974.

Degroote, Gilbert. "Erasmus en de Rederijkers van de zestiende eeuw." *Belgisch Tijdschrift voor Philologie en Geschiedenis* 29 (1951): 389–420, 1029–62.

Degroote, Gilbert, ed. Introduction to *Oude Klanken, Nieuwe Accenten; De Kunst van de Rederijkers.* Leiden, 1969.

Rens, Lieven. *Acht Eeuwen Nederlandse Letteren.* Antwerp, 1975.

Roose, Lode. "Waardering en invloed van Anna Bijns in de zestiende en zeventiende eeuw." *Spiegel der Letteren* 1 (1956–1957): 241–53.

————. *Anna Bijns, Een Rederijkster Uit De Hervormingstijd.* Series 6 of the Koninklijke Vlaamse Akademie voor Taal—en Letterkunde, Prize-winning works no. 93. Ghent, 1963.

Schneiderwirth, P. M. *Anna Bijns: Eine Flämische Lehrerin und Dichterin.* Paderborn, 1933.

Vinckenroye, F. Van. "Nieuwe varianten bij Anna Bijns." *Nieuwe Taalgids* 53 (1960): 264–69.

PART FIVE

pain

 aint Teresa of Jesus

CIRIACO MORÓN-ARROYO

Saint Teresa of Jesus was born in Avila, some sixty-five miles northwest of Madrid, on March 28, 1515. Her father was Alonso Sánchez de Cepeda, the son of a converted Jew from Toledo. In 1485, when Teresa's father was five years old, the Inquisition from Toledo subjected her grandfather and his family to a rite of reconciliation because of suspected Jewish practices. For seven consecutive Fridays the family had to participate in a procession of penance; they were dressed in a special outfit prescribed by the inquisitors (*sambenitillo*), had to endure the derision of the old Christians, and when the ritual ended, the dress remained displayed in the parish for generations as a reminder of the family's infamy.

In order apparently to distance himself from the awesome reminder, Teresa's grandfather moved his garment business to Avila around 1493. There Alonso Sánchez married for the first time in 1505; his wife, Catalina del Peso, died two years later, leaving him two children. In 1509 Alonso, now twenty-nine years old, married fifteen-year-old Beatriz de Ahumada, Teresa's mother. The couple had ten more children during their years together. Beatriz died in December 1528 at the age of thirty-three, after a short life full of sacrifice. Her only indulgence was her fondness for romances of chivalry, which she had to read secretly with her children because Alonso did not approve of them. The romances of chivalry so absorbed Teresa that she set out to write one herself. This drive to act is a fundamental feature of Teresa's character and one that is apparent from her early childhood. When at the age of five she heard of the Christian martyrs, she persuaded one of her brothers to flee the paternal house and go with her to "the land of the Moors" to seek martyrdom. In fact, they took the road to Salamanca, the famous university city. She writes of herself: "It is usually my nature that when I desire something I am impulsive in my desire for it."[1] In the height of her mystical quiet she would give to the episode of Martha and Mary in the Gospel (Luke 10:42) a personal interpretation quite different from the traditional one. Traditionally Martha and Mary represent the contemplative and active life. In praising Mary, Jesus presumably extolled the merits of the former over the latter. According to Teresa, the Lord praised Mary only after she had completed her chores and had been active in her own way. The ideal is to combine contemplation with action.

A "new Christian"—Christian of Muslim or Jewish ancestry—in sixteenth-century Spain was the subject of suspicion and discrimination. The biology of the period attributed to the Jews a particularly sharp brain shaped by the manna ingested in the desert. The effects of the manna were still visible three thousand years after the pilgrimage from Egypt. These ideas led to the establishment of statutes of "purity of blood," which denied new Christians high positions in the Church because of their "natural inclination" to Judaism. Teresa's reaction to the prevailing ideas on lineage is but one example of the creative position she took toward the values and conventions of her society. She wrote four long works: *The Book of Life* (1562), *The Way of Perfection* (1564), *Book of the Foundations* (1573), and *The Dwelling Places of the Interior Castle* (1577). All except the second one begin with an assertion of the advantages of good lineage as an omen of future accomplishments. The first chapter of *The Life* is titled: "To have had virtuous and God-fearing parents along with the graces the Lord granted me should have been enough for me to have led a good life, if I had not been so wretched."[2] *The Foundations* was written as the first entry in the pedigree of future nuns, who by knowing the virtues of the founders, would be stimulated to perfection. Finally, *The Dwelling Places* is based on the dignity of the human soul as a creature of God. Saint Teresa places herself above worldly values, and since the awareness of lineage was an obsession in sixteenth-century Spain—"the national illness" in the words of Karl Vossler—she demands that her nuns forget about family name and ties when they enter the convent. A Carmelite replaces the family name with a new one in which the new lineage is embraced: Teresa de Ahumada becomes Teresa of Jesus; this is her new identity.

As a young woman Teresa was extremely pleasant and attractive, fond of pretty dresses, open to flirting and even to love. These are the "great sins" referred to in *The Life*. At least, they were sufficient to cause concern in her father, who sent her to a boarding house—an Augustinian convent—under the vigilance of a virtuous nun. In the convent she practiced the required religious exercises, but her inclinations were "strongly against becoming a nun."[3] Nevertheless, on November 2, 1535, at the age of twenty, she escaped from her father's house and entered the Carmelite monastery in Avila. She forced herself to that decision in order to pay for her sins on earth rather than in Purgatory. The spiritual and possibly the corporal strain caused her to contract an illness that put her on the verge of death. In 1538 she appeared to be dead; her burial niche was opened, and only her father's refusal to part with the "corpse" prevented the family from burying her alive. She eventually regained consciousness but remained completely paralyzed for three years and in ill health for the rest of her life.

In the subsequent years she fulfilled her duties well; her goodness and charm were well known to all, but she did not show signs of spiritual perfectionism. As a matter of fact, her attractive character brought many visitors from outside the convent who distracted her from prayer. All this ended in 1554 when she experienced a conversion and gave herself wholly to the love of God. Two events converged in bringing about this rebirth: the reading of Saint Augustine's *Confessions,* and the contemplation of a Crucifix that awakened her to the sufferings of Christ. From that moment on, she severed all ties with worldly values and attitudes and followed the path to perfection.

Teresa says that she had a bad memory, was active and extroverted by temperament, and, as a result, was not capable of sustained concentration and meditation. She would pray vocally or read a fragment from a spiritual book and put herself in a receptive attitude in the presence of God. She advises her nuns to do the same without laboring with the faculties of the soul. In this she contradicts the mystical way of "recollection," sponsored by the Franciscans, which required an effort against the images of the senses and against the forms of the intellect. At the other extreme were the *alumbrados (illuminati),* who propounded total passivity. Teresa differs from them in that she demands from herself all that she can do and leaves the rest to the grace of God.

Her bad memory accounts for another feature of her style: the autobiographical character of her writings and the vitality that is associated with it. She is a woman, not a learned theologian. For this reason she considers herself incapable of making general statements on doctrine; she simply tells us what happens to her, without claiming that her particular experiences—or the mystical experience altogether—make her more perfect than any other person who fulfills his duties. The ultimate criterion of holiness for Teresa is to fulfill one's obligations to God and neighbor. For a person whose readings in religious literature were extensive, it is remarkable that her writings practically do not reflect, and certainly do not quote, such readings. This allows her personal style to flow without the impediment of extraneous quotations that make the reading of many spiritual books of the period so cumbersome.

After her conversion in 1554, Teresa experienced various mystical phenomena such as ecstasy and revelations. She consulted with priests and friars about these experiences, which eventually became the subject of gossip. The Catholic Church has always been suspicious of miracles and private revelations; around 1560 it was extremely dangerous to deviate from the sanctioned paths. In 1560 she perceived for the first time the possibility of restoring the Carmelite order to its original perfection. However, as a woman and a nun with a vow of obedience, she could not even dream of carrying out such a project. The dream, nonetheless, became a reality, and in 1562 the first monastery of reformed Carmelite nuns was inaugurated in Avila. The initial reaction of the city was harsh; the city council was determined to suppress the new foundation, but it did not succeed.

After the foundation of Avila, she waited a few years before continuing with her project. Then between 1567 and 1582 (the year of her death), she founded fifteen more reformed monasteries. She endured the Castilian winter and the Andalusian summer with an exemplary commitment to her task of founding, visiting, and reforming. In the meantime, a parallel reform of the Carmelite friars had been taking place since 1568. Teresa's most faithful collaborator in this endeavor was the famous mystic writer Saint John of the Cross (1542–1591).

Obviously the growth in numbers took its toll on the quality of the nuns and friars. Teresa had to endure persecution from her former superiors, rivalry among individuals of her own order, and a general deterioration of the high standards she had envisioned for her foundations. On March 28, 1581, she wrote: "I no longer have the power that I used to have, for things go according to the votes of the nuns."[4] The last days of her life resemble the passion of Christ. Rejected by her own niece, the Carmelite abbess of Valladolid, she arrived tired and hungry in Alba de Tormes. The abbess there also showed her similar disdain. In this state of abandonment, accompanied only by a few faithful nuns, she died on October 4, 1582.

Only once did Teresa aspire to be a writer: when as a teenager she took the pen to write a romance of chivalry of which no trace is left. In her mature years writing was always a matter of obedience to her spiritual directors or to the nuns of the early foundations. The time could not have been less propitious for a woman without formal education to begin writing on spiritual topics. In 1559 the Grand Inquisitor Fernando de Valdés had issued the *Index of Prohibited Books*. This list included some that Teresa had enjoyed reading. She recorded her reaction to the *Index* in the following words: "When they forbade the reading of many books in the vernacular, I felt that prohibition very much because reading some of them was an enjoyment for me, and I could no longer do so since only the Latin editions were allowed. The Lord said to me: Don't be sad, for I shall give you a living book. I was unable to understand why this was said to me, since I had not yet experienced any visions. Afterward, within only a few days, I understood very clearly, because I received so much to think about and such recollection in the presence of what I saw, and the Lord showed so much love for me by teaching me in many ways, that I had very little or almost no need for books."[5]

The Inquisition was particularly suspicious of devotional books for three reasons: the danger of Lutheranism, the fact that devotional books in the vernacular undermined the teaching authority of the clergy—another possible instance of Lutheranism—and the lack of precision in the language, which offended the clergy trained in the traditional scholastic formulas. Teresa's reaction to the *Index,* on the other hand, explains the freshness and originality of her style. She does not bring in abstract formulas or biblical quotations. If her lack of a good memory was a blessing from the inside, the Inquisition contributed from the outside by erasing the traces of ready-made learning.

Teresa wrote the first draft of her *Life* in 1562, just three years after the publication of the *Index.* Although the book went through several revisions and was not published until 1588, we know that it was scrutinized by theologians and inquisitors for several years. The book, after all, was devotional, narrated extraordinary experiences, was written by an "idiot"—a person who did not know Latin—and a woman. The fact that the most prestigious and suspicious theologians of the time, the Dominicans Bartolomé de Medina and Domingo Báñez, bowed before the simplicity and sublimity of Teresa's work is the best indication of her success. Both became her enthusiastic supporters.

Father Kieran Kavanaugh divides the book into four parts: the sins, graces, and vocation (ten chapters), the treatise on the degrees of prayer (twelve chapters), the mystical life (nine chapters), and the effects (nine chapters).

The first ten chapters narrate her life up to the moment of the definitive conversion, when she began to receive the mystical experiences. Chapter eleven (see the following translation) is devoted to a description of the degrees of prayer or mercies that she had received up to the moment of drafting the book. This chapter is emblematic of Teresa's mystic writing. She avoids abstract doctrine in favor of events; she avoids concepts and tries to be understood through images. The way of perfection is compared in this chapter to the irrigation of a garden, and the different stages along the way are four different modes of irrigation. The resort to images accounts for Teresa's literary mastery. At some points the images are so deep and sublime that the reader cannot anticipate the possibility of surpassing them. And yet, he is always surprised by Teresa's genius in finding new comparisons that convey ever greater intensity and beauty.

Four degrees of prayer are described in *The Life:* recollection, quiet, sleep of the faculties, and union. Recollection can be attained through human effort. It is not a struggle with the human faculties as it was in the Franciscan school; it is simply a decision to renounce worldly values and attitudes. The other three degrees are all "supernatural," that is, unattainable by natural means; they are mercies from God.

The Way of Perfection was written for the nuns of the reformed monastery of Avila in 1564. This first version is preserved in the Escorial manuscript, but it contains some statements that were suspicious to the theologians. Teresa rewrote the book in 1569 and made later other corrections in view of an eventual publication that did not take place until 1583, one year after her death. The Escorial version is the most important, since it contains a more spontaneous reaction to the religious and cultural situation of the period.

The book consists of two parts: chapters 1–42 contain the basis of spiritual perfection for the nuns. Humility is posited as the foundation of the spiritual edifice. All values of the world, especially honor in the sense of lineage, must be renounced. The second part (chapters 43–73) is a commentary on the *Pater noster,* but from a peculiar point of view. The fear of the Inquisition tended to deter people from prayer and from spiritual life altogether. It was most desirable to remain anonymous without ever being remembered by an inquisitor. Teresa reacted harshly against that attitude. If those who try to pray and struggle for perfection are deceived by the devil, those who do not care live in a state of permanent deception: "Should anyone tell you that prayer is dangerous, consider him the real danger and run from him."[6]

Lutherans and the Spanish groups called *alumbrados* tended to despise traditional prayers such as the Rosary or vocal prayer altogether in favor of meditation. Some theologians wrote books in defense of vocal prayer. Teresa, the master of mystic contemplation, solved the dilemma with another stroke of genius: "If they tell you that the prayer should be vocal, ask, for the sake of more precision, if in vocal prayer the mind and heart must be attentive to what you say. If the answer is 'yes'—for they cannot answer otherwise—you will see how they admit that you are forced to practice mental prayer and even experience contemplation if God should give it to you by such a means" (*The Way,* chapter 21, p. 121).

In Teresa's view the polemics over vocal versus mental prayer borders on the ridiculous. An attentive vocal prayer is already mental, and she sets out to demonstrate it with her commentary on the *Pater noster,* where she describes her mystical experience. The inquisitors may prohibit all imaginable books or prayers, but Teresa expects that they will not touch the words of the Gospel: "Hold fast, daughters, for they cannot take from you the Our Father and the Hail Mary" (*The Way,* chapter 21, p. 120). The preceding phrase was suppressed in the published version for fear of the Inquisition, which, indeed, becomes a target of Teresa's sarcasm.

The lucidity displayed in view of those intricate and frightening polemics—imprecision could bring one to the stake—is an example of Teresa's intimate sense of freedom. Her ideal was *andar en verdad* (to walk in truth). That "walking in truth" made her free. When word of her extraordinary experiences spread in Avila, some friends immediately mentioned the threat of the Inquisition. She describes her reaction in the following words: "Some persons came with great fear to tell me we were in trouble and that it could happen that others might accuse me of something and report me to the Inquisitors. This amused me and made me laugh, for I never had any fear of such a possibility. If anyone were to see that I went against the slightest ceremony of the Church in a matter of faith, I myself knew well that I would die a thousand deaths for the faith or for any truth of Sacred Scripture" (*The Life,* chapter 33, p. 222).

If prestigious theologians such as Father Luis de Granada and influential preachers such as Saint Francis of Borja and Saint Juan de Avila, both later canonized by the Catholic Church, were not spared the nuisance of the "holy tribunal," why was Teresa so sure of her immunity? The answer lies in the autobiographical character of her writings. She describes what she lives. Inquisitors and theologians may decide whether those experiences come from God or the devil, but they cannot deny the facts and her veracity as a narrator. She accepts the doctrine of the Church down to the slightest ceremony, but God is all powerful and can give from the abundance of his grace whatever he pleases. Perfection, however, will always lie in the fulfillment of the commandments, not in the extraordinary experiences.

Teresa's freedom in the face of the Inquisition is paralleled by her audacity in deflating social conventions. Chapter 21 of *The Life* criticizes the kings of this world for their shortcomings and injustices. In 1562 she spent a few months in Toledo in the house of Doña Luisa de La Cerda, one of the most noble ladies in Spain, and she noticed how often these ladies made themselves slaves to conventions devoid of any value. Instead, Teresa displayed her freedom in the form of a courteous spontaneity: "While I was there, the Lord granted me the most wonderful favors. These gave me such freedom and made me so despise all that I saw—and the greater the favors the greater the contempt—that I conversed with those noble ladies, whom it would have been an honor for me to serve, with the freedom I would have felt had I been their equal" (*The Life,* chapter 34, p. 228).

This intimate sense of freedom can be perceived as a secular value and by a secular reader. Teresa, on the other hand, bases it on her center, God. The glory of God is for her the aim of all creatures and the foremost obligation of all human beings. From that center as a vantage point, she evaluates everything according to its potential for bringing her closer to

God. She does not reject the world; the soul is made out of diamond and clear crystal; she enjoys water and flowers as beautiful creatures of God, but she places nature in a low rank when it is compared with God himself or his supernatural grace. Her last and most acclaimed book, *The Dwelling Places of the Interior Castle* (1577), describes the way of perfection as a quest for the center. The soul is portrayed as a castle with different mansions. In the innermost mansion or center of the soul God dwells with his infinite majesty, love, and light. Messages and inspirations radiate from that center to the faculties, inviting them to flee from the dangerous outskirts of the castle (sin) and from the exterior chambers (dispersion), and reach to God and themselves. For Teresa, the conquest of God is the conquest of our personal identity. Here again we perceive the secular value of this religious message, for to avoid dispersion and gain our center means to achieve maturity and a sense of purpose in life. Teresa's work is an art of overcoming alienation through commitment to a worthy cause.

The equation of the center with God and with the innermost part of the soul may tempt us to suspect pantheism in her text, but this suspicion is unfounded. The closer she comes to God, the more clearly she sees the distance between God and herself: "The union is like the joining of two wax candles to such an extent that the flame coming from them is but one, or that the wick, the flame, and the wax are all one. But afterward one candle can be easily separated from the other and there are two candles; the same holds for the wick."[7]

The Dwelling Places of the Interior Castle is divided into seven sections of different lengths, each one devoted to a set of dwelling places or mansions. The division of the book into seven sections may have been inspired by the popular septenaries of the Catholic Church: seven virtues, seven deadly sins, or seven sacraments. But the book is not an allegory based on numerical symbolism; in it Teresa narrates her own life, the nuances of her experiences being more important than the external frame of the book. The richness of the experiences makes a million out of the original seven mansions: "This castle has many dwelling places: some up above, others down below, others to the sides; and in the center and middle in the main dwelling place where the very secret exchanges between God and the soul take place" (*First Dwelling Places,* chapter 1, vol. 2, p. 284).

The castle in fact becomes a sphere or rather a shining globe. This image contrasts with two conceptions of mysticism: the popular one, associated with words such as progress or process along the spiritual path; and the traditional expression of mystical doctrine, found in male writers who were trained in scholastic theology. The way of perfection is described by these writers as a journey in three stages: purification, illumination, and perfection or union. Teresa knew that doctrine well, and although she would not attack it directly, she ignores it and attacks some of its conclusions (see *The Life,* chapter 22). In analyzing her own experiences, she discovers that human existence is not a line in which we make definitive conquests; it is rather a sphere of self-demand and concession, progress and return, elevation and failure.

In the first two groups of mansions the soul wrestles with the habits of sin and dispersion. The world shows its power in the form of sexual temptations, the attraction of wealth, and the social pressure against the individual who is determined to renounce worldly values. Still more subtle temptations await the soul in the third set of mansions: pride, self-complacency, and satisfaction in being recognized as a public saint. In the fourth group of dwelling places the soul begins to experience spiritual delights granted by God. Since these delights may be confused with natural and corporal affections, Teresa introduces subtle images to establish the difference. In these images both the psychological and literary mastery of the writer is displayed. Some 110 images can be cataloged in the book; they explain its beauty and modernity.

The fifth set of mansions deals with experiences called "union"; the sixth and longest section describes various types of ecstasy again by means of very original images. Finally, the seventh stage is the climax of mystic spirituality and for us, secular readers, an ideal portrait of human perfection. The soul has become aware of God as its center of repose and has reached the center of its own equilibrium. Sanctity becomes synonymous with mental sanity. The mystic at this stage knows the perfect balance between innocence and shrewdness, withdrawal and social commitment, obedience and freedom.

In all the dwelling places Teresa warns of possible falsifications and temptations that may occur in each stage: pride, excessive zeal, confusion of spiritual love with sentimentalism, and so forth. Paying too much attention to such phenomena may in turn bring about dread or narcissism. Her advice in these cases is to use the temptations of the devil against the devil. Temptations confront us with our weakness, thus inviting humility. Beyond that, Teresa proposes to disregard the temptations and proceed ahead with courage and fortitude (*ánimo*). *Animo* is the force that drives the soul along the spiritual journey; it is a key term of Teresa's anthropology, and consequently a key sign in this book.

Courage is a masculine, not a feminine, virtue. Greek philosophy and Saint Paul's statements about the role of women in the Church had reinforced each other for centuries in determining the biological and social inferiority of woman. Woman was inferior because the predominance of sensitivity did not allow the spiritual faculties of the soul—intellect and will—to act as freely as in man. Hence, the association of women with sexuality in the classical literature of Europe, and the proverbial inconsistency of women: "Frailty, thy name is woman" (*Hamlet*); "A piece of tender air, *mulier, mollis aer*" (*Cymbeline*).

Teresa had to contend with this idea of woman that, as the references from Shakespeare show, was common throughout Europe. What is more, she herself did not have a better philosophy; she accepted what the learned philosophers and theologians had determined in their wisdom. For this reason she frequently calls herself "*mujer y ruin*" (woman and base). But the general theory of woman does not prevent her from accepting her personal mission. She has a task to fulfill and is not daunted by ideological and social conventions. The Church must be defended against heresy and imperfection; if the Catholic armies fight in the battlefields and the learned theologians argue in the schools, the nuns can cooperate with a life of sacrifice and prayer. In this mission they have to be as courageous as men.

However, her specific activities, writing and founding monasteries, went far beyond the range of movements allowed women, especially in those "hard times" (*tiempos recios*). Teresa objects to the obligation of writing, imposed by her confessors, because it prevents her from spinning; and with regard to the foundations, when she began her reform all available philosophical and theological notions about the nature of women were brought to her attention. Anticipating Shakespeare's terms, the papal legate in Spain referred to Teresa as "a restless gadabout." Eventually she took the case directly to Christ and confronted him with Saint Paul's statement about the role of women in the Church:

> While thinking about whether they who thought it was wrong for me to go out to found monasteries might be right, and thinking that I would do better to be always occupied in prayer, I heard the words: "While one is alive, progress doesn't come from trying to enjoy Me more but by trying to do My will."
>
> I thought that their recommendation would be God's will because of what Saint Paul said about the enclosure of women (Titus 2:5), of which I was recently told and had even heard before. The Lord said to me: "Tell them they shouldn't follow just one part of Scripture but that they should look at other parts, and ask them if they can by chance tie My hands."[8]

This text shows how Teresa the woman challenged one of the most persistent assumptions of western philosophy and theology: the passive role of women in both society and Church. Once again, from a religious position we witness a cultural revolution in a secular sense. The last chapters of *The Dwelling Places* display that perfect combination of religious and secular wisdom that is apparent in all aspects of her life and writings.

In order to appreciate Teresa's cultural and literary originality, we must measure her accomplishments against the handicaps she had to overcome: she was a woman in sixteenth-century Spain, of Jewish descent, a nun in a monastery of closure, and severely ill since the age of twenty-two. Settled in God as her center, she had a clear hierarchy of values, was able to appreciate or deride social and religious institutions, had an exemplary sense of freedom, gave a new impulse to religious life and mystical literature, and through her insistence on courage, provides us with a formula that is still valid to banish the ghost of alienation.

NOTES

1. "Spiritual Testimonies," 1563. *The Collected Works of St. Teresa of Avila*, trans. Kieran Kavanaugh and Otilio Rodríguez (Washington, D.C.: 1976), vol. 1, p. 320. All quotations as well as the selections published in the anthological section are taken from this edition.

2. *The Life*, chapter 1, vol. 1, p. 33.

3. *The Life*, chapter 2, vol. 1, p. 38.

4. Letter 363. Santa Teresa de Jesús, *Obras completas*, ed. E. de la Madre de Dios and O. Stegginck (Madrid, 1971), p. 457. (My translation.)

5. *The Life*, chapter 26, vol. 1, pp. 172–73.

6. *The Way of Perfection*, chapter 21, vol. 2, p. 119.

7. *The Dwelling Places*, part 7, chapter 1, vol. 2, p. 434.

8. "Spiritual Testimonies," July 1571, vol. 1, p. 328.

From *The Book of Life*

PROLOGUE

1. Since my confessors commanded me and gave me plenty of leeway to write about the favors and the kind of prayer the Lord has granted me, I wish they would also have allowed me to tell very clearly and minutely about my great sins and wretched life. This would be a consolation. But they didn't want me to. In fact I was very much restricted in those matters. And so I ask, for the love of God, whoever reads this account to bear in mind that my life has been so wretched that I have not found a saint among those who were converted to God in whom I can find comfort. For I note that after the Lord called them, they did not turn back and offend Him. As for me, not only did I turn back and become worse, but it seems I made a study out of resisting the favors His Majesty was granting me. I was like someone who sees that he is obliged to serve more, yet understands that he can't even pay the smallest part of his debt.

2. May God be blessed forever, He who waited for me so long! I beseech Him with all my heart to give me the grace to present with complete clarity and truthfulness this account of my life which my confessors ordered me to write. And I know, too, that even the Lord has for some time wanted me to do this, although I have not dared. May this account render Him glory and praise. And from now on may my confessors knowing me better through this narration help me in my weakness to give the Lord something of the service I owe Him, whom all things praise forever. Amen.

CHAPTER I

(Treats of how the Lord began to awaken this soul to virtue in her childhood and of how helpful it is in this matter that parents also be virtuous.)

1. To have had virtuous and God-fearing parents along with the graces the Lord granted me should have been enough for me to have led a good life, if I had not been so wretched. My father was fond of reading good books, and thus he also had books in Spanish for his children to read. These good books together with the care my mother took to have us pray and be devoted to our Lady and to some of the saints began to awaken me when, I think, six or seven years old, to the practice of virtue. It was a help to me to see that my parents favored nothing but virtue. And they themselves possessed many.

My father was a man very charitable with the poor and compassionate toward the sick, and even toward servants. So great was his compassion that nobody was ever able to convince him to accept slaves. And his pity for them was such that once having in his home a slave owned by his brother, he treated her as though she were one of his children. He used to say that out of pity he couldn't bear seeing her held captive. He was very honest. No one ever saw him swear or engage in fault-finding. He was an upright man.

2. My mother also had many virtues. And she suffered much sickness during her life. She was extremely modest. Although very beautiful, she never gave occasion to anyone to think she paid any attention to her beauty. For at the time of her death at the age of thirty-three, her clothes were already those of a much older person. She was gentle and very intelligent. Great were the trials she suffered during her life. Her death was a truly Christian one.

3. We were in all three sisters and nine brothers. All resembled their parents in being virtuous, through the goodness of God, with the exception of myself—although I was the most loved of my father. And it seemed he was right—before I began to offend God. For I am ashamed when I

recall the good inclinations the Lord gave me and how poorly I knew how to profit by them.

4. My brothers and sisters did not in any way hold me back from the service of God. I had one brother about my age. We used to get together to read the lives of the saints. (He was the one I liked most, although I had great love for them all and they for me.) When I considered the martyrdoms the saints suffered for God, it seemed to me that the price they paid for going to enjoy God was very cheap, and I greatly desired to die in the same way. I did not want this on account of the love I felt for God but to get to enjoy very quickly the wonderful things I read there were in heaven. And my brother and I discussed together the means we should take to achieve this. We agreed to go off to the land of the Moors and beg them, out of love of God, to cut off our heads there. It seemed to me the Lord had given us courage at so tender an age, but we couldn't discover any means. Having parents seemed to us the greatest obstacle. We were terrified in what we read about the suffering and the glory that was to last forever. We spent a lot of time talking about this and took delight in often repeating: forever and ever and ever. As I said this over and over, the Lord was pleased to impress upon me in childhood the way of truth.

5. When I saw it was impossible to go where I would be killed for God, we made plans to be hermits. And in a garden that we had in our house, we tried as we could to make hermitages piling up some little stones which afterwards would quickly fall down again. And so in nothing could we find a remedy for our desire. It gives me devotion now to see how God gave me so early what I lost through my own fault.

6. I gave what alms I could, but that was little. I sought out solitude to pray my devotions, and they were many, especially the rosary, to which my mother was very devoted; and she made us devoted to it too. When I played with other girls I enjoyed it when we pretended we were nuns in a monastery, and it seemed to me that I desired to be one, although not as much as I desired the other things I mentioned.

7. I remember that when my mother died I was twelve years old or a little less. When I began to understand what I had lost, I went, afflicted, before an image of our Lady and besought her with many tears to be my mother. It seems to me that although I did this in simplicity it helped me. For I have found favor with this sovereign Virgin in everything I have asked of her, and in the end she has drawn me to herself. It wearies me now to see and think that I was not constant in the good desires I had in my childhood.

8. O my Lord, since it seems You have determined to save me, I beseech Your Majesty that it may be so. And since You have granted me as many favors as You have, don't You think it would be good (not for my gain but for Your honor) if the inn where You have so continually to dwell

were not to get so dirty? It wearies me, Lord, even to say this, for I know that the whole fault was mine. It doesn't seem to me that there was anything more for You to do in order that from this age I would be all Yours. If I start to complain about my parents, I am not able to do so, for I saw nothing but good in them and solicitude for my own good.

As I grew older, when I began to know of the natural attractive qualities the Lord had bestowed on me (which others said were many), instead of thanking Him for them, I began to make use of them all to offend Him, as I shall now tell.

CHAPTER 11

(Tells of the reason for the failure to reach the perfect love of God in a short time. Begins to explain through a comparison four degrees of prayer. Goes on to deal here with the first degree. The doctrine is very beneficial for beginners and for those who do not have consolations in prayer.)

1. Well, let us speak now of those who are beginning to be servants of love. This doesn't seem to me to mean anything else than to follow resolutely by means of this path of prayer Him who has loved us so much. To be a servant of love is a dignity so great that it delights me in a wonderful way to think about it. For servile fear soon passes away if in this first state we proceed as we ought. O Lord of my soul and my good! When a soul is determined to love You by doing what it can to leave all and occupy itself better in this divine love, why don't You desire that it enjoy soon the ascent to the possession of perfect love? I have poorly expressed myself. I should have mentioned and complained that we ourselves do not desire this. The whole fault is ours if we don't soon reach the enjoyment of a dignity so great, for the perfect attainment of this true love of God brings with it every blessing. We are so miserly and so slow in giving ourselves entirely to God that since His Majesty does not desire that we enjoy something as precious as this without paying a high price, we do not fully prepare ourselves.

2. I see clearly that there is nothing on earth with which one can buy so wonderful a blessing. But if we do what we can to avoid becoming attached to any earthly thing and let all our care and concern be with heavenly things, and if within a short time we prepare ourselves completely, as some of the saints did, I believe without a doubt that in a very short time this blessing will be given to us. But it seems to us that we are giving all to God, whereas the truth of the matter is that we are paying God the rent or giving Him the fruits and keeping for ourselves the ownership and the root. We resolve to be poor—and this is very meritorious—but then very

often turn back to being anxious and diligent about possessing not only the necessities but superfluities as well and about winning friends who might provide these things for us. And we are thereby placed in a state of greater anxiety—and perhaps danger—about not being in want than we were before when we had our own possessions.

It also appears to us that we are renouncing our status when we become religious or that we renounce it when we begin to live a spiritual life and follow the path of perfection. No sooner is some little point of etiquette concerning our status brought up than we forget we have already offered it to God; and we desire to take it right back out of His hands, so to speak, after having made Him, as it seemed, the Lord of our wills. So it is with everything else.

3. What a charming way to seek the love of God! And then we desire it with our hands full, as they say. We have our attachments since we do not strive to direct our desires to a good effect and raise them up from the earth completely; but to have many spiritual consolations along with attachments is incongruous, nor does it seem to me that the two can get along together. Since we do not succeed in giving up everything at once, this treasure as a result is not given to us all at once. May it please the Lord that drop by drop He may give it to us, even though it cost us all the trials in the world.

4. Indeed a great mercy does He bestow on anyone to whom He gives the grace and courage to resolve to strive for this good with every ounce of energy. For God does not deny Himself to anyone who perseveres. Little by little He will measure out the courage sufficient to attain this victory. I say "courage" because there are so many things the devil puts in the minds of beginners to prevent them in fact from starting out on this path. For he knows the damage that will be done to him in losing not only that one soul but many others. If the beginner with the assistance of God struggles to reach the summit of perfection, I believe he will never go to heaven alone; he will always lead many people along after him. Like a good captain he will give whoever marches in his company to God. The devil puts so many dangers and difficulties into the beginner's head that no little courage, but a great deal, is necessary in order not to turn back— and a great deal of assistance from God.

5. Speaking now of the initial stages of those who are determined to seek out this good and embark on this enterprise (for I shall speak afterward of the other stages I began to mention in regard to mystical theology, which I believe it is called), the greatest labor is in the beginning because it is the beginner who works while the Lord gives the increase. In the other degrees of prayer the greatest thing is enjoying; although whether in the beginning, the middle, or the end, all bear their crosses even though these crosses be different. For all who follow Christ, if they don't want to get

lost, must walk along this path that He trod. And blessed be the trials that even here in this life are so superabundantly repaid.

6. I shall have to make use of some comparison, although I should like to excuse myself from this since I am a woman and write simply what they ordered me to write. But these spiritual matters for anyone who like myself has not gone through studies are so difficult to explain. I shall have to find some mode of explaining myself, and it may be less often that I hit upon a good comparison. Seeing so much stupidity will provide some recreation for your Reverence.

It seems now to me that I read or heard of this comparison—for since I have a bad memory, I don't know where or for what reason it was used; but it will be all right for my purposes. The beginner must realize that in order to give delight to the Lord he is starting to cultivate a garden on very barren soil, full of abominable weeds. His Majesty pulls up the weeds and plants good seed. Now let us keep in mind that all of this is already done by the time a soul is determined to practice prayer and has begun to make use of it. And with the help of God we must strive like good gardeners to get these plants to grow and take pains to water them so that they don't wither but come to bud and flower and give forth a most pleasant fragrance to provide refreshment for this Lord of ours. Then He will often come to take delight in this garden and find His joy among these virtues.

7. But let us see now how it must be watered so that we may understand what we have to do, the labor this will cost us, whether the labor is greater than the gain, and for how long it must last. It seems to me the garden can be watered in four ways. You may draw water from a well (which is for us a lot of work). Or you may get it by means of a water wheel and aqueducts in such a way that it is obtained by turning the crank of the water wheel. (I have drawn it this way sometimes—the method involves less work than the other, and you get more water.) Or it may flow from a river or a stream. (The garden is watered much better by this means because the ground is more fully soaked, and there is no need to water so frequently—and much less work for the gardener.) Or the water may be provided by a great deal of rain. (For the Lord waters the garden without any work on our part—and this way is comparably better than all the others mentioned.)

8. Now, then, these four ways of drawing water in order to maintain this garden—because without water it will die—are what are important to me and have seemed applicable in explaining the four degrees of prayer in which the Lord in His goodness has sometimes placed my soul. May it please His goodness that I manage to speak about them in a way beneficial for one of the persons who ordered me to write this, because within four months the Lord has brought him further than I got in seventeen

years. This person has prepared himself better, and so without any labor of his own the flower garden is watered with all these four waters, although the last is still not given except in drops. But he is advancing in such a way that soon he will be immersed in it, with the help of the Lord. And I shall be pleased if you laugh should this way of explaining the matter appear foolish.

9. Beginners in prayer, we can say, are those who draw water from the well. This involves a lot of work on their own part, as I have said. They must tire themselves in trying to recollect their senses. Since they are accustomed to being distracted, this recollection requires much effort. They need to get accustomed to caring nothing at all about seeing or hearing, to practicing the hours of prayer, and thus to solitude and withdrawal—and to thinking on their past life. Although these beginners and the others as well must often reflect upon their past, the extent to which they must do so varies, as I shall say afterward. In the beginning such reflection is even painful, for they do not fully understand whether or not they are repentant of their sins. If they are, they are then determined to serve God earnestly. They must strive to consider the life of Christ—and the intellect grows weary in doing this.

These are the things we can do of ourselves, with the understanding that we do so by the help of God, for without this help as is already known we cannot have so much as a good thought. These things make up the beginning of fetching water from the well, and please God that it may be found. At least we are doing our part, for we are already drawing it out and doing what we can to water these flowers. God is so good that when for reasons His Majesty knows—perhaps for our greater benefit—the well is dry and we, like good gardeners, do what lies in our power, He sustains the garden without water and makes the virtues grow. Here by "water" I am referring to tears and when there are no tears to interior tenderness and feelings of devotion.

10. But what will he do here who sees that after many days there is nothing but dryness, distaste, vapidness, and very little desire to come to draw water? So little is the desire to do this that if he doesn't recall that doing so serves and gives pleasure to the Lord of the garden, and if he isn't careful to preserve the merits acquired in this service (and even what he hopes to gain from the tedious work of often letting the pail down into the well and pulling it back up without any water), he will abandon everything. It will frequently happen to him that he will even be unable to lift his arms for this work and unable to get a good thought. This discursive work with the intellect is what is meant by fetching water from the well.

But, as I am saying, what will the gardener do here? He will rejoice and be consoled and consider it the greatest favor to be able to work in the garden of so great an Emperor! Since he knows that this pleases the Lord and his intention must be not to please himself but to please the Lord, he gives the Lord much praise. For the Master has confidence in the gardener because he sees that without any pay he is so very careful about what he was told to do. This gardener helps Christ carry the cross and reflects that the Lord lived with it all during His life. He doesn't desire the Lord's kingdom here below or ever abandon prayer. And so he is determined, even though this dryness may last for his whole life, not to let Christ fall with the cross. The time will come when the Lord will repay him all at once. He doesn't fear that the labor is being wasted. He is serving a good Master whose eyes are upon him. He doesn't pay any attention to bad thoughts. He considers that the devil also represented them to Saint Jerome in the desert.

11. These labors take their toll. Being myself one who endured them for many years (for when I got a drop of water from this sacred well I thought God was granting me a favor), I know that they are extraordinary. It seems to me more courage is necessary for them than for many other labors of this world. But I have seen clearly that God does not leave one, even in this life, without a large reward; because it is certainly true that one of those hours in which the Lord afterward bestowed on me a taste of Himself repaid, it seems to me, all the anguish I suffered in persevering for a long time in prayer.

I am of the opinion that to some in the beginning and to others afterward the Lord often desires to give these torments and the many other temptations that occur in order to try His lovers and know whether they will be able to drink the chalice and help Him carry the cross before He lays great treasures within them. I believe His Majesty desires to bring us along this way for our own good so that we may understand well what little we amount to. The favors that come afterward are of such great worth that He desires first that before He gives them to us we see by experience our own worthlessness so that what happened to Lucifer will not happen to us.

12. My Lord, what do You do but that which is for the greater good of the soul You understand now to be Yours and which places itself in Your power so as to follow You wherever You go, even to death on the cross, and is determined to help You bear it and not leave You alone with it?

Whoever sees in himself this determination has no reason, no reason whatsoever, to fear. Spiritual persons, you have no reason to be afflicted. Once you are placed in so high a degree as to desire to commune in solitude with God and abandon the pastimes of the world, the most has been done. Praise His Majesty for that and trust in His goodness who never fails His friends. Conceal from your eyes the thought about why He gives devotion to one after such a few days and not to me after so many years. Let us believe that all is for our own greater good. Let His Majesty lead the way along the path He desires. We belong no longer to ourselves but to Him. He grants us a great favor in wanting us to desire to dig in His garden and be in the presence of its Lord who certainly is present with us. Should He desire that for some these plants and flowers grow by the water they draw, which He gives from this well, and for others without it, what difference does that make to me? Do, Lord, what You desire. May I not offend You. Don't let the virtues be lost, if You only out of Your goodness have already given me some. I desire to suffer, Lord, since You suffered. Let Your will be done in me in every way, and may it not please Your Majesty that something as precious as Your love be given to anyone who serves you only for the sake of consolations.

13. It should be carefully noted—and I say this because I know it through experience—that the soul that begins to walk along this path of mental prayer with determination and that can succeed in paying little attention to whether this delight and tenderness is lacking or whether the Lord gives it (or to whether it has much consolation or no consolation) has travelled a great part of the way. However much it stumbles, it should not fear that it will turn back, because the building has been started on a solid foundation. This is true because the love of God does not consist in tears or in this delight and tenderness, which for the greater part we desire and find consolation in; but it consists in serving with justice and for-titude of soul and in humility. Without such service it seems to me we would be receiving everything and giving nothing.

14. In the case of a poor little woman like myself, weak and with hardly any fortitude, it seems to me fitting that God lead me with gifts, as He now does, so that I might be able to suffer some trials He has desired me to bear. But when I see servants of God, men of prominence, learning, and high intelligence make so much fuss because God doesn't give them devotion, it annoys me to hear them. I do not mean that they shouldn't accept it if God gives it, and esteem it, because then His Majesty sees that this is appropriate. But when they don't have devotion, they shouldn't weary themselves. They should understand that since His Majesty doesn't give it, it isn't necessary; and they should be masters of themselves. They should believe that their desire for consolation is a fault. I have experienced and seen this. They should believe it denotes imperfection together with a lack of freedom of spirit and the courage to accomplish something.

15. Although I lay great stress on this because it is very important that beginners have such freedom and determination, I am not saying it so much for beginners as for others. For there are many who begin, yet they never reach the end. I believe this is due mainly to a failure to embrace the cross from the beginning; thinking they are doing nothing, they become

afflicted. When the intellect ceases to work, they cannot bear it. But it is then perhaps that their will is being strengthened and fortified, although they may not be aware of this.

We should think that the Lord is not concerned about these inabilities. Even though they seem to us to be faults, they are not. His Majesty already knows our misery and our wretched nature better than we do ourselves, and He knows that these souls now desire to think of Him and love Him always. This determination is what He desires. The other affliction that we bring upon ourselves serves for nothing else than to disquiet the soul, and if it was incapable before of engaging in prayer for one hour, it will be so now for four. Very often this incapacity comes from some bodily disorder. I have a great deal of experience in this matter, and I know that what I say is true because I have considered it carefully and discussed it afterward with spiritual persons. We are so miserable that our poor little imprisoned soul shares in the miseries of the body; the changes in the weather and the rotating of the bodily humors often have the result that without their fault souls cannot do what they desire, but suffer in every way. If they seek to force themselves more during these times, the bad condition becomes worse and lasts longer. They should use discernment to observe when these bodily disorders may be the cause, and not smother the poor soul. They should understand that they are sick. The hour of prayer ought to be changed, and often this change will have to continue for some days. Let them suffer this exile as best they can. It is a great misfortune to a soul that loves God to see that it lives in this misery and cannot do what it desires because it has as wretched a guest as is this body.

16. I have said they should use discernment because sometimes the devil is the cause. And so it isn't always good to abandon prayer when there is great distraction and disturbance in the intellect just as it isn't always good to torture the soul into doing what it cannot do.

There are other exterior things like works of charity and spiritual reading, although at times it will not even be fit for these. Let it then serve the body out of love of God—because many other times the body serves the soul—and engage in some spiritual pastimes such as holy conversations, provided they are truly so, or going to the country, as the confessor might counsel. Experience is a great help in all, for it teaches what is suitable for us; and God can be served in everything. His yoke is easy, and it is very helpful not to drag the soul along, as they say, but to lead it gently for the sake of its greater advantage.

17. So I return to the advice—and even if I repeat it many times this doesn't matter—that it is very important that no one be distressed or afflicted over dryness or noisy and distracting thoughts. If a person wishes to gain freedom of spirit and not be always troubled, let him begin by not

being frightened by the cross, and he will see how the Lord also helps him carry it and he will gain satisfaction and profit from everything. For, clearly, if the well is dry, we cannot put water into it. True, we must not become neglectful; when there is water we should draw it out because then the Lord desires to multiply the virtues by this means.

From *The Dwelling Places of the Interior Castle*

The First Dwelling Places

CHAPTER I

(Discusses the beauty and dignity of our souls. Draws a comparison in order to explain, and speaks of the benefit that comes from understanding this truth and knowing about the favors we receive from God and how the door to this castle is prayer.)

Today while beseeching our Lord to speak for me because I wasn't able to think of anything to say nor did I know how to begin to carry out this obedience, there came to my mind what I shall now speak about, that which will provide us with a basis to begin with. It is that we consider our soul to be like a castle made entirely out of a diamond or of very clear crystal, in which there are many rooms, just as in heaven there are many dwelling places. For in reflecting upon it carefully, Sisters, we realize that the soul of the just person is nothing else but a paradise where the Lord says He finds His delight. So then, what do you think that abode will be like where a King so powerful, so wise, so pure, so full of all good things takes His delight? I don't find anything comparable to the magnificent beauty of a soul and its marvelous capacity. Indeed, our intellects, however keen, can hardly comprehend it, just as they cannot comprehend God; but He Himself says that He created us in His own image and likeness.

Well if this is true, as it is, there is no reason to tire ourselves in trying to comprehend the beauty of this castle. Since this castle is a creature and the difference, therefore, between it and God is the same as that between the Creator and His creature, His Majesty in saying that the soul is made in His own image makes it almost impossible for us to understand the sublime dignity and beauty of the soul.

2. It is a shame and unfortunate that through our own fault we don't

understand ourselves or know who we are. Wouldn't it show great ignorance, my daughters, if someone when asked who he was didn't know,
and didn't know his father or mother or from what country he came? Well
now, if this would be so extremely stupid, we are incomparably more so
when we do not strive to know who we are, but limit ourselves to considering only roughly these bodies. Because we have heard and because faith
tells us so, we know we have souls. But we seldom consider the precious
things that can be found in this soul, or who dwells within it, or its high
value. Consequently, little effort is made to preserve its beauty. All our
attention is taken up with the plainness of the diamond's setting or the
outer wall of the castle; that is, with these bodies of ours.

3. Well, let us consider that this castle has, as I said, many dwelling
places: some up above, others down below, others to the sides; and in the
center and middle is the main dwelling place where the very secret exchanges between God and the soul take place.

It's necessary that you keep this comparison in mind. Perhaps God will
be pleased to let me use it to explain something to you about the favors
He is happy to grant souls and the differences between these favors. I shall
explain them according to what I have understood as possible. For it is
impossible that anyone understand them all since there are many; how
much more so for someone as wretched as I. It will be a great consolation
when the Lord grants them to you if you know that they are possible; and
for anyone to whom He doesn't, it will be a great consolation to praise
His wonderful goodness. Just as it doesn't do us any harm to reflect upon
the things there are in heaven and what the blessed enjoy—but rather we
rejoice and strive to attain what they enjoy—it doesn't do us any harm to
see that it is possible in this exile for so great a God to commune with
such foul-smelling worms; and, upon seeing this, come to love a goodness
so perfect and a mercy so immeasurable. I hold as certain that anyone
who might be harmed by knowing that God can grant this favor in this
exile would be very much lacking in humility and love of neighbor. Otherwise, how could we fail to be happy that God grants these favors to our
brother? His doing so is no impediment toward His granting them to us,
and His Majesty can reveal His grandeurs to whomever He wants. Sometimes He does so merely to show forth His glory, as He said of the blind
man whose sight He restored when His apostles asked Him if the blindness resulted from the man's sins or those of his parents. Hence, He
doesn't grant them because the sanctity of the recipients is greater than
that of those who don't receive them but so that His glory may be known,
as we see in Saint Paul and the Magdalene, and that we might praise Him
for His work in creatures.

4. One could say that these favors seem to be impossible and that it is
good not to scandalize the weak. Less is lost when the weak do not believe

in them than when the favors fail to benefit those to whom God grants them; and these latter will be delighted and awakened through these favors to a greater love of Him who grants so many gifts and whose power and majesty is so great. Moreover, I know I am speaking to those for whom this danger does not exist, for they know and believe that God grants even greater signs of His love. I know that whoever does not believe in these favors will have no experience of them, for God doesn't like us to put a limit on His works. And so, Sisters, those of you whom the Lord doesn't lead by this path should never doubt His generosity.

5. Well, getting back to our beautiful and delightful castle we must see how we can enter it. It seems I'm saying something foolish. For if this castle is the soul, clearly one doesn't have to enter it since it is within oneself. How foolish it would seem were we to tell someone to enter a room he is already in. But you must understand that there is a great difference in the ways one may be inside the castle. For there are many souls who are in the outer courtyard—which is where the guards stay—and don't care at all about entering the castle, nor do they know what lies within that most precious place, nor who is within, nor even how many rooms it has. You have already heard in some books on prayer that the soul is advised to enter within itself; well that's the very thing I'm advising.

6. Not long ago a very learned man told me that souls who do not practice prayer are like people with paralysed or crippled bodies; even though they have hands and feet they cannot give orders to these hands and feet. Thus there are souls so ill and so accustomed to being involved in external matters that there is no remedy, nor does it seem they can enter within themselves. They are now so used to dealing always with the insects and vermin that are in the wall surrounding the castle that they have become almost like them. And though they have so rich a nature and the power to converse with none other than God, there is no remedy. If these souls do not strive to understand and cure their great misery, they will be changed into statues of salt, unable to turn their heads to look at themselves, just as Lot's wife was changed for having turned her head.

7. Insofar as I can understand the door of entry to this castle is prayer and reflection. I don't mean to refer to mental more than vocal prayer, for since vocal prayer is prayer it must be accompanied by reflection. A prayer in which a person is not aware of whom he is speaking to, what he is asking, who it is who is asking and of whom, I do not call prayer however much the lips move. Sometimes it will be so without this reflection, provided that the soul has these reflections at other times. Nonetheless, anyone who has the habit of speaking before God's majesty as though he were speaking to a slave, without being careful to see how he is speaking, but saying whatever comes to his head and whatever he has learned from

saying at other times, in my opinion is not praying. Praise God, may no Christian pray in this way. Among yourselves, Sisters, I hope in His Majesty that you will not do so, for the custom you have of being occupied with interior things is quite a good safeguard against falling and carrying on in this way like brute beasts.

8. Well now, we are not speaking to these crippled souls, for if the Lord Himself doesn't come to order them to get up—as He did the man who waited at the side of the pool for thirty years—they are quite unfortunate and in serious danger. But we are speaking to other souls that, in the end, enter the castle. For even though they are very involved in the world, they have good desires and sometimes, though only once in a while, they entrust themselves to our Lord and reflect on who they are, although in a rather hurried fashion. During the period of a month they will sometimes pray, but their minds are then filled with business matters which ordinarily occupy them. They are so attached to these things that where their treasure lies their heart goes also. Sometimes they do put all these things aside, and the self-knowledge and awareness that they are not proceeding correctly in order to get to the door is important. Finally, they enter the first, lower rooms. But so many reptiles get in with them that they are prevented from seeing the beauty of the castle and from calming down; they have done quite a bit just by having entered.

9. You may have been thinking, daughters, that this is irrelevant to you since by the Lord's goodness you are not among these people. You'll have to have patience, for I wouldn't know how to explain my understanding of some interior things about prayer if not in this way. And may it even please the Lord that I succeed in saying something, for what I want to explain to you is very difficult to understand without experience. If you have experience you will see that one cannot avoid touching upon things that—please God, through His mercy—do not pertain to us.

The Fourth Dwelling Places

CHAPTER 3

. . . You, Sisters, are free of dangers, from what we can know. From pride and vainglory may God deliver you. If the devil should counterfeit God's favors, this will be known by the fact that these good effects are not caused, but just the opposite.

11. There is one danger I want to warn you about (although I may have mentioned it elsewhere) into which I have seen persons of prayer fall, especially women, for since we are weaker there is more occasion for what I'm about to say. It is that some have a weak constitution because of a

great amount of penance, prayer, and keeping vigil, and even without these; in receiving some favor, their nature is overcome. Since they feel some consolation interiorly and a languishing and weakness exteriorly, they think they are experiencing a spiritual sleep (which is a prayer a little more intense than the prayer of quiet) and they let themselves become absorbed. The more they allow this, the more absorbed they become because their nature is further weakened, and they fancy that they are being carried away in rapture. I call it being carried away in foolishness because it amounts to nothing more than wasting time and wearing down one's health. These persons feel nothing through their senses nor do they feel anything concerning God. One person happened to remain eight hours in this state. By sleeping and eating and avoiding so much penance, this person got rid of the stupor, for there was someone who understood her. She had misled both her confessor and other persons, as well as herself—for she hadn't intended to deceive. I truly believe that the devil was trying to gain ground, and in this instance indeed he was beginning to gain no small amount.

12. It must be understood that when something is truly from God there is no languishing in the soul, even though there may be an interior and exterior languishing, for the soul experiences deep feelings on seeing itself close to God. Nor does the experience last so long, but for a very short while—although one becomes absorbed again. In such prayer, if the cause of it is not weakness, as I said, the body is not worn down nor is any external feeling produced.

13. For this reason let them take the advice that when they feel this languishing in themselves they tell the prioress and distract themselves from it insofar as they can. The prioress should make them give up so many hours for prayer so that they have only a very few and try to get them to sleep and eat well until their natural strength begins to return, if it has been lost through a lack of food and sleep. If a Sister's nature is so weak that this is not enough, may she believe me that God does not want her to practice anything but the active life, which also must be practiced in monasteries. They should let her get busy with different duties; and always take care that she not have a great deal of solitude, for she would lose her health completely. It will be quite a mortification for her; in how she bears this absence is the way the Lord wants to test her love for Him. And He will be pleased to give her strength back after some time. If He doesn't, she will gain through vocal prayer and through obedience and will merit what she would have merited otherwise, and perhaps more.

14. There could also be some persons with such weak heads and imaginations—and I have known some—to whom it seems that everything they think about they see. This is very dangerous. Because I shall perhaps treat of it later on, I'll say no more here. I have greatly enlarged upon this

dwelling place because it is the one which more souls enter. Since it is, and since the natural and the supernatural are joined in it, the devil can do more harm. In those dwelling places still to be spoken of, the Lord doesn't give him so much leeway. May His Majesty be forever praised, amen.

The Seventh Dwelling Places

CHAPTER 4

(Concludes by explaining what she thinks our Lord's purpose is in granting such great favors to the soul and how it is necessary that Martha and Mary join together. This chapter is very beneficial.)

You must not think, Sisters, that the effects I mentioned are always present in these souls. Hence, where I remember, I say "ordinarily." For sometimes our Lord leaves these individuals in their natural state, and then it seems all the poisonous creatures from the outskirts and other dwelling places of this castle band together to take revenge for the time they were unable to have these souls under their control.

2. True, this natural state lasts only a short while, a day at most or a little more. And in this great disturbance, usually occasioned by some event, the soul's gain through the good company it is in becomes manifest. For the Lord gives the soul great stability and good resolutions not to deviate from His service in anything. But it seems this determination increases, and these souls do not deviate through even a very slight first movement. As I say this disturbance is rare, but our Lord does not want the soul to forget its being, so that, for one thing, it might always be humble; for another, that it might better understand the tremendous favor it receives, what it owes His Majesty, and that it might praise Him.

3. Nor should it pass through your minds that, since these souls have such determination and strong desires not to commit any imperfection for anything on earth, they fail to commit many imperfections, and even sins. Advertently, no; for the Lord must give souls such as these very particular help against such a thing. I mean venial sins, for from what these souls can understand they are free from mortal sins, although not immune. That they might have some sins they don't know about is no small torment to them. They also suffer torment in seeing souls go astray. Even though in some way they have great hope that they themselves will not be among these souls, they cannot help but fear when they recall some of those persons Scripture mentions who, it seems, were favored by the Lord, like Solomon, who communed so much with His Majesty, as I have said. The one among you who feels safest should fear more, for *blessed is*

the man who fears the Lord, says David. May His Majesty protect us always. To beseech Him that we not offend Him is the greatest security we can have. May He be praised forever, amen.

4. It will be good, Sisters, to tell you the reason the Lord grants so many favors in this world. Although, if you have paid attention, you will have understood this in learning of their effects, I want to tell you again here lest someone think that the reason is solely for the sake of giving delight to these souls; that thought would be a serious error. His Majesty couldn't grant us a greater favor than to give us a life that would be an imitation of the life His beloved Son lived. Thus I hold for certain that these favors are meant to fortify our weakness, as I have said here at times, that we may be able to imitate Him in His great sufferings.

5. We have always seen that those who were closest to Christ our Lord were those with the greatest trials. Let us look at what His glorious Mother suffered and the glorious apostles. How do you think Saint Paul could have suffered such very great trials? Through him we can see the effects visions and contemplation produce when from our Lord, and not from the imagination or the devil's deceit. Did Saint Paul by chance hide himself in the enjoyment of these delights and not engage in anything else? You already see that he didn't have a day of rest, from what we can understand, and neither did he have any rest at night since it was then that he earned his livelihood. I like very much the account about Saint Peter fleeing from prison and how our Lord appeared to him and told him "I am on my way to Rome to be crucified again." We never recite the office of this feast, where this account is, that I don't find particular consolation. How did this favor from the Lord impress Saint Peter or what did he do? He went straight to his death. And it was no small mercy from the Lord that Peter found someone to provide him with death.

6. O my Sisters! How forgetful this soul, in which the Lord dwells in so particular a way, should be of its own rest, how little it should care for its honor, and how far it should be from wanting esteem in anything! For if it is with Him very much, as is right, it should think little about itself. All its concern is taken up with how to please Him more and how or where it will show Him the love it bears Him. This is the reason for prayer, my daughters, the purpose of this spiritual marriage: the birth always of good works, good works.

7. This is the true sign of a thing, or favor, being from God, as I have already told you. It benefits me little to be alone making acts of devotion to our Lord, proposing and promising to do wonders in His service, if I then go away and when the occasion offers itself do everything the opposite. I was wrong in saying it profits little, for everything having to do with God profits a great deal. And even though we are weak and do not carry out these resolutions afterward, sometimes His Majesty will give us

the power to do so, even though, perhaps, doing so is burdensome to us, as is often true. Since He sees that a soul is very faint-hearted He gives it a severe trial, truly against its will, and brings this soul out of the trial with profit. Afterward, since the soul understands this, the fear lessens and one can offer oneself more willingly to Him. I meant "it benefits me little" in comparison with how much greater the benefit is when our deeds conform with what we say in prayer; what cannot be done all at once can be done little by little. Let the soul bend its will if it wishes that prayer be beneficial to it, for within the corners of these little monasteries there will not be lacking many occasions for you to do so.

8. Keep in mind that I could not exaggerate the importance of this. Fix your eyes on the Crucified and everything will become small for you. If His Majesty showed us His love by means of such works and frightful torments, how is it you want to please Him only with words? Do you know what it means to be truly spiritual? It means becoming the slaves of God. Marked with His brand, which is that of the cross, spiritual persons, because now they have given Him their liberty, can be sold by Him as slaves of everyone, as He was. He doesn't thereby do them any harm or grant them a small favor. And if souls aren't determined about becoming His slaves, let them be convinced that they are not making such progress, for this whole building, as I have said, has humility as its foundation. If humility is not genuinely present, for your own sake the Lord will not construct a high building lest that building fall to the ground. Thus, Sisters, that you might build on good foundations, strive to be the least and the slaves of all, looking at how or where you can please and serve them. What you do in this matter you do more for yourself than for them and lay stones so firmly that the castle will not fall.

9. I repeat, it is necessary that your foundation consists of more than prayer and contemplation. If you do not strive for the virtues and practice them, you will always be dwarfs. And, please God, it will be only a matter of not growing, for you already know that whoever does not increase decreases. I hold that love, where present, cannot possibly be content with remaining always the same.

10. It will seem to you that I am speaking with those who are beginning and that after this beginner's stage souls can rest. I have already told you that the calm these souls have interiorly is for the sake of their having much less calm exteriorly and much less desire to have exterior calm. What, do you think, is the reason for those inspirations (or to put it better, aspirations) I mentioned, and those messages the soul sends from the interior center to the people at the top of the castle and to the dwelling places outside the center where it is? Is it so that those outside might fall asleep? No, absolutely not! That the faculties, senses, and all the corporeal will not be idle; the soul wages more war from the center than it

did when it was outside suffering with them, for then it didn't understand the tremendous gain trials bring. Perhaps they were the means by which God brought it to the center, and the company it has gives it much greater strength than ever. For if here below, as David says, in the company of the saints we will become saints, there is no reason to doubt that, being united with the Strong One through so sovereign a union of spirit with spirit, fortitude will cling to such a soul; and so we shall understand what fortitude the saints had for suffering and dying.

11. It is very certain that from that fortitude which clings to it there the soul assists all those who are in the castle, and even the body itself which often, seemingly, does not feel the strength. But the soul is fortified by the strength it has from drinking wine in this wine cellar, where its Spouse has brought it and from where He doesn't allow it to leave; and strength flows back to the weak body, just as food placed in the stomach strengthens the head and the whole body. Thus the soul has its share of misfortune while it lives. However much it does, the interior strength increases and thus, too, the war that is waged; for everything seems like a trifle to it. The great penances that many saints—especially the glorious Magdalene, who had always been surrounded by so much luxury—performed must have come from this center. Also that hunger which our Father Elijah had for the honor of his God and which Saint Dominic and Saint Francis had so as to draw souls to praise God. I tell you, though they were forgetful of themselves, their suffering must have been great.

12. This is what I want us to strive for, my Sisters; and let us desire and be occupied in prayer not for the sake of our enjoyment but so as to have this strength to serve. Let's refuse to take an unfamiliar path, for we shall get lost at the most opportune time. It would indeed be novel to think of having these favors from God through a path other than the one He took and the one followed by all His saints. May the thought never enter our minds. Believe me, Martha and Mary must join together in order to show hospitality to the Lord and have Him always present and not host Him badly by failing to give Him something to eat. How would Mary, always seated at His feet, provide Him with food if her sister did not help her? His food is that in every way possible we draw souls that they may be saved and praise Him always.

13. You will make two objections: one, that He said that Mary had chosen the better part. The answer is that she had already performed the task of Martha, pleasing the Lord by washing His feet and drying them with her hair. Do you think it would be a small mortification for a woman of nobility like her to wander through these streets (and perhaps alone because her fervent love made her unaware of what she was doing) and enter a house she had never entered before and afterward suffer the criticism of the Pharisee and the very many other things she must have suf-

fered? The people saw a woman like her change so much—and, as we know, she was among such malicious people—and they saw her friendship with the Lord whom they vehemently abhorred, and that she wanted to become a saint since obviously she would have changed her manner of dress and everything else. All of that was enough to cause them to comment on the life she had formerly lived. If nowadays there is so much gossip against persons who are not so notorious; what would have been said then? I tell you, Sisters, the better part came after many trials and much mortification, for even if there were not other trial than to see His Majesty abhorred, that would be an intolerable one. Moreover, the many trials that afterward she suffered at the death of the Lord and in the years that she subsequently lived in His absence must have been a terrible torment. You see she wasn't always in the delight of contemplation at the feet of the Lord.

14. The other objection you will make is that you are unable to bring souls to God, that you do not have the means; that you would do it willingly but that not being teachers or preachers, as were the apostles, you do not know how. This objection I have answered at times in writing, but I don't know if I did so in this *Castle*. Yet since the matter is something I believe is passing through your minds on account of the desires God gives you I will not fail to respond here. I already told you elsewhere that sometimes the devil gives us great desires so that we will avoid setting ourselves to the task at hand, serving our Lord in possible things, and instead be content with having desired the impossible. Apart from the fact that by prayer you will be helping greatly, you need not be desiring to benefit the whole world but must concentrate on those who are in your company, and thus your deed will be greater since you are more obliged toward them. Do you think such deep humility, your mortification, service of all and great charity toward them, and love of the Lord is of little benefit? This fire of love in you enkindles their souls, and with every other virtue you will be always awakening them. Such service will not be small but very great and very pleasing to the Lord. By what you do in deed— that which you can—His Majesty will understand that you would do much more. Thus He will give you the reward He would if you had gained many souls for Him.

15. You will say that such service does not convert souls because all the Sisters you deal with are already good. Who has appointed you judge in this matter? The better they are the more pleasing their praises will be to our Lord and the more their prayer will profit their neighbor.

In sum, my Sisters, what I conclude with is that we shouldn't build castles in the air. The Lord doesn't look so much at the greatness of our works as at the love with which they are done. And if we do what we can, His Majesty will enable us each day to do more and more, provided that we do not quickly tire. But during the little while this life lasts—and perhaps it will last a shorter time than each one thinks—let us offer the Lord interiorly and exteriorly the sacrifice we can. His Majesty will join it with that which He offered on the cross to the Father for us. Thus even though our works are small they will have the value our love for Him would have merited had they been great.

16. May it please His Majesty, my Sisters and daughters, that we all reach that place where we may ever praise Him. Through the merits of His Son who lives and reigns forever and ever, may He give me the grace to carry out something of what I tell you, amen. For I tell you that my confusion is great, and thus I ask you through the same Lord that in your prayers you do not forget this poor wretch.

BIBLIOGRAPHY

Primary Works

Teresa of Avila. *The Collected Works of St. Teresa of Avila*. Trans. Kieran Kavanaugh and Otilio Rodríguez. 2 vols. Washington, D.C., 1976–1980.
————. *The Complete Works of St. Teresa of Jesus*. Trans. E. Allison Peers. New York, 1946.
————. *Obras completas de Santa Teresa*. Ed. Efrén de la Madre de Dios and Otger Steggink. Madrid, 1967.

Related Works

Auclair, Marcelle. *Teresa of Avila*. Trans. Kathleen Pond. New York, 1953.
Clissold, Stephen. *St. Teresa of Avila*. New York, 1982.
Efrén de la Madre de Dios and Otger Steggink. *Tiempo y vida de Santa Teresa*. Madrid, 1977.
Egido, Teófanes. "The Historical Setting of St. Teresa's Life." *Carmelite Studies* 1 (1980): 122–82.
Gabriel de Santa María Magdalena. *Saint Teresa of Jesus: Mistress of Spiritual Life*. Trans. a Benedictine of Stanbrook Abbey. Cork, 1949.
García de la Concha, Victor. *El arte literario de Santa Teresa*. Barcelona, 1978.
Hatzfeld, Helmut. *Santa Teresa de Avila*. New York, 1969.
Lincoln, Victoria. *Teresa: A Woman*. Edited, with an introduction, by Elias Rivers and Antonio T. de Nicolás. Albany, N.Y., 1984.
Llamas Martínez, Enrique. *Santa Teresa de Jesús y la Inquisición española*. Madrid, 1972.
Papasogli, Giorgio. *St. Teresa of Avila*. Trans. G. Anzilotti. New York, 1958.
Peers, E. Allison. *Handbook of the Life and Times of St. Teresa and St. John of the Cross*. London, 1954.
Ramge, Sebastian. *An Introduction to the Writings of St. Teresa*. Chicago, 1963.
Sullivan, John, ed. "Centenary of Saint Teresa." *Carmelite Studies* 4 (1984).
Trueman Dicken, E. W. *The Crucible of Love*. New York, 1963.
Walsh, William Thomas. *Saint Teresa of Avila*. Milwaukee, 1943.

PART SIX

ungary

A DOMINICAN AUTHOR

ea Ráskai

SUZANNE FONAY WEMPLE

The legend of Blessed Margaret, or *Margit* in Hungarian, was transmitted to us in that language by the first woman writing in Hungarian, Lea Ráskai. She penned the *Legend of Blessed Margaret* in 1510, some 240 years after the death of the virgin. The story she told was extremely popular, relating in full detail the life of the holy maiden. But the writer did not divulge anything about herself. We know only that she was a Dominican nun in the early sixteenth century in the very same monastery where Blessed Margaret spent most of her life.[1] The monastery was located on the isle of the Danube at Budapest, one that still today is called Isle of Margaret or *Margit sziget* in Hungarian. Scholars, literators, and philologists have tried to discover about her more than her name but have been unable to find anything of substance.

Lea Ráskai was the daughter of a noble family living in the province of Zemplén in northeast Hungary, in the villages of Kis and Nagyráska. Members of the family were the bearers of courtly and national honors since the days of King Endre II. The religious institution on the Isle of Margaret was the refuge of noble girls from marriage ever since the days of Blessed Margaret. Lea probably became a nun quite early in her life. She is completely silent on her family and herself, modeling her virtues after Blessed Margaret.

Between 1510 and 1525 she was the scribe of nearly five codices. She copied with two other sisters the *Book of Examples* (*Példák könyve*, 1510), containing fables from the apostles that were frequently used by teachers in the years thereafter. She transcribed, however, alone the *Legend of Saint Dominique* (1517), the *Cornides Codex* (1514–1519), the *Horvát Codex* (1522), in addition to the *Legend of Blessed Margaret* (around 1510).

The *Legend of Saint Dominique* is a very long codex describing the life examples, miracles, and the visions of the saint. The founder of the Hun-

garian order is also mentioned: Blessed Paul, who before joining the
order, was teaching canon law at Bologna. Paul's deeds in Hungary were
also significant. They show his power over the devil, the veneration of the
Blessed Mary, and the force of prayers that were his bulwark. If we add to
this the strength of Parisian university teachers and the vigor of preaching,
we have the goals of the Dominican order. The first part of the *Legend of
Saint Dominique* was based on Antoninus, monsignor of Florence, who
died in 1459, and part two on Gerardus de Fracheto, whose work was
more contemporary—he lived until 1270. There are, though, sections in
both parts which depend on the thirteenth-century Theodoric de Appol-
dia, Thuringian narrator of Saint Dominique's life. In each part, however,
the talented copyist Lea Ráskai included quite a bit of Hungarian
background.

The life, death, and prayers of the Virgin Mary are told in some detail in
the *Horvát Codex*. But not all the background of the narration has been
recorded by the thirteenth-century author David of Augsburg. Both the
language and some of the color have a Hungarian taste, which we must
attribute to Lea Ráskai.

The *Cornides Codex* is the most interesting from the viewpoint of the
narrator's thoughts. It contains fourteen sermons for the main feast days:
the sanctity of Mary and her visitation day, all saints' day, Christmas,
Easter, Ascension, Whit Sunday, Holy Trinity, Lord's Sunday, and others.
Their main source is the fifteenth-century anonymous collection of exhortations whose author called himself Paratus. In addition, it includes
eleven legends that for the most part came from the *Legenda Aurea*. From
the sermons and the lives of the saints, we get some of the symbolic origins
of the ecclesiastical sacraments, liturgy, ideology, and sanctifications. Even
more important, from this codex we get a feeling of Lea Ráskai's political
fears. She writes with sadness of the 1514 rebellion of the peasants; she
bemoans the unhappy consequences of the rule of the Jagellows in Hungary; and she trembles before the impending Turkish peril. We do not
know anything else of her despite the efforts of the learned people of Hungary to bring to the surface more information about her life.

After the battle of Mohács in 1526, the central part of Hungary was
occupied by the Turks. Lea Ráskai's activities came to an end. The
Dominican sisters first went to Nagyvárad, taking their codices along.
Around 1567 they wander to Nagyszombathely, and in 1615 one finds
them at Pozsony at the cloister of the Clarisse sisters. The last we hear of
them is in 1637, when only one Dominican sister was living.

The Royal Hungarian University Press printed the Margaret Codex,
The Legend of Blessed Margaret, in over two hundred pages.[2] It contains
six books but can be divided into four parts: her life, her miracles while
she was alive, miracles she performed after her death, and the list of nuns

at the monastery in her lifetime.

The Legend of Blessed Margaret tells the story of Margaret, daughter of King Béla IV and Queen Margaret, beginning with her birth in 1242. The country was threatened by the Tatars and the royal parents offered the not yet born child to God if He would allow the Hungarian nation to escape the armies of Batu, the Tatar leader. The queen delivered her child in the castle of Clissa in Dalmacia. As a small child, when Margaret could barely speak and certainly did not know the alphabet, they placed her in the monastery of the Dominican sisters at Veszprém, between the Danube and Vienna. Her governess, Olimpiádis, accompanied her. Ten years later, in 1252, the parents had her transferred to the monastery they built at Buda, on the island of the Danube known as Rabbit's Island, later called Margaret's Island.

Margaret was humble and obedient even as a small child. When someone dared to address her as the daughter of the king, she ran to Olimpiádis and complained to her. Once when her parents came to visit her, her clothes were soiled and torn, as if she was the lowest servant. This was because she chose always the most disparaging tasks in the cloister. Cleaning, sweeping with the broom, were no problems to her, and when she was finished with these dirty duties, she started to wash and weave the fibers. She did not behave like the king's daughter but like God's bride. Even her voice and laughter were not very loud but reminded one of submissiveness. The worst drudgeries, which the other sisters performed reluctantly, she executed willingly. For example, she emptied the water made filthy by handwashing out of the refectorium. When it was too heavy to carry out, she asked another sister, Csenge, the daughter of *ispán* Boldoldy,[3] for help. Once they were outside, not visible to the others, this sister hit Margaret with the water. She bore it patiently and said to her: "My dear relative, what are you doing?" On Good Thursday, she volunteered to wash the sisters' feet, wiping them dry with her veil and kissing them. The prioress, who allowed her to do this, was very happy to escape this function herself.

Not only did she help in the kitchen and served the sisters at their meals, but she also nursed the critically sick among the sisters and looked after the dying in the hospital that was adjacent to the community. Those who were ill felt much better if she came near them. Some even regained their health through her prayers. Those who died were not abandoned, as Margaret stayed near them until they were buried.

As she grew up, Margaret became a beautiful young woman. At age eighteen, the Czech king saw her and became enamored of her exquisite face, body, and spirit. Despite the fact that she grew up in a monastery, he asked to marry her. Her father was flattered and decided to ask the pope for an absolution from her vows. But Margaret was adamant. Despite the anger of her father, she requested through the Dominican provincial to call the primate from Esztergom and the bishops from Vác and Nyitra to consecrate her as a Dominican nun. The holy men did her bidding, and with three other nuns, they dressed her in the Dominican black habit in the presence of her brother and relatives on the third day after Whit Sunday at the altar of Saint Elizabeth.

The greatest worry to Margaret occurred when she heard that her brother turned against their father and engaged him in war. The virgin saint had herself beaten and tortured because this war was a terrible danger to the Hungarian nation. Her fellow sisters inquired in vain: "Why do you torment yourself for every story?" And it was of no avail. Margaret chose to live like God's pauper and martyr. Every day she arose before dawn and went to church to pray. And she did not miss the common prayers and songs with her fellow sisters. After working and asking for divine favor all day, she suffered at night by wearing the *cilicium*[4] and begged her fellow sisters to strike her flesh. She died in this manner, asking the provincial father, Michael, to hear her confession and to give her Christ's body and the last unction. Father Marcellus was also present at her bedside. After the last unction, she handed the prioress the keys to the box of her personal effects. There were two *cilicii* in it. One was ripped because of the frequent wearing, the other was quite new. There was also a belt made out of iron and a twig with which, together with a skin full of bristles of the hedgehog, she had beaten herself every night. There were also nails with which the two leg-wrappings[5] were driven into her legs. This way, after thirteen days of illness, Margaret died in the year 1271, in her twenty-ninth year.

Lea Ráskai also wrote a great deal about the miracles performed by Margaret. She cured people of their sickness, she gave beautiful dreams to friars who wanted to see paradise, and she helped people in their daily lives and with the governing of the kingdom. Of the nuns that lived in the monastery, Lea recorded only forty. Probably she had no time left to do more, as she had to flee from the island when the Turks advanced. But it is certain that all seventy nuns were of the aristocracy.

Lea Ráskai used primarily two narratives in writing *The Legend of Blessed Margaret.*[6] The first one was composed, according to most scholars, by John of Vercelli, the Dominican prior and professor at Paris University who traveled to Buda in 1273 to visit Margaret's monastery, just two years after her death. His main purpose was to gather a sufficient number of miracles performed by Margaret to expedite her canonization. He wrote her life in 1275 or early 1276. Unfortunately the manuscript was lost; scholars found only a brief Latin record of it in the Gömöry codex.[7] A German version of history in the fifteenth century by Jorg Valter is also extant in the Munich archives. This was all that was known about the manuscript until 1937 when Kornél Böle published the 1275–1276 legend of Margaret from a Bolognese codex of the fourteenth century and disputed John of Vercelli's authorship. Böle believed it was written by an old Hungarian Dominican monk, who was instrumental in saving the virgin's iron belt and twig. The opinion of Jorg Valter, who was the provincial of the Dominican female monastery of Vienna, however, was not discarded. The author of the original manuscript was probably the Dominican father, Marcellus, the confessor of Blessed Margaret. Wishing to have the same respect accorded to these stories by the papacy as he imparted to them, Marcellus handed them over to John, the prior of the Dominican order, who agreed for greater credibility to claim the writing as his own. On the basis of this manuscript, in 1490 Petrus Ranzanus, a Dominican bishop of Lucera and the ambassador of the pope in 1490 to the wedding of John Corvinus, also wrote a significant analysis.[8]

In addition to the manuscript of Marcellus, Lea Ráskai relied on the second hearing of the miracles of the maiden, which became the narrative of Garinus de Giaco, the head of the Dominicans, at Avignon in 1340. Lea transformed the two sources into her own Hungarian composition. As an additional source, some scholars are pointing to the anonymous Margaret legend that was written in Naples by a Franciscan in the service of Queen Mary, wife of Charles II of Anjou.[9] Mary's sister was Elizabeth, a nun in Margaret's monastery, from whom the queen could have gotten many of the stories about the female community. In the Viennese archives there is a fifteenth-century Italian work, *Specchio dell' anima semplice*, also composed by a spiritual Franciscan of Naples. I doubt, however, that Lea Ráskai could have been acquainted with it. Some of the heretical beliefs in it, which originated with the author, are attributed to Margaret. For example, that prayer, confession, and eucharist are immaterial after a person has become one with God are concepts that could not have entered Margaret's mind.

The sanctification of Margaret, even though expedited in 1306 by King Charles Robert and in the 1460s by King Matthias, was only accomplished by the bull of Pius XII, "Maxima inter munera," on November 19, 1943.

The translations that follow are from *Boldog Margit legendája* (Budapest, 1938). This book was published by the Kiralyi Magyar Egyetemi Nyomda and the foreword was by P. Kornél Böle, O.P. My translations are from pages 3–93 and are in modern English and do not attempt to preserve all grammatical phrases used in the Hungarian language of the time.

NOTES

1. The story of Lea Ráskai, the five codices which bear her name, and their sources are contained in János Horváth, *A magyar irodalmi müveltség kezdetei: Szent Istvántól Mohácsig*, pp. 219–27, 319–20. See also Piroska Szemző, "Ráskai Lea, a magyar középkor irónöje," *Katolikus szemle* 57 (1943): 108–13, and Damján Vargha, "Ráskai Lea irása a három lándzsárol," and "Csodatételek a Margit-legendájából," *Elet* 8 (July–December 1916): 396–99, 610–12, respectively. The last section of the manuscript, the nuns list, was composed at a later date, but remains unfinished because the nuns had to leave Buda, after the Turks defeated the Hungarians at Mohács in 1526.

2. *Boldog Margit legendája* (Budapest, 1938).

3. The Hungarian term *ispán* means the overseer of a county.

4. The *cilicium* is an underslip of rough thread worn for penance.

5. Leg-wrapping was an ancient practice to keep warm and protect the naked leg with a piece of linen or wool, which was wrapped around the leg, and usually worn in the shoe or the boot. *A magyar nyelv értelmezö szótára*, vol. 3 (Budapest, 1960), pp. 736–37.

6. Cyrill Horváth, *A Margit-legenda forrásai*. He published Johannes de Vercellis or frater Marcellus, *De vita et miraculis b. Margaritae virg. Belae IV regis Hung. filiae*, translated into German by Jorg Valter in Bibliotheca Monacensis Regia, ms. 750. See also Olga Vas, *A misztika hatása kódexirodalmunkra*, and Erzsébet Kozma, *A misztika és boldog Margit*.

7. About the Gömöry codex see Kálmán Timár, *Prémontrei kódexek*, p. 63.

8. János Horváth, *A magyar irodalmi müveltség kezdetei*, pp. 319–20.

9. Jacob Echard and Jacob Quetif, *Scriptores ordinis Praedicatorum*, vol. 1, pp. 619–20.

The Legend of Blessed Margaret

In this manner the queen left them in the monastery and she went away. Four days later, Olimpiádis put on the dress of the saintly order. At the time, saint lady Margaret could not express herself well. She had just begun to study the abc's and the Ave Maria, and after a short period, she managed to learn to sing it with the other little girls quite well.

The child, saint lady Margaret, took a crucifix into her hands and began asking her companions what it symbolized. Her companions replied that our Lord Jesus was killed in this manner for the sake of humanity. Hearing this, the saintly child cried. It was here that the saintly child, saint lady Margaret, put on the dress of the saintly order, with the utmost reverence according to the practice of the time, so that from her delicate childhood she should live according to the principles of the rule.

When this holy virgin was five years old, she saw that some of the sisters went about in their *cilicium*. She begged lady Olimpiádis, whom she called at all times mother, to give her a *cilicium;* Olimpiádis gave it to her but saint lady Margaret could not endure it. Growing taller quickly, she began to dress in stiffer dresses and gradually, for short periods, she would wear *cilicium* patches next to her bare flesh. Oh! what a great feat this is, that such a high noble offspring undertook to torture herself in this manner during her tender childhood!

Whenever saint lady Margaret was given an outer garment, it was of much better texture than that of her companions and she was ashamed to wear it. When she was forced to take the garment from the prioress because of the veneration accorded to her father and mother, saint lady Margaret went to the kitchen and washing the pots and pans and the rest of the dishes that were in the kitchen and sweeping the dust, she purposely darkened it. . . . When someone called saint lady Margaret the daughter of the king, with tears she went to lady Olimpiádis saying: "My sweet mother, they are being greatly offensive to me. They say that I am the daughter of the king."

Thus, when this holy virgin, saint lady Margaret, was already ten years old, she was taken from the cloister of Saint Catherina in Veszprém in the right reverend company of her parents and the preaching brothers and with the gathering of the good sisters who remained with her, and she was transported to the monastery that her parents built on the island of the Danube. The island was called Saint Mary's Island or Blessed Lady's Island; somewhat earlier it was said to be the Island of Rabbits. For the reverence of all powerful God and in the name and guardianship of God's Mother, the Blessed Virgin Mary, they built the monastery from the foundation, erected and completed it in every respect, and they endowed it with noble, royal gifts as was suitable for royal highnesses. . . .

The holy virgin was satisfied with little conversation. She was the lover of silence and never did she give herself over to loud laughter or ridicule. Under no circumstances did she allow herself to be praised; self-commendation and the words of compliments she despised altogether. This noble and holy virgin was kindled with the fire of God's love which intensified to the point that she prayed without stopping, with hardly any interference, concentrating on uninterrupted prayers from the first hours of the day until lunch in the convent. With such zeal she frequently watered with her tears the five wounds of the crucifix of our Lord Jesus Christ and kissed them with her mouth. In a similar fashion, she approached the image of the Holy Mother, venerating this also with great reverence. The saint crucifix was at all times on her or next to her and was adored by her, not only when awake but also when asleep. When she went to the refectory, she continuously genuflected in venerating most humbly the images of the saints. Elsewhere also, wherever the Lord Jesus, our Lady Mary and the rest of the saints' imagery were hanging, she revered them while genuflecting. Even though it may have been necessary to leave in a hurry, she did not abandon this reverence.

She was satisfied with the food of the community; she never ate away except if her mother or her aunts, the wives of the princes, came to the monastery. But this was infrequent and only because it was required of her. Many nights, the better part was spent in prayer and without sleeping in the company of one sister or two who were very pleased to converse with her. She asked her companions in a gentle tone that was not irritating to any of the sisters not to allow her to offend them in her prayers. Frequently her prayers were full of distasteful groaning of the heart, implorations, and hiccuping, as the sisters undoubtedly already knew from the manner in which she said the orations in an outwardly compelling but wonderful and mournful voice.

This virgin had great desire for fasting for the Beloved, and with great love, she attempted going nearly beyond the limits of her strength, trying to adhere to the most stringent hardships, sufferings, and fastings of the rule of the order. For this reason her body was emaciated. . . .

Good Thursday arriving she washed the feet of the sisters with great humility. There were seventy sisters at that time in the monastery. And she washed not only the sisters' feet but also the feet of the servants with great humility, piety, and sorrow. Genuflecting, she proceeded from one sister's feet to the next sister's feet, and she washed them and dried them with the veil from her head and kissed them; afterward she wore the same dress and veil. Saint lady Margaret asked the prioress' permission every year to wash their feet, so dedicated was saint lady Margaret to this function. And the prioress left it to her gladly.

After the supper of the Lord, following the washing of feet, this saint virgin did not go to bed but prayed with great piety and read the psalms standing on her feet in the choir. And at the midnight religious service and at other psalters she stood with the rest of the sisters and on Good Saturday continued in this position until the afternoon service. She did not eat, drink, or sleep on Good Friday; she did not say anything to any human being, marking the whole day with great devotion and mournful prayers, crying over the undeserved saintly death of Jesus. . . .

To the rest of the sisters she taught devoutness. One sister of excellent character was a choir singer, sister Catherina, the daughter of master András Várady. Quite frequently this sister asked the lady virgin to teach her how God should be worshiped, served, and implored. This holy virgin, saint lady Margaret, said to sister Catherina: "Offer your body and soul to the Lord God; your heart should always be with the Lord God so that death or whatever reason will be incapable of taking you from the love of God."

So very sweetly prayed this holy virgin at all times that no matter how cold it was and the rest of the sisters, after divine reverence, went to warm themselves, saint lady Margaret remained in the choir only in one garment or cape despite the great cold, so that she became blue all over as if she were dead. That was the way the sisters found her in the choir, in front of the saint altar of the Holy Cross. . . .

For having genuflected so much and so frequently bending her knees, the caps of her knees became swollen and calloused. Her mistress, the noble widow Olimpiádis, and the other sisters reported this with conviction, having looked at the knees while she was alive only secretly and after her death with great fondness. On account of her innocence and chastity, taking a bath or washing the legs above the ankles were entirely unknown to her. . . .

On one occasion when sister Sabina, daughter of master Donát, cooked crab for the dinner of the sisters, the pot of crabs caught on fire and sister Sabina did not dare to lift the pot from the ashes. When saint lady Margaret came to the kitchen and saw this sister did not dare to lift the pan, immediately saint lady Margaret thrust her hand in the midst of the flame and withdrew the pot from the middle of the ashes. But it did not burn either the hand or the thread of the dress of saint lady Margaret. . . .

During the holy virgin's turn for a week in the refectory, she swept the refectory and served everyone at the table with great affection and humility, not eating herself until the rest of the sisters rose from the table. When there was nothing further to serve the sisters for lunch, she went into the *capitulum* (the chamber where the sisters held meetings) and prayed until the sisters left the table. Saint lady Margaret ate at the second table with the servants, as a servant. At times this saint virgin carried out the water in which the sisters washed their hands, their wastewater. Oh my dear brothers, it is a miracle, that our hard heart does not split into two when we hear of the meekness of the holy virgin, especially when we reflect that we are nothing compared to her; but we cannot degrade ourselves nevertheless as the holy virgin has done. . . .

When this saint virgin swept the dormitory, she also swept and cleaned underneath the beds of the sisters. But my beloved brother, not only these things were done by this saint virgin. In addition, she cleaned quite often the place of personal necessity, which we call toilet, so much so that when this humble sister finished this chore, her dress was contaminated from excrement and was repulsive. Some of the sisters seeing her so terribly contaminated ran away from her. But the saint virgin did all this with great affection and meekness, so that everybody wondered about her; she did not appear the daughter of the king; she appeared a despicable person. My dear brother, this was the magnificent life of the Hungarian king's daughter. I beg you, think about it, if you saw her there, would you have left her doing all this? You should have seen her yourself!

When the ancient enemy, the devil from hell, saw that for the sake of divine mercy the holy virgin did these things and similar ones, he became jealous of the good deeds of the holy virgin and with his deceitfulness started a war against the holy virgin. At that time King Béla and his son István and the Czech king after great warfare made peace on the boundaries of Transylvania, where the Tatars caused much damage. For the sake of peace and friendship, the Czech king gave a present to King Béla, as friends do; King Béla together with the queen took the Czech king to the islands of the Danube and when they arrived to this island where the monastery of Our Blessed Lady was located, they wanted to see saint lady Margaret, their relative.

Upon seeing saint lady Margaret, the Czech king was immediately taken by her beauty. Although she wore an unpretentious garment, her virgin body was very attractive, but her real beauty was in her faith and humility. The Czech king became so captured by the beautiful saint lady Margaret, that he was willing to put himself and his country and all of his talent together with his country under King Béla's will and power to get saint lady Margaret as his wife.

Saint lady Margaret was eighteen years of age at this time. King Béla said to the Czech king that this was not possible, that he could not marry saint lady Margaret because from childhood on she was consecrated to the Lord God and gave her promise to the preaching order, pledging herself. But the Czech king said: "My previous wife was also a nun, a sister of the preaching order. I do not think anything of it." At this, the father of saint lady Margaret thought very much of the peace and of his livestock, that the danger of warfare would decrease, and of the excellent Czech help against the Tatars, whose return in this period was still very frightening. Convinced of his promises, King Béla said to the Czech king: "If my daughter Margaret permits this marriage and if I win the blessing of the pope, I will do what you are asking." . . .

. . . King Béla visited very often saint lady Margaret in regard to the wedding and gave her many talks attempting to bring his virgin daughter to this marriage. Saint lady Margaret with great reverence and firmness in her stand, as was appropriate toward her parents, but herself abhorring the wedding, answered this way: "Why do you tire yourselves for this detestable thing for so long? I want you to know with the firmness of my stand that my profession, my vow that I gave, the cleanliness of my virginity that you well know, I consecrated out of my heart and soul to our Lord God already in small infancy, and the cleanliness of my order I would not contradict or defile for the glory of this world and for my life and death."

. . . The queen called to her Father Marcellus, the provincial, and said to him: "Go my good father to my daughter Margaret, because the king wants to marry her, and get to know her will." Therefore the provincial went to saint lady Margaret at the request of the queen and saw lady

Margaret and gave the message of her mother, before the prioress, Olimpiádis, and the brother of saint lady Margaret, and asked her about her will. Then the blessed virgin, saint lady Margaret, answered thus and said to the provincial: "Certainly you know, my father, that I rather suffer the pain that I should be cursed, but I will not permit my parents in this matter and I will not go counter to my profession for any kind of reason." And at the same time the holy virgin said to the sisters, addressing the good Olimpiádis: "My parents disturb me so much with this marriage that I think that I will cut down my nose together with my lip." . . .

Saint lady Margaret wanted and begged that she be veiled with the holy veil and that she be given the black robe to wear for the sake of eliminating these harmful and shrill causes. For these reasons they called the reverend fathers and the excellent lords, the archbishop of Esztergom and the bishop of Vác and the bishop of Nyitra, for the dressing of saint lady Margaret in black. And the holy virgin, saint lady Margaret, together with three sisters, in the presence of her relatives and brother, with very great honor and great festivity, they dressed her in black and they sanctified in the presence of many monks and ecclesiastical personages, three days after Whit Sunday, in front of Saint Elizabeth's altar. . . .

. . . To her mistress, Olimpiádis, and some of the older sisters she told when she will die; it was already near when her flesh will be spoiled; and it happened so. When a sister died and saint lady Margaret was in the infirmary by her side, she said to her mistress: "My beloved mother, I will be the first after this sister who will die"; and it so happened. And she spoke of her death to her brothers: "My beloved brothers, I will die shortly, and I ask you to bury me in the choir, in front of the altar of the Holy Cross. If the choir is becoming too restricted for the sisters, then bury me in my place of prayer and do not be afraid that out of my body some kind of stench will rise; no stench will rise out of my body." Everything happened this way. She hardly lived twelve days when the innocent holy virgin got cold shivers. . . .

When this saintly virgin reached the thirteenth day of her illness, on a Saturday after the prayer in the evening was said in common, surrounded by the throng of the brothers and sisters in the year 1271 after the birth of Christ, in her twenty-ninth year, in the month of February on the fifteenth day, this excellent virgin was enflamed by the love her heavenly groom, whom she wished to see, whom she had served, whom she had loved above everybody else, for the love of whom she left her father, mother, and her worldly country's realm. She gave her blameless soul, her saintly, excellent soul to her Creator, her sweetest and most desirable Groom, and she rested in God. . . .

When the coffin was ready and after two or three months the masters took the raw stone from the tomb, wanting to place the red marble coffin in the tomb, they opened the tomb and from the coffin where saint lady Margaret was lying came such sweet smelling vapor, smoke, and smell as if many roses were placed there. The Lombard stone masons surely have testified to this. In this manner happened the funeral of this holy virgin saint lady Margaret, daughter of Béla, in the cathedral of the Blessed Lady before the altar of the Blessed Lady, on the island of the Blessed Lady which is known also as the Isle of the Rabbits, to the great reverence of our Lord God, to the gladness of the Holy Virgin Mary and showing the worthiness of saint lady Margaret.

Amen, Alleluia, Jesus, Maria!

BIBLIOGRAPHY

Primary Work

Boldog Margit legendája (The legend of Blessed Margaret). Budapest, 1938.

Related Works

Echard, Jacob, and Jacob Quétif. *Scriptores ordinis Praedicatorum.* Vol. 1. Lutetia (Paris), 1719.

Horváth, Cyrill. *A Margit-legenda forrásai* (The sources of the Margaret legend). Budapest, 1908.

Horváth, János. *A magyar irodalmi müveltseg kezdetei: Szent Istvántól Mohácsig* (The beginnings of Hungarian literary culture: from Saint Stephen to Mohács). A Magyar Szemle könyvei, IV. Budapest, 1944.

Kozma, Erzsébet. *A misztika és boldog Margit* (Mysticism and the Blessed Margaret). Vác, 1930.

Szemzö, Piroska. "Ráskai Lea, a magyar középkor irónöje" (Lea Ráskai, writer of the Hungarian Middle Ages). *Katolikus szemle* 57 (1943): 108–13.

Timár, Kálmán. *Prémontrei kódexek* (Manuscript of the Premonstratensians). Kalocsa, 1924.

Vargha, Damján. "Csodatételek a Margit-legendájából" (Miraculous acts from the Margaret legend). *Elet* 8 (July–December 1916): 610–12.

————. "Ráskai Lea irása a három lándzsárol" (The writing of Lea Ráskai about the three lances). *Elet* 8 (July–December 1916): 396–99.

Vas, Olga. *A misztika hatása kodexiródalmunkra* (The influence of mysticism on our manuscript literature). Budapest, 1937.

PART SEVEN

ngland

THE LEARNED WOMAN
IN TUDOR ENGLAND

 argaret More Roper

ELIZABETH MCCUTCHEON

In 1527 or early 1528 Hans Holbein the Younger made a drawing of his portrait of Sir Thomas More and his household. The portrait, probably commissioned by More himself, has disappeared, though later versions exist.[1] But—thanks to the pen and ink drawing, which More sent to Erasmus, his fellow humanist and longtime friend—we can still see Margaret Roper, then twenty-two years old. Of the ten figures in the group, she is the closest to the observer and the dominant figure on the right-hand side of the picture. Elegantly gowned, she is seated on the floor in the foreground of a handsomely paneled room. She holds an open book on her lap; another book lies nearby on the floor. Her younger sister, Cicely, is slightly behind her on one side; her stepmother, Alice More, is behind her on the other. Her father, Thomas More, sits magisterially in the center of the picture, with his father, John More, to his right, while his son (also John), his fool (Henry Patenson), his other daughter, Elizabeth, his foster daughter, Margaret Giggs, and a ward, Anne Cresacre, stand nearby.

Two strong visual images are established for Margaret, then: Margaret with books and Margaret with family. These images are proleptic. Already praised for her piety and learning at a time when such learning was extraordinary in a woman, Margaret Roper has continued to be admired for her erudition and loved for her devotion to her father.

The latter image—of devoted daughter—may not seem surprising. We often see Renaissance women through their fathers, their husbands, or their sons.[2] But father and daughter were so close, Sir Thomas More so famous, and his execution on Tower Hill in 1535 so tragic, that there is both a loss and a gain for the would-be biographer of Margaret Roper. On the one hand, there is a danger of losing sight of her or of seeing her only vis-à-vis her father.[3] On the other, we know much more about her than we otherwise would because of the biographies of More that were written before the end of the sixteenth century by people who were part of the family or knew people who were. On balance, the gain outweighs the loss. We would not have William Roper's life of his father-in-law, for example, which, as E. E. Reynolds points out, is a portrait of Margaret Roper, too (*Margaret Roper,* p. 132; cf. *Field,* p. 170). Nor would we know nearly so much about Margaret's education or her early writings without Thomas Stapleton's life, with its eight letters from More to his children for which it is the sole source. To read these letters is to reconstruct the story of Margaret's schooling and some part of the relationship between More and Margaret. For she was not only her father's favorite daughter but the person to whom he felt closest, and their correspondence and conversations illuminate aspects of self that we would not otherwise have.

Margaret was the oldest daughter and first child of Jane Colt More, who died in 1511, leaving four young children, and Thomas More. Margaret was born in 1505 and died in 1544, a few months after her thirty-ninth birthday.[4] She was well educated at home and soon became an exemplar of the new humanistic learning and of the learned woman. On July 2, 1521, when she was not quite sixteen, she married William Roper (1498?–1578).[5] The son of a wealthy landowner and lawyer, Roper, who followed his father as Clerk of the Pleas or Prothonotary, a lucrative office, had become a student at Lincoln's Inn in 1518, probably joining the large More household at about the same time. The Ropers continued to live with the Mores after their marriage, although William inherited considerable property after his father's death in 1524 and was successful in his suits for more. (Despite the simple image of self that Roper so successfully creates in the biography of his father-in-law, he was a litigious and sometimes headstrong man.)[6]

The Ropers' first child was born in 1523, an occasion that Erasmus commemorated by dedicating his commentary on Prudentius's Christmas and Epiphany hymns to Margaret. We do not know how many children Margaret gave birth to, but two sons and three daughters are known by name. The two sons, like their father, attended Lincoln's Inn and all the children were well educated. Margaret wanted Roger Ascham to teach Greek and Latin to her children (Reynolds, *Margaret Roper,* pp. 116–17), and Harpsfield tells how, when her husband was imprisoned in the Tower, officers of the king, sent to search her house, "founde her, not puling and lamenting, but full busily teaching her children" (p. 79).

The most famous of Margaret's children, Mary Clarke, later Basset, was a lady-in-waiting to Queen Mary and, like her mother, a woman of letters. John Morwen, Reader in Greek at Corpus Christi College, was her tutor (McConica, p. 267), and she presented her translation of Eusebius and other patristic historians to the then Princess Mary (Harpsfield, pp. 83, 334). But she is better known as the translator of More's *De Tristitia*, one of his Tower works. Rastell published her translation as *An Exposicion of a Parte of the Passion of Our Sauiour Iesus Christe* in his edition of More's works (1557). Of Mary Basset he writes: "The gentlewoman (who for her pastyme translated it) is no nerer to hym in kynred, vertue and litterature, than in hys englishe tongue: so that it myghte seme to haue been by hys own pen indyted fyrst, and not at all translated: suche a gyft hath she to folowe her graundfathers vayne in wryting" (More, *De Tristitia*, part 2, p. 1078). She had her mother's vein in writing, too.

Two aspects of Margaret Roper's life are extensively, if not fully, documented: her education and her relationship with her father, especially while he was under arrest (from 1534 until his execution on July 6, 1535) because of his opposition to the king and his refusal to swear to the oath that became associated with the Act of Succession. Margaret was the stellar pupil in what is sometimes called the "school of More": a group that included More's four children, his wards, foster daughter, and step-daughter, other relatives, husbands and wives of the pupils, and friends.[7] The tutors included John Clement, later an eminent physician, William Gonell, a Master Drew, Richard Hyrde, and Nicholas Kratzer, who became astronomer to King Henry VIII in 1519. More himself oversaw the children's education and is eloquent on the subject of what they should study and why. Roper cites as a commonplace his exhortation to "take virtue and learning for their meat, and play for their sauce" (*Two Lives*, p. 199). And the letter that More wrote to Gonell (1518?), in which he speaks of Gonell's estimation of "Margaret's lofty and exalted character of mind [which] should not be debased" (*Selected Letters*, p. 104), is a major statement about education for women in Renaissance England. In characteristically Christian humanist fashion, More joins "moral probity" with learning, later defining his goals as "piety towards God, charity to all, and modesty and Christian humility in themselves" (*Selected Letters*, p. 105). With respect to learning in women, he adds:

> Since erudition in women is a new thing and a reproach to the sloth of men, many will gladly assail it, and impute to learning what is really the fault of nature, thinking from the vices of the learned to get their own ignorance esteemed as virtue. On the other hand, if a woman (and this I desire and hope with you as their teacher for all my daughters) to eminent virtue of mind should add even moderate skill in learning, I think she will gain more real good than if she obtain the riches of Croesus and the beauty of Helen. Not because that learning will be a glory to her, though learning will accompany virtue as a shadow does a body, but because the reward of

wisdom is too solid to be lost with riches or to perish with beauty, since it depends on the inner knowledge of what is right. (*Selected Letters,* pp. 103–4)

Later in this same letter More addresses the question of woman's capacity to learn even more specifically:

> Nor do I think that the harvest is much affected whether it is a man or a woman who does the sowing. They *both* have the name of human being whose nature reason differentiates from that of beasts; *both,* I say, are *equally suited* for the knowledge of learning by which reason is cultivated, and, like plowed land, germinates a crop when the seeds of good precepts have been sown. But if the soil of a woman be naturally bad, and apter to bear fern than grain, by which saying many keep women from study, I think, on the contrary, that a woman's wit is the more diligently to be cultivated, so that nature's defect may be redressed by industry. (*Selected Letters,* p. 105; italics mine)

Taking into account one opinion of women's intellectual potential and their human nature, More answers misogynist objections by emphasizing the importance of their nurture. But he himself here seems to view the two sexes as equal in their native rational capacity and in their ability to learn and to exercise what he would have thought of as "right reason"—at once an intellectual and ethical operation of the mind.[8]

The actual curriculum that More oversaw was a rigorous one, grounded in a mastery of Latin and Greek and embracing the liberal and humane arts—grammar, rhetoric, poetry, logic, mathematics, philosophy, and astronomy—as well as theology and medicine. He encouraged a system of double translation, anticipating later Renaissance humanist educators. He put this to particularly apt, if ironic, use when one of his daughters translated the Latin letter he had written to Oxford University in 1518, defending Greek and liberal learning in general from an attack by a barbarous preacher, and another daughter turned it back into Latin (Stapleton, p. 92). The letter More's daughters translated is especially important because it defends a program of humanistic education that is very close to one they themselves were then following. In it, More states the case for the study of the "laws of human nature and conduct," best learned "from the poets, orators, and historians" (*Selected Letters,* p. 99), and of Greek, essential for reading and understanding Holy Scripture and the church fathers. More also encouraged dialogue, disputations, and declamations—and the energy and activity of the mind they stimulated. Arguing (as Vives paraphrases him) that "the art of writing might be disclosed more openly by contradiction, and, as it were, by conflict" (cited in Watson, p. 17), More introduced his children to Quintilian's declamations. And at some point Margaret and one of her sisters "disputed of philosophy" before King Henry VIII (Coke, in Gibson, p. 190).

The "school" was pious as well as learned, reflecting More's own deep commitment to Catholic doctrine and practice and the temper of early Tudor England. With the rest of the household they would have observed the seasonal round of the liturgical calendar. There were daily prayers (both morning and evening), and at meals one of the children read a passage from the Bible that the family subsequently discussed. They would have attended mass on Sundays and holy days, and Erasmus, writing in 1521 to the great French humanist, Budé, tells how carefully More's daughters listened to and evaluated the sermons they heard (*Letters,* 4:579). But we should be wary of drawing too somber a picture of this "school," which would have included dramatic performances; music; games; jokes and jests of the sort that surface in the stories Walter Smyth (Thomas More's personal servant) tells about the widow Edith, a sixteenth-century con artist; and observations of the heavens and of More's aviary and menagerie (a mischievous monkey is part of the Holbein sketch). And the "school" would have metamorphosed over the years, reflecting the development of the household and increasing maturity of the children. In 1521 More writes Margaret, urging her to continue to find time for "humane letters" and "liberal studies," acknowledging her wish "to give yourself diligently to philosophy," and hoping that she will "devote the rest of your life to medical science and sacred literature, so that you may be well furnished for the whole scope of human life, (which is to have a sound mind in a sound body)" (*Selected Letters,* pp. 148–49). She and her husband continued their studies together after they were married—anticipating later sixteenth-century couples like the Lumleys and Anne Cooke Bacon and her husband, Sir Nicholas Bacon.

By 1524 More's "school" was already well known among humanist circles in Europe. In part, this reflects the "public relations" side of humanism, quick to promote its own cause. More important, it shows how More's practice encouraged the recognition of woman's intellectual and ethical potential and gave the lie to the old idea that learning would corrupt a woman. More's daughters, in general, and Margaret, in particular, became exemplars of learning and virtue for other humanists, notably Vives and Erasmus. In 1523 the former singled them out for special praise in his *Instruction of a Christian Woman* (Watson, p. 53). Two years earlier Erasmus had complimented them in his letter to Budé, commenting on the style and substance of their Latin letters and remarking that their education had convinced him of the value of education for women (*Letters,* 4:578–79). Still more telling, however, is Erasmus's lively colloquy (first printed in 1524) between the abbot and the learned woman, probably based upon Margaret Roper (*Colloquies,* p. 218). There is a massive reversal of roles here. Antronius, "synonymous with 'ass' " (p. 217), is an ignorant, stupid, superstitious monk who boasts that, "You won't find a single book in my cell" (p. 221), and is appalled to discover the young Magdalia surrounded with books in Greek and Latin. Magdalia, as vivacious as she is intelligent, learned, and pious, is a keen disputant with a lively sense of humor; she has no trouble refuting the abbot's notion that "learning doesn't fit a woman" (p. 222). Among other things she argues for true pleasures, those of the mind, and, with a touch of self-reflexive wit, singles out the "More girls" in England and the Pirckheimers and Blauers in Germany (p. 223).

Erasmus's colloquy also illuminates social roles that are implicit in the humanists' idea of a humane education for women. For though Magdalia half-jokingly warns the abbot that, "If you're not careful, the net result will be that we'll preside in the theological schools, preach in the churches, and wear your miters" (p. 223), she herself speaks as a wife and mother. And she counters the abbot's argument that the distaff and spindle are women's proper tools with the rejoinder that "a wife's business [is] to manage the household and rear the children" (p. 221)—an important job she can hardly do well without wisdom. In practice, then, the humanists thought of woman's social sphere in the context of home and family. Since they were so concerned with good nurture and saw the family as the basis of society, they exalted this sphere, from one point of view. But they also viewed it paternalistically.[9]

The Holbein painting of the More household and More's relationship with Margaret, and hers with him, are a case in point, although their personal relationship came to have major political implications when More was imprisoned. We can never hope to recover the evidence of all that Margaret meant to More. But there is the comment he made after she recovered from the sweating sickness, probably in 1528: "If it had pleased God at that time to have taken [her] to His mercy . . . he would never have meddled with worldly matters after" (*Two Lives,* p. 213). And one of his last requests is that "my daughter Margaret may be at my burial" (*Two Lives,* p. 253). The earliest record comes from a charming Latin poem More wrote to Margaret and his other children. Recollecting their early years, he tells them how he "regularly fed you cake and gave you ripe apples and fancy pears." He gave them "silken garments," too, and "never could endure to hear you cry" (*Latin Poems,* p. 281). Characteristically, he adds that although he has always loved them intensely, he loves them more now because of their "genuine learning" and the "grace and eloquence" of their speech.

This is a recurrent theme in More's letters to Margaret, "whom virtue and learning have made so dear to my heart" (*Selected Letters,* p. 110).

Two letters from the early 1520s enlarge our view of the proud father and Margaret's learning (though we need to allow for More's hyperboles). In the first, he tells Margaret how impressed the bishop of Exeter was by one of her letters, which he admired "for its pure Latinity, its correctness, its erudition, and its expressions of tender affection" (*Selected Letters*, p. 152). He was equally impressed by her other writings (which More just happened to have with him) and sent a gold coin as a token of his goodwill. In the second letter More explains how dazzled the young Reginald Pole was by her "most charming letter," finding it "nothing short of marvelous" (*Selected Letters*, p. 154).[10]

Margaret's learning was itself an expression of daughterly affection, although it was much more than that. Margaret also became an agent for her father's piety and religious practices. Stapleton tells how More "hired a house" in Chelsea where he supported "many who were infirm, poor, or old," whom Margaret looked after "in her father's absence" (p. 67). She was also privy to her father's private devotional life and his penitential practices, and washed his shirt of hair, which he sent her the day before his execution (Roper, *Two Lives*, p. 252; cf. Stapleton, pp. 69–70). More tried to keep the hair shirt a secret from the rest of the family (although his wife, the down-to-earth Alice, begged More's confessor to urge him to put it away [Roper, *Lyfe*, p. 125]). Roper tells how, one summer day, the young Anne Cresacre saw More in his doublet, hose, and a plain shirt, without ruff or collar. Catching sight of the hair shirt beneath, she "began to laugh at it" (*Two Lives*, p. 224). Margaret alerted More, her gesture revealing both her sensitivity to the nuances of a social situation and her concern for her father.

But such things, while important, fade into insignificance in comparison with More's prison years. Roper records some of his wife's visits to her father. Prayer (the seven psalms and the litany) was followed by conversations that included such worldly business as how the queen (Anne Boleyn) did, the new statutes, "the oath confirming the Supremacy and matrimony," and the unlawfulness of More's imprisonment (*Two Lives*, p. 240). Margaret was with her father when monks from the Charterhouse were led from the Tower to their execution on May 4, 1535. Standing together at the window, they would have seen five priests, one a good friend of More's, tied down to hurdles. Reynolds surmises that the king or Cromwell allowed this visit in hopes of shaking More's resolve through Margaret (*Margaret Roper*, pp. 101–2). We can guess at their feelings and the pressures on them through More's conversation, as Roper records it: "Lo, dost thou not see, Meg, that these blessed fathers be now as cheerfully going to their deaths as bridegrooms to their marriage? Wherefore thereby mayst thou see, mine own good daughter, what a great difference there is between such as have in effect spent all their days in a strait, hard, penitential, and painful life religiously, and such as have in the world, like worldly wretches, as thy poor father hath done, consumed all their time in pleasure and ease licentiously" (*Two Lives,* p. 242). More's self-characterization is patently untrue. But he was passionately committed to the idea behind it—that this life is a testing ground for the world to come—and he had been attracted to a monastic life. So he told Meg, when first she visited him in the Tower, that "God maketh me a wanton, and setteth me on His lap and dandleth me" (*Two Lives,* p. 239).

In a letter that he wrote from the Tower in 1534 "To All My Loving Friends," More made his "well-beloved daughter" his personal representative, saying that anything she asked of them on his behalf should be regarded as if "I moved it unto you and required it of you personally present myself" (*Selected Letters,* p. 227). This does not mean that Margaret alone had access to him the whole time that he was in prison; More was visited by his wife and others and he was attended by his own servant, John a Wood, and by Margaret's. But Margaret first obtained license from the king to see him and their correspondence was both a personal and a political act. Cresacre More adds that she "meant to put her father's works in print" (p. 183).

This makes it virtually impossible to interpret the motives behind a "lamentable letter" in which Margaret urged her father to swear to the oath promising obedience to the Act of Succession and other acts of Parliament.[11] Her letter is not extant, but in May? 1534, More answered it. Reminding her that he cannot swear to the oath without violating his conscience, he begs her "to leave off such labor" and hold herself "content" with his "former answers" (*Selected Letters,* pp. 224–25). Rastell claims that Margaret's letter was just a ruse, to "win thereby credence with Master Thomas Cromwell" and get access to her father (*Selected Letters,* p. 224). Stapleton is of two minds. At one point he agrees with Rastell, arguing that "no one understood and sympathized with her father's mind more fully than she" and that she "expected that as usual her letter would be intercepted and examined by the King's Council" (p. 104). Elsewhere he says he is unsure of her "true sentiments" but that More was deeply grieved (pp. 148–49; cf. Reynolds, *Margaret Roper,* pp. 68–70). Roper (followed by Harpsfield) says only: "Now when he had remained in the Tower a little more than a month, my wife, longing to see her father, by her earnest suit at length got leave to go to him" (*Two Lives,* p. 239). Thomas More's most recent biographer, Richard Marius, comments that we "cannot know" if Rastell was right, but that Margaret "adored her father; she most certainly wanted him to live; she probably would have been relieved for many reasons had he followed her example" (p. 465). (Like almost everyone in England, she did accept the oath.)[12]

In any case, their correspondence allowed More to record his point of view, writing ostensibly, and from one perspective genuinely, in personal terms. He reports events, conversations, interrogations, and attempts at intimidation that amount to a sixteenth-century equivalent of brainwashing, setting down his recollections in scrupulous detail and making his own stand as clear as he can without giving his reasons for refusing to swear to the oath. Three long letters to Margaret are particularly important, recording an early interrogation at Lambeth and two interrogations in the spring of 1535. Another letter, answering hers on the cause of his "close keeping" (see below), includes parts of an ominous conversation with Thomas Cromwell and a warning of sudden searches "that may hap to be made in every house of ours as narrowly as is possible," since "some folk" think "that I was not so poor as it appeared in the search" (*Selected Letters*, p. 235).

He must have hoped that Margaret would save these letters and that eventually they would be published or otherwise circulated. As Marius puts it, they "do not seem to be letters of comfort; they seem rather like efforts to get his own view of these conversations before the world—or at least before his family circle—as clearly as he could, and we may suppose that they were copied and passed around in a sort of sixteenth-century *samizdat*" (p. 503). Certainly the government had its suspicions about Margaret's role, then and later. On June 14, 1535, More was questioned by members of the council about his letters to Margaret. He explained that he wrote out of worry that his daughter, "being (as he thought) with child, should take some harm" when she heard that the council had interrogated him. Stressing his obedience, he added that she "had written to him before divers letters, to exhort him and advertise him to accommodate himself to the king's pleasure" (*State Papers*, as cited in Reynolds, *Margaret Roper*, p. 103). Reynolds guesses that More wanted to protect Margaret, who "might get into trouble for writing more frequently than Cromwell permitted," and points out that "an even closer watch was kept to prevent further communications" (*Margaret Roper*, p. 103).

Stapleton tells how, after More's death, Margaret "was brought before the King's Council, and charged with keeping her father's head as a sacred relic, and retaining possession of his books and writings. She answered that she had saved her father's head from being devoured by the fishes, with the intention of burying it: that she had hardly any books and papers but what had been already published, except a very few *personal letters,* which she humbly begged to be allowed to keep for her own consolation" (p. 193; italics mine). Unfortunately, Margaret's bold answer cannot be otherwise substantiated, as there is no official account of the council proceedings for this period (Reynolds, in Stapleton, p. 193). But in 1538 Sir Geoffrey Pole, the younger brother of Reginald (Cardinal) Pole, was imprisoned and interrogated. He was asked, among other things, how often within the last twelve months or two years he had been in company with Mrs. Roper and Margaret Giggs Clement, where they had met, what they had talked about, and "What communication you have had with either of them touching the death of Sir Thos. More and others, and the causes of the same?" (*Letters and Papers,* p. 267).

Margaret's "daughterly dealings" had obvious political implications, then, during More's Tower years and afterward, although we could not guess this by what she wrote to her father. But there is the letter to Alice Alington (see below), and Roper's life of More records political conversations before and during More's imprisonment. Thus we hear Margaret relaying Roper's message that More "was put out of the Parliament bill," and her father's grim response that what is postponed is not withdrawn ("Quod differtur non aufertur," *Two Lives,* p. 237).

Their letters also give glimpses of the relationship between them, her love for her father, and her fear for his life. Writing to Margaret in 1534, More several times cites what he calls her "daughterly loving letter" (no longer extant) and tries to comfort and strengthen her. He reminds her of their heavenly home and repeats her words to him: "But good father, I wretch am far, far, farthest of all other from such point of perfection, our Lord send me the grace to amend my life, and continually to have an eye to mine end, without grudge [fear] of death, which to them that die in God, is the gate of a wealthy life to which God of his infinite mercy bring us all. Amen. Good Father strenght [strengthen] my frailty with your devout prayers" (*Selected Letters,* p. 240). The crucial word is "frailty," and More acknowledges his own frailty even as he urges her to "depend and hang upon the hope and strength of God" (p. 241). He adds, "Surely Megge a fainter heart than thy frail father hath, canst you not have. And yet I verily trust in the great mercy of God, that he shall of his goodness so stay me with his holy hand that he shall not finally suffer me to fall wretchedly from his favor. And the like trust (dear daughter) in his high goodness I verily conceive of you" (p. 241).

More's last known letter is to Margaret. Writing "with a coal" the day before his execution, he tells her: "I cumber [trouble] you good Margaret much, but I would be sorry, if it should be any longer than tomorrow, for it is Saint Thomas even, and the utas [octave] of Saint Peter and therefore tomorrow long I to go to God. . . . I never liked your manner toward me better than when you kissed me last for I love when daughterly love and dear charity hath no leisure to look to worldly courtesy" (*Selected Letters,* p. 257). This letter takes us back to Roper's biography, with its poignant evocation of Margaret's final farewell to her father, following his arraignment at Westminster. She waited for him near Tower wharf to seek his blessing. Then she broke through the guard surrounding him, ran to him, and embraced him, not once but twice, "and divers times together most lovingly kissed him—and at last, with a full heavy heart, was fain to depart from him" (*Two Lives,* pp. 251–52).

This scene, and the relationship it dramatizes—created through a triple bond of Christian charity, natural love, and "very daughterly dealing" (*Selected Letters,* pp. 240–41)[13]—has frequently shaped our sense of Margaret Roper. From the sixteenth century on, in fact, she has been far better known for the roles she fulfilled than as a writer. The *Paris News Letter,* an account of More's trial and death that quickly circulated on the Continent, includes Margaret's farewell to her father (Harpsfield, p. 265). And Harpsfield says much about her as "the excellent, learned and vertuous matrone" (p. 5), the "so good, so debonaire, and so gentle a wife" (p. 80), and the "good, loving and tender daughter" (p. 199). Stapleton writes more specifically still: "More than all the rest of his [More's] children, she resembled her father, as well in stature, appearance, and voice, as in mind and in general character" (p. 103). Catching the imagination and sympathy of artists and writers alike, she has subsequently appeared in plays, fiction, and poems. She is, for example, one of the tragic heroines in Tennyson's "Dream of Fair Women," imagined as one "who clasped in her last trance / Her murdered father's head" (p. 452). The Victorians also admired her as a good woman and were enthralled by *The Household of Sir Thomas More,* a diary, purportedly by Margaret Roper, that Anne Manning wrote (Marc'hadour, "Anne Manning"). In Robert Bolt's popular play, *A Man for All Seasons,* she is "a beautiful girl of ardent moral fineness" who "both suffers and shelters behind a reserved stillness which it is her father's care to mitigate" (p. xxi). Most recently she has been turned into the feminist and ahistorical heroine of Paula Vogel's *Meg* (Murphy, pp. 113–16).

To further complicate our view of Margaret Roper as writer, many of her works are lost, and we know about them through incidental references in her father's letters or through Stapleton, of More's early biographers the most interested in Margaret's learning. Many, perhaps most, of these lost works (other than the many letters no longer extant) were apprentice pieces. Stapleton speaks of prose and verse written in Greek and Latin and praises two Latin speeches, "written as an exercise" (p. 103), along with another speech, first written in English and subsequently translated into Latin by both father and daughter. He himself had one of these speeches—written in response to a declamation, attributed to Quintilian, about the poor man's bees, killed by poison sprinkled on flowers in the rich man's garden. "Quintilian" defended "the cause of the poor man: Margaret of the rich," which, Stapleton points out, was the more difficult position to take and gave "greater scope for Margaret's eloquence and wit" (p. 107). She also emended a corrupt passage in Saint Cyprian, and thus acquired a small but secure place in sixteenth-century scholarship.

And she and her father wrote, in friendly competition, on the subject of the four last things (death, judgment, hell, and heaven), probably in 1522, though only her father's treatment, unfinished, has survived.

In 1523 her father could still address her as one who expected an audience of two: her husband and her father. In this letter, written just before her first child was born, More treats her, however, as more than an apprentice. He comments that men would never believe "that you had not often availed yourself of another's help: whereas of all the writers you least deserved to be thus suspected. Even when a tiny child you could never endure to be decked out in another's finery." And he adds, "But, my sweetest Margaret, you are all the more deserving of praise on this account. Although you cannot hope for an adequate reward for your labor, yet nevertheless you continue to unite to your singular love of virtue the pursuit of literature and art. Content with the profit and pleasure of your conscience, in your modesty you do not seek for the praise of the public, nor value it overmuch even if you receive it, but because of the great love you bear us, you regard us—your husband and myself—as a sufficiently large circle of readers for all that you write" (*Selected Letters*, p. 155).

Obviously such a notion was rethought before Margaret Roper's translation of Erasmus's commentary on the Lord's Prayer, *Precatio Dominica* (1523), appeared in print: the first edition is lost, but it almost certainly appeared in 1524.[14] Since Margaret Roper is not named, her modesty was, in some sense, preserved. Yet a small circle of readers would have known who the translator was. And the dedicatory letter by Richard Hyrde, a family tutor, to Frances Staverton, More's niece and Margaret's cousin, gives further hints as to the identity of the "yong vertuous and well lerned gentylwoman of .xix. yere of age," described on the title page.[15]

Notwithstanding the modesty (or apparent modesty) of its presentation, Margaret Roper's translation of Erasmus's *Precatio Dominica* is a major work. To begin with, it is one of the earliest examples of the Englishing of Erasmian piety. And it was a popular one; by the early 1530s there were three editions, from which only three copies have survived. "Breaking new ground" as part of what McConica calls a "broader campaign directed at the English-reading public" (p. 67), it domesticates and disseminates Erasmus's view of the devotional life.[16] For Erasmus, the Lord's Prayer was a model for all prayer, and petition (asking for help from God), its fundamental form. His paraphrases of the Lord's Prayer were designed to bring about "a change of inner attitudes, the raising of one's sight from immediate, selfish desires to a more noble and exalted concern for the common welfare of all of God's sons," to appropriate Snyder's characterization of Erasmus's basic notion of prayer (p. 26) to this devout treatise.

Margaret Roper's translation is also a fine example of early Tudor English prose; Hyrde's point about her skill in "expressing lively the Latin" is well taken. Like other Tudor translations, hers is longer than the original. In part, this reflects the difference between English and Latin, but she also likes doublets, used primarily for emphasis (though she is also conscious of rhythm). Unity and concord, or servants and bondmen, or head and ruler, or verity and truth, replace a single noun. But she avoids recondite words, and her syntax is natural and cumulative. While she is clearly aware of Erasmus's elegant parallelism, she often softens it, achieving an easier and more expansive English rhythm. Amplification reveals a perceptive eye for Tudor life: Erasmus's *ambitio* becomes "ambitious desire of worldly promotion" (*Moreana* 7 [1965]: 14, 15, modernized). And at least twice she slightly expands a potentially dramatic scene involving a relationship between God and man.

Taking a historical perspective, Gee sees the Roper piece as a remarkable instance of an interim stage in the development of modern English. He calls special attention to the significance of translation to and from the Latin as the More "school" practiced it, suggesting that skill in writing *English* was an unintentional but real result ("Margaret Roper's English Version," pp. 264–71). From a broader perspective, M. C. Bradbrook points to the "absolutely central role" translation had in the Renaissance and its real "service to the language" (p. 90), a point of particular importance since so many women in the Renaissance made translations.

Finally, this devout treatise is almost unprecedented as a work written and published by a woman in Renaissance England. A very few works by women had appeared in print before 1524, but these were either published posthumously or were associated with royalty: Margaret Beaufort is a case in point. By contrast, Margaret Roper was still a very young woman, she was unknown to the world at large, and her connections were with neither the court nor the Church but with the new humanistic movement, through her father and Erasmus.[17] This little book ultimately makes a large claim, then, as concrete proof of the fruit of the new learning for women. The claim is visualized for its readers in the woodcut from the first known edition, which shows a woman at her desk, turning the pages of an open book in a book lined room (Hodnett, p. 397; *Moreana* 9 [1966]: 65). It is made even more emphatically by Hyrde's prefatory letter. Hyrde was deeply interested in the question of woman's education and translated Vives's *Instruction of a Christian Woman* sometime before his death in 1528. Here he argues the case for the learned woman in what Foster Watson calls "the first reasoned claim of the Renascence period, written in English, for the higher education of women" (p. 14). More's letter to Gonell (1518, discussed above) is intellectually more sophisticated; where More is concise and philosophical, Hyrde is diffuse and pragmatic. And the values he articulates are more domestic, his idea of the connection between learning and the moral life simpler, than More's. Hyrde is, so to speak, domesticating humanism for an English-reading public. The point remains, though; Margaret's translation (with its preface by Hyrde) can be seen as a prototype of the piety associated with learned women throughout the sixteenth century.

Obviously such piety could become a way to refute charges that learning would corrupt a woman—a point that much exercises Hyrde in his prefatory letter to the young Frances Staverton. We know nothing about the actual circumstances surrounding Margaret Roper's translation of Erasmus's treatise, however. It may be, as DeMolen suggests, that she was returning the honor Erasmus had paid her the year before, when he dedicated his commentary on Prudentius to her (p. 93). She would have been interested in his paraphrase of the Lord's Prayer in any case, given her own piety. And its concern for Christian faith and practice day by day makes it singularly appropriate for her. In particular it allowed her to reflect upon a relationship between child and father (here a heavenly one). The most striking aspect of her Englishing, in fact, is how she heightened this relationship: by the position of vocatives, by an increased number of "father's" or "good father's" (where Erasmus has nothing or only "pater"), by a more personal rendering of salvation—his "denique et uitam conferet aeternam" becomes "finally bring *us* to everlasting life" (*Moreana* 7 [1965]: 46, 47, modernized; italics mine), and by a more intimate address. Erasmus's work is already meditative and conversational; Margaret Roper makes it more so. Here is Erasmus: "Quis enim ferat esse mundi ludibrium, relegari, protrudi in carcerem, uinciri, damnari, torqueri, exui facultatibus, spoliari uxore charissima ac dulcissimis liberis: denique crudeli morte perimi, nisi fuerit tuo coelesti pane subinde confirmatus." And here is Margaret Roper: "For who, Father, might abide to be had in derision of the world, to be outlawed and banished, to be put in prison, to be fettered and manacled, to be spoiled of all his goods, and by strong hand be deprived of the company of his most dear wife and well-beloved children, but if now and then he were heartened with thy heavenly and ghostly bread?" (pp. 48, 49, modernized).[18]

Less than ten years later, Thomas More was himself in prison, in danger of death. The correspondence between Margaret Roper and her father has already been discussed. But one other letter, to her stepsister, Alice Alington, needs to be treated here.[19] It is an answer to Lady Alington, who wrote Margaret about her fruitless attempt to obtain the goodwill of Sir Thomas Audley, then lord chancellor, in More's case. It is also an apologetic for More's refusal to swear to the oath (McConica, p. 467). And it is a portrait of More, Margaret, and the relationship between them.

The letter begins by recounting Margaret's latest visit to her father, but it soon becomes a dialogue between them. Margaret, half-teasingly cast as Eve, asks a series of increasingly painful questions about her father's position. She plays her part well, as More himself observes (*Correspondence*, p. 524). But she is finally no Eve, and her questions allow her father to clarify the tragic gap between his conscience and the cost, in human terms, of obeying it. She starts with a point raised by Lady Alington's letter: unless More changes his mind, he can count on no support from friends in high places. More does not so much answer this question as subsume it: what is at stake is his conscience and his relationship with God. Margaret presses harder: what if what he calls conscience is just a "right simple scruple" (p. 516), as Audley said. After all, almost everyone else in England—including many wise and learned men—have sworn to the oath. Finally, she voices the fears weighing upon them. Her father may well be "in merueilous heavy trouble" (p. 529) or change his mind when it is too late: "It is not lyke to thinke upon a thinge that may be, and to see a thinge that shall be" (p. 530).

For More, such a change would be failure, a sign of fear and loss of faith.[20] And his final answer is at once defiant (despite its humility) and transcendental: all is in the hands of God. When we last see Margaret, she sits "very sadde," her heart "full heavye for the peryll of his person" (p. 529). But she has no fears for the well-being of his soul. In fact, there is a studied ambiguity throughout much of the letter about her own position—she frequently reports other people's opinions. Moreover, she accepts her father's basic principle: he should do nothing that would imperil his soul (although she would have him save his life, if he could). Thus her role as Eve is transformed; instead of bringing the apple to Adam, and with it death and separation from God, Margaret seeks to save her father from death—but not at the cost of eternal life. In other ways, too, her role is a complex one. It probably does reflect her hope that More could, in good conscience, sign the oath (see the beginning of this letter, where he alludes to earlier conversations between them). It also reflects a shared love of dialectic; Margaret's position allows her father to clarify conflicting claims of obligation, love, and conscience. From a temporal perspective it protects her. In addition, Margaret must have represented a real temptation for More—not so much in what she reported but in who she was, the daughter he loved so dearly. Finally, Margaret's questions are acutely thought and felt. By asking them she humanizes More; when he talks to her, we hear the human being behind the presence.

When this letter (or dialogue) was first printed, in 1557, the headnote pointed out that "it is not certainely knowen" whether Margaret wrote this letter or whether More wrote it in her name (*Correspondence*, p. 514). In some sense it must have been what Marius calls a "joint effort, something that she and her father carefully worked out together" (p. 467). Margaret's questions allowed her father to articulate his stand in the name of conscience, while her presence made palpable their love for each other. As so often for Margaret Roper, what she wrote about, the role she played, and the life she lived met in her relationship with her father.

NOTES

1. Reproduced in J. B. Trapp and Hubertus Schulte Herbrüggen, *"The King's Good Servant": Sir Thomas More,* p. 84; discussed, pp. 85–86; cf. Parker, pp. 16–21. For a miniature of Margaret Roper, aged thirty, see Trapp and Herbrüggen, pp. 87–89.

2. See Minna F. Weinstein, "Reconstructing Our Past: Reflections on Tudor Women," pp. 133–35, with its illustration by way of Margaret Roper.

3. E. E. Reynolds, *Margaret Roper: Eldest Daughter of St. Thomas More,* p. ix, addresses this problem. In addition, those who wrote about Margaret Roper in the sixteenth century were so concerned to defend her virtue (and the virtue of the learned woman, in general) that much that would individualize her or make her more accessible has been irretrievably lost. A third problem is the loss of so much of what she wrote.

4. My sources for the discussion of her life which follows include: Harpsfield, Cresacre More, Ro. Ba., Roper, and Stapleton; More and Margaret's correspondence; Marius, Reynolds's *Margaret Roper,* and Routh.

5. For William Roper's life, I have depended upon Harpsfield, Marius, Reynolds's *Margaret Roper,* and Roper, supplemented with Pearl Hogrefe ("Sir Thomas More's Connection with the Roper Family"), and Reginald G. Rigden.

6. Hogrefe, "Sir Thomas More's Connection with the Roper Family," pp. 529–33; Roper, *Lyfe,* p. xlii.

7. More's "school" and his ideas about education have been much written about. Secondary studies consulted include Bayne, Dunn, Garanderie, Hogrefe (*The Sir Thomas More Circle*), Kelso, McConica, Marius, Masek, Murray, Reynolds (*Margaret Roper*), Routh, Schoeck, Warnicke, and Watson. The list of books included in A. W. Reed, "John Clement and His Books," gives telling evidence of the sophisticated learning of one of the family tutors.

8. But More's attitude varies with the situation; see Richard Marius, *Thomas More: A Biography,* pp. 8–9, 41, and 92 and Judith P. Jones and Sherianne Sellers Seibel, "Thomas More's Feminism: to Reform or Re-Form."

9. Both Catherine M. Dunn and Ruth Kelso address this issue in some detail. Dunn, in particular, argues that the improvement of women's lot was "irregular" in the sixteenth century, but "nonetheless clearly discernible," and stresses the effect of the new learning ("The Changing Image of Woman in Renaissance Society and Literature," p. 34). At the same time she admits that "in general the woman's role continued to be primarily that of wife and mother" (p. 16).

10. Such praise, though sincere, is also patronizing from a twentieth-century perspective.

11. For more on this oath, see the extensive discussions in Marius's biography and Reynolds's *The Field Is Won.*

12. It is possible that Margaret's reason for taking the oath is among those More itemizes in their dialogue in the letter to Lady Alington; see, in particular, *Correspondence,* p. 521.

13. This bond is discussed in Germain Marc'hadour, *"Funiculus Triplex*: Margaret Roper and Thomas More."

14. For more on the dating problem, see E. J. Devereux's *Renaissance English Translations of Erasmus*, pp. 176–78, and "Some Lost English Translations of Erasmus," pp. 256–57.

15. See A. W. Reed, "The Regulation of the Book Trade Before the Proclamation of 1538," pp. 166–67, with evidence by Thomas Berthelet that confirms the name of the translator.

16. See, too, Richard L. DeMolen's introduction to Roper's *A Devout Treatise*, pp. 93–95.

17. These points are explored in detail in John A. Gee, "Margaret Roper's English Version of Erasmus' *Precatio Dominica* and the Apprenticeship Behind Early Tudor Translation," pp. 259–61.

18. Whether by accident or design, Margaret Roper omits the culmination of Erasmus's text: death. In effect, then, the relationship with wife and children is further heightened.

19. This letter has been variously interpreted. See, in particular, Chambers (in Harpsfield, p. clxii); Walter Gordon, "Tragic Perspective in Thomas More's Dialogue with Margaret in the Tower"; Marius, pp. 466–71; Louis L. Martz, "Thomas More: The Tower Works," pp. 63–66; Henri Meulon, "La Pensée du ciel chez Thomas More"; Reynolds, *Margaret Roper*, pp. 73–98.

20. See, too, the fine discussion by Gordon, pp. 5–6, 8.

A Devout Treatise upon the "Pater Noster"

Richard Hyrde, unto the most studious and virtuous young maid Frances S. sendeth greeting and well to fare.[1]

I have heard many men put great doubt, whether it should be expedient and requisite or not, a woman to have learning in books of Latin and Greek. And some utterly affirm that it is not only neither necessary nor profitable, but also very noisome and jeopardous: alleging for their opinion that the frail kind of women, being inclined of their own disposition[2] unto vice, and mutable at every novelty, if they should have skill in many things that be written in the Latin and Greek tongue, compiled and made with great craft and eloquence, where the matter is haply sometime more sweet unto the ear than wholesome for the mind, it would of likelihood both inflame their stomachs a great deal the more to that vice that men say they be too much given unto of their own nature already, and instruct them also with more subtlety and sleight of hand[3] to set forward and accomplish their froward intention and purpose. . . .

And where they find fault with learning, because they say it engendereth wit and craft, there they reprehend it for that that it is most worthy to be commended for, and the which is one singular cause wherefore learning ought to be desired, for he that had liefer have his wife a fool than a wise woman, I hold him worse than twice frantic. Also, reading and studying of books so occupieth the mind that it can have no leisure to muse or delight in other fantasies, when in all handiworks that men say be more meet for a woman the body may be busy in one place and the mind walking in another: and while they sit sewing and spinning with their fingers, may cast and compass many peevish fantasies in their minds, which must needs be occupied either with good or bad so long as they be waking. And those that be evil disposed, will find the means to be nought though they have knowledge of[4] never a letter on the book, and she that will be good, learning shall cause her to be much the better. For it showeth the image and ways of good living even right as a mirror showeth the similitude and proportion of the body. And doubtless the daily experience proveth that such as are nought are those that never knew what learning meant. For I never heard tell, nor read of any woman well learned, that ever was (as plenteous as evil tongues be) spotted or notorious[5] as vicious. But, on the other side, many by their learning take such increase of goodness, that many may bear them witness of their virtue, of which sort I could rehearse a great number, both of old time and late, saving that I will be content, as for now, with one example of our own country and time, that is: this gentlewoman which translated this little book hereafter following: whose virtuous conversation, living, and serious[6] demeanor, may be proof evident enough what good learning doth, where it is surely rooted: of whom other women may take example of prudent, humble, and wifely behavior, charitable and very Christian virtue, with which she hath, with God's help, endeavored herself no less to garnish her soul than it hath liked his goodness with lovely beauty and comeliness to garnish and set out her body: And undoubted is it, that to the increase of her virtue she hath taken and taketh no little occasion of her learning, besides her other manifold and great benefits[7] taken of the same, among which benefits this is not the least: that with her virtuous, worshipful, wise, and well-learned husband, she hath by the occasion of her learning and his delight therein, such especial comfort, pleasure, and pastime, as were not well possible for one unlearned couple either to take together or to conceive in their minds what pleasure is therein.

Therefore, good Frances, seeing that such fruit, profit, and pleasure cometh of learning, take no heed unto the foolish[8] words of those that dispraise it, as verily no man doth save such as neither have learning, nor knoweth[9] what it meaneth, which is indeed the most part of men; and as the most part and the best part be not always of one mind, so if this matter should be tried, not by wit and reason, but by heads or hands, the greater part is like, as it often doth, to vanquish and overcome the better, for the best part (as I reckon) whom I account the wisest of every age, as among the Gentiles the old philosophers, and among the Christian men the ancient doctors of Christ's Church, all affirm learning to be very good and profitable, not only for men but also for women, the which Plato the wise philosopher calleth a bridle for young people against vice. Where-

fore, good Frances, take you the best part and leave the most, follow the
wise men and regard not the foolish sort, but apply all your might, will,
and diligence to obtain that especial treasure which is delectable in youth,
comfortable in age, and profitable at all seasons: of whom without doubt
cometh much goodness and virtue. Which virtue whoso lacketh, he is
without that thing that only maketh a man: yea and without the which a
man is worse than an unreasonable beast, nor once worthy to have the
name of a man. . . .

And as a token of my good mind, and an instrument toward your success and furtherance, I send you this book, little in quantity but big in
value, turned out of Latin into English by your own forenamed
kinswoman, whose goodness and virtue, two things there be that prevent[10] me much to speak of. The one, because it were a thing superfluous
to spend many words unto you about that matter which yourself know
well enough, by long experience and daily use. The other cause is, for I
would eschew the slander of flattery: howbeit I count it no flattery to
speak good of them that deserve it, but yet I know that she is as loath to
have praise given her as she is worthy to have it, and had liefer her praise
to rest in men's hearts than in their tongues, or rather in God's estimation
and pleasure than any man's words or thought. And as touching the book
itself, I refer and leave it to the judgments of those that shall read it, and
unto such as are learned. The only name of the maker putteth out of
question the goodness and perfection of the work, which as to mine own
opinion and fantasy, cannot be amended in any point. And as for the
translation thereof, I dare be bold to say it, that whoso list and well can
confer and examine the translation with the original, he shall not fail to
find that she hath showed herself not only erudite and elegant in either
tongue, but hath also used such wisdom, such discreet and substantial
judgment in expressing lively the Latin, as a man may peradventure miss
in many things translated and turned by them that bear the name of right
wise and very well learned men. . . .

THE THIRD PETITION

Fiat voluntas tua sicut in caelo et in terra.[11] O Father which art the nourisher and orderer of all whom it pleaseth thy Son to acknowledge as his
brethren, and he so acknowledgeth all those that in pure faith professeth
his name in baptism: Thy children here in earth call and cry to thee dwelling in heaven, a place far out of all changeable mutability of things created, desiring indeed to come to thy heavenly and celestial company,
which is defiled[12] with no manner spot of evil, saving they know well that
none can be taken and received into so great a tranquility and quietness,
but only they which with busy study, while they live here, labor to be such

as there must be. Therefore it is all one realm, both of heaven and earth, saving this difference: that here we have sore and grievous conflict with the flesh, the world, and the devil, and there, although there is nothing that might diminish or defile[13] the wealth of blessed souls: Yet, as touching the full perfection of felicity, there is some manner miss, which is, that all the members and parts of thy Son be gathered together, and that the whole body of thy Son safe and sound be joined to his head, whereby neither Christ shall lack any of his parts and members, nor good men's souls their bodies: which, likewise as they were ever here in earth partakers of their punishments and afflictions, so their desire is to have them companions of their joy in heaven. And they finally in this world go about to follow the unity and concord of the heavenly kingdom, which, all the time they live bodily in earth, as it becometh natural and obedient children, study with all diligence to fulfill those things which they know shall content thy mind and pleasure, and not what their own sensual appetite giveth them, nor judging or disputing why thou wouldst this or that to be done, but thinking it sufficient that thus thou wouldst it, whom they know surely to will nothing but that that is best. And what thy will is we learned sufficiently of thy only begotten and most dear Son. He was obedient to thy will, even to his own death, and thus he said for our learning and instruction. "Father, if it may conveniently be, suffer this drink of my passion to be withdrawn from me; howbeit, yet thy will be fulfilled and not mine." So that then needs must man be ashamed to prefer and set forth his own will, if Christ our master was content to cast his own will away and subdue it to thine.

The flesh hath his proper will and delight, which man naturally desireth to keep and follow. The world also hath a will by itself, and the devil his will, far contrary to thine. For the flesh coveteth against the spirit, which we have received of thee; and the world enticeth us to set our love on frail and vanishing things; and the devil laboreth about that, that might bring man to everlasting destruction. Nor it is not enough that in baptism we have professed that we will be obedient to thy precepts, and there to have renounced the devil's service, except we labor all our life to perform steadfastly that which we have professed. But that we cannot perform, but if thou give us strength to help forth our purpose: so that our will have no place in us, but let thy will, Father, work in us that which thy wisdom judgeth and thinketh best for us. Whosoever liveth after the fleshly and carnal appetite, they are dead to thee, and then not as thy children. Yea, and we thy children also, as long as we are here bodily in earth, have from time to time[14] not a little business and ado in vanquishing the fleshly delight, which laboreth to prevent thy will. But grant, good Father, that thine ever overcome and have the better, whether it like thee we live or die, or to be punished for our correction, or be in prosperity to the intent we should give thee thanks for thy liberal goodness.

And they follow and obey the will of the devil, which do sacrifice and homage to idols, which slanderously backbite thy most honorable Son, and for envy and evil will go about to bring their neighbor into peril and destruction: and so they may shortly wax rich, care not whether they do right or wrong, and are all fulfilled with corrupt and unclean thoughts. But this is thy will, Father, that we should keep both our body and mind chaste and pure from all uncleanness of the world, and that we should prefer and set more by thine honor and thy Son's than all other things beside. And that we should be angry with no man, nor envy or revenge any man, but always be ready to do good for evil: yea, and to be content rather with torments, hunger, imprisonment, banishment, and death than in anything to be contrary to thy pleasure. And that we may be able every day more and more to perform all this, help us, O Father in heaven, that the flesh may ever more and more be subject to the spirit, and our spirit of one assent and one mind with thy spirit.

And likewise as now, in divers places, thy children, which are obedient to the gospel, obey and do after thy will: so grant they may do in all the world beside, that every man may know and understand that thou alone art the only head and ruler of all things; and that in like wise as there are none in heaven which mutter and rebel against thy will, so let every man here in earth with good mind and glad cheer obey thy will and godly precepts. Nor we cannot effectually and fully mind what thou, good Lord, willest, except it will please thee to pluck and draw us thereto. Thou commandest us to be obedient to thy will and pleasure, and indeed they are not worthy to be called children, but if in all points they follow and obey their father's bidding: but since it hath liked thy goodness to take us, although far unworthy, into so great an honor of thy name: let it please thee also of thy gentleness to give us a ready and steadfast will, that in nothing we pass over[15] or be against that which thy godly and divine will hath appointed us, but that we kill and mortify our fleshly and carnal lusts, and by thy spirit be led to the doing of all good works and all thing that is pleasant under thy sight. Whereby thou, Father, mayst acknowledge us as thy children natural, and not out of kind; and thy Son as kind and good brethren: that is to say, that both twayne may acknowledge in us his own proper benefit, to whom with the Holy Ghost equal and indifferent glory is due forever. Amen.

THE FOURTH PETITION

Panem nostrum quotidianum da nobis hodie.[16] O Father in heaven, which of thy exceeding goodness most plenteously feedest all things that thou hast so wonderously created, provide for us thy children, which are chosen to dwell in thy celestial and heavenly house and that hang wholly and only of thy Son, some spiritual and ghostly food, that we, obeying thy will and precepts, may daily increase and wax bigger in virtue, until after the course of nature we have obtained and gathered a full and perfect strength in our Lord Jesus Christ.

The children of this world, so long as they are not banished nor out of their friends' favor, all that time they take little care of their meat and drink, since their fathers of their tender love toward them make sufficient provision for them. Then much less ought we to be careful or studious, whom thy Son Jesus taught should cast away all care of the morrow's meal, persuading and assuring us, that so rich a Father, so gentle, so loving, and that had so great mind of us, and which sent meat to the little birds, and so nobly clotheth the lilies in the meadow, would not suffer his children which he hath endued with so honorable a name to lack meat and bodily apparel; but all thing set aside that belongeth to the body, we should specially and above all seek and labor about those things which pertaineth and belongeth to thy realm and the justice thereof. For as touching the justice of the Pharisees that savoreth all carnally, thou utterly despisest and settest nought by: for the spiritual justice of thy realm standeth by pure faith and unfeigned charity. And it were no great matter or show of thy plenty to feed with bread made of corn the body, which although it perished not for hunger, yet it must needs die and perish within short space, either by sickness, age, or other chance. But we, thy spiritual and ghostly children, desire and crave of our spiritual Father that spiritual and celestial bread whereby we are verily relived which be verily and truly called thy children.

That bread is thy word, full of all power, both the giver and nourisher of life: which bread thou vouchsafest to send us down from heaven, what time we were like to have perished for hunger. For verily the bread and teaching of the proud philosophers and Pharisees could not suffice and content our mind. But that bread of thine, which thou sendest us, restored dead men to life, of which whosoever doth eat shall never die. This bread relived us; by this bread we are nourished and fatted; and by this we come up to the perfect and full strength of the spirit. This bread, though day by day it be eaten and distributed to every bowel of the soul, yet but if thou, Father, dost give it, it is not wholesome nor anything availeth.

The blessed Body of thy dear Son is the bread whereof we be all partakers that dwell within thy large house of the Church. It is one bread that indifferently belongeth to us all, likewise as we are but one body, made of sundry and diverse members, but yet quickened with one spirit. And though all take of this bread, yet to many it hath been death and destruction, for it cannot be relief but to such as thou reachest it unto, mingling it with thy heavenly grace, by the reason whereof it may be wholesome to the receivers. Thy Son is verity and truth; truth also is the bread and teaching of the gospel, which he left behind him for our spiritual food.

And this bread likewise to many hath been unsavory, which have had the mouth of their soul out of taste by the fever of corrupt affections. But and it will please thee, good Father, to give forth this bread, then it must of necessity be sweet and pleasant to the eaters: then it shall comfort those that be in tribulation, and pluck up those that be slidden and fallen down, and make strong those that be sick and weak, and finally bring us to everlasting life.

And forasmuch as the imbecility and weakness of man's nature is ever ready and apt to decline into the worse, and the soul of man so continually assaulted and laid at with so many subtle engines, it is expedient and necessary that thou daily make strong and hearten thy children with thy bread, which else are far unable to resist so many and so strong enemies, so many assaults, and so many fearful and terrible darts. For who, Father, might abide to be had in derision of the world, to be outlawed and banished, to be put in prison, to be fettered and manacled, to be spoiled of all his goods, and by strong hand be deprived of the company of his most dear wife and well-beloved children, but if now and then he were heartened with thy heavenly and ghostly bread? He that teacheth the learning of the gospel, he is he that giveth us forth this bread, which yet he giveth all in vain, except it be also given by thee. Many there are, which receive the body of thy Son, and that hear the word and doctrine of the gospel, but they depart from thence no stronger than they came, because they have not deserved that thou, good Father, shouldst privily and invisibly reach it forth unto them. This bread, O most benign Father, give thy children every day, until that time come in which they shall eat of it at thy heavenly and celestial table: whereby the children of thy realm shall be fulfilled with the plenteous abundance of everlasting truth. And to take fruition thereof, it were a marvelous felicity and pleasure, which hath need of none other thing at all, neither in heaven nor earth: For in thee, O Father, alone is all thing, out of whom is right nought to be desired, which together with thy Son and the Holy Ghost reignest forever. Amen.

To Sir Thomas More

Mine own good father.[17]

It is to me no little comfort, since I cannot talk with you by such means as I would, at the least way to delight myself from time to time[18] in this bitter time of your absence, by such means as I may, by as often writing to you as shall be expedient, and by reading again and again your most fruitful and delectable letter, the faithful messenger of your very virtuous and ghostly mind, rid from all corrupt love of worldly things, and fast knit only in the love of God and desire of heaven, as becometh a very true worshiper and a faithful servant of God, which I doubt not, good father, holdeth his holy hand over you and shall (as he hath) preserve you both body and soul (ut sit mens sana in corpore sano)[19] and namely, now when you have cast away[20] all earthly consolations and resigned yourself willingly, gladly, and fully for his love to his holy protection.

Father, what think you hath been our comfort since your departing from us? Surely the experience we have had of your life past, and godly conversation, and wholesome counsel, and virtuous example, and a surety not only of the continuance of the same, but also a great increase by the goodness of our Lord to the great rest and gladness of your heart devoid of all earthly dregs, and garnished with the noble vesture of heavenly virtues, a pleasant palace for the Holy Spirit of God to rest in, who defend you (as I doubt not, good father, but of his goodness he will) from all trouble of mind and of body, and give me your most loving obedient daughter and handmaid, and all us your children and friends, to follow that that we praise in you, and to our only comfort remember and talk[21] together of you, that we may in conclusion meet with you, mine own dear father, in the bliss of heaven to which our most merciful Lord hath brought us with his precious blood.

Your own most loving obedient daughter and beadswoman, Margaret Roper, which desireth above all worldly things to be in John Wood's stead to do you some service.[22] But we live in hope that we shall shortly receive you again; I pray God heartily we may, if it be his holy will.

"As Written to the Lady Alington"

When I came next unto my father after, me thought it both convenient and necessary to show him your letter.[23] Convenient, that he might thereby see your loving labor taken for him. Necessary, that since he might perceive thereby, that if he stand still in this scruple of his conscience (as it is at the leastwise called by many that are his friends and wise) all his friends that seem most able to do him good either shall finally forsake him, or peradventure not be able in deed to do him any good at all. . . .

"But for the conclusion, daughter Margaret, of all this matter, as I have often told you, I take not upon me neither to define nor dispute in these matters, nor I rebuke not nor impugne any other man's deed, nor I never wrote, nor so much as spake in any company, any word of reproach in anything that the Parliament had passed, nor I meddled not with the conscience of any other man, that either thinketh or saith he thinketh contrary unto mine. But as concerning mine own self, for thy comfort shall I say, daughter, to thee, that mine own conscience in this matter (I damn none other man's) is such, as may well stand with mine own salvation, thereof am I, Megge, so sure, as that is, God is in heaven. And therefore as for all the remnant, goods, lands, and life both (if the chance should so fortune), since this conscience is sure for me, I verily trust in God, he shall rather strengthen me to bear the loss, than against this conscience to swear and put my soul in peril, since all the causes that I perceive move other men to the contrary, seem not such unto me, as in my conscience make any change."

When he saw me sit with this very sad, as I promise you, sister, my heart was full heavy for the peril of his person, for in faith I fear not his soul, he smiled upon me and said: "How now, daughter Marget? What how, mother Eve? Where is your mind now? Sit not musing with some serpent in your breast, upon some new persuasion, to offer father Adam the apple yet once again?"

"In good faith, father," quod I,[24] "I can no further go, but am (as I think Criseyde saith in Chaucer) come to dulcarnoun, even at my wits' end.[25] For since the example of so many wise men cannot in this matter move you, I see not what to say more, but if I should look to persuade you with the reason that Master Harry Patenson made.[26] For he met one day one of our men, and when he had asked where you were, and heard that you were in the Tower still, he waxed even angry with you and said, 'Why? What aileth him that he will not swear? Wherefore should he stick to swear? I have sworn the oath myself.' And so I can in good faith go now no further neither, after so many wise men whom ye take for no sample, but if I should say like Master Harry, 'Why should you refuse to swear, father? For I have sworn myself.'"

At this he laughed and said, "That word was like Eve, too, for she offered Adam no worse fruit than she had eaten herself."

"But yet, father," quod I, "by my troth, I fear me very sore, that this matter will bring you in marvelous heavy trouble. You know well that, as I showed you, Master Secretary sent you word as your true[27] friend, to remember, that the Parliament lasteth yet."

"Margaret," quod my father, "I thank him right heartily. But as I showed you then again, I left not this gear unthought on. And albeit I know well that if they would make a law to do me any harm, that law could never be lawful, but that God shall I trust keep me in that grace, that concerning my duty to my prince, no man shall do me hurt but if he do me wrong (and then as I told you, this is like a riddle, a case in which a man may lose his head and have no harm), and notwithstanding also that I have good hope, that God shall never suffer so good and wise a prince, in such wise to requite the long service of his true faithful servant, yet since there is nothing impossible to fall, I forgot not in this matter, the counsel of Christ in the gospel, that ere I should begin to build this castle for the safeguard of mine own soul, I should sit and reckon what the charge would be. I counted, Marget, full surely many a restless night, while my wife slept, and supposed[28] that I had slept too, what peril was possible for to fall to me, so far forth that I am sure there can come none above. And in devising, daughter, thereupon, I had a full heavy heart. But yet (I thank our Lord) for all that, I never thought to change, though the very uttermost should hap me that my fear ran upon."

"No, father" (quod I), "it is not like to think upon a thing that may be, and to see a thing that shall be, as ye[29] should (our Lord save you) if the chance should so fortune. And then should you peradventure think, that you think not now, and yet then peradventure it would be too late."

"Too late, daughter" (quod my father), "Margaret? I beseech our Lord, that if ever I make such a change, it may be too late indeed. For well I know[30] the change cannot be good for my soul, that change I say that should grow but by fear. And therefore I pray God that in this world I never have good of such change. For so much as I take harm here, I shall have at the leastwise the less therefore when I am hence. And if so were that I knew[31] well now, that I should faint and fall, and for fear swear hereafter, yet would I wish to take harm by the refusing first, for so should I have the better hope for grace to rise again. . . .

"Mistrust him, Megge, will I not, though I feel me faint, yea, and though I should feel my fear even at point to overthrow me, too, yet shall I remember how Saint Peter, with a blast of wind, began to sink for his faint faith, and shall do as he did, call upon Christ and pray him to help. And then I trust he shall set his holy hand unto me, and in the stormy seas, hold me up from drowning. Yea and if he suffer me to play Saint Peter further, and to fall full to the ground, and swear and forswear too (which our Lord for his tender passion keep me from, and let me lose[32] if it so fall, and never win thereby), yet after shall I trust that his goodness will cast upon me his tender piteous eye, as he did upon Saint Peter, and make me stand up again and confess the truth of my conscience afresh, and abide the shame and the harm here of mine own fault.

"And finally, Marget, this know[33] I well, that without my fault he will not let me be lost. I shall therefore with good hope commit myself wholly to him. And if he suffer me for my faults to perish, yet shall I then serve for a praise of his justice. But in good faith, Meg, I trust that his tender pity shall keep my poor soul safe and make me commend his mercy. And therefore, my own good daughter, never trouble thy mind for anything that ever shall hap me in this world. Nothing can come but that that God will. And I make me very sure that whatsoever that be, seem it never so bad in sight, it shall in deed be the best. And with this, my good child, I pray you heartily, be you and all your sisters and my sons, too, comfortable and serviceable to your good mother, my wife. And of your good husbands' minds I have no manner doubt. Commend me to them all, and to my good daughter Alington, and to all my other friends, sisters, nieces, nephews, and relatives by marriage,[34] and unto all our servants, man, woman, and child, and all my good neighbors and all our acquaintances abroad. And I right heartily pray both you and them, to serve God and be merry and rejoice in him. And if anything hap me that you would be loath, pray to God for me, but trouble not yourself: as I shall full heartily pray for us all, that we may meet together once in heaven, where we shall make merry forever, and never have trouble after."

To Sir Thomas More

Mine own most entirely beloved father.

I think myself never able to give you sufficient thanks, for the inestimable comfort my poor heart received in the reading of your most loving and godly letter, representing to me the clear shining brightness of your soul, the pure temple of the Holy Spirit of God, which I doubt not shall perpetually rest in you and you in him. Father, if all the world had been given to me, as I be saved it had been a small pleasure, in comparison of the pleasure I conceived of the treasure of your letter, which though it were written with a coal, is worthy in mine opinion to be written in letters of gold.

Father, what moved them to shut you up again, we can nothing hear. But surely I conjecture that when they considered that you were of so temperate mind, that you were contented to abide there all your life with such liberty, they thought it were never possible to incline you to their will, except it were by restraining you from the Church, and the company of my good mother your dear wife and us your children and beadsfolk. But, father, this chance was not strange to you. For I shall not forget how you told us when we were with you in the garden, that these things were like enough to chance shortly after. Father, I have many times rehearsed to mine own comfort and divers others, your fashion and words ye had to us when we were last with you: for which I trust by the grace of God to be the better while I live, and when I am departed out of this frail life, which, I pray God, I may pass and end in his true obedient service, after the wholesome counsel and fruitful example of living I have had (good father) of you, whom I pray God give me grace to follow; which I shall the better through the assistance of your devout prayers, the special stay of my frailty. Father, I am sorry I have no longer leisure at this time to talk with you, the chief comfort of my life; I trust to have occasion to write again shortly. I trust I have your daily prayer and blessing.

Your most loving obedient daughter and beadswoman, Margaret Roper, which daily and hourly is bounden to pray for you, for whom she prayeth in this wise, that our Lord of his infinite mercy give you of his heavenly comfort, and so to assist you with his special grace that ye never in anything decline from his blessed will, but live and die his true obedient servant. Amen.

NOTES TO THE TEXT

1. Selections from *A Devout Treatise upon the "Pater Noster"* are based upon DeMolen's diplomatic reprint of the British Library copy and Marc'hadour's reprint, *Moreana* 7 and 13 (which used the Yale University copy for the Roper translation and the British Library copy for Hyrde's preface), together with the microfilm (Reel 37 in the STC series). Spelling and punctuation have been modernized, contractions expanded, paragraphing regularized, and archaic and obsolete words replaced: notes give the original words, in modernized spelling.

Richard Hyrde (died 1528) graduated from Oxford in 1519; he was learned in Greek, Latin, and physic, and was a member of the household of Sir Thomas More, whom he called "my singular good master and bringer up" (Watson, pp. 31, 159–60; DeMolen, ed., p. 96). Diane Valeri Bayne's "Instruction of a Christian Woman" brings together almost everything that is known about him. Frances Staverton, whom Hyrde tutored, was the daughter of More's sister, Joan, and Richard Staverton, and thus Margaret Roper's cousin.

2. Courage.
3. Conveyance.
4. Can.
5. Infamed.
6. Sad.
7. Commodities (twice).
8. Lewd.
9. Wotteth.
10. Let.
11. From the Lord's Prayer: "Thy will be done on earth as it is in heaven."
12. Defouled.
13. Minish or defoyle.
14. Among.
15. Overhip.
16. From the Lord's Prayer: "Give us this day our daily bread."
17. The letters are based upon More's *Correspondence*, ed. Rogers. Spelling and punctuation have been modernized, contractions expanded, paragraphing regularized, and (with exceptions noted below) archaic and obsolete words replaced: for original words, see notes. This and the last letter are to Sir Thomas More from Margaret Roper in 1534; numbers 203 and 209 in Rogers.
18. Among.
19. Juvenal, satire 10, line 356: "That there may be a sound mind in a sound body." The larger context is important; this is the key line in the conclusion of a poem about the vanity of human wishes.
20. Abjected.
21. Comin.
22. As noted earlier, John a Wood was More's personal servant.

23. Written in August 1534 by Sir Thomas More in his daughter's name, by Margaret Roper, or by both; number 206 in Rogers.

24. *Quod:* said (used to indicate direct discourse and therefore kept, here and hereafter).

25. *Trow* (replaced by *think*). Chaucer, *Troilus and Criseyde,* book 3, line 931: "At dulcarnoun," completely perplexed.

26. Patenson was Sir Thomas More's fool. This is probably ironic, then.

27. Very. The Master Secretary is Thomas Cromwell.

28. Weened.

29. *Ye:* you; normally the *you* form is used; it is possible, then, that *ye* is used for special emphasis, which is why I have kept it here and in the following letter.

30. Wot.

31. Wist.

32. Leese.

33. Wot.

34. Allies.

BIBLIOGRAPHY

Primary Works

Erasmus. *The Colloquies of Erasmus.* Trans. Craig R. Thompson. Chicago, 1965.
————. "Correspondance entre Erasme et Margaret Roper." Trans. Soeur Marie-Claire Robineau, Sister Gertrude-Joseph Donnelly, and E. E. Reynolds. *Moreana* 12 (1966): 29–46, 121.
————. *Opera Omnia.* 10 vols. 1703–1706. Reprint. Hildesheim, 1961–1962.
————. *Opus Epistolarum Des. Erasmi Roterodami.* Ed. P. S. Allen and H. M. Allen. 12 vols. Oxford, 1906–1958.
Harpsfield, Nicholas. *The Life and Death of Sr. Thomas Moore.* Ed. Elsie V. Hitchcock and R. W. Chambers. Early English Text Society Original Series 186. London, 1932.
Hyrde, Richard. "Défense et illustration des humanités féminines." Ed. Germain Marc'hadour. Trans. Marie-Claire Robineau, O.P. *Moreana* 13 (1967): 5–24.
Letters and Papers, Foreign and Domestic, of the Reign of Henry VIII. Ed. J. S. Brewer, J. Gairdner, and R. Brodie. 21 vols. 1862–1910. Reprint. Vaduz, 1965.
More, Cresacre. *The Life of Sir Thomas More.* 1726. Reprint, ed. J. L. Kennedy. Athens, Pa., 1941.
More, Thomas. *The Correspondence of Sir Thomas More.* Ed. Elizabeth Frances Rogers. Princeton, 1947.
————. *De Tristitia Christi.* Ed. and trans. Clarence H. Miller. Vol. 14, parts 1 and 2 of *The Complete Works of St. Thomas More.* New Haven, Conn., 1976.
————. *Latin Poems.* Ed. Clarence H. Miller, Leicester Bradner, Charles A. Lynch, and Revilo P. Oliver. Vol. 3, part 2 of *The Complete Works of St. Thomas More.* New Haven, Conn., 1984.
————. *Selected Letters.* Ed. Elizabeth Frances Rogers. Vol. 1 of *Selected Works of St. Thomas More.* New Haven, Conn., 1961.
————. *The Workes of Sir Thomas More Knyght.* 1557. Reprint, 2 vols., with an introduction by K. J. Wilson. London, 1978.
Ro. Ba. *The Lyfe of Syr Thomas More, Sometymes Lord Chancellor of England.* Ed. Elsie V. Hitchcock, P. E. Hallett, and A. W. Reed. Early English Text Society Original Series 222. London, 1950.

Roper, Margaret More, trans. *A Devout Treatise upon the "Pater Noster"* . . . *by Erasmus.* London, 1526. STC 10477. Reel 37.

———. *A Devout Treatise upon the "Pater Noster."* Edited, with an introduction, by Richard L. DeMolen. In *Erasmus of Rotterdam: A Quincentennial Symposium,* ed. Richard L. DeMolen, pp. 93–124, 139–46, and errata. New York, 1971.

———. *A Devout Treatise upon the "Pater Noster."* Modernized by Germain Marc'hadour. With "Paraphrase sur le *Pater Noster*." Trans. Soeur Marie-Claire Robineau, O.P. *Moreana* 9 (1966): 65–92; 10 (1966): 91–110; 11 (1966): 109–18.

———. *Erasmus' Paraphrase of the "Pater Noster" (1523) with Its English Translation by Margaret Roper (1524).* Ed. Germain Marc'hadour. *Moreana* 7 (1965): 9–64.

Roper, William. *The Life of Sir Thomas More. Two Early Tudor Lives.* Ed. Richard S. Sylvester and Davis P. Harding. New Haven, Conn., 1962.

———. *The Lyfe of Sir Thomas Moore, Knighte.* Ed. Elsie V. Hitchcock. Early English Text Society Original Series 197. London, 1935.

Stapleton, Thomas. *The Life and Illustrious Martyrdom of Sir Thomas More.* Trans. Philip E. Hallett. Ed. E. E. Reynolds. Sussex, 1966.

Related Works

Bayne, Diane Valeri. "The Instruction of a Christian Woman: Richard Hyrde and the Thomas More Circle." *Moreana* 45 (1975): 5–15.

Bolt, Robert. *A Man for All Seasons.* New York, 1960.

Bradbrook, M. C. Review of *The Paradise of Women,* ed. Betty Travitsky. *Tulsa Studies in Women's Literature* 1 (1982): 89–93.

Chambers, R. W. *Thomas More.* 1935. Reprint. Ann Arbor, Mich., 1958.

Devereux, E. J. *Renaissance English Translations of Erasmus: A Bibliography to 1700.* Toronto, 1983.

———. "Some Lost English Translations of Erasmus." *The Library,* 5th ser., 17 (1962): 255–59.

Dunn, Catherine M. "The Changing Image of Woman in Renaissance Society and Literature." In *What Manner of Woman: Essays on English and American Life and Literature,* ed. Marlene Springer, pp. 15–38. New York, 1977.

Fuller, Thomas. *The History of the Worthies of England.* Ed. P. Austin Nuttall. 3 vols. 1840. Reprint. New York, 1965.

Garanderie, M. M. de la. "Le Féminisme de Thomas More et d'Erasme." *Moreana* 10 (1966): 23–29.

Gartenberg, Patricia. "A Checklist of English Women in Print, 1475–1640." *Bulletin of Bibliography* 34 (1977): 1–13.

Gee, John A. "Hervet's English Translation, with Its Appended Glossary of Erasmus' *De Immensa Dei Misericordia.*" *Philological Quarterly* 15 (1936): 136–52.

———. "Margaret Roper's English Version of Erasmus' *Precatio Dominica* and the Apprenticeship Behind Early Tudor Translation." *Review of English Studies* 13 (1937): 257–71.

Gibson, R. W. *St. Thomas More: A Preliminary Bibliography of His Works and of Moreana to the Year 1750.* New Haven, Conn., 1961.

Gordon, Walter. "Tragic Perspective in Thomas More's Dialogue with Margaret in the Tower." *Cithara* 17 (1978): 3–12.

Greco, Norma, and Ronaele Novotny. "Bibliography of Women in the English Renaissance." *University of Michigan Papers in Women's Studies* 1 (1974): 29–57.

Hageman, Elizabeth H. "Recent Studies in Women Writers of Tudor England. Part 1: Women Writers, 1485–1603, Excluding Mary Sidney, Countess of Pembroke." *English Literary Renaissance* 14 (1984): 409–25.

Hodnett, Edward. *English Woodcuts: 1480–1535.* 1935. Reprint. Oxford, 1973.

Hogrefe, Pearl. *The Sir Thomas More Circle.* Urbana, Ill., 1959.

———. "Sir Thomas More's Connection with the Roper Family." *PMLA* 47 (1932): 523–33.

———. *Tudor Women: Commoners and Queens.* Ames, Iowa, 1975.

Hughey, Ruth Willard. "Cultural Interests of Women in England from 1524 to 1640." Master's thesis abstract, Cornell University, 1932.

Jones, Judith P., and Sherianne Sellers Seibel. "Thomas More's Feminism: To Reform or Re-Form." In *Quincentennial Essays on St. Thomas More,* ed. Michael J. Moore, pp. 67–77. Boone, N.C., 1978.

Juvenal and Persius. Trans. G. G. Ramsay. Loeb Classical Library. Rev. ed. Cambridge, Mass., 1979.

Kelso, Ruth. *Doctrine for the Lady of the Renaissance.* 1956. Reprint. Urbana, Ill., 1978.

Khanna, Lee Cullen. "No Less Real Than Ideal: Images of Women in More's Work." *Moreana* 55–56 (1977): 35–51.

Maber, Richard G. "Une Machabée moderne: Margaret Roper vue par le Père Pierre Le Moyne (1647)." *Moreana* 82 (1984): 33–40.

———. "Pierre Le Moyne's Encomium of Margaret Roper, Translated by John Paulet, Marquis of Winchester (1652)." *Moreana* 90 (1986): 47–52.

McConica, James Kelsey. *English Humanists and Reformation Politics.* Oxford, 1965.

Manning, Anne. *The Household of Sir Thomas More.* Introduction by Richard Garnett. Philadelphia, n.d.

Marc'hadour, Germain. "Anne Manning." *Gazette Thomas More* 1 (1979): 83–90.

———. "*Funiculus Triplex:* Margaret Roper and Thomas More." *Moreana* 78 (1983): 93–97.

Marius, Richard. *Thomas More: A Biography.* New York, 1984.

Martz, Louis L. "Thomas More: The Tower Works." In *St. Thomas More: Action and Contemplation,* ed. Richard S. Sylvester, pp. 59–83. New Haven, Conn., 1972.

Masek, Rosemary. "Women in an Age of Transition: 1485–1714." In *The Women of England: From Anglo-Saxon Times to the Present,* ed. Barbara Kanner, pp. 138–82. Hamden, Conn., 1979.

Meulon, Henri. "La Pensée du ciel chez Thomas More." *Moreana* 27–28 (1970): 5–13.

Morison, Stanley. *The Likeness of Thomas More: An Iconographical Survey of Three Centuries.* Ed. Nicolas Barker. London, 1963.

Murphy, Clare M. "On the Women in More's Life: Two Recent Works." *Moreana* 82 (1984): 109–17.

Murray, Francis G. "Feminine Spirituality in the More Household." *Moreana* 27–28 (1970): 92–102.

Norrington, Ruth. *In the Shadow of a Saint: Lady Alice More.* Waddesdon, Eng., 1983.

Parker, K. T. *The Drawings of Hans Holbein in the Collection of H. M. the King at Windsor Castle.* London, 1945.

Plowden, Alison. *Tudor Women: Queens and Commoners.* New York, 1979.

Reed, A. W. "John Clement and His Books." *The Library,* 4th ser., 6 (1926): 329–39.

———. "The Regulation of the Book Trade Before the Proclamation of 1538." *Transactions of the Bibliographical Society* 15 (1917–19): 157–84.

———. "The Wydow Edyth." *The Library,* 3rd ser., 9 (1918): 186–99.

Reynolds, E. E. *The Field Is Won: The Life and Death of Saint Thomas More.* London, 1968.

———. *Margaret Roper: Eldest Daughter of St. Thomas More.* New York, 1960.

Rigden, Reginald G. *Well Hall.* London, 1970.

"Roper, William." *Dictionary of National Biography.*

Routh, Enid M. G. *Sir Thomas More and His Friends.* 1934. Reprint. New York, 1963.

Schoeck, R. J. "The School of More." *New Catholic Encyclopedia.* 17 vols. New York, 1967–1979.

A Short-Title Catalogue of Books Printed in England, Scotland, and Ireland: 1475–1640. Comp. A. W. Pollard and G. R. Redgrave. London, 1956.

Smith, Hilda L. *Reason's Disciples: Seventeenth-Century English Feminists.* Urbana, Ill., 1982.

Smyth, Walter. *XII Mery Jests of the Wydow Edyth.* Vol. 3 of *Shakespeare Jest-Books,* ed. William C. Hazlitt, pp. 27–108. 3 vols. London, 1864.

Snyder, Lee Daniel. "Erasmus on Prayer: A Renaissance Reinterpretation." *Renaissance and Reformation* 12 (1976): 21–27.

Sullivan, Frank, and Majie Sullivan. *Moreana: Materials for the Study of Saint Thomas More.* 4 vols. Los Angeles, 1964–1968.

Sullivan, Majie. *Moreana: Materials for the Study of Saint Thomas More: Supplement and Chronology to 1800.* Los Angeles, 1977.

Tennyson, Alfred. *The Poems of Tennyson.* Ed. Christopher Ricks. London, 1969.

Trapp, J. B., and Hubertus Schulte Herbrüggen. *"The King's Good Servant": Sir Thomas More.* London, 1977.

Travitsky, Betty, ed. *The Paradise of Women: Writings by Englishwomen of the Renaissance.* Westport, Conn., 1981.

Verbrugge, Rita M. "Margaret More Roper's Personal Expression in the *Devout Treatise upon the 'Pater Noster.'"* In *Silent but for the Word: Tudor Women as Patrons, Translators, and Writers of Religious Works,* ed. Margaret Patterson Hannay, pp. 30–42, 260–64. Kent, Ohio, 1985.

Vogel, Paula A. *Meg: A Play in Three Acts.* New York, 1977.

Warnicke, Retha M. *Women of the English Renaissance and Reformation.* Westport, Conn., 1983.

Watson, Foster. *Vives and the Renascence Education of Women.* London, 1912.

Weinstein, Minna F. "Reconstructing Our Past: Reflections on Tudor Women." *International Journal of Women's Studies* 1–2 (1978): 133–58.

White, Helen C. *The Tudor Books of Private Devotion.* Madison, Wisc., 1951.

Wiesner, Merry E. *Women in the Sixteenth Century: A Bibliography.* Sixteenth-Century Bibliography 23. St. Louis, 1983.

Williams, Franklin. "Margaret Roper Charms Washington Irving." *Gazette Thomas More* 2 (1980): 47–50.

COUNTESS OF PEMBROKE

ary Sidney

COBURN FREER

Few authors in the history of English literature have affected so many other writers in their own time as Mary Herbert. Born Mary Sidney in Worcestershire in 1561, she had on each side parents who were members of the new Elizabethan aristocracy, and shared fully in that society's sense of national responsibility and boundless opportunity. Her mother was a Dudley, descended from John Dudley, Duke of Northumberland; she was an intimate of the queen, and her brother Robert, Earl of Leicester, was alternately one of the queen's most trusted and despised confidants. Mary Sidney's father, Henry, came from a family that had served the Crown in several different capacities, for which the family had come to hold Penshurst Place, one of the finest manor houses in England, later celebrated by Ben Jonson. She was raised in Penshurst and in her father's official state residence of Ludlow Castle, later to be the setting of Milton's masque best known today as *Comus*. She had three sisters, all of whom died in childhood, and she appears to have been closest to her eldest brother, Philip, who was seven years older than she; the two lived in the same household until at the age of fourteen Mary took up residence in the household of Queen Elizabeth. Although she had been trained in French, Italian, Latin, Greek, and possibly Hebrew, it is probable that in court her knowledge of music and skill at embroidery—of which much is made in one of her epitaphs—may have provided a somewhat steadier set of credentials.

In 1577 she married Henry Herbert, the second earl of Pembroke, and took up residence in her husband's grand estate, Wilton Place. That year her brother came to visit her, and he came then for a longer stay in 1580, after some high-spirited behavior at court had made him unwelcome there. Over the next year or two the pair spent many hours together, reading in the large library of English and Continental authors that the Countess had already begun to assemble. By Philip Sidney's account, the writing of the *Arcadia* was begun at his sister's request and "is done for you, only to you . . . being done on loose sheets of paper, most of it in your presence, the rest by sheets sent unto you as fast as they were done."[1] Even allowing here for the influence of the Renaissance cult of *sprezzatura* or nonchalance, writing for the two must have been an easy and natural kind of transaction, and it would be no exaggeration to say that the older brother's example informed the later work of the Countess on every level. It was probably at this time that Philip Sidney also began a translation of the Book of Psalms into English, employing as a model the varied and highly wrought stanzas of the contemporary French translation by Clément Marot and Théodore de Bèze. Later the Countess was to complete this collection, but it is not certain that as of this time she had begun to do any writing of her own. In the years 1580–1584 she had two sons and two daughters, to whom she was extremely devoted.

While it is always risky to guess at the source of any artistic motive, there is a good possibility that the deaths, within one year, of the Countess's father and mother may have determined her rather generally in her literary vocation; but the death of her brother that same year of 1586, in one of Elizabeth's Dutch wars, could only have reinforced her sense of the specific jobs she had to do. In any event she soon undertook the completion of the translation of the Psalms (Philip Sidney had done only the first forty-three); a thorough revision and expansion of the *Arcadia,* which had been published in an incomplete and unauthorized version in 1590; a translation of the *Discourse of Life and Death* by her brother's friend Philippe de Mornay; a translation of Petrarch's *Trionfo della morte;* and a translation of Robert Garnier's French neoclassical tragedy *Marc Antoine,* a selection from which follows this introduction.

Soon after the death of her brother, the Countess also began to show the attention to other writers that was to earn her a reputation as one of the most intelligent patrons of this or any other age. "In her time," according to John Aubrey, "Wilton House was like a College, there were so many learned and ingenious persons. She was the greatest patroness of wit and learning of any lady in her time."[2] The Countess's taste and hospitality were celebrated by Francis Meres, Edmund Spenser, Abraham Fraunce, Nicholas Breton, Thomas Moffet, Fulke Greville, Thomas Nashe, Gabriel Harvey, Samuel Daniel, Michael Drayton, John Davies of Hereford, Ben Jonson, John Donne—it would be hard to find a major writer of the period who, though he may not have had some acquaintance with the Countess, at least had friends who did. Her son William was of course one of Shakespeare's most important patrons, and it has often been conjectured that the "W.H." to whom the *Sonnets* are dedicated was the third earl of Pembroke, Mary's son. At this date the interesting thing about such lists of names is the remarkably varied tastes and styles they represent: clearly the patron who prompted praise from such varied quarters must have seemed to have a receptive mind and an interest in what was new. In this regard it should not be surprising that the Countess was also greatly interested in the natural sciences, to the extent that she had a laboratory built at Wilton and supported a chemist in his research.

All the while the Countess maintained her friendships in the court (though for the most part she resided still in the West country) and she remained a favorite of the queen. When the Earl of Pembroke died in 1601, Wilton Place went by law to the eldest son, and while there is a record of King James I and his wife Queen Anne having visited the Countess there in 1603, for many years Mary Herbert appears to have lived principally in London at Crosby Castle, which she rented from the Duke of Northampton. She never remarried. In 1615 James granted her for life a royal manor in Bedfordshire, where she built a grand home and was visited by numerous figures in the court, including the king. In her declining years she took the waters at various spas, with various results; she died in London in 1621, and is buried in Salisbury Cathedral beside her husband.

Invariably the terms "major writer" and "minor writer" will be used to separate the Countess from the more illustrious writers with whom she associated, but these terms used by themselves may lead us to overlook several important aspects of Elizabethan literary history. The Countess was one of those few people—rare enough in any age—who have a conscious grasp of literary evolution as it occurs, who sense the major changes in genres, subjects, and stance as they occur, and in crystallizing those in a few carefully built works, make a whole new range of opportunities for expression available to their contemporaries. Her translation of the Psalms is a case in point: there is no previous collection of lyrics in English so varied metrically as these 150 poems, and the 107 by the Countess are if anything more complex stylistically, more sophisticated in technique, than their counterparts by her brother. Taken as a whole, the Sidney psalter has been rightly described as "a school of English versification,"[3] and it influenced, directly or indirectly, a good number of English poets of the seventeenth century, chief among them the Countess's kinsman by marriage George Herbert. Her translation of de Mornay shows the discursive side of her religious concerns and reveals as well her sympathy with a strongly Protestant form of piety.

Her revision of the *Arcadia* seems in retrospect one of her most ambitious undertakings. This fantastic work of narrative, pastoral romance, lyric song, and political as well as artistic doctrine, stands at the beginning of much that is central, surfacing and resurfacing, in the history of English narrative and fiction. To undertake its thorough revision demonstrates that the Countess had (as Spenser said) "a brave mind" and a "heroic spirit."[4] Her task might be roughly analogous to rewriting Joyce's *Ulysses*, and to her great credit the Countess was anything but timid. Comparison of her version with her brother's not only reveals much about the mind of each writer: it also shows two widely differing conceptions of the pastoral mode, artistic order, and physical reality. That the Countess's departures from her received text were deliberate cannot be doubted, given the detail and extent of her revisions, and comparison of the two should long continue to illuminate our understanding of the genre and the period as a whole.

The work selected for inclusion in this anthology was written in the fall of 1590, while the Countess was residing in her husband's house at Ramsbury, about thirty miles northeast of Wilton. The play was first published in 1592 under the title of *Antonius: a tragedie*, and then was reprinted in 1595 as *The Tragedie of Antonie*, in the same volume as the translation of de Mornay. It is of special importance that on the title page the Countess is acknowledged as the author, because at this time members of the nobility who wrote (and particularly women) circulated their manuscripts in private and discreetly avoided any appearance of cultivating a reading public. This was a bold step for a person who was by all accounts modest and retiring.

As noted earlier, the source of the Countess's work is Robert Garnier's *Marc Antoine* (1578), and her translation should be viewed as part of the general reawakening of interest in classical models for Elizabethan literature. In 1581 Thomas Newton had published the first complete collection of Seneca's tragedies in English translation; and the next twenty years were to see a number of English plays inspired either directly by Seneca or indirectly by his French translator Garnier. The Countess's *Antonie* provided the inspiration for at least three plays, including Thomas Kyd's *Cornelia* (1594), and Samuel Daniel's *The Tragedie of Cleopatra* (1594) and *Philotas* (1595). Numerous other plays in this period went to various classical subjects for their topics and developed them in the five-act, highly rhetorical, and nobly conceived Senecan mode; typical subjects included the pantheon of Roman heroes and heroines, usually laboring in heroic struggles involving self-definition and the future of their nation. Many direct translations from Seneca were also published and reprinted during this time, and the last English edition of Seneca in the Renaissance was that by Thomas Lodge in 1620, although this collection was a good ten or fifteen years beyond the heyday of Senecan drama.

The term often applied to these plays is "closet drama," and like many other such phrases, the adjective would seek not only to define but to kill. "Closet drama" suggests willful obscurity and terminal stuffiness. Nothing can live much less grow in a closet; and closets are usually full of objects we cannot use but, through some fault of our own, cannot bear to throw away. The Countess's play and others like it have labored under this term or mind-set for several centuries, and it might be salutary to take a step back from our own preconceptions before getting down to particulars.

Senecan tragedy is based first of all upon a value system that is stoic, self-sacrificing, and highly idealistic, while incorporating an ethic that would understand the nature of circumstance and power in this world. It offers a tragic view of human life, and we should probably not anticipate its revival during the latter decades of the twentieth century. This is not to say that it lacks elements one might find admirable and even appealing. Recognizing the brevity of life, the importance of true friendship and the poverty of most social relations, the futility of seeking merely material goods, the necessity of mercy and balanced judgment, and the call to heroic action—which may include, under very special circumstances, the obligation of suicide: this value system would understandably appeal to a writer whose dearest relative had just died in a war of uncertain purpose in a foreign country. Couple all this with the grandeur of a system that sees a total congruence or correspondence between the ideal and material worlds, and we have in addition a powerful and all-mastering framework for poetic metaphor: our every action will resonate to the most distant star.

Senecan values answered to the personal needs of the Countess, just as they helped focus the values of an Elizabethan nobility that was very conscious of its own role in building a nation only recently emerged from comparative anarchy, with the violence of civil wars and religious persecution. Literary histories often remark wryly that the Countess and her friends rather mistook the direction the theater was to take, and missed by a fairly wide margin the road laid down by Marlowe, Shakespeare, Jonson, and the rest; but the point is that plays like *The Tragedy of Antony* were not conceived or written as popular theater, any more than the people who attended the popular theater would have relished a drama based on self-control, logic, and intellectual passion. No doubt the Countess would have been appalled at any effort by the vulgar entrepreneurs on the Bankside to stage her play, just as in later life this very private noblewoman was said to have torn her hair out when she heard that her unruly son Philip had been switched in the face by a Scot at a public horserace. One constant theme in all her work is the necessity of idealism and the virtue of the fixed soul in a world of chaos; *Antony* implicitly assumes that the highest aim of art is to appeal to the noblest instincts in man, and as for what those were, Seneca could provide a model that had held up as well as any and better than most.

Inevitably the question is asked whether such a play is in fact a play at all, or is only a set of extended meditations in verse. We cannot with any degree of confidence say how Seneca's plays were performed, nor can we be sure what Elizabethan literary circles may have done with such plays in court, but we can make some educated guesses as to how classical drama and imitations of classical drama were handled in the universities, and these might give us at least a provisional answer to the question. One might infer from that analogy that a play like *Antony* would have been read in the manner of a production in reader's theater, with different voices taking different parts, and treating them as if they were the expression of dramatic characters undergoing changes in their lives. It is most unlikely that in such a performance there would have been either costumes or action, but in a sense this is liberating, and to those dubious as to how effective this would be, one might recommend listening to a recording of a modern work for reader's theater, such as Dylan Thomas's *Under Milk Wood*.

To come to specifics in the play at hand: Garnier's *Marc Antoine* is typical of sixteenth-century tragedies based upon the Senecan model. The plot of the play is grounded in the dramatic unities, and the principal characters are given long monologues unpunctuated by even the rumor of action. There are the obligatory five acts, in this case separated by four choruses, and to Cleopatra alone is given the final summing-up. Garnier's play is written in rhymed alexandrines with lyrical stanzas for the choruses; the Countess, however, despite her demonstrated facility with complex forms in other works, here translates Garnier's couplets into blank verse, while retaining intricate rhyme schemes in most of the choruses. The complete translation runs to just over two thousand lines, or about four-fifths the length of *Macbeth*.

It would be possible to fault Garnier's play on two counts, the first for being what it is, a play based upon the Senecan model, and second for taking liberties with that model. Arguments of this kind being largely circular, we might focus instead upon what the Countess was (apparently) attempting to do, and point out some of the ways in which she succeeds, using as a point of departure her decision to translate Garnier's rhymed alexandrines into blank verse. The results of this change are most evident in the heightened contrast between the speeches of the principal characters and the choruses. The self-control of the principals seems at once looser and subtler because of the contrast between their blank verse and the choric stanzas. The gain in a naturalistic range of expression is enormous, and it seems likely that this looseness was calculated, especially in view of the way the Countess has broken her syntax across the line endings: the ratio of enjambed lines to end-stopped lines in the blank verse of *Antony* is much closer to that in Shakespeare's final period than it is to that in his plays contemporary with *Antony*.[5] More impressive, this openness occurs within a translation that stays quite close to the original, often

so close as to constitute a reliable crib for Garnier's French. The Countess's total competence with these virtuoso pieces makes all the more interesting her decision to depart from Garnier's couplets in the body of the
play. No heroic spirit would forgo that much labor for nothing.

To understand why the Countess has heightened the contrast between
the verse of the choruses and that of the main characters we need to look
at the ideas they discuss. The main theme in the play is the working of
Fortune, on which the characters' views range widely. Antony begins by
saying the heavens are obstinate against him, but gradually he moves into
a position of personal responsibility; Cleopatra is tempted by her advisors
to blame her destiny, and does, although eventually she comes to accept
the conjunction of a controlling destiny and personal decision; and
Caesar stands in contrast to the two lovers, convinced as he is of his own
moral superiority, a view encouraged by the timeservers who surround
him.

Opposed to Antony's and Cleopatra's ideas of freedom and the importance of the individual life are the four choruses, who steadily advance a
series of dismal oversimplifications. The first chorus, a group of Egyptians, replies to Antony's opening lament by calling all human effort folly,
saying that the heavens hate us all, and adding with infallible logic that
wretchedness always pursues the wretch. When Cleopatra has her turn to
lament in the second act, the chorus has two speeches, the first noting that
mourning is satisfaction of a kind, even if the system of destiny is irrevers-
ible. As Cleopatra's anguish then reaches greater heights, the chorus bursts
into praise for the fertility of Egypt and the glories of the natural cycle.
The logic of this slowly dawns as the chorus continues: because of these
two lovers, the Egyptians may have lost their political freedom and may
be facing what we would call a balance of payments deficit, but they are
consoled by thinking that time overthrows all, even Romans. This Egyptian chorus puts in its last appearance at the end of act III, after Antony
has been contemplating suicide; here they say that blind desire is torture,
and thank the heavens for death. Man has at least enough freedom to kill
himself, which in this case would allow Antony to avoid an inevitable
humiliation greater than that he feels now. Only one chorus remains, that
at the end of act IV, and this time a chorus of Roman soldiers speaks after
Caesar, saying that the gods are indifferent to the spectacle of human
suffering. This chorus has the homey realism of one of W. H. Auden's
military lyrics, for although the soldiers say that they really want to hang
up their armor and see the destruction stop, in the meantime they are glad
that they are going to have just one general to obey. Their main worry
now is that Rome's pride in being outside the laws of temporal change
may eventually cause the gods to overthrow the Empire. This is what the
Egyptian chorus had said before, but since it now comes out in a tighter

poetic form, it looks like an old premonition which might now be coming true. The soldiers still agree with the Egyptians, though, that there is no possibility for heroism or achievement in this world.

The principals all explore the ideas of Fortune and freedom in greater detail than these choruses can imagine. Much of the pleasure of reading a play of this kind lies in our watching the character go through a maze of assorted evasions, alibis, and half-truths, meanwhile resisting over-simplifications and temptations from outside, to emerge finally into a heightened state of self-knowledge. Again, the poetic technique the Countess brings to the play corresponds fully to the development of character: while the choruses argue, in elaborate and interlocking forms, that man is a prisoner of fate, the principals are left to work out their own destinies in the freedom of blank verse.

The characterization of Caesar helps to illuminate this contrast. Act IV is an interlude with Caesar and his aides, and as this is omitted from the selection presented below, a summary of it might be useful here, along with some comment about its place in the play's design. Caesar and his company are in no uncertainty as to their place in Fortune's design. Caesar announces early on that to praise the gods is to praise him, for he is "Fortune's king and lord" (line 1365). Antony's problem, as Caesar and Agrippa diagnose it, was that he "thought he held / (By overweening) Fortune in his hand" (1398–99), while it was perfectly evident that Caesar held it. Antony also dared the gods when he gave his children the names of divinities (1420–27). It was only appropriate, Caesar observes, that "fortune, in my stead, / Repulsing him his forces disarrayed" (1468–69). After establishing the Roman party line, however, Caesar is prepared to tamper with circumstance himself, by planning the murder of all his remaining opponents. It is when Agrippa is urging the consistency of Caesar's egotism—not to mention the utility of a pious restraint—that Dercetas enters with the news of Antony's death. This news mollifies Caesar somewhat, sending him into a formal eulogy which Agrippa commonsensically interrupts to suggest that Caesar might first thank the gods, and then seize Cleopatra's treasure and jewels. On this note the act ends, and we might feel that we have been let in by the back door, so to speak, to the idea that controls Cleopatra's final scene. Although fortune may give certain blessings as well as certain burdens, one still has choices to make. Yet when selfish choices are made in the name of an external fortune, the results cannot be happy, either in Cleopatra's case or, as the Roman chorus intimates after act IV, in Caesar's. If Rome falls, it will fall as much because of bad choices by individuals (including Caesar) as by fate. There is, in short, a large element of unresolved self-deception in Caesar's speeches, a self-deception in which he shows no particular interest and which provides an ironic commentary on the searching in the speeches of Antony and Cleopatra.

Throughout the play the Countess's attention to the detail of poetic technique is both scrupulous and thoughtful. Beside the major change of adopting blank verse, she has made countless adjustments in Garnier's individual speeches, fine-tuning them to register better with the mind of the speaker. These changes could be discovered by close comparison of the two texts, but one illustration might be suggestive. In the chorus of Roman soldiers, their infantryman's hope for one general with one mind was expressed in Garnier's play by an *a a b b c d c d* stanza, but when the Countess translated this she went to closed couplets. It is the only long speech so translated in the play, and it is perfectly suited to the lockstep mentality of this particular chorus. The Countess had the gift for being able to hear each voice in each place in her design.

This finally remains one of the great contributions that this play and this writer offered to English literature. She is one of the first to understand (as the authors of such other landmarks as *Gorboduc* [1590] did not understand) that the poetic form of a play should mirror the speakers' mental states, and further, the poetry given an individual character might reasonably undergo some changes as the character develops. Beyond that, she is also one of our first dramatists to demonstrate some understanding of the way single speeches might be prepared for, and might form a running commentary upon one another. In these ways she is perhaps the first author in English to show a method of dramatic exposition working directly through poetry, and whatever the popularity of her own work with a public audience, *Antony* proves conclusively that the English literary imagination was prepared for the great achievements in drama that lay in the generation ahead.

As for the literary fortunes of the Countess, her translation of the Psalms remained known to a good number of churchmen, and selections were reprinted in anthologies of religious lyrics during the eighteenth and nineteenth centuries. Her other works fell into comparative obscurity. Until this century, literary histories tended to stress instead her importance as a patron; her reputation was attached to, and in many ways the result of, her devotion to her brother and her interest in seeing his works completed and printed. In the later nineteenth century, Ruskin in particular recommended her Psalm translations, but the rest of her poetry and *Antony* remained largely unread. A typical contemporary explanation of the reasons for this might be found in George Saintsbury's *History of Elizabethan Literature* (London, 1901), which claimed that the spirit of Seneca was simply inimical to "the genius of the English nation." Renewed interest in the literary career of the Countess has been part of a general

revival of interest in the whole Sidney group. To judge from recent mono-
graphs and dissertations, a full reassessment of the Countess's career and
literary milieu may be underway now; this should demonstrate from
many different perspectives that the Countess was not simply one of the
chief patrons of the Elizabethan era, but also one of its most original
literary minds as well.

NOTES

1. "To my dear lady and sister the Countess of Pembroke," in *The Countess of
Pembroke's Arcadia*, ed. Jean Robertson (Oxford, 1973), p. 3.
2. John Aubrey, *Brief Lives*, ed. Anthony Powell (New York, 1949), p. 33. Much in
Aubrey's biographical sketch is highly implausible, however, and Waller nicely sifts out what
can be confirmed from other sources.
3. Hallett Smith, "English Metrical Psalms in the Sixteenth Century and Their Literary
Influence," *Huntington Library Quarterly* 9 (1946): 269.
4. See the dedicatory sonnet prefixed to *The Faerie Queene*, and cf. *Colin Clout's Come
Home Again*, line 488.
5. These comparative figures are offered by Alice Luce in her edition of the play.

At Ramsbury. 26 of November. 1590.

The Tragedy of Antony by Robert Garnier. Translated by Mary Herbert, Countess of Pembroke

THE ARGUMENT

After the overthrow of Brutus and Cassius, the liberty of Rome now being
utterly oppressed and the Empire settled in the hands of Octavius Caesar
and Mark Antony (who for knitting a straiter bond of amity between
them, had taken to wife Octavia, the sister of Caesar), Antony undertook
a journey against the Parthians, with the intent to regain on them the
honor won from them by the Romans, at the discomfiture and slaughter
of Crassus. But coming in his journey into Syria, the places renewed in his
remembrance the long intermitted love of Cleopatra, queen of Egypt, who
before time had both in Cilicia and at Alexandria entertained him with all
the exquisite delights and sumptuous pleasures which a great prince and
voluptuous lover could to the uttermost desire. Whereupon omitting his
enterprise, he made his return to Alexandria, again falling to his former
loves, without any regard of his virtuous wife Octavia, by whom nev-

ertheless he had excellent children. This occasion Octavius took of taking
arms against him, and preparing a mighty fleet, encountered him at Actium, who also had assembled to that place a great number of galleys of
his own, besides sixty which Cleopatra brought with her from Egypt. But
at the very beginning of the battle, Cleopatra with all her galleys betook
her to flight, which Antony seeing could not but follow, by his departure
leaving to Octavius the greatest victory which in any sea battle had been
heard of. Which he not negligent to pursue, follows them the next spring
and besiegeth them within Alexandria, where Antony finding all that he
had trusted to fail him, beginneth to grow jealous and to suspect
Cleopatra. She thereupon enclosed herself with two of her women in a
monument she had before caused to be built, thence sends him word she
was dead; which he believing for truth, gave himself with his sword a
deadly wound, but died not until a messenger came from Cleopatra to
have him brought to her to the tomb. Which she not daring to open lest
she should be made a prisoner to the Romans, and carried in Caesar's
triumph, cast down a cord from a high window, by the which (her women
helping her) she trussed up Antony half dead, and so got him into the
monument. The stage supposed Alexandria; the chorus first Egyptians,
and after, Roman soldiers; the history to be read at large in Plutarch in the
Life of Antony.

THE ACTORS

Antony
Cleopatra
Iras *and*
Charmian, Cleopatra's *women*
Philostratus, *a philosopher*
Lucilius
Diomed, *secretary to* Cleopatra
Octavius Caesar
Agrippa
Euphron, *teacher of* Cleopatra's *children*
Children of Cleopatra
Dercetas, *the messenger*

ACT I

   Antony.   Since cruel Heaven's against me obstinate,
Since all mishaps of the round engine do
Conspire my harm; since men, since powers divine,
Air, earth, and sea are all injurious;
And that my Queen herself, in whom I lived,

The idol of my heart, doth me pursue,
It's meet I die. For her have I foregone
My country, Caesar unto war provoked
(For just revenge of sister's wrong, my wife,
Who moved my Queen—ay me!—to jealousy),   10
For love of her, in her allurements caught
Abandoned life, I honor have despised,
Disdained my friends, and of the stately Rome
Despoiled the Empire of her best attire,
Condemned that power that made me so much feared,
A slave become unto her feeble face.
O cruel traitress, woman most unkind,
Thou dost, forsworn, my love and life betray,
And giv'st me up to rageful enemy,
Which soon (O fool!) will plague thy perjury.   20
    Yielded Pelusium on this country's shore,
Yielded thou hast my ships and men of war,
That nought remains (so destitute am I)
But these same arms which on my back I wear.
Thou should'st have had them too, and me unarmed
Yielded to Caesar naked of defense.
Which while I bear let Caesar never think
Triumph of me shall his proud chariot grace
Not think with me his glory to adorn,
On me alive to use his victory.   30
    Thou only, Cleopatra, triumph hast,
Thou only hast my freedom servile made,
Thou only hast me vanquished: not by force
(For forced I cannot be) but by sweet baits
Of thy eyes' graces, which did gain so fast
Upon my liberty that nought remained.
None else henceforth, but thou my dearest Queen,
Shall glory in commanding Antony.
    Have Caesar fortune and the gods his friends,
To him have love and the fatal sisters given   40
The scepter of the earth; he never shall
Subject my life to his obedience.
But when that death, my glad refuge, shall have
Bounded the course of my unsteadfast life,
And frozen corpse under a marble cold
Within tomb's bosom, widow of my soul,
Then at his will let him it subject make:
Then what he will let Caesar do with me.

Make me limb after limb be rent, make me
My burial take in sides of Thracian wolf.   50
   Poor Antony! Alas what was the day,
The days of loss that gained thee thy love!
Wretch Antony! Since Maegara pale
With snaky hairs enchained thy misery,
The fire thee burnt was never Cupid's fire
(For Cupid bears not such a mortal brand),
It was some fury's torch, Orestes' torch,
Which sometime burnt his mother-murdering soul
(When wandering mad, rage boiling in his blood,
He fled his fault which followed as he fled),   60
Kindled within his bones by shadowy pale
Of mother slain returned from Stygian lake.
   Antony, poor Antony! Since that day
Thy good old hap did fair from thee retire.
Thy virtue dead, thy glory made alive
So oft by martial deeds is gone in smoke;
Since then the bays so well thy forehead knew
To Venus' myrtles yielded have their place;
Trumpets to pipes; field tents to courtly bowers;
Lances and pikes to dances and to feasts.   70
Since then, O wretch! Instead of bloody wars
Thou shouldst have made upon the Parthian kings
For Roman honor filed by Crassus' foil,
Thou threw thy cuirass off, and fearful helm,
With coward courage unto Egypt's queen
In haste to run, about her neck to hang
Languishing in her arms thy idol made;
In sum given up to Cleopatra's eyes.
Thou break'st at length from thence, as one encharmed
Breaks from th'enchanter that him strongly held.   80
For thy first reason (spoiling of their force
The poisoned cups of thy fair sorceress)
Recured thy spirit; and then on every side
Thou mad'st again the earth with soldiers' swarm.
All Asia hid: Euphrates' banks do tremble
To see at once so many Romans there
Breathe horror, rage, and with a threatening eye
In mighty squadrons cross his swelling streams.
Nought seen but horse, and fiery sparkling arms;
Nought heard but hideous noise of muttering troops.   90
The Part, the Mede, abandoning their goods,

Hide them for fear in hills of Hircanie,
Redoubting thee. Then willing to besiege
The great Phraate, head of Medea,
Thou campedst at her walls with vain assault,
Thy engines (mishap!) not thither brought.
  So long thou stayest, so long thou dost thee rest,
So long thy love with such things nourished
Reframes, reforms itself and stealingly
Retakes his force and rebecomes more great.   100
For of thy Queen the looks, the grace, the words,
Sweetness, allurements, amorous delights,
Entered again thy soul, and day and night,
In watch, in sleep, her image followed thee:
Not dreaming but of her, repenting still
That thou for war had such a goddess left.
  Thou carest no more for Parth, nor Parthian bow,
Sallies, assaults, encounters, shocks, alarms,
For ditches, ramparts, wards, entrenched grounds;
Thy only care is of Nilus' streams,   110
Sight of that face whose guileful semblant doth
(Wandering in thee) infect thy tainted heart.
Her absence thee besots: each hour, each hour
Of stay, to thee impatient seems an age.
Enough of conquest, praise thou deem'st enough,
If soon enough the bristled fields thou see
Of fruitful Egypt, and the stranger flood
Thy Queen's fair eyes (another Pharos) lights.
  Returned lo, dishonored, despised,
In wanton love a woman thee misleads   120
Sunk in foul sink; meanwhile respecting nought
Thy wife Octavia and her tender babes,
Of whom the long contempt against thee whets
The sword of Caesar now thy lord become.
  Lost thy great Empire, all those goodly towns
Reverenced thy name as rebels now thee leave,
Rise against thee, and to the ensigns flock
Of conquering Caesar, who enwalls thee round
Caged in thy hold, scarce master of thyself,
Late master of so many nations.   130
  Yet, yet, which is of grief extremest grief,
Which is yet of mischief highest mischief,
It's Cleopatra alas! Alas it's she,
It's she augments the torment of thy pain,

Betrays thy love, thy life alas! Betrays,
Caesar to please, whose grace she seeks to gain,
With thought her crown to save and fortune make
Only thy foe which common ought have been.
    If her I always loved, and the first flame
Of her heart-killing love shall burn me last,   140
Justly complain I she disloyal is,
Nor constant is, even as I constant am,
To comfort my mishap, despising me
No more, than when the heavens favored me.
    But ah! By nature women wavering are,
Each moment changing and rechanging minds.
Unwise, who blind in them, thinks loyalty
Ever to find in beauty's company.

ACT II, SCENE I

    Philostratus.   What horrible fury, what cruel rage,
O Egypt so extremely thee torments?
Hast thou the gods so angered by thy fault?
Hast thou against them some such crime conceived,   240
That their engrained hand lift up in threats
That they should desire thy heart in blood to bathe?
And that their burning wrath which nought can quench
Should pitiless on us still light down?
    We are not hewn out of the monstrous mass
Of giants, those which heaven's wrack conspired;
Ixion's race, false prater of his loves;
Nor yet of him who fained lightnings found;
Nor cruel Tantalus, nor bloody Atreus,
Whose cursed banquet for Thyestes' plague   250
Made the beholding sun for horror turn
His back, and backward from his course return;
And hastening his wing-footed horse's race,
Plunge him in sea for shame to hide his face:
While sullen night upon the wondering world
For midday's light her starry mantle cast.
    But what we be, whatever wickedness
By us is done, alas! With what more plagues,
More eager torments could the gods declare
To heaven and earth that they us hateful hold?   260
With soldiers, strangers, horrible in arms
Our land is hid, our people drowned in tears.

But terror here and horror, nought is seen,
And present death prising our life each hour.
Hard at our ports and at our porches waits
Our conquering foe: hearts fail us, hopes are dead;
Our Queen laments; and this great emperor
Sometime (would now they did) whom worlds did fear
Abandoned, betrayed, now minds no more
But from his evils by hastened death to pass.   270
   Come you poor people tired with ceaseless plaints,
With tears and sighs make mournful sacrifice
On Isis' altars, not ourselves to save,
But soften Caesar and him piteous make
To us, his prey; that so his lenity
May change our death into captivity.
   Strange are the evils the fates on us have brought;
O but alas! How far more strange the cause!
Love, love (alas, whoever would have thought?)
Hath lost this realm inflamed with his fire.   280
Love, playing love, which men say kindles not
But in soft hearts, hath ashes made our towns.
And his sweet shafts, with whose shot none is killed,
Which ulcer not, with deaths our lands have filled.
   Such was the bloody, murdering, hellish love
Possessed thy heart, fair false guest Priam's son,
Firing a brand which after made to burn
The Trojan towers by Grecians ruinate.
By this love, Priam, Hector, Troilus,
Memnon, Deiphobus, Glaucus, thousands more   290
Whom red Scamander's armor clogged streams
Rolled into seas, before their dates are dead.
So plaguey he, so many tempests raiseth,
So murdering he, so many cities razeth,
When insolent, blind, lawless, orderless,
With mad delights our sense he entertains.
   All-knowing gods our wracks did us foretell
By signs in earth, by signs in starry spheres,
Which should have moved us, had not destiny
With too strong hand warped our misery.   300
The comets flaming through the scattered clouds
With fiery beams, most like unbraided hairs;
The fearful dragon whistling at the banks;
And holy Apis' ceaseless bellowing
(As never erst) and shedding endless tears;

Blood raining down from heaven in unknown showers;
Our god's dark face overcast with woe,
And dead men's ghosts appearing in the night.
Yea, even this night while all the city stood
Oppressed with terror, horror, servile fear,   310
Deep silence over all: the sounds were heard
Of diverse songs, and diverse instruments,
Within the void of air, and howling noise,
Such as mad Bacchus' priests in Bacchus' feasts
On Nisa make; and (seemed) the company,
Our city lost, went to the enemy.
  So we forsaken both of Gods and men,
So are we in the mercy of our foes,
And we henceforth obedient must become
To laws of them who have us overcome.   320

ACT II, SCENE 2

  Cleopatra.   That I have thee betrayed, dear Antony,
My life, my soul, my sun? I had such thought?
That I have thee betrayed, my lord, my king?
That I would break my vowed faith to thee?   390
Leave thee? Deceive thee? Yield to thee the rage
Of mighty foe? I ever had that heart?
Rather sharp lightning lighten on my head;
Rather may I to deepest mischief fall;
Rather the opened earth devour me;
Rather fierce tigers feed them on my flesh;
Rather, O rather let our Nilus send,
To swallow me quick, some weeping crocodile.
  And didst thou then suppose my royal heart
Had hatched, thee to ensnare, a faithless love?   400
And changing mind, as Fortune changed cheer,
I would weak thee, to win the stronger, loose.
O wretch! O caitiff! O too cruel hap!
And did not I sufficient loss sustain
Losing my realm, losing my liberty,
My tender offspring, and the joyful light
Of beamy sun, and yet, yet losing more
Thee Antony my care, if I lose not
What yet remained? Thy love alas! Thy love
More dear than scepter, children, freedom, light.   410
  So ready I to row in Charon's barge,

Shall lose the joy of dying in thy love;
So the sole comfort of my misery
To have one tomb with thee is me bereft.
So I in shady plains shall plain alone,
Not (as I hoped) companion of thy moan,
O height of grief!
    Iras.   Why with continual cries
Your grievous harms do you exasperate?
Torment yourself with murdering complaints,
Strain your weak breast so oft, so vehemently?   420
Water with tears this fair alabaster?
With sorrow's sting so many beauties wound?
Come of so many kings, want you the heart
Bravely, stoutly, this tempest to resist?
    Cleopatra.   My evils are wholly unsupportable,
No human force can them withstand but death.
    Iras.   To him that strives nought is impossible.
    Cleopatra.   In striving lies no hope of my mishaps.
    Iras.   All things do yield to force of lovely face.
    Cleopatra.   My face too lovely caused my wretched case.   430
My face hath so entrapped, to cast us down,
That for his conquest Caesar may it thank,
Causing that Antony one army lost,
The other wholly did to Caesar yield.
For not enduring (so his amorous spirit
Was with my beauty fired) my shameful flight,
Soon as he saw from rank wherein he stood
In hottest fight, my galleys making sail,
Forgetful of his charge (as if his soul
Unto his lady's soul had been enchained),   440
He left his men, who so courageously
Did leave their lives to gain him victory,
And careless both of fame and army's loss
My oared galleys followed with his ships,
Companion of my flight, by this base part
Blasting his former flourishing renown.
    Iras.   Are you therefore cause of his overthrow?
    Cleopatra.   I am sole cause: I did it, only I.
    Iras.   Fear of a woman troubled so his spirit?
    Cleopatra.   Fire of his love was by my fear inflamed.   450
    Iras.   And should he then to war have led a queen?
    Cleopatra.   Alas! This was not his offense but mine.
Antony (ay me! Who else so brave a chief!)

Would not I should have taken seas with him,
But would have left me fearful woman far
From common hazard of the doubtful war.
   O that I had believed! Now, now of Rome
All the great Empire at our beck should bend.
All should obey, the vagabonding Scyths,
The feared Germans, back-shooting Parthians,   460
Wandering Numidians, Britons far removed,
And tawny nations scorched with sun.
But I cared not: so was my soul possessed
(To my great harm) with burning jealousy,
Fearing lest in my absence Antony
Should leaving me retake Octavia.
   Charmian.   Such was the rigor of your destiny.
   Cleopatra.   Such was my error and obstinacy.
   Charmian.   But since gods would not, could you do withal?
   Cleopatra.   Always from gods good haps, not harms, do fall.   470
   Charmian.   And have they not all power on men's affairs?
   Cleopatra.   They never bow so low as worldly cares,
But leave to mortal men to be disposed
Freely on earth whatever mortal is.
If we therein sometimes some faults commit,
We may them not to their high majesties
But to ourselves impute, whose passions
Plunge us each day in all afflictions.
Wherewith when we our souls do thorned feel,
Flattering ourselves we say they destinies are,   480
That gods would have it so, and that our care
Could not impeach but that it must be so.
   Charmian. Things here below are in the heavens begot,
Before they be in this our world borne,
And never can our weakness turn awry
The stalless course of powerful destiny.
Nought here—force, reason, human providence,
Holy devotion, noble blood—prevails,
And Jove himself whose hand doth heavens rule,
Who both to gods and men as king commands,   490
Who earth (our firm support) with plenty stores,
Moves air and sea with twinkling of his eye,
Who all can do, yet never can undo
What once hath been by their hard laws decreed.
   When Trojan walls, great Neptune's workmanship,
Environed were with Greeks, and Fortune's wheel

Doubtful ten years now to the camp did turn,
And now again toward the town returned,
How many times did force and fury swell
In Hector's veins egging him to the spoil   500
Of conquered foes, which at his blows did fly,
As fearful sheep at feared wolves' approach,
To save (in vain: for why? It would not be)
Poor walls of Troy from adversaries' rage,
Who dyed them in blood, and cast to ground
Heaped them with bloody burning carcasses.
   No, Madam, think that if the ancient crown
Of your progenitors that Nilus ruled
Force take from you, the gods have willed it so,
To whom ofttimes princes are odious.   510
They have to everything an end ordained:
All worldly greatness by them bounded is;
Some sooner, some later, as they think best;
None their decree is able to infringe.
But, which is more, to us disastered men
Which subject are in all things to their will,
Their will is hid: nor while we live, we know
How, or how long we must in life remain.
Yet must we not for that feed on despair,
And make us wretched ere we wretched be,   520
But always hope the best, even to the last,
That from ourselves the mischief may not grow.
   Then, Madam, help yourself, leave off in time
Antony's wrack, lest it your wrack procure:
Retire you from him, save from wrathful rage
Of angry Caesar both your realm and you.
You see him lost, so as your amity
Unto his evils can yield no more relief.
You see him ruined, so as your support
No more henceforth can him with comfort raise.   530
Withdraw you from the storm; persist not still
To lose yourself; this royal diadem
Regain of Caesar.
   Cleopatra.   Sooner shining light
Shall leave the day, and darkness leave the night;
Sooner moist currents of tempestuous seas
Shall wave in heaven, and the nightly troops
Of stars shall shine within the foaming waves,
Than I thee, Antony, leave in deep distress.

I am with thee, be it thy worthy soul
Lodge in my breast, or from that lodging part   540
Crossing the joyless lake to take her place
In place prepared for men demigods.
    Live, if thee please, if life be loathsome die;
Dead and alive, Antony, thou shalt see
Thy princess follow thee, follow, and lament
Thy wrack, no less her own than was thy weal.
    Charmian.   What helps his wrack this everlasting love?
    Cleopatra.   Help or help not, such must, such ought I prove.
    Charmian.   Ill done, to lose yourself, and to no end.
    Cleopatra.   How ill think you to follow such a friend?   550
    Charmian.   But this your love nought mitigates his pain.
    Cleopatra.   Without this love I should be inhumane.
    Charmian.   Inhuman he, who his own death pursues.
    Cleopatra.   Not inhumane who miseries eschews.
    Charmian.   Live for your sons.
    Cleopatra.   Nay for their father die.
    Charmian.   Hardhearted mother!
    Cleopatra.   Wife, kindhearted, I.
    Charmian.   Then will you them deprive of royal right?
    Cleopatra.   Do I deprive them? No, it's destiny's might.
    Charmian.   Do you not them deprive of heritage,
That give them up to adversaries' hands,   560
A man forsaken fearing to forsake,
Whom such huge numbers hold environed?
T'abandon one 'gainst whom the frowning world
Banded with Caesar makes conspiring war?
    Cleopatra.   The less ought I to leave him least of all.
A friend in distress should most assist.
If that when Antony great and glorious
His legions led to drink Euphrates' streams,
So many kings in train redoubting him,
In triumph raised as high as highest heaven;   570
Lord-like disposing as him pleased best,
The wealth of Greece, the wealth of Asia:
In that fair fortune had I him exchanged
For Caesar, then men would have counted me
Faithless, unconstant, light: but now the storm
And blustering tempest driving on his face,
Ready to drown, alas! what would they say?
What would himself in Pluto's mansion say?
If I, whom always more than life he loved,

If I, who am his heart, who was his hope,   580
Leave him, forsake him (and perhaps in vain)
Weakly to please who him hath overthrown?
Not light, unconstant, faithless should I be,
But vile, forsworn, of treacherous cruelty.
    Charmian.   Cruelty to shun you self-cruel are.
    Cleopatra.   Self-cruel him from cruelty to spare.
    Charmian.   Our first affection to ourself is due.
    Cleopatra.   He is my self.
    Charmian.   Next it extends unto
Our children, friends, and to our country soil.
And you for some respect of wifely love,   590
(Albeit scarce wifely) lose your native land,
Your children, friends, and (which is more) your life.
With so strong charms doth love bewitch our wits:
So fast in us this fire once kindled flames.
Yet if his harm by yours redress might have—
    Cleopatra.   With mine it may be closed in darksome grave.
    Charmian. And that, as Alcest to herself unkind,
You might exempt him from the laws of death.
But he is sure to die: and now his sword
Already moisted is in his warm blood,   600
Helpless for any succor you can bring
Against death's sting, which he must shortly feel.
    Then let your love be like the love of old
Which Carian queen did nourish in her heart
Of her Mausolus: build for him a tomb
Whose stateliness a wonder new may make.
Let him, let him have sumptuous funerals:
Let grave thereon the horror of his fights;
Let earth be buried with unburied heaps.
Frame the Pharsaly, and discolored streams   610
Of deep Enipeus; frame the grassy plain,
Which lodged his camp at siege of Mutina.
Make all his combats and courageous acts,
And yearly plays to his praise institute;
Honor his memory; with doubled care
Breed and bring up the children of you both
In Caesar's grace, who as a noble prince
Will leave them lords of this most glorious realm.
    Cleopatra.   What shame were that! Ah gods! What infamy!
With Antony in his good haps to share,   620
And overlive him dead, deeming enough

To shed some tears upon a widow tomb!
The after-livers justly might report
That I him only for his empire loved,
And high estate, and in that hard estate
I for another did him lewdly leave.
Like to those birds wafted with wandering wings
From foreign lands in springtime here arrive,
And live with us so long as summer's heat
And their food lasts, then seek another soil.   630
And as we see with ceaseless fluttering
Flocking of silly flies a brownish cloud
To vintaged wine yet working in the tun,
Not parting thence while they sweet liquor taste,
After, as smoke, all vanish in the air,
And of the swarm not one so much appear.
    Iras.   By this sharp death what profit can you win?
    Cleopatra.   I neither gain nor profit seek therein.
    Iras.   What praise shall you of after-ages get?
    Cleopatra.   Nor praise, nor glory in my cares are set.   640
    Iras.   What other end ought you respect, than this?
    Cleopatra.   My only end my only duty is.
    Iras.   Your duty must upon some good be founded!
    Cleopatra.   On virtue it, the only good, is founded.
    Iras.   What is that *virtue*?
    Cleopatra.   That which us beseems.
    Iras.   Outrage ourselves? Who that beseeming deems?
    Cleopatra.   Finish I will my sorrows dying thus.
    Iras.   'Minish you will your glories doing thus.
    Cleopatra.   Good friends I pray you seek not to revoke
My fixed intent of following Antony.   650
I will die. I will die: must not his life,
His life and death by mine be followed?
    Meanwhile, dear sisters, live: and while you live,
Do often honor to our loved tombs.
Strew them with flowers, and sometimes haply
The tender thought of Antony your lord
And me poor soul to tears shall you invite,
And our true loves your doleful voice commend.
    Charmian.   And think you, Madam, we from you will part?
Think you alone to feel death's ugly dart?   660
Think you to leave us? And that the same sun
Shall see at once you dead, and us alive?
We'll die with you, and Clotho pitiless

Shall us with you in hellish boat embark.
   Cleopatra.   Ah live, I pray you: this disastered woe
Which wracks my heart, alone to me belongs;
My lot 'longs not to you; servants to be
No shame, no harm to you, as is to me.
   Live, sisters, live, and seeing his suspect
Hath causeless me in sea of sorrows drowned,   670
And that I cannot live, if so I would,
Nor yet would leave this life, if so I could,
Without his love: procure me, Diomed,
That 'gainst poor me he be no more incensed.
Wrest out of his conceit that harmful doubt,
That since his wrack he hath of me conceived
Though wrong conceived: witness you reverent gods,
Barking Anubis, Apis bellowing.
Tell him, my soul burning, impatient,
Forlorn with love of him, for certain seal   680
Of her true loyalty my corpse hath left,
T'increase of dead the number numberless.
   Go then, and if as yet he me bewail,
If yet for me his heart one sigh forth breathe,
Blest shall I be, and with far more content
Depart this world, where so I me torment.
Mean season us let this sad tomb enclose,
Attending here till death conclude our woes.
   Diomed.   I will obey your will.
   Cleopatra.   So the desert
The gods repay of thy true faithful heart.   690
Diomed. And is't not pity, gods, ah gods of heaven!
To see from love such hateful fruits to spring?
And is't not pity that this firebrand so
Lays waste the trophies of Philippi fields?
Where are those sweet allurements, those sweet looks,
Which gods themselves right heartsick would have made?
What doth that beauty, rarest gift of heaven,
Wonder of earth? Alas! What do those eyes?
And that sweet voice all Asia understood,
And sunburnt Afric wide in deserts spread?   700
Is their force dead? Have they no further power?
Cannot by them Octavius be surprised?
Alas, if Jove in midst of all his ire,
With thunderbolt in hand some land to plague,
Had cast his eyes on my queen, out of hand

His plaguing bolt had fallen out of his hand;
Fire out of his wrath into vain smoke should turn,
And other fire within his breast should burn.
    Nought lives so fair. Nature by such a work
Herself should seem in workmanship hath past.   710
She is all heavenly: never any man
But seeing her was ravished with her sight.
The alabaster covering of her face,
The coral color her two lips ingrains,
Her beamy eyes, two suns of this our world,
Of her fair hair the fine and flaming gold,
Her brave straight stature, and her winning parts
Are nothing else but fires, fetters darts.
    Yet this is nothing [to] th'enchanting skills
Of her celestial spirit, her training speech,   720
Her grace, her majesty, and forcing voice,
Whether she it with fingers' speech consort,
Or hearing sceptered kings' ambassadors
Answer to each in his own language make.
    Yet now at need it aids her not at all
With all these beauties, so her sorrow stings.
Darkened with woe, her only study is
To weep, to sigh, to seek for loneliness.
Careless of all, her hair disordered hangs;
Her charming eyes whence murdering looks did fly,   730
Now rivers grown, whose wellspring anguish is,
Do trickling wash the marble of her face.
Her fair discovered breast with sobbing swollen
Self-cruel she still martyreth with blows.
    Alas! It's our ill hap, for if her tears
She would convert into her loving charms,
To make a conquest of the conqueror
(As well she might, would she her force employ),
She should us safety from these ills procure,
Her crown unto her, and to her race assure.   740
Unhappy he, in whom self-succor lies,
Yet self-forsaken wanting succor dies.

ACT III

   Antony.   Lucil sole comforter of my bitter case,
The only trust, the only hope I have
In last despair, ah is not this the day

That death should me of life and love bereave?
What wait I for that have no refuge left,
But am sole remnant of my fortune left?
All leave me, fly me; none, no not of them   870
Which of my greatness greatest good received,
Stands with my fall; they seem as now ashamed
That heretofore they did me aught regard:
They draw them back, showing they followed me
Not to partake my harms, but cozen me.
    Lucilius.   *In this our world nothing is steadfast found,*
In vain he hopes, who here his hopes doth ground.
    Antony.   Yet nought afflicts me, nothing kills me so,
As that I so my Cleopatra see
Practice with Caesar, and to him transport   880
My flame, her love, more dear than life to me.
    Lucilius.   Believe it not; too high a heart she bears,
Too princely thoughts.
    Antony.   Too wise a head she wears
Too much inflamed with greatness, evermore
Gaping for our great Empire's government.
    Lucilius.   So long time you her constant love have tried.
    Antony.   But still with me good fortune did abide.
    Lucilius.   Her changed love what token makes you know?
    Antony.   Pelusium lost, and Actium's overthrow,
Both by her fraud: my well-appointed fleet,   890
And trusty soldiers in my quarrel armed,
Whom she, false she, instead of my defense,
Came to persuade to yield them to my foe;
Such honor Thyre[us] done, such welcome given,
Their long close talks I neither knew, nor would,
And treacherous wrong Alexas hath me done,
Witness too well her perjured love to me.
But you O gods, if any faith regard,
With sharp revenge her faithless change reward.
    Lucilius.   The dole she made upon our overthrow,   900
Her realm given up for refuge to our men,
Her poor attire when she devoutly kept
The solemn day of her nativity,
Again the cost and prodigal expense
Showed when she did your birthday celebrate,
Do plain enough her heart unfeigned prove,
Equally touched, you loving, as you love.
    Antony.   Well, be her love to me or false or true,

Once in my soul a cureless wound I feel,
I love, nay burn in fire of her love: 910
Each day, each night her image haunts my mind.
Herself my dreams; and still I tired am,
And still I am with burning pincers nipped.
Extreme my harm; yet sweeter to my sense
Than boiling torch of jealous torment's fire;
This grief, nay rage, in me such stir doth keep,
And thorns me still, both when I wake and sleep.
    Take Caesar conquest, take my goods, take he
Th'honor to be lord of the earth alone,
My sons, my life bent headlong to mishaps: 920
No force, so not my Cleopatra take.
So foolish I, I cannot her forget,
Though better were I banished her my thought.
Like to the sick whose throat the fever's fire
Hath vehemently with thirsty drought inflamed,
Drinks still, albeit the drink he still desires
Be nothing else but fuel to his flame.
He cannot rule himself; his health's respect
Yieldeth to his distempered stomach's heat.
    Lucilius.   Leave off this love, that thus renews your woe. 930
    Antony.   I do my best, but ah! Cannot do so.
    Lucilius.   Think how you have so brave a captain been,
And now are by this vain affection fallen.
    Antony.   The ceaseless thought of my felicity
Plunges me more in this adversity.
For nothing so a man in ill torments,
As who to him his good state represents.
This makes my rack, my anguish, and my woe
Equal unto the hellish passions grow,
When I to mind my happy puissance call 940
Which erst I had by warlike conquest won,
And that good fortune which me never left,
Which hard disaster now hath me bereft.
    With terror tremble all the world I made
At my sole word, as rushes in the streams
At water's will; I conquered Italy,
I conquered Rome, that nations so redoubt,
I bore (meanwhile besieging Mutina)
Two consuls' armies for my ruin brought;
Bathed in their blood, by their deaths witnessing 950
My force and skill in matters martial.

   To wreak thy uncle, unkind Caesar, I
With blood of enemies the banks imbrued
Of stained Enipeus, hindering his course
Stopped with heaps of piled carcasses;
When Cassius and Brutus ill betide
Marched against us, by us twice put to flight,
But by my sole conduct: for all the time
Caesar heartsick with fear and fever lay.
Who knows it not? and how by everyone
Fame of the fact was given to me alone.   960
   There sprang the love, the never-changing love,
Wherein my heart hath since to yours been bound;
There was it, my Lucil, you Brutus saved,
And for your Brutus Antony you found.
Better my hap in gaining such a friend,
Than in subduing such an enemy.
Now former virtue dead doth me forsake,
Fortune engulfs me in extreme distress;
She turns from me her smiling countenance,   970
Casting on me mishap upon mishap.
Left and betrayed of thousand thousand friends,
Once of my suit, but you Lucil are left,
Remaining to me steadfast as a tower
In holy love, in spite of fortune's blasts.
But if of any god my voice be heard,
And be not vainly scattered in the heavens,
Such goodness shall not gloryless be lost,
But coming ages still thereof shall boast.
   Lucilius.   Men in their friendship ever should be one,   980
And never ought with fickle fortune shake,
Which still removes, nor will, nor knows the way,
Her rolling bowl in one sure state to stay.
Wherefore we ought as borrowed things receive
The goods light she lends us to pay again,
Not hold them sure, nor on them build our hopes
As on such goods as cannot fail, and fall;
But think again, nothing is durable,
Virtue except, our never-failing host:
So bearing sail when favoring winds do blow,   990
As frowning tempests may us least dismay
When they on us do fall, not over-glad
With good estate, nor over-grieved with bad,
Resist mishap.

Antony.   Alas! It is too strong.
Mishaps ofttimes are by some comfort borne,
But these, ay me! whose weights oppress my heart,
Too heavy lie, no hope can them relieve.
There rests no more, but that with cruel blade
For lingering death a hasty way be made.
    Lucilius.   Caesar, as heir unto his father's state,   1000
So will his father's goodness imitate,
To you ward; whom he knows allied in blood,
Allied in marriage, ruling equally
Th'Empire with him, and with him making war
Have purged the earth of Caesar's murderers.
You into portions parted have the world
Even like coheirs their heritages part,
And now with one accord so many years
In quiet peace both have your charges ruled.
    Antony.   Blood and alliance nothing do prevail   1010
To cool the thirst of hot ambitious breasts;
The son his father hardly can endure,
Brother his brother, in one common realm.
So fervent this desire to command,
Such jealousy it kindleth in our hearts,
Sooner men will permit another should
Love her they love, than wear the crown they wear.
All laws it breaks, turns all things upside down:
Amity, kindred, nought so holy is
But it defiles. A monarchy to gain   1020
None cares which may, so he may it obtain.
    Lucilius.   Suppose he monarch be and that this world
No more acknowledge sundry emperors,
That Rome him only fear, and that he join
The east with west, and both at once do rule:
Why should he not permit you peaceably
Discharged of charge and Empire's dignity,
Private to live reading philosophy,
In learned Greece, Spain, Asia, any land?
    Antony.   Never will he his Empire think assured   1030
While in this world Mark Antony shall live.
Sleepless suspicion, pale distrust, cold fear
Always to princes company do bear
Bred of reports, reports which night and day
Perpetual guests from court go not away.
    Lucilius. He hath not slain your brother Lucius,

Nor shortened hath the age of Lepidus,
Albeit both into his hands were fallen,
And he with wrath against them both inflamed.
Yet one, as lord in quiet rest doth bear   1040
The greatest sway in great Iberia;
The other with his gentle princes retains
Of highest priest the sacred dignity.
    Antony.   He fears not them, their feeble force he knows.
    Lucilius.   He fears no vanquished overfilled with woes.
    Antony.   Fortune may change again.
    Lucilius.   A downcast foe
Can hardly rise, which once is brought so low.
    Antony.   All that I can is done; for last assay
(When all means failed) I to entreaty fell
(Ah coward creature!) whence again repulsed   1050
Of combat I unto him proffer made,
Though he in prime, and I by feeble age
Mightily weakened both in force and skill.
Yet could not he his coward heart advance,
Basely afraid to try so praiseful chance.
This makes me plain, makes me myself accuse,
Fortune in this her spiteful force doth use
'Gainst my gray hairs; in this unhappy I
Repine at heavens in my haps pitiless.
A man, a woman both in might and mind,   1060
In Mars's school who never lesson learned,
Should me repulse, chase, overthrow, destroy,
Me of such fame, bring to so low an ebb?
Alcides' blood, who from my infancy
With happy prowess crowned have my praise,
Witness thou Gaul unused to servile yoke,
Thou valiant Spain, you fields of Thessaly,
With millions of mourning cries bewailed,
Twice watered now with blood of Italy.
    Lucilius.   Witness may Afric, and of conquered world   1070
All four quarters witnesses may be.
For in what part of earth inhabited,
Hungry of praise have you not ensigns spread?
    Antony.   Thou knowest rich Egypt (Egypt of my deeds
Fair and foul subject), Egypt ah! Thou knowest
How I behaved me fighting for thy king,
When I regained him his rebellious realm,
Against his foes in battle showing force,

And after fight in victory remorse.
   Yet if to bring my glory to the ground,   1080
Fortune had made me overthrown by one
Of greater force, of better skill than I,
One of those captains feared so of old,
Camill, Marcellus, worthy Scipio,
This late great Caesar, honor of our state,
Or that great Pompey aged grown in arms,
That after harvest of a world of men
Made in a hundred battles, fights, assaults,
My body through pierced with push of pike
Had vomited my blood, in blood my life,   1090
In midst of millions, fellows in my fall;
The less her wrong, the less should be my woe,
Nor she should pain, nor I complain me so.
   No, no, whereas I should have died in arms,
And vanquished oft new armies should have armed,
New battles given, and rather lost with me
All this whole world submitted unto me,
A man who never saw enlaced pikes
With bristled points against his stomach bent,
Who fears the field, and hides him cowardly   1100
Dead at the very noise the soldiers make,
His virtue, fraud, deceit, malicious guile,
His arms the arts that false Ulysses used
(Known at Modena, where the consuls both
Death-wounded were, and wounded by his men
To get their army, war with it to make
Against his faith, against his country soil.
Of Lepidus, which to his succors came,
To honor whom he was by duty bound,
The Empire he usurped, corrupting first   1110
With baits and bribes the most part of his men),
Yet me hath overcome, and made his prey,
And state of Rome with me hath overcome.
   Strange! One disordered act at Actium
The earth subdued, my glory hath obscured.
For since, as one whom heaven's wrath attaints,
With fury caught, and more than furious
Vexed with my evils, I never more had care
My armies lost, or lost name to repair:
I did no more resist.
    Lucilius.   All war's affairs,   1120

But battles most, daily have their success
Now good, now ill; and though that fortune have
Great force and power in every worldly thing,
Rule all, do all, have all things fast enchained
Unto the circle of her turning wheel,
Yet seems it more than any practice else
She doth frequent Bellona's bloody trade,
And that her favor, wavering as the wind,
Her greatest power therein doth oftenest show.
Whence grows, we daily see, who in their youth   1130
Got honor there, do lose it in their age,
Vanquished by some less warlike than themselves,
Whom yet a meaner man shall overthrow.
Her use is not to lend us still her hand,
But sometimes headlong back again to throw,
When by her favor she hath us extolled
Unto the top of highest happiness.
   Antony.   Well ought I curse within my grieved soul,
Lamenting day and night, this senseless love,
Whereby my fair enticing foe entrapped   1140
My headless reason, could no more escape.
It was not fortune's ever-changing face,
It was not destiny's changeless violence
Forged my mishap. Alas! Who doth not know
They make, nor mar nor anything can do.
Fortune, which men so fear, adore, detest,
Is but a chance whose cause unknown doth rest,
Although ofttimes the cause is well perceived,
But not th'effect the same that was conceived.
Pleasure, nought else, the plague of this our life,   1150
Our life which still a thousand plagues pursue,
Alone hath me this strange disaster spun,
Fallen from a soldier to a chamberer,
Careless of virtue, careless of all praise.
Nay, as the fatted swine in filthy mire
With glutted heart I wallowed in delights,
All thoughts of honor trodden under foot.
So I me lost, for finding this sweet cup
Pleasing my taste, unwise I drank my fill,
And through the sweetness of that poison's power   1160
By steps I drove my former wits astray.
I made my friends, offended, me forsake,
I helped my foes against myself to rise.

I robbed my subjects, and for followers
I saw myself beset with flatterers,
Mine idle arms fair wrought with spiders' work,
My scattered men without their ensigns strayed;
Caesar meanwhile who never would have dared
To cope with me, me suddenly despised,
Took heart to fight, and hoped for victory   1170
On one so gone, who glory had forgone.
    Lucilius.   Enchanting pleasure, Venus' sweet delights
Weaken our bodies, over-cloud our spirits,
Trouble our reason, from our hearts out-chase
All holy virtues lodging in their place,
Like as the cunning fisher takes the fish
By traitor bait whereby the hook is hid;
So pleasure serves to vice instead of food
To bait our souls thereon too liquorish.
This poison deadly is alike to all,   1180
But on kings doth greatest outrage work,
Taking the royal scepters from their hands,
Thenceforward to be by some stranger borne;
While that their people charged with heavy loads
Their flatterers pill, and suck their marrow dry,
Not ruled but left to great men as a prey,
While this fond prince himself in pleasure drowns
Who hears nought, sees nought, doth nought of a king
Seeming himself against himself conspired.
Then equal justice wandereth banished,   1190
And in her seat sits greedy tyranny.
Confused disorder troubleth all estates,
Crimes without fear and outrages are done.
Then mutinous rebellion shows her face,
Now hid with this, and now with that pretense,
Provoking enemies, which on each side
Enter at ease, and make them lords of all.
The hurtful works of pleasure here behold.
    Antony.   The wolf is not so hurtful to the fold,
Frost to the grapes, to ripened fruits the rain,   1200
As pleasure is to princes full of pain.
    Lucilius.   There needs no proof but by th'Assyrian king,
On whom that monster woeful wrack did bring.
    Antony.   There needs no proof but by unhappy I,
Who lost my empire, honor, life thereby.
    Lucilius.   Yet hath this ill so much the greater force

As scarcely any do against it stand,
No, not the demigods the old world knew,
Who all subdued, could pleasure's power subdue.
    Great Hercules, Hercules once that was   1210
Wonder of earth and heaven, matchless in might,
Who Antaeus, Lycus, Geryon overcame,
Who drew from hell the triple-headed dog,
Who Hydra killed, vanquished Achelous,
Who heaven's weight on his strong shoulders bore,
Did he not under pleasure's burden bow?
Did he not captive to this passion yield,
When by his captive, so he was inflamed,
As now yourself in Cleopatra burn?
Slept in her lap, her bosom kissed and kissed,   1220
With base unseemly service bought her love,
Spinning at distaff, and with sinewy hand
Winding on spindle's thread, in maid's attire?
His conquering club at rest on wall did hang;
His bow unstrung he bent not as he used;
Upon his shafts the weaving spiders spun;
And his hard cloak the fretting moths did pierce.
The monsters free and fearless all the time
Throughout the world the people did torment,
And more and more increasing day by day   1230
Scorned his weak heart become a mistress' play.
    Antony.   In only this like Hercules am I;
In this I prove me of his lineage right,
In this himself, his deeds I show in this:
In this, nought else, my ancestor he is.
    But go we; die I must, and with brave end
Conclusion make of all foregoing harms;
Die, die I must; I must a noble death,
A glorious death unto my succor call;
I must deface the shame of time abused,   1240
I must adorn the wanton loves I used
With some courageous act, that my last day
By mine own hand my spots may wash away.
    Come, dear Lucil; alas! Why weep you thus?
This mortal lot is common to us all.
We must all die, each doth in homage owe
Unto that god that shared the realms below.
Ah sigh no more, alas! appease your woers,
For by your grief my grief more eager grows.

ACT IV

(Caesar describes himself as sole master of fortune, which affects all other beings on earth; he and Agrippa condemn Antony's pride and his infatuation with Cleopatra. While they discuss the role of the gods in human affairs, Dercetas enters carrying the sword that Antony has just used to kill himself. He tells Caesar how Cleopatra had retreated to her monument and had given out word that she was dead; he also describes Antony's suicide and his lingering death as Cleopatra raised him into the tomb. Caesar laments Antony briefly, and he then orders that Cleopatra's treasure is to be seized and she is to be taken to Rome and exhibited in triumph. A chorus of Roman soldiers then asks that war and discord might end, and that Rome's glory not affront Jove and the heavens.)

ACT V

    Cleopatra.   O cruel fortune! O accursed lot!
O plaguy love! O most detested brand!
O wretched joys! O beauties miserable!
O deadly state! O deadly royalty!
O hateful life! O queen most lamentable!
O Antony by my fault buriable!
O hellish work of heaven! Alas! The wrath
Of all the gods at once on us is fallen.   1800
Unhappy queen! O would I in this world
The wandering light of day had never seen!
Alas! Of mine the plague and poison I
The crown have lost my ancestors me left,
This realm I have to strangers subject made,
And robbed my children of their heritage.
    Yet this is nought (alas!) unto the price
Of you dear husband, whom my snares entrapped:
Of you, whom I have plagued, whom I have made
With bloody hand a guest of moldy tomb;   1810
Of you, whom I destroyed, of you, dear lord,
Whom I of empire, honor, life have spoiled.
    O hurtful woman! And can I yet live,
Yet longer live in this ghost-haunted tomb?
Can I yet breathe? Can yet in such annoy,
Yet can my soul within this body dwell?
O sisters you that spin the threads of death!
O Styx! O Phlegethon! You brooks of hell!
O imps of night!
    Euphron.   Live for your children's sake:
Let not your death of kingdom them deprive.   1820

Alas what shall they do? Who will have care?
Who will preserve this royal race of yours?
Who pity take? Even now me seems I see
Those little souls to servile bondage fallen,
And born in triumph.
    Cleopatra.   Ah most miserable!
    Euphron.   Their tender arms with cursed cord fast bound
At their weak backs.
    Cleopatra.   Ah gods, what pity more!
    Euphron.   Their seely necks to ground with weakness bend.
    Cleopatra.   Never on us, good gods, such mischief send.
    Euphron.   And pointed at with fingers as they go.   1830
    Cleopatra.   Rather a thousand deaths.
    Euphron.   Lastly his knife
Some cruel caitiff in their blood imbrue.
    Cleopatra. Ah my heart breaks. By shady banks of hell,
By fields whereon the lonely ghosts do tread,
By my soul, and the soul of Antony
I you beseech, Euphron, of them have care.
Be their good father, let your wisdom let
That they fall not into this tyrant's hands.
Rather conduct them where their freezed locks
Black Ethiopes to neighbor sun do show;   1840
On wavy ocean at water's will;
On barren cliffs of snowy Caucasus;
To tigers swift, to lions and to bears,
And rather, rather, unto every coast,
To every land and sea, for nought I fear
As rage of him, whose thirst no blood can quench.
    Adieu dear children, children dear adieu;
Good Isis you to place of safety guide,
Far from our foes, where you your lives may lead
In free estate devoid of servile dread.   1850
    Remember not, my children, you were born
Of such a princely race: remember not
So many brave kings which have Egypt ruled
In right descent your ancestors have been;
That this great Antony your father was,
Hercules' blood, and more than he in praise.
For your high courage such remembrance will,
Seeing your fall with burning rages fill.
    Who knows that if your hands false destiny
The scepters promised of imperious Rome,   1860

Instead of them shall crooked sheephooks bear,
Needles or forks, or guide the cart or plough?
Ah learn t'endure: your birth and high estate
Forget, my babes, and bend to force of fate.
 Farewell, my babes, farewell my heart is closed,
With pity and pain, my self with death enclosed,
My breath doth fail. Farewell forevermore,
Your sire and me you shall see nevermore.
Farewell sweet care, farewell.
 Children.   Madame adieu.
 Cleopatra. Ah this voice kills me. Ah good gods! I swoon.
I can no more, I die.   1870
 Iras.   Madame, alas!
And will you yield to woe? Ah speak to us.
 Euphron. Come children.
 Children.   We come.
 Euphron.   Follow we our chance.
The gods shall guide us.
 Charmian.   O too cruel lot!
O too hard chance! Sister what shall we do,
What shall we do, alas! If murdering dart
Of death arrive while in that slumbering swoon
Half dead she lie with anguish overgone?
 Iras. Her face is frozen.
 Charmian.   Madam for gods' love
Leave us not thus: bid us yet first farewell.   1880
Alas! Weep over Antony: let not
His body be without due rites entombed.
 Cleopatra. Ah, ah.
 Charmian.   Madame.
 Cleopatra.   Ay me!
 Charmian.   How faint she is!
 Cleopatra. My sisters, hold me up. How wretched I,
How cursed am: and was there ever one
By fortune's hate into more dolors thrown?
 Ah weeping Niobe, although thy heart
Beholds itself enwrapped in causeful woe
For thy dead children, that a senseless rock
With grief become, on Sipylus thou standest   1890
In endless tears; yet didst thou never feel
The weights of grief that on my heart do lie.
Thy children thou, mine I poor soul have lost,
And lost their father, more than them I wail,

Lost this fair realm; yet me the heavens' wrath
Into a stone not yet transformed hath.
    Phaeton's sisters, daughters of the sun,
Which wail your father fallen into the streams
Of stately Po: the gods upon the banks
Your bodies to bank-loving alders turned.   1900
For me, I sigh, I ceaseless weep, and wail,
And heaven pitiless laughs at my woe,
Revives, renews it still: and in the end
(Oh cruelty!) doth death for comfort lend.
    Die Cleopatra then, no longer stay
From Antony, who thee at Styx attends:
Go join thy ghost with his, and sob no more
Without his love within these tombs enclosed.
    Iras.   Alas! Yet let us weep, lest sudden death
From him our tears, and those last duties take   1910
Unto his tomb we owe.
    Charmian.   Ah let us weep
While moisture lasts, then die before his feet.
    Cleopatra.   Who furnish will mine eyes with streaming tears
My boiling anguish worthily to wail,
Wail thee Antony, Antony my heart?
Alas, how much I weeping liquor want!
Yet have mine eyes quite drawn their conduits dry
By long beweeping my disastered harms.
Now reason is that from my side they suck
First vital moisture, then the vital blood.   1920
Then let the blood from my sad eyes outflow,
And smoking yet with thine in mixture grow.
Moist it, and heat it new, and never stop,
All watering thee, while yet remains one drop.
    Charmian.   Antony take our tears: this is the last
Of all the duties we to thee can yield
Before we die.
    Iras.   These sacred obsequies
Take Antony, and take them in good part.
    Cleopatra.   O goddess thou whom Cyprus doth adore,
Venus of Paphos, bent to work us harm   1930
For old Iulus brood, if thou take care
Of Caesar, why of us tak'st thou no care?
Antony did descend, as well as he,
From thine own son by long enchained line,
And might have ruled by one and selfsame fate,

True Trojan blood, the stately Roman state.
   Antony, poor Antony, my dear soul,
Now but a block, the booty of a tomb,
Thy life, thy heat is lost, thy color gone,
And hideous paleness on thy face hath seized.   1940
Thy eyes, two suns, the lodging place of love,
Which yet for tents to warlike Mars did serve,
Locked up in lids (as fair day's cheerful light
Which darkness flies) do winking hide in night.
   Antony by our true loves I thee beseech,
And by our hearts sweet sparks have set on fire,
Our holy marriage, and the tender ruth
Of our dear babes, knot of our amity:
My doleful voice thy ear let entertain,
And take me with thee to the hellish plain,   1950
Thy wife, thy friend: hear Antony, O hear
My sobbing sighs, if here thou be, or there.
   Lived thus long, the winged race of years
Ended I have as destiny decreed,
Flourished and reigned, and taken just revenge
Of him who me both hated and despised.
Happy, alas too happy: if of Rome
Only the fleet had hither never come.
And now of me an image great shall go
Under the earth to bury there my woe.   1960
What say I? Where am I? O Cleopatra,
Poor Cleopatra, grief thy reason reaves.
No, no, most happy in this hapless case,
To die with thee, and dying thee embrace:
My body joined with thine, my mouth with thine,
My mouth, whose moisture burning sighs have dried
To be in one self tomb, and one self chest,
And wrapped with thee in one self sheet to rest.
   The sharpest torment in my heart I feel
Is that I stay from thee, my heart, this while.   1970
Die will I straight now, now straight will I die,
And straight with thee a wandering shade will be,
Under the cypress trees thou haunt'st alone,
Where brooks of hell do falling seem to moan.
But yet I stay, and yet thee overlive,
That ere I die due rites I may thee give.
   A thousand sobs I from my breast will tear,
With thousand plaints thy funerals adorn:

My hair shall serve for thy oblations,
My boiling tears for thy effusions,   1980
Mine eyes thy fire: for out of them the flame
(Which burnt thy heart on me enamored) came.
   Weep my companions, weep, and from your eyes
Rain down on him of tears a brinish stream.
Mine can no more, consumed by the coals
Which from my breast as from a furnace rise.
Martyr your breasts with multiplied blows,
With violent hands tear off your hanging hair,
Outrage your face: alas! Why should we seek
(Since now we die) our beauties more to keep?   1990
   I spent in tears, not able more to spend,
But kiss him now, what rests me more to do?
Then let me kiss you, you fair eyes, my light,
Front* seat of honor, face most fierce, most fair!
O neck, O arms, O hands, O breast where death
(O mischief) comes to choke up vital breath.
A thousand kisses, thousand thousand more
Let you my mouth for honors farewell give:
That in this office weak my limbs may grow,
Fainting on you, and forth my soul may flow.   2000

    * Forehead.

BIBLIOGRAPHY

Primary Works

Sidney, Mary. *A Discourse of Life and Death; Antonius: A Tragedie.* London, 1592.
————. *The Psalms of Sir Philip Sidney and the Countess of Pembroke.* Ed. J. C. A.
    Rathmell. New York, 1963.
————.*The Tragedie of Antonie.* London, 1595.
————.*The Tragedie of Antonie.* Ed. A. A. Luce. Weimar, 1897.
————.*The Tragedie of Antonie.* Ed. Geoffrey Bullough. In *Narrative and Dramatic
    Sources of Shakespeare.* Vol. 5. New York, 1964.
————.*"The Triumph of Death" and Other Unpublished and Uncollected Poems.* Ed. G. F.
    Waller. Salzburg, 1977.

Related Works

Beauchamp, V. W. "Sidney's Sister as Translator of Garnier." *Renaissance Notes* 10 (1957):
    8–13.
Charlton, H. B. *The Senecan Tradition in Renaissance Tragedy.* Manchester, 1946.
Clemen, Wolfgang. *English Tragedy Before Shakespeare.* London, 1955.

Eliot, T. S. "Seneca in Elizabethan Translation." In *Essays on Elizabethan Drama*. New York, 1960.

Herington, C. J. "Senecan Tragedy." *Arion* 5 (1966): 422–71.

Jondorf, Gillian. *Robert Garnier and the Themes of Political Tragedy in the Sixteenth Century.* Cambridge, 1969.

Lucas, F. L. *Seneca and Elizabethan Tragedy.* Cambridge, 1922.

Rossiter, A. P. *English Drama from Early Times to the Elizabethans.* London, 1950.

Schanzer, Ernest. *The Problem Plays of Shakespeare.* London, 1953. Chapter 3 contains a detailed comparison of *Antony* and Shakespeare's *Antony and Cleopatra.*

Stone, Donald F., Jr. *French Humanist Tragedy.* Manchester, 1974.

Waller, G. F. *Mary Sidney, Countess of Pembroke: A Critical Study of Her Writings and Literary Milieu.* Salzburg, 1979.

Witherspoon, A. M. *The Influence of Robert Garnier on Elizabethan Drama.* New Haven, Conn., 1924.

Young, Frances Berkeley. *Mary Sidney, Countess of Pembroke.* London, 1912.

lizabeth I

FRANCES TEAGUE

Queen Elizabeth I is a legendary figure. Anyone who has read about her reign treasures a favorite anecdote about her, an anecdote which can range from stern dignity to earthy raillery. On the one hand, there is her rebuke of William Cecil: "The word 'must' is not to be used to princes"; on the other, there is her greeting to Edward de Vere when he returned to court after exiling himself seven years for committing an indiscretion in her presence: "My lord, I had forgot the fart."[1] How difficult it becomes to sum up succinctly so rich a life—yet she herself managed the feat. Speaking to her ladies-in-waiting about her epitaph, Queen Elizabeth said: "I am no lover of pompous title, but only desire that my name may be recorded in a line or two, which shall briefly express my name, my virginity, the years of my reign, the reformation of religion under it, and my preservation of peace."[2] In this speech Elizabeth summarized nicely the main points of her life that a biographer must discuss: her virginity, her religion, and her power.

Elizabeth Tudor was a clever child. Intelligent, articulate, and well be-haved, she proved an apt pupil for the lessons in languages taught her by her tutor, Roger Ascham, and the lessons in power taught her by her father, Henry VIII. More important, perhaps, she lived her childhood by the motto she would adopt as queen: *Video, et taceo*—I see and hold my tongue. Though she was not unduly taciturn—possessing personal charm and a gift for language—on dangerous subjects such as religion, politics, and flirtation, she remained silent. Thus she survived King Henry, unlike her mother Anne Boleyn, and was loved by the public, unlike her sister Queen Mary.

Born on September 7, 1533, Elizabeth's infancy was spent in a separate royal household as the legitimate daughter of a monarch. With the fall and execution of her mother three years later, Elizabeth was reduced to bastardy and her bright prospects dimmed. This is not to suggest that she was neglected as a child, however, since Henry VIII continued to love and support her. In fact, when he married his last wife, Catherine Parr, in 1543, the new queen took both Elizabeth and her stepbrother Edward into the queen's household where Sir John Cheke and Roger Ascham educated the two children.

Cheke and Ascham belonged to a new school of thought, humanism, which had developed in fifteenth-century Italy and spread to England. Humanism sought to reform the Roman Catholic Church, revive the classics, and exalt human nature, and it is no surprise to learn that Elizabeth's writing as queen shows the effects of her early training. We know quite a lot about her education during 1548 and 1549 because Ascham, her tutor in these years, recorded her work and her abilities in his treatise on education, *The Scholemaster* (1570). Each day she studied Greek, classical authors like Sophocles and Demosthenes as well as the New Testament, and Latin, especially Cicero and Livy. Not only did she read such authors; she also translated their work into English, then translated her English versions back into Greek or Latin under Ascham's watchful eye.

Clearly, then, Ascham concentrated on training the princess in the language skills she would use so well as monarch, and he is chiefly responsible for her well-known fluency in Greek and Latin. But these were not her only languages, nor was he her only tutor. Elizabeth knew French, Italian, Spanish, Flemish, Welsh, and German as well;[3] though we do not know who all of her early tutors were, she studied the classics with another brilliant young humanist, William Grindall, until his death in 1548, and Italian with Baptista Castiglione. Whoever Ascham's predecessors were, at the age of eleven she wrote Catherine Parr a graceful letter in Italian and later that same year she sent the queen an original translation of the French poem by Marguerite of Navarre, *The Mirror of the Sinful Soul*. In addition to Elizabeth's training in languages, she probably studied astronomy, geography, natural philosophy, and mathematics.[4] Like any Renaissance girl of good family, Elizabeth also knew something of riding, music, and needlework. For example, the original manuscript of *The Mirror of the Sinful Soul* came in an elaborately embroidered cover of blue corded silk decorated with red, silver, and gold, a cover which seems to be Elizabeth's handiwork. Thomas Heywood described the years she spent with Edward in Catherine Parr's household this way:

> So pregnant ingenious were either [Elizabeth or Edward], that they desired to looke upon bookes as soone as the day began to breake. Their *horae matutinae* [morning hours] were so welcome, that they seemed to prevent the nights sleeping for the entertainment of the morrows schooling. . . .
> And when hee was cal'd out to any youthfull exercise becomming a Child of his age, . . . she in her private Chamber betooke her selfe to her Lute or violl, and (wearyed with that) to practise her needle.[5]

Heywood offers a pretty picture of an intelligent and industrious child who studied with her brother and passed her lonely hours with music and needlework. But the picture has a darker side, for Elizabeth spent the latter part of her girlhood under suspicion and investigation.

Aside from occasional disapproval from her father, Elizabeth led a serene life until she reached the age of thirteen, a suitable age for marriage. That same year the king died, and Elizabeth became a possible route to the throne of England. Thomas Seymour was quick to notice this political fact, but unable to take advantage of it because his brother Edward Seymour, the Lord Protector, stopped him from wooing the princess. Thomas then successfully courted and wed Elizabeth's guardian, Dowager Queen Catherine Parr. After this marriage he continued his flirtation with the child until 1548, when Elizabeth was sent away to establish her own household. Soon after, Catherine Parr died, and Thomas Seymour renewed his courtship of Elizabeth. Edward Seymour was outraged by his brother's scandalous behavior: in 1549 he had Thomas arrested and began an investigation into Elizabeth's part in the wooing.

Elizabeth's conduct under this investigation was remarkable. Although only fifteen, Elizabeth answered her interrogators with discretion and self-assurance; no one could break down her protestations of innocence: Seymour may have wished to woo her, but she in no way countenanced his suit. Though one of her servants tried to implicate her, the princess was exonerated while Seymour went to the scaffold. Again in 1553, when there were rumors that she might be involved in a plot undertaken by Northumberland, Elizabeth successfully defused suspicion by her conduct. After 1553, when Edward died and the fervently Catholic Mary came to the throne, however, the rumors and plots multiplied until it was only a matter of time until the Protestant Elizabeth was in serious trouble. Elizabeth tried to allay her sister's doubts by studying Catholicism and withdrawing from the court. All her efforts came to naught when Sir Thomas Wyatt rebelled in early 1554; despite her discreet silence on dangerous subjects, Elizabeth was suspected of involvement and was taken prisoner, first in the Tower of London, then at the royal manor of Woodstock. She remained under guard at Woodstock from May 1554 until April 1555. During this year of captivity, she wrote two poems about her position: one, scratched on her window with a diamond, sums up her strategy for dealing with her accusers; the other, written on a shutter, is a meditation on Fortune modeled after Boethius. Despite Mary's suspicions and the continued Protestant intrigues against the Catholic regime, Elizabeth rode out the rest of her sister's reign safely, her life preserved as long as she held her tongue. When Mary died in November of 1558, Elizabeth's discreet silence came to an end. From then until her own death, Elizabeth spoke and wrote as a queen.

On January 15, 1559, about two months after Mary Tudor's death, Elizabeth rode from the Tower of London to Westminster, stopping along the way to watch a series of pageants that wished her well and urged Protestantism on her. Halfway along her route she was met by the Lord Mayor, and there she spoke her thanks to him and all her subjects; the following day she was crowned in Westminster. Reading the short speech and prayer spoken during the procession, one is struck by Elizabeth's self-assurance and her remembrance of her earlier troubles. Although she had been a disinherited bastard and a prisoner suspected of treason, time had brought her to the crown and she was grateful. Her subjects rejoiced in Elizabeth, lovely and intelligent, because they knew that when she married, England would be more secure than it had been under either Edward or Mary.

For there could be no question that she would marry. Every Renaissance lady was supposed to marry, for marriage was a woman's destiny. As Elizabeth told the Spanish ambassador, "The world, when a woman remains single, assumes that there must be something wrong about her, and that she has some discreditable reason for it."[6] Furthermore, Elizabeth had no lack of suitors; she was the best match in Europe, and dozens of men hoped to catch her fancy and her kingdom.

But although she liked to flirt, she did not want to wed and showed it by her comments and her actions. While she consistently said that she was ready to wed for the good of her nation, she also said repeatedly that if she were to follow her own desires, she would live and die a virgin. To modern ears, this declaration sounds odd, yet in the Renaissance a woman's chastity was her highest virtue, much as a man's honor was his. For Elizabeth, virginity defined her relationship with God and with her nation. As a devout Christian, she believed Saint Paul's distinction: "The unmarried woman careth for the things of the Lord, that she may be holy both in body and spirit; but she that is married careth for the things of the world, how she may please *her* husband" (1 Corinthians 7:34). When she spoke to Parliament about marriage in 1559, the first point she made was that her spinsterhood was the way of life "most acceptable unto God," and there seems no reason to doubt her sincerity. Certainly Elizabeth had little patience with doctrinal differences, but of her Christianity there can be no doubt.

In another sense, Elizabeth was married already. According to William Camden, she showed a Parliamentary delegation the ring she had worn at the accession and said, "I have already joined myself in marriage to a husband, namely, the kingdom of England. And behold the pledge of this my wedlock and marriage with my kingdom."[7] To protect that marriage and preserve her nation in safety, Elizabeth was willing to take a human husband, if one could be found who would balance the claims of English

Protestants and Catholics, France, Spain, the papacy, the Netherlands—in short, she would marry to keep the succession safe and the nation out of trouble. Quite simply, despite dozens of suitors over two decades, no such husband came along. It quickly became apparent that England's safety lay not in Elizabeth's marriage, but rather in her courtship; by playing one suitor off against another, Elizabeth and her advisors were able to extract concessions from and stave off conflicts with other nations. By remaining unmarried Elizabeth preserved her relationship to God, her personal independence and power, and a useful tool of diplomacy. Under the circumstances, a husband could have been a foolish mistake; Elizabeth was no fool.

Still there were men she almost married: Robert Dudley; Archduke Charles of Austria; and finally, Francis, Duke of Alençon. Dudley would have been a good choice. She had known him since childhood, marriage to an English Protestant would please her subjects, and members of the court thought the two were deeply in love. The insuperable difficulty was his wife, Amy Robsart. When this poor woman died suddenly in a terrible fall, rumors sprang up that she had been murdered.[8] Once again under suspicion, Elizabeth wavered between intelligent discretion and incautious desire, sometimes preferring Dudley and sometimes turning him away. While she wavered, she fell out of love with him and instead paid attention to his chief rival, Archduke Charles of Austria. Charles offered an excellent political match, allying England with the Hapsburgs; but he was Catholic, which was a liability, and he proved reluctant to come and woo her in person. Despite the diplomatic soundness of the match, nothing came of his courtship by proxy. Elizabeth's last suitor was Francis, Duke of Alençon. A lukewarm Catholic, homely, and twenty years younger than Elizabeth, "Monsieur," as she called him, wooed her as eagerly as if she were twenty-five instead of forty-five. It would have been a sound political alliance and Elizabeth felt genuine affection for the young man, but the age difference was too great and the public response too hostile for his suit to succeed. Although Francis, unlike Archduke Charles, came to woo her himself, she put him off, and in 1582 he left England. "On Monsieur's Departure" may mark the end of his courtship. (Unfortunately we cannot tell if the poem is about Francis or Robert Devereaux, the earl of Essex, a great favorite of Elizabeth who ultimately betrayed her and had to be executed. Until we can date the poem with greater certainty, we cannot know the circumstances of its composition or gauge its sincerity.)

Because Elizabeth never married, she had no children to succeed her on the throne. There was no shortage of possible heirs, however, and the most dangerous of these was Mary Stuart, exiled queen of Scotland. Whatever the truth of the matter, Mary was suspected of adultery and murder; further, she was a devout Catholic in a Protestant Scotland. In

1568 her own people drove her into England where Elizabeth defended and protected her, despite the fact that the English government was closely allied with the Scottish rebels. Elizabeth's position was an awkward one: she wanted peace and Protestantism in Scotland, but she recognized the threat to all monarchs posed by the Scottish rebellion. Therefore Elizabeth refused to turn Mary over to the rebels, refused to meet her in person, and held her in custody at a series of country houses. Mary remained in custody for the next eighteen years, plotting all the while to raise a Catholic army, overthrow Elizabeth, and seize the throne of England. In 1586 the situation finally came to crisis. Mary was caught urging a group of young courtiers not merely to overthrow Elizabeth, but to assassinate her; the plot was discovered and in October she was tried and condemned to die. Elizabeth delayed the execution. Parliament sent a deputation to petition the queen to sign the death warrant. After receiving the deputation and making a speech to them, Elizabeth sent a message asking Parliament to find another way than death for Mary. A second deputation returned and insisted on Mary's death. Still Elizabeth delayed the execution. Another plot on Elizabeth's life was revealed and rumors swept through the land. No longer could Elizabeth delay, so on February 1, 1587, Elizabeth signed Mary's death warrant. Six days later Elizabeth wept bitterly when the news arrived of Mary's death. To kill a woman of royal blood went against everything she believed.

Elizabeth was not the only one distressed by Mary's execution. France, Scotland, and Spain all protested the sentence and the death, but while Scotland and France expressed indignation without taking action, Philip of Spain thought the occasion a good excuse for war on England. He built and armed a fleet of ships, then sent it to support an invasion to take over England. Philip's Armada, despite delays caused by Francis Drake's raids and a great storm, set sail for England in July 1588. The Armada was 130 ships strong; England's navy had only 34 ships, which were much smaller vessels. Yet the people of England offered other ships, bringing the size of the navy to 197, and the smaller size made the English ships easier to maneuver. Thus when the Armada arrived, it was soundly defeated. The threat of an invasion remained, however, so part of the British land forces stayed in camp at Tilbury to defend the city of London. Ten days after the Armada's defeat, while new rumors of an invasion were circulating, Elizabeth rode out to review her troops. Here she made her famous speech to her soldiers; Camden said of it, "Incredible it is how much she encouraged the hearts of her captains and soldiers by her presence and speech to them."[9] Reading the speech today, one can see why her soldiers cheered her: it is a masterful statement of courage and national pride.

Although the war with Spain dragged on until Philip's death in 1598, the defeat of the Armada had brought England safety. Spain continued to fight through these years, but her wars were waged against France and the Netherlands as well as England. This division of effort as well as the enormous drain on finances weakened Spain greatly. In the late 1590s it was not Spain that concerned Elizabeth, but war in Ireland and the Essex rebellion. By 1603, the year she died, England was at peace, although that peace had cost her not only the life of her favorite, Essex, but also the men and money needed to subdue the Irish rebels. Bad weather in March 1603 and grief over the death of her old friend, the Countess of Nottingham, made Elizabeth ill. Weak and feverish, she refused to go to bed despite the pleas of her courtiers. Finally, she was carried to bed, too weak to resist any longer. After she had designated James, King of Scotland, as her heir and after the archbishop of Canterbury had come and prayed for her, she rested. Early the next morning, March 24, Elizabeth was dead.

Two years before in a speech to Parliament which became known as the Golden Speech, Elizabeth said, "To be a King and wear a crown is a thing more glorious to them that see it, than it is pleasant to them that bear it." She made the Crown glorious by her wit, her poise, and her love of England. That glory is reflected in her writing.

Included here are the six poems which are almost certainly by Elizabeth; there are ten other poems sometimes attributed to her, which have been omitted, as well as several verse translations. Only one of the poems is in the queen's handwriting, but the poems are found in contemporary books and manuscripts, such as Holinshed's *Chronicles* and Harington's papers, and there is no reason to doubt their attribution.

Two were written during her confinement at Woodstock in 1554–1555. The first of these is of interest for the light it sheds on her state of mind; the second also offers insight to her feelings and introduces the theme of Fortune, which occurs in another poem as well. The childhood poem in the French Psalter, like "The Doubt of Future Foes," deals with discord caused by false minds, while "On Monsieur's Departure" sums up the paradoxes of love.

The three very short poems tell us very little. The longer poems, all written on specific occasions, display a uniformity of style and theme. As Leicester Bradner says, "They show her courage, her scorn of fortune, her belief in herself, and her hatred of sedition."[10] The poem written on a shutter at Woodstock derives from this passage in Boethius's *Consolation of Philosophy:*

> All things thou holdest in strict bounds,—
> To human acts alone denied
> Thy fit control as Lord of all.
> Why else does slippery Fortune change
> So much, and punishment more fit
> For crime oppress the innocent?

Corrupted men sit throned on high;
By strange reversal evilness
Downtreads the necks of holy men.
Bright virtue lies in dark eclipse
By clouds obscured, and unjust men
Heap condemnation on the just;
No punishment for perjury
Or lies adorned with speciousness.
                    (Book 1, poem 5)[11]

Like Boethius, Elizabeth was a prisoner when she wrote her poem. In the lyric, her love for Boethius combines with her sense of unjust treatment. Following the Christian Stoicism of Boethius, Elizabeth believes that Fortune governs human affairs and that the rule of Fortune sometimes allows freedom for the guilty and imprisonment for the innocent (like herself). But since men are caught on Fortune's wheel, little can be done to alter this state of affairs. This viewpoint is an orthodox one, though one notes that the last line of her shutter poem and the couplet "On Fortune" both express faith that God will recognize her virtue and send her foes "all they have taught."

The poems "The Doubt of Future Foes" and "On Monsieur's Departure" both use natural imagery, not surprisingly since Elizabeth loved the out of doors and tried to walk or ride every day. "The Doubt of Future Foes" is thought to concern Mary Queen of Scots and to have been written soon after Mary, "The foreign banished wight," fled to England. To contemporary ears, Elizabeth's poem may sound clumsy, since it is written in the then-popular "poulter's measure." A number of inversions make the poem difficult. The speaker can feel no "present joy" because her wit warns her that in this imperfect world her future is threatened by sedition. Next she predicts the ultimate downfall of those ambitious minds that hope to try ruling in her place; her rule has brought peace to the kingdom and her people will support her. Given Mary's plotting during her confinement, the poem seems prescient. The natural metaphors, which compare treason to bad weather and traitors to barren plants, remind one of the garden scene in *Richard II*, particularly the Gardener's lines, "Go thou and, like an executioner, / Cut off the heads of too-fast-growing sprays" (III.iv.34–35); the poem and play have the same *topos*.

The poem "On Monsieur's Departure," is at once easier to read and more difficult to assess. Written in iambic pentameter, the poem laments a love that can be neither expressed nor escaped. The last stanza pleads for a resolution to the lover's dilemma, for the stability that comes from the fulfillment or death of passion. But how seriously is one to take this little poem? The poem is sometimes thought to refer to the departure of Elizabeth's last suitor, the Duke of Alençon, whom she nicknamed "Monsieur." If this is so, one must ask if she was in love and this poem was an expression of private feelings, or if she wrote it "for political effect"[12] and offered the lyric as a love token like the purple and gold garter she gave the French ambassador to pass on to "Monsieur."[13] A further complication arises because an early manuscript of the poem is placed among materials relating to the Earl of Essex. However one decides to understand this, or the other poems, it seems likely that one will prefer the speeches to the poetry.

Throughout her reign, Elizabeth made speeches or had them read in her name. She made more speeches herself later in her reign; in the early years she seems to have felt uncomfortable speaking publicly, and so she often asked Sir Nicholas Bacon, Lord Keeper of the Great Seal, to deliver speeches for her. When one considers Elizabeth's intelligence and education, as well as her recorded conversation, one must conclude that she wrote most of her speeches herself. To scholars' ears, the speeches sound highly characteristic, and most have concluded that the speeches express Elizabeth's ideas and arguments in her own words. This is not to say that her writing went unedited. George P. Rice, Jr., has described the process that a speech went through:

> It is altogether likely that [an amanuensis] took Elizabeth's dictation on state papers and for speeches; such drafts, in whole or in part, would then have passed along to [William] Cecil for final checking. The latter's approving initials are found on the lower right-hand corner of certain state papers which survive. A few of the queen's addresses, in some scholarly opinion, were written *in toto* by Cecil for Elizabeth's delivery. A few were, of course, impromptu, and occasionally in a foreign tongue, as exemplified by her Latin rebuke to de Ialines in 1597; others were read by the queen seated, either from notes or a manuscript.[14]

Thus William Cecil, Elizabeth's chief adviser until his death in 1598, helped her compose these speeches.

Although some of the speeches were written down for the official record, most are preserved in a listener's notes; when two or more versions of a speech survive, they may vary widely. Certain features of the speeches remain constant, however: the plain diction; the long, balanced sentences; and the insistent reverence for God and love of her people. Few of the words in Elizabeth's speeches need glossing today, few are polysyllabic. What difficulty there is in reading them comes in following the careful balance of clause against clause or the string of coordinate elements. These stylistic features were, of course, highly valued in the Renaissance, and Elizabeth, while never Euphuistic, was very much a product of her time. Generally she avoids figures of speech, preferring to go directly to the point. From time to time she uses short, blunt sentences for emphasis, as in this famous passage from a speech she made to Parliament in 1566.

> As for mine own part I care not for death, for all men are mortal, and though I be a woman I have as good a courage, answerable to my place, as ever my father had. I am your anointed Queen. I will never be by violence constrained to do anything. I thank God I am endued with such qualities that if I were turned out of the realm in my petticoat I were able to live in any place in Christendom.[15]

In this passage Elizabeth answers Parliament's fears about the succession. She shifts the ground of concern to fears about death in the first long sentence, acknowledging that she is a woman (which is what has caused their concern), but insisting on her personal courage and her royal descent. (She may also hope to shame them—a woman is unafraid, but they are fearful—and to make them uneasy by hinting at the succession problems caused by her father's many marriages.) She then drives home her chief point in a short, blunt sentence: she is the monarch; by extension, they are merely her subjects. In another short sentence, she reminds them that they have overstepped their bounds. In her last sentence, she uses a homely illustration which shows her pride and independence; in this, as in the preceding sentence, the hyperbole of a monarch coerced or exiled in her petticoat is intended to elicit startled denials from her listeners. The rhetorical strategy of this passage is superb.

In Elizabeth's speeches, we see her writing at its best. Paul Corts has argued:

> Elizabeth's speeches . . . , speeches of which we still possess original drafts, show us her deep interest in rhetorical technique. The drafts show that Elizabeth worked hard on word choice and phraseology, changing words and phrases repeatedly before finding satisfaction. Elizabeth's rhetorical style can best be summed up in her own words that "a silent thought may serve." She did not tell all that she knew, rather she told as little as she could. What she said appeared less important than how she said it as she charmed her subjects with her well-intentioned but substantively empty appeals.[16]

There may be little substance on political issues in these speeches, but on two points the substance is clear and unvaried from her Coronation Speech in 1588 to her Golden Speech in 1601. She loved and tried to serve God. She loved and tried to serve her people. Again and again she returns to these points as an explanation for her actions: her love of God and country governed all she said and did.

In addition to her poems and her speeches, Elizabeth's writing includes letters, prayers, and translations. Most of the letters are concerned with affairs of state; G. B. Harrison says, "The most personal are, for the most part, letters of rebuke, condolence or congratulation."[17] In her correspondence, as in her speeches, one may catch a glimpse of the private woman, but generally one sees the public personage only. This is not to say that the letters are overly formal or uncharacteristic, of course. Some of the letters are quite coy, and as in the speeches, there is more technique than substance in them. Others are blunt when the queen wishes her will to be done without delay. In any given letter, the writing reveals more about monarchy than about the person who was monarch. Harrison makes a nice distinction:

> Though few rulers have on occasion written better letters, she was not a good correspondent, for the famous letter writers are those who record intimate experiences and share secrets and observations; they are seldom men of action. The Queen wrote to command, to exhort, to censure, to persuade, and sometimes to prevaricate: but she had no familiar confidant, man or woman. It was this loneliness which gave her strength, but prevented her from opening her heart to anyone.[18]

The letters are expressions of that strength, even when most playful.

If the letters express strength, the prayers express humility.[19] Written in Latin, Greek, Italian, and French, as well as English, they are direct and unequivocal statements of Elizabeth's faith. In them she thanks God for raising her to the throne, acknowledges her weakness, and asks for guidance and protection. There is no pride in them. The prayers Elizabeth wrote for her own use are orthodox in their Protestantism, but unlike some of the more extreme English Protestants, she never prays against Catholicism. Elizabeth asks God to strengthen the English church, but does not attack the faith of others. She once told the French ambassador, "There is only one Jesus Christ and one faith, and all the rest is a dispute over trifles."[20] This spirit of toleration is evident in her private devotions as well as her public actions.

In her translations, though, Elizabeth's pride came forward once again. She was vain about her linguistic skill, telling the archbishop of Saint Andrews, "I am more afraid of making a fault in my Latin than of the Kings of Spain, France, Scotland, the whole House of Guise, and all of their confederates."[21] Translation had been an important part of her education, and she continued to translate her favorite authors all her life. At age eleven she translated *The Mirror of the Sinful Soul* for Catherine Parr; as an adult she translated Boethius's *De Consolatione Philosophiae*, Plutarch's *De Curiositate,* a fragment of Horace's *De Arte Poetica,* a dialogue of Xenophon, and epistles of Seneca and Cicero.[22] Other translations, though mentioned, have not survived. The translation of Boethius is of particular interest. Elizabeth undertook the work when she was sixty and tried to work as quickly as possible. Three independent accounts claim she translated the work in a space of time ranging from twenty-four to twenty-seven hours. Even allowing for courtly flattery, such speed is amazing and indicates remarkable facility. Her work is closer to a metaphrase than a good translation, since it is literal even to word order. The Boethius is generally accurate, if clumsy; her other surviving translations are less exact. Earlier I quoted a section from Boethius that probably influenced one of Elizabeth's poems; here is Elizabeth's translation of the same passage:

Al giding with assured end,
Mans workes alone thou dost dispice [despise].
O gidar by right desart from meane to kipe [keep].
for why so many slipar fortune
turnes doth make? oppressing fautles
dew paine for wicked mete,
but in hy Seatz the wicked factz abide,
and wicked stamps on holy necks with uniust turne.
And Cleare vertu dimmed
with thick blackenis Lurketh,
And iust man the wickeds crime doth beare.
fals othe in fraude doth thè annoy.[23]

With an effort, one can adjust to the peculiar spelling and make sense of this. The line beginning, "O gidar by . . ." does not come from Boethius; it seems to summarize the two preceding lines, but what exactly it means is obscure. Elizabeth could speak clearly in Latin and other languages when she wished. On one such occasion she made a crisp extempore Latin rebuke to the Polish ambassador, de Ialines, when he threatened her. Generally speaking, however, as a translator, Elizabeth was an excellent monarch.

During her lifetime, only Elizabeth's speeches were made public; after her death some of her speeches, poems, and translations were published in works like Sir John Harington's *Nugae Antiquae,* William Camden's *Annals of Elizabeth,* and later editions of Raphael Holinshed's *Chronicles of England.* Given Elizabeth's enormous personal popularity among her people, sixteenth- and seventeenth-century response to her work was enthusiastic, if uncritical, approbation. In succeeding generations, her writing has been studied principally by historians interested in her reign.[24] Since she lived during a period in which English literature exploded into brilliance and since her subjects included such artists as Spenser, Sidney, Jonson, and Shakespeare, most literary critics have discussed the writing she inspired rather than the writing she produced. Spenser's *Faerie Queene,* Sidney's masque *The Lady of the May,* Jonson's *Cynthia's Revels,* and Shakespeare's *Midsummer Night's Dream* all owe something to Elizabeth; there are many other works that are Elizabethan in subject as well as period. Her own writing has inevitably been overshadowed. Only in the twentieth century have such scholars as G. B. Harrison, J. E. Neale, and Leicester Bradner begun to edit and evaluate her work. Much remains to be done, particularly with the speeches, which are often models of rhetorical excellence as well as important historical documents.

NOTES

1. The first is given in Frederick Chamberlin's *The Sayings of Queen Elizabeth*, p. 311; the second is in John Aubrey's *Brief Lives*, ed. Oliver Dick (Ann Arbor, Mich., 1957), p. 305. Unfortunately, because Elizabeth *was* a legendary figure, the stories that have grown up around her are often legends. Neither Chamberlin nor Aubrey is completely trustworthy; cf. J. E. Neale, "The Sayings of Queen Elizabeth," *History*, n.s., 10 (1925): 212–33.

2. Chamberlin, p. 310.

3. Percy Ames, introduction to *The Mirror of the Sinful Soul*, p. 15; Elizabeth Jenkins, *Elizabeth the Great*, p. 13; J. E. Neale, *Queen Elizabeth I*, pp. 13, 128.

4. These were the subjects Mary Tudor studied (Ames, ed., p. 25).

5. Thomas Heywood, *Englands Elizabeth*, ed. Rider, pp. 25–26.

6. Chamberlin, p. 64.

7. William Camden, *The History of . . . Princess Elizabeth*, p. 27. I have modernized spelling. For the authenticity of this quotation, however, see the discussion in J. E. Neale's *Elizabeth and Her Parliaments*, vol. 1, p. 47ff.

8. Neale doubts murder and thinks it most likely Amy Robsart committed suicide (*Queen Elizabeth I*, p. 81).

9. Camden, p. 416.

10. Leicester Bradner, ed., *The Poems of Queen Elizabeth*, p. xiii.

11. Boethius, *Consolation of Philosophy*, trans. V. E. Watts (Baltimore, 1969), p. 47.

12. Bradner, ed., p. xiii.

13. Neale, *Queen Elizabeth I*, p. 256.

14. George P. Rice, ed., *The Public Speaking of Queen Elizabeth*, p. 44. The speech texts that Rice gives are unreliable. The best and most complete texts can be found in Neale's *Elizabeth I and Her Parliaments*.

15. *English Historical Review* 36 (1921): 516. I have modernized spelling.

16. Paul Richard Corts, "Governmental Persuasion in the Reign of Queen Elizabeth I, 1558–1563," pp. 209–10.

17. G. B. Harrison, ed., *The Letters of Queen Elizabeth*, p. ix.

18. Ibid., p. xiv.

19. For a fuller account see Tucker Brooke, "Queen Elizabeth's Prayers," *Huntington Library Quarterly* 2 (1938): 69–77.

20. Chamberlin, p. 116.

21. Chamberlin, p. 18.

22. Caroline Pemberton, ed., *Queen Elizabeth's Englishings*, p. vii.

23. Pemberton, ed., p. 14.

24. The best available guide to this scholarship is Conyers Read, *Bibliography of British History: Tudor Period, 1485–1603*, pp. 50–65.

Woodstock: The Window Poem

. . . The Lady Elizabeth at her departing out from Woodstock wrote these verses with her diamond in a glass window very legibly as here followeth:

Much suspected by me,[1]
Nothing proved can be;
    Quoth Elizabeth prisoner.

Woodstock: The Shutter Poem

Oh Fortune, thy wresting, wavering state
Hath fraught with cares my troubled wit,
Whose witness this present prison late
Could bear, where once was joy's loan quit.[2]
Thou causedst the guilty to be loosed
From bands where innocents were enclosed,
And caused the guiltless to be reserved,
And freed these that death had well deserved.
But all herein can be nothing wrought,
So God send to my foes all they have taught.

French Psalter Poem

No crooked leg, no bleared eye,
No part deformed out of kind,
Nor yet so ugly half can be
As is the inward, suspicious mind.

Doubt of Future Foes

The doubt of future foes exiles my present joy,
And wit me warns to shun such snares as threaten mine annoy,
For falsehood now doth flow and subjects' faith doth ebb,
Which would not be if reason ruled or wisdom weaved the web.
But clouds of joys untried do cloak aspiring minds,
Which turn to rain of late repent by changed course of winds;[3]
The top of hope supposed, the root of rue shall be
And fruitless all their grafted guile, as shortly ye shall see.

Then dazzled eyes with pride, which great ambition blinds,
Shall be unsealed by worthy wights whose foresight falsehood finds,
The daughter of debate, that discord aye doth sow,
Shall reap no gain where former rule hath taught still peace to grow.
No foreign banished wight shall anchor in this port.
Our realm brooks no seditious sects; let them elsewhere resort.
My rusty sword through rest shall first his edge employ
To poll the tops that seek such change or gape for future joy.[4]

On Fortune

Never think you fortune can bear the sway
Where virtue's force can cause her to obey.

On Monsieur's Departure

I grieve, and dare not show my discontent;
   I love, and yet am forced to seem to hate;
I do, yet dare not say I ever meant;
   I seem stark mute, but inwardly do prate;
      I am and not; I freeze and yet am burn'd;
      Since from myself, my other self I turn'd.
My care is like my shadow in the sun,
   Follows me flying, flies when I pursue it,
Stands and lies by me, doth what I have done;
   His too familiar care doth make me rue it:
      No means I find to rid him from my breast
      Till by the end of things it be suppress'd.
Some gentler passions slide into my mind,
   For I am soft and made of melting snow;
Or be more cruel, Love, and so be kind—
   Let me or float or sink, be high or low,
      Or let me live with some more sweet content,
      Or die and so forget what love ere meant.[5]

Coronation Prayer and Speech

Before entering her chariot at the Tower of London to begin her coronation procession through the city, Elizabeth "lifted up her eyes to Heaven
and said:

"O Lord, Almighty and Everlasting God, I give Thee most hearty thanks that Thou hast been so merciful unto me as to spare me to behold this joyful day. And I acknowledge that Thou hast dealt as wonderfully and as mercifully with me as Thou didst with Thy true and faithful servant, Daniel, Thy prophet, whom Thou deliveredst out of the den from the cruelty of the greedy and raging Lions: even so was I overwhelmed and only by Thee delivered. To Thee therefore only be thanks, honor, and praise for ever. Amen."

During the procession she was met by the Lord Mayor of London who welcomed her. Her response:

"I thank my Lord Mayor, his brethren, and you all. And whereas your request is that I should continue your good lady and queen, be ye ensured that I will be as good unto you as ever queen was to her people. No will in me can lack, neither do I trust shall there lack any power. And persuade yourselves that for the safety and quietness of you all I will not spare if need be to spend my blood. God thank you all."

Marriage Speech

On Saturday, February 4, 1559, the House of Commons decided to ask the new queen to marry. The following Monday a delegation, headed by Sir Thomas Gargrave, Speaker of the House, presented their petition to her. (That petition is now lost.) She then sent this reply, which was read to the House by John Mason on Friday, February 10:

"As I have good cause, so do I give you all my hearty thanks for the good zeal and loving care you seem to have—as well towards me as to the whole estate of your country. Your petition, I perceive, consisteth of three parts, and my answer to the same shall depend of two.

"And to the first part, I may say unto you that from my years of understanding sith I first had consideration of myself to be born a servant of Almighty God, I happily chose this kind of life in the which I yet live: which, I assure you, for mine own part hath hitherto best contented myself and, I trust, hath been most acceptable unto God. From the which, if either ambition of high estate offered to me in marriage by the pleasure and appointment of my Prince[6]—whereof I have some record in the presence, as you, our Treasurer, well know[7]—or if eschewing the danger of mine enemies or the avoiding of the peril of death, whose messenger or rather a continual watchman, the Prince's indignation, was no little time daily before mine eyes (by whose means—although I know or justly may suspect—yet I will not now utter, or if the whole cause were in my sister herself, I will not now burthen her therewith because I will not charge the dead), if any of these, I say, could have drawn or dissuaded me from this kind of life, I had not now remained in this estate wherein you see me. But so constant have I always continued in this determination (although my youth and words may seem to some hardly to agree together, yet is it most true), that at this day I stand free from any other meaning that either I have had in times past or have at this present; with which trade of life I am so thoroughly acquainted that I trust God, who hath hitherto therein preserved and led me by the hand, will not of His goodness suffer me to go alone.

"For the other part, the manner of your petition I do well like and take it in good part because it is simple and containeth no limitation of place or person.[8] If it had been otherwise, I must needs have misliked it very much and thought it in you a very great presumption: being unfit and altogether unmeet for you to require them that may command; or those to appoint, whose parts are to desire; or such to bind and limit, whose duties are to obey; or to take upon you to draw my love to your liking, or to frame my will to your fantasy. For a guerdon constrained and gift freely given can never agree together. Nevertheless, if any of you be in suspect,[9] whensoever it may please God to incline my heart to another kind of life, you may very well assure yourselves, my meaning is not to determine anything wherewith the realm may or shall have just cause to be discontented. And therefore put that clean out of your heads. For I assure you (what credit my assurance may have with you, I cannot tell; but what credit it shall deserve to have, the sequel shall declare), I will never in that matter conclude anything that shall be prejudicial to the realm. For the well, good, and safety whereof, I will never shun to spend my life. And whomsoever my chance shall be to light upon, I trust he shall be such as shall be as careful for the realm and you[10]—I will not say as myself because I cannot so certainly determine of any other, but by my desire he shall be such as shall be as careful for the preservation of the realm, and you, as myself. And albeit it might please Almighty God to continue me still in this mind to live out of the state of marriage, yet is it not to be feared; but He will so work in my heart and in your wisdom, as good provision by His help may be made whereby the realm shall not remain destitute of an heir that may be a fit governor and peradventure more beneficial to the realm than such offspring as may come of me. For though I be never so careful of your well doing, and mind ever so to be, yet may my issue grow out of kind and become perhaps ungracious. And in the end, this shall be for me sufficient: that a marble stone shall declare that a queen, having reigned such a time, lived and died a virgin. And here I end and take your coming to me in good part and give unto you all my hearty thanks—more yet for your zeal and good meaning than for your petition."

Speech on Mary, Queen of Scots

Distrusting Mary, queen of Scots, the Parliament of 1584–1585 had passed a bill for Elizabeth's safety, which said anyone who plotted against the monarch forfeited all title to the crown. Furthermore, in 1584 the Privy Council had devised the Bond of Association; those who signed it agreed to vengeance on those who tried to harm Elizabeth. In this atmosphere, Mary was caught urging Elizabeth's assassination. A deputation from Parliament went to Elizabeth on Saturday, November 12, to petition for Mary's execution. This is her reply:

"The bottomless graces and immeasurable benefits bestowed upon me by the Almighty are and have been such, as I must not only acknowledge them but admire them, accounting them as well miracles as benefits; not so much in respect of His Divine Majesty—with whom nothing is more common than to do things rare and singular—as in regard of our weakness, who cannot sufficiently set forth His wonderful works and graces, which to me have been so many, so diversely folded and embroidered one upon another, as in no sort am I able to express them.

"And although there liveth not any that may more justly acknowledge themselves infinitely bound unto God than I, whose life He hath miraculously preserved at sundry times (beyond my merit) from a multitude of perils and dangers, yet is not that the cause for which I count myself the deepliest bound to give Him my humblest thanks, or to yield Him greatest recognition; but this which I shall tell you hereafter, which will deserve the name of wonder, if rare things and seldom seen be worthy of account. Even this it is: that as I came to the crown with the willing hearts of subjects, so do I now, after twenty-eight years' reign, perceive in you no diminution of goodwills, which, if haply I should want, well might I breathe but never think I lived.

"And now, albeit I find my life hath been full dangerously sought, and death contrived by such as no desert procured it, yet am I thereof so clear from malice—which hath the property to make men glad at the falls and faults of their foes, and make them seem to do for other causes, when rancor is the ground—as I protest it is and hath been my grievous thought that one, not different in sex, of like estate, and my near kin, should be fallen into so great a crime. Yea, I had so little purpose to pursue her with any color of malice, that as it is not unknown to some of my Lords here—for now I will play the blab—I secretly wrote her a letter upon the discovery of sundry treasons, that if she would confess them, and privately acknowledge them by her letters unto myself, she never should need be called for them into so public question. Neither did I it of mind to circumvent her, for then I knew as much as she could confess; and so did I write.

"And if, even yet, now the matter is made but too apparent, I thought she truly would repent—as perhaps she would easily appear in outward show to do—and that for her none other would take the matter upon them; or that we were but as two milkmaids, with pails upon our arms; or that there were no more dependency upon us, but mine own life were only in danger, and not the whole estate of your religion and well doings; I protest—wherein you may believe me, for although I may have many vices, I hope I have not accustomed my tongue to be an instrument of untruth—I would most willingly pardon and remit this offense. Or if by my death other nations and kingdoms might truly say that this Realm had attained an ever prosperous and flourishing estate, I would (I assure you) not desire to live, but gladly give my life, to the end my death might procure you a better Prince. And for your sakes it is that I desire to live: to keep you from a worse. For, as for me, I assure you I find no great cause I should be fond to live. I take no such pleasure in it that I should much wish it, nor conceive such terror in death that I should greatly fear it. And yet I say not but, if the stroke were coming, perchance flesh and blood would be moved with it, and seek to shun it.

"I have had good experience and trial of this world. I know what it is to be a subject, what to be a Sovereign, what to have good neighbors, and sometime meet evil-willers. I have found treason in trust, seen great benefits little regarded, and instead of gratefulness, courses of purpose to cross. These former remembrances, present feeling, and future expectation of evils, (I say), have made me think an evil is much the better the less while it dureth, and so them happiest that are soonest hence; and taught me to bear with a better mind these treasons, than is common to my sex—yea, with a better heart perhaps than is in some men. Which I hope you will not merely impute to my simplicity or want of understanding, but rather that I thus conceived—that had their purposes taken effect, I should not have found the blow, before I had felt it; nor, though my peril should have been great, my pain should have been but small and short. Wherein, as I would be loath to die so bloody a death, so doubt I not but God would have given me grace to be prepared for such an event; which, when it shall chance, I refer to His good pleasure.

"And now, as touching their treasons and conspiracies, together with the contriver of them. I will not so prejudicate myself and this my Realm as to say or think that I might not, without the last statute, by the ancient laws of this land have proceeded against her; which was not made particularly to prejudice her,[11] though perhaps it might then be suspected in respect of the disposition of such as depend that way. It was so far from being intended to entrap her, that it was rather an admonition to warn the danger thereof. But sith it is made, and in the force of a law, I thought good, in that which might concern her, to proceed according thereunto rather than by course of common law. Wherein, if you the judges have not deceived me, or that the books you brought me were not false—which God forbid—I might as justly have tried her by the ancient laws of the land.

"But you lawyers are so nice and so precise in sifting and scanning every word or letter, that many times you stand more upon form than matter, upon syllables than the sense of the law. For, in this strictness and exact following of common form, [Mary] must have been indicted in Staffordshire, been arraigned at the bar, holden up her hand, and then been tried by a jury: a proper course, forsooth, to deal in that manner with one of her estate! I thought it better, therefore, for avoiding of these and more absurdities, to commit the cause to the inquisition of a good number of the greatest and most noble personages of this Realm, of the judges and others of good account, whose sentence I must approve.

"And all little enough: for we Princes, I tell you, are set on stages, in the sight and view of all the world duly observed. The eyes of many behold our actions; a spot is soon spied in our garments, a blemish quickly noted in our doings. It behoveth us, therefore, to be careful that our proceedings be just and honorable.

"But I must tell you one thing more: that in this late Act of Parliament you have laid an hard hand on me—that I must give direction for her death, which cannot be but most grievous, and an irksome burden to me. And lest you might mistake mine absence from this Parliament—which I had almost forgotten: although there be no cause why I should willingly come amongst multitudes (for that amongst many, some may be evil), yet hath it not been the doubt of any such danger or occasion that kept me from thence, but only the great grief to hear this cause spoken of, especially that such one of state and kin should need so open a declaration, and that this nation should be so spotted with blots of disloyalty. Wherein, the less is my grief for that I hope the better part is mine; and those of the worse not much to be accounted of, for that in seeking my destruction they might have spoiled their own souls.

"And even now could I tell you that which would make you sorry. It is a secret; and yet I will tell it you (although it be known I have the property to keep counsel but too well, oftentimes to mine own peril). It is not long since mine eyes did see it written that an oath was taken within few days either to kill me or to be hanged themselves; and that to be performed ere one month were ended. Hereby I see your danger in me, and neither can or will be so unthankful or careless of your consciences as to take no care for your safety.

"I am not unmindful of your oath made in the [Bond of] Association, manifesting your great goodwills and affections, taken and entered into upon good conscience and true knowledge of the guilt, for safeguard of my person; done (I protest to God) before I ever heard it, or ever thought of such a matter, till a thousand hands, with many obligations, were showed me at Hampton Court, signed and subscribed with the names and seals of the greatest of this land. Which, as I do acknowledge as a perfect argument of your true hearts and great zeal to my safety, so shall my bond be stronger tied to greater care for all your good.

"But, for that this matter is rare, weighty and of great consequence, and I think you do not look for any present resolution—the rather for that, as it is not my manner in matters of far less moment to give speedy answer without due consideration, so in this of such importance—I think it very requisite with earnest prayer to beseech His Divine Majesty so to illuminate mine understanding and inspire me with His grace, as I may do and determine that which shall serve to the establishment of His Church, preservation of your estates, and prosperity of this Commonwealth under my charge. Wherein, for that I know delay is dangerous, you shall have with all conveniency our resolution delivered by our message. And whatever any Prince may merit of their subjects, for their approved testimony of their unfeigned sincerity, either by governing justly, void of all partiality, or sufferance of any injuries done (even to the poorest), that do I assuredly promise inviolably to perform, for requital of your so many deserts."

Tilbury Speech

After the defeat of the Armada, while the nation still feared a land invasion, Elizabeth reviewed her troops in their camp at Tilbury:

"My loving people: we have been persuaded by some that are careful of our safety to take heed how we commit ourself to armed multitudes for fear of treachery, but I assure you I do not desire to live to distrust my faithful and loving people. Let tyrants fear. I have always so behaved myself that, under God, I have placed my chiefest strength and safeguard in the loyal hearts and goodwill of my subjects. And therefore I am come amongst you, as you see, at this time, not for my recreation and disport, but being resolved in the midst and heat of the battle to live or die amongst you all, to lay down for my God, and for my kingdom, and for my people, my honor and my blood, even in the dust. I know I have the body but of a weak and feeble woman, but I have the heart and stomach of a king—and of a king of England too—and think foul scorn that Parma, or Spain, or any prince of Europe should dare to invade the borders of my realm. To which, rather than any dishonor shall grow by me, I myself will take up arms, I myself will be your general, judge, and rewarder of every one of your virtues in the field. I know already for your forwardness you have deserved rewards and crowns, and we do assure you, in the word of a prince, they shall be duly paid you."

The Golden Speech

During the last Parliament of her reign, Elizabeth revoked many patents of monopoly at Parliament's request. On November 30, 1601, the members of Parliament came to her to express their thanks. As they knelt before her, she made this speech.

"Mr. Speaker: we have heard your declaration and perceive your care of our estate, by falling into a consideration of a grateful acknowledgment of such benefits as you have received; and that your coming is to present thanks to us, which I accept with no less joy than your loves can have desire to offer such a present.

"I do assure you there is no prince that loves his subjects better, or whose love can countervail our love. There is no jewel, be it of never so rich a price, which I set before this jewel: I mean your love. For I do esteem it more than any treasure or riches; for that we know how to prize, but love and thanks I count unvaluable. And, though God hath raised me high, yet this I count the glory of my crown, that I have reigned with your loves. This makes me that I do not so much rejoice that God hath made me to be a Queen, as to be a Queen over so thankful a people. Therefore, I have cause to wish nothing more than to content the subject; and that is a duty which I owe. Neither do I desire to live longer days than I may see your prosperity; and that is my only desire. And as I am that person that still yet under God hath delivered you, so I trust, by the almighty power of God, that I shall be His instrument to preserve you from every peril, dishonor, shame, tyranny, and oppression; partly by means of your intended helps [the subsidies they were granting] which we take very acceptably, because it manifesteth the largeness of your good loves and loyalties unto your sovereign.

"Of myself I must say this: I never was any greedy, scraping grasper, nor a strait, fast-holding Prince, nor yet a waster. My heart was never set on any worldly goods, but only for my subjects' good. What you bestow on me, I will not hoard it up, but receive it to bestow on you again. Yea, mine own properties I account yours, to be expended for your good; and your eyes shall see the bestowing of all for your good. Therefore, render unto them, I beseech you, Mr. Speaker, such thanks as you imagine my heart yieldeth, but my tongue cannot express.

"Mr. Speaker, I would wish you and the rest to stand up, for I shall yet trouble you with longer speech.

"Mr. Speaker, you give me thanks, but I doubt me I have a greater cause to give you thanks than you me, and I charge you to thank them of the Lower House from me. For, had I not received a knowledge from you, I might have fallen into the lapse of an error, only for lack of true information.

"Since I was Queen, yet did I never put my pen to any grant but that, upon pretext and semblance made unto me, it was both good and beneficial to the subject in general, though a private profit to some of my ancient servants who had deserved well at my hands. But the contrary being found by experience, I am exceedingly beholding to such subjects as would move the same at the first. And I am not so simple to suppose, but that there be some of the Lower House whom these grievances never touched: and for them, I think they spake out of zeal to their countries, and not out of spleen or malevolent affection as being parties grieved; and I take it exceeding gratefully from them, because it gives us to know that no respects or interest had moved them, other than the minds they have to suffer no diminution of our honor and our subjects' love unto us. The zeal of which affection, tending to ease my people and knit their hearts unto me, I embrace with a princely care, for above all earthly treasure I esteem my people's love, more than which I desire not to merit.

"That my grants should be grievous to my people and oppressions privileged under color of our patents, our kingly dignity shall not suffer it. Yea, when I heard it, I could give no rest unto my thoughts until I had reformed it. Shall they, think you, escape unpunished that have thus oppressed you, and have been respectless of their duty, and regardless of our honor? No, I assure you, Mr. Speaker, were it not more for conscience' sake than for any glory or increase of love that I desire, these errors, troubles, vexations, and oppressions, done by these varlets and lewd persons, not worthy the name of subjects, should not escape without condign punishment. But I perceive they dealt with me like physicians who, ministering a drug, make it more acceptable by giving it a good aromatical savor, or when they give pills do gild them all over.

"I have ever used to set the Last Judgment Day before mine eyes, and so to rule as I shall be judged to answer before a higher Judge, to whose judgment seat I do appeal, that never thought was cherished in my heart that tended not unto my people's good. And now, if my kingly bounties have been abused, and my grants turned to the hurt of my people, contrary to my will and meaning, and if any in authority under me have neglected or perverted what I have committed to them, I hope God will not lay their culps and offenses to my charge; who, though there were danger in repealing our grants, yet what danger would I not rather incur for your good, than I would suffer them still to continue?

"I know the title of a King is a glorious title; but assure yourself that the shining glory of princely authority hath not so dazzled the eyes of our understanding, but that we well know and remember that we also are to yield an account of our actions before the great Judge. To be a King and wear a crown is a thing more glorious to them that see it, than it is pleasant to them that bear it. For myself, I was never so much enticed with the glorious name of a King or royal authority of a Queen, as delighted that God hath made me His instrument to maintain His truth and glory, and to defend this Kingdom (as I said) from peril, dishonor, tyranny, and oppression.

"There will never Queen sit in my seat with more zeal to my country, care for my subjects, and that will sooner with willingness venture her life for your good and safety, than myself. For it is my desire to live nor reign no longer than my life and reign shall be for your good. And though you have had and may have many princes more mighty and wise sitting in this seat, yet you never had nor shall have any that will be more careful and loving.

"Shall I ascribe anything to myself and my sexly weakness? I were not worthy to live then; and, of all, most unworthy of the mercies I have had from God, who hath given me a heart that yet never feared any foreign or home enemy. And I speak it to give God the praise, as a testimony before you, and not to attribute anything to myself. For I, oh Lord! what am I, whom practices and perils past should not fear? Or what can I do? That I should speak for any glory, God forbid.

"This, Mr. Speaker, I pray you deliver unto the House, to whom heartily recommend me. And so I commit you all to your best fortunes and further counsels. And I pray you, Mr. Comptroller, Mr. Secretary, and you of my Council, that before these gentlemen go into their countries, you bring them all to kiss my hand."

NOTES TO THE TEXT

In his edition of Elizabeth's poems, Bradner gives a full account of the textual problems. For this edition I have modernized spelling and punctuation; generally I am in agreement with Bradner. The texts I used were these: "Woodstock: The Window Poem," in Raphael Holinshed, *The Chronicles* (Microfilm), 2d ed. (London, 1587), vol. 3, p. 1158; "Woodstock: The Shutter Poem," in Paul Hentzner, *Itinerarium* (Nuremberg, 1612), pp. 144–45, and John Nichols, *The Progresses of Queen Elizabeth* (1823; reprint, New York, 1965), vol. 1, p. 10; "French Psalter Poem," in J. H. Plumb, *Royal Heritage* (New York, 1977), p. 75; "Doubt of Future Foes," in Ruth Hughey, *The Arundel Harington Manuscript* (Columbus, Ohio, 1960), vol. 1, pp. 276–77, and George Puttenham, *Arte of English Poesy* (1589; reprint, Menston, Eng., 1968), p. 208; Folger manuscript V.h. 317, folio 20v; "On Fortune," in Puttenham, p. 197; "On Monsieur's Departure," in Nichols, vol. 2, p. 346. I wish to thank Laetitia Yeandle for directing me to the Folger Shakespeare Library's manuscript and helping me read it.

In his book *Elizabeth I and Her Parliaments,* J. E. Neale gives the fullest account of her speeches. For this edition I have used American spellings. For the speeches I edited, I have used the following texts: "Coronation Prayer and Speech," *The Quenes Maiesties Passage Through the Citie of London to Westminster the Day Before Her Coronacion,* ed. James M. Osborn (1559; reprint, New Haven, Conn., 1960); "Marriage Speech," in Sir Simonds D'Ewes, *A Compleat Journal of the [Parliaments] . . . of Queen Elizabeth* (1693; reprint, Wilmington, Del., 1974); and "Tilbury Speech," *Cabala* (Microfilm; London, 1691). The texts of the speech on Mary, Queen of Scots, and of the Golden Speech are Neale's, vol. 2, pp. 116–20 and 388–91 respectively.

    1. "Suspected by" means "suspected about."

    2. Lines 3–4 are unclear. They might be paraphrased this way: this present prison (Woodstock), where once I gave up the joy loaned me by Fortuna, can bear witness lately to my troubled wit.

    3. Puttenham spells "rain" as "raigne," suggesting a pun.

    4. The texts of this poem vary widely; see Bradner, pp. 72–73, for a fuller discussion.

> 1 doubt] dread exiles] exile A-H MS., FSL MS.
> 3 subjects'] subject AEP.
> 4 would] should A-H MS. FSL MS., weaved] wove A-H MS.
> 5 joys] toys AEP. do] doth A-H MS.
> 6 rain] rage A-H MS. FSL MS. repent] report winds] minds A-H MS.
> 7 top] topps supposed] suppose A-H MS. rue] ruth AEP.
> 8 all] of A-H MS. ye] you FSL MS. yow A-H MS.
> 9 Then] Their FSL MS. The A-H MS. which] with blinds] blinde A-H MS.
> 11 discord aye] eek discord AEP.
> 12 hath . . . grow] still peace hath taught to know FSL MS. AEP.
> 14 brooks . . . sects] it brookes no strangers force AEP.
> 15 My] Our through] with AEP. first] finderst FSL MS..
> 16 poll . . . that] pull their tops who FSL MS. seek] seekes A-H MS.
>   gape . . . joy] gape for ioy AEP gapes for further Ioy A-H MS.

    5. Bradner gives the variants (pp. 73–74). Leonard Forster has a useful discussion of the poem's Petrarchanism and the role Petrarchanism played in Elizabeth's politics in *The Icy Fire* (Cambridge, 1969), pp. 122–47.

    6. Elizabeth here refers to the fervent wish of Mary Tudor and her consort, Philip of Spain, to see Elizabeth safely married.

    7. Probably William Paulet, the Lord High Treasurer.

    8. That is, the House of Commons had not tried to limit Elizabeth's choice of a husband by insisting on an Englishman or prince.

    9. That is, suspicion.

    10. And] as D'Ewes.

    11. She refers here to the Act for the Queen's Safety of 1584–1585.

BIBLIOGRAPHY

Primary Works

Ames, Percy, ed. *The Mirror of the Sinful Soul.* London, 1897.
Bradner, Leicester, ed. *The Poems of Queen Elizabeth.* Providence, 1964.
Harrison, G. B., ed. *The Letters of Queen Elizabeth.* New York, 1935.
Osborn, James M., ed. *The Quenes Maiesties Passage Through the Citie of London to*

Westminster the Day Before Her Coronacion. New Haven, Conn., 1960. Facsimile of 1559 edition.

Pemberton, Caroline, ed. *Queen Elizabeth's Englishings.* London, 1899.

Rice, George P., ed. *The Public Speaking of Queen Elizabeth.* New York, 1951.

Related Works

Brooke, Tucker. "Queen Elizabeth's Prayers." *Huntington Library Quarterly* 2 (1938): 69–77.

Camden, William. *The History of . . . Princess Elizabeth.* Ed. Wallace T. MacCaffrey. Chicago, 1970.

Chamberlin, Frederick. *The Sayings of Queen Elizabeth.* London, 1923.

Christy, Miller. "Queen Elizabeth's Visit to Tilbury in 1588." *EHR* 34 (1919): 43–61.

Corts, Paul Richard. "Governmental Persuasion in the Reign of Queen Elizabeth I, 1558–1563." Ph.D. diss., Indiana University, 1971.

D'Ewes, Sir Simonds. *A Compleat Journal of the [Parliaments] . . . of Queen Elizabeth.* 1693. Facsimile edition. Wilmington, Del., 1974.

Forster, Leonard. *The Icy Fire.* Cambridge, Eng., 1969.

Hageman, Elizabeth. "Renaissance Women Writers" (s.v. Elizabeth). *ELR* (1984). This bibliography includes Elizabeth as an author.

Haigh, Christopher, ed. *The Reign of Elizabeth I.* Athens, Ga., 1986.

Heywood, Thomas. *Englands Elizabeth* Ed. Philip R. Rider. New York, 1982.

Jenkins, Elizabeth. *Elizabeth the Great.* New York, 1958.

Neale, J. E. *Elizabeth I and Her Parliaments.* 2 vols. New York, 1958.

———. *Queen Elizabeth I.* New York, 1934. This is the standard biography of her life.

———. "The Sayings of Queen Elizabeth." *History,* n.s., 10 (1925): 212–33.

Nichols, John. *The Progresses of Queen Elizabeth.* London, 1823.

Read, Conyers. *Bibliography of British History: Tudor Period, 1485–1603.* 2d ed. Oxford, 1959. This book includes Elizabeth's political career.

Schleiner, Winfried. "*Divina virago:* Queen Elizabeth as an Amazon." *Studies in Philology* 75 (1978): 163–80.

Yates, Frances A. *Astraea.* London, 1975.

LADY WROTH

ary Sidney

MARGARET PATTERSON HANNAY

Mary Sidney Wroth was born into a remarkable literary family. Her uncle, Sir Philip Sidney, is the author of the *Arcadia,* a prose romance that remained the most popular book of English fiction for two centuries; of the sonnet sequence *Astrophil and Stella;* and of *The Defense of Poesie,* the most influential essay on literary theory written during the English Renaissance. Her aunt, Mary Sidney Herbert, Countess of Pembroke, was celebrated in her own day and in ours as one of the most important woman writers and patrons of the Elizabethan period. The Countess's best-known work is her metric translation of the Psalms, which influenced the devotional poetry of John Donne and George Herbert, both of whom were family friends. Recently, the work of Philip and Mary's younger brother, Robert Sidney, Earl of Leicester, was discovered in a manuscript. Like Philip, Robert wrote a sequence of love sonnets—*Rosis and Lysa.*

Lady Mary, born in 1586 or 1587, was the eldest daughter of Robert Sidney and of his wife, Barbara Gamage, a Welsh heiress. Although her father was often away during her childhood, serving as commander of the English garrison across the English channel at Flushing, Mary grew up in an unusually affectionate home. Her mother preserved hundreds of letters Robert wrote to her.[1] A typical letter, sent to Barbara at Wilton, home of the Countess of Pembroke, reads: "You must excuse mee for our matters bee so busied as I can not write so often as I would. But you shall ever bee most deer to me, and whyle I live I will have the same care of you as of mine own life. Sweete wenche farewell till I can see you."[2] Young Mary was apparently with her mother on this and on many subsequent visits to the Countess's palatial homes at Wilton and at Baynard's Castle; Robert and Barbara made Baynard's Castle their London home even when the Countess was not in residence.[3] Because the couple had eleven children, the letters frequently concern plans for lying-in and christenings; on at least one occasion, Barbara stayed with the Countess for her delivery.[4]

Barbara and the children joined her husband in Flushing whenever she could, but her nearly constant state of pregnancy, her concern for her children, and the intermittent threat of war in the Lowlands made those visits less frequent than she would have liked. For example, in 1595 Robert wrote, "If you were not as you are I would put you to the trouble to come to me: but considering how neere your time you are I would not do it for anything."[5] Even when she was not pregnant, bringing the family to Flushing was a logistical nightmare. Robert's agent Rowland Whyte reported in 1597, "The 2 ships you send for my Lady are at Gravesend. . . . Upon Monday godwilling she begins her journey to you. She will [embarke] her nursery [the four little ones] at Gravesend. She herself with the three greater will go to Margate, where are the Queen's ships by my Lord Admiral's speciall care doth attend her."[6] On that occasion, when she was about ten years old, Mary traveled with her mother to the Continent; these occasional journeys gave her closer European ties than most other Englishwomen had. During the long separations of the family, however, her father followed her growth only through reports. For example, Whyte wrote on December 22, 1599, "Mrs. Mary is growne so tall and so goodly . . . that yr Lordship cannot believe until ye see yt. . . . My lady sees them [all the children] well. They are all in good health, well taught, and brought up in learning and qualiteis fit for their birth and condition."[7]

During Elizabeth's reign, Robert Sidney had relatively little influence at court and relied on his sister, the Countess of Pembroke, to intercede for permission to return home on leave.[8] Barbara frequently spent her time with her sister-in-law. The real affection between them is indicated in the one letter which has survived, explaining that the Countess is sending Barbara her own nurse during one of Barbara's visits to Flanders:

> Sister, How yow are guided of a midwife I know not butt I hope well & dowt not. for a Nurse I will asuer you for that time till it pleased God to free her from that charge I found so good Cawse to lyke of her in euery respect as I doo not thinke you coold have bin better furnished any way. You shall find her most quiet and most carefull. . . . God send yow a goodly boy & I assuer my self she will doo her part to your content if the sea deliuer her no worse to yow than from home she departeth. the same god send yow a blessed and a happy time. I wisshe it from my hart with my blessing to my pretty Daughter my good Barbara farewell as my self. . . . Yr most loueing Sister, M. Pembroke.[9]

The "daughter" the Countess mentions would be young Mary, who was then about four years old. Because it was customary for a child to be named after her godmother and for the godmother to call her "daughter," it is highly probable that Mary Wroth was the goddaughter and under the special care of the Countess of Pembroke.

The Countess no doubt encouraged Mary, along with her own sons William and Philip Herbert, to write poetry as their uncle had done. Mary did not know her famous uncle Sir Philip Sidney, who died in the year of her birth. While Robert had assumed Philip's role as administrator and commander in the Lowlands, the Countess had devoted herself to preserving Philip's memory as a Protestant martyr and to completing or editing his unfinished works, works that later provided the model for the writings of Lady Wroth. The first authorized edition of *The Countess of Pembroke's Arcadia* (so named because Philip wrote it for his sister and dedicated it to her) was published in 1593; in 1598, when Mary was about twelve, her aunt brought out a collected edition of Philip Sidney's works, including the *Arcadia* and *Astrophil and Stella*.[10] Mary certainly knew these works from childhood and must have been with her aunt at various times when the Countess was editing the manuscripts for publication.

During the reign of Elizabeth, Robert Sidney received no significant promotions or titles, but remained stuck in Flushing. On his accession, James I made Robert the first of the Sidneys to rise to the nobility by creating him Baron Sidney of Penshurst. Queen Anne appointed him as her chamberlain, and the family was thereafter much at court.

Mary became part of the court circle in 1604 and acted in several masques, including Ben Jonson's *The Masque of Blackness*. She apparently had been writing poetry for some time, for her work was praised by such contemporary writers as Nathaniel Baxter, Joshua Sylvester, and George Chapman. Ben Jonson was a particular friend, saying that he had become "a better lover and a much better Poet" after reading her sonnets.[11] Jonson dedicated his drama *The Alchemist* to her and praised her as "a Sydney" (*Epigrams* 103) who incorporated the virtues of all the goddesses (*Epigrams* 105).

Mary's family continued to prosper under James. Her father inherited the title and estates of his uncle, the Earl of Leicester. Her cousin William Herbert, Earl of Pembroke, acted with her in court masques and was given many valuable grants by James. Her younger cousin Philip Herbert was made Earl of Montgomery and given vast wealth as a favorite of the king. In 1604, all three cousins were married. Philip's marriage to Susan de Vere, Mary's friend, was considered one of the most brilliant social occasions in the early Stuart years.[12] William married Mary Talbot, daughter of the seventh earl of Shrewsbury. Mary herself made what seemed an excellent marriage to Sir Robert Wroth, a hunting companion of James I, and was settled on his primary estate at Loughton,[13] which she repaired with funds granted her by Queen Anne.[14] In his poem "To Sir Robert Wroth," Jonson praised Mary's husband and estate, much as he had praised her parents in "To Penshurst." The young couple was not happy, for shortly after their marriage Robert Sidney told his wife that "my son Wroth" finds "some what that doth discontent him: but the particulars I could not get out of him, onely that hee protests that hee cannot take any exceptions to his wife, nor her carriage towards him. It were very soon for any unkindness to begin."[15] Robert felt a particular affection for his oldest daughter; his letters frequently mention visits with "my daughter Wroth."

In 1614 Mary's husband died, leaving her with an infant son (James, who died in 1616) and a staggering debt of twenty-three thousand pounds. She undertook to pay off the debt herself and, despite King James's repeated pardoning of various debts, by 1624 she had paid off just half of the total. She was in financial difficulties for the rest of her life. It may have been the need for money that prompted her to publish the first part of her *Urania;* as was fashionable in the court, her other work circulated in manuscript and remains unpublished, including the rest of *Urania* and a pastoral tragicomedy, *Loves Victorie.*

Urania, the first known full-length work of fiction by an English-woman, concerns the love of Queen Pamphilia, the image of Constancy, for Amphilanthus, "Lover-of-two." The female protagonist is condemned to passive suffering more often than active redress, reflecting gender roles. Love is usually false, and the romance has a disillusioned, even cynical, tone; inconstancy appears an almost inevitable male attribute, which is sometimes presented comically: "Being a man, it was necessary for him to exceede a woman in all things, so much as inconstancie was found fit for him to excell her in, hee left her for a new" (p. 264). In the published version, Pamphilia, like Queen Elizabeth, eventually chose to marry only her kingdom; however, in the unpublished second part, she and Amphilanthus each marry someone else. Since it supposedly satirized various court intrigues, *Urania* caused such a scandal that Lady Wroth was forced to apologize and withdraw the book from sale; it has never been reprinted.

The printed version stops in the middle of a sentence; the Newberry manuscript contains the second part of the text, which also, like Sidney's *Arcadia,* stops mid-sentence. In addition to poems scattered through the text in the manner of the *Arcadia,* a series of over one hundred songs and sonnets entitled *Pamphilia to Amphilanthus* is appended to the text, presenting the Petrarchan courtly love traditions from the perspective of Pamphilia, a learned woman "excellent in writing." Significantly, Wroth wrote in an Elizabethan mode like her father's *Rosis and Lysa* and her uncle's *Astrophil and Stella.* The full title makes the family references clear: *The Countess of Mountgomeries* URANIA. *Written by the Right Honourable the Lady* MARY WROATH. *Daughter to the Right Noble Robert Earle of Leicester. And Neece to the Ever Famous, and Renowned*

Sr Phillips Sidney Knight. And to Ye Most Exelent Lady Mary Countesse of Pembroke Late Deceased.[16]

The poems have a melancholy tone; Pamphilia is constant in her love to the faithless Amphilanthus. "Let no other new love invite you . . . But purely shine / On, me, who have all truth preserved" (poem 61). Much of the imagery is Petrarchan, but the tone of suffering seems from the heart. Pamphilia finally turns from love of Amphilanthus to the love of God. The concluding poem speaks of Venus's praise as proper to "young beginners"; Pamphilia vows to progress now to "truth, which shall eternal goodness prove; / Enjoying of true joy, the most and best / The endless gain which never will remove" (poem 103).

Although the love poetry may not refer to a specific person, there are hints that Amphilanthus may be Mary's cousin, William Herbert. She never remarried, but a genealogical manuscript by Sir Thomas Herbert of Tintern, William Herbert's cousin, states that she bore two illegitimate children to William: "He had two natural children by the Lady Mary Wroth the Earl of Leicester's Daughter, William who was a Captain under Sir Hen Herbert, Collonell under Grave Maurice, and dyed unmarried and Catherine the wife of Mr. Lovel near Oxford."[17] The authority of Sir Thomas and the names of the children make it quite probable that she did bear him these children.[18] Robert Sidney wrote to his wife in 1615, "You have done very well in putting Wil away, for it had bin to grete a shame he should have stayde in the hous."[19] Although her sexual indiscretions with her cousin undoubtedly humiliated her parents and her godmother, they would not have been terribly unusual for the Stuart court. Other scandals, particularly those involving the Hay family and those leading to the Overbury murder, surely overshadowed her liaison, but she was not wise to allude to those scandals in her *Urania*.

Lady Mary Wroth, the first Englishwoman to write a full-length work of prose fiction and the first to write a significant body of secular poetry, was castigated for that achievement. Lord Denny admonished her to imitate her "vertuous & learned Aunt, who translated so many godly bookes, & especially the holy Psalms of David" rather than creating "lascivious tales & amarous toyes"; translation, not creation, was the province of a learned woman. Denny's admonition is ironic, since it was probably her aunt, the Countess of Pembroke, who encouraged her to imitate the model of Sir Philip Sidney's works, as her father Robert had done. Wroth gave a spirited reply to Denny, but she apparently was forced to learn the womanly virtue of silence; if she did write more after her *Urania*, it has not survived. She died in 1651 or 1653.

The following selections are taken from *Pamphilia to Amphilanthus*. In addition to her treatment of the usual Petrarchan themes such as the debate between day and night or the complaints against Venus and her son

Cupid, Wroth gives us glimpses of a lady's amusements at court—hawking, hunting, singing, embroidery—and of the more tragic side of love—pregnancy and abandonment. Many of the poems echo the work of her uncle and father, and poem 25 refers to Jonson's *Masque of Blackness*.

I have modernized the spelling and punctuation of the 1621 edition, after consulting the pioneering textual work of Gary Waller and the more recent authoritative edition by Josephine Roberts. The poems are numbered by their position in the Pamphilia sequence; I have supplied titles from the words of the poems.

NOTES

1. De L'Isle manuscripts U1475, correspondence series 81, letters 1–323. These letters span the years from 1587 until Barbara's death in 1621. Letters from the De L'Isle collection are published by permission of Viscount De L'Isle V.C., K.G. from his collection at Penshurst Place.

2. July 27, 1588, De L'Isle manuscripts, correspondence series 81, letter 6. Barbara was at Wilton during that July through September, apparently with her children.

3. See, for example, the Household book at Baynard's Castle (October 1600–March 1601), which begins with the item "milke for Mrs. Barbar Sidney" and contains many more references to her household. De L'Isle manuscripts U1475, accounts 27, item 4.

4. De L'Isle correspondence series 12, letters 188 and 190, both written on November 29, 1599. Robert's letters show regret that "I kannot be with you in your paine."

5. December 5, 1595, De L'Isle correspondence series 81, letter 36.

6. June 2, 1595, De L'Isle correspondence series 12, letter 100.

7. De L'Isle correspondence series 12, letter 198. Whyte was with Barbara and the children at Baynard's Castle.

8. Rowland Whyte to Robert Sidney, January 14, 1597/1598, De L'Isle correspondence series 12, letter 121. "My lady Pembroke did me the favor to wryte. . . . She hast taken ocasion to wryte again and to renew her suite to my Lord Treasurer. The copies of her letter unto him she did vouchsafe to send unto me of her own hand writing. I never reade any thing that culd express an earnest desire like unto this. . . . My Lady Pembroke hast again sent order to [clean] and make ready Baynards Castell for your Lordship and my Lady for she seeming to believe that this letter of hers will [prevail] in your [suite]. I pray you take knowledge of this grat favor she does you." Addressed to Robert Sidney, governor of Flushing.

9. September 9, 1590, British Library Additional Manuscripts shelfmark 15,232. Inscribed by the countess, "To my beloved Sister, the Lady Sidney, these."

10. A manuscript copy of poems from the *Arcadia* and of the Astrophel sonnets are bound with Barbara's letter from the countess and may well have belonged to Barbara Sidney. British Library Additional Manuscripts shelfmark 15,232.

11. "A Sonnet to the Noble Lady, the Lady Mary Wroth," *Ben Jonson: The Complete Poems*, ed. George Parfitt (New Haven, 1982), p. 165.

12. Dudley Carleton to John Chamberlain, January 7, 1604, Public Record Office, State Papers 14 (James I), volume 12, folio 6.

13. Her marriage portion was three thousand pounds, the same sum given to her sister, Katherine. The extravagance of the wedding celebration forced her father to borrow money.

See the special accounting of "your honor's extraordinary charge in the marriage of your daughter" for the exact expenses. Her cousin William, earl of Pembroke, supplied one thousand pounds of the dowry. "Income and Expenses of the First Earl of Leicester," British Library Additional Manuscripts shelfmark 12,066.

14. Josephine Roberts, introduction to *The Poems of Lady Mary Wroth*, pp. 13–14.

15. October 10, 1604, De L'Isle correspondence series 81, letter 117.

16. By her marriage to Mary's cousin Philip Herbert, earl of Montgomery, Susan de Vere had become wealthy enough to patronize the arts. *The Countess of Mountgomeries* URANIA may have been so designated purely out of friendship, but it is likely that the impoverished Lady Wroth was hoping for financial reward from her old friend.

17. Cited in Roberts, introduction to *The Poems of Lady Mary Wroth*, p. 24.

18. William would obviously be named for his father. Catherine was the name of the countess of Huntington, who helped raise so many of the Sidney children, and of Mary's cousin, the countess of Pembroke's daughter who died in childhood.

19. August 16, 1615, De L'Isle correspondence series 81, letter 265.

From *Pamphilia to Amphilanthus*

1. THE VISION

When night's black mantle could most darkness prove,
   And sleep (death's image) did my senses hire
   From knowledge of myself, then thoughts did move
   Swifter than those most swiftness need require:

In sleep, a Chariot drawn by winged Desire
   I saw, where sat bright Venus, Queen of love,
   And at her feet her son, still adding fire
   To burning hearts which she did hold above,

But one heart flaming more than all the rest
   The goddess held, and put it to my breast.
   "Dear son, now shut," said she, "thus must we win."

He her obeyed, and martyred my poor heart.
   I, waking, hoped as dreams it would depart
   Yet since—O me—a lover I have been.

7. SONG: A SHEPHERDESS

The spring now come at last
   To trees, fields, to flowers,
And meadows makes to taste
   His pride, while sad showers
Which from mine eyes do flow

    Makes known with cruel pains
      Cold winter yet remains
No sign of spring we know.

The Sun which to the Earth
    Gives heat, light, and pleasure,
Joys in spring, hateth dearth,
    Plenty makes his treasure.
His heat to me is cold,
    His light all darkness is
    Since I am barred of bliss
I heat nor light behold.

A shepherdess thus said
    Who was with grief oppressed
For truest love betrayed
    Barred her from quiet rest,
And weeping thus said she
    My end approaches near
    Now willow must I wear
My fortune so will be.

With branches of this tree
    I'll dress my hapless head
Which shall my witness be
    My hopes in love are dead;
My clothes embroidered all
    Shall be with Garlands round
    Some scattered, others bound,
Some tied, some like to fall.

The bark my book shall be
    Where daily I will write
This tale of hapless me
    True slave to Fortune's spite;
The root shall be my bed
    Where nightly I will lie,
    Wailing inconstancy
Since all true love is dead.

And these lines I will leave
    If some such lover come
Who may them right conceive
    And place them on my tomb:

She who still constant loved
  Now dead with cruel care
  Killed with unkind despair
And change, her end here proved.

11. THE WEARY TRAVELER

The weary traveler, who, tired, sought
  In places distant far, yet found no end
  Of pain or labor, nor his state to mend,
  At last with joy is to his home back brought,

Finds not more ease, though he with joy be fraught,
  When past his fear, content like souls ascend,
  Than I, on whom new pleasures do descend,
  Which now as high as firstborn bliss is wrought.

He tired with his pains, I with my mind;
  He all content receives by ease of limbs;
  I, greatest happiness that I do find,
  Belief for faith, while hope in pleasure swims.

Truth saith 'twas wrong conceit bred my despite,
Which once acknowledged, brings my heart's delight.

12. ENDLESS TORMENTS

You endless torments that my rest oppress,
  How long will you delight in my sad pain?
  Will never Love your favor more express?
  Shall I still live, and ever feel disdain?

Alas now stay, and let my grief obtain
  Some end; feed not my heart with sharp distress.
  Let me once see my cruel fortunes gain
  At least release, and long-felt woes redress.

Let not the blame of cruelty disgrace
  The honored title of your god-head, Love:
  Give not just cause for me to say, a place
  Is found for rage alone on me to move.

O quickly end, and do not long debate
My needful aid, lest help do come too late.

13. WELCOME NIGHT

Cloyed with the torments of a tedious night
  I wish for day; which come, I hope for joy:
  When cross I find new tortures to destroy
  My woe-killed heart, first hurt by mischief's might,

Then cry for night, and once more day takes flight
  And brightness gone; what rest should here enjoy
  Usurped is; hate will her force employ;
  Night cannot grief entomb though black as spite.

My thoughts are sad; her face as sad doth seem:
  My pains are long; her hours tedious are:
  My grief is great, and endless is my care:
  Her face, her force, and all of woes esteem.

Then welcome Night, and farewell flattering day
Which all hopes breed, and yet our joys delay.

16. FAREWELL LIBERTY

Am I thus conquered? have I lost the powers
  That to withstand, which joys to ruin me?
  Must I be still while it my strength devours
  And captive leads me prisoner, bound, unfree?

Love first shall leave men's fantasies to them free,
  Desire shall quench love's flames, spring hate sweet showers,
  Love shall loose all his darts, have sight, and see
  His shame, and wishings hinder happy hours.

Why should we not Love's purblind charms resist?
  Must we be servile, doing what he list?
  No, seek some host to harbor thee. I fly

Thy babyish tricks, and freedom do profess;
  But O, my hurt makes my lost heart confess
  I love, and must: So farewell liberty.

21. SONG: STAY, MY THOUGHTS

Stay, my thoughts, do not aspire
  To vain hopes of high desire:
  See you not all means bereft

To enjoy? No joy is left;
　　Yet still methinks my thoughts do say
　　Some hopes do live amid dismay.

Hope then once more hope for joy;
　　Bury fear which joys destroy;
　　Thought hath yet some comfort given
　　Which despair hath from us driven;
　　Therefore dearly my thoughts cherish
　　Never let such thinking perish.

'Tis an idle thing to plain
　　Odder far to die for pain;
　　Think and see how thoughts do rise
　　Winning where there no hope lies,
　　Which alone is lovers' treasure
　　For by thoughts we love do measure:

Then kind thought my fancy guide
　　Let me never hapless slide;
　　Still maintain thy force in me,
　　Let me thinking still be free:
　　Nor leave thy might until my death,
　　But let me thinking yield up breath.

22. COME, DARKEST NIGHT

Come, darkest night, becoming sorrow best;
　　Light, leave thy light, fit for a lightsome soul;
　　Darkness doth truly suit with me oppressed
　　Whom absence power doth from mirth control.

The very trees with hanging heads condole
　　Sweet summer's parting, and of leaves distressed
　　In dying colors make a grief-ful role;
　　So much (alas) to sorrow are they pressed.

Thus of dead leaves her farewell carpet's made:
　　Their fall, their branches, all their mournings prove
　　With leafless, naked bodies, whose hues fade
　　From hopeful green, to wither in their love.

If trees and leaves for absence, mourners be,
No marvel that I grieve, who like want see.

23. THE SUN WHICH GLADS

The sun which glads the earth at his bright sight,
  When in the morn he shows his golden face,
  And takes the place from tedious drowsy night,
  Making the world still happy in his grace,

Shows happiness remains not in one place,
  Nor may the Heavens alone to us give light,
  But hide that cheerful face, though no long space,
  Yet long enough for trial of their might.

But never sunset could be so obscure
  No desert ever had a shade so sad,
  Nor could black darkness ever prove so bad,
  As pains which absence makes me now endure.

The missing of the sun a while makes night,
But absence of my joy sees never light.

24. WHEN LAST I SAW THEE

When last I saw thee, I did not thee see,
  It was thine Image, which in my thoughts lay
  So lively figured, as no time's delay
  Could suffer me in heart to parted be;

And sleep so favorable is to me,
  As not to let thy loved remembrance stray,
  Lest that I waking might have cause to say
  There was one minute found to forget thee;

Then since my faith is such, so kind my sleep
  That gladly thee presents into my thought;
  And still true lover like thy face doth keep
  So as some pleasure shadow-like is wrought.

Pity my loving, nay of conscience give
Reward to me in whom thy self doth live.

25. LIKE TO THE INDIANS

Like to the Indians, scorched with the sun,
  The sun which they do as their God adore,

So am I used by love, for evermore
I worship him, less favors have I won.

Better are they who thus to blackness run,
    And so can only whiteness' want deplore,
    Than I who pale and white am with griefs store,
    Nor can have hope, but to see hopes undone.

Besides their sacrifice received in sight
    Of their chose saint; mine hid as worthless rite.
    Grant me to see where I my offerings give,

Then let me wear the mark of Cupid's might
    In heart, as they in skin of Phoebus' light,
    Not ceasing off'rings to love while I live.

26. FOND PLEASURES

When every one to pleasing pastime hies
    Some hunt, some hawk, some play, while some delight
    In sweet discourse, and music shows joy's might,
    Yet I my thoughts do far above these prize.

The joy which I take is that free from eyes
    I sit, and wonder at this day-like night,
    So to dispose themselves, as void of right,
    And leave true pleasure for poor vanities.

When others hunt, my thoughts I have in chase;
    If hawk, my mind at wished end doth fly;
    Discourse, I with my spirit talk and cry;
    While others music choose as greatest grace.

O God, say I, can these fond pleasures move?
Or music be but in sweet thoughts of love?

37. THE HIVE OF LOVE

How fast thou fliest, O Time, on love's swift wings
    To hopes of joy, that flatters our desire
    Which to a lover, still, contentment brings!
    Yet, when we should enjoy thou dost retire.

Thou stayest thy pace, false Time, from our desire,
    When to our ill thou hastest with Eagle's wings,

Slow, only to make us see thy retire
Was for despair, and harm, which sorrow brings.

O slack thy pace, and milder pass to love.
    Be like the Bee, whose wings she doth but use
    To bring home profit, master's good to prove,
    Laden, and weary, yet again pursues,

So lade thy self with honey of sweet joy,
And do not me the hive of love destroy.

40. FALSE HOPE

False hope which feeds but to destroy, and spill
    What it first breeds; unnatural to the birth
    Of thine own womb; conceiving but to kill,
    And plenty gives to make the greater dearth,

So Tyrants do who falsely ruling earth
    Outwardly grace them, and with profits fill
    Advance those who appointed are to death
    To make their greater fall to please their will.

Thus shadow they their wicked vile intent
    Coloring evil with a show of good,
    While in fair shows their malice so is spent;
    Hope kills the heart, and tyrants shed the blood.

For hope deluding brings us to the pride
Of our desires, the farther down to slide.

45. FRAMED WORDS

If I were given to mirth t'would be more cross
    Thus to be robbed of my chiefest joy,
    But silently I bear my greatest loss—
    Who's used to sorrow, grief will not destroy.

Nor can I as those pleasant wits enjoy
    My own framed words, which I account the dross
    Of purer thoughts, or reckon them as moss
    While they (wit sick) themselves to breath employ.

Alas, think I, your plenty shows your want,
    For where most feeling is, words are more scant,
    Yet pardon me, Live, and your pleasure take,

Grudge not, if I neglected, envy show.
　'Tis not to you that I dislike do owe,
　But crossed my self, wish some like me to make.

47. YOU BLESSED STARS

You blessed stars which do heaven's glory show,
　And at your brightness make our eyes admire,
　Yet envy not though I on earth below
　Enjoy a sight which moves in me more fire.

I do confess such beauty breeds desire;
　You shine, and clearest light on us bestow,
　Yet doth a sight on earth more warmth inspire
　Into my loving soul, his grace to know.

Clear, bright, and shining as you are, is this
　Light of my joy, fixed steadfast nor will move
　His light from me, nor I change from his love,
　But still increase as th'height of all my bliss.

His sight gives life unto my love-ruled eyes
My love content because in his, love lies.

61. SONG: NO OTHER NEW LOVE

Dearest if I by my deserving
May maintain in your thoughts my love,
　Let me it still enjoy
　　Nor faith destroy
Pity love where it doth move.

Let no other new love invite you
To leave me who so long have served,
　Nor let your power decline
　　But purely shine
On me, who have all truth preserved.

Or had you once found my heart straying
Then would not I accuse your change,
　But being constant still
　　It needs must kill
One, whose soul knows not how to range;

Yet may you love's sweet smiles recover
Since all love is not yet quite lost,

But tempt not love too long
   Lest so great wrong
Make him think he is too much crossed.

64. THE JUGGLER

Love like a juggler comes to play his prize
   And all minds draw his wonders to admire,
   To see how cunningly he (wanting eyes)
   Can yet deceive the best sight of desire.

The wanton child, how he can feign his fire
   So prettily, as none sees his disguise!
   How finely do his tricks, while we fools hire
   The badge and office of his tyrannies.

For in the end such juggling he doth make
   As he our hearts instead of eyes doth take.
   For men can only by their sleights abuse

The sight with nimble and delightful skill,
   But if he play, his gain is our lost will,
   And, childlike, we cannot his sports refuse.

77. THIS STRANGE LABYRINTH

In this strange Labyrinth how shall I turn?
   Ways are on all sides, while the way I miss:
   If to the right hand, there in love I burn;
   Let me go forward, therein danger is;

If to the left, suspicion hinders bliss;
   Let me turn back, shame cries I ought return
   Nor faint, though crosses which my fortunes kiss;
   Stand still is harder, although sure to mourn.

Thus let me take the right, or left-hand way,
   Go forward, or stand still, or back retire:
   I must these doubts endure without allay
   Or help, but travail find for my best hire.

Yet that which most my troubled sense doth move,
Is to leave all and take the thread of Love.*

  *This is the first of "A Crown of Sonnets Dedicated to Love," a series of fourteen in-
terlocked sonnets.

103. MY MUSE NOW HAPPY

My muse now happy, lay thyself to rest,
    Sleep in the quiet of a faithful love.
    Write you no more, but let these fancies move
    Some other hearts, wake not to new unrest.

But if you study, be those thoughts addressed
    To truth, which shall eternal goodness prove;
    Enjoying of true joy, the most, and best,
    The endless gain which never will remove.

Leave the discourse of Venus and her son
    To young beginners, and their brains inspire
    With stories of great love, and from that fire
    Get heat to write the fortunes they have won,

And thus leave off; what's past shows you can love,
Now let your constancy your honor prove.
                                                        Pamphilia

BIBLIOGRAPHY

Primary Works

Sidney, Mary (Lady Wroth). *The Countess of Mountgomeries* URANIA. *Written by the Right Honourable the Lady* MARY WROATH. *Daughter to the Right Noble Robert Earle of Leicester. And Neece to the Ever Famous, and Renowned Sir Phillips Sidney Knight. And to Ye Most Exelent Lady Mary Countesse of Pembroke Late Deceased.* Printed for John Marriott and John Grismand, 1621.
———. *Pamphilia to Amphilanthus.* Ed., with an introduction, Gary Waller. Salzburg, 1977.
———. *Pamphilia to Amphilanthus.* In *The Poems of Lady Mary Wroth*, ed., with an introduction, Josephine A. Roberts. Baton Rouge, 1983.

Related Works

Beilin, Elaine V. "'The Onely Perfect Vertue': Constancy in Mary Wroth's *Pamphilia to Amphilanthus.*" *Spenser Studies* 2 (1981):229–45.
Parry, Graham. "Lady Mary Wroth's *Urania.*" *Proceedings of the Leeds Philosophical and Literary Society* 16 (1975):51–60.
Paulissen, May Nelson. "Forgotten Love Sonnets of the Court of King James: The Sonnets of Mary Wroth." *Publications of the Missouri Philological Association* 3 (1978):24–31.
———. *The Love Sonnets of Lady Mary Wroth: A Critical Introduction.* Salzburg, 1982.
Roberts, Josephine A. "Lady Mary Wroth's Sonnets: A Labyrinth of the Mind." *Journal of Women's Studies in Literature* 1 (1979):319–29.
———. "An Unpublished Literary Quarrel Concerning the Suppression of Mary Wroth's *Urania* (1621)." *Notes and Queries* 222 (1977):532–35.

Salzman, Paul. "Contemporary References in Mary Wroth's *Urania.*" *Review of English Studies* 29 (1978):178–81.

Swift, Carolyn Ruth. "Feminine Identity in Lady Mary Wroth's *Urania.*" *English Literary Renaissance* 14 (1984):328–46.

Witten-Hannah, Margaret A. "Lady Mary Wroth's *Urania:* The Work and the Tradition." Unpublished Ph.D. dissertation, University of Auckland, 1978.

THE MATCHLESS ORINDA

atherine Philips

ELIZABETH H. HAGEMAN

Because her poem "On the First of January 1657" includes the statement that God has "By moments number'd out the precious sands, / Till [the poet's life] is swell'd to six and twenty years" (lines 4–5), students of Katherine Philips have assumed that her actual birth date was January 1, 1631/1632. The accuracy of that precise date remains unvalidated, but church records do reveal that the future poet was baptized at Saint Mary Woolchurch in London on January 11 of that year. Her mother was Katherine Fowler, née Katherine Oxenbridge, daughter of Daniel Oxenbridge, a doctor of physic and fellow of the Royal College of Physicians in London; her father was James Fowler, a prosperous London cloth merchant. In his *Brief Lives,* Philips's contemporary John Aubrey indicates that after receiving early training at home—she learned to read from "her cozen Blackett, who had lived with her from her swadling clothes to eight"—young Katherine Fowler was enrolled in the Presbyterian Mrs. Salmon's school for girls in nearby Hackney. Aubrey reports that Katherine Fowler was a pious, intelligent child. "She was," he writes, "very religiously devoted when she was young; prayed by herself an hower together, and tooke sermons *verbatim* when she was but 10 yeares old." She "Loved poetrey at schoole, and made verses there." Mrs. Blackett, in particular, had favorable memories of her former charge, whom she remembered as "Very good-natured; not at all high-minded"—even if she was "pretty fatt; not tall; reddish faced."[1]

In December 1642, John Fowler died, leaving his wife, his daughter, and his son Joshua a combined legacy of some 3,300 pounds. A few years later, probably in 1646, Fowler's widow married Sir Richard Phillips of Picton Castle in Pembrokeshire, the southernmost county of Wales, and in August of 1648, young Katherine Fowler married James Philips, a relative by birth and by marriage to Sir Richard.[2] She was then sixteen years old; her new husband was fifty-four.

From 1648 until 1664, the year of her death, Katherine Philips's home was the Priory in Cardigan, on the banks of the River Teify, not far from the sea. Among her best-known works are the poems to Lucasia, five of which—"Friendship's Mystery. To My Dearest Lucasia," "A Dialogue of Absence 'twixt Lucasia and Orinda," "To My Excellent Lucasia, on Our Friendship," and "Parting with Lucasia, a Song"—are printed in this anthology. Orinda is Philips's name for herself in her poems and letters; Lucasia is Anne Owen, who lived some twenty-five miles away and who was a close friend of Philips from at least as early as 1651 until Philips's death. "To My Dear Sister Mrs. C.P. on Her Marriage" celebrates the marriage in 1653 of Philips's sister-in-law Cicily Philips to John Lloyd in Saint Mary's Church, next door to Cardigan Priory; the "Epitaph on Mr. John Lloyd" was written three years later to be carved on Lloyd's funeral monument in the church in Cilgerran, a few miles from Cardigan. Even some of Philips's poems on political subjects can be related to her life in Wales. "Upon the Double Murther of King Charles I," for example, responds to verses written by the Welsh republican Vavasor Powell when he was visiting the priory; and "On the Third of September 1651" moralizes on an event that certainly pleased Philips's Parliamentarian husband: Cromwell's defeat of Charles II at the Battle of Worcester—a defeat which effectively ended the second and final tide of the English Civil War.

The genres Philips chose for the bases of her poems include many that were popular among her contemporaries: the pastoral dialogue, the wooing poem, the poem of parting, the epithalamion, the epitaph, and the elegy. Time and again her approach to those genres is that of an intelligent poet writing to an audience she expects to appreciate her exploitation of traditional poetic conventions and her deft manipulation of language. For example, in a number of the poems she wrote during the 1650s, Philips expresses a longing for a quiet life of ordered peace: in "A Retir'd Friendship. To Ardelia," she explicitly contrasts a secluded life of "kindly mingling Souls" with the world of "Bloud and Plots"; in the Lucasia poems she reiterates the idea that personal friendship offers joy superior to that of "Crown-conquerors" ("To My Excellent Lucasia, on Our Friendship"); and in "To Mr. Henry Lawes," she imagines the musician's holy power to "repair a State." Highly traditional in their echoing pastoral motifs established by classical poets like Virgil and Horace and developed throughout the English sixteenth century, Philips's poems of retirement are most timely in their nostalgic longing for a lost golden age and then in their celebrating the return of the monarchy as a revival of a pastoral paradise.[3] Both royalist and Parliamentarian poets of the seventeenth century, it should be noted, wrote pastoral verse: Katherine Philips's age was the age of Milton's "Lycidas," of Herrick's *Hesperides*, of Vaughan's *Olor Iscanus,* and of Marvell's "The Garden." The latter two works, in fact, include tributes to Philips: in *Olor Iscanus* (1651), Vaughan presents a poem in praise of Katherine Philips, for whom "No *Lawrel* growes, but for [her] *Brow*," and "The Garden" incorporates perhaps the greatest compliment of all—two, possibly three, echo allusions to lines from Philips's work.[4]

In her two most moving poems on death—the epitaph for the tomb of her infant son and "Orinda upon Little Hector Philips"—Philips uses the conventional *topos* of the metaphoric relationship between the "numbers" of time and the "numbers" of poetry to convey the pain of a bereaved parent. In the latter poem, the number forty, which is associated in Christian numerology with periods of privation and trial,[5] reinforces her theme of the untimeliness of the boy's death: the long-awaited child—born after "Twice forty months" of marriage—died "in forty days." Unsustained by any muse but her "Tears" and unaided by any "Art" but her grief, this mother offers only "gasping numbers" for her child's elegy. Those "gasping numbers" are appropriate to the occasion, for the poem is "Too just a tribute for [the child's] early Herse." In the "Epitaph" Philips writes of having been "Seven years childless" and puns on the words *morning* and *mourning* as she predicts that "if" the Sun (significant here because the sun heralds new days and new beginnings) should be "Half so glorious as [the child's] eyes," it will, like the child, be shrouded in a "morning Cloud." If the mark of a successful poem about death is, as many think, the poet's ability to find consolation, then Philips has failed. But if the poet's task is to find a verbal formulation of a state of mind, then few poems are more successful than these two.

In her epithalamion for Cicily Philips and the verses written in her behalf three years later when her husband died, Philips again uses the theme of time in interestingly appropriate ways. She begins "To My Dear Sister Mrs. C.P. on Her Marriage" by defining the kind of verses she will not write: she announces that she is not so naïve as to think that celebrating a marriage in traditionally festive ways (with the cups, garlands, and altars invoked by poets like Edmund Spenser in his "Epithalamion") is anything but indulgence in "wild toyes [which] / Be but a troublesome and empty noise." Orinda, a more serious poet, will offer instead "great Solemnities"—her "wishes for *Cassandra's* bliss." The phrase "those men" to name the poets whose mode Orinda rejects is of course apt in a poem whose persona is the female Orinda in an age when most poets were men and most marriage poems celebrated the groom's joy. Orinda takes for granted her society's notion of the new wife's duties to her husband and to the marriage and prays "May her Content and Duty be the same." Content will come, Orinda continues, if the marriage is the kind of companionate marriage that Protestant writers of sixteenth- and seventeenth-century England recommended[6]—if it is the kind of loving marriage that Philips's poems to her own husband (Antenor in the verses) suggest she enjoyed. In the second line of her poem, Orinda rejects the idea that those who "crown the cup" really do "crown the day" in favor of a different kind of wish expressed at the end of her poem: she hopes this couple "may count the hours as they pass, / By *their own* Joys and not by Sun or Glass" (italics mine). Far less ornate than the kind of epithalamion this poet refuses to emulate, Philips's poem is remarkable for her careful adoption of a plain style as a vehicle for a poem that advocates a marriage characterized by "Friendship, Gratitude, and strictest Love."

Written, as its subtitle says, "in the person of his wife," the "Epitaph on Mr. John Lloyd" is poignant in its sympathetic expression of the wife's sorrow for a husband who "so untimely dy'd / And living pledges was deny'd." Knowing that even her "Grief at length must dy" and fully aware that future generations will look at the monument with "unconcerned Eys," the widow begs the funeral monument to use its persuasive powers to teach them not only to admire John Lloyd for his virtue, but to pity her for her grief. The effect of the epitaph is multifaceted: literally "inscribed on his Monument / in Kilgarron" (subtitle), it images a widow's successful search for relief. The stone *can* "Preserve," at least for some time, her grief, and its words *do* articulate the message she intends. In providing the widow with words with which to bid the "abiding faithful stone" to instruct those who will read it "then," Philips has given her a way to assert that her husband has a "name [that] can live" after all.

Radically different in tone, but similarly successful in their wit, are the three poems about wooing printed in this anthology: the companion poems "To Regina Collier, on Her Cruelty to Philaster" and "To Philaster, on His Melancholy for Regina" and the poem printed at the end of this selection, "An Answer to Another Perswading a Lady to Marriage." In the latter, the poet addresses a callow youth who wastes his time wooing a lady whom he sees as the goddess of love herself. Philips treats both lady and lover with comic scorn: if he really believed her to be a goddess, he would not presume to confine her in a domestic love—to make her a "petty Houshold God"; if she really were as lovely as he thinks, she would not be so publicly and indiscriminately flirtatious. In the companion poems, the poet chides each lover in turn: first the "Triumphant Queen of scorn," and then her disconsolate suitor. Regina, she asserts, has become a "Round-head"—a Parliamentarian (here a term of dispraise for a person who "insult[s] upon" a subject she has conquered with her own seductive beauty). But unlike those poets who content themselves with poems urging ladies to submit to their men, Orinda then turns to the unsuccessful wooer and calls him a "vain / And double Murtherer"—a murder in that his self-indulgent grief is suicidal and in that his pain "wounds" Regina too. As she urges him to give up Regina, this poet expresses disdain for the "Queen" who does not deserve Philaster's loyalty and also for the lover whose "dulness"—stupidity—allows him to mourn an undeserving mistress.

The same temperament that led to those witty poems is evident in a manuscript in Philips's hand now in the National Library of Wales.[7] Inscribed before her marriage to James Philips, the manuscript is a single sheet on which are written two poems and a snippet of prose—all on the subject of love and marriage. On one side of the sheet is a playful dispraise of marriage, which "affords but little Ease / The best of husbands are so hard to please" (lines 1–2), and "A recipt to cure a Love sick Person who cant obtain the Party desired":

> Take two oz: of the spirits of reason three oz: of the Powder of experiance five drams of the Juce of Discretion three oz: of the Powder of good advise & a spoonfull of the Cooling watter of Consideration make these all up into Pills & besure to drink a little content affter y^m & then the head will be clear of maggotts & whimsies & you restored to y^r right sences but the persons that wont be ruld must become a sacrifise to cupid & dye for love for all the Doctors in the world cant cure y^m.

> If this wont do apply the plaister & if that wont do itts out of my power to find out what will.

On the other side of the sheet are sixteen lines in the couplets that Philips would use in many of her later verses—in panegyrics to members of the royal family and to her fellow poets, in verse letters to her husband, in moral poems with titles like "Happiness," "The Soul," and "The World." The speaker of this poem claims that "If himans rites shall call me hence / It shall be with some man of sence" (lines 3–4). Her requirements that her husband be "Nott with the great butt with the good estate" (line 5) and that he stand "Ready to serve his friend his country & his king" (line 12) indicate how thoroughly the young poet had assimilated the values of seventeenth-century neoclassical poetry. For in this poem young Katherine Fowler has transformed the formulaic description of the loyal, sensible, and moderate friend advocated by poets like Ben Jonson[8] into a description of the ideal husband.

The fact is that while Philips's poems and letters suggest that she did enjoy a companionate marriage with James Philips and that she found congenial friends among her neighbors and relatives in Wales, many of her closest connections were with Londoners—and, in spite of the fact that many of the members of her family were Parliamentarians, with royalists. As a Member of Parliament, James Philips made extended trips to London; in all likelihood Katherine Philips accompanied him in his sojourns there. She must have been in London in the spring of 1655, for their only son Hector was buried then in the church of Saint Benet-Sherehog in Syth's Lane in London. Among her many London friends were two, Mary Aubrey and Mary Harvey, who had been Philips's classmates at Mrs. Salmon's school. Mary Aubrey (later Mrs. Montague) appears as Rosania in Philips's verses. Whether any of Philips's poems refer to Mary Harvey, we do not know, but one—"To Sir Edward Dering (the Noble Silvander) on His Dream and Navy, Personating Orinda's Preferring Rosania Before Solomon's Traffic to Ophir"—is addressed to the man Mary Harvey married in 1648, and two of Philips's poems are printed in Henry Lawes's *Second Book of Ayres and Dialogues* (1655), which is dedicated to Lady Dering.

Sir Edward's name appears several times in letters Philips wrote to Sir Charles Cotterell in the early 1660s. Moreover, six of the letters that survive in Dering's letterbook, now owned by the University of Cincinnati, are addressed to Philips; others are written to their mutual friends the Countess of Roscommon, Mary Montague, Lady Gifford, and Lady Dungannon (Anne Owen, who in 1662 was remarried to Marcus Trevor, Lord Dungannon). In those letters, also written in the early 1660s, Dering uses the same classical names that Philips used to refer to their mutual friends, and his admiration for Philips is a constant theme.[9] In a letter written to Philips on January 3, 1662, for instance, he writes of "Orinda's pen, whose every line gives more lasting honour than Egyptian Pyramids, though they alone of all the wonders of the world, seem to despise the injuries of time." In July of 1664, Dering writes to Lady Roscommon that "Since Orindas death, I am growne so cold & stupid, and my complexion not very active and spirituall at the best, is now so dull & frozen, that I hardly know what I do or say, I entertaine nothing with delight, even the satisfactions of sincere & vertuous friendship, which among humane joyes I did esteeme the most, have not the sweetnesse which they had. . . . Sure, another wound like this, would make me alltogether insensible, and leave me (allmost) as unconcerned for the world, as if I had never been." The following February, when he writes to Lucasia of his slow recovery from that sorrow, he includes a statement of the significance of their friend's life:

> But not to dwell too long upon so melancholy reflexions, your Ladyship could not but observe that Orinda had conceived the most generous designe, that in my opinion ever entred into any breast, which was to unite all those of her acquaintance which she found worthy or desired to make so, (among which later number she was pleased to give me a place) into one societie, and by the bands of friendship to make an alliance more firme than what nature, our country or equall education can produce: and this would in time have spread very farr, and have been improved with great and yet unimagind advantage to the world: for it would have been of great use sure, to show the world that there were satisfactions in vertuous friendship farr transcending all those delights, which the most specious follyes

> can tempt us with; and doubtlesse many would have quitted the extrava-
> gancies of their inclinations for feare of being banishd so happy a conversa-
> tion, that would have resisted more pressing arguments, and all the
> instruments of a more rugged discipline.

Dering's words here might seem to support those who have read in Philips's friendship poems evidence that she organized and headed a Society
of Friendship that met to discuss literary and/or philosophical questions.[10] Surely, however, if Philips had founded such a society, Dering
would not be using words that would suggest that Lady Dungannon
might not have noticed its existence. In the absence of better evidence that
Philips had organized a society with a membership list or a definite program, it seems more reasonable to believe that the word "society" in her
poems and in this letter refers to her social set—what we might now call
her network of friends. What Dering's statement *does* show is the reality
and significance of the close ties between members of the social circle to
which they both belonged.

Dering's words also suggest that Philips's contemporaries agreed with
the judgment of twentieth-century anthologists that the poems on friendship are her best—or, if not her best, then certainly her most characteristic—works. In those poems, Philips appropriates the language love
poets of the mid-seventeenth century had inherited from the Elizabethans
and Jacobeans and applies it to a new subject: female friendship. Her
friendship poems abound with echo allusions to poems like John Donne's
"Canonization," "The Sun Rising," "The Ecstasy," and "A Valediction:
Forbidding Mourning." In, for example, "Friendship in Embleme, or the
Seal. To My Dearest Lucasia" (a poem not printed in this volume), Philips
transforms the conceit of the compass from Donne's "A Valediction: Forbidding Mourning" into an insignia of her friendship. Donne worked
with his compass image for the last three of the nine stanzas in his poem;
Philips rings changes on it for ten of her sixteen stanzas, all written, as are
Donne's, in tetrameter lines rhyming *a b a b*. In "A Valediction: Forbidding Mourning," Donne says his "love [is] so much refin'd / That our
selves know not what it is." Orinda goes further, maintaining that
"Friendship hearts so much refines, / It nothing but itself designs." And
while Donne contrasts his love with that of "Dull sublunary lovers,"
Orinda asserts that the only reason for explicating her emblematic image
is "that we may the mind reveal / To the dull eye."

In "Friendship's Mystery. To My Dearest Lucasia," Orinda echoes
Donne's "The Canonization," in which the poet demonstrated that he and
his lady "prove / Mysterious by this love," when she bids Lucasia,

> Come, my *Lucasia*, since we see
>   That Miracles Mens faith do move,

By wonder and by prodigy
    To the dull angry world let's prove
    There's a Religion in our Love.

In his "Sun Rising," Donne asserts of himself and his lady: "She is all States, all Princes, I, / Nothing else is." Orinda declares an even more complete equality between herself and her friend when she says that "all our Titles [are] shuffled so, / Both Princes, and both Subjects too." The "shuffling" of those friends' "Titles" is nowhere more clear than in "A Dialogue of Absence 'twixt Lucasia and Orinda," where, rather than teach Lucasia what to think, Philips allows her to teach Orinda. Orinda's sorrow is lightened at least a little by Lucasia's assurance that

Our Souls, without the help of Sense,
    By wayes more noble and more free
    Can meet, and hold intelligence.

In the end, Orinda admits that parting is—if not joyful—then "sadly sweet," and the friends join to sing the chorus, which looks forward to a final union when "we shall come where no rude hand shall sever, / And there wee'l meet and part no more for ever."

The theme of Platonic friendship, of course, may be found throughout Renaissance literature. In 1560, for example, the English writer George Turberville had written that true friends as "two in bodies twaine / Possessing but one heart."[11] Seventeenth-century poets like William Cartwright had also conflated the theme of friendship with the vocabulary of Platonic love.[12] But most Renaissance writers followed the classical assumption that when they wrote of friends they were celebrating relationships between men. Turberville, for instance, cited Tullie and Atticus, Theseus and Pirithous, Damon and Pythias, Pylades and Orestes, Titus and Gysippus, Laellius and Scipio, Achilles and Patroclus, and Nysus and Aeurialus as illustrations of true friendship. When women appeared in literary works about friendship, they were, as a rule, the seductresses who wooed men like John Lyly's Euphues away from his true friend Philautus.[13] It remained for Katherine Philips to assert a philosophy of friendship that took for granted the notion that women could be friends with each other and with men.

We can see both how well-known Philips was for her poems on friendship and how atypical her idea of female friendship was when we read Jeremy Taylor's *A Discourse of the Nature and Offices of Friendship. In a Letter to the Most Ingenious and Excellent M.K.P.* (1657; republished in the same year and again in 1662 as *The Measures and Offices of Friendship*). His essay is organized as a series of answers to questions from Orinda herself.[14] Taylor credits her with being "so eminent in friendships [that she] could also have given the best answer to [her] own enquires"; he even suggests she "could have trusted [her] own reason, because it is not only greatly instructed by the direct notices of things, but also by great experience in the matter of which [she] now enquire[s]" (p. 301). The poet who had hoped that Cassandra and her husband would enjoy a life so intertwined that "we may not know / Who most Affection or most Peace engrost" would probably have been glad to read Taylor's assertion that "marriage is the queen of friendships" (p. 325), and surely Orinda would approve of the judgments that "some wives have been the best friends in the world" and that a woman "can die for her friend as well as the bravest Roman knight" (p. 330). But Taylor's belief in women's value in times of true need is not complete. "I cannot say," he writes, "that women are capable of those excellencies by which men can oblige the world; and therefore a female friend in some cases is not so good a councellor as a wise man, and cannot so well defend my honour, nor dispose of reliefs and assistances if she be under the power of another" (p. 330). Taylor writes, here, in a practical vein; knowing full well women's limited power in seventeenth-century society, he continues, "A man is the best friend in trouble, but a woman may be equal to him in the days of joy" (p. 331). And then Taylor's tone becomes wittily patronizing as he concludes that section of his essay and moves on to its next topic. "I hope you will pardon me," he writes, "that I am a little gone from my undertaking: I went aside to wait upon the women and to do countenance to their tender virtues; I am now returned, and if I were to do the office of a guide to uninstructed friends, would add the particulars following" (p. 331). Nothing has been said in this essay about the possibility of women's being friends with one another. And the comments on women's ability to be friends to men, it turns out, was only a digression that briefly impeded the progress of Taylor's real task.

Having read Taylor's *Discourse* and not knowing of any other piece on friendship addressed to Orinda, some writers have believed that Taylor must be the Palaemon whom Orinda addresses in a poem printed below, "To the Noble Palaemon, on His Incomparable Discourse of Friendship"—even though the title of another of her poems identifies Sir Francis Finch as Palaemon. In 1939, however, W. G. Hiscock published his discovery, in the library of Christ Church College, Oxford, of an essay on friendship by Finch dated October 1653 and published the following March.[15] In fact, there are at least two extant copies of Finch's essay—the second owned by Yale University. The existence of Finch's essay clarifies the question of the title of Philips's poem and provides another interesting example of her creativity. For the verse letter occasioned by Palaemon's "incomparable Discourse of friendship" responds quite directly to an essay that Orinda obviously (and rightly) sees as a genial compliment to her.

Finch's piece is prefaced by a letter to "the truly honourable Mrs. A.O." (A2r) and signed "Your most devoted, faithfull *Palaemon*" (A2v). That "Mrs. A.O." is Philips's friend Anne Owen is made clear by Palaemon's saying he wrote the piece at the command of "the onely Names I *reverence* to such a height as it takes off all colour and thoughts of dispute, *Lucasia* and *Orinda*" (p. 1). The title of Orinda's poem is a genial response to Palaemon's humility: "How to begin," he says, "I know not; and if I find it difficult to end, I may possibly swell this into a *bulk incongruous* for a *letter,* and I am sure aforehand it will neither have *Method* nor *Solidity* enough to deserve the appellation of a *Treatise,* or *Discourse*" (p. 2). Finch's essay does have *Method:* he systematically discusses "The *Nature* of [friendship], the *Causes* of it, and the *Benefit* and *Use* of it" (p. 2). That its *Solidity* makes it worthy of the title "discourse" Orinda affirms by calling it a one—and by claiming it is "incomparable." Indulging as surely as had Palaemon in friendly overstatement, Orinda credits him with discovering and then rescuing friendship from oblivion and wishes "for a voice which loud as thunder were" to declare Palaemon's "conquering truths." Her assertion that his written words create a "glorious Monument more permanent than a temple, statue, or a tomb" wittily aligns Finch's essay with works as significant as Shakespeare's sonnet "Not marble, nor the gilded monuments / Of princes" and asserts that Finch can be compared to poets like Shakespeare to whom Ben Jonson had written in 1623, "Thou art a Moniment, without a tombe, / And art alive still, while thy Booke doth live" ("To the Memory of My Beloved, the Author Mr. William Shakespeare: And What He Hath Left Us").

Philips's name can be associated with Finch's as early as 1651, for in that year they both contributed commendatory poems for the posthumous edition of the poems and plays of William Cartwright. John Berkenhead, too, contributed a poem to the 1651 volume, as did Philips' countryman Henry Vaughan, the musician Henry Lawes, and their mutual acquaintance Sir Edward Dering. All but Vaughan also contributed pieces for the 1655 edition of Lawes's *Second Book of Ayres and Dialogues*.[16] Two songtexts by Edmund Waller, who was to become Philips's rival in the 1660s, and one by William Cartwright appear in the 1655 volume. In his poem to Cartwright, Berkenhead asks, "Where are such Flames, such Puissance and Sway, / As thy Cratander, or Lucasia?" Cratander and Lucasia are both characters in dramas by Cartwright. Lucasia, of course, is also Philips's name for Anne Owen; and Cratander is the name she calls Berkenhead in "To Mr. J.B. the Noble Cratander, upon a Composition of His Which He Was Not Willing to Own Publickly."

Indeed, one of the five songs by Berkenhead in the 1655 volume is addressed to a Lucasia. As the author of a recent book on Berkenhead points out, study of English writers of the 1650s makes it increasingly clear that "the Cavaliers were a comparatively small group of people, united by political and cultural, and, very often, by family ties, who naturally sought out each others' company during the Interregnum."[17] "Little wonder, with such friends," that same author says two pages earlier, "that Orinda was a staunch Episcopalian by the Restoration."[18]

It may be going too far to call Philips a "staunch Episcopalian" in 1660, but it is true that by the time the monarchy was restored to England she had left her Presbyterian childhood far enough behind that she could celebrate the coronation of Charles II with enthusiastic phrases and that her last poem, dated July 10, 1664, should be addressed to the archbishop of Canterbury. A number of Philips's poems, some written during the Interregnum, some after the Restoration, show her royalist sympathies. Thanks to the collection of her letters published in 1705 and reissued (with the addition of one letter) in 1729, we know that some of her poems were written under the direct encouragement of her friend "Poliarchus," Sir Charles Cotterell, Master of Ceremonies in the court of Charles II. On May 3, 1662, Philips sent Cotterell verses which she proposes he edit and return so she may "send the Duchess [of Gloucester] another Copy, in obedience to the Command she was pleas'd to lay upon me, that I should let her see all my Trifles of this nature." And then Orinda adds with obvious pleasure, "I have been told, that when her Highness saw my Elegy on the queen of Bohemia, she graciously said, it surpriz'd her." On June 4, 1662, Philips thanks Cotterell for his account of the queen's arrival in Portsmouth—an account that she would turn into her "To the Queen's Majesty on Her Arrival at Portsmouth, May 14, 1662." And in November of 1663, she sends "To the Queen's Majesty, on Her Late Sickness and Recovery" in response to his account of the queen's recovery from an illness that had seemed to be fatal.

A month later, on December 24, Philips responds to a letter in which Cotterell has told her of his showing that poem to the royal family: "now give me leave," she says, "to quarrel with you heartily, for presenting the Copy of Verses to the Queen, and that too without making any Alteration in them, contrary to the Request I made you, when at the same time you knew very well that Mr. Waller had employ'd his Muse on the same subject." Ironically, she imagines that "Mr. Waller has, it may be, contributed not a little to encourage me in this Vanity, by writing on the same Subject the worst Verses that ever fell from his Pen. . . . But sure he, who is so civil to the Ladies [Waller was well known for not being civil] had heard that I design'd such an Address, and contenting himself with having got so much the Advantage of me in *Pompey*, was willing to yield me this Mate at Chess, and to write ill on purpose to keep me in Countenance." Nonetheless, Philips admits, she is "not . . . so mortify'd to this World as to be insensible of the infinite Honour their Majesty's have done me in receiving so very graciously that worthless Tribute from the humblest of their Subjects."

The story to which Philips refers when she writes of Waller's "having got so much the Advantage of me in *Pompey*" is also told in the letters. In 1662, having accompanied the newly remarried Lucasia to Dublin, Philips became acquainted with the earl of Orrery who, she reports to Cotterell in a letter of August 20, encouraged her to complete a translation of Corneille's *Pompey*. In October she wrote to Cotterell of having sent him a copy of her work "which I fear will not be deem'd worthy to breathe in a place where so many of the greatest Wits have so long clubb'd for another of the same Play," and in December she expresses concern that "the other Translation, done by so many eminent Hands, will . . . appear first, and throw this [her *Pompey*] into everlasting Obscurity." In January 1661/1662 Philips hopes "to hear what becomes of the other Translation of *Pompey,* and what Opinion the Town and Court have of it: I have laid out several ways to get a Copy, but cannot yet procure one, except only of the first Act that was done by Mr. Waller. Sir Edward Filmore did one, Sir Charles Sedley another, and my Lord Buckhurst another; but who the fifth I cannot learn, pray inform your self as soon as you can, and let me know it." Later in the month, she writes that Lord Orrery has decided to produce her translation in Dublin and that Lord Roscommon has written a prologue and Sir Edward Dering an epilogue for it. No account of the performance survives, but we do know that it was a great success and that soon thereafter Philips's translation was printed in Dublin by John Crooke and performed in London. In a letter of April 15, 1663, we learn that Henry Herringman had written to Philips "to give him leave to reprint it at London" and that she commissioned her brother-in-law Hector Philips "to treat with him about it." But before the end of the year Crooke had reprinted Philips's play in London, and in 1664 Herringman printed the other translation, announcing on its title page that it had been "Translated out of French by Certain Persons of Honour." Pleased by her success with *Pompey,* Philips began a translation of Corneille's *Horace*. She reached act 4, scene 6, before her sudden death in 1664. Completed by John Denham, the play was performed at court in 1668 and at the Theatre Royal the following year.

Given her obvious interest in the production and subsequent publication of *Pompey,* one might expect Philips to have been eager to see her poems in print. That, however, seems not to have been the case, for after a quarto volume of seventy-five of her poems was printed by Richard Marriott in January 1663/1664, letters from Philips to Cotterell and to Lady

Dorothy Temple express her dismay.[19] In fact, on January 29, Orinda addressed two letters to Cotterell: one in which she agreed with his proposal that the best response to the publication might be "to hasten to London and vindicate my self by publishing a true Copy." "Mean while," she wrote, "I have sent you inclos'd my true Thoughts on that Occasion in Prose, and have mix'd nothing else with it, to the end that you may; if you please, shew it to any body that suspects my Ignorance and Innocence of that false Edition of my Verses; and I believe it will make a greater Impression on them, than if it were written in Rhyme: Besides, I am yet in too great a Passion to solicite the Muses, and think I have at this time more reason to rail at them than court them; only that they are very innocent of all I write, and I can blame nothing but my own Folly and Idleness for having expos'd me to this Unhappiness; but of this no more till I hear from you again." Philips did indeed go to London in 1664, but she contracted smallpox and died in June of that year—without issuing an authorized edition of her work.

In 1667, however, a folio edition of 116 poems, 5 verse translations, and Philips's *Pompey* and her *Horace* was published by Henry Herringman. The preface to the volume is unsigned, but students of Philips have assumed it to have been written by Cotterell, because it includes a transcription of the letter Philips had written for him to let others read.[20] In that public document Philips maintains that she now finds herself "that unfortunate person that cannot so much as think in private, that must have my imaginations rifled and exposed to play the Mountebanks, and dance upon the Ropes to entertain all the rabble; to undergo all the raillery of the Wits, and all the severity of the Wise, and to be the sport of some that can, and some that cannot read a Verse." Her principal concern seems to derive from a sense of having lost control of her work. "The truth is," she writes, "I have an incorrigible inclination to that folly of riming, and intending the effects of that humour, only for my own amusement in a retir'd life; I did not so much resist it as a wiser woman would have done; but some of my dearest friends having found my Ballads, (for they deserve no better name) they made me so much believe they did not dislike them, that I was betray'd to permit some Copies for their divertisement; but this, with so little concern for them, that I have lost most of the originals, and that I suppose to be the cause of my present misfortune." In addition to the understandably disturbing fact of having poems she had written for a limited audience circulating for the amusement and criticism of all England, Philips is (again understandably) concerned that the 1664 volume contains errors—the poems, she has heard, are "abominably transcrib'd," and that it includes poems "that are not mine."[21] The poet is also conscious of having inadvertently invaded the privacy of some of her friends and relatives. As she says, there are "worthy persons that had the ill luck of my converse, and so their Names expos'd in this impression without their leave [and] few things in the power of Fortune could have given me so great a torment as this most afflictive accident." There are those who have taken Philips's statements as the pretty complaints of a lady falling victim to the error of one who protests too much.[22] It is more likely, I should think, that Philips means what she says: she did not choose to publish a collection of her verse. Moreover, had she anticipated a volume of her work, she would have wanted control over which poems would appear—and in what form.

It is of course true that a seventeenth-century woman writer would have particular reason to dread making herself public in such a way; indeed, in the letter published in 1667, Philips says that a "wiser woman" would have refrained from making herself a possible object of scandalous talk. According to the ethic of Philips's age, *any* talk about a woman is by definition scandalous, and we might wonder that Philips would have agreed to enter the public arena by permitting the production and publication of *Pompey*—and of course, to a lesser extent, by allowing the publication of the poems in the volume of Cartwright's works and in Lawes's *Second Book of Ayres and Dialogues*. During the Interregnum, one J. Jones, perhaps the republican Jenkin Jones, had threatened to publish "Upon the Double Murther of King Charles I," in which she expresses sympathy for the executed king and disdain for the Welsh republican Vavasor Powell's "Libellous Copy of Rimes" against Charles I. Exactly how severe the repercussions against James Philips would have been is difficult to say; but we do know that in a verse letter written to her husband after Jones's threat Philips argued that it would be no more fair to blame him for her work than it is to blame Eve for Adam's fall.[23] Philips of course well knew that in the seventeenth century it was common wisdom that the fall of humanity *was* caused by Eve's seduction of Adam—and that husbands *are* responsible for their wives' actions. Surely her words here are heavily and consciously ironic.

In the mid sixties, Philips's concern is somewhat different from what it would have been in the 1650s when Jones made his threat. For Philips's poems are bold in a number of ways—in their confident claim that Orinda's friendships are as wondrous and wonderful as the romantic love Donne had celebrated earlier in the century; in her focusing on Cicily Lloyd, rather than on her new husband, both in her epithalamion and then in his epitaph; in her most "cavalier" verses, the poems in which she chides Regina Collier for her cruelty to her suitor and then chides the suitor for allowing himself to be victimized by her; and in the clever lines in which she mocks not only a lovesick youth but his lady who thinks she is the sun itself. In conception and execution, much of Katherine Philips's work is quite remarkable. Had it been less remarkable, less irreverent about seventeenth-century mores and less personal in its being written to and for individuals whom she cared about, Philips might have been more willing to present it to all of England. As it was, Philips' choice had been to circulate her poems within a restricted circle of friends. Having written for Lucasia and Palaemon, for Rosania and Silvander, and for the king and his family, Philips could only have been startled to think of herself being read by the likes of Samuel Pepys.[24]

That Philips' works were a commercial success is verified by the 1667 edition's being reprinted in 1669, 1678, and 1710. In addition to the printed texts, a number of manuscript versions of her works survive. Most important are two manuscripts (NLW 775b and 776b) now in the National Library of Wales and one owned by the Harry Ransom Humanities Research Center, the University of Texas at Austin. NLW 775b is a quarto-sized manuscript book in its original calf binding with the initials "K.P." stamped on the front and back covers. Used, evidently, by Philips to record fair copies of her poems, the volume contains fifty-one poems, two fragments, and the titles of two additional poems. NLW 776b is a slightly larger quarto manuscript, also bound in calf, in which Philips's translations of *Pompey, Horace,* and the five shorter pieces that appear in the 1667 volume precede copies of ninety of her poems. An introductory dedication "To the Excellent Rosania" (Mary Aubrey) indicates that the book was transcribed after Orinda's death but before the edition of 1667 was published.[25] The Texas manuscript contains seventy-four of Philips' poems and the titles of two more—all in the hand of Philips's friend Sir Edward Dering. Three other seventeenth-century manuscripts—County of South Glamorgan Libraries, Cardiff MS 2. 1073; Bodleian Library MS Locke e. 17; and University of Nottingham Library, Portland Manuscript MS Pw V 338—provide variant readings of some of the poems printed below.[26]

The nineteen poems that appear here are a representative selection of some 126 surviving poems by Katherine Philips. Except for the "Epitaph on Mr. John Lloyd," which was not published until 1905 and which I have, therefore, transcribed from Philips's holograph, NLW 775b, they have as their copytext a copy of the 1667 edition of the *Poems* now owned by the Folger Shakespeare Library. They appear here in the order they are printed in the 1667 volume. I have transcribed (except in the titles) capitals, italics, spelling, and punctuation as in the copytexts—except that I have silently emended the few spelling errors corrected in the 1669 edition, I have omitted ornamental initials and capital letters in the second letter of each poem, and I have made no attempt to reproduce the long *s* of seventeenth-century type.

In the notes to each poem I have listed variant titles and substantive variants from the six seventeenth-century manuscripts noted above and from the two relevant volumes printed prior to 1667: Lawes's 1655 *Second Book of Ayres* and the 1664 selection of Philips's *Poems*. In my transcription of the "Epitaph on Mr. John Lloyd" and in the manuscript variants listed in the notes, I have expanded abbreviations and contractions such as the following: & (and), y^e (the), y^t (that), w^{ch} (which), wth (with), and w^t (what).

I am indebted to the Folger Shakespeare Library for permission to quote from the printed editions of Philips's poems and letters and to the National Library of Wales; the Harry Ransom Humanities Research Center, the University of Texas at Austin; the County of South Glamorgan Libraries; the Bodleian Library, Oxford University; the University of Nottingham Library; and the Archives and Rare Books Department, University Libraries, University of Cincinnati for permission to quote from manuscripts in their collections. In the notes to the poems I use the following abbreviations for the manuscript and printed texts:

775	National Library of Wales MS 775b
776	National Library of Wales MS 776b
Texas	Harry Ransom Humanities Research Center, the University of Texas at Austin, Philips MS (uncatalogued)
Cardiff	County of South Glamorgan Libraries, Cardiff MS 2. 1073
Locke	Bodleian Library, Oxford University, MS Locke e. 17
Nottingham	University of Nottingham Library, Portland Manuscript Pw V 338
1655	Henry Lawes, *Second Book of Ayres and Dialogues* (1655)
1664	*Poems. By the Incomparable, Mrs. K. P.* (1664)
1667	*Poems. By the most deservedly Admired Mrs. Katherine Philips* (1667)

NOTES

1. Aubrey, vol. 2, pp. 153–54.

2. Souers, pp. 10–23. Souers's study remains the most complete and accurate account of Philips's family and her life.

3. Røstvig, *The Happy Man*, presents the theme of retirement in seventeenth-century poetry as "the result of the fusion, in the first half of the seventeenth century, of a Stoic philosophy with intense religious emotion. Add to this mixture a generous feeling of resentment at the victory of the Puritans in the Civil War, and the prescription is fairly complete" (pp. 15–16). Røstvig sees Philips as the popularizer of retirement poetry (pp. 348–57). See also Turner, *The Politics of Landscape*, and—for the classical background of the tradition— Michael O'Loughlin, *The Garlands of Repose: The Literary Celebration of Civic and Retired Leisure; The Traditions of Homer and Vergil, Horace and Montaigne* (Chicago and London, 1978).

4. Vaughan's "To the Most Excellently Accomplished, Mrs. K. Philips" is the penultimate poem in *Olor Iscanus* (1651); his *Thalia Rediviva* (1678) includes "To the Editor of the

Matchless Orinda." For Marvell's echoes of Philips, see Pritchard, "Marvell's 'The Garden':
A Restoration Poem?"

5. For the number forty in Christian numerology, see Vincent Foster Hopper, *Medieval
Number Symbolism: Its Sources, Meaning, and Influence on Thought and Expression* (New
York, 1969), pp. 15, 25–26. Cornelius Agrippa, *Three Books of Occult Philosophy*, trans.
J.F. (London, 1651), pp. 223–24, notes the significance of the number forty in biblical events
and says, "It doth conduce to the account of birth, for in so many daies the seed is fitted, and
transformed in the womb, untill it be by its due, and harmonicall proportions brought unto
a perfect organicall body, being disposed to receive a rationall soul. And so many dayes they
say women be, after they have brought forth, before all things are setled within them, and
they purified, and so many dayes infants refrain from smiling, are infirme, and live with a
great deal of hazard." Whether young Hector Philips lived exactly forty days is uncertain, for
in manuscript 775b in the National Library of Wales Philips writes that he was born on
April 23 and died on May 2.

6. For a standard study of ideas about marriage in Protestant England see William Haller
and Malleville Haller, "The Puritan Art of Love," *Huntington Library Quarterly* 5 (1941–
1942): 235–72. As the Hallers note, however, the male writers they quote dictate a marriage
that will provide men with the contentment derived from a loving and obedient wife: "The
man," they write, "was the head, but the head must love, and the preachers, themselves
married men, proposed to learn and to tell how this should be done." Whether Philips
actually enjoyed the happy relationship she represents in the poems and letters is not possible
to say.

7. I am indebted to the National Library of Wales for permission to quote from the two
poems and to transcribe, in its entirety, the prose piece from Orielton manuscript, parcel 24.
Below the second poem are the words "Humbly Dedicated to Mrs. Anne Barlow / C
Fowler." Thomas, "An Edition of the Poems and Letters of Katherine Philips, 1632–1664,"
pp. 545–56, identifies Anne Barlow as the eldest daughter of Dorothy and John Barlow of
Slebech. Her first husband was Nicholas Lewis of Hean Castle; her second, Lewis Wogan of
Wiston—both in Pembrokeshire. I should like to thank Claudia Limbert for calling the
Orielton manuscript and Thomas's dissertation to my attention. Limbert's transcription of
the manuscript appears in her "Two Poems and a Prose Receipt: The Unpublished Juvenilia
of Katherine Philips," *English Literary Renaissance*, forthcoming. Ronald Lockely, *Orielton: The Human and Natural History of a Welsh Manor* (London, 1977), 19–20, tran-
scribes portions of the manuscript, but he does not seem to have realized the identity of "C
Fowler."

8. For the theme of friendship in Cavalier verse, see Miner, esp. pp. 250–305. Although
both he and Latt treat Philips's poems on female friendship, they do not comment on her
poems about marriage as friendship poems. I know of no male poets of Philips's period who
present their marriages in terms of friendships, but the idea that married love is a form of
friendship appears in classical, medieval, and Renaissance discussions of friendship—in, for
example, Aristotle's *Nicomachean Ethics*, VIII.x.5, xi.4, xii.7; Thomas Aquinas's *Summa
Contra Gentiles*, III.123, 124; and Jeremy Taylor's *Discourse of the Nature and Offices of
Friendship*, p. 90. In his *Friendship*, Francis Finch contrasts love between married people and
that between friends: "If any *Love* may stand in competition with that of *Friends*, it is the
Conjugal, and that, if any where, where the *Marriage* was purely the choice and congruity of
the Persons united, without the *Byasse* of other *Interests* which usually bear a great sway in
that Union" (p. 7).

9. Letterbook of Sir Edward Dering, Archives and Rare Books Department, University
Libraries, University of Cincinnati. The quotations from the letters in this paragraph are
from letters 4, 37, and 47 in part 1 of the letterbook.

10. Clark, pp. 50–51, cites the letter to demonstrate that Philips's Society included men and that it existed after the Restoration. Thomas, "An Edition of the Poems and Letters," p. xxii, presents the letter as evidence that "the 'societie' that Dering describes is not very different from that which Gosse imagined, though the latter embroidered his picture with some rather improbable details." Thomas does not mention the telling fact that this letter is addressed to Lucasia.

11. Laurens J. Mills, *One Soul in Bodies Twain: Friendship in Tudor Literature and Stuart Drama* (Bloomington, 1937), traces the theme in English Renaissance literature. He does not, however, mention Philips.

12. Souers, pp. 255–64, presents Philips as one of a group of poets that "marched under the banner of Cartwright" and argues that she follows him "not only in manner but in matter. In him she found expressed completely the one distinctive theme forever to be associated with her name, the theme of Platonic Friendship." See also Evans, esp. pp. 52–53. Souers and Evans (and, following them, Patrick Thomas) see Philips as a *précious* poet.

13. Mills, pp. 182–87. Curiously, Mills sees *Euphues* as a book that appealed to women readers (p. 182). Female friends are, of course, represented in Renaissance drama; one thinks immediately of Helena and Hermia in *Midsummer Night's Dream*. See, however, Louis Adrian Montrose, "Shaping Fantasies: Figurations of Gender and Power in Elizabethan Culture," *Representations* 1 (1983): 61–94, for the observation that their friendship is presented as a childish state: "Hermia's farewell to Helena is also a farewell to their girlhood friendship, a delicate repudiation of youthful homophilia" (p. 68).

14. For the possibility that Philips and Taylor were personally acquainted, see Souers, pp. 73–74. Quotations from Taylor's essay are from *The Whole Works of the Right Rev. Jeremy Taylor . . . with a Life of the Author*, ed. Reginald Heber (London, 1828), vol. 11.

15. See Hiscock, pp. 466–68. In his *Life* of Taylor, Heber speculated that Finch had written such a discourse (vol. 1, p. lxxvii).

16. See Souers, p. 59, for the conjunction of these writers' works.

17. P. W. Thomas, p. 141. Patrick Thomas, "Orinda, Vaughan and Watkyns," demonstrates that even Philips's Anglo-Welsh literary connections are rooted in London, rather than in Wales.

18. P. W. Thomas, p. 139.

19. Philips's letter to Dorothy Temple, now in the Theater Collection, Houghton Library, Harvard University, is transcribed by Souers, pp. 220–23.

20. This letter appears in slightly different forms in the 1705 edition and in the 1667 volume; the quotations in this paragraph are from the 1667 version.

21. Although there are indeed errors in the 1664 volume, all of the poems ascribed to Philips there are in fact hers.

22. See, for example, Brashear.

23. In "To Antenor, on a Paper of Mine Which J.J. Threatens to Publish to Prejudice Him," lines 11–12, Philips writes, "For *Eve's* Rebellion did not *Adam's* blast, / Until himself forbidden Fruit did taste." Noting that the 1664 text gives the name "J. Jones," J. R. Tutin, ed., *Katherine Philips: "The Matchless Orinda": Selected Poems*, p. 46, n. 18, suggests Philips refers to a local Puritan, Jenkins Jones. Thomas, "An Edition of the Poems and Letters," pp. 158–59, concurs and observes that the title of the poem on Vavasor Powell in manuscript 776b indicates it is the poem to which Philips refers in the piece to Antenor: the title there is "On the double murther of the King (In answer to a libellous paper written by V. Powell, at my house) These verses were those mention'd in the precedent coppy." The "precedent coppy" in manuscript 776b is "To Antenor On a Paper of mine, which an unworthy Adversity of his threatned to publish, to prejudice him, in Cromwels time."

24. On September 16, 1667, Pepys (*The Diary of Samuel Pepys,* ed. Robert Latham and

William Matthews [Berkeley and Los Angeles, 1974] 8:439) writes that he "stayed [evidently at Henry Herringman's bookshop] reading Mrs. Philips's poems till my wife and Mercer called me . . . to dinner." He says nothing about purchasing a copy of the volume.

25. Mambretti reads the signature at the end of the letter as "Pole:ʳ," an abbreviation for "Poliarchus." Thomas, "An Edition of the Poems and Letters," p. lxxii, indicates, however, that the name seems to be "Polex:ʳ," possibly an abbreviation for "Polexander." In any case, the dedication to Mary Aubrey so soon after Philips's death does confirm Mambretti's belief that the manuscript "seems a valuable witness to the Philips canon."

26. Thomas, "An Edition of the Poems and Letters," pp. lxvii–lxxvii, lists extant seventeenth-century manuscripts containing poems by Philips. To his list of poems by Philips should be added "To Rosania and Lucasia, Articles of Friendship," H. E. Huntington manuscript HM 183, No. 17a, printed in *The Female Spectator: English Women Writers Before 1800*, ed. Mary R. Mahl and Helene Koon (Bloomington and London, 1977), pp. 158–59.

Upon the Double Murther of King Charles I. In Answer to a Libellous Copy of Rimes by Vavasor Powell

I think not on the State, nor am concern'd[1]
Which way soever the great Helm[2] is turn'd:
But as that son whose father's danger nigh
Did force his native dumbness, and untie
The fetter'd organs; so this is a cause
That will excuse the breach of Nature's laws.[3]
Silence were now a sin, nay Passion now
Wise men themselves for Merit would allow.
What noble eye could see (and careless pass)
The dying Lion kick'd by every Ass?
Has *Charles* so *broke God's Laws,* he must not have
A quiet Crown, nor yet a quiet Grave?
Tombs have been Sanctuaries; Thieves lie there
Secure from all their penalty and fear.
Great *Charles* his double misery was *this,*
Unfaithful Friends, ignoble Enemies.
Had any Heathen been this Prince's foe,
He would have wept to see him injur'd so.
His Title was his Crime, they'd reason good
To quarrel at the Right they had withstood.
He broke God's Laws, and therefore he must die;
And what shall then become of thee and I?
Slander must follow Treason; but yet stay,
Take not our Reason with our King away.
Though you have seiz'd upon all our defence,

Yet do not sequester[4] our common Sense.
Christ will be King, but I ne're understood
His Subjects built his Kingdom up with blood,
Except their own; or that he would dispence
With his commands, though for his own defence.
Oh! to what height of horrour are they come
Who dare pull down a Crown, tear up a Tomb?

On the Fair Weather Just at the Coronation, It Having Rained Immediately Before and After

So clear a season, and so snatch'd from storms,[5]
Shews Heav'n delights to see what Man performs.
Well knew the Sun, if such a day were dim,
It would have been an injury to him:
For then a Cloud had from his eye conceal'd
The noblest sight that ever he beheld.
He therefore check'd th'invading Rains we fear'd,
And in a bright *Parenthesis* appear'd.
So that we knew not which look'd most content,
The King, the People, or the Firmament.
But the Solemnity once fully past,
The storm return'd with an impetuous[6] hast.
And Heav'n and Earth each other to out-do,
Vied both in Cannons and in Fire-works too.
So *Israel* past through the divided flood,
While in obedient heaps the Ocean stood:
But the same Sea (the Hebrews once on shore)
Return'd in torrents where it was before.[7]

On the Third of September 1651

As when the glorious Magazine[8] of Light[9]
Approches to his Canopy of Night,
He with new splendour clothes his dying Rays,
And double brightness to his Beams conveys;
And (as to brave and check[10] his ending fate)
Puts on his highest looks in's lowest state,
Drest in such terrour as to make us all
Be *Anti-Persians,*[11] and adore his Fall;

Then quits the world depriving it of Day,
While every Herb and Plant does droop away:
So when our gasping *English* Royalty
Perceiv'd her Period[12] was now drawing nigh,
She summons her whole strength to give one blow,
To raise her self, or pull down others too,
Big with revenge and hope she now spake more
Of terror than in many months before;
And musters her Attendants, or to save
Her from, or else attend her to, the Grave:
Yet but enjoy'd the miserable fate
Of setting Majesty, to die in State.
Unhappy Kings, who cannot keep a Throne,
Nor be so fortunate to fall alone!
Their weight sinks others: *Pompey* could not fly,
But half the World must bear him company;[13]
And captiv'd *Sampson* could not life conclude,
Unless attended with a multitude.[14]
Who'd trust to Greatness now, whose food is air,[15]
Whose ruine sudden, and whose end despair?
Who would presume upon his Glorious Birth,
Or quarrel for a spacious share of Earth
That sees such Diadems become so cheap,
And Heros tumble in a common heap?
Oh give me Vertue then, which sums up all,
And firmly stands when Crowns and Scepters fall.

To the Noble Palaemon, on His Incomparable Discourse of Friendship

We had been still undone, wrapt in disguise,[16]
Secure, not happy; cunning, and not wise;
War had been our design, Interest our trade;
We had not dwelt in safety, but in shade,
Hadst thou not hung our Light more welcome far
Than wand'ring Sea-men think the Northern-star;
To shew, lest we our happiness should miss,
'Tis plac'd in Friendship, Mens and Angels bliss.
Friendship, which had a scorn or mask been made,
And still had been derided or betray'd;
At which the great Physician still had laugh'd,

The Souldier stormed, and the Gallant scoff'd;
Or worn not as a Passion, but a Plot,[17]
At first pretended, and at last forgot;
Hadst thou not been her great Deliverer,
At first discover'd, and then rescu'd her,
And raising what rude Malice had flung down,
Unveil'd her Face, and then restor'd her Crown:
By so august an action to convince,
'Tis greater to support than be a Prince.
Oh for a Voice which loud as Thunder were,
That all Mankind thy conqu'ring truths might hear!
Sure the Litigious as amaz'd would stand,
As Fairy Knights touch'd with *Cambina's* Wand,[18]
Drawn by thy softer, and yet stronger Charms,
Nations and Armies would lay down their Arms,
And what more honour can on thee be hurl'd,
Than to protect a Vertue, save a world?
But while great Friendship thou hast copied out,
Thou'st drawn thy self so well, that we may doubt
Which most appears, thy Candour or thy Art,
Whether we owe more to thy Brain or Heart.
But thus we know without thine own consent,
Thou'st rais'd thy self a glorious Monument;
Temples and Statues Time will eat away,
And Tombs (like their Inhabitants) decay;
   But there *Palaemon* lives, and so he must
   When Marbles crumble to forgotten dust.

To Mr. Henry Lawes

Nature, which is the vast Creation's Soul,[19]
That steddy curious[20] Agent in the whole,
The Art of Heaven, the Order of this Frame,
Is only Number in another name.
For as some King conqu'ring what was his own,
Hath choice of several Titles to his Crown;
So harmony on this score now, that then,
Yet still is all that takes and governs Men.
Beauty is but Composure, and we find
Content is but the Concord of the Mind,
Friendship the Unison of well-tun'd Hearts,

Honour the *Chorus* of the noblest parts,
And all the World on which we can reflect
Musick to th'Ear, or to the Intellect.
If then each man a Little World must be,
How many Worlds are copied out in thee,
Who art so richly formed, so compleat
T'epitomize all that is Good and Great;
Whose Stars this brave advantage did impart,
Thy Nature's as harmonious as thy Art?
Thou dost above the Poets praises live,
Who fetch from thee th'Eternity they give.
And as true Reason triumphs over sense,
Yet is subjected to intelligence:
So Poets on the lower World look down,
But *Lawes* on them; his Height is all his own.
For, like Divinity it self, his Lyre
Rewards the Wit it did at first inspire.[21]
And thus by double right Poets allow
His and their Laurel[22] should adorn his brow.
Live then, great Soul of Nature, to asswage
The savage dulness of this sullen Age.
Charm us to Sense; for though Experience fail
And Reason too, thy Numbers may prevail.
Then, like those Ancients, strike, and so command
All Nature to obey thy gen'rous hand.
None will resist but such who needs will be
More stupid than a Stone, a Fish, a Tree.[23]
Be it thy care our Age to new-create:
What built a World may sure repair a State.

Friendship's Mystery. To My Dearest Lucasia.

Come, my *Lucasia*,[24] since we see
    That Miracles Mens faith do move,
By wonder and by prodigy
    To the dull angry world let's prove
    There's a Religion in our Love.

2

For though we were design'd t'agree,
    That Fate no liberty destroyes,

But our Election is as free
    As Angels, who with greedy choice
    Are yet determin'd to their joyes.[25]

3

Our hearts are doubled by the loss,
    Here Mixture is addition grown;
We both diffuse, and both ingross:[26]
    And we whose minds are so much one,
    Never, yet ever are alone.

4

We court our own Captivity
    Than Thrones more great and innocent:
'Twere banishment to be set free,
    Since we wear fetters whose intent
    Not Bondage is, but Ornament.

5

Divided joyes are tedious found,
    And griefs united easier grow:
We are our selves but by rebound,[27]
    And all our Titles shuffled so,
    Both Princes, and both Subjects too.[28]

6

Our Hearts are mutual Victims laid,
    While they (such power in Friendship lies)
Are Altars, Priests, and Off'rings made:
    And each Heart which thus kindly[29] dies,
    Grows deathless by the Sacrifice.

A Dialogue of Absence 'Twixt Lucasia and Orinda. Set by Mr. Henry Lawes

Luc. Say my *Orinda,* why so sad?[30]
  Orin. Absence from thee doth tear my heart;
Which, since with thine it union had,

Each parting splits. *Luc.* And can we part?
Orin. Our Bodies must. *Luc.* But never we:
   Our Souls, without the help of Sense,
By wayes more noble and more free
   Can meet, and hold intelligence.[31]
Orin. And yet those Souls, when first they met,
   Lookt out at windows through the Eyes.[32]
Luc. But soon did such acquaintance get,
   Not Fate nor Time can them surprize.
Orin. Absence will rob us of that bliss
   To which this Friendship title brings:
Love's fruits and joys are made by this
   Useless as Crowns to captiv'd Kings.
Luc. Friendship's a Science,[33] and we know
   There Contemplation's most employ'd.
Orin. Religion's so, but practick too,
   And both by niceties destroy'd.
Luc. But who ne're parts can never meet,
   And so that happiness were lost.
Orin. Thus Pain and Death are sadly sweet,
   Since Health and Heav'n such price must cost.

Chorus

But we shall come where no rude hand shall sever,
And there wee'l meet and part no more for ever.

To My Dear Sister Mrs. C.P. on Her Marriage

We will not like those men our offerings pay[34]
Who crown the cup, then think they crown the day.
We make no garlands, nor an altar build,
Which help not Joy, but Ostentation yield.
Where mirth is justly grounded these wild toyes[35]
Be but a troublesome, and empty noise.

2

But these shall be my great Solemnities,
Orinda's wishes for *Cassandra's* bliss.
May her Content be as unmix'd and pure
As my Affection, and like that endure;

And that strong Happiness may she still find
Not owing to her Fortune, but her Mind.

3

May her Content and Duty be the same,
And may she know no Grief but in the name.
May his and her Pleasure and Love be so
Involv'd and growing, that we may not know
Who most Affection or most Peace engrost;
Whose Love is strongest, or whose Bliss is most.

4

May nothing accidental e're appear
But what shall with new bonds their Souls endear;
And may they count the hours as they pass,
By their own Joys, and not by Sun or Glass:
While every day like this may sacred prove
To Friendship, Gratitude, and strictest Love.

Epitaph on Mr. John Lloyd of Kilrhewy in Pembrokeshire (Who Dy'd July the 11, 1656), Inscribed on His Monument in Kilgarron (in the Person of His Wife)

Preserve thou sad, and sole Trustee[36]
Of my dear husbands Memory
These reliques of my broken heart
Which I am forced to impart
For since he so untimely dy'd
And living pledges was deny'd
Since days of mourning soon are done
And Tears do perish as they run,
Nay since my Grief at length must dy
(For that's no longer liv'd then I)
His name can live no way but one,
In an abiding faithfull Stone.
   Tell then the unconcerned Eys
   The value of thy Guest and prize

How good he was, usefull, and Just
How kind, how faithfull to his trust,
Which known, and when their sence propounds[37]
How mournfully a widdow sounds
They may instructed go from thee
To follow him, and pitty me.

A Retir'd Friendship. To Ardelia

Come, my *Ardelia,* to this Bower[38]
  Where kindly mingling Souls awhile
Lets innocently spend an hour,
  And at all serious follies smile.

2

Here is no quarrelling for Crowns,
  Nor fear of changes in our Fate;
No trembling at the great ones frowns,
  Nor any slavery of State.

3

Here's no disguise nor treachery,
  Nor any deep conceal'd design;
From Bloud and Plots this Place is free
  And calm as are those looks of thine.

4

Here let us sit and bless our Stars
  Who did such happy quiet give,
As that remov'd from noise of Wars
  In one anothers hearts we live.

5

Why should we entertain a fear?
  Love cares not how the World is turned:
If crouds of dangers should appear,
  Yet Friendship can be unconcern'd.

6

We wear about us such a charm,
    No horrour can be our offence;
For mischief's self can do no harm
    To Friendship or to Innocence.

7

Let's mark how soon *Apollo's*[39] beams
    Command the flocks to quit their meat,
And not entreat the neighbouring streams
    To quench their thirst, but coole their heat.

8

In such a scorching Age as this
    Who would not ever seek a shade,
Deserve their Happiness to miss,
    As having their own peace betray'd.

9

But we (of one anothers mind
    Assur'd)[40] the bois'trous World distain;
With quiet Souls and unconfin'd
    Enjoy what Princes wish in vain.

To My Excellent Lucasia, on Our Friendship

I did not live until this time[41]
    Crown'd my felicity.
When I could say without a crime,
    I am not thine, but Thee.

This Carcass breath'd, and walkt, and slept,
    So that the World believ'd
There was a Soul the Motions kept;
    But they were all deceiv'd.

For as a Watch by art is wound
    To motion, such was mine:

But never had *Orinda* found
    A Soul till she found thine;

Which now inspires,[42] cures and supplies,
    And guides my darkned Breast:
For thou art all that I can prize,
    My Joy, my Life, my Rest.

No Bridegrooms nor Crown-conquerors mirth
    To mine compar'd can be:
They have but pieces of this Earth,
    I've all the World in thee.

Then let our Flames still light and shine,
    And no false fear controul,
As innocent as our Design,
    Immortal as our Soul.

To Regina Collier, on Her Cruelty to Philaster

Triumphant Queen of scorn![43] how ill doth fit
In all that Sweetness, such injurious Wit?
Unjust and Cruel! what can be your prize,
To make one heart a double Sacrifice?
Where such ingenious Rigour you do shew,
To break his Heart, you break his Image too;[44]
And by a Tyranny that's strange and new,
You murder him because he worships you.
No pride can raise you, or can make him start,
Since Love and Honour do enrich his heart.
Be Wise and Good, lest when Fate will be just,
She should o'rethrow those glories in the dust,
Rifle[45] your Beauties, and you thus forlorn
Make a cheap Victim to another's scorn;
And in those Fetters which you do upbraid,
Your self a wretched Captive may be made.
Redeem the poyson'd Age, let it be seen
There's no such freedom as to serve a Queen.
But you I see are lately Round-head[46] grown,
And whom you vanquish you insult upon.

To Philaster, on His Melancholy for Regina

Give over now thy tears, thou vain
    And double Murtherer;[47]
For every minute of thy pain
    Wounds both thy self and her.
Then leave this dulness;[48] for 'tis our belief,
Thy Queen must cure, or not deserve, thy Grief.

Parting with Lucasia, a Song

1

Well, we will do that rigid thing[49]
    Which makes Spectators think we part;
Though Absence hath for none a sting
    But those who keep each others heart.

2

And when our Sense is dispossest,[50]
    Our labouring Souls will heave and pant,
And gasp for one anothers breast,
    Since their Conveyances[51] they want.

3

Nay, we have felt the tedious smart
    Of absent Friendship, and do know
That when we die we can but part;
    And who knows what we shall do now?

4

Yet I must go: we will submit,
    And so our own Disposers be;
For while we nobly suffer it,
    We triumph o're Necessity.

5

By this we shall be truly great,
  If having other things o're come,
To make our victory compleat
  We can be Conquerors at home.

6

Nay then to meet we may conclude,
  And all Obstructions overthrow,
Since we our Passion[52] have subdu'd,
  Which is the strongest thing I know.

To My Dearest Antenor, on His Parting

Though it be just to grieve when I must part
With him that is the Guardian of my Heart;[53]
Yet by an happy change the loss of mine
Is with advantage paid[54] in having thine.
And I (by that dear Guest[55] instructed) find
Absence can do no hurt to Souls combin'd.
As we were born to love, brought to agree
By the impressions of Divine Decree:[56]
So when united nearer we became,
It did not weaken, but encrease, our Flame.
Unlike to those who distant joys admire,
But slight them when possest of their desire.
Each of our Souls did its own temper fit,
And in the other's Mould so fashion'd it,
That now our Inclinations[57] both are grown,
Like to our Interests and Persons, one;
And Souls whom such a Union fortifies,
Passion[58] can ne're destroy, nor Fate surprize.
Now as in Watches, though we do not know
When the Hand moves, we find it still doth go:
So I, by secret Sympathy inclin'd,
Will absent meet, and understand thy mind;
And thou at thy return shalt find thy Heart
Still safe, with all the love thou dids't impart.
For though that treasure I have ne're deserv'd,
It shall with strong Religion be preserv'd.

And besides this thou shalt in me survey
Thy self reflected while thou art away.
For what some forward Arts do undertake,
The Images of absent Friends to make,
And represent their actions in a Glass,
Friendship it self can only bring to pass,
That Magick which both Fate and Time beguiles,
And in a moment runs a thousand miles.
So in my Breast thy Picture drawn shall be,
My Guide, Life, Object, Friend, and Destiny:
And none shall know, though they employ their wit,
Which is the right *Antenor,* thou, or it.

To the Queen's Majesty, on Her Late Sickness and Recovery

The publick Gladness that's to us restor'd,[59]
For your escape from what we so deplor'd,
Will want as well resemblance as belief,
Unless our Joy be measur'd by our Grief.
When in your Fever we with terrour saw
At once our Hopes and Happiness withdraw;
And every *crisis* did with jealous fear
Enquire the News we scarce durst stay to hear.
Some dying Princes have their Servants slain,
That after death they may not want a Train.
Such cruelty were here a needless sin;
For had our fatal Fears prophetick been,
Sorrow alone that service would have done,
And you by Nations had been waited on.
Your danger was in ev'ry Visage seen,
And onely yours was quiet and serene.
But all our zealous Grief had been in vain,
Had not Great *Charles's* call'd you back again:
Who did your suff'rings with such pain discern,
He lost three Kingdoms[60] once with less concern.
Lab'ring your safety he neglected his,
Nor fear'd he Death in any shape but this.
His *Genius*[61] did the bold Distemper tame,
And his rich Tears quench'd the rebellious Flame.
At once the *Thracian* Hero[62] lov'd and griev'd,

Till he his lost Felicity retriev'd;
And with the moving accents of his woe
He Spouse recover'd from the Shades below.
So the King's grief your threatned loss withstood,
Who mourn'd with the same fortune that he woo'd:
And to his happy Passion we have been
Now twice oblig'd for so ador'd a Queen.
But how severe a Choice had you to make,
When you must Heav'n delay or Him forsake?
Yet since those joys You made such haste to find
Had scarce been full if he were left behind,
How well did Fate decide your inward strife,
By making him a Present of your Life?
Which rescu'd Blessing he must long enjoy
Since our Offences could it not destroy.
For none but Death durst rival him in you;
And Death himself was baffled in it too.

Epitaph. On Her Son H.P. at St. Syth's Church, Where Her Body also Lies Interred

What on Earth deserves our trust?[63]
Youth and Beauty both are dust.
Long we gathering are with pain,
What one moment calls again.
Seven years childless, marriage past,
A Son, a Son is born at last:
So exactly limb'd and fair,
Full of good Spirits, Meen, and Air,
As a long life promised,
Yet, in less than six weeks dead.
Too promising, too great a mind
In so small room to be confin'd:
Therefore, as fit in Heav'n to dwell,
He quickly broke the Prison shell.
So the subtle Alchimist,
Can't with *Hermes* Seal[64] resist
The powerful spirit's subtler flight,
But t'will bid him long good night.
And so the Sun if it arise

Half so glorious as his Eyes,
Like this Infant, takes a shrowd,
Buried in a morning Cloud.

Orinda upon Little Hector Philips

1

Twice forty months of Wedlock I did stay,[65]
Then had my vows crown'd with a Lovely boy.
And yet in forty days he dropt away,
O swift Vicissitude of humane joy.

2

I did but see him and he dis-appear'd,
I did but pluck the Rose-bud and it fell,
A sorrow unforeseen and scarcely fear'd,
For ill can mortals their afflictions spell.

3

And now (sweet Babe) what can my trembling heart
Suggest to right my doleful fate or thee,
Tears are my muse and sorrow all my Art,
So piercing groans must be thy Elogy.

4

Thus whilst no eye is witness of my mone,
I grieve thy loss (Ah boy too dear to live)
And let the unconcerned World alone,
Who neither will, nor can refreshment give.

5

An Off'ring too for thy sad Tomb I have,
Too just a tribute to thy early Herse,
Receive these gasping numbers to thy grave,
The last of thy unhappy Mothers verse.

An Answer to Another Perswading
a Lady to Marriage

1

Forbear bold Youth, all's Heaven here,[66]
    And what you do aver,
To others Courtship may appear,
    'Tis Sacriledge to her.

2

She is a publick Deity,
    And were't not very odd
She should despose herself to be
    A petty Houshold God?

3

First make the Sun in private shine,
    And bid the World adieu,
That so he may his beams confine
    In complement to you.[67]

4

But if of that you do despair,
    Think how you did amiss,
To strive to fix her beams[68] which are
    More bright and large than this.

NOTES TO THE TEXT

1. An itinerant Welsh preacher, Vavasor Powell was a Fifth Monarchist who believed in the imminent coming of Christ to establish a Fifth Monarchy (following those of Assyria, Persia, Greece, and Rome). As a republican, Powell was adamant in his dislike of Charles I (and, later, of Cromwell). Although Powell's verses evidently have not survived, it is clear from the subtitle in manuscript 776b in the National Library of Wales that they were written while he was a guest as Cardigan Priory. Philips's lines indicate that Powell had attempted to justify the execution of Charles I by maintaining that the monarch had usurped God's power in England. Her argument is that Christ, the Prince of Peace, would never approve of His followers using violence—even to depose usurpers of His kingdom.

Texts: 776, Texas, Cardiff, 1664, 1667.

Variants: Title On the double murther of the King (In answer to a libellous paper written by V. Powell, at my house) These verses were those mention'd in the precedent coppy. (776), Upon the double murther of K. Charles in answer to a libellous rime made by V. P. (Texas), Upon the double Murther of Charles the First In answeare to a libellous Copy of rimes made by V. P. (Cardiff), Upon the double Murther of K. CHARLES I. in Answer to a Libellous Copy of Rimes made by Vavasor Powell. (1664). 2 the / that (776, Texas). 5 this / here (Texas); this is a / here's a fair (1664). 7 now a sin / criminal (776). 8 would / will (776). 9 noble / humane (776). 11 Has / Hath (776, Texas). 12 Crown / Scepter (776); yet / *omitted* (776). 13 their / heere (Cardiff). 20 the / a (776). 22 thee / you (776). 24 Reason / Judgment (776). Between 26 and 27: But I admire not at the new supply: / No bounds will hold those who at Sceptres fly (776, Cardiff, 1664); the / this (776, Texas). 29 or / nor (776) 30 own / *omitted* (776). 32 tear / pull (Cardiff).

2. *The great Helm:* with this phrase, Philips refers to the "ship" of state that she does not claim to "steer."

3. For lines 1–6: Angeline Goreau, *Reconstructing Aphra: A Social Biography of Aphra Behn* (New York, 1980), p. 89, suggests that the law of nature Orinda has determined to break is the law that women not speak on public matters. For the Renaissance dictum that women remain silent, see Ruth Kelso, *Doctrine for the Lady of the Renaissance* (1956; reprint, Urbana, Ill., 1978), and Suzanne W. Hull, *Chaste, Silent, & Obedient: English Books for Women, 1475–1640* (San Marino, Calif., 1982). I am indebted to Lois Schwoerer for calling Goreau's comment to my attention.

4. *Sequester:* excommunicate or confiscate.

5. Other contemporary accounts of the coronation of Charles II note the good omen of Coronation Day, April 23, 1661, being a day of good weather between two storms. See, for example, James Heath, *The Glories and Magnificent Triumphs of the Blessed Restitution of His Sacred Majesty K. Charles II* (London, 1662), p. 197. The representation of the moment of the coronation as a sunny interlude in the midst of a storm is, as far as I have been able to determine, original with Philips.

Texts: Locke, 776, Texas, 1664, 1667.

Variants: Title The faire weather at the Coronation betwixt 2 great storms which preceded and followed it. (Locke), On the Fayre weather at the Coronation. (776, Texas), On the Fair Weather just at Coronation (1664). 5 his / the (Locke). 6 he / eye (Locke). 7 check'd / stopt (Locke). 8 in a / a more (1664) 12 an impetuous / its accustomed (Locke); storm returned with an impetuous hast / intermitted Storms return'd as fast (776, Texas); replaced by line of stars (1664). 13 And / When (Locke) 14 Cannons / Cannon (776, Texas); Fire-works / Bonefires (Locke). 16 While / Whilst (776, Texas). Between 16 and 17: On this side and on that the waves retreate / Whilst not one dropp an Hebrews foot did wet (Locke). 17 Hebrews once on shore / Jews once set a shoare (Locke); on shore / ashoare (776). 18 Return'd / Came back (776, Texas).

6. *Impetuous:* forceful, violent.

7. Lines 15–18: for the story of the Israelites' passage through the Red Sea, see Exodus 14:21–30.

8. *Magazine:* storehouse, sometimes for gunpowder or explosives. Here the "Magazine of Light" is a metaphor for the sun.

9. Cromwell's defeat of Charles II at the Battle of Worcester on September 3, 1651, was tantamount to ending the second phase of the Civil War. Charles and his forces fought bravely and well, but they were outnumbered two to one by the Commonwealth army, and they were severely defeated. Charles himself escaped and was restored to the English throne by Parliamentary action in 1660.

Texts: 775, 776, Texas, 1664, 1667.

Variants: Title On the 3d September 1651. (775), On the 3d of September 1651. (Texas). 2 Approaches / Approacheth (Texas). 5 And as / As if (775, Texas). 6 in's / in (Texas). 10 does / doth. 12 was now / now was (775, Texas). 18 else attend / wait upon (775, Texas); the / her (Texas). 20 setting / sitting (775). 24 bear / keep (Texas). 25 And captiv'd / Thus Captive (775). 31 so / thus (775). 32 a / the (775, Texas).

10. *Brave and check:* meet courageously and stop abruptly.

11. *Anti-Persians:* since Persians were thought to be sun worshipers, an Anti-Persian could be said to worship a falling, or setting, sun.

12. *Period:* the end or conclusion of the monarchy.

13. *Pompey:* Cneis Pompeius Magnus, Pompey the Great, was defeated by Julius Caesar at the Battle of Pharsalus in 48 B.C. Fifteen thousand of Pompey's men were killed, and twenty-four thousand taken prisoner. Pompey then fled to Egypt, where he was assassinated by Photinus.

14. *Sampson:* the Israelite hero who, having been blinded by the Philistines, pulled down the temple at Gaza, destroying himself and his enemies. See Judges 14–16.

15. *Whose food is air:* who live on false hopes.

16. Sir Francis Finch's *Friendship* (1654) is addressed "D. Noble Lucasia-Orinda" and is signed "Palaemon." The name Palaemon is associated with the theme of friendship in Chaucer's "Knight's Tale," Shakespeare's *Two Noble Kinsmen,* and in book IV of Spenser's *Faerie Queene,* where the sea god Palaemon, who in Greek mythology is said to be a protector of ships, is "Now hight *Palaemon,* and is saylers frend" (IV.xi.13.23–26). The sea god Palaemon also appears in Saint Amant's "La Solitude," which Philips translated; and, as Thomas notes in his dissertation, p. 57, Palaemon is a character in Honore D'Urfé's pastoral romance *L'Astrée* (1610–1627).

Texts: 775, 776, Texas, 1664, 1667.

Variants: Title To Palaemon on his discourse of friendship. (776), To the incomparable Palaemon on his noble discourse of friendship. (Texas). 2 and / but (775, 776); Secure not happy been, cunning not wise (Texas). 5 Hadst thou / Had you (776); our Light / out light (775), out lights (Texas). 11 the great Physician / the Politician (775, 776, Texas). 14 and / or (775, 776, 1664); last / least (1664). 15 Hadst thou / Had you (776); her / our (1664). 16 At / And (775). 19 so august an / that transcendent (776); so / such (1664). 20 greater / better (776). 21 which / as (776); loud / big (775, 776, Texas, 1664). 22 thy / these (776). 24 with / by (776, Texas). 25–26 reversed (775, 776, Texas). 25 thy / your (775, 776), replaced by line of stars (1664). 26 Armies / People (775, 776, Texas); lay down / let fall (775, 776, Texas). 27–28 omitted (776). 27 can / could (775). 29 while / whilst (776); thou / you (776); hast / have (776). 30 Thou'st / Y'have (776); thy / your (776). 31 thy / your (776); thy / your (776). 32 Whether / Or (775, 776, Texas, 1664); to / unto (775, 776, Texas, 1664); thy / your (776). 33 thine / thy (775, Texas), your (776). 34 Thou'st rais'd / Th'hast rear'd (775); Thou'st / Y'have (776); thy / your (776). Between 34 and 35: And that so lasting that all Fate forbids, / And will outlive Egyptian Pyramids (775, 1664), And that so solid as all Fate forbids, / And will outlast Egyptian Pyramids (776). And that so lasting as all fate forbids, / And will outlive Egyptian Pyramids (Texas). 37 there / here (776).

17. *Passion, but a Plot:* in contrasting friendship that derives from deep emotion (Passion) with that which is consciously designed or secretly contrived (Plot), Philips perhaps puns on the distinction between a Passion play, which treats religious matters, and a fictional drama which is "plotted" merely for effect.

18. *Cambina's Wand:* In "The Legend of Cambel and Triamond or of Friendship," book IV of Spenser's *Faerie Queene,* Cambina creates peace between two knights who are fighting for the hand of Canace: "Shee smote them lightly with her powrefull wand. / Then suddenly as if their hearts did faile, / Their wrathfull blades downe fell out of their hand / And they like men astonisht still did stand" (IV.iii.48.2–5).

19. One of six commendatory poems printed in Lawes's *Second Book of Ayres and Di-*

alogues (1655). Henry Lawes (1596–1662) was the foremost songwriter of mid-seventeenth-century England. For his place in the society of Interregnum and Restoration poets, see Souers, pp. 59–60, and Willa McClung Evans, *Henry Lawes: Musician and Friend of Poets* (New York, 1941). For the basic conceit of the poem, the idea that the universe is a harmonious whole created by a God of music, see Leo Spitzer, *Classical and Christian Ideas of World Harmony: Prolegomena to an Interpretation of the Word "Stimmung"* (Baltimore, 1963), and Gretchen Ludke Finney, *Musical Backgrounds for English Literature: 1589–1650* (New Brunswick, n. d.). Souers, p. 60, notes that John Dryden uses the same conceit in his "Ode on Saint Cecilia's Day." (Dryden, a relative by marriage to Philips, was a great admirer of her work.)

   Texts: 775, 776, Texas, 1655, 1664, 1667.

   Variants: Title To the truly noble Mr. Henry Lawes. (775, 776, 1664), To Mr Henry Lawes. (Texas), To the much honoured Mr. HENRY LAWES, On his Excellent Compositions in Musick. (1655). 2 That / The (Texas); in / through (Texas). 4 Number / Musick (1655). 5 For / And (1655). 10 Concord / accord (776, 1664). 11 Unison / Union (1664) 12 Honour / Honour's (775, 776, 1655, 1664). 17 formed / furnished (1655). 18 and / or (775, 1655). 20 Nature's / Nature (776); as / more (775); as / then (775). 30 Laurel / Laurells (775, Texas, 1655). 33 for / and (775, Texas). 34 may / will (775), can (1655). 38 Stone, a Fish / Fish a Stone (1655).

   20. *Curious:* careful, studious.

   21. For the *topos* of music and poetry as sister arts, see Ernst Robert Curtius, *European Literature and the Latin Middle Ages,* trans. Willard R. Trask (1953; reprint, New York, 1963), and Robert Toft, "Musicke a Sister to Poetrie: Rhetorical Artifice in the Passionate Airs of John Dowland," *Early Music* 12 (1984): 190–99.

   22. *Laurel:* the bay tree or bay laurel used to create a garland with which a victorious poet is to be crowned.

   23. Philips thus places Lawes in the tradition of poets like the Thracian Orpheus, whose song was so wondrous that savage beasts and even trees would come running to listen, and the Corinthian Arion, who, when he was thrown into the sea by pirates, was rescued by a dolphin whom he charmed with his music.

   24. Lucasia, to whom this poem is addressed, is Philips's name for her friend Anne Owen, later Lady Dungannon.

   Texts: 775, 776, Texas, 1655, 1664, 1667.

   Variants: Title Friendships Mysterys to my dearest Lucasia. (Set by Mr H. Lawes). (775), Friendships mystery set by Mr. Lawes. (776), Friendships mystery to my Dearest Lucasia: Set by Mr H Lawes. (Texas), Mutuall Affection between Orinda and Lucatia. (1655), Friendship's Mystery, To my dearest Lucasia. Set by Mr. Henry Lawes. (1664). 3 wonder / wonders (1664). 4 dull angry / enraged (776). dull / fierce (1655). 11 the / their (775, 776, Texas, 1655). 16 court / count (1664). 17 Thrones more great and / Greatest thrones more (1664). 19 Since / While (Texas), When (1655).

   25. *Election . . . joyes:* Like the Angels who joyfully (and paradoxically) seek the fate to which they are "determined," the poet and Lucasia happily choose the friendship to which they have been "elected"/chosen by God.

   26. *Diffuse* and *ingross:* terms from alchemy—to spread out and to collect together.

   27. Line 23: compare Lady Mary Wroth's *Pamphilia and Amphilanthus,* sonnet 82, for a similar statement of the power of loving another to teach one about oneself: "[Love] doth inrich the witts, and make you see / That in your self, which you knew nott before"—*The Poems of Lady Mary Wroth,* ed. Josephine A. Roberts (Baton Rouge and London, 1983), p. 130.

   28. Line 25: compare John Donne, "The Sunne Rising," lines 21–22: "She's all States, and all Princes, I, / Nothing else is."

   29. *Kindly:* readily, benevolently—also naturally. When the friends willingly give up their

hearts to one another in an act imaged as a religious sacrifice, each gains a kind of eternal life that proves "There's a religion in [their] Love."

30. As far as I have been able to determine, Lawes's setting for this poem has not survived.

Texts: 776, Texas, 1664, 1667.

Variants: Title A Dialogue of Absence betwixt Lucasia and Orinda Set by Mr. Lawes. (776), A Dialogue Between Lucasia and Orinda set by Mr H. Lawes. (Texas). 2 doth / will (776). 4 And / But (776). 8 Can / Will (776). 9 And / But (776); first they / they first (776) 10 windows / window (776). 14 this / such (776). 16 captiv'd / captive (776, Texas). 21 parts / part (776, Texas).

31. *Intelligence:* understanding, true comprehension. When Orinda's and Lucasia's souls "hold intelligence," they participate in a conversation more profound than those they could have by means of their five senses.

32. Line 10: A reference to the Neoplatonic idea that lovers first behold one another's souls as they are manifested in their physical appearances.

33. *Science:* knowledge acquired by study; a particular branch or area of learning.

34. Cicely Philips, Katherine Philips's sister-in-law, married John Lloyd at Saint Mary's Church, Cardigan, on October 31, 1653 (Thomas, "An Edition of the Poems and Letters," pp. 97–98). When she refers to her brother-in-law, Philips uses his given name, Hector. Perhaps she chose the name Cassandra for her sister-in-law because in Greek mythology Cassandra and Hector are sister and brother.

Texts: 775, 776, Texas, 1664, 1667.

Variants: Title Marriage / nuptials (775), Nuptial. (1664), To my dear Sister C. P. on her Nuptial. (776), To Mrs C. P. on her nuptialls. (Texas). 3 We / Wee'l (775, Texas). 6 *omitted* (776); Do but disturb, and not adorn our Joys (775, Texas); replaced by line of stars (1664). 20 new / the (Texas); bonds / bands (775, Texas). 21 they pass / they doe pass (775, Texas). 24 Gratitude, and strictest / duty, gratitude and (775, Texas).

35. The "wild toyes" Orinda lists in lines 1–3 are the ritual celebrations of marriage outlined in Virginia Tufte, *The Poetry of Marriage: The Epithalamium in Europe and Its Development in England,* University of Southern California Studies in Comparative Literature, vol. 2 (Los Angeles, 1970).

36. *Text:* 775.

First published by J. R. Tutin in 1905. In 775, a blank space is left in the title between "July the" and "1656." Thomas, "An Edition of the Poems and Letters," p. 529, provides the number "11" for the date in the title from the monument, which survives in Cilgerran Church.

37. *Propounds:* conceives, imagines.

38. It is not clear to whom Philips has addressed this poem.

Texts: 775, 776, Texas, 1664, 1667.

Variants: Title A retir'd friendship to Ardelia. 23d. Aug. 1651. (775, Texas), A retir'd friendship, to Ardelia 1651. (776). 2 Souls / thoughts (776). 4 all/ *omitted* (776). 7 frowns / frowne (776). 11 blood and / bloody (776). 20 Yet friendship can be / Our harmless souls are (776). 22 be our / give us (776). 23 For mischief's / Mischief it (776). 24 or / and (775, 776, Texas). 27 neighbouring streams / neighbour-streams (775, 776, Texas) neighbouring Springs (1664). 30 Who would not ever / Whoever would not (775, 776, Texas). 35 With quiet Souls and unconfin'd / And here can quiet be, and kind (776). 36 Enjoy what Princes / Which Princes wish, but (776).

39. *Apollo:* in classical mythology, the god of the sun.

40. Lines 33–34: compare John Donne, "A Valediction Forbidding Mourning," lines 16–20: "But we by'a love, so much refin'd, / That our selves know not what it is, / Inter-assured of the mind, / Care lesse, eyes, lips, and hands to misse."

41. *Texts:* 775, 776, Texas, 1664, 1667.

Variants: Title To My excellent Lucasia on our friendship. 17th July 1651 [final numeral possibly a 3]. (775), To my Excellent Lucasia on our mutuall friendship promis'd. 17. July 1651. (776), 17 July 1652. To the excellent Lucasia on our Friendship. (Texas). Not in stanzas (775, 776) 17 No / Nor (775, Texas); Crown-conquerors / crown'd conquerours (775, 776, Texas). 21 Flames / flame (775, 776, Texas, 1664). 22 false / bold (775), damp (776).

42. *Inspires:* breathes life into, animates.

43. This poem is addressed to Regina Collier, whose husband John Collier had died in 1649. For Philaster, see note 47 below.

Texts: 776, Texas, Cardiff, 1664, 1667.

Variants: Title For Regina. (Texas), For the Queen of Hearts. (Cardiff). 1 fit / sit (776, Texas). 5 Where / When (776). 6 his / your (776).

44. Line 6: When Regina breaks Philaster's heart, she also breaks the image emblazoned there—the image he worships, of course, is of Regina herself.

45. *Rifle:* plunder, despoil, strip bare.

46. *Round-head:* a Parliamentarian—so called because of their custom of wearing their hair cut close to their heads. In this context a Roundhead is a traitor—ironically, here, to her own cause.

47. Souers's supposition that Philaster was Philips's name for Colonel John Jeffries, who fought on the royalist side in the Civil War (p. 234n), is verified in manuscript 775b by her identification of him in the title of another Philaster poem: Philips's holograph of "To Mrs. Mary Carne when Philaster Courted Her" is entitled "To Mrs M. Karne when J. Jeffreys Esq courted her."

Texts: 775, 776, Texas, Cardiff, 1664, 1667.

Variants: Title To J. J. esq: upon his melancholly for Regina. (775), Orinda to Philaster. (Cardiff). 1 now / *omitted* (Cardiff). 5 Then leave / Quit quit (775); leave / hang (Cardiff).

48. *Dulness:* stupidity.

49. *Texts:* 775, 776, Texas, 1664, 1667.

Variants: Title Parting with Lucasia 13th Jann 1657/8 A Song. (775), A Parting with Lucasia. (776), Parting with Lucasia 13 January 1657/1658. (Texas), Parting with Lucasia, Jan 13. 1657. A Song. (1664). 3 hath / has (776). 13 Yet I / Yet since I (775, 776, Texas); we will / wee'le (775, 776, Texas). 15 nobly / noblier (1664).

50. *Dispossest:* dislodged, expelled.

51. *Conveyances:* the bodies that carry the souls from place to place.

52. *Passion:* strong emotion—here the anguish felt by friends who have parted.

53. Similar to the previous poem in being a poem of parting, this poem is addressed to Philips's husband, whom she calls Antenor (the name of an elderly counsellor in Troy) in the poems and letters. Here, as in the verses on the man she hoped to marry (quoted in the introductory essay, above) and in the marriage poem she wrote for her sister-in-law, Philips presents married love as a form of friendship.

Texts: 775, 776, Texas, 1664, 1667.

Variants: Title on his / At (776), To Antenor parting. (Texas). 3 an / a (775, 776, Texas), change / chance (776). 7 As / And (775, 776, Texas). 10 our / the (776). 13 its own / in its (1664). 16 Like to our / As well as (776). 17–18 *omitted* (776). 17 a / an (775, Texas). 18 destroy / betray (775, Texas). 20 we find it still doth / and yet we find they (776). 25 For / And (776). 27 And / But (775); besides this thou shalt in me / that Deare Spy, shall in my heart (776). 28 while / when (Texas); art / wert (776). 29 what / though (776). 32 Friendship it self can only bring to / Nothing but kindness can bring this (776). 35 So / Thus (776). 36 Life, Object, Friend, and / My Guide, my Object, and my (776).

54. *With advantage paid:* the poet has given her heart to Antenor, but in receiving his, she has gained a greater heart than the one she "lost."

55. *That dear Guest:* Antenor's heart, now residing in her breast.

56. Line 8: the poet and her husband/lover have been "impressed"—called into service—by the "Decree" of the God of Love. For a similar notion of fate controlling human relationships, see "Friendship's Mystery" above.

57. *Inclinations:* dispositions. Also, perhaps, an echo allusion to the image of the compass in John Donne's "A Valediction Forbidding Mourning," in which one foot of the compass "leanes, and harkens after" the other.

58. *Passion:* deeply felt emotion. Compare note 52 above.

59. In the autumn of 1663, when Queen Catherine was dangerously ill of spotted fever, Charles II became, for some three weeks, a devoted husband and nursed her back to health. (Samuel Pepys reports that, despite his anxiety over Catherine, the king found time to have supper with his mistress, Lady Castlemain, every evening during the queen's illness: *The Diary of Samuel Pepys,* ed. Robert Latham and William Matthews [Berkeley and Los Angeles, 1971], vol. 4, p. 342.)

Texts: 776, Nottingham, 1664, 1667.

Variants: 1 that's / is (776). 9 have / had (Nottingham). 10 may / might (776). 11 were / was (Nottingham). 18 *Charles* / Charls his (Nottingham). 19 suffering / sufferings (776). 25 At / As (776). 30 that / as (776). 32 for / to (Nottingham). 36 full / so (776). 39 he / we (Nottingham, 1664). 41 durst / could (Nottingham).

60. *Three kingdoms:* England, Scotland, and Wales, which Charles lost in 1653 at the Battle of Worcester. In his poem on the queen's recovery from her illness, "To the queen, upon her Majesties Birth'day, after Her happy recovery from a dangerous illness," Edmund Waller uses the same conceit: "He that was never known to Mourn, / So many kingdoms from him torn, / His tears reserved for You, more dear, / More priz'd than all those Kingdoms were" (lines 31–34).

61. *Genius:* spirit. In this line Philips juxtaposes Charles's power and that of the "bold Distemper," who is now the king's rival for the queen's soul. At the end of the poem, the rival wooer is Death himself.

62. *Thracian Hero:* Orpheus, the Thracian poet of Greek mythology who descended to the Underworld to free his wife, Eurydice. He won her liberty by charming Hades and Persephone with his music.

63. The title of "Orinda upon Little Hector Philips" in Philips's holograph, National Library of Wales, manuscript 775b, indicates that Philips's only son Hector was born on April 23 and died on May 2, 1655. If those dates are correct, Philips had indeed been married for the seven years that she mentions in line 5 of this poem—the eighty months that she numbers in line 1 of "Orinda upon Little Hector Philips," but unless "May" is a slip of the pen and the child really died on June 2, he lived for nine days, not forty. The child was buried near Philips's father and his family in the church of Saint Benet-Sherehog on Syth's Lane in London. As the last six words of the printed title to this poem indicate and as John Aubrey confirms, p. 153, Philips was buried in the same church when she died in 1664. The church burned in the Great Fire of 1666 and was never rebuilt.

Texts: 776, 1667.

Variants: Title EPITAPH ON HECTOR PHILLIPS at St. Sith's Church. (776). 13 as / omitted (776). 14 He / omitted (776). 19 And / omitted (776).

64. *Hermes* Seal: Hermetic seal—an airtight closure of a vessel. Named for Hermes Trismegistus, Eygptian god said to be the author of mysterious doctrines including alchemy, and his namesake the Greek god of science, Hermes.

65. *Texts:* 775, 1667.

Variants: Title On the death of my first and dearest childe, Hector Philipps borne the 23d of April and dy'd the 2d of May 1655 Set by Mr. Lawes. (775). Only the first eight lines are transcribed in 775. 1 of / in (775). 6 pluck / touch (775). 8 For / Soe (775).

66. *Text:* 1667.

67. Stanza 3: an example of the impossibility *topos*. For the early history of this *topos* as it is used in anti-feminist lying songs, see Susan Schibanoff, "Creseyde's 'Impossible' Aubes," *Journal of English and Germanic Philology* 76 (1977): 326–33.

68. *Beams:* eye beams. The lady casts her eyes on even more men than does the sun; the bold youth will never be able to keep this flirtatious lady to himself.

BIBLIOGRAPHY

Primary Works

Ferguson, Moira, ed. "Katherine Fowler Philips." In *First Feminists: British Women Writers, 1578–1799*, pp. 102–13. Bloomington, Ind., 1985.

Limbert, Claudia, ed. "Two Poems and a Prose Receipt: The Juvenilia of Katherine Philips." *English Literary Renaissance*, forthcoming.

Mahl, Mary R., and Helene Koon, eds. "Katherine Phillips." In *The Female Spectator: English Women Writers Before 1800*, pp. 154–64. Bloomington, Ind., 1977.

Philips, Katherine. *Familiar Letters. Written by the Right Honourable John, Late Earl of Rochester, and Several Other Persons of Honour and Quality. With Letters Written by Mr. Thomas Otway and Mrs. K. Philips.* London, 1697.

———. *Letters from Orinda to Poliarchus.* 1705. Reprint, with one additional letter. London, 1729.

———. *Poems. By the Incomparable, Mrs. K.P.* London, 1664.

———. *Poems. By the Most Deservedly Admired Mrs. Katherine Philips, the Matchless Orinda. To Which Is Added, Monsieur Corneille's Pompey and Horace, Tragedies. With Several Other Translations out of French.* 1667. Reprints. London, 1669, 1678, and 1710.

———. *Pompey: A Tragedy.* Dublin, 1663. Reprint. London, 1663.

Saintsbury, George, ed. "Katherine Philips." In *Minor Poets of the Caroline Period*, vol. 1, pp. 485–612. 1905. Reprint. Oxford, 1968.

Tutin, J. R., ed. *Katherine Philips ("Orinda"): Selected Poems.* Orinda Booklets (Extra Series), no. 1. Hull, Eng., 1905.

———. *Katherine Philips: "The Matchless Orinda": Selected Poems.* Orinda Booklets, no. 1. Cottingham near Hull, Eng., 1904.

Related Works

Aubrey, John. *"Brief Lives," Chiefly of Contemporaries, Set Down Between the Years 1669 and 1696, Edited from the Author's MSS. by Andrew Clark.* Vol 2. Oxford, 1898.

Bond, Maurice F., ed. *The Diaries and Papers of Sir Edward Dering Second Baronet, 1644 to 1684.* London, 1976.

Brashear, Lucy. "The Forgotten Legacy of the 'Matchless Orinda.'" *Anglo-Welsh Review* 65 (1979): 68–79.

Canfield, Dorothea Frances. *Corneille and Racine in England.* 1904. Reprint. New York, 1966.

Clark, William Smith. *The Early Irish Stage: The Beginnings to 1720.* Oxford, 1955.

Cotton, Nancy. *Women Playwrights in England, c. 1363–1750.* Lewisburg, Pa., 1980.

Crum, Margaret, ed. *First-Line Index of English Poetry, 1500–1800, in Manuscripts of the Bodleian Library.* 2 vols. Oxford, 1969.

Day, Cyrus Lawrence, and Eleanore Boswell Murrie. *English Song-Books, 1651–1702: A Bibliography with a First-Line Index of Songs.* London, 1940.

Elmen, Paul. "Some Manuscript Poems by the Matchless Orinda." *Philological Quarterly* 30 (1951): 53–57.

Evans, G. Blakemore, ed. *The Plays and Poems of William Cartwright.* Madison, Wisc., 1951.

Gosse, Edmund. "The Matchless Orinda." *Cornhill Magazine* 44 (1881): 407–20. Reprinted in *Seventeenth Century Studies*, pp. 229–58. London, 1883.

Hiscock, W. G. "Friendship: Francis Finch's Discourse and the Circle of the Matchless Orinda." *Review of English Studies* 15 (1939): 466–68.

Latt, David Jay. "The Progress of Friendship: The *Topoi* for Society and the Ideal Experience in the Poetry and Prose of Seventeenth-Century England." Ph.D. dissertation, University of California at Los Angeles, 1971.

Lennep, William van, Emmett L. Avery, and Arthur Scouten, eds. *The London Stage, 1660–1800. Part I: 1660–1700.* Carbondale, Ill., 1965.

Mambretti, Catherine Cole. "'Fugitive Papers': A New Orinda Poem and Problems in Her Canon." *Papers of the Bibliographical Society of America* 71 (1977): 443–52.

––––––. "Orinda on the Restoration Stage." *Comparative Literature* 37 (1985): 233–51.

Miner, Earl. *The Cavalier Mode from Jonson to Cotton.* Princeton, 1971.

Price, Curtis A. "The Songs for Katherine Philips' *Pompey* (1663)." *Theater Notebook* 33 (1979): 61–66.

Pritchard, Allan. "Marvell's 'The Garden': A Restoration Poem?" *Studies in English Literature* 23 (1983): 371–88.

Roberts, William. "The Dating of Orinda's French Translations." *Philological Quarterly* 49 (1970): 56–67.

––––––. "Saint-Amant, Orinda and Dryden's Miscellany." *English Language Notes* 1 (1964): 191–96.

––––––. "Sir William Temple on Orinda: Neglected Publications." *Papers of the Bibliographical Society of America* 57 (1963): 328–36.

Røstvig, Maren-Sofie. *The Happy Man: Studies in the Metamorphoses of a Classical Ideal, 1600–1700.* Oslo Studies in English 2. Oxford, 1954.

Souers, Philip Webster. *The Matchless Orinda.* Harvard Studies in English 5. 1931. Reprint. Johnson Reprint Corp., 1968.

Thomas, Patrick Hungerford Bryan. "An Edition of the Poems and Letters of Katherine Philips, 1632–1664." Ph.D. dissertation, University College of Wales, 1982.

––––––. "Orinda, Vaughan and Watkyns: Anglo-Welsh Literary Relationships During the Interregnum." *Anglo-Welsh Review* 62 (1976): 96–102.

Thomas, P[eter]. W[illiam]. *Sir John Berkenhead, 1617–1679: A Royalist Career in Politics and Polemics.* Oxford, 1969.

Turner, James. *The Politics of Landscape: Rural Scenery and Society in English Poetry, 1630–1660.* Cambridge, Mass., 1979.

Waller, Jennifer. "'My Hand a Needle Better Fits': Anne Bradstreet and Women Poets in the Renaissance." *Dalhousie Review* 54 (1974): 436–50.

Chronology of Literary and Historical Figures and Major Events

CHRONOLOGY OF LITERARY AND HISTORICAL FIGURES
AND MAJOR EVENTS

	General	Italy	France
1400–1410	Hundred Years War (1337–1453)	E. S. Piccolomini b. Aeneas Sylvius b. L. Valla b.	Froissart, *Chronicles* Deschamps d.
1410–1420	Council of Constanz End of Great Schism Johann Hus Battle of Agincourt	*Catherine of Bologna b.*	
1420–1430	Joan of Arc	School of Vittorino da Feltre Pontano b.	
1430–1440		School of Guarino Veronese L. Pulci b.	Gaguin b. Christine de Pizan d. F. Villon b.
1440–1450	Battle of Crécy Jack Cade's rebellion	Boiardo b. *Catherine of Genoa b.* L. Bruni d.	
1450–1460	End of Hundred Years War Gutenberg discovers printing press (1500) Constantinople falls to the Turks (1553) War of the Roses (1455–1485)	Leonardo da Vinci b. Sannazaro b. Savonarola b. Poliziano b.	
1460–1470	Ivan the Great rules Russia	Piccolomini d. Pico della Mirandola b. *Catherine of Bologna d.*	F. Villon d. G. Budé b. Crétin b.

Spain and Portugal	German Principalities/ Hapsburg Empire and the Netherlands	Central and Eastern Europe	England
		János Vitéz b.	Death of Chaucer (1400) Wakefield Cycle
J. de Mena b. G. Manrique b.	Johannes von Templ d.		
			Paston Letters
		Nil Sorsky b.	
	Helene Kottanner fl.		
J. de Mena d.	Celtis b. Reuchlin b. Sebastian Brant b.	Menčetić b.	
Juan del Encina b. F. de Rojas b.	*Caritas Pirckheimer b.* Erasmus b.	János Vitéz d. Janus Pannonius d.	Skelton b.

(continued)

CHRONOLOGY OF LITERARY AND HISTORICAL FIGURES
AND MAJOR EVENTS (*continued*)

	General	Italy	France
1460–1470		Aeneas Sylvius d. Tebaldeo b. Bembo b. Bibbiena b. Machiavelli b.	
1470–1480		Michelangelo b. Aristo b. Trissino b. Castiglione b.	
1480–1490		*Veronica Gambara b.* Girolamo Vida b. Straparola b. Bandello b. Pulci d. Raphael b.	Saint-Gelais b. Scaliger b.
1490–1500	Columbus discovers America Expulsion of Moors from Spain Vasco da Gama sails to India Cabral discovers Brazil	*Vittoria Colonna b.* Agnolo Firenzuola b. Ficino d. Boiardo d. Cellini b. Savonarola d. Speroni b. Poliziano d. Aretino b. B. Tasso b.	*Marguerite of Navarre b.* Marot b. Rabelais b. *Pathelin*
1500–1510	Pope Julius II Columbus d. Maximilian I, Holy Roman Emperor	Palingenius d. Giraldi b. Grazini b.	*Dianne de Poitiers b.* Gaguin d. John Calvin b.

Spain and Portugal	German Principalities/ Hapsburg Empire and the Netherlands	Central and Eastern Europe	England
Boscán b.	Albrecht Dürer b. Copernicus b. Thomas Murner b. Thomas a Kempis d.		Caxton prints first book in England Thomas More b.
Bartolomé de Torres Naharro b. Ribeiro b. G. Manrique d.	Ulrich von Hutten b. *Margaret of Austria b.* Martin Luther b. Ulrich Zwingli b. Niklaus Manuel b.	Lucić b.	*Le Morte d'Arthur*
Ignatius of Loyola b. *La Celestina* Vives b. Juan de Valdes b.	Hans Sachs b. *Anna Bijns b.* *Ship of Fools* Agricola b. Burkard Waldis b. Paracelsus b. Sebastian Franck b.		*Everyman*
G. dela Vega b. H. de Mendoza b. L. de Rueda b.	Conrad Celtis d.	M. Rej b. N. Sorsky d.	*Margaret Roper b.*

(*continued*)

CHRONOLOGY OF LITERARY AND HISTORICAL FIGURES
AND MAJOR EVENTS (*continued*)

	General	Italy	France
1500–1510	Henry VIII, King of England	Castelvetro b. Ruzante b. Benvenuto Cellini b.	Scève b.
1510–1520	Magellan circumnavigates the globe Luther posts his thesis Charles V, Holy Roman Emperor Cortez conquers Mexico Francis I, King of France	Vasari b. *Catherine of Genoa d.* *Orlando Furioso* Bibbiena d. *The Prince* Leonardo d.	*Madeleine Neveu b.* J. Amyot b. de Bèze b. Bonaventure des Periers b. *Louise Labé b.*
1520–1530	Diet of Augsburg Edict of Worms Turkish victory at the Battle of Mohács German Peasants War Adrian VI, pope Clement VII, pope Henry VIII proclaimed head of the Church of England	*Gaspara Stampa b.* Raphael d. *The Book of the Courtier* Castiglione d. Sannazaro d. Machiavelli d.	Noël du Fail b. du Bellay b. Ronsard b. *Pernette du Guillet b.*
1530–1540	Jesuit order established Anglican Church separates from Rome Dissolution of English monasteries	*Vittoria Colonna d.* Ariosto d. Correggio d. Aretino d. T. Tasso b. Tebaldeo d.	*Pantagruel* Marot d. *Marguerite de Navarre d.* Jodelle b. Grévin b. *Marie Dentière fl.*

Spain and Portugal	German Principalities/ Hapsburg Empire and the Netherlands	Central and Eastern Europe	England
Saint Teresa b.	*Lea Ráskai fl.* *Praise of Folly* Reuchlin d. Neogeorg b. *Dyl Ulenspiegel* Johannes Secundus b. Dürer d.	Držic b.	*Utopia* Roger Ascham b.
Jorge de Monte Mayor b. de Camões b. Luis de Leon b. J. del Encina d. Naharro d.	Nikolaus Manuel d. Coornhert b. Sebastian Brant d. Ulrich von Hutten d. Luther's *New Testament* *Margaret of Austria d.*	Kurbsky b. J. Kochanowski b.	Tyndale's Bible Skelton d.
Francisco de Aldana b. Saint John of the Cross b. dela Vega d. Juan de Herrera b. Vives d.	*Caritas Pirckheimer d.* Paracelsus d. Murner d. Cranach d. Erasmus d. J. van der Noot b.	Peter Bornemissan b.	*Queen Elizabeth I b.* Thomas More d.

(*continued*)

CHRONOLOGY OF LITERARY AND HISTORICAL FIGURES
AND MAJOR EVENTS (*continued*)

	General	Italy	France
1530–1540			Montaigne b.
			Hélisenne de Crenne fl.
1540–1550	Council of Trent	Giordano Bruno b.	Charron b.
	King Philip II of Spain	Agnolo Firenzuola d.	Marot d.
	Papacy begins issuing	*Vittoria Colonna d.*	*Pernette du Guillet d.*
	the *Index*	*Veronica Gambara d.*	Garnier b.
	King Edward VI of	Folengo d.	*Catherine Fradomet b.*
	England	Trissino d.	Budé d.
		Palingenius d.	Guillaume du Bartas b.
		Ruzante d.	des Periers d.
		Bembo d.	*Marguerite of*
		C. Bruno b.	*Navarre d.*
1550–1560	Establishment of	*Gaspara Stampa d.*	Scève d.
	Colonies in America	Michelangelo d.	du Bellay d.
	Queen Mary Tudor	Straparola d.	Agrippa d'Aubigne b.
	Reign of Elizabeth I	Aretino d.	Malherbe b.
	begins		Rabelais d.
			J. C. Scaliger d.
			Saint Gelais d.
			Louise Labé d.
1560–1570	Queen Elizabeth I of	Galileo b.	d'Urfé b.
	England	Girolamo Vida d.	F. de Sales b.
		Bandello d.	*Dianne de Poitiers d.*
		Marino b.	
		Campanella b.	

Spain and Portugal	German Principalities/ Hapsburg Empire and the Netherlands	Central and Eastern Europe	England
Guevara d.	Georg	Klonovic b.	*Margaret Roper d.*
Cervantes b.	Rollenhagen b.	Sep-Szaryński b.	Gascoigne b.
Boscan d.	Paracelsus d.		
Fernando de	Copernicus d.		
Rojas d.	Luther d.		
Mateo de	Fischart b.		
Alemán b.	Frischlin b.		
Valdes d.	H. L. Spiegel b.		
Lazarillo de Tormes	Waldis d.	B. Balassa b.	*Mirror for*
Ignatius of Loyola d.	Melanchton d.	Simonides b.	*Magistrate*
		Palitsyn b.	Raleigh b.
			Sidney b.
			Spenser b.
Gongora b.	Heinrich Julius von	Držic d.	*Mary Sidney,*
Monte Mayor d.	Braunschweig	Pázmany b.	*Countess of*
Luis de Leon fl.	Wolfenbüttel b.	M. Rej d.	*Pembroke b.*
Rueda d.			Marlowe b.
			Shakespeare b.
			Chapman b.
			Bacon b.

(continued)

CHRONOLOGY OF LITERARY AND HISTORICAL FIGURES
AND MAJOR EVENTS (*continued*)

	General	Italy	France
1570–1580	Drake circumnavigates the globe	Torquato Tasso fl. Giraldo d. Vasari d. Cellini d.	Jodelle d.
1580–1590	Defeat of Spanish Armada Calendar reform of Pope Gregory XIII Execution of Mary Queen of Scots	Grazzini d.	*Madeleine Neveu d.* *Catherine Fradomet d.* Ronsard d. Jansen b.
1590–1600	Edict of Nantes	T. Tasso d. Giordano Bruno d.	Guillaume du Bartas d. Garnier d. Noël du Fail d. J. Amyot d. Descartes b. Balzac b.
1600–1610	King James I of England Settlement at Jamestown Bodleian Library founded		de Bèze d. F. H. Aubignac b. Mairet b. Corneille b. M. de Scudery b.
1610–1620	Mayflower Thirty Years War between French and Hapsburgs (1618–1648)		Scarron b. La Rochefoecauld b. Cyrano b.

Spain and Portugal	German Principalities/ Hapsburg Empire and the Netherlands	Central and Eastern Europe	England
de Camões d. Francisco de Aldana d. Mendoza d.	J. Boehme b. *Anna Owena Hoyers b.* *Anna Bijns d.* Kepler b. Rubens b. Hans Sachs d. J. Cats b.		*Mary Wroth b.* Gascoigne d. *Gorboduc* Ben Jonson b. Donne b.
Saint Teresa d. Cervantes fl.	Heinsius b. *Faustbuch* Frishlin d. P. C. Hooft b. Vondel b.	Comenius b. Gundulić b. Kochanowski d. Kurbsky d.	*Dr. Faustus* Sidney d. Fletcher b. *Mary Sidney, Lady Wroth b.*
de Herrera d. Luis de Leon d. Saint John of the Cross d.	Fishart d. Coornhert d. J. van der Noot d. Huygens b. F. von Spcc b. Opitz b.	Balassa d. Sarbiesvwski b.	*Romeo and Juliet* Marlowe d. *Richard II* Herrick b.
Don Quixote, part 1	Georg Rollenhagen d. Moscherosch b. J. J. Scaliger d. J. Balde b.	Klonovic d.	*Queen Elizabeth I d.*
Mateo de Alemán d. *Don Quixote,* part 2 Cervantes d.	Heinrich Julius d. H. L. Spiegel d. Gryphius b.		Shakespeare d. King James Bible

(*continued*)

CHRONOLOGY OF LITERARY AND HISTORICAL FIGURES
AND MAJOR EVENTS (*continued*)

	General	Italy	France
1620–1630	King Charles I of England		Molière b. Agrippa d'Aubigné d. Pascal b. Malherbe d. Mme de Sévigné b. d'Urfé d. Bossuet b. de Sales d. Corneille b. N. de Leclos b. La Fontaine b.
1630–1640			Jansen d. Mme de Lafayette b. Boileau b. Racine b.
1640–1650	King Charles of England executed Oliver Cromwell		Descartes d. La Bruyère b.

Spain and Portugal	German Principalities/ Hapsburg Empire and the Netherlands	Central and Eastern Europe	England
Gongora d.	J. Boehme d. Angelus Silesius b. Grimmelshausen b.	M. Zrinyi b.	Dekker fl. Bunyan b. *Mary Sidney, Countess of Pembroke d.*
	Spinoza b. Opitz d.	Gundulic d. Pázmány d.	*Katherine Philips b.* Chapman d. Donne d. Ben Jonson d.
	Abraham à Santa Clara b.		*Mary Wroth d.*

Contributors

KRISTIAAN P. G. AERCKE holds a licentiate from the University of Antwerp and is a doctoral candidate in the Comparative Literature Department of the University of Georgia. His publications include works on Belgian and English literature and studies on medieval, Renaissance, and seventeenth-century literature.

BRIGITTE EDITH ARCHIBALD is an associate professor of foreign languages at North Carolina A&T State University, Greensboro. Her specialty lies in the area of German Reformation, German Renaissance, and German Baroque literature.

JOSEPH R. BERRIGAN is a professor of history at the University of Georgia. His research interests include Franciscan mysticism, Renaissance humanism, and historiography.

MAYA C. BIJVOET is an assistant professor of French and German at the University of Colorado, Colorado Springs. Her research interests include the novel, women writers, and Romanticism.

GWENDOLYN BRYANT is an assistant professor in the Fine Arts Department of Bishop's University, Lennoxville, Quebec. Her research interests are Renaissance literary and art history.

COBURN FREER is a professor of English at the University of Georgia. He is the author of *Music for a King,* a study of George Herbert, and *The Poetics of Jacobean Drama.*

JOSEPH GIBALDI is associate director of book publications and research programs at the Modern Language Association of America. Author and editor of numerous scholarly and professional books and articles, he has taught comparative literature at, among others, New York University, the University of Georgia, Fairleigh Dickinson University, and the Juilliard School.

ELIZABETH H. HAGEMAN is an associate professor of English at the University of New Hampshire. Her bibliographical essay "Recent Studies in English Women Writers of Tudor England" appeared in the autumn 1984 issue of *English Literary Renaissance;* a companion piece, "Recent Studies in Women Writers of the Seventeenth Century," is forthcoming.

MARGARET PATTERSON HANNAY is an associate professor of English literature at Siena College. She is the editor of *Silent But for the Word: Tudor Women as Patrons, Translators, and Writers of Religious Works* and is completing a biography of Mary Sidney, Countess of Pembroke, under an NEH Fellowship for College Teachers.

THOMAS HEAD is an assistant professor of the history of Christianity at the School of Theology at Claremont. His major research interest is in the relationship of clerical and lay cultures in the Middle Ages and Reformation.

ANN ROSALIND JONES is an associate professor in the Comparative Literature Program at Smith College. Her research interests include contemporary literary theory, feminist critical methods, and love poetry written by women during the Renaissance.

ANNE R. LARSEN is an associate professor of French at Hope College. She has published articles on a number of Renaissance women writers.

ELIZABETH MCCUTCHEON is a professor of English at the University of Hawaii. Her special interests include rhetoric, Christian humanism, the lives of women in sixteenth-century England, and the works of Erasmus, Sir Thomas More, and others in the More circle.

CIRIACO MORÓN-ARROYO is Emerson Hinchliff Professor of Hispanic Studies and Comparative Literature at Cornell University. His publications deal with Spanish thought in the European context. His last book is a collection of essays by various contributors on *El erasmismo en España* (1986).

DONALD CHRISTOPHER NUGENT is an associate professor of history and religious studies at the University of Kentucky. He is the author of *Ecumenism in the Age of the Reformation* and *Masks of Satan: The Demonic in History.*

RICHARD POSS holds a doctorate in comparative literature from the University of Georgia. His major interests include Petrarch, Italian Renaissance art, and the role of Venice in the English Renaissance.

JEANNE PRINE is a doctoral candidate in the Comparative Literature Department at the University of Georgia.

KITTYE DELLE ROBBINS-HERRING is an associate professor of foreign languages at Mississippi State University, where she teaches French and women's studies. Her interests are in medieval and Renaissance literature.

SANDRA SIDER is Curator of Manuscripts and Rare Books at the Hispanic Society of America, where she has presented lectures on palaeography and cartographic history. Her publications include works on Renaissance emblems, hieroglyphs, and iconography.

FRANCES TEAGUE is an associate professor of English at the University of Georgia. Her research interests include stage history and Renaissance women writers.

MARCEL TETEL is a professor in the Department of Romance Languages at Duke University. He is particularly interested in French and Italian Renaissance literature.

FRANK J. WARNKE is professor and head of the Comparative Literature Department at the University of Georgia. His publications have been primarily concerned with Western European literature of the sixteenth and seventeenth centuries.

SUZANNE FONAY WEMPLE is a professor in the history department and the Medieval and Renaissance Studies Program of Barnard College at Columbia University. She is perhaps best known for her *Women in Frankish Society: Marriage and the Cloister, 500–900.*

CHARITY CANNON WILLARD is a professor emerita of Ladycliff College. Her publications include works on Christine de Pizan and late medieval and Renaissance social and cultural history.

KATHARINA M. WILSON is an associate professor of comparative literature at the University of Georgia. Her publications have been primarily concerned with early women writers, Austrian literature, and medieval and Renaissance cultural history.

Index

de Abbavilla, 178

Acta Sanctorum, 85–86, 95

Adorno, Giuliano, 68

"Advice to Widows" (Hoyers), 304, 308

Aeneid (Virgil), 50, 195

Aesop, 160

"L'Agnodice" (C. des Roches), 239, 250–53, 257

Agrippa, Cornelius, 215, 237, 582

Agrippa of Nettelsheim, xxi

Alamanni, Luigi, 25

Alberti, Leon Battista, 161

Albret, Henri de, (king of Navarre), 100

Albret, Jeanne de, 100

The Alchemist (Jonson), 550

Alençon, Charles, Duke of, 99

Alexander VI, Pope, 48

Allegri, Antonio, 47, 49

Amadis of Gaul, 160

L'Amant desconforté (Prevost), 180

Ambrose, Saint, 81

Amoretti (Spenser), 55

L'Amoureux transi sans espoir (Bouchet), 180

"de l'Amour Lesbienne" (Labé), 132

Amye de Court (de la Borderie), 222

Anduze, Clara d', 5

Angela of Foligno, 82, 84–86, 95

Les Angoysses douloureuses qui procedent d'amours (Briet), 177–85, 187, 189–95, 212–16

"Anna Owena Hoyers's Advice, Which She Has Given to All Old Widows to Live Thereafter," 316

"Anna Owena Hoyers's Brief Reflections on the Marriage of Old Women, Since God Has Nothing to Do with It," 321–23

"An Answer to Another Perswading a Lady to Marriage" (Philips), 569, 600

Anthony of Padua, 81

Anthony of Vienna, 88

Antonius: A Tragedie (M. Sidney, countess of Pembroke), pp. 484–89

Anvers, Chez Martin Lempereur, 265

Apologia Mulierum (Pompeo Colonna), 25

Arcadia (P. Sidney), 482–83, 548, 550–51, 553

Aretino, Pietro, 25, 28, 48

Ariosto, Ludovico, 22, 25, 28, 56, 257

Aristotle, 160, 216, 582

The Art of War (Machiavelli), 23

Ascham, Roger, 450, 522–23

Asola, Andrea di, 24, 28

L'Astrée (d'Urfe), 188

Astrophil and Stella (P. Sidney), 548, 550, 551

"As Written to the Lady Alington" (Roper), 472–75

Aubigné, Agippa d', xxi, 240

Aubrey, John, 566

Auden, W. H., 487

Aufzeichnungen des Malte Laurids Brigge (Rilke), 5–6

Augelier, Abel, 235

Augustine, Saint, 70, 84, 92, 403

Augustus, Emperor, 51

Austen, Jane, 11

Avalos, Alfonso de (marquis of Vasto), 24

Avalos, Constanza de, 31

Avalos, Ferrante Francesco d' (marquis
    of Pescara), 23–24, 29–30, 34–35
Avrillon, Mademoiselle d', 333

Bacon, Anne Cooke, xxx, 453
Bacon, Sir Nicholas, 453, 530
Baïf, Jean-Antoine de, 133, 233
Bascio, Matteo de, 27
Bassanese, Fiora A., 4, 10–11, 21
Batarnay, Imbert de, 158
Baxter, Nathaniel, 550
Beaujeu, Anne de, 351
Belarmine, Saint Robert, 67
Belges, Jean Lemaire de, 183, 187,
    213, 353, 354
Bellay, Joachim Du, 133, 160, 219
Bembo, Illuminata, 82, 85, 95
Bembo, Pietro, xiii, 24, 28, 47, 221
Berkenhead, John, 575, 576
Bernini, xv
Berulle, Cardinal de, 67
Bèze, Theodore de, 482
Bibliothèque d'Humanisme et
    Renaissance (Saulnier), 223
Biëncorf (1569), 374
Bijns, Anna, xii, xv, xxxi, xxxiii,
    365–87
Bilder aus der Deutschen
    Vergangenheit (Freytag), 335
Billon, François de, 183
Biography (Catherine of Genoa), 71,
    72–74
Boccaccio, 179–80, 183, 212
Boethius, 160, 524, 528–29, 532–33
Boldog Margit legendája (Ráskai),
    439–40
Boleyn, Anne (queen of England), 522
Bolt, Robert, 459
Bonaventura, 374
The Book of Life (Teresa of Jesus),
    402, 405, 407, 409, 411–21
The Book of the City of Ladies (de
    Pizan), xxx, iv, xxxv, 350, 355
Book of the Courtier (Castiglione),
    23–24
Book of the Foundations (Teresa of
    Jesus), 402

Borromeo, Charles, 81
Bossuet, 67
Bouchet, Jean, 180
Boudewijns, Katharina, 375
Bourges, Clémence de, 219, 222
Bracchart, Charlotte de, 240, 242
Brechtanus, 370, 373
Breton, Nicholas, 482
Brézé, Louis de (senechal of
    Normandy), 159
Briçonnet, Guillaume, 99
Bridget, Saint, xix
Brief Lives (Aubrey), 566
Briet, Marguerite (Hélisenne de
    Crenne), xii, xiv, 177–93, 212–16
Britonio, Givolamo, 24, 28
Brunetière, 222
Bruni, Leonardo, xx, xxxv
Budé, Guillaume, 453
Buonarroti, Michelangelo, 25–28, 30
Burckhard, Jacob, 25
Butler's Lives of the Saints, 95

Callimachus, 137
Calvin, John, xxvii–xxviii, xxxvi,
    132, 264–65
Camden, William: The History
    of . . . Princess Elizabeth, 525, 527,
    533
"Canonization" (Donne), 572
Canzoniere (Petrarch), 52
Capello, Bernardo, 48
"Caritas Pirckheimer to Conrad
    Celtis," 294–96
Caro, Annibale, 25
Cartwright, William, 573, 575
Castelein, Matthijs de, 369, 375
Castiglione, Baldassare, 23–24, 48,
    237
Castiglione, Baptista, 523
Catherine de Medicis, xviii, xxii
Catherine of Bologna, Saint, xii, xiii,
    87–95
Catherine of Genoa, Saint, xii, xiii,
    67–71
Catherine of Racconigi, Blessed, 68
Catherine of Ricci, Saint, 68

Catherine of Siena, Saint, xv, 68, 81
Catherine Tomas, Saint, 68
Catullus, 138–39
Caviceo, Jacobo, 183, 213
Cecil, William (Lord Burghley), 522, 530
Cellini, Benvenuto, 160–61
Celtis, Konrad, xvi, 287–89, 301
Cento Virgilianus (Proba), 242
Cereta, Laura, xvii, xxiii–xxvii
Champier, Symphorien, 159
The Champions of Ladies (Martin le Franc), 159
"Chanson" (Margaret of Austria), 358
"Chanson d'Amazones" (des Roches), 239, 249
Chansons Spirituelles (Marguerite of Navarre), 106
Chapman, George, 550
Charles (archduke of Austria), 526
Charles V (king of Spain), 23, 49
Chartier, Alain, 186
Cheke, Sir John, 523
Chrestien, Guillaume, 159
Chronicles of England, Scotland, and Ireland, 528, 533
Cicero, 160, 523, 532
Clarke, Mary (Basset), 450
Claudian, 241
Clémence de Bourges, 134–35
Clement VII, Pope, 24, 27
Colet, Claude, 183–84, 186–87
Colonna, Fabrizio, 23, 29
Colonna, Cardinal Pompeo, 25
Colonna, Vittoria, xii, xiii, xxviii, 3, 23–33, 53
Collaltino di Collalto, 5–9
Colloque de l'Abbé et la Femme Savante (Marot), 216
Colloquies (Erasmus), 454
Comédie des quatre femmes (Marguerite of Navarre), 107
Comédie du parfait amant (Marguerite of Navarre), 107
Complainte des Tristes Amours de Flammette a Son Amy Pamphile, 180

Comte, Béat, 265
Comus (Milton), 481
"Conde Clards de Adonis" (Du Guillet), 219
Confessions (Saint Augustine), 403
Coniugium (Erasmus), 238
The Consolation of Philosophy, 524, 528–29, 532–33
Contarini, Gasparo (1483–1542), 25, 27
"A Conversation Between Mother and Child" (Hoyers), 306
Cornaro, Catherine, xxii
Corneille, Pierre, 577
Cornelia (Kyd), 484
Cornides Codex, 435–36
Correggio (Antonio Allegri), 47, 49
Correr, Gregorio, 86
Correspondence (More), 463–64
Corso, Rinaldo, 56
Costanzo, Angelo di, 25
The Countess of Pembroke's Arcadia (P. Sidney), 550
Cousin, Jean, 160
Crashaw, Richard, 32
Croce, Benedetto, p. 21
Cymbeline (Shakespeare), 410
Cynthia's Revels (Jonson), 533
Cyprian, Saint, 459

Die Daemonen (von Doderer), 325
Daniel, Samuel, 482, 484
Dante Alighieri, 7, 24
Davies of Hereford, John, 482
Débat de Folie et d'Amour (Labé), 132, 135–37, 241
Decameron (Boccaccio), 100
de Crenne, Hélisenne, xii, xiv, 177–93, 212–16
Defence et Illustration de la Langue Françoyse (Du Bellay), 219
"A Defense of Women" (Dentière), 264, 267, 277–78
The Defense of Poetry (P. Sidney), 548
de la Cruz, San Juan, 31
de la Cruz, Sor Juana Inés, 7, 31
Dèlie (Scève), 220

Delorme, Philibert, 160–61
Demosthenes, 523
"Denkwürdigkeiten" (Pirckheimer), 289–91, 294, 296–301
Die Denkwürdigkeiten der Helene Kottanner (Kottanner), 327
Dentière, Marie, xii, xv, xxxi, 260–83
Dering, Sir Edward, 571, 580, 582
Desportes, Philippe, 32
des Roches, Catherine, ix, xii, xiv, xviii, xxiii, xxvii, 214, 232–40, 241
des Roches, Madeleine (Madeleine Neveu), ix, xii, xiv, xviii, xxiii, xxvii, 232–33, 234–40, 241
Deutsche Wahrheit (Hoyers), 308, 311–16
Devereaux, Robert (second earl of Essex), 526, 528, 530
A Devout Treatis upon the "Pater Noster" (Roper), 465–71
Dialoghi d'Amore (Bembo), 221
Diálogos de Roma (de Hollanda), 25
Dialogue (Saint Catherine), 67
"Dialogue de Placide et Severe" (des Roches), 237, 242
"Dialogue de Sincero et Charite" (des Roches), 234
"Dialogue d'Iris et Pasithee" (des Roches), 237–38, 241, 254–56
"A Dialogue of Absence 'Twixt Lucasia and Orinda" (Philips), 567
"A Dialogue of Absence 'Twixt Lucasia and Orinda. Set by Mr. Henry Lawes" (Philips), 589–90
Dialogue of the Gods (Lucian), 135
Dickinson, Emily, 11
Discourse of Life and Death (de Mornay), 482
A Discourse of the Nature and Offices of Friendship . . . (Taylor), 573, 574
Dissectin (Estienne), 159
Divine Comedy (Dante), 24
Dlugosz, Johann, 333
Doderer, Heimito von, 334
Donadoni, Eugenio, 21
Donne, John, 31–32, 482, 548, 572, 573, 579, 603

Dordtsche Bundel, 367
Drake, Sir Francis, 527
Drayton, Michael, 482
"Dream of Fair Women" (Tennyson), 459
"The Dream of Gerontius," (Cardinal Newman), 67
Dubois, Jacques, 159
Dudley, Robert (earl of Leicester), 526
Du Guillet, Pernette, xii, xiv, xviii, 133, 186, 219–23
Duino Elegies (Rilke), 5–6
Du Mans, Peletier, 240 (n. 2)
Du Moulin, Antoine, 219–20
Durand of Champaigne, xix
Dürer, Albrecht, 288, 293
The Dwelling Places of the Interior Castle (Teresa of Jesus), 402, 408, 410, 421–31

Ebreo, Leone, 223
Economicus (Xenophon), 237
"The Ecstasy" (Donne), 572
Edward VI (king of England), 523–25
Eleanor of Aragon, xxii
Eleanor of Austria, xxx
Eleanore, Marie (queen of Sweden), 307
Elegia de Madonna Fiammetta (Boccaccio), 180
Elégie sur le Trespas de Mesdames des Roches de Poitiers Mère et Fille (le Grand), 241
Elizabeth I (queen of England), xii, xiv, xviii, xxii, xxviii, xxi, 482, 522–47
Elizabeth of Hungary, Saint, xxii, 327–31, 334, 438
Elizabeth of Nassau-Saarbrücken, xxx
Eloge (Poliziano), 242
Eloges des Hommes Illustres (Sainte-Marthe), 241–42
Elzevieren, Ludwig, 306
Englands Elizabeth (Heywood), 523–24
"Epistle to Her Mother" (C. des Roches), 241, 253–54

"Epistle to My Daughter" (M. des Roches), 233, 241, 244–45

"Epistle to the Ladies" (des Roches), 243–44

Epistre très Utile (Dentière), 267

"Epitaph on Her Son H.P. at St. Syth's Church, Where Her Boy Also Lies Interred" (Philips), 598–99

"Epitaph on Mr. John Lloyd" (Philips), 567–69, 580–81

"Epitaph on Mr. John Lloyd of Kilrhewy in Pembrokeshire . . . " (Philips), 591–92

"Epithalamion" (Spenser), 568

Epîtres de l'Amant Vert (de Belges), 353

Erasmus, xviii, xx, 215, 237–38, 293, 354–55, 449–50, 453–54, 460–62

Ercolani, Agostino, 47

Este, Ercole, 27, 48

Este, Isabella d', xxii, 47–49

Este, Margaret d', 81

Este, Nicholas III d', 81

Estienne, Charles, 159

Etaples, Jacques Lefèvre, 99

Fabula (Hyginus), 239

Faerie Queene (Spenser), 533

Familiar and Invective Letters (Briet), 184, 189

Familiar Quotations (Bartlett), 213

Farel, Guillaume, 260–67

Farnese, Alexander (duke of Parma), 542

Fattucci, G. Francesco, 28

Fénelon, Françoise, 67

Ferdinand II (king of Naples), 23, 48

Fernel, Jean, 159

Fèvre, Jean de, 213

Fidele, Cassandra, xiv, xvii, xxii, xxvi, xxxii, 188, 242

Flaminio, Marcantonio, 25

Flaminius, Joannes Antonius, 85–86

Flore, Jeanne, 214

Flores, Juan de, 180

Floris ende Blanchefloer, 366

Le Fort inexpugnable de l'honneur du sexe féminin (de Billon), 183

Fournel, Philippe (seigneur de Crasnes), 178–80

Fradonnet, André, 233

Francis I (king of France), 23, 99, 48, 53

Francis (duke of Alençon), 526, 529–30

Francis of Assisi, Saint, 84, 93

Francis of Sales, Saint, 67

Fraunce, Abraham, 482

Frederigo III (duke of Mantua), 31

Freud, Sigmund, 184

Freytag, Gustav, 334

"Friendship in Embleme, or the Seal to My Dearest Lucasia" (Philips), 572

"Friendship's Mystery. To My Dearest Lucasia" (Philips), 567, 572, 588–89

Froment, Antoine, 261–62, 265–67

Furbiti, Guy, 262

Galindo, Beatriz, xviii

Gambara, Gianfrancesco da, 47–48

Gambara, Girolamo da, 50

Gambara, Ippolito da, 50

Gambara, Veronica, xii, xxii, 28, 47–66

"The Garden" (Marvell), 567–68, 582

Gargrave, Sir Thomas, 537

Garnier, Robert, 482, 484, 486–89

Gaston de Foix, 51

Genova, Bonzida, 69–71

Genovese, Paolo Interiano, 28

Gerard, Jean, 265

The Germ of Calvinism (de Jussie), 262

Germania Illustrata (Celtis), 289

Gerson, John, 301

Geuzen Liedtboeck, 375

Giberti, Matteo, 24, 27–28

Giberto X of Correggio, 48–49

Giovio, Paolo, 25

Golden Verse (Pythagoras), 257

Gonzaga, Saint Aloysius, 67

Gonzaga, Cecilia, 81, 86
Goujon, Jean, 160
Gournay, Marie de, 189, 240, 242
Grand, Louis de, 233, 241
Grassettus, Jacobus, S.J., 86
Graves, Robert, 7, 11, 21
Greene, Robert, 134
Greville, Fulke, 482
Grindall, William, 523
Gryphius, Andreas, 32
Guarino, 81
Guernelli, Giovanni, 10, 21
Guersens, Caye-Jules de, 234, 240–41
Guidiccioni, Giovanni, 25, 28

Hamlet (Shakespeare), 410
"Happiness" (Philips), 570
Harengue . . . (de Bracchart), 243
Harington, Sir John, 528
Harvey, Gabriel, 482
Hausset, Madame de, 333
"Hélisenne to Her Lady Readers"
    (Briet), 190, 196–208
Heloise, 5
Henry II (king of France), 5, 7, 158
Henry VIII (king of England), 522–24
Heptameron (Marguerite of Navarre),
    100–130
Herbert, George, 31–32, 483, 548
Herbert, Mary Sidney (countess of
    Pembroke), xii, xvi, xviii, xxx,
    481–521, 548–50, 552–53
Heroides (Ovid), 29, 141
Heywood, Thomas, 523–24
The History of Princess Elizabeth
    (Camden), 525, 527, 533
Holanda, Francisco de, 25
Holbein, Hans, the Younger, 449,
    453–54
Holinshed, Raphael, 528, 533
Horace, 214, 567, 532
Horace (Corneille), 577–78, 580
Horvát Codex, 435–36
Hoyers, Anna Owena, xii, xiv, xxxi
Hoyer, Hermann, 304, 308
Hrotsvit of Gandersheim, 288

Hügel, Friedrich von, 67
Hunnens, Wennecke, 304

Innocent VIII, Pope, 48
Institutio Oratoria (Quintilian), 214
Instruction of a Christian Woman
    (Vives), 241, 453, 461
The Invective Letters of my Lady
    Hélisenne de Crenne, 208–13, 215
Isabella I (queen of Spain), xxii, xvii

James I (king of England), 528
John, Saint, 87, 89
John of the Cross, Saint, 67, 69, 71,
    404
Jonson, Ben, 481–82, 485, 550, 553,
    570, 575
Joyce, James, 484
Julius II, Pope, 23, 48
Jussie, Sister Jeanne de, 262–63, 266
Juvenal, 476

Kempe, Margery, xxviii
Kilényi, Maria, 335
Kottanner, Helene, xii, xv, xxxi,
    327–35, 327–49
Kress, Christoph, 291
Kyd, Thomas, 484

Labé, Louise, xxiii, xxvi, xxvii, xii,
    xiv, xviii, 5, 179, 182, 186, 212,
    214, 219, 222–23, 232, 241
La Borderie, Bertrand de, 222
La Ceppède, Jean de, 31
The Lady of the May (P. Sidney), 533
Lafayette, Madame de, 188
Lapiz, Ulrich von, 332
Latin Poems (More), 454
Lawes, Henry, 575, 579, 581
Leben König Siegmunds (Windecke),
    333
Le Franc, Martin, 159
Legenda Aurea, 436
Legend of Blessed Margaret (Ráskai),
    435–38, 440–46
Legend of Saint Dominique, 435–36

Leo X, Pope, 23–24, 48
Letters (Cicero), 160
The Letters of Margaret of Austria,
 359–61
The Letters of Queen Elizabeth,
 531–32
"Libellous Copy of Rimes" (Powell),
 577
Libro del Pelegrino (Caviceo), 213
Life (Catherine of Genoa), 71, 72–74
"The Life and Deeds of Mark Antony
 and His Friend Cleopatra," 160
Life and Metamorphoses of Ovid, 160
Linck, Wenzel, 292
Livres des Trois Vertus (de Pizan),
 351, 353, 355
Livy, 523
Locke, Anne, xxx
Lodge, Thomas, 484
Loisel, Antoine, 236
Longinus, 215
Louise of Savoy, xv, xviii, xxii
"Love Poems" (Colonna), 29–32,
 35–38
Luther, Martin, xxvii–xxviii, xxxvi,
 264–65, 365, 369–72, 374
Luyken, Ian, 31
"Lycidas" (Milton), 567
Lyfe (Roper), 455
Lyly, John, 191, 573

McAuliffe, Dennis J., 30
Macbeth (Shakespeare), 486
Machiavelli, Nicolo, 23
Magny, Olivier de, 133, 160
Mann, Thomas, 6, 11, 21
Manning, Anne, 459
Marc Antoine (Garnier), 482, 484,
 486
Marcellus, 439
Margaret, Blessed, 435–39
Margaret of Austria, xii, xv, xvii, xxii,
 350–62
Margaret of Parma, xxii
Marguerite of Navarre, xxi, xxii, xxiii,

xxviii, 25, 28, 99–102, 104,
 106–7, 177–79, 189, 215, 260–61,
 356, 523
Marieken van Niemeghen, 366
Marino, Giambattista, 32
Marlowe, Christopher, 485
Marot, Clément, 132, 133, 162, 180,
 185, 212–13, 215, 221, 482
Marvell, Andrew, 32, 567, 582
*The Marvelous Acts and Deeds of the
 City of Geneva* (Froment), 262
Mary Magdalene, Saint, 31, 32
Mary of Hungary, xxii
Mary Stuart (queen of Scots), xxii,
 526–27, 529, 539–42
Mary Tudor (queen of England), 27,
 522, 524–25, 537–38
Mason, John, 537
The Masque of Blackness (Jonson),
 550, 553
Massignon, Louis, 67
Matthew, Saint, 90, 93
*The Measures and Offices of
 Friendship* (Taylor), 573
Medici, Lorenzo de' (the Magnificent),
 48
Medicina (Fernel), 159
Meg (Vogel), 459
Melanchton, Philip, 292
Memoirs (Kottanner), 328, 330–35,
 337–48
Meres, Francis, 482
*The Method of Treating Wounds
 Made by Arquebuses and Arrows*
 (Paré), 159
Meun, Jean de, 213
Michelangelo Buonarroti, xiii, 3, 10,
 53
Midsummer Night's Dream
 (Shakespeare), 533, 583
Milton, John, 481, 567
Minnermus, 137
Minturo, Antonio, 25
The Mirror of the Sinful Soul
 (Marguerite of Navarre), xvi, 99,
 523, 532

Les Missives (des Roches), 232, 241–42
Moderne, Jaques, 219
Moffet, Thomas, 482
Molière, 188
Molza, Francesco Maria, 25
De Monarchia et Sacra Corona Regni Hungariae (von Réva), 334
Montefeltro, Agnese di, 23
Montefeltro, Frederigo da (duke of Urbino), 23, 82
Monteverdi, 181
Morata, Olympia, 242
More, Sir Thomas, xx, xxiii, 237, 449–51, 453–64, 476–77
Morel, Diane de, 238, 242
Morel, Jean de, 237, 242
Mornay, Philippe de, 482–83
Morone, Giovanni (1509–1580), 25
A Most Beneficial Letter . . . (Dentière), 260–61, 264, 266–67, 275–80
Most Marvelous Victories of Women of the New World (Postel), 159
Motteville, Madame de, 333
Muziano, Girolamo, 25

Nashe, Thomas, 482
La Nativité de Jésus Christ (Marguerite of Navarre), 107
Nederduytsche Helicon, 375
Nevell, Madeleine, 232–35, 240
Newman, Cardinal, 67
Newton, Thomas, 484
Nicholas of Cusa, 71
Nicomachean Ethics (Aristotle), 582
de Nobilitate et Praecellentia Foeminei Sexus (Agrippa), 215
Nogarola, Ginevra, xxvi
Nogarola, Isotta, xxvi, xvii, xxii
"No *Laurel* Growes, but for her *Brow*" (Vaughan), 568
Norimberga (Celtis), 298
Northumberland, earl of, 524
"Not Marble, nor the Gilded Monuments of Princes" (Shakespeare), 575

Nottingham, Countess of, 528
Nugae Antiquae (Harrington), 333
Nützel, Kaspar, 289, 292, 302

Ochino, Bernadino (1487–1564), 27, 30
"Ode I" (des Roches), 245–47
Odysseus, 143
Olor Iscanus (Vaughan), 567, 568, 581
On Architecture (Alberti), 161
"On the Fair Weather Just at the Coronation . . . " (Philips), 585
"On the First of January 1657" (Philips), 566
On the Human Body (Vesalius), 159
On the Sublime (Longinus), 215
"On the Third of September 1651" (Philips), 567, 585–86
"Orinda upon Little Hector Philips" (Philips), 568, 599
Orlando Furioso (Ariosto), 22, 25, 56, 242, 257
Ovid, 29, 138–39, 160, 212–13
Owens, Hans, 304

Pamphilia to Amphilantus (M. Sidney), 551–52
Panthé (de Guersens), 234
Paré, Ambroise, 159
Parr, Catherine (queen of England), 523–24, 532
"Parting with Lucasia, a Song" (Philips), 567, 595–96
Pasithee, 241
Pasquier, Etienne, 184, 186, 236, 238, 240
The Passion of Al-Hallāj: Mystic and Martyr of Islam (Massignon), 67
Paul III (Pope), 27, 52
Paul, Saint, 82, 91, 525
Példák Könyve, 435
Pellejay, Claude, 234
Pelletier, Jacques, 233
Penelope, 143
Pèriers, Bonaventure de, 221

Petrarch, Francesco, 6, 10, 20–31, 47, 53–55, 180, 182, 212, 237, 482
Peutinger, Margaret, xviii
Phaedrus (Plato), 136–37
Philip II (king of Spain), 50, 527, 542
Philips, Katherine, xii, xvi, 566–608
Philotas (Daniels), 484
Pia, Alda, 48
Pia, Emilia, 48
Piccolomini, Aeneas Sylvius, 333
Pico, Galeotto, 51
Pico, Violante, 48
Pico della Mirandola, 48, 293
Pii, Marco de, 95
Pii, Taddea de, 95
Piombo, Sebastiano del, 25
Pippinck, Henrick, 372–73
Pirckheimer, Caritas, xviii, xii, xiv, xviii, 287–303
Pirckheimer, Katharina, 292
Pirckheimer, Willibald, 287–89, 292–93, 301
Pithou, Pierre, 238
Pizan, Christine de, xxii, xxv, xix, xx, 159, 180, 186, 189, 213, 330, 350–51, 353, 355–56
Plato, 221
Plutarch, 257, 532
Poitiers, Dianne de, xii, xiii, xxxii, 158–63
Pole, Reginald, 25, 27
Poliziano, Angelo, 242
Pompadour, Madame de, 333
Pompey (Corneille), 577–80
Postel, Guillaume de, 159
"Pour une mascarade d'Amazones" (des Roches), 239
Powell, Vavasor, 579
Praise of Folly (Erasmus), 135
Precatio Dominico (Erasmus), 460
Precepts of Marriage (Plutarch), 237
Les Precieuses Ridicules (Molière), 188
Prevost, Anthoine, 180
Prieelken der Gheestelijcker Wellusten, 375

La Princesse de Clèves (Madame de Lafayette), 189
Proba, Falconia, 242
Propertius, 138–39, 141
La Puce (des Roches), 241–42
Pythagoras, 215, 241, 257

Quintilian, 214, 452, 459

Rabelais, François, 184–85, 189
Rambaldo, Antonio, 10
Raphael, 47
de Raptu Proserpinae (Claudian), 241
Ráskai, Lea, xii, xvi, xxxi, 435–446
"Restitution de *La Guerre et Délivrance*" (Rilliet), 267
"A Retir'd Friendship. To Ardelia" (Philips), 567, 592–93
Réva, Peter von, 334
Revilliod, Gustave, 267
Ribera, Catherina, xxii
Richard II (Shakespeare), 529
Rilke, Rainer Maria, 5–6, 11, 21, 134–35
Rilliet, Albert, 267
Robert, Simon, 261
Robert of Blois, xix
Romance of the Rose (de Meun), 160
Romieu, Marie de, 240
Ronsard, Pierre de, 132–33, 160, 223, 375
Roper, Margaret More, xii, xvi, xviii, xxvi, xxxi, 449–80
Rosa, Scipione Montino della, 49
Rosis and Lyra (R. Sidney), 548, 551
Rossi, Ludovico, 49, 51
Rossom, Martin, 370–71
Rota, Bernardino, 25
Ruskin, John, 489
Les Rymes (Du Guillet), 219–30

Sacred Poems (Colonna), 39–42
Sadoleto, Jacopo (1477–1547), 24, 27
Sainte-Beuve, Charles Augustin, 222
Sainte-Marthe, Scévole de, 233–34, 238, 240–42
Saintsbury, George, 489

Saint-Vertunien, François de, 240
Salza, Abdelkader, 4, 10–11, 20
Sannazaro, Jacopa (d. 1530), 24
San Pedro, Diego de, 183
Saulnier, Verdun, 223
Savonarola, Girolamo, 31, 84–86
Scaliger, Joseph-Juste, 234, 240–41
Scève, Maurice, 132, 143, 161, 180,
    185, 212, 219–23, 230
Scheurl, Christoph, 289
Scholemaster (Ascham), 523
Second Book of Ayres and Dialogues
    (Lawes), 571–72, 575, 579, 581
Selected Letters (Roper), 451–60
Semiramis, 140
Seneca, 160, 484–86, 532
Seven Weapons of the Spirit (Catherine
    of Bologna), 82, 86–95
Seymour, Edward (duke of Somerset
    and Lord Protector), 524
Seymour, Thomas (lord of Sheffield
    Castle), 524
Sforza, Catherine, xxii
Sforza, Battista, 23
Sforza, Guidobaldo, 23
Shakespeare, William, 410, 482, 485,
    529, 533
Ship of Virtuous Ladies (Symphorien
    Champier), 159
Shurman, Anna Maria van, 240, 242
Sidney, Mary (Lady Wroth), xii, xvi,
    xxiii, 548–65
Sidney, Mary (countess of Pembroke),
    xii, xvi, xviii, xxx, 481–521,
    548–50, 552–53
Sidney, Sir Philip, xviii, 481–82, 533,
    548, 550–52
Sidney, Robert, 548–53
Sigea, Luisa, 242
Silvius, Aeneas, 213
Sint-Aldegonde, Marnix van, 374
Sintra (Sigea), 242
Sixtus IV, Pope, 48
Socrates, 6
Solitaire Premier (de Tyard), 241
"Song of Praise" (Hoyers), 307
Song of Songs, 69

"Sonnets de Sincero et Charite" (C.
    des Roches), 234
Sophocles, 523
*The Sorrowful Anguishes Which
    Proceed From Love . . .* (de
    Crenne),196–208
"The Soul" (Philips), 570
Southwell, Robert, 31–32
Specchio Dell' Anima Semplice, 439
Spee, Friedrich von, 31
Spenser, Edmund, 55, 482–83, 533,
    568
Speroni, Sperone, 223
Spiritual Dialogue (Catherine of
    Genoa), 70
Spiritual Poems (Gambara), 29–31
Staël, Madame de, 189
Stampa, Baldassare, 4
Stampa, Cassandra, 4, 9
Stampa, Gaspara, xii, xiii, 3–21, 56,
    135
Stapleton, 459
State Papers (More), 457
Summa Contra Gentiles (Aquinas),
    582
"The Sun Rising" (Donne), 572–73
Sylvester, Joshua, 550
Symbola (Pythagoras), 241, 257
Symeoni, Gabriel, 160

Tahureau, Jacques, 233
Tarzia, Galeazzo di (1520–1553), 25
Tasso, Bernardo (1483–1569), 25
Tasso, Torquato, 10, 25
Taurella, Hyppolita, 242 (n. 23)
Taylor, Jeremy, 573–74, 583
Tennyson, Lord Alfred, 459
Teresa of Jesus, Saint (Teresa of
    Ahumada), xii, xv, 401–31
Terracina Laura, 242
Thalia Rediviva (Vaughan), 581
Thomas, Dylan, 486
Three Books of Occult Philosophy
    (Agrippa), 582
Tibullus, 138, 141
Titian, 31, 47
Tolomei, Claudio, 25

Torre, Francesco della, 28

"To Mademoiselle Clémence de
Bourges of Lyon" (Labé), 149–50

"To Mr. Henry Lawes" (Philips), 567,
587–88

"To Mr. J.B. the Noble Cratander,
Upon a Composition of His Which
He Was Not Willing to Own
Publickly" (Philips), 575

"To My Daughter" (des Roches), 253

"To My Dearest Antenor, on His
Parting" (Philips), 596–97

"To My Dear Sister Mrs. C.P. on Her
Marriage" (Philips), 567–68,
590–91

"To My Distaff" (C. des Roches), 214,
239, 249–50

"To My Excellent Lucasia, on Our
Friendship" (Philips), 567, 593–94

"To Philaster, on His Melancholy for
Regina" (Philips), 569, 595

"To Regina Collier, on Her Cruelty to
Philaster" (Philips), 569, 594

To Sir Thomas More (Roper), 471–72,
475–76

"To the Christian Reader" (Hoyers),
311

"To the Excellent Rosaria" (Aubrey),
580

"To the Noble Palaemon, on His
Incomparable Discourse of
Friendship" (Philips), 586–87

"To the Queen's Majesty on Her
Arrival at Portsmouth, May 14,
1662" (Philips), 576

"To the Queen's Majesty, on Her Late
Sickness and Recovery" (Philips),
576, 597–98

"To the Very Christian Princess
Marguerite of France, Queen of
Navarre . . ." (Dentière), 275–77

"The Tragedy of Anthony" by Robert
Garnier. Translated by Mary
Herbert, Countess of Pembroke (M.
Sidney), 490–520

The Tragedy of Cleopatra (Daniels),
484

Trionfo della Morte (Petrarch), 482

de Tristitia (More), 451

Triumph of Christ's Cross (Colonna),
31, 42–44

The Triumph of the Cross
(Savonarola), 31

Triumphs (Petrarch), 31

Tucher, Anton, 289

Tucher, Apollonia, 289

Tucher, Sixtus, 289

Turberville, George, 573

Two Lives (Roper), 451, 454–56,
458–59

Tyard, Pontus de, 133, 241

Tyler, Margaret, xxx, xxxvii

Ubertino da Casale, 82

Ulysses (Joyce), 484

Upham, Thomas C., 67

"Upon the Double Murther of King
Charles I" (Philips), 567, 579,
584–85

Urania (M. Sidney), xvi, 551–52

"A Valediction: Forbidding
Mourning" (Donne), 572

Varano, Battista da, 81–82, 95

Varano, Constanza, 188

Varano, Gildlio Cesare da, 81

Varchi, Benedetto, 25

Vasto, Marchese del, 47

Vaughan, Henry, 567–68, 575, 581

Vega, Lope de, 32

Verdi, Giuseppe, 10

Vere, Edward de (earl of Oxford), 522

Veronese, Paolo, 25

Vesalius, Andreas, 159

Vigri, Catherine de. See Catherine of
Bologna

Viret, Pierre, 262–63

Virgil, 48, 50, 567

Virtuous Deeds of Women (Plutarch),
257

Vision of God (Nicholas of Cusa), 71

Vitiello, Justin, 4, 10–11, 21

Vitorino, 81

Vives, Juan Luis, xxi, 237, 241, 453, 461
Vocabulario di Cinquemila Vocabuli Toschi, 29
Vogel, Paula, 459
Vondel, Joost van den, 32

The War for and Deliverance of the City of Geneva . . . (Dentière), 260–64, 267 (n. 3), 270–75
The Way of Perfection (Teresa of Jesus), 402, 406

Wesley, John, 68
Windecke, Eberhard, 333
"The World" (Philips), 570
Wyatt, Sir Thomas, 524

Xenophon, 237, 532

Zayas y Sotomayor, Maria de, xxiii, xxv, xxxi
Zen, Bartolomeo, 9
Zvzorić, 264
Zwingli, 264, 293